D0602913

2750

ph

mary Joseph

Lectures on
Macroeconomics

June '89

Lectures on Macroeconomics

Olivier Jean Blanchard and
Stanley Fischer

The MIT Press
Cambridge, Massachusetts
London, England

© 1989 Massachusetts Institute of Technology

All rights reserved. No part of this book may be reproduced in any form by any electronic or mechanical means (including photocopying, recording, or information storage and retrieval) without permission in writing from the publisher.

This book was set in Palatino by Asco Trade Typesetting Ltd., Hong Kong and printed and bound by Halliday Lithograph in the United States of America.

Library of Congress Cataloging-in-Publication Data

Blanchard, Olivier (Olivier J.)
  Lectures on macroeconomics/Olivier Jean Blanchard and Stanley Fischer.

  p.   cm.
  Bibliography: p.
  Includes index.
  ISBN 0-262-02283-4
  1. Macroeconomics. I. Fischer, Stanley. II. Title.
HB172.5.B57 1989   88-13757
339—dc19   CIP

from Serena, 1988

Contents

329 - 337

Preface

On the surface, macroeconomics appears to be a field divided among schools, Keynesians, monetarists, new classical, new Keynesian, and no doubt others. Their disagreements, which often appear to be as much about methodology as about results, leave outsiders bewildered and skeptical.

This is not our assessment of the field. Behind the public relations gimmicks and the strong incentives that exist in academia to differentiate products, macroeconomics shares many basic models and views. We believe that macroeconomics exists as a science, an admittedly young, hesitant, and difficult one. Its inherent difficulties stem from the need to draw from all branches of microeconomics, deal with aggregation, make contact with data, and eventually make policy recommendations.

We have written this book to accomplish two goals. The first is to present the common heritage, the conceptual framework and the sets of models that are used and agreed upon by the large majority of macroeconomists. The second is to present life at the frontier, showing the various directions in which researchers are currently working. Because of the nature of research, it is at the frontier where disagreements are strongest and the debate most vocal. But even there, we see a scientific debate in which hypotheses are examined, tested, and, if they do not pass the test, eventually rejected.

We start in chapter 1 with the basic facts that need to be explained, the existence and persistence of economic fluctuations and their characteristics.

We then present in chapters 2 through 4 the workhorses of modern macroeconomics, the Ramsey growth model and the overlapping generations model, with or without money. These models serve as building blocks in much of modern macroeconomics. Even without additions, they shed light on the fundamental issues of the determinants of saving, the role of fiscal policy in affecting capital accumulation, and the difference between barter and monetary economics. We use them in chapter 5 to discuss issues of bubbles, multiple equilibria, and deterministic cycles. In chapters 6 and 7 we extend these basic models to allow for the presence of uncertainty and stochastic fluctuations.

By the end of chapter 7, we have in effect written a text on equilibrium economics. By then we are also at the frontiers of current research, where various groups of macroeconomists part company. Some believe that the equilibrium approach can explain the basic macroeconomic facts. Others, including us, believe that deviations from the competitive equilibrium paradigm are central to a full understanding of macroeconomic fluctuations. The proposition that goods, labor, and financial markets differ in important ways from the simple competitive paradigm is not controversial. What is controversial is whether those deviations can explain important aspects of aggregate fluctuations. This is the subject of chapters 8 and 9, which cover what is sometimes called new Keynesian economics. Developments in those chapters are sometimes tentative and not yet fully integrated, but we have little doubt that this is where the future lies.

Working macroeconomists, like doctors treating cancer, cannot wait for all the answers to analyze events and help policy. They have to take guesses and rely on a battery of models that cannot be derived from first principles but have repeatedly proved useful. We present such models in chapter 10, showing how they can be and have been used, and what shortcuts they implicitly take. The book concludes with chapter 11 on economic policy, which presents both traditional and game-theoretic analyses of monetary and fiscal policy.

Lectures on Macroeconomics is intended as a text and reference book both for graduate students in macro and monetary economics and for our fellow professionals. The earlier chapters can be and have been used in a first graduate course in macroeconomics, whereas the later chapters are more suited to advanced courses. We believe that the book presents a comprehensive view of modern macroeconomics and an objective view of the field.

The book requires some mathematics. We are tempted to make the usual claim that high school algebra will suffice, but that would have to be a good high school. We use statistics and econometrics sparingly, primarily in chapter 1. We have not been systematic in presenting proofs of results, presenting those we believe important and in other cases referring the reader to alternative sources.

We owe thanks to students and colleagues. Primarily, we thank successive generations of students at MIT, and some at Harvard, who have attended our courses, suffered through the drafts of the chapters, pointed out errors, and suggested expositional changes. Teaching those students is one of the great rewards of academic life. Although it would be invidious to single out particular students, we would like to mention those who have at different times worked as research assistants on the book and as teaching assistants for our courses in monetary economics in which it was used: among them Ricardo Caballero, Jordi Gali, Takeo Hoshi, Anil Kashyap, Athanasios Orphanides, John Shea, and David Wilcox.

Our colleagues at MIT and elsewhere have been generous in their willingness to read, to comment on, and to help improve the book. We thank in particular Laurence Ball, Robert Barro, Roland Benabou, Peter Diamond, Rudi Dornbusch, Peter Howitt, Nobu Kiyotaki, Mervin King, Richard Layard, N. Gregory Mankiw, Steve Nickell, Jim Poterba, Danny Quah, Christina Romer, David Romer, Julio Rotemberg, José Scheinkman, Dick Startz, Larry Summers, Lars Svensson, John Taylor, Jean Tirole, Mark Watson, and Philippe Weil. We are indebted too to Richard Layard and the Centre for Labour Economics at the London School of Economics for their hospitality, which enabled us to push the book over the hump in the summer of 1987.

Finally, we thank Thomas M. Dolan for his superb editorial assistance, and The MIT Press for a splendid all-around job.

1

Introduction

Underlying the existence of macroeconomics as a separate field of study are the phenomena of economywide movements in output, unemployment, and inflation. Although developed economies are characterized by growth, this growth is far from steady. Expansions and recessions alternate over time, associated with movements in unemployment. Occasionally, recessions turn into depressions, such as the U.S. depression from 1873 to 1878, the Great Depression of the 1930s, and the long period of high unemployment in Europe in the 1980s. Periods of price deflation, such as the prolonged price level decline in the last two decades of the nineteenth century, the recession of 1920–21, and the Great Depression, appear to be something of the past: most economies now alternate between periods of low and high, sometimes very high, inflation. It is the main purpose of macroeconomics, and of this book, to characterize and explain these movements of output, unemployment, and prices.

In this chapter we introduce the major issues of macroeconomics by characterizing the basic facts that call for explanation. We then provide a preview of the book, and end by stating some of our goals and choices in writing it.

1.1 Macroeconomic Facts

Growth, Employment, and Productivity

The dominant macroeconomic fact in developed economies in the last two centuries is that of output growth.[1] Figure 1.1 shows the behavior of U.S. real GNP from 1874 to 1986.[2] Using Maddison's first estimate of U.S. real GNP, U.S. growth averaged 3.7% per year for the period 1820 to 1986. The average rate of growth has been 3.4% since 1874, 3.0% since 1919, and 3.2% since 1950. Equivalently, real GNP is about 37 times larger than it was

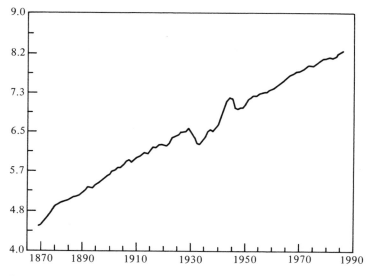

Figure 1.1
Logarithm of real GNP (1982 dollars). Sources for GNP: 1874–89, Romer (1986b, table 3);
1890–1908, Romer (1986b, table 5); 1909–28, Romer (1987, table 5); 1929–47,
Commerce Dept. (1986, table 1.4); 1948–86, Economic Report of the President (1987).

in 1874, 7 times larger than in 1919, and 3 times larger than in 1950.
Extrapolating backward leads to the well-known conclusion that economic
growth at these rates cannot have been taking place for more than a few
centuries.

What are the sources of this growth? Here are the stylized facts as laid
out by Solow in 1970. First, output growth reflects growth in both the labor
force and labor productivity: total labor hours have increased 1.4% per year
and output per hour by 2.0% per year since 1874. Thus output growth has
come more from increasing labor productivity than from increases in the
labor force; this is shown in figure 1.2 which gives total man-hours and
output per man-hour for the private domestic sector (i.e., excluding the
government) since 1874.[3] Growth in output per man-hour, labor productivity, has been 2.1% since 1919 and 2.1% since 1950; output per
man-hour is now nine times higher than it was in 1874, and double its 1950
level.[4]

Where does this growth in living standards, reflected in output per
man-hour, come from? How much of it is due to increases in capital and
applied knowledge, and to increased specialization? Solow (1957) suggested

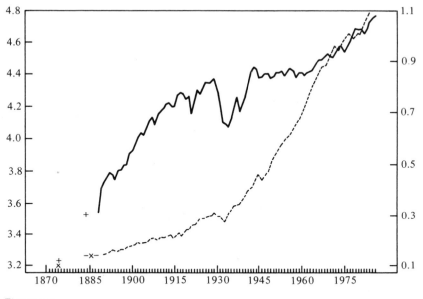

Figure 1.2
Logarithm of man-hours (solid line, left-hand scale) and output per man-hour (dashed line, right-hand scale, 1977 ≡ 1.0). Crosses indicate annual data not available. Sources for GPDP: 1870–1928, Commerce Dept. (1973, LTEG, series A13); 1929–47, Commerce Dept. (1973, LTEG, series A14); 1948–86, Commerce Dept. (1987, table 1). For man-hours: 1870–1947, Commerce Dept. (LTEG, series A59); 1948–86, Commerce Dept. (1987, table 1).

a simple decomposition that, though not theory-free, provides a useful description of the data. Under the assumptions of constant returns to scale and competitive markets, the rate of growth of output can be written as

$$g_y = ag_n + (1 - a)g_k + q,$$

where g_y, g_n, and g_k are the growth rates of output, labor, and capital, respectively, and a is the share of labor in output; q then measures that part of growth that cannot, under the maintained assumptions, be explained by either growth of labor or growth of capital.[5] This term has been dubbed *multifactor productivity growth*, or less formally, the Solow residual.

The data suggest that the Solow residual plays an important role in growth. We can rewrite the above equation as

$$(g_y - g_n) = \left(\frac{1 - a}{a}\right)(g_k - g_y) + \left(\frac{1}{a}\right)q.$$

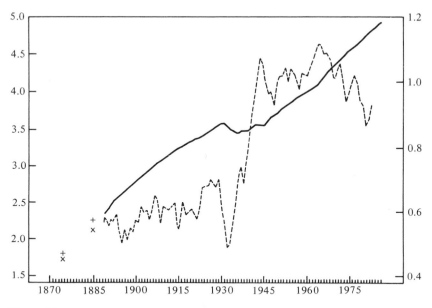

Figure 1.3
Logarithm of capital services (solid line, left-hand scale) and output per unit of capital
(dashed line, right-hand scale, 1977 ≡ 1.0). Crosses indicate annual data not available.
Sources for GPDP: see figure 1.2. For capital: 1870–1947, Commerce Dept. (1973, series
A59); 1948–86, Commerce Dept. (1987, table 1).

The rate of growth of output per man-hour depends positively on the rate
of growth of the capital–output ratio and on the Solow residual. There
can be labor productivity growth, even if q is equal to zero, as long as
the capital–output ratio increases. Existing measures of capital suggest,
however, that capital has grown at a rate roughly similar to that of output,
so that $g_k - g_y$ has been close to zero. This can be seen in figure 1.3, which
shows the evolution of capital as well as the output–capital ratio for the
private domestic sector since 1874.[6] The average rate of growth of capital
has been 2.8% since 1874, 2.1% since 1919, and 3.4% since 1950.

The relative constancy of the output–capital ratio implies a positive
Solow residual, equal roughly to the labor share times the rate of growth of
labor productivity. Multifactor productivity, for the private domestic sector,
is plotted in figure 1.4. Its rate of change averages 1.9% since 1874, 2.0%
since 1919, and 1.7% since 1950, accounting for approximately half of the
growth in the private economy over the whole period. Despite the detailed

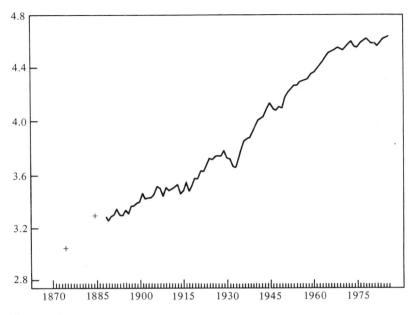

Figure 1.4
Logarithm of multifactor productivity. Crosses indicate annual data not available. Sources
for GPDP: see figure 1.2. For total input: 1870–1947, Commerce Dept. (1973, series A59);
1948–86, Commerce Dept. (1987, table 1).

work of Denison and others, we have only a limited understanding of
where this residual comes from, and of why it is higher in some countries
than in others, or higher during some periods than during others. In seeking
to explain the interactions among output, employment, and capital accumulation, we shall for the most part take as given the long-term movements in
multifactor productivity.

Both the figures and the data we have presented emphasize the most
important fact of modern economic history: persistent long-term growth.
But, as the large fluctuations in figures 1.1 to 1.4 make clear, this growth is
far from steady. We turn now to the fluctuations.

The Stochastic Behavior of Output and Unemployment

Figure 1.1 shows substantial fluctuations in GNP growth over time. Associated with these movements in output are movements in unemployment,
which are plotted for the period since 1890 in figure 1.5. There is little

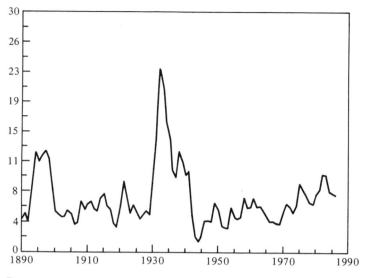

Figure 1.5
Unemployment rate. Sources: 1890–1930, Romer (1986a, table 9); 1931–40, Darby (1976, p. 8); 1940–86, Economic Report of the President (1987).

question that these movements are associated with fluctuations in welfare: periods of boom, expansion, and declining unemployment are widely perceived as happy times in which governments win reelection; periods of recession and depression are often times of crisis and despair.

Explaining booms and recessions will be the object of several chapters of this book, but at this stage we limit ourselves to describing them.[7] Although it is of interest to look at actual movements in output and to see whether fluctuations can be related to specific events or policies, our goal is to describe the general characteristics of fluctuations rather than to study specific episodes. We want to know, for example, how long typical recessions or expansions last, whether fluctuations in output are largely transitory or largely permanent. To do so, we must look at the series for output and other variables as time series with well-defined characteristics and thus use time series methods to uncover those characteristics.

Macroeconomists are, and should be, schizophrenic about the use of time series methods. On the one hand, there is no hope of discovering empirical regularities unless variables follow stable stochastic processes over time. On the other, it is clear that there are episodes, such as depressions or hyperinflations, during which some variables behave abnormally and where a straightforward use of time series methods would be inappropriate. (Even if there existed a stable Kondratieff process that generated depressions on average every 50 years, this would not help us much given the average length of our macroeconomic time series.) The intellectually uncomfortable attitude of most macroeconomists has been to study these episodes separately, and to use time series methods for times when the assumption that variables follow some stable process is not obviously unacceptable. This is what we do below by focusing on the U.S. postwar period, thus ignoring the Great Depression.

The first systematic time series study of business cycles was that of Burns and Mitchell (1946). Their approach was to treat each cycle as a separate episode, terminating and starting at a trough and going from trough to peak through an expansion, and from peak to trough through a contraction. The typical business cycle was then characterized by the mean lengths of expansions and contractions, the amplitude of fluctuations, and the behavior of economic variables relative to the business cycle chronology. This business cycle chronology was used creatively by researchers in the NBER tradition, for instance, by Friedman and Schwartz (1963) in their monumental *Monetary History*.

Most macroeconometricians, however, have abandoned the Burns-Mitchell methodology. This is because the approach is partly judgmental and the statistics it generates do not have well-defined statistical properties. Much of the recent work has proceeded, instead, under the assumption that variables follow linear stochastic processes with constant coefficients. As we shall see later in the book, this has had the advantage of allowing for a better integration of macroeconomic theory and econometrics. In return for this integration and for well-understood statistical properties, some of the richness of the Burns-Mitchell analysis, such as its focus on asymmetries between recessions and expansions or its notion of business cycle time (as opposed to calendar time) may well have been lost.[8] For the postwar United States, however, the assumption that major economic variables follow linear (or loglinear) stochastic processes does not appear too strongly at variance with the data.

Trends versus Cycles, Permanent and Transitory Shocks
The main problem macroeconomists have struggled with in characterizing output fluctuations has been that of separating trend from cycle. This decomposition can be seen as a purely statistical issue devoid of economic significance.[9] Most economists, however, believe that, behind short-run

fluctuations, the economy evolves along an underlying growth path, which can be thought of as the trend. The issue is then how to characterize that trend.

A useful way of approaching the issue is to think of the economy as being affected by two types of shocks. Some shocks have permanent effects on output—we shall call them permanent shocks. Prime candidates are improvements in productivity or increases in the labor force. Some shocks have transitory effects, effects on output that disappear over time; they may include bad crops, temporary increases in government spending, changes in the money. We may then think of the trend as that part of output that is due to permanent shocks; by construction, this series is nonstationary. That part of output that comes from transitory shocks can be thought of as the cycle; by construction, that series is stationary.

We now present three decompositions. The first, and traditional approach, assumes that the trend component of output is smooth so that most of the short-run fluctuations in output come from transitory shocks. This decomposition has recently been challenged on the grounds that the assumption of a smooth trend is not justified. We thus present a second decomposition that assumes, instead, that all fluctuations are due to permanent shocks, that actual output and trend output are the same. We then discuss those results and present a third decomposition, which we find more reasonable, that uses information from both output and unemployment movements.

The Traditional Decomposition

The traditional business cycle approach characterizes the economy as growing along a smooth trend path from which it is disturbed by cyclical fluctuations.

Several methods have been used to define the trend, the simplest being an exponential growth path that best fits the historical data. But there appear to be long-run changes in productivity growth that are badly captured by such a trend. Okun (1962) developed an alternative approach to capture such changes. He defined the trend, or "potential output," as that level of output that would prevail if the unemployment rate was equal to 4% instead of its actual value. To derive the relation between actual output and unemployment required to get from actual to potential output, he examined alternative methods. One consisted of regressing first differences of output on first differences of unemployment. Okun found that a 1% decrease in the unemployment rate was associated with a 3% increase in output. This ratio of 3 to 1 has become known as Okun's law.

Many decompositions of output between trend and cycle have followed the spirit of Okun's computation. Some construct the trend by fitting a piecewise linear trend through the logarithm of GNP in years with similar levels of unemployment. Some use a smoothed version of the potential output series constructed using Okun's law. Those decompositions all lead to an estimated trend growth rate that is lower in the 1970s and the 1980s than in earlier decades.[10]

We now give the results of such a decomposition, using data on U.S. quarterly GNP, measured at an annual rate, for the period 1947-I to 1987-II. Based on the results described above, we allow trend growth to differ pre- and post-1973. Thus we first regress the logarithm of GNP on a piecewise linear trend; we then fit an ARMA process to the deviations of the logarithm of GNP from the estimated trend, the cyclical component. Estimated trend growth is 3.4% for 1947-I to 1973-I and 2.3% from 1973-I to 1987-II. The behavior of the cyclical component is well captured by an ARMA(2, 2) process:

$$y = 1.31y(-1) - 0.42y(-2) + e - 0.06e(-1) + 0.25e(-2),$$

$$\sigma_e = 1\%.$$

(1)

The term e, which we will refer to as the shock, is, by construction, that part of the deviation of current GNP from trend that cannot be predicted from past GNP. It is therefore serially uncorrelated. The standard deviation of the quarterly movements in GNP that cannot be predicted from past values is equal to 1% of GNP, which is large.

A useful way of seeing what equation (1) implies is to look at the moving average representation of the process, or equivalently to trace out the dynamic effects of a shock e on GNP over time. This is done in figure 1.6. The graph of the dynamic effects of a shock in e on output is hump shaped, increasing initially and eventually fading out. A shock has an effect on GNP that increases for three quarters and then decreases slowly over time. After 10 quarters, the effect is still 40% of the initial impact; after 20 quarters, all but 3% of the effect has disappeared.[11] The view that reversible cyclical fluctuations account for most of the short-term movements of real GNP and unemployment has been dominant for most of the last half century.

An Alternative Decomposition

The traditional approach proceeds on the assumption that the part of output that is due to permanent shocks is smooth. But this assumption has recently been challenged, most forcefully by Prescott (1986). There is no reason to

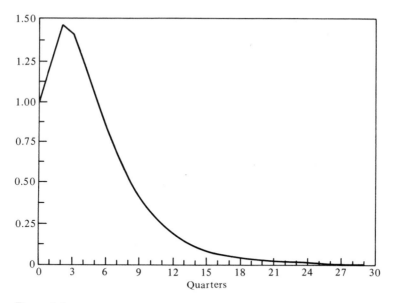

Figure 1.6
Dynamic response of GNP to a shock under the assumption of trend stationarity

believe, the argument goes, that productivity shocks, for example, lead to smooth growth in output; the process for productivity growth itself may not be smooth and may lead to fluctuations in output as well as in employment.

An extreme view along these lines is that all fluctuations are the results of the dynamic effects of permanent shocks, that actual and trend outputs are the same. Therefore, removing a deterministic or even a smooth trend from output makes no economic sense, and the output process must be thought of (and estimated as) a nonstationary process in which all shocks have permanent effects.[12]

Campbell and Mankiw (1987a), building on work by Nelson and Plosser (1982), have shown that the behavior of the logarithm of quarterly real GNP is well captured, for the postwar United States, by an ARIMA(1, 1, 2), which implies that the growth rate of output itself follows an ARMA(1, 2) process. Let Δy denote $y - y(-1)$, the change in the logarithm of real GNP and thus the growth rate. (Note that the growth rate is per quarter.) The ARIMA process, estimated over the same period as equation (1) is

$$\Delta y = c + 0.2\Delta y(-1) + e + 0.08e(-1) + 0.24e(-2), \qquad \sigma_e = 1\%, \qquad (2)$$

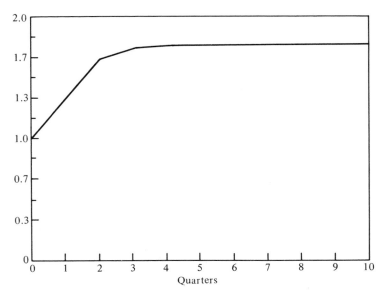

Figure 1.7
Dynamic response of GNP to a shock under the assumption of difference stationarity

where c, the drift term, is a positive constant, reflecting the fact that output growth is on average positive. Note that the standard error in equation (2) is roughly the same as that in (1).

The dynamic effect of a shock on output, an increase in e, is in this case presented in figure 1.7. By construction, shocks have permanent effects. This does not, however, a priori rule out dynamic effects that are larger in the short run than in the long run. But what emerges is a dynamic response of shocks that steadily increases through time: the effect on GNP of a shock of 1 in the first quarter builds up to reach 1.7 after four quarters, and remains equal to 1.7 permanently thereafter.

This approach leads to a very different description of movements in GNP. Movements in GNP result from the accumulation of shocks, each of which is on average positive (when the drift term is taken into account) and has large permanent effects on output. Slowdowns in growth result from small or even negative shocks, expansions from large positive ones. There is no sense in which recessions or expansions are temporary, no sense in which there are cyclical fluctuations.

Interpreting the Time Series Representations
Under the traditional decomposition, transitory shocks account for nearly all fluctuations in output. Under the alternative decomposition, permanent shocks account instead for all movements in output. What are we to conclude?

The first step may be to test which decomposition fits the data better. This has been done by Campbell and Mankiw (1987a), who have compared equation (2) to a deterministic-trend-plus-stationary-ARMA representation. They found that the data were unable to give a clear answer, that both representations gave approximately the same fit. But the problem is actually more serious than that. Equation (2) tells us that output is well represented by a nonstationary process; there are infinitely many ways of decomposing a nonstationary process as the sum of a nonstationary process (the trend) and a stationary process (the cycle). In particular, we can always decompose the series for output into a trend that is arbitrarily smooth and a stationary series.[13]

Where does this leave us? There is clearly no hope of making further progress by looking only at the behavior of output. But progress can be made by looking at other variables in addition to output and by assuming that different shocks affect them differently.[14] We now present one such decomposition that uses information from both unemployment and output.

The Stochastic Process of Output and Unemployment
Our approach is related to Okun's method of obtaining a time series for potential output. But rather than attempting to disentangle trend and cycle, we use the joint behavior of GNP and unemployment to try to disentangle the effects of permanent and transitory shocks.[15] We assume the presence of two types of shocks in the economy. The first type, transitory shocks, has no long-run effect on either output or the unemployment rate. The second type, permanent shocks, has a long-run effect on output but no long-run effect on the unemployment rate. This set of assumptions clearly implies that because neither type of shocks has a long-run effect on the unemployment rate, the unemployment rate is stationary, an assumption that appears consistent with the postwar evidence.[16] Under these assumptions, one can recover the time series for each type of shock and thus obtain the components of output and unemployment movements that are a result of permanent and transitory shocks, respectively.[17]

Figure 1.8 gives the two output series that would have obtained had there been no transitory or no permanent shocks. The top graph can be thought

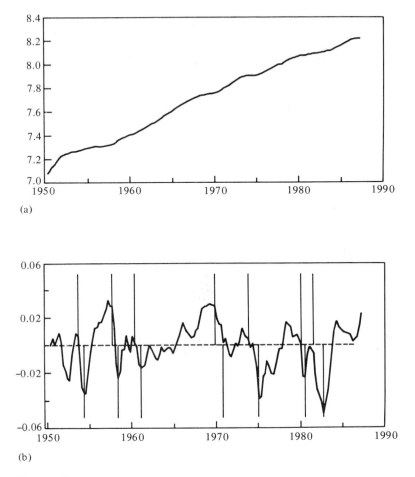

Figure 1.8
Output fluctuations: (a) due to permanent shocks; (b) due to transitory shocks

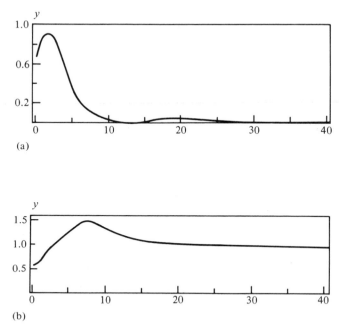

(a)

(b)

Figure 1.9
Moving average responses of output: (a) to transitory shocks; (b) to permanent shocks

of as the trend component, the bottom graph as the cyclical component of output. The moving average responses of output to each type of shock are presented in figure 1.9.

The picture that emerges from these figures is that of an economy in which both types of shocks play an important role. Transitory shocks matter and have a hump-shaped effect on output before their effects die out. But the path of output would be far from smooth even in the absence of those transitory shocks. What emerges is a more complex image of fluctuations than is implied by either of the two earlier decompositions, with temporary shocks moving output around a stochastic trend that itself contributes significantly to movements in real GNP.

We return in subsequent chapters to this characterization of the business cycle. Because the leading candidate as a cause of permanent shocks to the economy is changes in technical knowledge, we see the movements in output due to permanent shocks as evidence of the importance of movements in aggregate supply; because aggregate demand shocks (e.g., those caused by changes in the money stock in the face of imperfectly adjusting wages and prices) have largely transitory effects on output, we see the presence of temporary shocks as consistent with theories that emphasize the role of aggregate demand in the business cycle. The issue of the relative importance of aggregate demand and supply shocks in economic fluctuations is one of the recurrent themes of the book.

Comovements of GNP and Other Variables

The stylized facts of macroeconomic behavior extend beyond those of long-term growth and the dynamics of output and unemployment to the comovements of output and other variables. Both to set out the facts that need explanation, and to help discriminate among theories, we describe these comovements here.

Because researchers differ in the questions they want to answer and in the implicit theories that guide them through the data, there is a plethora of reported statistics on covariations in macroeconomic variables. We will draw on these results and compute our own set of statistics. These are correlations, at various leads and lags, of innovations obtained from estimation of univariate ARIMA processes for each series.[18] They have a simple interpretation. For example, a high positive contemporaneous correlation between innovations in consumption and innovations in GNP indicates that unexpected movements in GNP—that is, movements that cannot be predicted from past values of GNP—are usually associated with unexpected movements in consumption of the same sign.

Comovements in GNP and Its Components
Table 1.1 gives estimated ARIMA processes for the logarithms of GNP, consumption, fixed investment, and government spending and for the level of inventory investment.[19] It also reports the correlations between the innovations in GNP and the innovations in each component at lags -3 to $+3$.

Table 1.1 confirms that all components of spending move with output.[20] The contemporaneous correlation between innovations in GNP and each component is large and significant; correlations between innovations in GNP and innovations in each component one period later and one period earlier are smaller but also significant (except in one case). Correlations at other leads and lags are usually insignificant.

From the information in the table one can also compute the coefficient from a regression of the innovation in each component on the contem-

Table 1.1
Comovements in GNP and its components: correlations between innovations[a]

Innovations at time 0 in:	Innovations in GNP at time:[b]						
	-3	-2	-1	0	$+1$	$+2$	$+3$
Consumption[c]	-0.09	0.00	0.14	0.48	0.16	0.00	0.02
Fixed investment[d]	-0.01	0.03	0.10	0.52	0.16	0.01	-0.12
Government spending[e]	-0.01	0.13	0.15	0.23	-0.06	0.06	-0.01
Inventory investment[f]	0.00	0.07	0.21	0.57	-0.15	-0.03	0.06

a. Residuals from ARIMA processes for GNP and its components. Quarterly data, at annual rates, billions of 1982 dollars, from 1947-IV to 1987-II.
b. $\Delta y = 0.6 \times 10^{-2} + 0.24\Delta y(-1) + e + 0.08e(-1) + 0.24e(-2), s = 0.10 \times 10^{-1}$, where y is the logarithm of GNP and s is the estimated standard error of the innovation.
c. $\Delta c = 0.8 \times 10^{-2} + e + 0.02e(-1) + 0.24e(-2), s = 0.8 \times 10^{-2}$, where c is the logarithm of personal consumption expenditures.
d. $\Delta i_{\text{fix}} = 0.6 \times 10^{-2} + 0.31\Delta i_{\text{fix}}(-1) + e + 0.22e(-1), s = 0.25 \times 10^{-1}$, where i_{fix} is the logarithm of fixed investment.
e. $\Delta g = 0.3 \times 10^{-2} + 0.57\Delta g(-1) + e + 0.01e(-1) + 0.11e(-2), s = 0.18 \times 10^{-1}$, where g is the logarithm of government purchases of goods and services.
f. $\Delta i_{\text{inv}} = 0.28 - 0.14\Delta i_{\text{inv}}(-1) + e - 0.23e(-4), s = 15.7$, where i_{inv} is the level of inventory investment, with heteroscedasticity correction (divided by the estimated time trend of absolute value of first difference).

poraneous innovation in GNP.[21] Though one must be careful not to interpret such a regression as causal, the regression coefficient, which has the dimension of an elasticity, gives an idea of how much a particular component moves with GNP. The elasticity of consumption to GNP, so defined, is equal to 35%, and thus is much smaller than 1. The elasticity of fixed investment to GNP is equal to 1.2. Because inventory investment is in levels, it would make no sense to report the regression coefficient in that case. However, movements in inventory investment can be very large compared to those in GNP. In particular, recessions are usually accompanied by inventory disinvestment. In those periods after 1948 when GNP declines relative to a deterministic trend, the average share of the fall attributable to a decline in inventory investment is about 50%.[22]

The strong covariation of GNP and both consumption and investment is one of the best established facts characterizing economic fluctuations. It is this set of facts that led early on to the development of the multiplier-accelerator model of fluctuations. The positive covariation of inventory investment and GNP has proved harder—although, as we shall see, not impossible—to reconcile with demand-driven models of fluctuations: one would expect transitory increases in sales to come partly out of inventories and partly out of production, generating a negative correlation between inventory investment and sales.

Comovements in GNP and Relative Prices

Table 1.2 characterizes the comovements between output and relative prices. The first two are indexes of real wages in terms of consumption ("consumption wages" for short): hourly earnings in manufacturing and in the private sector, both deflated by the CPI. The third is a "product wage," with hourly earnings in manufacturing deflated by the price index relevant for firms, the PPI. The next two are the relative prices of crude fuels and of nonfuel-nonfood materials, deflated by the CPI. The sixth is an intertemporal price, the nominal interest rate, measured as the yield on three-month treasury bills. The last is a real interest rate, r, constructed as the yield on three-month treasury bills minus the one-period-ahead forecast of CPI inflation, itself obtained from ARMA estimation of the inflation process.

The table presents estimated ARIMA processes for the logarithms of the three real wages and the logarithms of the two relative prices. Because it is not clear whether the process for the nominal interest rate is stationary, we give the results of estimation of both ARMA and ARIMA processes for the nominal interest rate. The real rate is clearly stationary and is thus estimated by an ARMA model. We then report the correlations at lags $+3$ to -3 between the various innovations and innovations in the logarithm of GNP.

There is very little correlation at any lead or lag betwen economywide real wages and output, but there is a significant positive contemporaneous correlation between manufacturing wages and output. The correlation is stronger for the consumption wage than for the product wage. These two findings are representative of the results of the large amount of research on the cyclical behavior of consumption or product wages since Keynes' *General Theory*. The *General Theory* assumption that firms are always on the demand curve for labor implies, together with the assumption of decreasing returns to labor, a negative correlation between real wages and output or employment. It was soon found, in particular by Dunlop (1938), that real wages are, if anything, procyclical rather than countercyclical, and this led Keynes (1939) to doubt his own characterization of the transmission mechanism of demand shocks to output. This initial finding has been largely confirmed by subsequent research, at least for the United States, at the aggregate level (Sargent 1978; Kennan 1988), at the industry level (Bernanke and Powell 1986), and at the individual level, using panel data (Bils 1985).

Table 1.2
Comovements in GNP and relative prices: correlations between innovations[a]

Innovations at time 0 in:	Innovations in GNP at time:						
	−3	−2	−1	0	+1	+2	+3
Real consumption wage w[b]	−0.03	−0.02	−0.13	0.19	0.06	0.02	−0.03
Real consumption wage in manufacturing w_m[c]	0.06	0.09	−0.09	0.41	0.05	0.00	0.00
Real product wage in manufacturing w_{mp}[d]	0.12	−0.01	−0.09	0.26	0.11	−0.03	0.06
Relative price of crude fuel p_f[e]	−0.08	−0.02	−0.18	−0.04	−0.04	−0.13	−0.06
Relative price of nonfuel-nonfood materials p_{nf}[f]	−0.16	0.08	0.12	0.22	0.13	−0.02	−0.10
Nominal interest rate i							
Level[g]	0.00	0.15	0.13	0.14	−0.01	−0.30	−0.14
First differences[h]	0.00	0.17	0.17	0.18	0.02	−0.26	−0.12
Real interest rate r[i]	−0.03	−0.15	−0.10	0.04	0.11	−0.11	−0.01

a. Residuals from ARIMA processes as estimated for relative prices. Quarterly data, 1948-IV to 1987-II. See table 1.1 for estimated GNP process.

b. $\Delta w = 0.10 \times 10^{-2} + 0.66\Delta w(-1) + e - 0.19e(-1) + 0.27e(-3)$, $s = 0.48 \times 10^{-2}$, where w is the logarithm of average hourly earnings in the private sector corrected for overtime and interindustry shifts divided by the CPI.

c. $\Delta w_m = 0.10 \times 10^{-2} + 0.60\Delta w_m(-1) + e - 0.35e(-1)$, $s = 0.75 \times 10^{-2}$, where w_m is the logarithm of average hourly earnings in manufacturing, corrected for overtime and interindustry shifts, and divided by the CPI.

d. $\Delta w_{mp} = 0.20 \times 10^{-2} + 0.52\Delta w_{mp}(-1) + e - 0.26e(-1)$, $s = 0.98 \times 10^{-2}$, where w_{mp} is the logarithm of average hourly earnings in manufacturing corrected for overtime and interindustry shifts, divided by the producer price index (PPI) for finished goods in manufacturing.

e. $\Delta p_f = 0.57 \times 10^{-2} + 0.04\Delta p_f(-1) + e + 0.18e(-1) + 0.31e(-4)$, $s = 0.26 \times 10^{-1}$, where p_f is the logarithm of the producer price index for crude fuels divided by the CPI.

f. $\Delta p_{nf} = -0.13 \times 10^{-2} + 0.33\Delta p_{nf}(-1) + e + 0.25e(-1)$, $s = 0.31 \times 10^{-1}$, where p_{nf} is the logarithm of the producer price index for nonfuel-nonfood crude materials divided by the CPI.

g. $i = 0.30 + 0.67i(-1) + 0.03i(-2) + 0.24i(-3) + e + 0.63e(-1)$, $s = 0.75$, where i is the average yield on three-month Treasury bills.

h. $\Delta i = 0.04 - 0.22\Delta i(-1) - 0.26\Delta i(-2) + 0.09\Delta i(-3) + e + 0.57e(-1)$, $s = 0.74$.

i. $r = 0.61 - 0.17r(-1) + 0.36r(-2) + 0.44r(-3) + e + 0.63e(-1)$, $s = 2.06$, where r is the average yield on three-month Treasury bills minus the one period ahead forecast of CPI inflation based on an ARMA(1, 2) process.

The correlation between changes in real wages and changes in output or employment is usually slightly positive but often statistically insignificant.

There is a small but consistently negative correlation in table 1.2 between the price of crude fuel and GNP. This is consistent with the finding by Hamilton (1983) that there have been sharp rises in the price of crude oil before every post-World War II recession in the United States except in 1960. It is clear, in particular, that in both 1974 and 1980, major increases in oil prices were associated with sharp recessions in output. By contrast, nonfood-nonfuel prices are procyclical: cross correlations with GNP are small but mostly positive.

The behavior of both the nominal and the real interest rates is worth noting.[23] Nominal interest rate innovations are positively correlated with current and lagged GNP innovations but negatively correlated with GNP two to five quarters later (the table reports results only up to three quarters ahead). Under the assumption that money shocks are a major source of fluctuations, this set of correlations implies that if nominal interest rates play a major role in the transmission mechanism of money shocks to output, they do so with a lag of two or more quarters.[24] Due to the difficulties involved in constructing an expected inflation series, one must interpret the real interest rate results with caution; in any case they do not suggest any strong relation between real rates and GNP innovations.

Comovements of GNP and Nominal Variables
In table 1.3 we present the correlations between innovations in GNP and the innovations in price inflation measured by the rate of change of the CPI, wage inflation measured by the rate of change of the manufacturing wage, and money growth defined as the rate of growth of M1. Here again it is not clear whether price and wage inflation are themselves stationary (nominal wage and price levels surely are not). Thus correlations are reported using innovations from both ARMA and ARIMA estimations.

There is, perhaps surprisingly, little contemporaneous correlation between innovations in GNP and innovations in inflation. The only (marginally) significant correlation is between GNP innovations and inflation one quarter later. The contemporaneous correlation between innovations in wage inflation and GNP is, however, positive and significant: it is this correlation that underlies the Phillips curve, which plays a central role in theories of the business cycle that allow aggregate demand disturbances to affect output.

Money growth exhibits less serial correlation than either wage or price inflation. Innovations in money growth are positively contemporaneously correlated with innovations in GNP. That correlation—as well as the wealth

Table 1.3
Comovements in GNP and nominal variables: correlations between innovations from ARIMA processes[a]

Innovations at time 0 in:	Innovations in GNP at time:						
	−3	−2	−1	0	+1	+2	+3
Price inflation							
π Level[b]	0.05	0.02	0.19	−0.06	−0.03	−0.09	−0.06
First differences[c]	0.07	0.04	0.23	0.00	0.02	0.03	0.03
Wage inflation							
w Level[d]	0.05	0.12	−0.06	0.38	−0.04	−0.13	−0.07
First differences[e]	0.09	0.19	−0.03	0.39	−0.03	−0.13	−0.10
Money growth $m_1{}^d$	0.14	0.02	−0.09	0.26	0.14	0.11	−0.12

a. All variables at annual rates. See table 1.1 for estimated GNP process.
b. $\pi = 0.10 \times 10^{-2} + 0.89\pi(-1) + e - 0.06e(-1) - 0.26e(-2)$, $s = 0.5 \times 10^{-2}$, where π is the rate of change of the CPI.
c. $\Delta\pi = -0.7 \times 10^{-4} + e - 0.06e(-1) - 0.31e(-2) + 0.37e(-3)$, $s = 0.5 \times 10^{-2}$.
d. $w = 0.27 \times 10^{-2} + 0.8w(-1) + e - 0.44e(-1) + 0.03e(-2)$, $s = 0.5 \times 10^{-2}$, where w is the rate of change of the manufacturing wage.
e. $\Delta w = -0.10 \times 10^{-3} + e - 0.62e(-1) - 0.13e(-2)$, $s = 0.5 \times 10^{-2}$.
f. $m = 0.47 \times 10^{-2} + 0.55m(-1) + e - 0.11e(-1)$, $s = 0.75 \times 10^{-2}$, where m is the rate of growth of nominal M1.

of qualitative and other quantitative evidence to the same effect accumulated in particular by Friedman and Schwartz (1963)—has led to wide acceptance of the view that movements in money can have large effects on output. The recent evidence from the disinflations of the 1980s, both in the United States and abroad, has also convinced many that sharp contractions in money lead to sharp contractions in output.[25] The positive correlation between money growth and output innovations must, however, be juxtaposed with the positive contemporaneous correlation between short nominal rates and innovations in GNP presented above. If money is the major source of fluctuations in GNP, then its contemporaneous effect on GNP cannot be explained through interest rates.[26]

This concludes our first pass at the facts. The reader should remember the major correlations and conclude that no simple monocausal theory can easily explain them. Equilibrium theories based on supply shocks have to confront the weak correlations between real wages and GNP, as well as the positive relation between nominal variables and activity. Theories in which the cycle is driven by demand shocks have to give convincing explanations for the behavior of real wages. Theories that emphasize money shocks have to confront the correlations among interest rates, money, and output.

1.2 An Overview of the Book

Our theoretical starting points are the two basic real models that provide the frameworks for most optimizing models in macroeconomics: the Ramsey model in chapter 2 and the overlapping generations model in chapter 3.

In chapter 2 we analyze an economy where there is no uncertainty, people are infinitely lived, firms maximize their value, all markets are competitive and clear instantaneously, and there is no money. This perfectly operating economy provides a benchmark with which to compare other economies whose behavior is based on alternative assumptions.

We start the chapter by studying the optimal allocation of resources, the optimal consumption and investment decisions that would be chosen by a central planner maximizing the utility of the representative individual in the model (a problem first analyzed by Ramsey 1928). We then show the equivalence of this central planning allocation to that implied by a competitive economy in which individuals make optimal consumption and investment decisions based on the sequences of current and anticipated market-clearing wage and interest rates. This equivalence is hardly surprising, given our assumptions, but it turns out nevertheless to be very useful: it is often much simpler to solve the central planning problem directly rather than to solve for the equilibrium of the decentralized economy.

The Ramsey model is more than a benchmark. We show its usefulness by characterizing the equilibrium of a small open economy that has access to international capital markets in which it can borrow and lend at the world interest rate; we proceed to describe the optimal dynamic responses of saving, investment, and the current account to adverse supply shocks.

In chapter 3 we focus again on the dynamics of saving, investment, and capital accumulation, this time taking into account the fact that people are less than infinitely lived and that they may not care about what happens after they die. We develop two models. The first is a discrete time model, the overlapping generations model of Diamond (1965), in which people live for two periods, and the second a continuous time model, developed by Blanchard (1985), in which people face a constant probability of death.

We study the issue of dynamic efficiency, whether it is possible for such an economy to accumulate too much capital. We then turn to how government policies, including deficit-financed fiscal policy and the introduction of social security, affect capital accumulation and welfare. We examine the issue of the elasticity of saving with respect to the interest rate. In addition we discuss a question raised by Barro (1974), whether the fact that parents care for their children makes the economy behave like the infinite horizon Ramsey economy described in chapter 2.

Money is introduced in chapter 4. We consider a variety of approaches but spend a good part of the chapter developing a model, due to David Romer (1986), that extends to general equilibrium the Baumol-Tobin approach to the demand for cash balances. In that economy people have to use money to buy goods and thus have to keep money in addition to interest-paying bonds; we trace the flow of transactions through the economy and characterize the equilibrium and the effects of money and inflation on the real equilibrium. We then study, in a simpler version of the Romer model and in an earlier model developed by Sidrauski (1967), the dynamic effects of changes in money growth on real variables when all markets are competitive and prices perfectly flexible. We conclude that the real effects of changes in money growth are unlikely to be large if prices are perfectly flexible.

Issues of nonuniqueness are swept under the rug at various points in the first three chapters, either by assumption or by relegating them to discrete notes at the end of each chapter. Chapter 5 returns to the nonuniqueness issue. One type of nonuniqueness that arises in dynamic models with rational expectations is associated with bubbles, cases in which variables differ from their fundamental values. Well-known examples include bubbles on asset prices such as stocks, whereby the price is high because it is expected to increase further, and indeed does increase, validating initial expectations. We discuss, in a partial equilibrium framework, the circumstances under which such bubbles can arise and the form they may take. Then, following work by Tirole (1985) and Weil (1987), we discuss when and how general equilibrium considerations allow us to rule out such bubbles; the conditions turn out to be closely related to the conditions for dynamic efficiency discussed in chapter 3.

We then examine other issues that arise from nonlinearities. Among these the most interesting is that of deterministic cycles, explored by Grandmont (1985). We present this possibility and explain why we do not think that it provides convincing foundations for a theory of macroeconomic fluctuations.

Moving to fluctuations, we introduce stochastic shocks and uncertainty in the economy in chapter 6. Following the early lead of Slutsky (1937) and Frisch (1933), fluctuations are analyzed in terms of impulses (or shocks) and propagation mechanisms. Throughout the rest of the book we allow for uncorrelated (and unexplained) shocks to tastes, technology, nominal money, government behavior, and the like, and trace out their dynamic effects on the main macroeconomic variables. The ultimate goal is to find a plausible set of shocks and propagation mechanisms that can explain actual fluctuations.

In chapter 6 we examine, within a partial equilibrium context, consumption, investment, and production-inventory decisions. Our intention in each case is to show the effects of uncertainty on behavior and the dynamic effects of different types of shocks.

In chapter 7 we examine the dynamic effects of shocks in the general equilibrium real models developed in chapters 2 and 3. In doing so, we are studying real equilibrium business cycle models, which have been advocated in particular by Prescott (1986). We consider Diamond- and Ramsey-like models with technological shocks and study the behavior of output, consumption, fixed investment, and inventory investment. We show that such models can easily explain the joint behavior of output and its components as dynamic responses to plausible processes for productivity. However, the approach runs into severe difficulties in explaining the behavior of employment, even when the models are extended to allow for decentralized labor markets and search. These difficulties stem largely, and not surprisingly, from the inability to explain the joint behavior of output, employment, and real wages characterized earlier in this chapter.

At the end of chapter 7 we extend the equilibrium business cycle approach to models with money in which imperfect information about nominal magnitudes provides a potential channel for aggregate demand shocks to affect output, along the lines of Lucas (1973). We conclude that such an extension does not provide a convincing explanation of the effects of demand shocks on output.

In chapter 8 we explore the Keynesian approach, based on the view that suppliers are slow to adjust prices and wages and that supply accommodates long-lasting movements in aggregate demand.[27] In the 1970s the disequilibrium approach was to study the implications of slowly adjusting prices and wages, taking such slow adjustment as both given and unexplained. This strategy has run out of steam, making it clear that to make progress, the behavior of prices and quantities must be simultaneously explained.

The chapter starts by exploring the old notion that coordination problems are in large part responsible for economic fluctuations. Constructing a general equilibrium model of monopolistic competition, we show that the social return to price adjustment exceeds the private return and that small costs of price adjustment can therefore lead to large fluctuations of output, an argument first formalized by Akerlof and Yellen (1985) and Mankiw (1985). We then show that the larger the proportion of price-setters who do not adjust, the smaller is the private cost of not adjusting for those remaining; we also explore the possibility of multiple equilibria.

We then extend the analysis to a dynamic economy in which price-setters change prices infrequently. We study the choice of price rules and the macroeconomic implications of such rules. Three well-known models along those lines are the models developed by Fischer (1977), Taylor (1979), and Caplin and Spulber (1987); we show how and when they can generate persistent effects of aggregate demand on output and how results can be quite different under alternative price rules.

Although this approach must be part of any model that explains effects of aggregate demand on output, we conclude, however, that it cannot by itself explain such effects. Put simply, if fluctuations are associated with unemployment and if the unemployed are worse off than those with jobs, small costs of decreasing nominal wages do not provide a convincing explanation of why the unemployed do not bid down nominal wages.

This leads us, in chapter 9, to examine the potential role of further imperfections in goods, labor, and credit markets. Throughout, the focus is on macroeconomic implications, in particular, on why unemployment may not lead to a decrease in wages given prices and why in goods markets firms may prefer to satisfy demand at a constant markup of prices over wages, even in the presence of increasing marginal cost. In each case we draw the main implications from the imperfection and show its aggregate implications within a macroeconomic model, with or without nominal rigidities.

In examining labor markets, we explore three separate directions of research. The first is whether the presence of contracts modifies the behavior of real wages and employment, in particular, whether the provision of insurance under imperfect information may lead to real wage rigidity and larger employment fluctuations. The second is whether the ability of some workers to organize formally (in unions) or informally can also lead to more real wage rigidity and larger or more persistent employment fluctuations. The third covers efficiency wage theories, which have in common the implication that the productivity of labor depends on the wage or the relative wage paid by the firm. We conclude that both the second and third avenues hold promise for explaining real wage rigidity in the face of movements in unemployment.

We then turn to goods markets. There we explore theories based on imperfect competition, which have in common that firms are sometimes willing to supply higher output at approximately constant markups. We also explore the possibility that if marginal costs decrease with the level of activity, the economy may have multiple equilibria; we analyze two models along these lines, one based on trading externalities, the other based on increasing returns to scale. Finally, we turn to credit markets. If, as is obviously often the case, loans are risky and the characteristics of borrowers are not known, credit markets may be characterized by moral hazard and adverse selection. Changes in credit conditions may take place without changes in interest rates; we show how, in the presence of nominal rigidities or in some cases even in the absence of such rigidities, monetary policy can affect activity but have little effect on interest rates.

Although chapter 9 takes us to the frontiers of current research, it does not leave us with a single unified framework in which we an analyze all questions in macroeconomics. Thus for the time being, and probably forever, we have to rely on a variety of models to analyze current issues and current policies. Chapter 10 presents such a battery of models and shows how each can be used to shed light on current events.

Some of the models are or can be derived from first principles. Among these is the model of asset pricing developed by Lucas (1978), which can be used, for example, to analyze why stocks pay on average more than bonds or how the term structure of interest rates should behave under different sources of shocks. But most of the models are not derived from first principles. These include (1) the money demand model of Cagan (1956), which, supplemented by a government budget constraint, allows a simple analysis of the interaction between fiscal policy and inflation, (2) the IS-LM model, which can be used to analyze the effects of current as well as anticipated policies in the presence of price rigidities, (3) the Mundell-Fleming-Dornbusch model, which can be used to look at the same issues in an open economy, and (4) the aggregate supply–aggregate demand model, along the lines of Taylor (1979) and Layard and Nickell (1986). Whether the shortcuts that underlie these models are acceptable or misleading is for current and future research to decide. They have all repeatedly proved useful in allowing macroeconomists to think about complex events in an organized way.

Our approach to the analysis of policy in chapter 11 is similarly pragmatic. We cannot wait for "the true model" to give policy advice. Similarly, we cannot recommend that, because of our ignorance, policy be inactive: Is it inactive fiscal policy to raise tax rates in recessions so as to balance the budget or to leave tax rates unchanged and run countercyclical deficits? Using the models developed earlier in the book, we consider in turn issues of monetary and fiscal policy, and then the more general issue of dynamic inconsistency which was first raised by Kydland and Prescott (1977).

Our discussion of monetary policy takes place mostly within sticky price models in which money can have strong effects on output. Taking this as a given, we analyze first the consequences for the inflation rate and the price level of alternative operating rules for monetary policy, such as fixed money growth or a fixed nominal interest rate. We examine particularly the question of whether accommodating policies may render the price level or inflation rate indeterminate and what that might mean. We then turn to issues associated with the active use of policy, in the absence of either complete current information or exact knowledge of the structure of the economy, to ask whether the best practicable policy is one of keeping the growth rate of money constant.

Fiscal policy, such as changes in the level of taxes, is likely to have real effects even in equilibrium models. Because the fiscal policy questions in sticky price models are not very different from the monetary policy issues, we study fiscal policy mainly in equilibrium models. We focus, in particular, on the issue of whether the government should try to balance the budget or run, instead, countercyclical deficits when it has only distortionary taxes at its disposal.

Finally, we turn to issues of dynamic consistency. If private actions depend on expectations of future policies, the government typically has an incentive to announce policies but, when the time comes, to follow others. We present the structure of the argument and then analyze the role of reputation and other devices in alleviating the problem. We conclude by assessing the empirical relevance and policy implications of the dynamic consistency issue.

1.3 Prelude

We end this introductory chapter with a description of our goals in writing this book and our approach to macroeconomics, and of the prerequisites for assimilating its contents.

On Contents

As should be clear from the guided tour, we have not written a treatise nor presented a unified view of the field. That was possible when Patinkin wrote *Money, Interest and Prices*, which integrated the Keynesian revolution into macroeconomics while pointing to future developments. But the field is now too large and too fragmented. The Keynesian framework embodied in the "neoclassical synthesis," which dominated the field until the mid-

1970s, is in theoretical crisis, searching for microfoundations; no new theory has emerged to dominate the field, and the time is one of explorations in several directions with the unity of the field apparent mainly in the set of questions being studied.

That macroeconomics is in crisis should not be taken to mean that the field is starting from scratch. Indeed, we hope to show that there is much known and even much agreed on. We do believe that there now exists a useful macroeconomics. At the same time neither the microfoundations nor the evidence is strong enough for any reasonable researcher to feel at ease. The questions that macroeconomics tries to answer are inherently difficult ones; the fact that modern approaches can be defined as the study of dynamic general equilibrium under uncertainty, with incomplete (and possibly imperfect) markets gives a flavor of that difficulty. We believe that macroeconomics is at one of its most creative and productive stages, and we try to reflect that sense of excitement.

That we present alternative theories as honestly as we can does not imply that we are theoretical wimps. We believe that most (not all) current theories do capture important aspects of reality; we do not believe in monocausal or monodistortion accounts of fluctuations. We believe that eclecticism in the pursuit of truth is no crime; we are sure, however, that our preferences, which are obviously reflected in our own research, will be clear to the careful reader.

On Our Approach

One of our main choices has been to start from a neoclassical benchmark, with optimizing individuals and competitive markets. As our guided tour indicates, this is not because we believe that such a benchmark describes reality or can account for fluctuations. We are sure that incomplete markets and imperfect competition are needed to account for the main characteristics of actual fluctuations. We also believe that such nonneoclassical constructs as bounded rationality (in the discussion of the existence of bubbles) or interdependent utility functions (in some versions of efficiency wage theories) may be needed to understand important aspects of financial and labor markets. We believe, however, that looking at their effects as arising from deviations from a well-understood benchmark is the best research strategy.[28] Alternative strategies that have started squarely from a different benchmark have for the most part proved unsuccessful.

If and when one specific deviation from the benchmark model appears to be an essential ingredient of any macroeconomic theory, an alternative model may arise as a benchmark for macroeconomics.[29] If, for example, imperfect competition and increasing returns turn out to be essential, much of what is in chapters 2 and 3, such as the process of capital accumulation and growth or the form of the golden rule, will need to be reconsidered.[30] We are not there yet.

Our neoclassical bent does not extend to thinking that the only valid macroeconomic models are those explicitly based on maximization. The models presented in chapter 10 make this point. We are aware of the danger of shortcuts, which can prove in the end to have been highly misleading: the crisis of Keynesian economics comes precisely from having used such shortcuts for too long. However, we believe that waiting for a model based on first principles before being willing to analyze current events and give policy advice is a harmful utopia that leaves the real world to the charlatans rather than to those who recognize the uncertainties of our current knowledge. Thus we see no alternative to using shortcuts, at least for the time being and probably forever.

For lack of space and because this would require more knowledge of econometrics than we want to assume, we do not present much formal empirical work. Such work, and the integration of theory and empirical work, is nonetheless essential to macroeconomics, defined as the field that analyzes and tries to understand economywide movements in output, employment, and prices. The integration of empirical and theoretical work on fluctuations, through the common use of the impulse-propagation mechanism framework and its associated time series implications, is certainly one of the most important achievements of postwar macroeconomics.

Finally, and despite first impressions to the contrary, we have for lack of space left out topics that we would have liked to cover. We will mention three.

The first, which we touched on earlier in this chapter, is that of productivity growth and productivity movements. Although most of the increase in our standard of living comes from productivity growth, we are remarkably ignorant about its determinants, about why it differs across time and across countries. Recent real business cycle models rely on productivity shocks to generate dynamics, but we have little direct evidence on such shocks and how they propagate. Recent work on increasing returns has looked at such issues in a novel way and would be included in a longer book.

The second is that of asset pricing. Many theoretical developments have taken place—such as the development of the consumption asset-pricing model—that have clarified the link between macroeconomics and finance.

Given our primary focus on macroeconomic fluctuations, we have for the most part omitted them, except for a brief presentation in chapter 10.[31]

The third is open economy macroeconomics. It is common to note that all major economies, including the United States, are now open to trade in both goods and assets markets. Although we present some open economy models and issues, in chapter 2 and again in chapter 10, we have made no attempt to give a complete review of the issues within an open economy.[32]

On the Prerequisites

This book has evolved from lectures to graduate students specializing in macroeconomics at both Harvard and MIT. This roughly defines the level of the book. It requires some maturity in macroeconomics so that, for example, a thorough understanding of the issues at the level of the Dornbusch and Fischer textbook (1987) is a strict minimum. Several chapters can be used in a first-year graduate course, but we do not think that the book should be used as a textbook in such courses. We would and do build a first-year course differently, going earlier to the models of chapter 10 to provide motivation for what macroeconomics is in the end about. We think of the book as a textbook for students specializing in the field and as a reference book for researchers.

We have tried throughout to deemphasize techniques in favor of intuition. Nevertheless, most of the arguments are formal, and the book assumes a number of specific prerequisites.[33] Knowledge of calculus and some basic knowledge of calculus of variations are essential. Basic knowledge of statistics (distributions, conditional distributions, commonly used distributions, Bayes' rule) is required. Basic knowledge of time series, essentially ARIMA models, is useful. Other techniques are introduced when needed; we present them briefly, together with references to more thorough treatments.

Notes

1. Maddison (1982) reviews the historical record, for some countries since 1700, for most of the members of the OECD.

2. We limit ourselves to the United States, but the features we emphasize are common to developed economies. The earliest starting year for consistent data for both GNP and the various measures of inputs is 1874 (actually the average of the decade 1869–1878).

3. Annual data for the series presented in figures 1.2 to 1.4 are available only from 1889. Estimates are available for 1874 and 1884.

4. Although labor productivity growth appears roughly constant over the specified periods, there are of course substantial variations over shorter periods. For instance, output per hour grew 2.7% per year from 1950 to 1973 and only 0.9% per year from 1973 to 1986.

5. If one believes, however, that part of growth comes from the exploitation of returns to scale and that markets may not be competitive, the Solow residual is no longer the correct measure of that part of growth that does not come from growth of inputs. Denison (1974) in his calculations of the sources of growth assumed that the production function exhibited scale economies of 10%; that is, an increase in all inputs by 100% would increase output by 110%. Denison recognized that there was no firm statistical basis for this estimate, but he did review earlier studies of the issue. For two recent approaches, see Hall (1986) and Romer (1987).

6. Note, however, the large increase in the output-capital ratio during 1933 to 1945. Part of the increase appears to come from undermeasurement of investment during the war (Gordon 1969). Part of the increase appears genuine, however, suggesting a step change in the output-capital ratio pre-1930 and post-1945.

7. Nevertheless, what follows touches on many conceptual and technical issues, to which we will return more formally and more precisely later. All that is needed to follow the basic argument is some knowledge of time series, in particular of ARMA and ARIMA processes. A good introduction, sufficient for those purposes, is given in Pindyck and Rubinfeld (1981).

8. Recent work has returned to exploring those aspects. See, for example, Neftci (1984) and DeLong and Summers (1986) on asymmetries, and Stock (1987) on time deformation.

9. This is, for example, the approach taken by Prescott (1986).

10. See, for example, Perloff and Wachter (1979) and Gordon (1984).

11. The discussion in the text proceeds as if there was only one type of shock affecting output. This is surely not the case. There are likely to be many types of shocks, each of them with a different dynamic effect on GNP. We can think of the moving average representation given in figure 1.6 as being roughly a weighted average of the dynamic responses of GNP to each of those shocks, with the weights being proportional to the relative importance of the shocks. See Granger and Morris (1976) for a more formal discussion of the relation between univariate and multivariate moving average representations.

12. By nonstationary processes we mean processes with a unit root. These processes are such that shocks have a permanent but bounded effect on output.

13. By arbitrarily smooth we mean a process such that the variance of the shock is arbitrarily small. We know of no simple reference for this result. Although a proof would take us too far afield, the intuition behind the result is a simple one for readers

with some background in time series: though the nonstationary component has to account for all fluctuations in output at zero frequency, we can attribute all fluctuations in output at positive frequencies to the stationary component. In this way we can make the nonstationary component, the trend, arbitrarily smooth.

14. The NBER itself bases the dating of cycles on the behavior of many series—in contradiction to the widely held view that a recession is defined by two consecutive quarters of decline in real GNP.

15. The methodology follows Blanchard and Quah (1987). Other related decompositions of the behavior of output have been given by Evans (1987) and Campbell and Mankiw (1987b).

16. The evidence is less clear-cut than this sentence may suggest. Over the postwar period, unemployment has trended upward slowly. So we cannot think of the unemployment rate as stationary around a constant mean. If we look at longer time periods and at evidence from other countries, the unemployment rate seems sometimes to remain very high or very low for long periods of time. This is suggestive of some form of nonstationarity. We return to this issue later in the book.

17. Explaining how this is done would take us too far afield. See Blanchard and Quah (1987).

18. These correlations are not very sensitive to whether an ARIMA process is fitted to the original series or whether an ARMA process is fitted to deviations from a smooth trend, for example, an exponential trend. There is a close relation between the correlations presented here and the results of Granger-Sims causality tests, popularized by Sims (1972) and often used to describe the joint behavior of time series: a variable x will Granger-cause variable y if the set of correlations between current innovations in y and lagged innovations in x is significant.

19. We cannot take the logarithm of inventory investment because the series is sometimes negative. The innovations for inventory investment are from a process estimated in levels, with a heteroscedasticity correction.

20. Since output is the sum of its components, it should come as no surprise that the average contemporaneous correlation is positive in table 1.1.

21. The regression coefficient is equal to the correlation coefficient multiplied by the ratio of the standard deviation of the innovation in the specific component to the standard deviation of the innovation in GNP.

22. The data are presented in Dornbusch and Fischer (1987). The percentage is even higher (68%) if one calculates inventory disinvestment as a percentage of the peak to trough decline in GNP (Blinder and Holtz-Eakin 1986).

23. The process for the nominal interest rate exhibits substantial subsample instability. In particular, it appears to be sharply different in the 1980s. Thus the estimated process is at best an average process.

24. The joint behavior of nominal interest rates, nominal money, and output has been examined within the framework of vector autoregressions by Sims (1980) and Litterman and Weiss (1985). Both studies find that given nominal money, there is a positive correlation between innovations in interest rates and future innovations in GNP. What theories this finding rules out is still unclear, however.

25. The quantitative evidence on the role of money growth in the 1980s U.S. disinflation is, however, less than conclusive. Although the 1982 recession was preceded by a period of very low money growth, money grew faster on average in the eighties than earlier. The major sign of monetary tightness preceding the recession was very high nominal interest rates. Thus one must argue that these episodes were associated with shifts in money demand. Although such arguments are reasonable, they cannot be supported by looking only at money growth-output correlations.

26. There is a limit to what can be learned from simple bivariate correlations. If, for example, the economy is well described by the Keynesian model, and if fiscal and monetary shocks are roughly of equal importance in affecting output, the correlation between innovations in interest rates and output may well be close to zero. This zero correlation does not imply that money does not affect output, only that there are two types of shocks in that economy, with opposite effects on interest rates.

27. Although we call the approach Keynesian, it long predates Keynes. Monetarists have emphasized the slow adjustment of wages and prices to monetary shocks.

28. The same point is made by Solow in his American Economic Association presidential address (1980).

29. Stiglitz and Weiss (1987) argue for a new benchmark model based on imperfect information about buyers' and sellers' characteristics.

30. See, for example, Romer (1987) for how increasing returns and monopolistic competition may modify the "neoclassical" theory of growth.

31. Sargent (1987) has an extensive discussion of asset pricing.

32. This is done masterfully in Dornbusch (1988).

33. It is traditional at this stage to claim that nothing more is needed than high school algebra, but that would not be right.

References

Akerlof, George, and Janet Yellen (1985). "A Near Rational Model of the Business Cycle with Price and Wage Inertia." *Quarterly Journal of Economics* 100, supplement, 176–213.

Barro, Robert (1974). "Are Government Bonds Net Wealth?" *Journal of Political Economy* 81, 6 (Dec.), 1095–1117.

Bernanke, Ben, and James Powell (1986). "The Cyclical Behavior of Industrial Labor Markets: A Comparison of the Prewar and Postwar Eras." In Robert Gordon (ed.), *The American Business Cycle: Continuity and Change*. NBER and University of Chicago Press, 583–621.

Bils, Mark (1985). "Real Wages over the Business Cycle: Evidence from Panel Data." *Journal of Political Economy* 93, 4 (Aug.), 666–689.

Blanchard, Olivier (1985). "Debt, Deficits and Finite Horizons." *Journal of Political Economy* 93, 2 (April), 223–247.

Blanchard, Olivier, and Danny Quah (1987). "The Dynamic Effects of Aggregate Demand and Supply Shocks." MIT Working Paper. September.

Blinder, Alan, and Douglas Holtz-Eakin (1986). "Inventory Fluctuations in the United States Since 1929." In Robert Gordon (ed.), *The American Business Cycle: Continuity and Change*. NBER and University of Chicago Press, 183–214.

Burns, Arthur, and Wesley C. Mitchell (1946). *Measuring Business Cycles*. New York: National Bureau of Economic Research.

Cagan, Philip (1956). "The Monetary Dynamics of Hyperinflation." Reprinted in Milton Friedman (ed.), *Studies in the Quantity Theory of Money*. University of Chicago Press.

Campbell, John, and N. Gregory Mankiw (1987a). "Are Output Fluctuations Transitory?" *Quarterly Journal of Economics* 102, 4 (Nov.), 857–880.

Campbell, John, and N. Gregory Mankiw (1987b). "Permanent and Transitory Components in Macroeconomic Fluctuations." *American Economic Review* (May), 111–117.

Caplin, Andrew, and Daniel Spulber (1987). "Menu Costs and the Neutrality of Money." *Quarterly Journal of Economics* 102, 4 (Nov.), 703–726.

Darby, Michael (1976). "Three-and-a-half Million U.S. Employees Have Been Mislaid. Or, an Explanation of Unemployment 1934–1941." *Journal of Political Economy* 84, 1 (Feb.), 1–16.

DeLong, Brad, and Lawrence H. Summers (1986). "Are Business Cycles Symmetrical?" In Robert Gordon (ed.), *The American Business Cycle*." University of Chicago Press, 166–179.

Denison, Edward F. (1974). *Accounting for United States Economic Growth 1929–1969*. Washington, DC: Brookings Institution.

Diamond, Peter (1965). "National Debt in a Neoclassical Growth Model." *American Economic Review* 55 (Dec.), 1126–1150.

Dornbusch, Rudiger (1988). *Open Economy Macroeconomics*, 2d ed. New York: Basic Books.

Dornbusch, Rudiger, and Stanley Fischer (1987). *Macroeconomics*, 4th ed. New York: McGraw-Hill.

Dunlop, John (1938). "The Movement of Real and Money Wages." *Economic Journal*, 413–434.

Evans, George (1987). "Output and Unemployment in the United States." Mimeo. Stanford University.

Fischer, Stanley (1977). "Long Term Contracts, Rational Expectations and the Optimal Money Supply." *Journal of Political Economy* 85, 1 (Feb.), 191–206.

Friedman, Milton, and Anna J. Schwartz (1963). *A Monetary History of the United States, 1867–1960*. Princeton University Press.

Frisch, Ragnar (1933). "Propagation and Impulse Problems in Dynamic Economics." In *Economic Essays in Honor of Gustav Cassel*. London: Allen and Unwin, 171–205.

Gordon, Robert J. (1969). "45 Billion Dollars of U.S. Private Investment Have Been Mislaid." *American Economic Review* 59, (June), 221–238.

Gordon, Robert J. (1984). "Unemployment and Potential Output in the 1980s." *Brookings Papers on Economic Activity* 2, 537–564.

Grandmont, Jean Michel (1985). "On Endogenous Competitive Business Cycles." *Econometrica* 53, 5 (Sept.), 995–1046.

Granger, Clive W., and M. J. Morris (1976). "Time Series Modeling and Interpretation." *Journal of the Royal Society* 139, part 2, 246–257.

Hall, Robert E. (1986). "Productivity and the Business Cycle." Hoover Institute Working Paper. November.

Hamilton, James D. (1983). "Oil and the Macroeconomy since World War II." *Journal of Political Economy* 91, 2 (April), 228–248.

Kennan, John (1988). "Equilibrium Interpretations of Employment and Real Wage Fluctuations." *NBER Macroeconomics Annual*, forthcoming.

Keynes, John Maynard (1939). "Relative Movements in Real Wages and Output." *Economic Journal*, 34–51.

Kydland, Finn, and Edward Prescott (1977). "Rules Rather Than Discretion: The Inconsistency of Optimal Plans." *Journal of Political Economy* 85, 3 (June), 473–492.

Layard, Richard, and Steve Nickell (1986). "The Performance of the British Labour Market." London School of Economics. Mimeo. May.

Litterman, Robert, and Lawrence Weiss (1985). "Money, Real Interest Rates and Output: A Reinterpretation of Postwar U.S. Data." *Econometrica* 53, 1 (Jan.), 129–156.

Lucas, Robert E. (1973). "Some International Evidence on Output-Inflation Trade-offs." *American Economic Review* 63 (June), 326–334.

Lucas, Robert E. (1978). "Asset Prices in an Exchange Economy." *Econometrica* 46, 1429–1445.

Maddison, Angus (1982). *Phases of Capitalist Development*. Oxford University Press.

Mankiw, N. Gregory (1985). "Small Menu Costs and Large Business Cycles: A Macroeconomic Model of Monopoly." *Quarterly Journal of Economics* 100, 2 (May), 529–539.

Neftci, Salih N. (1984). "Are Economic Times Series Asymmetric over the Business Cycle?" *Journal of Political Economy* 92, 307–328.

Nelson, Charles, and Charles Plosser (1982). "Trends and Random Walks in Macro-economic Time Series." *Journal of Monetary Economics* 10 (Sept.), 139–162.

Okun, Arthur M. (1962). "Potential GNP: Its Measurement and Significance." Reprinted in J. Pechman (ed.), *Economics for Policymaking*. Cambridge, MA: MIT Press, 1983.

Patinkin, Don (1965). *Money, Interest and Prices*. 2d ed. New York: Harper and Row.

Perloff, Jeffrey, and Michael Wachter (1979). "A Production Function, Nonaccele-rating Inflation Approach to Potential Output." In K. Brunner and A. Meltzer (eds.), *Three Aspects of Policy and Policymaking: Knowledge, Data and Institutions*. Volume 10. Carnegie-Rochester Conference Series.

Pindyck, Robert S., and Daniel L. Rubinfeld (1981). *Econometric Models and Economic Forecasts*. New York: McGraw-Hill.

Poterba, James, and Lawrence Summers (1987). "Mean Reversion in Stock Prices: Evidence and Implications." NBER Working Paper 2343.

Prescott, Edward (1986). "Theory Ahead of Business Cycle Measurement." *Federal Reserve Bank of Minneapolis Quarterly Review* 10, 4 (Fall).

Ramsey, Frank (1928). "A Mathematical Theory of Saving." *Economic Journal* 38, 152 (Dec.), 543–559. Reprinted in Joseph Stiglitz and Hirofumi Uzawa (eds.), *Readings in the Modern Theory of Economic Growth*. Cambridge: MIT Press, 1969.

Romer, Christina (1986a). "Spurious Volatility in Historical Unemployment Data." *Journal of Political Economy* 94 (Feb.), 1–37.

Romer, Christina (1986b). "The Prewar Business Cycle Reconsidered: New Estimates of Gross National Product, 1869–1918." NBER Working Paper 1969. July.

Romer, Christina (1987). "Gross National product, 1909–1928: Existing Estimates, New Estimates and New Interpretations of World War I and Its Aftermath." NBER Working Paper 2187.

Romer, David (1986). "A General Equilibrium Version of the Baumol-Tobin Model." *Quarterly Journal of Economics* 101, 4 (Nov.), 663–686.

Romer, Paul M. (1987). "Crazy Explanations for the Productivity Slowdown." *NBER Macroeconomics Annual*, 163—202.

Sargent, Thomas (1978). "Estimation of Dynamic Labor Demand Schedules under Rational Expectations." *Journal of Political Economy* 86, 6 (Dec.), 1009—1044.

Sargent, Thomas (1987). *Dynamic Macroeconomic Theory*. Cambridge: Harvard University Press.

Sidrauski, Miguel (1967). "Rational Choice and Patterns of Growth in a Monetary Economy." *American Economic Review* (May), 534—544.

Sims, Christopher (1972). "Money, Income and Causality." *American Economic Review* 62, 540—542.

Sims, Christopher (1980). "Comparison of Interwar and Postwar Business Cycles: Monetarism Reconsidered." *American Economic Review* 70, 2 (May), 250—257.

Slutsky, Eugen (1937). "The Summation of Random Causes as the Source of Cyclic Processes." *Econometrica*, 105—146.

Solow, Robert (1957). "Technical Change and the Aggregate Production Function." *Review of Economic Studies* 39 (Aug.), 312—330.

Solow, Robert (1970). *Growth Theory: An Exposition*. Oxford University Press.

Solow, Robert (1980). "On Theories of Unemployment." *American Economic Review* 70, 1 (March), 1—11.

Stiglitz, Joseph, and Andrew Weiss (1987). "Keynesian, New Keynesian and New Classical Economics." NBER Working Paper 2160.

Stock, James H. (1988). "Measuring Business Cycle Time." *Journal of Political Economy*, forthcoming.

Taylor, John (1980). "Aggregate Dynamics and Staggered Contracts." *Journal of Political Economy* 88, 1 (Feb.), 1—24.

Tirole, Jean (1985). "Asset Bubbles and Overlapping Generations." *Econometrica* 53, 5 (Sept.), 1071—1100.

Weil, Philippe (1987). "Confidence and the Value of Money in an Overlapping Generations Economy." *Quarterly Journal of Economics* 102, 1 (Feb.), 1—22.

2

Consumption and Investment: Basic Infinite Horizon Models

In this chapter and the next we focus on the fundamentals of consumption and capital accumulation in dynamic nonmonetary equilibrium models. We introduce basic models—in this chapter, the Ramsey infinite horizon optimizing model, and in the next, overlapping generations models with finite horizon maximizers—and begin to analyze economic issues such as how much interest rates affect savings and whether the choice between tax and deficit financing affects capital accumulation.

Individuals are assumed in this chapter to have an infinite horizon, or to live forever.[1] The infinite horizon assumption turns out to have strong implications: together with the assumptions of competitive markets, constant returns to scale in production, and homogeneous agents, it typically implies that the allocation of resources achieved by a decentralized economy will be the same as that chosen by a central planner who maximizes the utility of the representative economic agent in the model. We demonstrate here the equivalence between the allocation of resources in the decentralized economy and in a planned economy.

We start this chapter by developing the Ramsey (1928) analysis of optimal economic growth under certainty, by deriving the intertemporal conditions that are satisfied on the optimal path that would be chosen by a central planner. We then show, in section 2.2, the equivalence of the optimal path to the equilibrium path of the decentralized economy. In section 2.3 we examine the effects of both lump-sum and capital taxation on the rate of saving and the equilibrium interest rate in the framework of the decentralized infinite horizon economy.

In section 2.4 we analyze the economy of a small country, showing how the evolution of the current account is determined by investment and saving behavior. We examine the response of the economy to supply shocks, showing under what circumstances a country will respond to an adverse shock by borrowing abroad.

In the final section, section 2.5, we discuss some of the special features and implications of the intertemporally separable utility function with constant rate of time preference used in the chapter, and examine alternative formulations.

2.1 The Ramsey Problem

Frank Ramsey[2] posed the question of how much a nation should save and solved it using a model that is now the prototype for studying the optimal intertemporal allocation of resources. The model presented in this section is essentially that of Ramsey.

The population, N_t, grows at rate n; it can be thought of as a family, or many identical families, growing over time. The labor force is equal to the population, with labor supplied inelastically. Output is produced using capital, K, and labor. There is no productivity growth.

The output is either consumed or invested, that is, added to the capital stock. Formally,

$$Y_t = F(K_t, N_t) = C_t + \frac{dK_t}{dt}. \tag{1}$$

For simplicity, we assume that there is no physical depreciation of capital, or that Y_t is net rather than gross output.[3] The production function is homogeneous of degree one: that is, there are constant returns to scale.

In per capita terms

$$f(k_t) = c_t + \frac{dk_t}{dt} + nk_t, \tag{2}$$

where lowercase letters denote per capita (equal to per worker) values of variables so that k is the capital-labor ratio and $f(k_t) \equiv F(K_t/N_t, 1)$; we assume $f(\cdot)$ to be strictly concave and to satisfy the following conditions, known as Inada conditions:

$$f(0) = 0, \qquad f'(0) = \infty, \qquad f'(\infty) = 0.$$

We also assume that the economy starts with some capital so that it can get production off the ground:

$$k_0 > 0.$$

The preferences of the family for consumption over time are represented by the utility integral:

$$U_s = \int_s^\infty u(c_t) \exp[-\theta(t - s)] \, dt. \tag{3}$$

The family's welfare at time s, U_s, is the discounted sum of instantaneous utilities $u(c_t)$. The function $u(\ )$ is known as the instantaneous utility function, or as "felicity"; $u(\ )$ is nonnegative and a concave increasing function of the per capita consumption of family members. The parameter θ is the rate of time preference, or the subjective discount rate, which is assumed to be strictly positive.[4]

The Command Optimum

Suppose that a central planner wants at time $t = 0$ to maximize family welfare. The only choice that has to be made at each moment of time is how much the representative family should consume and how much it should add to the capital stock to provide consumption in the future. The planner has to find the solution to the following problem:

$$\max U_0 = \int_0^\infty u(c_t) \exp(-\theta t) \, dt \tag{4}$$

subject to (2) and the constraints

k_0 given; $k_t, c_t \geqslant 0$ for all t.

We characterize the solution using the maximum principle.[5] The optimal solution is obtained by setting up the present value Hamiltonian function:

$$H_t = u(c_t) \exp(-\theta t) + \mu_t[f(k_t) - nk_t - c_t]. \tag{5}$$

The variable μ is called the *costate* variable associated with the *state* variable k; equivalently it is the multiplier on the constraint (2). The value of μ_t is the marginal value as of time zero of an additional unit of capital at time t.

It is often more convenient to work, instead, with the marginal value, as of time t, of an additional unit of capital at time t, $\lambda_t \equiv \mu_t \exp(\theta t)$; we shall do so here. Replacing μ_t by λ_t in (5) gives

$$H_t = [u(c_t) + \lambda_t(f(k_t) - nk_t - c_t)] \exp(-\theta t). \tag{5'}$$

We do not explicitly impose the nonnegativity constraints on k and c.

Necessary and sufficient conditions for a path to be optimal under the assumptions on the utility and production functions made here are that[6]

$$H_c = 0,$$

$$\frac{d\mu_t}{dt} = -H_k,$$

$$\lim_{t \to \infty} k_t \mu_t = 0.$$

Using the definition of $H(\cdot)$ and replacing μ by λ, we get

$$u'(c_t) = \lambda_t, \tag{6}$$

$$\frac{d\lambda_t}{dt} = \lambda_t [\theta + n - f'(k_t)], \tag{7}$$

$$\lim_{t \to \infty} k_t u'(c_t) \exp(-\theta t) = 0. \tag{8}$$

Equations (6) and (7) can be consolidated to remove the costate variable λ, yielding

$$\frac{du'(c_t)/dt}{u'(c_t)} = \theta + n - f'(k_t), \tag{7'}$$

or equivalently

$$\left[\frac{c_t u''(c_t)}{u'(c_t)} \right] \left(\frac{dc_t/dt}{c_t} \right) = \theta + n - f'(k_t).$$

The expression $cu''(c)/u'(c)$ will recur often in this book. It reflects the curvature of the utility function. More precisely, it is equal to the elasticity of marginal utility with respect to consumption. If utility is nearly linear and if marginal utility is nearly constant, then the elasticity is close to zero. This elasticity is itself closely related to the *instantaneous elasticity of substitution*. The elasticity of substitution between consumption at two points in time, t and s, is given by

$$\sigma(c_t) \equiv -\frac{u'(c_s)/u'(c_t)}{c_s/c_t} \frac{d(c_s/c_t)}{d[u'(c_s)/u'(c_t)]}.$$

Taking the limit of that expression as s converges to t gives $\sigma = -u'(c_t)/u''(c_t)c_t$ so that $\sigma(c_t)$ is the inverse of the negative of the elasticity of marginal utility. When utility is nearly linear, the elasticity of substitution is very large. Using the definition of σ, (7') can be rewritten as

$$\frac{dc_t/dt}{c_t} = \sigma(c_t)[f'(k_t) - \theta - n]. \tag{7''}$$

The key conditions are (7) [or (7′) or (7″)] and (8). Equation (7) is the Euler equation, the differential equation describing a necessary condition that has to be satisfied on any optimal path. It is the continuous time analogue of the standard efficiency condition that the marginal rate of substitution be equal to the marginal rate of transformation, as we shall show shortly. The condition is also known as the Keynes-Ramsey rule. It was derived by Ramsey in his classic article, which includes a verbal explanation attributed to Keynes. We now develop an intuitive explanation of this repeatedly used condition.

The Keynes-Ramsey Rule

The easiest way to understand the Keynes-Ramsey rule is to think of time as being discrete and to consider the choice of the central planner in allocating consumption between time t and $t + 1$. If he decreases consumption at time t by dc_t, the loss in utility at time t is equal to $u'(c_t)\, dc_t$. This decrease in consumption at time t, however, allows for more accumulation and thus more consumption at time $t + 1$: consumption per capita can be increased by $(1 + n)^{-1}[1 + f'(k_t)]\, dc_t$, leading to an increase in utility at $t + 1$ of $(1 + n)^{-1}[1 + f'(k_t)]u'(c_{t+1})\, dc_t$. Along the optimal path small reallocations in consumption must leave welfare unchanged so that the loss in utility at time t must be equal to the discounted increase in utility at time $t + 1$. Thus

$$u'(c_t) = (1 + \theta)^{-1}(1 + n)^{-1}[1 + f'(k_t)]u'(c_{t+1}).$$

This condition can be rewritten as

$$\frac{(1 + \theta)^{-1}u'(c_{t+1})}{u'(c_t)} = \frac{1 + n}{1 + f'(k_t)}, \tag{9}$$

which states that the marginal rate of substitution (MRS) between consumption at times t and $t + 1$ is equal to the marginal rate of transformation (MRT), from production, between consumption at times t and $t + 1$. If the period is short enough, this condition reduces to equation (7′).

A more rigorous argument runs as follows: Consider two points in time, t and s, $s > t$. We now imagine reallocating consumption from a small interval following t to an interval of the same length following s. Decrease c_t by amount Δc_t at time t for a period of length Δt, thus increasing capital accumulation by $\Delta c_t \Delta t$. That capital is allowed to accumulate between $t + \Delta t$ and s, with consumption over that interval unchanged from its

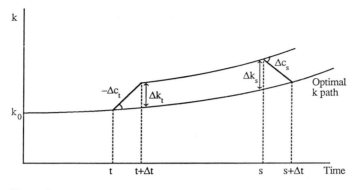

Figure 2.1
The Keynes-Ramsey rule

original value. All the increased capital is consumed during an interval of length Δt starting at s, with consumption thereafter being unchanged from the level on the original path. This variation from the optimal path is illustrated in figure 2.1.

For sufficiently small Δc and Δt, such a reallocation should have no effect on welfare, provided the path is optimal. Thus

$$u'(c_t)\Delta c_t \Delta t + u'(c_s) \exp[-\theta(s-t)]\Delta c_s \Delta t = 0.$$

The relation between Δc_t and Δc_s is implied by

$$\Delta c_t \Delta t = \Delta k_t, \qquad \Delta c_s \Delta t = \Delta k_s,$$

and

$$\Delta k_s = -\Delta k_t \exp\left\{ \int_{t+\Delta t}^{s} [f'(k_v) - n]\, dv \right\}.$$

Capital accumulated in the first interval Δt grows at the rate $f'(k) - n$ between $t + \Delta t$ and s.

Eliminating Δc's and Δk's from the preceding relations gives

$$\frac{u'(c_t)}{u'(c_s) \exp[-\theta(s-t)]} = \exp\left\{ \int_{t+\Delta t}^{s} [f'(k_v) - n]\, dv \right\}. \tag{10}$$

Equation (10) has the same interpretation as equation (9), namely, that marginal rates of substitution and transformation are equal.

As this equality must hold for all t and s, it follows that

$$\lim_{s \to t} \frac{d\text{MRS}(t, s)}{ds} = \lim_{s \to t} \frac{d\text{MRT}(t, s)}{ds}.$$

Applying this to (10) gives equation (7′).

The Keynes-Ramsey rule, in discrete or continuous time, implies that consumption increases, remains constant, or decreases depending on whether the marginal product of capital (net of population growth) exceeds, is equal to, or is less than the rate of time preference. This rule is quite fundamental and quite intuitive: the higher the marginal product of capital relative to the rate of time preference, the more it pays to depress the current level of consumption in order to enjoy higher consumption later. Thus, if initially the marginal product of capital is high, consumption will be increasing over time on the optimal path. Equation (7″) shows the specific role of the elasticity of substitution in this condition: the larger this elasticity, the easier it is, in terms of utility, to forgo current consumption in order to increase consumption later, and thus the larger the rate of change of consumption for a given value of the excess of the marginal product over the subjective discount rate.

The Transversality Condition

Equation (8), the transversality condition, is best understood by considering the same maximization problem with the infinite horizon replaced by a finite horizon T. In this case, if $u'(c_T) \exp(-\theta T)$ were positive (i.e., if the present value of the marginal utility of terminal consumption were positive), it would not be optimal to end up at time T with a positive capital stock because it could, instead, be consumed.[7] The condition would be

$$k_T u'(c_T) \exp(-\theta T) = 0.$$

The infinite horizon transversality condition (TVC) can be thought of as the limit of this condition as T becomes large.[8]

Two Useful Special Cases

CRRA
Two instantaneous utility functions are frequently used in intertemporal optimizing models. The first is the constant elasticity of substitution, or isoelastic, function:[9]

$$u(c) = \frac{c^{1-\gamma}}{1 - \gamma}, \qquad \text{for } \gamma > 0, \gamma \neq 1,$$

$$= \ln c, \qquad \text{for } \gamma = 1.$$

The basic economic property of this function is implied by its name. The elasticity of substitution between consumption at any two points in time, t and s, is constant and equal to $(1/\gamma)$. Thus, in equation (7″), σ is no longer a function of consumption. The elasticity of marginal utility is equal to $-\gamma$.

When this instantaneous utility function is used to describe attitudes toward risk, something we shall do later in the book when we allow for uncertainty, γ has an alternative interpretation. It is then also the coefficient of relative risk aversion, defined as $-u''(c)c/u'(c)$. Thus this function is also called the constant relative risk aversion (CRRA) utility function.[10]

Substantial empirical work has been devoted to estimating σ under the assumption that it is indeed constant, by looking at how willing consumers are to shift consumption across time in response to changes in interest rates. Estimates of σ vary substantially but usually lie around or below unity: the bulk of the empirical evidence suggests a relatively low value of the elasticity of substitution.

CARA
The second often used class of utility functions is the exponential, or constant absolute risk aversion (CARA), of the form

$$u(c) = -\left(\frac{1}{\alpha}\right) \exp(-\alpha c), \qquad \alpha > 0.$$

Under this specification the elasticity of marginal utility is equal to $-\alpha c$, and the instantaneous elasticity of substitution is equal to $(\alpha c)^{-1}$; thus σ is decreasing in the level of consumption.

When interpreted as describing attitudes toward risk, this function implies constant absolute risk aversion, with α being the coefficient of absolute risk aversion, $-u''(c)/u'(c)$. Constant absolute risk aversion is usually thought of as a less plausible description of risk aversion than constant relative risk aversion; the CARA specification is, however, sometimes analytically more convenient than the CRRA specification and thus also belongs to the standard tool kit.

For the CARA utility function, the Euler equation becomes

$$\frac{dc}{dt} = \alpha^{-1}[f'(k) - n - \theta]. \tag{7‴}$$

In this case the change in consumption is proportional to the excess of the marginal product of capital (net of population growth) over the discount rate.

Steady State and Dynamics

The optimal path is characterized by equations (7'), (8), and the constraint (2). We start with the steady state. In steady state both the per capita capital stock, k, and the level of consumption per capita, c, are constant. We denote the steady state values of these variables by k^* and c^*, respectively.

The Modified Golden Rule

From (7), with dc/dt equal to zero, we have the modified golden rule relationship:

$$f'(k^*) = \theta + n. \tag{11}$$

The marginal product of capital in steady state is equal to the sum of the rate of time preference and the growth rate of population. Corresponding to the optimal capital stock k^* is the steady state level of consumption, implied by (2):

$$c^* = f(k^*) - nk^*. \tag{12}$$

The *golden rule* itself is the condition $f'(k) = n$: this is the condition on the capital stock that maximizes *steady state* consumption per capita.[11] The modification in (11) is that the capital stock is reduced below the golden rule level by an amount that depends on the rate of time preference. Even though society or the family could consume more in a steady state with the golden rule capital stock, the impatience reflected in the rate of time preference means that it is not optimal to reduce current consumption in order to reach the higher golden rule consumption level.

The *modified golden rule* condition is a very powerful one: it implies that ultimately the productivity of capital, and thus the real interest rate,[12] is determined by the rate of time preference and n. Tastes and population growth determine the real interest rate ($\theta + n$), and technology then determines the capital stock and level of consumption consistent with that interest rate.[13] Later in the chapter we will explore the sensitivity of the modified golden rule result to the formulation of the utility function $u(\cdot)$ in (1).

Dynamics

To study dynamics, we use the phase diagram in figure 2.2, drawn in (k, c) space.[14] All points in the positive orthant are feasible, except for points on

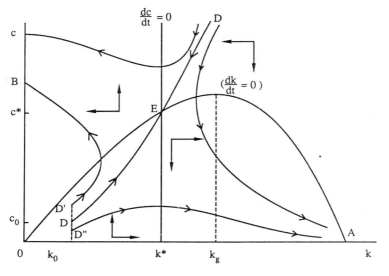

Figure 2.2
The dynamics of capital and consumption

the vertical axis above the origin: without capital (i.e., if $k = 0$), output is zero, and thus positive c is not feasible.

The locus $dk/dt = 0$ starts from the origin, reaches a maximum at the golden rule capital stock k_g at which $f'(k_g) = n$, and crosses the horizontal axis at point A where $f(k) = nk$. The $dc/dt = 0$ locus is, from (7'), vertical at the modified golden rule capital stock, k^*.

Anywhere above the $dk/dt = 0$ locus, the capital–labor ratio k is decreasing: consumption is above the level that would just maintain k constant (i.e., the level of c on the $dk/dt = 0$ curve.) Similarly, k is increasing at points below the $dk/dt = 0$ locus. In the case of the $dc/dt = 0$ locus, consumption is increasing to the left of the locus, where $f'(k) > \theta + n$, and decreasing to the right of the locus. The vertical arrows demonstrate these directions of motion.[15]

There are three equilibria, the origin, if $\sigma^{-1}(0)$ is different from zero (see note 15), point E, and point A. In appendix A we show that only the trajectory DD, the *saddle point path*, that converges to E satisfies the necessary conditions (2), (7'), and (8). On all other paths, either the Keynes-Ramsey condition eventually fails or the transversality condition is not satisfied.[16]

The central planner's solution to the optimizing problem (1) is fully summarized by the path DD. For each initial capital stock, this implies a unique initial level of consumption. For instance, with initial capital stock k_0, the optimal initial level of consumption is c_0. Convergence of c and k to c^* and k^* is monotonic. Note that in this certainty model the central planner knows at time 0 what the level of consumption and the capital stock will be at every moment in the future.

Local Behavior around the Steady State

Linearization of the dynamic system (2) and (7') yields further insights into the dynamic behavior of the economy. Linearizing both equations in the neighborhood of the steady state gives

$$\frac{dc}{dt} = -\beta(k - k^*), \qquad \beta \equiv [-f''(k^*)c^*]\sigma(c^*) > 0, \tag{13}$$

and

$$\frac{dk}{dt} = [f'(k^*) - n](k - k^*) - (c - c^*)$$
$$= \theta(k - k^*) - (c - c^*). \tag{14}$$

The solution to this system of linear differential equations is most easily found by reducing it to a single second-order equation in k. Differentiating (14) with respect to time, and using (13) to substitute for dc/dt, gives

$$\frac{d^2k}{dt^2} - \theta\left(\frac{dk}{dt}\right) - \beta k = -\beta k^*. \tag{15}$$

The roots of the characteristic equation associated with the second-order differential equation are $\theta \pm (\sqrt{\theta^2 + 4\beta})/2$. One root is positive and the other negative, implying the saddle point property: the presence of a positive root implies that for arbitrary initial conditions, the system explodes; for any given value of k_0, there is a unique value of dk/dt such that the system converges to the steady state (see appendix B).

Let λ be the negative, stable root. The solution for k_t such that, starting from k_0, the system converges to k^* is

$$k_t = k^* + (k_0 - k^*)\exp(\lambda t).$$

The speed of convergence is thus given by $|\lambda|$. In turn $|\lambda|$ is an increasing function of f'' and of σ, and a decreasing function of θ. The higher the elasticity of substitution, the more willing people are to accept low consumption early on in exchange for higher consumption later and the faster capital accumulates and the economy converges to the steady state.[17]

2.2 The Decentralized Economy

Suppose that the economy is decentralized rather than centrally planned. There are two factor markets, one for labor and one for capital services. The rental price of labor, the wage, is denoted w_t; r_t is the rental price of capital. There is a debt market in which families can borrow and lend.

There are many identical families, each with a welfare function given by equation (3). Each family decides, at any point in time, how much labor and capital to rent to firms and how much to save or consume. They can save by either accumulating capital or lending to other families. Families are indifferent as to the composition of their wealth, so the interest rate on debt must be equal to the rental rate on capital.[18]

There are many identical firms, each with the same technology as described by equation (2); firms rent the services of capital and labor to produce output.[19] The constant returns assumption means that the number of firms is of no consequence, provided the firms behave competitively, taking the prices (the real wage and rental rate on capital) facing them as given.[20]

Both families and firms have perfect foresight; that is, they know both current and future values of w and r and take them as given. (Under certainty, perfect foresight is the equivalent of rational expectations, an assumption we will discuss at length later.) More formally, let $\{w_t, r_t\}$, $t = [0, \infty)$, be the sequence of wages and rental rates. Then, given this sequence, each family maximizes at any time s

$$U_s = \int_s^\infty u(c_t) \exp[-\theta(t - s)] \, dt$$

subject to the budget constraint,

$$c_t + \frac{da_t}{dt} + na_t = w_t + r_t a_t, \qquad \text{for all } t, \, k_0 \text{ given,} \qquad (16)$$

where

$$a_t \equiv k_t - b_{pt}.$$

Family wealth, or more precisely nonhuman wealth, is given by a_t, which is equal to holdings of capital, k_t, minus family debt, b_{pt}.

At any time t, the family supplies both capital and labor services inelastically: capital is the result of previous decisions and is given at time t; by assumption, labor is supplied inelastically. Thus the only decision the family has to make at each point in time is how much to consume or save.

Firms in turn maximize profits at each point in time. Since their technology is characterized by the production function (2), first-order conditions for profit maximization imply that

$$f'(k_t) = r_t,$$
$$f(k_t) - k_t f'(k_t) = w_t.$$
(17)

Consider an arbitrary path of wages and rental rates. This sequence will lead each family to choose a path of consumption and wealth accumulation. Given that private debt must always be equal to zero in the aggregate, wealth accumulation will determine capital accumulation. The path of capital will in turn imply a path of wages and rental rates. The equilibrium paths of wages and rental rates are defined as those paths that reproduce themselves given optimal decisions by firms and households. We now characterize the equilibrium path of the economy.[21]

The No-Ponzi-Game Condition

In stating the maximization problem of a family, we have not imposed the constraint that family nonhuman wealth, which is given by a_t at time t, be nonnegative. In the absence of any restrictions on borrowing, the solution to the maximization problem is then a trivial one. It is for the family to borrow sufficiently to maintain a level of consumption such that the marginal utility of consumption equals zero (or an infinite level of consumption if marginal utility is always positive) and to let the dynamic budget constraint determine the dynamic behavior of a. From the budget constraint it follows that this path of consumption will lead to higher and higher levels of borrowing (negative a), borrowing being used to meet interest payments on the existing debt. Ultimately, net indebtedness per family member will be growing at rate $r_t - n$.

We need therefore an additional condition that prevents families from choosing such a path, with an exploding debt relative to the size of the family. At the same time we do not want to impose a condition that rules out temporary indebtedness.[22] A natural condition is to require that family debt not increase asymptotically faster than the interest rate:

$$\lim_{t \to \infty} a_t \exp\left[-\int_0^t (r_v - n)\, dv \right] \geq 0.$$
(18)

This condition is sometimes known as a no-Ponzi-game (NPG) condition.[23] Although (18) is stated as an inequality, it is clear that as long as marginal utility is positive, families will not want to have increasing wealth forever at rate $r - n$, and that the condition will hold as an equality. Thus in what follows we use the condition directly as an equality.

To see what the condition implies, let us first integrate the budget constraint from time 0 to some time T. This gives

$$\int_0^T c_t \exp\left[\int_t^T (r_v - n)\, dv\right] dt + a_T$$

$$= \int_0^T w_t \exp\left[\int_t^T (r_v - n)\, dv\right] dt + a_0 \exp\left[\int_0^T (r_v - n)\, dv\right].$$

Multiplying both sides by $\exp[-\int_0^T (r_v - n)\, dv]$, that is, discounting to time zero, letting T go to ∞, and using the NPG condition, gives

$$\int_0^\infty c_t \exp\left[-\int_0^t (r_v - n)\, dv\right] dt = a_0 + h_0,$$

where

$$h_0 \equiv \int_0^\infty w_t \exp\left[-\int_0^t (r_v - n)\, dv\right] dt.$$

This condition implies that the present value of consumption is equal to total wealth, which is the sum of nonhuman wealth, a_0, and of human wealth, h_0, the present value of labor income. Thus condition (18) allows us to go from the dynamic budget constraint (16) to an intertemporal budget constraint.[24]

The Decentralized Equilibrium

Maximization of (3) subject to (16) and (18), carried out by setting up a Hamiltonian, implies the following necessary and sufficient conditions:

$$\frac{du'(c_t)/dt}{u'(c_t)} = \theta + n - r_t, \tag{19}$$

$$\lim_{t\to\infty} a_t u'(c_t) \exp(-\theta t) = 0. \tag{20}$$

In equilibrium, aggregate private debt b_{pt} must always be equal to zero: though each family assumes it can freely borrow and lend, in equilibrium there is neither lending nor borrowing. Thus $a_t = k_t$. Using this and equations (17) for w_t and r_t and replacing in (16) and (19) gives

$$c_t + \frac{dk_t}{dt} + nk_t = f(k_t), \tag{21}$$

$$\frac{du'(c_t)/dt}{u'(c_t)} = \theta + n - f'(k_t). \tag{22}$$

Equations (20), (21), and (22) characterize the behavior of the decentralized economy. Note that they are identical to equations (8), (2), and (7′) which characterize the behavior of the economy as chosen by a central planner. Thus the dynamic behavior of the decentralized economy will be the same as that of the centrally planned one. Our analysis of dynamics carries over to the decentralized economy.[25]

The Role of Expectations

Equation (19), the Euler equation, gives the rate of change of consumption as a function of variables known at the current moment. It could be interpreted as suggesting that households need not form expectations of future variables in making their consumption/saving decisions and that the assumption of perfect foresight is not necessary. However, it is clear from the intertemporal budget constraint that the household cannot plan without knowing the entire path of both the wage and the interest rate. Expectations thus are crucial to the allocation of resources in the decentralized economy. In terms of the Euler equation, equation (19) only determines the rate of change, not the level of consumption.

Although it is difficult in general to solve explicitly for the level of consumption, this can be done easily when the utility function is of the CRRA family. In this case equation (19) gives

$$\frac{dc_t/dt}{c_t} = \sigma(r_t - n - \theta).$$

For a given value of initial consumption c_0, we can integrate this equation forward to get

$$c_t = c_0 \exp\left[\int_0^t \sigma(r_v - n - \theta)\, dv\right].$$

Replacing in the intertemporal budget constraint gives the value of c_0 consistent with the Euler equation and the budget constraint

$$c_0 = \beta_0(a_0 + h_0),$$

where

$$\beta_0^{-1} \equiv \left[\int_0^\infty \exp \left\{ \int_0^t [(\sigma - 1)(r_v - n) - \theta\sigma] \, dv \right\} dt \right].$$

Consumption is a linear function of wealth, human and nonhuman. The parameter β_0 is the propensity to consume out of wealth. It is generally a function of the expected path of interest rates. An increase in interest rates, given wealth, has two effects. The first is to make consumption later more attractive: this is the substitution effect. The second is to allow for higher consumption now and later: this is the income effect. In general, the net effect on the marginal propensity to consume is ambiguous. For the logarithmic utility function, however, $\sigma = 1$, and the two effects cancel; the propensity to consume is then exactly equal to the rate of time preference, θ, and is independent of the path of interest rates.

In general, expectations of interest rates affect both the marginal propensity to consume out of wealth and the value of wealth itself, through h_0. Expectations of wages also affect c_0 through h_0. Given these expectations, families decide how much to consume and save. This in turn determines capital accumulation and the sequence of factor prices.

What happens if expectations are incorrect? Agents will choose a different plan from our hypothetical central planner. When the divergence between actual and expected events causes them to revise their expectations, they will choose a new path that is optimal given their expectations. To pursue this line, we would have to specify how expectations are formed and revised. We defer that for later treatment.

2.3 The Government in the Decentralized Economy

In this section we introduce the government into the model. We assume that the government's spending requirements are fixed exogenously,[26] and we examine the effects on the economy's equilibrium of, first, changes in the level of government spending and, second, different ways of financing a given level of government spending—either through taxation or borrowing.

Balanced Budget Changes in Government Spending

Suppose that a government is consuming resources and paying for them with taxes. The government's per capita demand for resources g_t is exogenous and, further, does not directly affect the marginal utility of consumption of the representative household.[27] To begin with, let the government levy per capita lump-sum taxes $\tau_t = g_t$, so that the government budget is balanced at every moment.

The household flow budget constraint now becomes

$$c_t + \frac{da_t}{dt} + na_t = w_t + r_t a_t - \tau_t, \qquad a_t = k_t - b_{pt},$$

which, using the NPG condition, integrates to

$$\int_0^\infty c_t R_t \, dt = k_0 - b_{p0} + \int_0^\infty w_t R_t \, dt - \int_0^\infty \tau_t R_t \, dt,$$

or equivalently,

$$\int_0^\infty c_t R_t \, dt = k_0 - b_{p0} + h_0 - G_0, \qquad (23)$$

where $R_t = \exp[-\int_0^t (r_v - n) \, dv]$ is the factor by which future spending is discounted to the present and G_0 is the present discounted value of government spending, which is equal, by virtue of the assumption that $\tau_t = g_t$, to the present discounted value of lump-sum taxes.

Government spending enters the intertemporal budget constraint, affecting the decisions of the family, the real equilibrium of the economy, and thus the time paths of w_t and r_t (and hence R_t). Suppose that the government demands a constant amount of resources, g, per capita, where g is small. Using the equivalence between the decentralized and the centrally planned economy, we draw figure 2.3 to show the dynamics. The diagram is the same as figure 2.2, except that the output available for the private sector is reduced by the uniform amount g, accounting for the vertical shift downward of the $dk/dt = 0$ locus to $(dk/dt = 0)'$.

There is no equilibrium at low levels of the capital stock. But once there is sufficient capital to produce goods for the government, beyond k', the analysis is similar to that in figure 2.2. The economy will proceed to a steady state at E' with the modified golden rule capital stock, and with consumption $c^{*'}$ smaller by an amount g than it was in the steady state in figure 2.2. In steady state government spending completely crowds out private consumption but has no effect on the capital stock.

Does a change in government spending have dynamic effects on capital accumulation? If the economy is in steady state initially, the change in government spending is reflected instantaneously in consumption with no dynamic effect on capital accumulation. If the economy is not initially in

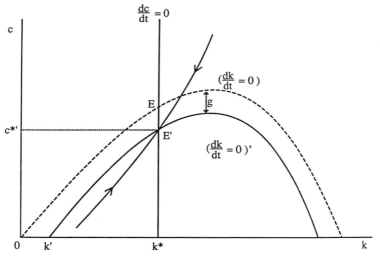

Figure 2.3
The effects of an increase in public spending

steady state, whether or not the change in spending has a transitory effect depends on the characteristics of the felicity function. If, for example, felicity belongs to the CARA class, there is no dynamic effect on capital accumulation.

Debt Financing

Instead of financing itself through taxes with $\tau_t = g_t$, the government may borrow from the private sector. Government debt must pay the same rate as capital, if agents are to hold it in their portfolios. Let b_t be per capita government debt. The government faces the following dynamic budget constraint:

$$\frac{db_t}{dt} + nb_t = g_t - \tau_t + r_t b_t.$$

The left-hand side is government borrowing per capita, which is equal to the increase in the per capita debt (db_t/dt) plus the amount of debt (nb_t) that can, as a result of the growing population, be floated without increasing the amount of debt per capita. The right-hand side is the excess of government outlays, consisting of its purchases of goods and services and interest payments, over its tax receipts. The flow constraint says only that the government has to borrow when its outlays exceed its tax receipts, or that it repays debt or lends to the private sector when tax receipts exceed outlays.

Integrating this budget constraint and imposing the NPG condition this time on the government (that debt not increase faster asymptotically than the interest rate) gives an intertemporal budget constraint for the government:

$$b_0 + \int_0^\infty g_t R_t \, dt = \int_0^\infty \tau_t R_t \, dt. \tag{24}$$

The present value of taxes must be equal to the present value of government spending plus the value of the initial government debt b_0, given the NPG condition. Equivalently, the government must choose a path of spending and taxes such that the present value of $g_t - \tau_t$, which is sometimes referred to as the primary deficit, equals the negative of initial debt, b_0; if the government has positive outstanding debt, it must anticipate running primary surpluses at some point in the future. For instance, it is consistent with (24) that the government maintain the initial value of the per capita debt, b_0, forever, running a primary surplus just large enough to pay the interest net of the amount of debt that can be financed by selling b_0 to each newborn person.

The presence of government debt also modifies the dynamic budget constraint of the family, which becomes

$$c_t + \frac{da_t}{dt} + na_t = w_t + r_t a_t - \tau_t, \tag{25}$$

with a_t now equal to $k_t - b_{pt} + b_t$. Note that there is an implicit assumption in (25) that the family can borrow and lend at the same interest rate, r_t, as the government.

Integrating this budget constraint subject to the NPG condition gives the following intertemporal budget constraint:

$$\int_0^\infty c_t R_t \, dt = k_0 - b_{p0} + b_0 + \int_0^\infty w_t R_t \, dt - \int_0^\infty \tau_t R_t \, dt. \tag{26}$$

The present value of consumption must be equal to the sum of nonhuman wealth, which is the sum of $k_0 - b_{p0}$ and b_0, and of human wealth, which is the present value of wages minus taxes.

The government budget constraint shows that for a given pattern of government spending (and given b_0), the government has to levy taxes of a given present value: equivalently, the government need not run a balanced budget at every moment of time. For instance, starting from a balanced budget, it can reduce taxes at some point, borrow from the public, and raise future taxes to repay the interest and the debt.

What then is the effect of a change in the timing pattern of the taxes raised to finance a given pattern of government expenditures? The answer is given by replacing the intertemporal budget constraint of the government in (26). This gives

$$\int_0^\infty c_t R_t \, dt = k_0 - b_{p0} + \int_0^\infty w_t R_t \, dt - \int_0^\infty g_t R_t \, dt. \tag{27}$$

Equation (27) is exactly the same as equation (23). Neither taxes nor government debt appear in the budget constraint of the family. Only government spending matters. This has a strong implication: *for a given path of government spending, the method of finance, through lump-sum taxation or deficit finance, has no effect on the allocation of resources.*

The intuition for this result is obtained by looking at the intertemporal budget constraints of the government and families. A decrease in taxes, and thus a larger deficit today, must according to the government budget constraint lead to an increase in taxes later. According to the family budget constraint, the current decrease and the anticipated future increase exactly offset each other in present value, leaving the budget constraint unaffected. Families thus do not modify their paths of consumption. They willingly save the increase in current income, exactly offsetting the dissaving of the government.

This conclusion is remarkable, for it provides one instance in which, so long as the government ultimately meets its NPG condition, the size of the national debt is of no consequence, and neither is deficit finance. We will return several times to the issue of the effects of the national debt and deficit finance and study the robustness of this strong neutrality result.

Distortionary Taxation of Capital

Distortionary taxation certainly affects the allocation of resources. Suppose that the government taxes the return to capital at the rate τ_k, and remits the proceeds in lump-sum fashion to the private sector. If r_t is the pre-tax rate of return on capital, $(1 - \tau_k)r_t$ is the aftertax return on capital and must also be the rate of return on private debt as capital and debt are perfect substitutes in the family's portfolio. The family's flow budget constraint is now

$$c_t + \frac{da_t}{dt} + na_t = w_t + (1 - \tau_k)r_t a_t + z_t, \tag{28}$$

where z_t is the per capita lump-sum transfers (equal to the government's receipts from the taxation of capital) made to the family.

Setting up the Hamiltonian for this problem yields a modification of (19):

$$\frac{du'(c_t)/dt}{u'(c_t)} = \theta + n - (1 - \tau_k)r_t. \tag{19'}$$

Note first that the taxation of capital affects the steady state capital stock. With $r_t = f'(k_t)$, the steady state capital stock (when $dc/dt = 0$) is given by

$$k^* = f'^{-1}\left(\frac{\theta + n}{1 - \tau_k}\right).$$

The aftertax rate of return to capital will still be equal to the rate of time preference adjusted for population growth $\theta + n$; for that reason the pre-tax rate of return is higher than $\theta + n$. The marginal product of capital in steady state is accordingly higher, meaning that the steady state capital stock is lower than when capital is not taxed.

Figure 2.4 shows how the taxation of capital affects the economy. The steady state moves from E to E', the steady state capital stock falls from k^* to $k^{*'}$, and the steady state rate of consumption is lower than it was in the

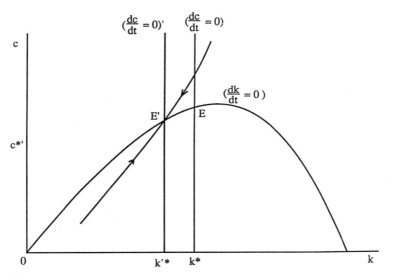

Figure 2.4
The effects of capital taxation

absence of distortionary taxation. Equivalently, if the government instead subsidized capital using lump-sum taxation, it could increase the steady state capital stock and level of consumption, as long as the steady state capital stock was below the golden rule level.

2.4 Application: Investment and Saving in the Open Economy

In this section we extend the closed economy optimizing model to the open economy. The extension not only sheds light on the optimal and actual responses of an economy to shocks, such as a reduction in productivity, but it also provides further insights into investment and saving behavior.

We extend the original model in two directions. In the closed economy model used so far, there was no cost to installing capital; whatever was saved could be added to the capital stock at no cost, and investment was purely passive. We now introduce costs of installation. This will be seen to imply that there is now both a well-defined saving decision and a well-defined investment decision.

If we maintained the assumption that the economy was closed, interest rates would have to adjust so that saving would be equal to investment at all points in time, or equivalently so that the demand for goods, consumption plus investment, would be equal to the supply of goods.[28] Instead, we open up the economy, allowing international trade in both goods and assets. It is then possible for saving and investment not to be equal at any moment of time: temporary imbalances, current account deficits, can be financed by foreign borrowing. In this way we show most clearly the separate dynamics of investment and saving.[29]

As before, there is equivalence between the command optimum and the decentralized equilibrium. We describe the command optimum in the text, and demonstrate its equivalence to the decentralized equilibrium in appendix C.

The Command Optimum

The optimization problem is

$$\max U_0 = \int_0^\infty u(c_t) \exp(-\theta t)\, dt \tag{29}$$

subject to

$$\frac{db_t}{dt} = c_t + i_t\left[1 + T\left(\frac{i_t}{k_t}\right)\right] + \theta b_t - f(k_t), \tag{30}$$

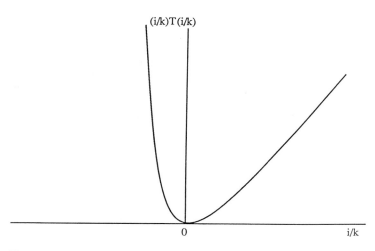

Figure 2.5
Costs of installation for investment

$$\frac{dk_t}{dt} = i_t, \tag{31}$$

$$T(0) = 0,$$

$$T'(\cdot) > 0,$$

$$2T'(\cdot) + \frac{i}{kT''(\cdot)} > 0.$$

All variables are in per capita terms, and population is assumed here to be constant; b denotes per capita debt. The felicity and production functions $u(\cdot)$ and $f(\cdot)$ have the same properties as in earlier sections.

There are two changes from the previous analysis. First, there are now costs of installing investment goods.[30] It takes $i[1 + T(\cdot)]$ units of output to increase the capital stock by i units. The amount $T(\cdot)$ per unit of investment is used up in transforming goods into capital. The properties of $T(\cdot)$ make the installation cost function $(i/k)T(\cdot)$, shown in figure 2.5, nonnegative and convex, with a minimum value of zero when investment is equal to zero: both investment and disinvestment are costly. For simplicity, we assume that there is no depreciation.[31]

The other difference is that the economy can now borrow and lend freely abroad at the constant world interest rate θ.[32] This implies the flow budget constraint (30): the change in foreign debt (db/dt) is equal to spending (on consumption, investment, and interest payments) minus output. The change in foreign debt is the current account deficit, so that (30) is equivalent to the statement that the current account deficit is equal to the excess of absorption over production.

There is a simple relation among the current account deficit, saving, and investment that will be useful later. A brief refresher in national income accounting identities and definitions may be useful at this point. The current account deficit is equal to the change in foreign debt, which is in turn equal to interest payments minus net exports of goods, the trade surplus (nx):

$$\frac{db}{dt} = \theta b - nx.$$

Per capita GDP and GNP are given by

$$GDP = c + i[1 + T(\cdot)] + nx,$$

$$GNP = GDP - \theta b.$$

Saving is equal to GNP minus consumption:

$$s = GNP - c = i[1 + T(\cdot)] + nx - \theta b = i[1 + T(\cdot)] - \frac{db}{dt}$$

so that

$$\frac{db}{dt} = \text{current account deficit} = i[1 + T(\cdot)] - s.$$

The maximization problem as now stated has a simple solution. It is again a Ponzi-like solution, but now on the part of the central planner vis-à-vis the rest of the world. The country should borrow until the marginal utility of consumption is equal to zero, and then borrow further to meet interest payments on its debt. It is unlikely that the lenders would be willing to continue lending if the country's only means of paying off its debt were to borrow more. Accordingly, we impose the NPG condition[33]

$$\lim_{t \to \infty} b_t \exp(-\theta t) = 0. \tag{32}$$

To solve the intertemporal problem, we set up the present value Hamiltonian:

$$H_t = \left[u(c_t) - \mu_t \left\{ c_t + i_t \left[1 + T\left(\frac{i_t}{k_t}\right) \right] + \theta b_t - f(k_t) \right\} + \mu_t q_t i_t \right] \exp(-\theta t). \tag{33}$$

The costate variables on the flow budget constraint (30) and the capital accumulation equation (31) are $-\mu_t \exp(-\theta t)$ and $\mu_t q_t \exp(-\theta t)$.[34]

Necessary and sufficient conditions for a maximum are

$$u'(c_t) = \mu_t \qquad \text{(from } H_c = 0\text{)}, \tag{34}$$

$$1 + T\left(\frac{i_t}{k_t}\right) + \left(\frac{i_t}{k_t}\right) T'\left(\frac{i_t}{k_t}\right) = q_t \qquad \text{(from } H_i = 0\text{)}, \tag{35}$$

$$\frac{d[-\mu_t \exp(-\theta t)]}{dt} = \theta \mu_t \exp(-\theta t), \tag{36}$$

$$\frac{d[\mu_t q_t \exp(-\theta t)]}{dt} = -\left\{\mu_t \left[f'(k_t) + \left(\frac{i_t}{k_t}\right)^2 T'\left(\frac{i_t}{k_t}\right)\right]\right\} \exp(-\theta t), \tag{37}$$

$$\lim_{t \to \infty} -\mu_t b_t \exp(-\theta t) = 0, \tag{38}$$

$$\lim_{t \to \infty} \mu_t q_t k_t \exp(-\theta t) = 0. \tag{39}$$

Equations (36) and (37) are the Euler equations associated with b and k, respectively. Equations (38) and (39) are the transversality conditions associated with b and k, respectively. We are now ready to characterize the solution. We start with consumption.

Consumption

Carrying out the differentiation in (36), we obtain

$$\frac{d\mu_t}{dt} = 0, \tag{40}$$

which implies that μ is constant. In turn, this implies from (34) that consumption is constant on the optimal path. That is precisely what should be expected given the findings in sections 2.1 and 2.2 on the effects of the relationship between the interest rate and the rate of time preference on the profile of the consumption path.

To obtain the level of consumption, we integrate the flow constraint (30) using condition (38), which yields

$$\int_0^\infty c_t \exp(-\theta t)\, dt = \int_0^\infty \left\{f(k_t) - i_t\left[1 + T\left(\frac{i_t}{k_t}\right)\right]\right\} \exp(-\theta t)\, dt - b_0$$

$$= v_0. \tag{41}$$

The present discounted value of consumption is equal to net wealth at time 0, v_0, the present discounted value of net output [the contents of the braces in (41)] minus the initial level of debt. Since consumption is constant, (41) implies that[35]

$$c_t = c_0 = \theta v_0. \tag{42}$$

Investment

Equation (35) contains a very strong result, namely, that the rate of investment (relative to the capital stock) is a function only of q_t, which is the shadow price in terms of consumption goods of a unit of installed capital. Equation (35) implies a relation $q = \Psi(i/k)$, with $\Psi' > 0$ and $\Psi(0) = 1$. Thus we can define an inverse function $\varphi(\cdot)$ such that $i/k = \varphi(q)$. From the properties of $\Psi(\cdot)$, it follows that $\varphi' > 0$ and $\varphi(1) = 0$. Replacing in (31) gives

$$\frac{dk_t}{dt} = i_t = k_t\varphi(q_t), \qquad \varphi'(q) > 0, \; \varphi(1) = 0. \tag{43}$$

Investment is, from (43), an increasing function of q, the shadow price of capital. At the margin the planner equates the value of an addition to the capital stock with its marginal cost, which rises with the rate of investment. It makes sense to incur the higher marginal cost of investing faster only when the shadow value of capital is higher. Note that the rate of investment is zero when $q = 1$, when the shadow price of capital is the same as that of goods "on the hoof," so that positive rates of investment require $q > 1$. Note finally that the level of q determines the rate of investment relative to the capital stock, i_t/k_t.

What in turn determines q? From (37), given (40),

$$\frac{dq_t}{dt} = \theta q_t - f'(k_t) - \varphi(q_t)^2 T'[\varphi(q_t)]. \tag{37'}$$

Integrating (37') subject to (39),[36]

$$q_t = \int_t^\infty \{f'(k_v) + \varphi(q_v)^2 T'[\varphi(q_v)]\} \exp[-\theta(v - t)] \, dv. \tag{44}$$

The shadow price of capital is equal to the present discounted value of future marginal products. Marginal product is itself the sum of two terms: the first is the marginal product of capital in production; the second is the reduction in the marginal cost of installing a given flow of investment due to the increase in the capital stock (because the installation cost depends on the ratio of investment to capital). The higher the current or future expected marginal products or the lower the discount rate, the higher are q and the rate of investment.[37]

The most significant feature of (44) is that q, and thus the rate of investment, does not depend at all on the characteristics of the utility function or on the level of debt. The investment decision is independent of the saving or consumption decisions in this open economy framework with an exogenous real interest rate.

Saving, Investment and the Current Account

Saving is given by

$$s_t = f(k_t) - c_t - \theta b_t.$$

From the derivation of consumption above, $c_t = \theta v_t$ so that

$$s_t = f(k_t) - \theta \int_t^\infty \left\{ f(k_z) - i_z \left[1 + T\left(\frac{i_z}{k_z}\right) \right] \right\} \exp[-\theta(z - t)]\, dz. \qquad (45)$$

Thus saving is high when output is high compared to future expected output. The other distinctive result is that saving is independent of the level of debt: the equality of the marginal propensity to consume and of the interest rate implies that a higher level of debt leads to equal decreases in income and consumption, leaving saving unaffected.

Since the current account surplus is equal to saving minus investment, neither of which is affected by the stock of debt, the current account is also independent of the stock of debt.

Steady State and Dynamics

The dynamic system characterizing the behavior of the economy is recursive, with (43) and (37′) determining investment, capital, and output. The level of consumption and debt dynamics are then determined by (42) and (30).

Investment and Capital

In steady state $dk/dt = dq/dt = 0$. Accordingly, from (31), from $\varphi(1) = 0$, and from (37′),

$$q^* = 1, \qquad f'(k^*) = \theta, \qquad (46)$$

where the asterisks denote steady state values.

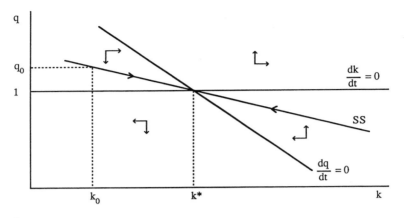

Figure 2.6
Dynamics of investment and capital

In steady state the rate of investment is zero.[38] The shadow price of capital must therefore be equal to its replacement cost, or $q = 1$; in turn, the marginal product of capital has to be equal to the interest rate, which is itself equal to the rate of time preference.

We limit our analysis of the dynamics of investment and capital to a neighborhood around the steady state. To do so, we linearize (43) and (37') around $q^* = 1$ and k^*:

$$\begin{bmatrix} \dfrac{dk}{dt} \\[2mm] \dfrac{dq}{dt} \end{bmatrix} = \begin{bmatrix} 0 & k^*\varphi'(1) \\[1mm] -f''(k^*) & \theta \end{bmatrix} \begin{bmatrix} k - k^* \\[1mm] q - 1 \end{bmatrix}. \tag{47}$$

Figure 2.6 gives the phase diagram corresponding to (47). The $dk/dt = 0$ locus is horizontal at $q = 1$; the $dq/dt = 0$ locus is downward sloping.[39] The arrows indicate directions of motion. There is therefore a unique path converging to the steady state, the downward-sloping path SS.[40]

The dynamics of investment are implied by the saddle point path SS. Given an initial capital stock k_0, the initial value of q, q_0 is read off SS, and the associated level of investment follows from (43). Since q_0 in this case exceeds unity, capital accumulates over time. Output increases and so does net output, which is equal to $f(k) - i[1 + T(i/k)]$: output increases while investment decreases over time.

c, net output

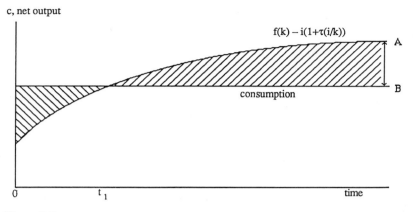

Figure 2.7
Consumption, net output, trade and current accounts

Consumption and Debt

We have already seen that the level of consumption is constant, determined by the path of net output (which is itself determined by the path of investment) and by the initial stock of debt.

Figure 2.7 shows a path of net output that increases over time as the capital stock increases to its steady state level. We will now determine the level of consumption in figure 2.7. Assume that the initial stock of debt b_0 was zero. The constant level of consumption must then, from (41), be such that the present discounted value of net output minus consumption is zero, or equivalently that the present discounted value of current and future trade surpluses is zero.[41] Graphically, the discounted values of the two hatched areas in figure 2.7 must be equal and opposite in sign; the level of consumption is determined by drawing a horizontal line such that the two areas are equal in present value.

In figure 2.7 net output increases over time. Net output accordingly starts out below and eventually exceeds consumption. The initial excess of consumption over net output is achieved by foreign borrowing, or by running a current account deficit. Debt accumulates during this phase. Eventually, net output rises sufficiently so that the trade balance shows a surplus. In steady state the current account must be balanced. The trade surplus is offset by interest payments on debt. The steady state level of debt b^* is positive and such that θb^* is equal to AB, the trade surplus, in figure 2.7. The presence of the debt reflects the decision to consume at a rate above the level of net output early in time.

Productivity Shocks and the Current Account

The paths of consumption and the current account in the preceding analysis can serve as a baseline for the analysis of the effects of shocks to productivity on the economy. Suppose that output is given by

$$y = (1 - z_0)f(k) - z_1.$$

Here z_0 is a multiplicative shock, and z_1 is an additive shock. Reflecting the experience of oil shocks in the 1970s, we take the shocks to be adverse, and consider increases in either z_0 or z_1 that reduce output given the capital stock.[42]

A Permanent Additive Shock

We start by considering an unexpected permanent increase in z_1, from a value of zero, with the economy initially in steady state.[43] An increase in z_1 has no effect on the marginal product of capital and thus no effect on investment and the capital stock. Since the change is both unexpected and permanent, the increase in z_1 leads to an unexpected and permanent reduction in net output by the same amount, z_1. From (41) it follows that consumption falls by exactly the same amount. Saving therefore remains unchanged. Further, with both savings and investment unchanged, the current account is unaffected by the productivity shock.

In this case of an unexpected permanent reduction in z_1, the economy takes its losses immediately, and with no further consequences for the allocation of resources.[44]

A Transitory Additive Shock

Suppose now that z_1 increases unexpectedly but temporarily at time 0 for a period of length T. There is still no effect on investment, but there will now be a change in saving and the current account. The change in the present discounted value of net output is given by

$$-z_1 \int_0^T \exp(-\theta t)\, dt,$$

or equivalently

$-z_1 \theta^{-1}[1 - \exp(-\theta T)]$

so that the change in consumption is given by $-z_1[1 - \exp(-\theta T)]$.

This change in consumption is permanent. If T is small, the change in consumption is also small. Agents cut consumption only a little, and most of the decrease in output translates into a reduction in saving and a current account deficit. After output returns to normal, the economy runs a permanent trade surplus to pay for the increased interest payments on the debt. If T is large, the change in consumption is larger, the reduction in saving and the increase in debt smaller. As T tends to infinity, we obtain the same results as in the permanent case.

A Permanent Multiplicative Shock

Finally, let z_0 increase from zero to a positive value at $t = 0$. Because the marginal product of capital is $(1 - z_0) f'(k)$, a change in z_0 affects investment. We start by analyzing the effects of the change on investment and output.

As figure 2.8 shows, the increase in z_0 shifts the $dq/dt = 0$ locus to the left. The $dk/dt = 0$ locus is unaffected. The steady state of the economy shifts from E to E'. At E' the steady state capital stock $k^{*\prime}$ is lower than k^*, the initial steady state capital stock; the marginal product of capital $(1 - z_0) f'(k)$ is again equal to θ.

The new saddle point path is SS'. With the initial capital stock given by k^*, the path of adjustment is composed of a jump at time 0 from E to A, and a movement over time from A to E'. The rate of investment is negative on

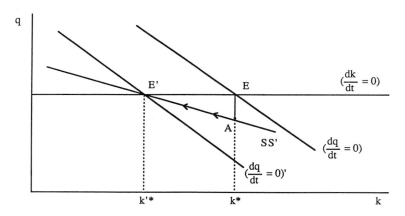

Figure 2.8
Effects of an adverse supply shock on investment and capital

the adjustment path, returning to zero as the economy moves to the new lower steady state capital stock.

Net output, which is equal to $(1 - z_0)f(k) - i[1 + T(i/k)]$, may either increase or decrease initially, depending on whether the fall in output when z_0 increases is larger or smaller than the decline in investment. In the long run, however, the effect is unambiguous. As investment returns to zero and the capital stock falls to a lower level, net output must be lower in the new steady state, because the initial effect of the adverse shock is compounded by lower capital accumulation.

In figure 2.9 we show net output falling initially, and then declining further to its new steady state level. The new level of consumption is determined again by the condition that the present value of the hatched areas above and below it be equal.

With net output above consumption immediately after the shock, the economy is saving in anticipation of lower net output later. In figure 2.9 the economy runs current account and trade surpluses immediately after the shock and becomes a net owner of foreign assets in steady state.

These examples show that there is no simple relation between adverse supply shocks and the current account even in the simple model developed in this section. What happens depends on the nature of the shocks affecting the economy, for example, whether they are additive or multiplicative, temporary or permanent. Sachs (1981) has used a closely related model to study the effects of the oil shocks of the 1970s on the current accounts of different groups of countries. He argues that the response of the indus-

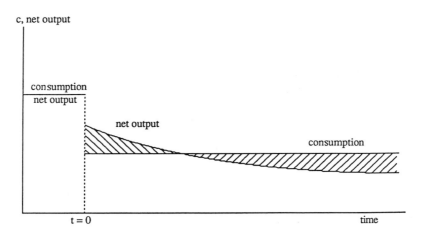

Figure 2.9
Dynamic effects of an adverse multiplicative shock

trializing developing countries, which borrowed extensively abroad during that period, conforms roughly to the predictions of the model.

2.5 The Utility Function

The assumption that the utility function is additively separable, with exponential discounting, produces strong results. In particular, because the modified golden rule relation (11) fixes the steady state real interest rate, the model of this chapter implies that no policy changes or shocks to the production function can affect the steady state aftertax real interest rate.

There is, however, no strong reason, beyond analytical convenience, to assume additive separability or a constant rate of time preference. Marginal utility of current consumption may well depend on past consumption through habit or through boredom effects. One may well have a rate of time preference that changes through life or, say, between summers and winters. What happens when we allow for such complications? This is the question we briefly explore in this last section.

Relaxation of the assumption of additive separability may lead to far more complex dynamics. Assume, for instance, the following form of the felicity function at time t:

$$u(c_t, z_t),$$

where z_t depends on past rates of consumption. The assumption here is that the history of consumption affects the marginal utility of current consumption. Ryder and Heal (1973) have shown that, with only this modification to the standard Ramsey model, optimal paths may overshoot the modified golden rule steady state, and that oscillatory approaches to the steady state are possible.

In this section we continue, however, to assume that the felicity function takes the form $u(c_t)$ and examine, instead, the assumption of a constant rate of time preference.[45] We first show a further implication of constant rates of time preference and then explore the rationale for that formulation and present an alternative representation.

Differences in Rates of Time Preference

We have assumed until now that all families have the same discount rate θ. There is no reason why this should generally be so. Consider the alternative in which there are m different types of families, ordered by decreasing impatience, with rates of time preference $\theta_1 > \cdots > \theta_m > 0$. The economy is in other respects identical with that of section 2.2, except that for expositional simplicity we assume zero population growth.

We now show that in steady state the interest rate r must be equal to the lowest rate of time preference θ_m. Suppose that this is not the case, and that r is smaller than θ_m. Then with r smaller than all rates of time preference, all families have decreasing consumption over time, by equation (19); but if all families have decreasing consumption and there is no population growth, the economy cannot be in steady state with constant aggregate consumption.

Suppose, instead, that r is greater than θ_m. All families with discount rate smaller than r have increasing consumption, and others have decreasing consumption. The share of total consumption accounted for by families with increasing consumption must be increasing over time. Indeed, the share of total consumption accounted for by the families with the lowest discount rate must eventually tend to one. Total consumption must therefore eventually be increasing; this is again inconsistent with being in steady state.

In steady state therefore the interest rate r equals θ_m.[46] The consumption of the most patient consumers is constant. The consumption of all other families is declining so that eventually their share in total consumption is zero. Slow and steady wins the race, and all the wealth; not only do the most patient families own all physical capital, but they also "own" the human capital of others who pay over all their labor income in return for past borrowing.[47] The model paints a somber, though unrealistic, picture of the dynamics of income and wealth distribution.

A slightly less extreme result is obtained if consumers are prohibited from borrowing against labor income and thus are constrained to have non-negative financial wealth. The steady state will still have $r = \theta_m$. The most patient families will hold all nonhuman wealth; all others will have a level of consumption equal to their labor income.[48] This result, though less drastic, is still not a good description of income distribution dynamics.[49]

There are many simplifications in this model, including the absence of uncertainty and the existence of infinitely lived families. These are possible directions in which to search for better models of income distribution dynamics. Another direction, to which we turn below, is the specification of preferences. What happens when we relax the assumption that the discount rate is constant?

Calendar Time, Time Distance, and Time Consistency

Suppose that, instead of the assumption of a constant rate of time preference, the utility integral is given by

$$U_s = \int_s^\infty u(c_t)D[t,\, t-s,\, x(t)]\, dt. \tag{48}$$

Utility is a weighted integral of felicities at different times, with the weighting function, $D(\cdot)$, referred to as a discount function. In (48) we make the discount function potentially a function of calendar time, t, of *time distance*, $t - s$, and possibly other variables, $x(t)$, for instance, the rate of consumption itself. Note that the formulation (1) makes the discount factor between any two periods purely a function of time distance: the rate of discount applied to utility for any particular number of years (say, T) in the future is always the same [in this case $\exp(-\theta T)$].

In any optimal program the marginal rate of substitution between consumption at any two dates is equal to the marginal rate of transformation. Using (48),[50] we now characterize the optimal program. Consider two planning dates, τ_1 and τ_2, and two points in time about which plans are made, t_1 and t_2: assume that

$$t_2 > t_1 > \tau_2 > \tau_1.$$

As of planning date τ_1, the marginal rate of substitution between consumption at time t_1 and consumption at time t_2 is given by

$$\frac{u'(c(t_1))D(t_1,\, t_1 - \tau_1)}{u'(c(t_2))D(t_2,\, t_2 - \tau_1)}. \tag{49}$$

Now consider the same marginal rate of substitution between consumption at time t_1 and consumption at time t_2 viewed as of planning date τ_2, $\tau_2 > \tau_1$:

$$\frac{u'(c(t_1))D(t_1,\, t_1 - \tau_2)}{u'(c(t_2))D(t_2,\, t_2 - \tau_2)}. \tag{50}$$

Comparison of (49) and (50) indicates that since $D(t, t - \tau_1)$ is generally different from $D(t, t - \tau_2)$, there is no reason for the rates of substitution between consumptions at times t_1 and t_2 to be the same from the two different planning dates. This implies that the optimal plan chosen at time τ_1 will no longer be optimal as of time τ_2. The optimal plan is therefore *time inconsistent*: the family's optimal plan changes over time even though no new information becomes available.

There are now two issues: First, under what restrictions on the discount function $D(\cdot)$ is the optimal plan time consistent? And second, what happens when the optimal plan is time inconsistent?

For the optimal plan to be the same as of time τ_1 and time τ_2, the marginal rates of substitution (49) and (50) must be the same. This can happen if the discount function $D(\cdot)$ is *either* an exponential function of time distance, $\exp[-\theta(t-s)]$ [check that this form ensures that the rates of substitution (49) and (50) are the same], *or* purely a function of calendar time or calendar values of other variables.[51] The first instance gives one possible rationale for assuming exponential discounting.

Dealing with Inconsistency

What happens, though, if people do have a discount function that leads to time inconsistency?[52] This question can be handled at many levels, but we do not dig deeply.[53] One possibility is that of *precommitment*. Consumers, having solved their optimal plan at time $t = 0$, may find a way of committing themselves to the plan to prevent what they then (at $t = 0$) would regard as backsliding. For instance, they could commit themselves to a savings path by entering a savings plan.

Another possibility is that consumers recognize that their tastes will be changing and make their plans assuming that they will at each future moment follow their tastes of that moment. They then choose a consistent plan in the sense that all future actions are correctly taken into account in the planning process.[54] If their discount function is only a function of time distance, this will lead them to act as if they had a constant rate of time preference through life.

This gives two possible rationales for assuming exponential discounting. The first is that exponential discounting leads to optimal programs that are time consistent. The other is that even if families do not exponentially discount the future but behave in time-consistent fashion, they may act as if they had exponential discounting. As we have seen, however, exponential discounting is not the only form of discounting that leads to time consistency. We now examine a formulation of the discount function in which the discount rate depends on the level of consumption. This formulation leads to a rate of time preference that changes through time but still implies time consistency of the optimal program.

Dependence of the Discount Rate on Utility

Uzawa (1968) considered the possibility that the rate of time preference depends on the level of utility or consumption. Uzawa's utility functional is

$$\int_0^\infty u(c_t) \exp\left\{-\int_0^t \theta[u(c_v)]\, dv\right\} dt.$$

The innovation is that the instantaneous rate of time preference is a function of the current level of utility, and thus of consumption.[55] Uzawa specified that

$$\theta'(\cdot) > 0. \tag{51}$$

The implication of (51) is that a higher level of consumption at time v increases the discount factor applied to utility at and after v. In steady state a higher level of consumption implies a higher rate of time preference. The assumption $\theta'(\cdot) > 0$ is difficult to defend *a priori*; indeed, we usually think it is the rich who are more likely to be patient. Assumption (51) is, however, needed for stability: if the rate of time preference fell with the level of consumption, the rich would become richer over time. That problem does not arise when, as in (51), the rate of time preference increases with the level of consumption.

We do not analyze the dynamics of this growth model but briefly characterize the steady state. Setting up the full model as in section 2.1, and deriving optimality conditions for the family, we obtain[56]

$$[u'(c_t) - \lambda_t] - \frac{\theta'[u(c_t)]u'(c_t)}{\theta[u(c_t)]} \{u(c_t) - \lambda_t[f(k_t) - nk_t - c_t]\} = 0,$$

$$\frac{d\lambda_t/dt}{\lambda_t} = \theta[u(c_t)] + n - f'(k_t), \tag{52}$$

$$\lim k_t \lambda_t \exp\left\{-\int_0^t \theta[u(c_v)]\, dv\right\} = 0. \tag{53}$$

The first equation gives the relation between the costate variable and consumption. Note that the dependence of the discount rate considerably complicates this relation, which we shall not discuss further. Note also that if $\Theta(\cdot)$ is constant, this relation reduces to $u'(c) = \lambda$, as in the Ramsey model. Equation (52) gives the relation between the rate of change of the costate variable the discount rate, and the marginal product; this relation is as in the Ramsey model. Equation (53) is the standard transversality condition.

The other equation is the capital accumulation equation:

$$\frac{dk_t}{dt} = f(k_t) - nk_t - c_t.$$

In steady state $d\lambda/dt = dk/dt = 0$ so that

$$\theta[u(c^*)] = f'(k^*) - n,$$

$$c^* = f(k^*) - nk^*.$$

These two loci are drawn in figure 2.10.

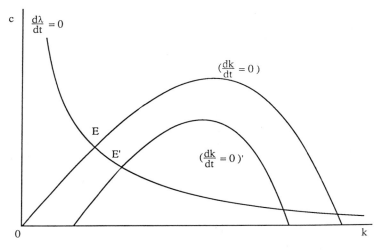

Figure 2.10
Dynamics with endogenous time preference

The $dk/dt = 0$ locus is the same as in section 2.1. The $d\lambda/dt = 0$ locus however, is now downward sloping rather than vertical. The saddle point steady state equilibrium is at point E.

Consider now an additive productivity shock, an increase in z_1, that shifts the $dk/dt = 0$ locus down uniformly. The new equilibrium is at E'. The steady state capital stock rises so that the reduction in consumption caused by lower productivity is compensated for by an increase in capital. The rate of time preference and the real interest rate are lower in the new equilibrium at E' than they were at E.

The results in figure 2.10 contrast sharply with those that would occur in the model of section 2.1. In that case the fall in productivity would leave the steady state real interest rate unaffected and would result in a reduction in consumption exactly equal to the decrease in output.

Returning to the issue that motivated our look at the Uzawa formulation, consider the situation where families have different discount rate functions. In steady state all discount rates will be equal. This implies a distribution of consumption across families and an associated steady state distribution of wealth. Families with more patience, in the sense that at a given level of consumption their rate of time preference is lower, achieve higher steady state wealth and consumption.

This specification avoids the pathological results of the constant discount rate case. Nonetheless, the Uzawa function, with its assumption $\theta'(\cdot) > 0$, is not particularly attractive as a description of preferences and is not recommended for general use. A nondegenerate steady state, when individual tastes differ, can also be achieved by assuming that agents have finite lives; this is a more plausible avenue which we develop in chapter 3.

Appendix A: Ruling Out Explosive Paths in the Ramsey Model

To show that the saddle point path DD in figure 2.2 is the optimal path, suppose that the initial capital stock is k_0, $0 < k_0 < k^*$. Consider any trajectory that starts above point D, at D', say. This path implies that the economy reaches zero capital in finite time. The proof turns on the fact that on such a path d^2k/dt^2 eventually becomes negative. Differentiating (2) gives

$$\frac{d^2k}{dt^2} = [f'(k) - n]\left(\frac{dk}{dt}\right) - \frac{dc}{dt} < 0, \quad \text{as} \quad \frac{dc}{dt} > 0, \quad f'(k) - n > 0.$$

Thus $k_t = k_0 + \int_0^t (dk_v/dv)\, dv$ will reach zero in finite time.

Note that c is rising on the path starting at D' all the time until it hits the axis at point B. But when the path reaches B, k is zero, and the economy has to move to the origin. Thus c has to jump from a positive value to zero. But such a jump violates the necessary condition (7'), and it thus cannot have been optimal to start at D'.

Consider, alternatively, a trajectory starting below D, for example, at D''. This path converges asymptotically to A. But such a path violates the transversality condition. At points close to A, k is approximately constant, whereas from (7') and $k > k_g$,

$$\frac{du'(c)/dt}{u'(c)} = \theta + n - f'(k) > 0.$$

Thus as t tends to infinity and the trajectory approaches A, the transversality condition is violated.

Similar arguments apply if the initial capital stock is larger than k^*. It follows that the saddle point path DD is the unique path that satisfies conditions (2), (7'), and (8).

Appendix B: Local Behavior of Capital around the Steady State in the Ramsey Model

The characteristic equation associated with equation (15) is

$$x^2 - \theta x - \beta = 0.$$

It has two roots:

$$\lambda \equiv \frac{\theta - \sqrt{\theta^2 + 4\beta}}{2} < 0$$

and

$$\mu \equiv \frac{\theta + \sqrt{\theta^2 + 4\beta}}{2} > 0.$$

Thus paths that satisfy equation (15) are given by

$$k_t - k^* = c_0 \exp(\lambda t) + c_1 \exp(\mu t),$$

where c_0 and c_1 are arbitrary constants.

As k_0 is given from history, c_0 and c_1 must satisfy

$$k_0 - k^* = c_0 \exp(0) + c_1 \exp(0) = c_0 + c_1.$$

In addition, as μ is positive, c_1 must be equal to zero for k to converge to k^*. Thus $c_1 = 0$ and $c_0 = k_0 - k^*$. This implies in turn that

$$k_t = k^* + (k_0 - k^*) \exp(\lambda t).$$

Appendix C: Command Optimum and Decentralized Equilibrium in the Open Economy Model

We show here the equivalence of the command optimum and the decentralized competitive equilibrium in the open economy model of section 2.4. For notational simplicity, we assume that there are as many firms as families so that the same symbol denotes the ratio of a variable per capita or per firm.

The structure of the economy is the following: Firms rent labor services in the labor market but own the capital stock; they finance investment through retained earnings. Families supply labor services and own the firms, receiving profits net of investment expenses. They allocate their income between consumption and saving, where saving takes the form of lending to the rest of the world.[57]

Value Maximization by Firms

For simplicity, we do not explicitly model the labor market. Labor is supplied inelastically so that labor market equilibrium implies that each firm hires one worker, paying wages of $\{w_t\}$ $t = [0, \infty)$. The decision problem of a representative firm at time zero is then to choose the time path of investment that maximizes the present discounted value of cash flows:

$$\max V_0 = \int_0^\infty \left\{ f(k_t) - i_t \left[1 + T\left(\frac{i_t}{k_t}\right) \right] - w_t \right\} \exp(-\theta t) \, dt \tag{C1}$$

subject to $dk_t/dt = i_t$ and the same technology as the central planner.

By letting $q_t \exp(-\theta t)$ be the Lagrange multiplier associated with the capital accumulation equation and setting up a present value Hamiltonian, the first-order conditions lead to equations identical to (43), (37'), and (44). Firms invest until the marginal cost of investment is equal to the shadow value of installed capital, q. This shadow value is itself equal to the present discounted value of future marginal products. Firms choose the same path of investment and capital accumulation as the central planner.

Given our assumption that firms finance investment through retained earnings, dividends paid by firms are therefore equal to net cash flows[58]

$$\pi_t = f(k_t) - i_t \left[1 + T\left(\frac{i_t}{k_t}\right) \right] - w_t. \tag{C2}$$

Utility Maximization by Families

Each family supplies one unit of labor inelastically, receiving wage w_t and dividends π_t. Its only decision problem is to choose a path of consumption that maximizes

$$U_0 = \int_0^\infty u(c_t) \exp(-\theta t) \, dt. \tag{C3}$$

It can borrow and lend on the world market at the rate θ. The dynamic budget constraint is therefore

$$\frac{db_t}{dt} = c_t + \theta b_t - \pi_t - w_t. \tag{C4}$$

To this we add the NPG condition:

$$\lim_{t \to \infty} b_t \exp(-\theta t) = 0. \tag{C5}$$

The solution to this maximization problem is given by

$$c_t = c_0 = \theta \int_0^\infty (\pi_t + w_t) \exp(-\delta t) \, dt. \tag{C6}$$

Replacing π_t by its value from (C2) in (C6) gives the same path of consumption as equation (42). Families will choose the same path of consumption as the central planner.

Appendix D: Saddle Point Equilibrium in the Linearized (k, q) System

Equation (47) linearizes the dynamic system that describes the behavior of q and k around the steady state values. The solution to such a linear system is given by

$$k_t - k^* = c_{11} \exp(y_1 t) + c_{12} \exp(y_2 t),$$
$$q_t - 1 = c_{21} \exp(y_1 t) + c_{22} \exp(y_2 t), \tag{D1}$$

where y_1 and y_2 are the roots of the characteristic equation associated with (47), namely,

$$\begin{vmatrix} 0 - y & k^* \varphi'(1) \\ -f''(k^*) & \theta - y \end{vmatrix} = 0,$$

and where $[c_{11} \; c_{21}]$ and $[c_{12} \; c_{22}]$ are eigenvectors associated with each of these two roots.

The roots are given by

$$y = \frac{\theta \pm \sqrt{\theta^2 - 4f''(k^*)k^*\varphi'(1)}}{2}.$$

Both roots are real, with one root negative and the other positive. The positive root exceeds θ.

Denote the negative root by y_1. The eigenvector associated with y_1 is given by

$$\begin{bmatrix} -y_1 & k^*\varphi'(1) \\ -f''(k^*) & \theta - y_1 \end{bmatrix} \begin{bmatrix} c_{11} \\ c_{21} \end{bmatrix} = 0, \tag{D2}$$

so that $c_{21} = \{y_1[k^*\varphi'(1)]^{-1}\}c_{11}$. Examining (A7), we see that for the path that converges to $(k^*, 1)$, both c_{12} and c_{22} must be equal to zero. (Zero is always an eigenvector.)

To calculate the constants c_{11} and c_{21}, note that at time zero, the first row of (D1) is

$$k_0 - k^* = c_{11}. \tag{D3}$$

Replacing the c's by their values in (D1) gives the converging path for k and q.

On all paths other than the converging path, c_{12} and/or c_{22} are different from zero. Thus q and k eventually increase at rate y_2. This implies that qk eventually increases at rate no less than y_2, which is itself greater than θ. Thus they all violate the transversality condition (39).

Of course, the proof that the transversality condition is violated on all but the saddle point path in the linearized system does not establish the fact that the paths of the original system that are not saddle point paths explode at a rate greater than θ. A complete proof requires a characterization of the dynamics of the original nonlinear system along the lines of the proof presented in appendix A.

Problems

1. *The Solow growth model. (This follows Solow 1956.)*

(a) Consider an economy with a population growth rate equal to n, with constant returns to scale in production, and in which individuals save a constant fraction, s, of their income. Show that the differential equation describing the behavior of the capital stock per capita is given by

$$\frac{dk}{dt} = sf(k) - nk,$$

where $f(\cdot)$ is the production function per capita and s is the savings rate.

(b) Characterize the steady state capital stock per capita in this model.

(c) Examine the stability of the system, and characterize the adjustment of the capital stock toward its steady state.

(d) Can a constant saving rate along the path of adjustment be consistent with intertemporal utility maximization by infinitely long-lived individuals?

(e) Assume that factor markets are competitive. Show that the savings rate that leads to the golden rule capital stock is equal to the share of capital in production. Explain.

2. *Growth with exogenous technological progress.*

Suppose that, in a Ramsey economy, production is given (as in note 13) by the function

$$Y_t = F(K_t, \exp(\phi t)N_t),$$

where ϕ is the constant and exogenous rate of technical progress. Assume that the population grows at rate n and that the utility function is of constant relative risk aversion form, with a coefficient of relative risk aversion equal to γ.

(a) Derive and interpret the modified golden rule condition in this case.

(b) Characterize the dynamics of consumption and capital accumulation.

(c) Suppose that the economy is in steady state and that ϕ decreases permanently and unexpectedly. Describe the dynamic adjustment of the economy to this adverse supply shock.

3. *Optimal consumption with exponential utility.*

Consider a family, growing at rate n and with discount rate θ, that faces a given path of future wages and interest rates and has a constant absolute risk aversion utility function, with a coefficient of risk aversion α. Solve for the path of consumption, as is done in the text for the CRRA utility function.

4. *Government spending in the Ramsey model.*

(a) In the Ramsey model, suppose that the government unexpectedly increases government spending, raising it from a base level g_0 to the level g_1 (per capita in both cases), starting from steady state. Analyze the effects of this increase on the paths of consumption and capital accumulation.

Note: You may want to use the equivalence between the command and market solutions and treat the increase in g as a negative additive productivity shock.

(b) Do the same exercise, assuming that the economy is not initially in steady state. Characterize the dynamic effects when utility is of the CARA form. Explain.

(c) Suppose, instead, that the increase in government spending is announced at time t_0 to take place at time t_1, with $t_1 > t_0$. Characterize the dynamic effects on consumption and capital accumulation from t_0.

Note: Phase diagrams are convenient to use when characterizing the effects of such anticipated changes. Note that between t_0 and t_1 the equations of motion are given by the dynamic system with $g = g_0$, and that after t_1 the equations of motion are given by the dynamic system with $g = g_1$. Note further that c cannot jump anticipatedly at time t_1. Note finally that k at time t_0 is given and that the system must converge to the new equilibrium. Show that these conditions uniquely define the path of adjustment. (Abel 1981 characterizes the effects of anticipated or temporary changes in taxation on investment within the q theory using such phase diagrams.)

5. *Savings and investment with costs of adjustment in a closed economy.*
(This follows Abel and Blanchard 1983.)

Assume that there are costs of adjusting the capital stock, as in section 2.4, but that the economy is closed. Derive the optimal paths of consumption and capital accumulation in this case and provide an explanation of the difference between the Euler equation for this case and equation (7).

6. *Foreign debt and trade surpluses.*

(a) Using the relevant budget constraint, show that b_0, the initial value of external debt, is equal to the present value of net exports, provided an NPG condition is satisfied.
(b) Suppose that for some period of time a country's external debt is growing more rapidly than at the rate $r - n$. What can you conclude about the likelihood that the NPG condition will be violated in the long run? What then is the relevance of the NPG condition?

7. Suppose that in a closed economy there is an unexpected permanent reduction in the efficiency of production, represented in the symbols in the text as an increase in z_0. Assuming that the economy started in a steady state, derive and explain its optimal dynamic adjustment toward the new steady state.

8. *Growth with increasing returns, I.*

Consider an economy with the production function

$$Y = K^{a+b}N^{1-a}, \qquad b > 0, a + b < 1$$

so that there are increasing returns to scale but decreasing returns to capital given labor. Population is growing at the rate n, and there is no depreciation.
(a) Show that it is possible for capital, output, and consumption all to grow at the same rate g. This is known as *balanced growth*. Derive the balanced growth rate g, and explain its dependence on a, b, and n.
(b) Suppose that the felicity function for the representative family is

$$u(c_t) = \ln c_t$$

and that the family has a constant discount rate θ.
   Assuming that the economy converges to a balanced growth path, characterize the steady state marginal product of capital. Compare it to the modified golden rule level that would obtain under constant returns (i.e., with $b = 0$). Explain the difference.

9. *Growth with increasing returns, II. (This follows Rebelo 1987.)*

Consider the following economy: Population is constant and normalized to unity, and the representative individual maximizes

$$\int_0^{\infty} U(C) \exp(-\theta t) \, dt.$$

K is the capital stock in the economy and can be used either to produce consumption goods or new capital goods. Let x, $0 \leqslant x \leqslant 1$, be the proportion of capital used in the production of consumption goods. The two production functions for consumption and investment goods are given by

$$C = F(xK),$$

$$F(0) = 0, \qquad F'(\cdot) > 0, \, F''(\cdot) < 0.$$

$dK/dt = I = B(1 - x)K$; B is a positive constant. Capital does not depreciate.

(a) What is the maximum growth rate of capital in this economy? What is the associated level of consumption?

(b) Derive the first-order conditions associated with this maximization problem. Interpret them. Give, in particular, an interpretation of the Lagrange multipliers and costate variables as shadow prices.

(c) Assume that $F(xK) = A(xK)^a$, where $0 < a < 1$, and that $U(C) = \ln(C)$. Show that if the economy converges to a balanced growth path, the rate of growth of consumption is given by $a(B - \theta)$. Explain in words.

What happens to the relative price of capital goods in terms of consumption goods along the balanced growth path?

(d) Contrast your results with those obtained in the conventional Ramsey model. Explain why they differ.

(e) How does this model do in terms of explaining the basic facts of growth as laid out by Kaldor and Solow, and summarized in chapter 1? What is the relation of consumption to income along the balanced growth path? What is the relation of output to capital? (Be careful about how you define capital—value or volume—here.)

Notes

1. In chapter 3 we show that people who have finite lives may still act as if they in effect had infinite lives.

2. Frank Ramsey was a Cambridge, England, mathematician and logician who died at the age of 26. His genius is evidenced by the fact that he had written three classic articles in economics by the age at which many economists are contemplating leaving graduate school. J. M. Keynes (1930) eulogizes Ramsey.

3. If depreciation is exponential at the rate λ, then gross output is $Y + \lambda K = F(K, N) + \lambda K = G(K, N)$. If $F(K, N)$ is degree one homogeneous, so is $G(K, N)$.

4. An alternative plausible formulation is the so-called Benthamite welfare function in which the felicity function becomes $N_t u(c_t)$ so that the number of family members receiving the given utility level is taken into account. Recognizing that $N_t = N_0 e^{nt}$, we see that the Benthamite formulation is equivalent to reducing the rate of time preference to $(\theta - n)$ because the larger size of the family at later dates in effect

increases the weight given to the utility of the representative individual in a later generation.

In assuming that $\theta > 0$, we depart from Ramsey who, interpreting the maximization problem as the problem solved by a central planner, argued that there was no ethical case for discounting the future.

5. Ordinary calculus optimization methods have to be augmented to handle the presence of a time derivative in constraint (2). Intriligator (1971) provides an introduction to intertemporal optimization methods.

6. A warning is in order here. First, under weaker assumptions than those made in the text, for example, a linear production function or no discounting, an optimum may not exist. Even if an optimum does exist, the transversality condition, equation (8), may not be necessary. But if one is ready to set sufficiently strong conditions for the maximization problem, these problems can usually safely be ignored. For a more careful statement and further discussion, see Shell (1969) and Benveniste and Scheinkman (1982).

7. Note from the formulation of the central planner's problem that it is implicitly assumed that capital can be consumed.

8. We emphasize again that as intuitive as this argument for the transversality condition is, there are infinite horizon problems in which the transversality condition is not necessary for the optimal path. See Shell (1969) and Michel (1982).

9. To show that the utility function converges to the logarithmic function as γ tends to unity, use L'Hospital's rule.

10. On the basic measures of risk aversion, see J. Pratt in Diamond and Rothschild (1978); see also the following articles in Diamond and Rothschild by Yaari and by Rothschild and Stiglitz.

Behavior toward risk and the degree of substitution between consumption at different times are conceptually two different issues. Under the assumption that the von Neumann-Morgenstern utility integral is additively separable over time, however, the two depend only on the curvature of the instantaneous utility function and are thus directly related. See chapter 6 for further discussion.

11. In steady state, with $dk/dt = 0$, we have from (2),

$c^* = f(k^*) - nk^*$.

Maximization of c^* with respect to k^* gives the golden rule, that the marginal product of capital (or interest rate) is equal to the growth rate of population.

12. We freely interchange the marginal product and interest rates. We show later that in the decentralized Ramsey economy, the two are indeed equal.

13. The result that the steady state interest rate does not depend on the utility function can, however, be easily overturned. If labor-augmenting (Harrod-neutral) technical progress is taking place at the rate μ, so that

$Y_t = F[K_t, \exp(\mu t)N_t]$

and if the utility function is of the CRRA class, then the modified golden rule condition becomes $f'(k^*) = \theta + \sigma\mu + n$. [In this case k^* is the ratio of capital to effective labor, i.e., $K_t/\exp(\mu t)N_t$, and the steady state is one in which consumption per capita is growing at the rate μ.]

14. The analysis can also be undertaken in (k, λ) space, using the first-order condition (6).

15. The behavior of consumption on the horizontal axis, where $c = 0$, depends on the value of the instantaneous elasticity of substitution $\sigma(c)$ for $c = 0$. Equation (7″) implies that

$$\frac{dc}{dt} = \sigma(c)[f'(k) - \theta - n]c.$$

If $\sigma^{-1}(0)$ is not zero, then $dc/dt = 0$ when $c = 0$. We assume this to be the case. If the condition is not met, one must examine the behavior of $c\sigma(c)$ at $c = 0$.

16. Throughout the book we will encounter phase diagrams in which there is only one convergent path. Although we will often simply assume that the economy proceeds on this converging path, an argument must be made in each case that the converging path is the only one that satisfies the conditions of the problem. As we will see in chapter 5, there are cases in which we cannot rule out some of the diverging paths.

17. Changes in f'' and θ affect both the rate of convergence to the steady state and the steady state capital stock itself.

18. The condition that the rental rate on capital is equal to the interest rate is special to this one-good model. If the relative price of capital, p_k, could vary, asset market equilibrium would ensure that the expected rate of return from holding capital would be equal to the interest rate. The rate of return from holding capital is the rental rate, r_k plus any capital gains on capital minus depreciation, all expressed relative to the price of the capital:

$$\text{rate of return} = \frac{r_k + (dp_k/dt) - \delta p_k}{p_k} = \text{real interest rate},$$

where δ is the rate of depreciation. In the single-good model, p_k is identically one, so there are no changes in the relative price of capital, and we are assuming that δ is zero; accordingly, the rate of return on capital is r_k, which is equal to the interest rate. (We are implicitly assuming that the economy never specializes completely; if it did not save at all, the relative price of capital goods could be less than one; if it did not consume at all, the relative price of capital could exceed one.)

19. For notational convenience we shall assume that there is just one family and one firm, both acting competitively.

20. There are many alternative ways of describing the decentralized economy. For example, firms can own the capital and finance investment by either borrowing or issuing equity. Or, instead of operating with spot factor markets, the economy may

operate in the Arrow-Debreu complete market framework in which markets for current and all future commodities, including services, are open at the beginning of time; all contracts are made then, and the rest of history merely executes these contracts. Under perfect foresight, all these economies will have the same allocation of resources.

21. We limit ourselves in what follows to paths of wages and rental rates such that the following condition is satisfied:

$$\lim_{t \to \infty} \exp \left[- \int_0^t (r_v - n) \, dv \right] = 0.$$

This condition says, roughly, that asymptotically the interest rate must exceed the rate of population growth. We will show that the equilibrium path indeed satisfies this condition. A complete argument would show that if this condition is not satisfied, there is no equilibrium. See note 25 below for further elaboration.

22. In the present model, in which all families are the same, they will in equilibrium have the same wealth position and hold the same fraction of the capital stock. Since the aggregate capital stock must be positive, each family will, in equilibrium, have positive wealth. This is, however, a characteristic of equilibrium, not a constraint that should be imposed a priori on the maximization problem of each family. In an economy with heterogeneous families, or families with different paths of labor income, positive aggregate capital may coexist with temporary borrowing by some families.

23. Charles Ponzi, one of Boston's sons, made a quick fortune in the 1920s using chain letters. He was sent to prison and died poor.

24. This raises the question of how the no-Ponzi-game condition is actually enforced. The fact that parents cannot, for the most part, leave negative bequests to their children implies that family debt cannot increase exponentially. It may in fact impose a stronger restriction on borrowing than the no-Ponzi-game condition used here.

25. Following up on note 21, there is one loose end in our proof of equivalence, which we now tie up. We have restricted ourselves to paths where the interest rate exceeds asymptotically the population growth rate. Given this restriction, we showed that there is an equilibrium path, which is the same as the central planning one, so that r converges asymptotically to $n + \theta$. We now need to show that paths on which the interest rate is asymptotically less than n, cannot be equilibria. To see why, rewrite the budget constraint facing the family as

$$\frac{da_t}{dt} = (r_t - n)a_t + (c_t - w_t).$$

Consider then two paths of consumption, which have the same level of consumption after some time T, so that $c_t - w_t$ is the same on both paths after T. Then, if $r_t - n$ is asymptotically negative, both paths will lead to the same asymptotic value of a (the same level of net indebtedness if a is negative). If one path satisfies the no-Ponzi-game condition, so will the other. But this implies that the family will always want to have very high (possibly infinite) consumption until time T. This cannot be an equilibrium.

26. We consider endogenous government spending in chapter 11.

27. Government spending, for instance, on education, might substitute for private spending, in which case the utility function would have to be amended appropriately. Similarly, government spending on defense and public safety might contribute to the economy's productive capacity, but we do not model any such effects.

28. The dynamics of investment and savings in a closed economy with adjustment costs are studied in Abel and Blanchard (1983).

29. Blanchard (1983), Fischer and Frenkel (1972), and Svensson (1984) have used similar models to examine the dynamics of foreign debt and the current account.

30. Investment decisions based on adjustment costs have been modeled by Abel (1981), Eisner and Strotz (1963), Lucas (1967), and Tobin (1969). Our specification is that of Hayashi (1982).

31. The conditions specified after equation (31) ensure the properties of the installation cost function $iT(i/k)$. Note that, in practice, when capital depreciates, the costs of small rates of disinvestment, which can take place through depreciation, are likely to be very small or zero.

Instead of defining both a production and an installation cost function, we could have defined a 'net' production function that gives output available for consumption or export, $H(K, N, I)$. This is the approach taken, for example, by Lucas (1967). In our case $H(K, N, I) = F(K, N) - I[1 + T(I/K)]$, where uppercase letters are total amounts of corresponding per capita variables. The function $H(\cdot)$ has constant returns to scale if $F(\cdot)$ does.

32. If the world interest rate had differed from the rate of time preference, the country would either accumulate or decumulate forever. This follows from the Euler equation in the absence of population growth, which from section 2.2 will give $[du'(c_t)/dt]/u'(c_t) = \theta - r$, where r is the interest rate. If the country accumulates forever because $\theta < r$, then it eventually becomes a large economy and begins to affect the world interest rate; if $\theta > r$, then the country runs its wealth down as far as it can. To avoid these difficulties, we set $\theta = r$. We could also obtain convergence to a steady state if we specified a time path for the world interest rate that converges to θ, rather than always being equal to θ. We assume $r = \theta$ for simplicity.

33. We state the NPG condition as an equality. We could again state it as an inequality, requiring the present discounted value of debt to be nonnegative. But if marginal utility is positive, the central planner will not want to accumulate increasing claims on the rest of the world forever. Thus the NPG condition will hold with equality.

34. Defining the costate variable on (31) as $\mu_t q_t \exp(-\theta t)$ rather than as a single variable is a matter of convenience, as will become clear later when we show that q plays a key role in determining investment.

35. Note that because of the equality of the interest rate and the subjective discount rate, the marginal propensity to consume out of wealth is equal to θ independently of the form of the felicity function.

36. Note that given constant μ_t, equation (39) implies that $\lim q_t k_t \exp(-\theta t) = 0$ as t goes to ∞. This is, however, not the same as $\lim q_t \exp(-\theta t) = 0$ as t goes to ∞, which is the condition needed to derive (44). To derive (44), one must characterize the phase diagram associated with equations (37') and (43) and show that the only path that satifies these equations and the transversality condition (39) is a path where both k and q tend to k^* and q^*, respectively, so that $\lim q_t \exp(-\theta t) = 0$ as t goes to ∞.

37. This way of thinking about the investment decision was developed by Tobin. For that reason, q is often called Tobin's q. See Hayashi (1982) for a discussion of the relation of q to its empirical counterparts; in particular, Hayashi discusses the conditions under which average q, as reflected, say, in the stock market valuation of a firm, is equal to marginal q, the shadow value of an additional unit of installed capital. Marginal and average q are equal, leaving aside tax issues, if the firm's production function and the adjustment cost function $iT(\cdot)$ are each first-degree homogeneous and firms operate in competitive markets. Under those assumptions one would expect a tight relation between the market valuation of firms and their investment decisions. Empirically, although average q and investment rates are indeed correlated, the relation is far from tight (see Hayashi 1982).

38. If there is population growth at the rate n, then q^* is given by $n = \phi(q^*)$ so that $q^* > 1$, and k^* is given by

$$\theta q^* = f'(k^*) - n^2 T'(n).$$

39. The restriction to local dynamics ensures that $dq/dt = 0$ is negatively sloped; away from the steady state there is no assurance that the slope of $dq/dt = 0$ is negative without imposing more conditions on the $T(\cdot)$ function. However, the restrictions imposed on $T(\cdot)$ are sufficient to ensure that there is a unique steady state in the neighborhood of which the $dq/dt = 0$ locus is negatively sloped.

40. In appendix D we show that the transversality condition suffices in the linearized system to rule out any divergent paths that satisfy the necessary conditions (47).

41. The current account always has present discounted value equal to zero when condition (32) is satisfied; it is only when the initial debt is zero that the same applies to the trade account.

42. Given the equivalence between the command optimum and the decentralized economy, the shocks can also be interpreted as taxes, where the government is using the proceeds of the taxes to finance government spending that does not affect the utility function, as in section 2.3.

43. This experiment raises the methodological issue of how unexpected changes can occur in a model in which there is perfect foresight. The correct way to analyze such changes would be to set up the maximizing problems of the central planner or economic agents explicitly as decision problems under uncertainty. This substantially complicates the analysis, and we defer this to chapter 6; we can think of the approach taken here as a shortcut in which the surprise is an event that was regarded as so unlikely as not to be taken into account up to the time it occurs.

44. If individuals dislike changes in the rate of consumption so that the felicity function is, for instance, $u(c, dc/dt)$, the reduction in z_1 would cause a smaller decline in consumption than in output initially; the country would in that case initially borrow abroad temporarily to cushion the shock of the reduction in the standard of living, and end up with permanently higher debt and lower consumption.

45. We briefly return in chapter 7 to the issue of nonseparability in the context of a discussion of labor supply.

As we shall see, however, the distinction between the felicity function and the discount factor becomes somewhat blurred when we allow for more general formulations of this discount factor.

46. The argument to this point does not eliminate the possibility that there is no steady state. The argument of this paragraph can be seen, however, to imply the existence of a steady state with $r = \theta_m$.

47. The no-Ponzi-game condition prevents the shortsighted from going further and further into debt.

48. Ramsey (1928) conjectured this result; it was proved by Becker (1980).

49. Note the similarity between the discussion here and that of the relationship between the world interest rate and rate of time preference of a small country in section 2.4.

50. Because the point we are about to make about the optimal program does not depend on the presence of $x(t)$ in the discount function, we omit that argument henceforth.

51. This result is due to Strotz (1956).

52. An example is $D(\cdot) = \max[0, A - \theta(t - s)]$.

53. See Elster (1979) and Schelling (1984) for more extensive discussion of how people do and should deal with inconsistencies. Issues of time consistency also arise in the context of games between agents or between agents and the government. We will study these in chapter 11.

54. There is no "correct" way to behave when tastes are dynamically inconsistent, for there is no way of knowing which is the right set of tastes: the title "Ulysses and the Sirens" (Elster 1979) refers to Ulysses's strategy of having himself tied to the mast to avoid succumbing to the Sirens' cry—but maybe the real Ulysses was the one who would have succumbed if the other Ulysses hadn't tied him to the mast.

55. Epstein and Hynes (1983) suggest an alternative specification, namely,

$$\int_0^\infty \exp\left[-\int_0^s u(c_v)\, dv \right] ds.$$

This specification has the same qualitative implication as Uzawa's but is more tractable analytically. Note that in this form there is no longer any distinction between the discount rate and the instantaneous felicity function.

56. Lucas and Stokey (1984) work with a model of this type.

57. Once again, there are many alternative ways of describing the decentralized economy. Firms could, instead, finance investment by issuing shares or by borrowing either abroad or domestically. The real allocation would be the same in all cases.

58. If investment is so high that net cash flows are negative, the firm is, in effect, issuing equity by paying a negative dividend, that is, making a call on stockholders for cash.

References

Abel, Andrew (1981). "Dynamic Effects of Permanent and Temporary Tax Policies in a q Model of Investment." *Journal of Monetary Economics*, 353–373.

Abel, Andrew, and Olivier Blanchard (1983). "An Intertemporal Equilibrium Model of Saving and Investment." *Econometrica* 51, 3 (May), 675–692.

Arrow, Kenneth J., and Mordecai Kurz (1970). *Public Investment, the Rate of Return, and Optimal Fiscal Policy*. Johns Hopkins Press.

Becker, Robert A. (1980). "On the Long-Run Steady State in a Simple Dynamic Model of Equilibrium with Heterogeneous Households." *Quarterly Journal of Economics* 95, 2 (Sept.), 375–382.

Benveniste, L. M., and José A. Scheinkman (1982). "Duality Theory for Dynamic Optimization Models of Economics: The Continuous Time Case." *Journal of Economic Theory* 27, 1 (June), 1–19.

Blanchard, Olivier (1983). "Debt and the Current Account Deficit in Brazil." In Pedro Aspe Armella et al. (eds.), *Financial Policies and the World Capital Market: The Problem of Latin American Countries*. University of Chicago Press.

Diamond, Peter A., and Michael Rothschild (1978). *Uncertainty in Economics*. Academic Press.

Eisner, Robert, and Robert H. Strotz (1963). "Determinants of Business Investment." In *Commission on Money and Credit: Impacts of Monetary Policy*. Prentice-Hall.

Elster, Jon (1979). *Ulysses and the Sirens*. Cambridge University Press.

Epstein, Larry G., and J. Allan Hynes (1983). "The Rate of Time Preference and Dynamic Economic Analysis." *Journal of Political Economy* 91, 4 (Aug.), 611−635.

Fischer, Stanley, and Jacob Frenkel (1972). "Investment, the Two-Sector Model, and Trade In Debt and Capital Goods." *Journal of International Economics* 2 (Aug.), 211−233.

Hall, Robert E. (1981). "Intertemporal Substitution in Consumption." NBER Working Paper 720.

Hayashi, Fumio (1982). "Tobin's Marginal and Average q: A Neoclassical Interpretation." *Econometrica* 50 (Jan.), 213−224.

Intriligator, Michael D. (1971). *Mathematical Optimization and Economic Theory.* Prentice-Hall.

Keynes, John Maynard (1930). "F. P. Ramsey." *Economic Journal* (Mar.). Reprinted in J. M. Keynes. *Essays in Biography.* London: Macmillan, 1972.

Lucas, Robert E. (1967). "Adjustment Costs and the Theory of Supply." *Journal of Political Economy* 75, 321−334.

Lucas, Robert E. Jr., and Nancy L. Stokey (1984). "Optimal Growth with Many Consumers." *Journal of Economic Theory* 32, 1 (Feb.), 139−171.

Michel, Philippe, (1982). "On the Transversality Condition in Infinite Horizon Optimal Problems." *Econometrica* 50, 4 (July), 975−986.

O'Connell, Stephen A., and Stephen P. Zeldes (1985). "Rational Ponzi Games." Department of Economics, University of Pennsylvania.

Ramsey, Frank P. (1928). "A Mathematical Theory of Saving." *Economic Journal* 38, No. 152 (Dec.), 543−559. Reprinted in Joseph E. Stiglitz and Hirofumi Uzawa (eds.). *Readings in the Modern Theory of Economic Growth*, MIT Press, 1969.

Rebelo, Sergio (1987). "Long Run Policy Analysis and Long Run Growth." Working paper. Rochester. November.

Ryder, Harl E., Jr., and Geoffrey M. Heal (1973). "Optimum Growth with Intertemporally Dependent Preferences." *Review of Economic Studies* 40, 1 (Jan.), 1−32.

Sachs, Jeffrey D. (1981). "The Current Account and Macroeconomic Adjustment in the 1970's." *Brookings Papers on Economic Activity* 1, 201−268.

Schelling, Thomas C. (1984). *Choice and Consequence.* Harvard University Press.

Shell, Karl (1969). "Applications of Pontryagin's Maximum Principle to Economics." In H. W. Kuhn and G. P. Szego (eds.), *Mathematical Systems Theory and Economics.* Vol. 1. Springer-Verlag, Berlin.

Solow, Robert (1956). "A Contribution to the Theory of Economic Growth." *Quarterly Journal of Economics* 70, 1 (Feb.), 65−94.

Strotz, Robert H. (1956). "Myopia and Inconsistency in Dynamic Utility Maximization." *Review of Economic Studies* 23, 165–180.

Svensson, Lars E.O. (1984). "Oil Prices, Welfare, and the Trade Balance." *Quarterly Journal of Economics* 99, 4 (Nov.), 649–672.

Tobin, James (1969). "A General Equilibrium Approach to Monetary Theory." *Journal of Money, Credit and Banking* 1, 1 (Feb.), 15–29.

Uzawa, Hirofumi (1968). "Time Preference, the Consumption Function and Optimum Asset Holdings." In J. N. Wolfe (ed.), *Value, Capital and Growth: Papers in Honour of Sir John Hicks*. University of Edinburgh Press.

3   The Overlapping
                                      Generations Model

The overlapping generations model of Allais (1947), Samuelson (1958), and Diamond (1965) is the second basic model used in micro-based macro-economics. The name implies the structure: at any one time individuals of different generations are alive and may be trading with one another, each generation trades with different generations in different periods of its life, and there are generations yet unborn whose preferences may not be registered in current market transactions.

The model is widely used because it makes it possible to study the aggregate implications of life-cycle saving by individuals. The capital stock is generated by individuals who save during their working lives to finance their consumption during retirement. The determinants of the aggregate capital stock as well as the effects of government policy on the capital stock and the welfare of different generations are easily studied. The model can be extended to allow for bequests, both intentional and unintentional.

Given the descriptive appeal of the life-cycle hypothesis, these uses of the model would alone justify its widespread popularity. But beyond that, the model provides an example of an economy in which the competitive equilibrium is not necessarily that which would be chosen by a central planner. There is an even stronger result: the competitive equilibrium may not be Pareto optimal. Life-cycle savers may overaccumulate capital, leading to equilibria in which everyone can be made better off by consuming part of the capital stock. This possible inefficiency of the equilibrium contrasts sharply with the intertemporal efficiency of the competitive equilibrium in the Ramsey model. One of the goals of this chapter is to elucidate the aspects of the life-cycle model that make inefficiency possible.

We start, in section 3.1, with the simplest version of the overlapping generations model in which individuals live for only two periods. Starting from individual maximization, we show how the aggregate capital stock evolves over time. We extend the model to consider the effects of altruism (or bequests) on the equilibrium. We then use the model in section 3.2 to examine the effects of the introduction of a social security system on the capital stock and the welfare of different generations.

The two-period-lived individuals in the simplest model appear very different from the infinite horizon maximizers of the Ramsey model. However, in section 3.3 we show, by developing a continuous time version of the overlapping generations model due to Blanchard (1985), that the Ramsey model can in a well-defined sense be viewed as a special case of the overlapping generations model. We then use this model to study two sets of issues. In section 3.4 we examine the effects of government deficit finance on capital accumulation and interest rates. Then in section 3.5 we use the model to analyze the effects of changes in the interest rate on aggregate saving.

3.1 Two-Period Lives

In the real world individuals at different stages of their life-cycles interact in markets, when young, dealing mainly with older people and later with mostly younger people. This feature is captured in the simplest overlapping generations model in which individuals live for two periods so that, at any point in time, the economy is composed of two cohorts, or generations, the young and the old.

This section presents a model of equilibrium initially developed by Diamond (1965), building on earlier work by Samuelson (1958). We first characterize the decentralized competitive equilibrium of the model. We then compare the market solution to the command optimum, the allocation that would be chosen by a central planner, and emphasize the significance of the golden rule. We finally consider how the decentralized equilibrium is modified if individuals care about the welfare of their heirs and parents.

The Decentralized Equilibrium

The market economy is composed of individuals and firms. Individuals live for two periods. An individual born at time t consumes c_{1t} in period t and c_{2t+1} in period $t + 1$, and derives utility[1]

$$u(c_{1t}) + (1 + \theta)^{-1} u(c_{2t+1}), \qquad \theta \geq 0, u'(\cdot) > 0, u''(\cdot) < 0.$$

Individuals work only in the first period of life, supplying inelastically one unit of labor and earning a real wage of w_t. They consume part of their first-period income and save the rest to finance their second-period retirement consumption.

The saving of the young in period t generates the capital stock that is used to produce output in period $t + 1$ in combination with the labor supplied by the young generation of period $t + 1$. The number of individuals born at time t and working in period t is N_t. Population grows at rate n so that $N_t = N_0(1 + n)^t$.

Firms act competitively and use the constant returns technology $Y = F(K, N)$. As in chapter 2, we assume that $F(\ )$ is a net production function, with depreciation already accounted for. Output per worker, Y/N, is thus given by the production function $y = f(k)$, where k is the capital–labor ratio. The production function is assumed to satisfy the Inada conditions. Each firm maximizes profits, taking the wage rate, w_t, and the rental rate on capital, r_t, as given.

We now examine the optimization problems of individuals and firms and derive the market equilibrium.

Individuals
Consider an individual born at time t. His maximization problem is

$$\max u(c_{1t}) + (1 + \theta)^{-1}u(c_{2t+1})$$

subject to

$$c_{1t} + s_t = w_t,$$

$$c_{2t+1} = (1 + r_{t+1})s_t,$$

where w_t is the wage received in period t and r_{t+1} is the interest rate paid on saving held from period t to period $t + 1$.[2] In the second period the individual consumes all his wealth, both interest and principal.[3]

The first-order condition for a maximum is

$$u'(c_{1t}) - (1 + \theta)^{-1}(1 + r_{t+1})u'(c_{2t+1}) = 0. \tag{1}$$

Substituting for c_{1t} and c_{2t+1} in terms of s, w, and r implies a saving function:

$$s_t = s(w_t, r_{t+1}), \qquad 0 < s_w < 1, s_r \gtrless 0. \tag{2}$$

Saving is an increasing function of wage-income, on the assumption of separability and concavity of the utility function, which ensures that both goods are normal. The effect of an increase in the interest rate is ambiguous, however. An increase in the interest rate decreases the price of second-period consumption, leading individuals to shift consumption from the first to the second period, that is, to substitute second- for first-period consumption. But it also increases the feasible consumption set, making it possible to increase consumption in both periods; this is the income effect. The net effect of these substitution and income effects is ambiguous. If the elasticity of substitution between consumption in both periods is greater than one, then in this two-period model the substitution effect dominates, and an increase in interest rates leads to an increase in saving.[4]

Firms

Firms act competitively, hiring labor to the point where the marginal product of labor is equal to the wage, and renting capital to the point where the marginal product of capital is equal to its rental rate:

$$f(k_t) - k_t f'(k_t) = w_t,$$

$$f'(k_t) = r_t. \tag{3}$$

Here k_t is the firm's capital–labor ratio.

Goods Market Equilibrium

The goods market equilibrium requires that the demand for goods in each period be equal to the supply, or equivalently that investment be equal to saving:

$$K_{t+1} - K_t = N_t s(w_t, r_{t+1}) - K_t.$$

The left-hand side is net investment, the change in the capital stock between t and $t + 1$. The right-hand side is net saving: the first term is the saving of the young; the second is the dissaving of the old.

Eliminating K_t from both sides tells us that capital at time $t + 1$ is equal to the saving of the young at time t. Dividing both sides by N_t gives

$$(1 + n)k_{t+1} = s(w_t, r_{t+1}). \tag{4}$$

Factor Markets Equilibrium

The services of labor are supplied inelastically; the supply of services of capital in period t is determined by the saving decision of the young made in period $t - 1$. Equilibrium in the factor markets obtains when the wage and the rental rate on capital are such that firms wish to use the available amounts of labor and capital services. The factor market equilibrium conditions are therefore given by equations (3), with k_t being the ratio of capital to the labor force.

Dynamics and Steady States

The capital accumulation equation (4), together with the factor market equilibrium conditions (3), implies the dynamic behavior of the capital stock:

$$k_{t+1} = \frac{s[w(k_t),\, r(k_{t+1})]}{1+n},\qquad (4)'$$

or

$$k_{t+1} = \frac{s[f(k_t) - k_t f'(k_t),\, f'(k_{t+1})]}{1+n}.$$

Equation (4′) implies a relationship between k_{t+1} and k_t. We will describe this as the saving locus.

The properties of the saving locus depend on the derivative:

$$\frac{dk_{t+1}}{dk_t} = \frac{-s_w(k_t)k_t f''(k_t)}{1 + n - s_r(k_{t+1})f''(k_{t+1})}.\qquad (5)$$

The numerator of this expression is positive, reflecting the fact that an increase in the capital stock in period t increases the wage, which increases saving. The denominator is of ambiguous sign because the effects of an increase in the interest rate on saving are ambiguous. If $s_r > 0$, then the denominator in (5) is positive, as is dk_{t+1}/dk_t.

The saving locus in figure 3.1 summarizes both the dynamic and the steady state behavior of the economy. The 45-degree line in figure 3.1 is

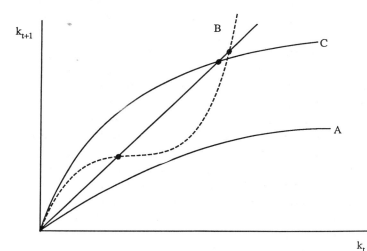

Figure 3.1
Saving and steady states

the line along which steady states, at which $k_{t+1} = k_t$, must lie. Any point at which the saving locus s crosses that line is a steady state. The possible shapes of the saving locus are not restricted much by the assumptions on tastes and technology we have made so far. Three possible saving loci are shown in figure 3.1. Locus A implies that no steady state with a positive capital stock exists. Locus B implies the existence of two equilibria, and locus C implies a unique equilibrium. The model does not, without further restrictions on the utility and/or production functions, guarantee either existence or uniqueness of a steady state equilibrium with positive capital stock.

Let us simply assume that there exists a unique equilibrium with positive capital stock. Will it be stable? To see this, we evaluate the derivative in (5) around the steady state:

$$\frac{dk_{t+1}}{dk_t} = \frac{-s_w k^* f''(k^*)}{1 + n - s_r f''(k^*)}.$$

(Local) stability requires that dk_{t+1}/dk_t be less than one in absolute value:

$$\left| \frac{-s_w k^* f''(k^*)}{1 + n - s_r f''(k^*)} \right| < 1. \tag{6}$$

Again, without further restrictions on the model, the stability condition may or may not be satisfied. How can instability arise? Take, for example, an economy with a low initial level of capital, $k_0 < k^*$, and thus high r and low w. If high interest rates reduce saving ($s_r < 0$), saving may be low and capital may further decrease rather than converge to a positive level over time.

To obtain definite results on the comparative dynamic and steady state properties of the model, it is necessary either to specify functional forms for the underlying utility and production functions or to impose conditions sufficient for uniqueness of a positive steady state capital stock, and then to invoke the correspondence principle to sign the relevant derivatives.[5] For instance, by assuming dynamic stability [i.e., that condition (6) is satisfied], it is easy to show that an increase in n will reduce the steady state capital stock per capita, just as it does in the Ramsey model. It will be found that the stability assumption makes it possible to derive definite results on the effects of policy changes, including, for example, fiscal policy.

In figure 3.2 we show the dynamic adjustment toward steady state in a case in which there is a unique, stable, nonoscillatory equilibrium. The assumption that the equilibrium is stable and nonoscillatory is equivalent to

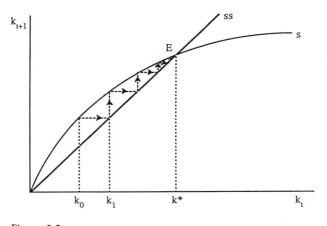

Figure 3.2
Dynamic adjustment

$$0 < \frac{-s_w k^* f''(k^*)}{1 + n - s_r f''(k^*)} < 1.$$

The economy starts out at k_0 and gradually moves toward the steady state capital stock. Each successive generation is better off than its predecessors, whose capital accumulation, undertaken in this model for purely selfish motives, raised wages for the next generation. Note, though, that we could have drawn the $s(\ )$ curve differently and allowed for an oscillatory but stable equilibrium, for an unstable equilibrium, or for multiple equilibria.

We next want to examine the optimality properties of the market equilibrium in the overlapping generations model. To do this, we have to develop an optimality criterion by which to evaluate alternative equilibria.

Optimality Properties

We now ask how the market allocation compares to that which would be chosen by a central planner who maximizes an intertemporal social welfare function. This raises a basic question, that of the relevant social welfare function. When individuals have infinite horizons, it is logical to take the social welfare function to be their own utility function. Here, however, each generation cares, at least in its private decisions, only about itself and not about future generations. Why should a central planner do otherwise?

The issue is not fundamentally different from that of defining a social welfare function in an atemporal context, when people have different endowments, abilities, and the like (an issue analyzed at length in the research on social choice). If, for example, we think of the social welfare optimum as that allocation of consumption which would be agreed upon by people before they know which generation they belong to, the social welfare function may be the utility of the representative generation, or the minimum, or the sum of utilities of all generations over some period of time. Or, perhaps, even if people do not care in their private behavior about future generations, they may still care, as members of society, about society's future. Thus they may ask the central planner to maximize the present discounted value of current and future utilities, using a social discount rate.[6] We consider the allocation chosen by a central planner maximizing such a welfare function. Given the difficulties associated with the choice of welfare functions, we then turn to a weaker optimality criterion, one that avoids having to specify a social welfare function; we ask whether the market outcome is Pareto optimal. The answer is that it may not be, and that this depends on whether the economy accumulates more or less capital than is implied by the golden rule.

The Command Optimum[7]

We assume, without discussing it further at this point, that the central planner discounts the utility of future generations at rate R. Also, for reasons that will become clear later, we start by assuming that the planner cares only about the utility of the $T + 1$ current and future generations.[8] This implies a social welfare function of the form

$$U = (1 + \theta)^{-1} u(c_{20}) + \sum_{t=0}^{T-1} (1 + R)^{-t-1} [u(c_{1t}) + (1 + \theta)^{-1} u(c_{2t+1})]. \quad (7)$$

If the planner cares less about future generations, R is positive. If he cares equally about all generations, R is equal to zero. If, in Benthamite fashion, he weights utility by the size of each generation, R is actually negative: $1 + R = (1 + n)^{-1}$.

The resource constraint on the planner is given by

$$K_t + F(K_t, N_t) = K_{t+1} + N_t c_{1t} + N_{t-1} c_{2t}. \quad (8)$$

The total supply of goods is allocated to the consumption of young and old and provides for the next period's capital stock. Dividing by the labor force N_t,

$$k_t + f(k_t) = (1 + n)k_{t+1} + c_{1t} + (1 + n)^{-1} c_{2t}. \quad (8')$$

The central planner maximizes (7) subject to the accumulation equation (8') and the two additional constraints that k_0 and k_{T+1} are both given. The initial capital stock k_0 is given by history; k_{T+1} is a terminal condition. If the central planner does not give weight to what happens at $T + 1$, k_{T+1} is equal to zero.

Replacing c_{1t}, $t = 0, \ldots, T - 1$, in the objective function by its value from the accumulation equation gives an unconstrained maximization problem. Collecting terms that include c_{2t} or k_t gives

$$\cdots + u(c_{1t-1}) + (1 + \theta)^{-1}u(c_{2t}) + (1 + R)^{-1}u(c_{1t}) + \cdots$$

$$= \cdots + u[k_{t-1} + f(k_{t-1}) - (1 + n)k_t - (1 + n)^{-1}c_{2t-1}]$$

$$+ (1 + \theta)^{-1}u(c_{2t}) + (1 + R)^{-1}u[k_t + f(k_t) - (1 + n)k_{t+1}$$

$$- (1 + n)^{-1}c_{2t}] + \cdots. \tag{9}$$

Differentiating (9) with respect to c_{2t} and k_t gives the first-order conditions for the centrally planned optimum:

c_{2t}: $(1 + \theta)^{-1}u'(c_{2t}) - (1 + R)^{-1}(1 + n)^{-1}u'(c_{1t}) = 0,$ (10)

k_t: $-(1 + n)u'(c_{1t-1}) + (1 + R)^{-1}[1 + f'(k_t)]u'(c_{1t}) = 0.$ (11)

Equation (10) is a condition for optimal allocation between young and old who are alive at the same time. It states that the marginal rate of substitution, from the point of view of the central planner, between consumption of the young and consumption of the old in period t must be equal to $1 + n$, the rate of transformation.

Equation (11) is a condition for optimal intertemporal allocation and is similar to that discussed in chapter 2. Decreasing consumption at $t - 1$ leads to a decrease in utility $u'(c_{1t-1})$ but makes possible through capital accumulation an increase in utility of $(1 + n)^{-1}[1 + f'(k_t)]u'(c_{1t})$. This increase, discounted to time $t - 1$ using the social discount rate $(1 + R)^{-1}$, must equal the initial decrease. Equivalently, equation (11) can be expressed in terms of the equality between the marginal rates of substitution and transformation.

Note that the central planner's first-order conditions respect the first-order conditions the individual chooses for himself in the market economy: combining (10) and (11) implies that

$$u'(c_{1t-1}) = [1 + f'(k_t)](1 + \theta)^{-1}u'(c_{2t}),$$

which is the first-order condition (1), with $r_t = f'(k_t)$. Since the planner is maximizing the weighted welfares of different generations, it is not surprising that he allocates consumption within an individual's lifetime in the same way as the individual himself would allocate it.

What do the planner's optimum conditions imply? We look first at the *steady state* associated with equations (10) and (11)[9] Let c_1^*, c_2^*, and k^* denote the steady state values of c_1, c_2, and k. They satisfy

$$(1 + \theta)^{-1} u'(c_2^*) = (1 + R)^{-1}(1 + n)^{-1} u'(c_1^*), \tag{12}$$

$$1 + f'(k^*) = (1 + R)(1 + n). \tag{13}$$

The steady state level of capital therefore satisfies the *modified golden rule*. If R and n are not too large, (13) implies that, to a close approximation, $f'(k^*) = R + n$. The marginal product is equal to the sum of the social discount rate and the rate of growth of population. If $R = 0$, that is, if the central planner gives equal weight to the utility of each generation, the marginal product is simply equal to n; the steady state is the golden rule steady state, at which the steady state level of per capita consumption is maximized. Note the similarity of these results to those of chapter 2. In the present case, however, the level of steady state capital does not depend on θ, the subjective individual discount rate, but on R, the social discount rate.

A Turnpike Theorem
Will the allocation chosen by the central planner be close to or converge over time to the steady state? To answer this, we consider the system composed of (8'), (10), and (11). As it is nonlinear, we first linearize it around the steady state. Some manipulation gives a second-order difference equation in $(k - k^*)$, the deviation of the capital stock from its steady state value:

$$(k_{t+1} - k^*) - (2 + R + a)(k_t - k^*) + (1 + R)(k_{t-1} - k^*) = 0, \tag{14}$$

where

$$a \equiv \left[\frac{f'' u_1'}{(1 + n)(1 + f')u_1''} \right] \left\{ 1 + \left[\frac{u_1''(1 + \theta)}{u_2''(1 + f')(1 + n)} \right] \right\} \geqslant 0,$$

$$f' \equiv f'(k^*),$$

$$u_i' \equiv u'(c_i^*),$$

$$f'' \equiv f''(k^*),$$

$$u_i'' \equiv u''(c_i^*), \qquad i = 1, 2.$$

The difference equation is to be solved subject to two terminal conditions, that both k_0 and k_{T+1} are given. To do so, we first write down the characteristic equation associated with (14):

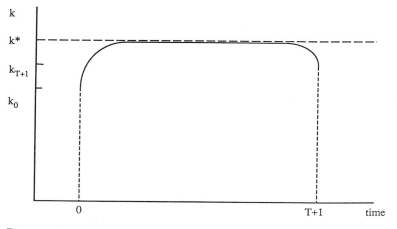

Figure 3.3
The turnpike

$$x^2 - (2 + R + a)x + 1 + R = 0. \tag{15}$$

The characteristic equation has two roots. One, x_1, is between zero and one; the other, x_2 is larger than $1 + R$.[10] A solution to (14) can thus be written as

$$(k_t - k^*) = \mu_1 x_1^t + \mu_2 x_2^t. \tag{16}$$

The values of μ_1 and μ_2 are determined by the initial and terminal conditions:

$$k_0 - k^* = \mu_1 + \mu_2,$$
$$k_{T+1} - k^* = \mu_1 x_1^{T+1} + \mu_2 x_2^{T+1}. \tag{17}$$

If T is large, then, as x_2 is larger than one, x_2^{T+1} is a very large number. Thus, for (17) to hold, μ_2 must be close to zero. In turn, (17) implies that μ_1 must be close to $(k_0 - k^*)$. Figure 3.3 characterizes the path of capital accumulation when T is large. Initial and terminal values for k are assumed to be less than the steady state value, so that the deviations $(k_0 - k^*)$ and $(k_{T+1} - k^*)$ are negative.

If T is large, the path of accumulation is such that capital is close to the steady state (modified golden rule) level for a long time. Capital rapidly rises from its initial value to a value close to k^* and diverges from this level only when t gets large in order to satisfy the terminal condition. This characteristic of the optimal path, visible in figure 3.3, is known as the *turnpike property*: the best way to go from any k_0 to a specified terminal capital stock k_{T+1}, if T is large, is to stay close to k^* for a long time.[11]

The turnpike theorem clarifies the normative significance of the modified golden rule: even in a finite horizon program, the economy should be close to the modified golden rule capital stock for much of the time.

What if the central planner cares about all future generations, so that T is equal to infinity? With R negative, the sum U does not converge. What about the borderline case $R = 0$? The sum in U still does not converge.[12] It turns out, however, that treating the infinite horizon case as the limit, as T goes to infinity, of the finite horizon problem is acceptable. The same is true when R is positive.

Thus, if R is nonnegative, the optimal path converges over time from k_0 to k^*, the modified golden rule level of capital. If the central planner cares equally about all generations, the economy tends to the golden rule and, in steady state, consumption per capita is maximized.

The Special Significance of the Golden Rule
We have shown at this stage that in the command optimum with $R > 0$, the economy converges to a steady state where

$$1 + f'(k^*) = (1 + n)(1 + R). \tag{13}$$

Since R is an arbitrary parameter—that is, unrelated to preferences as captured by the individual utility function—it is hardly surprising that k^* is generally not equal to the steady state level of capital chosen by the decentralized economy. We can, however, go further than just to note the difference between the two. We can ask if a steady state, even if it does not satisfy (13), is at least a Pareto optimum, that is, whether it is possible to reallocate resources in a way that makes at least some people better off while making none worse off.

To answer this, we return to the accumulation equation (8'). Define total consumption c_t as $c_{1t} + (1 + n)^{-1} c_{2t}$ and steady state values of c and k by c^* and k^*, respectively. The accumulation equation implies that in steady state

$$f(k^*) - nk^* = c^*.$$

Consider the effects of a change in k^* on c^*:

$$\frac{dc^*}{dk^*} = [f'(k^*) - n] \gtreqless 0 \qquad \text{depending on } f'(k^*) \gtreqless n.$$

This suggests the importance of the golden rule level of capital. If the steady state capital stock exceeds the golden rule level, a *decrease* in the capital stock *increases* steady state consumption. This is because the capital stock has become so large that its productivity is outweighed by the amount of resources that have to be used up each period just to provide the newborn with the existing level of capital per worker: the economy staggers under the weight of the need to maintain the per capita capital stock constant. This suggests that steady states with capital in excess of the golden rule are not Pareto optima, as we now prove.

Suppose that at time t the economy is in steady state. Consider increasing consumption in period t and reducing capital accumulation so that the capital stock is, from $t + 1$ on, permanently lower by $dk < 0$. The accumulation equation implies that

$$dc_t = -(1 + n)dk > 0,$$

$$dc_{t+i} = (f' - n)dk > 0, \qquad \text{if } f' < n, i > 0.$$

Total consumption goes up from t on. Thus, if this increase in consumption is divided between c_1 and c_2 in each period, the utility of each generation increases.

The allocation of resources in economies with capital stock in excess of the golden rule is therefore not Pareto optimal: everyone can be made better off by reducing the capital stock. Such economies are often referred to as *dynamically inefficient*: they have overaccumulated capital.[13] Note that the golden rule result depends on the assumption that the economy goes on forever, that there is no last generation. If there were a last generation, the reallocation would imply that it would have less capital and thus less consumption.

Inefficiency in the Market Economy

Is dynamic inefficiency more than a theoretical curiosum? Could actual economies indeed overaccumulate capital? Could the U.S. economy be dynamically inefficient?

Overaccumulation is surely more than a theoretical curiosum. To see this, consider the following example. Both the utility and production functions are Cobb-Douglas:

$$U = \ln c_1 + (1 + \theta)^{-1} \ln c_2,$$

$$f(k) = Ak^{\alpha} - \delta k.$$

Here δ is the depreciation rate so that $f(\cdot)$ is net rather than gross production.

In this case equation (4) implies that the steady state interest rate is

$$r^* = \left[\frac{\alpha(1 + n)(2 + \theta)}{(1 - \alpha)} \right] - \delta.$$

Reasonable values for these parameters are consistent with either $r^* > n$ or $r^* < n$.[14] Thus dynamic inefficiency cannot be simply dismissed as an exotic possibility.

When the model is extended to allow for productivity growth, it is easy to show that the golden rule level of capital is such that the rate of interest must be equal to the growth rate of the economy. This suggests a more direct way of checking whether the U.S. economy, for example, is or is not dynamically efficient, by simply comparing the growth rate and the interest rate. But what interest rate should one choose? There exists a wide spectrum of rates of return, from the profit rate of firms to the rate of return on equities to the nearly riskless rate on short-term Treasury bills. Although they are all the same in the model presented above, they are quite different in the data. And the answer depends very much on which rate is used: the average growth rate has, for the postwar period, been higher than the average riskless rate but considerably lower than the profit rate. Thus, to answer the question, one needs to introduce uncertainty explicitly in order to derive the form of the golden rule and the appropriate rate. Some progress has been made in that direction, and we return to the issue in chapter 6. We are far, however, from having a definite answer to the basic issue of whether the U.S. economy is dynamically efficient.[15]

The Market Economy and Altruism

The life-cycle consumers studied so far care only about their own welfare and leave no bequests. But this is unrealistic, for bequests do take place and probably account for an important part of individual wealth.[16]

The reasons why bequests are made affect their implications for intertemporal efficiency. Bequests do not necessarily imply that current generations care about the welfare of future generations. Uncertainty about time of death and the lack of annuity markets imply that many bequests are simply accidental.[17] More somber motives, such as the desire to manipulate children's behavior, may explain bequests (Bernheim, Shleifer, and Summers 1985).

In this section we assume that bequests reflect concern for the welfare of future generations and explore the implications for capital accumulation and dynamic efficiency. We also briefly examine the implications of two-sided altruism, in which in addition children are concerned about their parents' welfare.

We assume that parents care about their children's welfare by weighting the children's utility in their own utility function. Let the utility of a generation born at time t be denoted by V_t. V_t is given by

$$V_t = u(c_{1t}) + (1 + \theta)^{-1}u(c_{2t+1}) + (1 + R)^{-1}V_{t+1}. \tag{14}$$

Each generation cares about its own utility and the utility of the next generation, discounted at rate $R > 0$. Although R now reflects private preferences, there is clearly no reason for θ and R to be the same.[18]
    We can solve (14) recursively forward. This gives

$$V_t = \sum_{i=0}^{\infty}(1 + R)^{-i}[u(c_{1t+i}) + (1 + \theta)^{-1}u(c_{2t+i+1})]. \tag{15}$$

Note the similarity of this objective function to that of the command optimum.[19] Although each generation cares directly only about the next, this series of intergenerational links implies that each generation acts as if it cared about the utility of all future generations.
    What are the constraints faced by a generation born at time t? In addition to wage income, it receives a bequest from the previous generation in the first period of its life. It in turn leaves a bequest to the next generation in the second period. Thus

$$c_{1t} + s_t = w_t + b_t, \tag{16}$$

$$c_{2t+1} + (1 + n)b_{t+1} = (1 + r_{t+1})s_t, \tag{17}$$

where b_t is the bequest received by each member of generation t [corresponding to a bequest of $(1 + n)b_t$ given by each member of the smaller generation $t - 1$]. Bequests must be nonnegative.
    Competition in factor markets still implies that

$$w_t = f(k_t) - k_t f'(k_t),$$

$$r_t = f'(k_t).$$

Equilibrium in the goods market still implies the accumulation equation (8′).
    We are now ready to characterize equilibrium. An individual born in period t maximizes the following with respect to s_t and b_{t+1}:

$$u(c_{1t}) + (1 + \theta)^{-1}u(c_{2t+1}) + (1 + R)^{-1}u(c_{1t+1}) + \cdots.$$

Using (16) and (17), we obtain the following first-order conditions:

$$u'(c_{1t}) = (1 + \theta)^{-1}(1 + r_{t+1})u'(c_{2t+1}), \tag{18}$$

$$(1 + \theta)^{-1}(1 + n)u'(c_{2t+1}) \geqslant (1 + R)^{-1}u'(c_{1t+1}), \qquad b_{t+1} = 0, \tag{19}$$

or

$$(1 + \theta)^{-1}(1 + n)u'(c_{2t+1}) = (1 + R)^{-1}u'(c_{1t+1}), \qquad b_{t+1} > 0.$$

Recognizing that $r_t = f'(k_t)$, and assuming for a moment that bequests are positive, these conditions are identical to those of the command optimum. Thus we have what appears to be a very strong result. A market economy in which individuals have a bequest motive in the form of (14), and in which bequests are being made, replicates a command optimum. In this case the steady state level of capital is the modified golden rule level, with the relevant discount rate being the rate at which parents care about their childrens' utility; the overlapping generations model then behaves almost exactly like the Ramsey model.

It is, however, necessary to return to the nonnegativity constraint on bequests. If we assume that parents cannot require their children to make transfers to them, then they cannot leave negative bequests. We have then to examine the implications of the inequality constraint in (19). Because this is often difficult, we limit ourselves to an analysis of the steady state.[20]

In steady state, $c_{1t+1} = c_{1t}$; using this fact, we obtain from (18) and (19) the set of inequalities:

$$(1 + r^*) \leqslant (1 + n)(1 + R), \qquad \text{and } b = 0, \tag{20}$$

or

$$(1 + r^*) = (1 + n)(1 + R), \qquad \text{and } b \geqslant 0.$$

The steady state may therefore be such that either bequests are positive and the interest rate is equal to the modified golden rule or there are no bequests and the interest rate is less than the modified golden rule value. There is nothing that requires the interest rate to be greater than the population growth rate and thus the economy to be dynamically efficient.

Under what structural parameters will an economy reach a steady state with or without positive bequests? Consider an economy in which people have a bequest motive, and discount the utility of future generations at rate R, but are prevented by law from making bequests. The equilibrium is therefore the equilibrium of the Diamond economy. Suppose that the steady state interest rate under the no-bequest constraint, $1 + r^*$, is less than $(1 + n)(1 + R)$. If, in that steady state, the restriction on making bequests were lifted, would people want to make positive bequests? A simple variational argument shows the answer to be negative: the net change in utility from a small increase in bequests would be equal to $-1 + (1 + r^*)/[(1 + n)(1 + R)]$, which is negative under our assumptions. Thus an economy in which the constrained no-bequest equilibrium interest rate, $1 + r^*$, is less than $(1 + n)(1 + R)$ will be such that even when positive bequests are allowed, bequests will be equal to zero and the interest rate will be unchanged.

The nonnegativity condition on bequests therefore softens considerably our earlier proposition about the equivalence of an economy with a bequest motive and a command optimum. The presence of a bequest motive implies that the steady state interest rate, $1 + r^*$, cannot be greater than the modified golden rule, $(1 + n)(1 + R)$: the steady state capital stock cannot be too low. If the no-bequest equilibrium were such that that the interest rate exceeded the modified golden rule, bequests would take place until the two were equal, with positive bequests in equilibrium. The presence of a bequest motive does not, however, rule out that the interest rate may be less than $(1 + n)(1 + R)$. If the no-bequest equilibrium is such that the interest is less than the modified golden rule, allowing for bequests will not affect the equilibrium. The equilibrium will be one with no bequests and the same interest rate. In particular, the presence of a bequest motive does not exclude the possibility that the economy may be dynamically inefficient.

We can also see that it is not finite lives as such that generate possible inefficient equilibria but the fact that future generations' preferences do not affect current decisions.[21] When parents incorporate their childrens' utility in their own utility function to an extent sufficient to cause the parents to make bequests, the equilibrium becomes efficient; the steady state of the economy is at the modified golden rule.

Two-Sided Altruism
Intergenerational gifts move in fact in both directions, from children to parents and from parents to children. Does this two-sided altruism ensure that equilibria are Pareto optimal? The answer is, not necessarily. Before examining that result, though, we discuss the representation of two-sided altruism.[22]

Denote by W_t the direct utility of the *t*th generation,

$$W_t = u(c_{1t}) + (1 + \theta)^{-1}u(c_{2t+1}).$$

In equation (14) we represented the individual's utility function as

$$V_t = W_t + (1 + R)^{-1}V_{t+1} \tag{14'}$$

and showed that this was equivalent to

$$V_t = \sum_0^\infty (1 + R)^{-i}W_{t+i}.$$

With two-sided altruism the parents' utility is affected not only by the utility of their children but also by the utility of their parents. It is thus natural to write the utility function by analogy with (14') as

$$V_t = W_t + (1 + R)^{-1} V_{t+1} + (1 + \varphi)^{-1} V_{t-1},$$ (21)

where $(1 + \varphi)^{-1}$ is the weight placed by a child on the parent's utility. If (21) has a solution, it is of the form

$$V_t = \sum_{i=-\infty}^{\infty} \gamma_i W_{t+i}.$$ (22)

We may then ask when a solution exists and, if it does, what the relation of the γ_i's is to R and φ. This question has been analyzed by Kimball (1987). Suppose that we require the γ_i to be positive and finite, to go to zero as $|i|$ goes to infinity, and $\{\gamma_i\}$, $i \geqslant 0$, to be a geometric series. The first requirement is self-explanatory. The second requires that concern about distant relatives go to zero, both backward and forward. The third requires (22) to be such that the family behaves in a time consistent fashion.[23]

These restrictions on the γ_i imply the following restrictions on R and φ:

$$(1 + \varphi)^{-1} + (1 + R)^{-1} < 1,$$

$$(1 + \varphi)^{-1}(1 + R)^{-1} < \frac{1}{4}.$$

The intuition behind these conditions is that if altruism is too strong, the formulation (21) implies a "hall of mirrors" effect. People may care about their children, both directly and indirectly, as they care for their parents who care for their grandchildren, and so on. If the second inequality is not satisfied, there are no finite positive weights satisfying (22): altruism is too strong. If the first condition is not satisfied, altruism increases with distance, something we have ruled out a priori.

If these conditions on R and φ are satisfied, the γ_i are given by

$$\gamma_i = A^{-1} \mu^i, \qquad \text{for } i \geqslant 0,$$

$$\quad = A^{-1} \lambda^i, \qquad \text{for } i \leqslant 0,$$

where

$$A \equiv \sqrt{1 - 4(1 + \varphi)^{-1}(1 + R)^{-1}},$$

$$\lambda = (2\varphi)^{-1}(1 + A), \qquad \lambda > 1,$$

$$\mu = (2\varphi)^{-1}(1 - A), \qquad \mu < 1.$$

Consider now the first-order condition for an individual maximizing (22), taking as given the gifts and bequests he receives. The budget constraints for such an individual are

$$c_{1t} = w_t + b_t - g_t + s_t, \tag{23}$$

$$c_{2t+1} = s_t(1 + r_{t+1}) - (1 + n)b_{t+1} + (1 + n)g_{t+1}. \tag{24}$$

Here g_t is the gift made by a young person to the parents in period t.

The individual maximizes at time t:

$$\gamma_{-1}(1 + \theta)^{-1}u(c_{2t}) + \gamma_0[u(c_{1t}) + (1 + \theta)^{-1}u(c_{2t+1})] + \gamma_1 u(c_{1t+1}) + \cdots. \tag{25}$$

Using (23) and (24) and maximizing (25) with respect to s_t, g_t, and b_{t+1} implies the following first-order conditions:[24]

$$u'(c_{1t}) = (1 + \theta)^{-1}(1 + r_{t+1})u'(c_{2t+1}), \tag{26}$$

$$u'(c_{1t}) \geq \left(\frac{\gamma_{-1}}{\gamma_0}\right)(1 + \theta)^{-1}u'(c_{2t}), \qquad \text{with equality if } g_t > 0. \tag{27}$$

$$(1 + n)(1 + \theta)^{-1}u'(c_{2t+1}) \geq \left(\frac{\gamma_1}{\gamma_0}\right)u'(c_{1t+1}),$$

with equality if $b_{t+1} > 0$ \tag{28}

By examining steady states, we see that the three first-order conditions imply the following inequalities:

$$\frac{\gamma_{-1}}{\gamma_0} \leq 1 + r^* \leq (1 + n)\left(\frac{\gamma_0}{\gamma_1}\right), \tag{29}$$

or if we use the definitions of γ_i above,

$$\frac{1}{\lambda} \leq 1 + r^* \leq \frac{1 + n}{\mu}, \qquad \lambda > 1, \mu < 1.$$

The results are a straightforward extension of the results obtained under one-sided altruism. The second inequality tells us that, as before, the interest rate cannot be too high: if it were, bequests and further capital accumulation would be taking place until equality is restored. The first inequality tells us that now the interest rate cannot be too low. If it were, gifts would be taking place until equality is restored. If, however, the interest rate satisfies both inequalities, neither bequests nor gifts will take place. What is important to note is that the interval that satisfies both inequalities includes the golden rule interest rate, $r = n$.[25] Thus the inclusion of two-sided altruism, inter-

esting as it is, does not ensure Pareto optimality in the overlapping generations model.

3.2 Social Security and Capital Accumulation

In this section we focus on the effects of social security on capital accumulation and welfare. Social security programs to provide for retirement income
were not introduced to affect capital accumulation. The programs were
introduced partly for income distribution reasons, to ensure a minimum level
of income in retirement, partly because it was felt that individuals might
suffer from myopia and not provide adequately for their retirement. Nevertheless, any program that affects the path of income received by individuals
is likely to have an effect on savings and thus on capital accumulation. It is
this effect that we concentrate on.

From the previous section and without altruism, equilibrium in the decentralized economy is characterized by

$$u'(w_t - s_t) = (1 + \theta)^{-1}(1 + r_{t+1})u'[(1 + r_{t+1})s_t],\tag{1}$$

$$s_t = (1 + n)k_{t+1},\tag{4'}$$

$$w_t = f(k_t) - k_t f'(k_t),$$

$$r_t = f'(k_t).$$

We examine now how the introduction of social security modifies these
equilibrium conditions.[26] Individuals make a social security contribution
while they are young and receive payment from the social security system
when old. Let d_t be the contribution of a young person at time t, and let b_t
be the benefit received by an old person in period t.

There are two polar ways to run a social security system. It can be *fully
funded*: the contributions of the young at time t are invested and returned
with interest at time $t + 1$ to the then old. In this case $b_t = (1 + r_t)d_{t-1}$; the
rate of return on social security contributions is r_t. Or social security can be
run as an unfunded system, as a *pay-as-you-go system*, that transfers current
contributions made by the young directly to the current old so that $b_t =
(1 + n)d_t$; the "rate of return" on contributions is then equal to n. In practice,
the U.S. social security system is mostly unfunded.[27]

A Fully Funded System

In a fully funded system the government in period t raises d_t in contributions
from the young, invests the contributions d_t as capital, and pays $b_t =$

$(1 + r_t)d_{t-1}$ to the old, whose contribution was invested in period $t - 1$. Equations (1) and (4') thus become

$$u'[w_t - (s_t + d_t)] = (1 + \theta)^{-1}u'[(1 + r_{t+1})(s_t + d_t)], \tag{30}$$

$$s_t + d_t = (1 + n)k_{t+1}. \tag{31}$$

Comparison of (1) and (4') with (30) and (31) shows that if k_t is the solution to the first system, it is also the solution to the second. This is so provided that $d_t < (1 + n)k_{t+1}$ in the pre-social security economy, that is, that social security contributions do not exceed the amount of saving that would otherwise have occurred. With this proviso we reach a strong conclusion: *fully funded social security has no effect on total savings and capital accumulation.*

The explanation is that the increase in social security saving, d_t, is exactly offset by a decrease in private saving in such a way that the total, $s_t + d_t$, is equal to the previous level of s_t. The reason is clear: the social security system provides a rate of return equal to that on private saving so that it is as if the social security system were taking part of each individual's saving and investing that amount itself. The consumer is, however, indifferent to who does the saving, caring only about the rate of return; this means that consumers offset through private savings whatever savings the social security system does on their behalf.

A Pay-as-You-Go System

Things are quite different when social security is not funded. In this case equations (1) and (4') become, using $b_{t+1} = (1 + n)d_{t+1}$,

$$u'(w_t - s_t - d_t) = (1 + \theta)^{-1}u'[(1 + r_{t+1})s_t + (1 + n)d_{t+1}], \tag{32}$$

$$s_t = (1 + n)k_{t+1}. \tag{33}$$

From the point of view of each individual, the rate of return on social security savings is n rather than r. The government can pay a rate of return n because in each period there are more people alive to make contributions to the social security system. Because social security in the pay-as-you-go system is a pure transfer scheme, which does not save at all, the only source of capital for the economy in (33) is private saving s_t.

Consider the effects of social security on private saving, given wages and interest rates. Differentiating (32) and assuming that $d_t = d_{t+1}$ gives

$$\frac{\partial s_t}{\partial d_t} = -\frac{u_1'' + (1 + \theta)^{-1}(1 + n)u_2''}{u_1'' + (1 + \theta)^{-1}(1 + r_{t+1})u_2''} < 0, \tag{34}$$

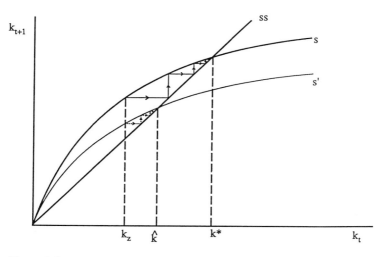

Figure 3.4
The effects of social security

so that $|\partial s_t / \partial d_t| \gtrless 1$ depending on $n \gtrless r$. The partial derivative signs indicate that the wage rate and interest rate are held constant.

Social security contributions decrease private savings. Whether they decrease private savings more or less than one for one depends on the relation of the interest rate to the rate of population growth.

However, this is only the partial equilibrium effect. The decrease in saving, and thus in capital, decreases wages and increases interest rates. The decrease in wages further decreases savings. The increase in interest rates has, as we have seen, an ambiguous effect. What is therefore the general equilibrium effect of an increase in social security on the capital stock?

In figure 3.4 we show the relationship between k_{t+1} and k_t implied by the saving function, assuming in this case that the steady state is unique and stable and that the dynamics are nonoscillatory. We are thus assuming that

$$0 < \frac{dk_{t+1}}{dk_t} < 1,$$

where dk_{t+1}/dk_t is as specified in equation (5).

Consider now the dynamic equation

$$(1 + n)k_{t+1} = s[w_t(k_t), r_{t+1}(k_{t+1}), d_t]. \tag{35}$$

We want to know how the saving locus in figure 3.4 changes when d_t increases from zero. The answer is obtained by differentiating (35), holding k_t constant, to obtain

$$\frac{dk_{t+1}}{dd_t} = \frac{\partial s_t / \partial d_t}{1 + n - s_r f''(\ )} < 0.$$

The numerator is negative; the denominator, by virtue of (5) and the assumption of stability, is positive. Therefore an increase in social security moves the saving locus in figure 3.4 down, from s to s'.[28]

The impact of social security on the dynamic adjustment of the economy is to slow the rate of capital accumulation while also reducing the steady state capital stock. Suppose that pay-as-you-go social security is introduced in period z, when the capital stock is k_z. The economy, which had been proceeding toward the steady state capital stock k^* along the solid line path, now moves to $\hat{k}$ along the dashed path. The steady state capital stock is reduced, as is the capital stock in each future period relative to what it would otherwise have been.

Is this a desirable outcome, leaving aside other reasons that explain the introduction of social security in the first place? Using a Pareto optimality criterion, the answer depends on whether the interest rate prevailing before the introduction of social security, r, was smaller or larger than n. If r was less than n, social security, by reducing or possibly eliminating dynamic inefficiency, is unambiguously welfare improving. If r was greater than n before the introduction of social security, then the scheme benefits the first old generation, which receives a positive transfer of d_t, at the expense of subsequent generations and is not Pareto improving.

The Bequest Motive and Ricardian Equivalence

The analysis so far assumes that individuals have no bequest motive. What is the effect of unfunded social security if current generations care about the welfare of future generations to the extent that they are making positive bequests?

The answer can be deduced from the fact that social security contributions are negative bequests, transfers from the young to the old. When the government takes amount d_t from a young person to give $(1 + n)d_t$ to each old person, who is at the same time making total bequests of $(1 + n)b_t$, giving b_t to each heir, the old person simply increases bequests by d_t per heir to produce exactly the same allocation as before.[29]

Social security thus has no effect on capital accumulation if the market economy has positive bequests before the introduction of social security, which in turn implies that r, the interest rate before the introduction of social security, is equal to $R + n$. Individuals offset the change in social security contributions by an offsetting change in bequests so that the net transfers between generations are unaffected. This is another case of *Ricardian equivalence*, in which some government fiscal actions are completely offset and their effects nullified by private sector responses.[30]

If, however, the market economy has no bequests before the introduction of social security, which implies that r is less than $R + n$, unfunded or pay-as-you-go social security has the same effect on capital accumulation as in an economy in which generations are selfish.

Other Effects of Social Security

In this simplest model of social security, the introduction of unfunded social security has either no effect or, more likely, a negative effect on capital accumulation. There are, however, other effects that we have not considered in the model.

The first, emphasized by Feldstein (1974) and Munnell (1974), is that social security may lead individuals to retire earlier. Their saving during their working years will have to be higher to finance a longer retirement, thus tending to offset the effects of social security in reducing private saving that we have examined in this section. The evidence of both Feldstein and Munnell is, though, that on balance capital accumulation is still reduced by social security. Munnell's evidence also bears on and contradicts an argument emphasized by Katona (1965), that the introduction of compulsory pension plans may make individuals more aware of the necessity to save for retirement and lead them to increase their savings, or at least not to decrease them by as much as their contributions to the plan.

In addition the introduction of social security may be expected to have effects on saving in an economy in which individuals face uncertainty about future incomes, which they cannot insure against.[31] For instance, if an economy lacks an annuities market, then the introduction of social security, which in effect creates annuities, is likely to affect saving. The effects will depend on the reasons why the private market could not support the relevant market. Abel (1987a) shows that the introduction of fully funded social security in an economy in which individuals have different mortality risks, known to themselves but not the insurance company, tends to reduce the equilibrium capital stock.[32]

The conclusion from theory is that the introduction of social security will have an effect on capital accumulation unless people are able to offset exactly the set of transfers implied by the social security program. When theory implies that social security has an effect, it is generally to decrease capital accumulation.

3.3. A Model of Perpetual Youth

Overlapping generations models with more than two generations tend to be analytically intractable. Generations at different stages of their life cycle have systematically different propensities to consume and different levels of wealth, making aggregation difficult or impossible.[33] Further, even the two-period discrete time overlapping generations model of sections 3.1 and 3.2 is unwieldy compared to the Ramsey model of chapter 2. In this section we introduce a tractable continuous time version of the overlapping generations model which we apply in the next two sections to an analysis of fiscal policy and the effects of interest rate changes on saving.

We start by describing the age structure of the population and the structure of markets and then go on to derive individual and aggregate consumption and saving behavior. The production side of the model is the same as that in section 3.1. We conclude by examining the dynamic adjustment of the economy toward the steady state. We should note in advance that there is a reward for the effort involved in formal aggregation: the derived aggregate model is extremely tractable.

The Structure of the Model

Population
Instead of living forever, each individual now faces a probability of dying at any moment. We assume that the probability of death per unit time, p, is constant throughout life. This implies, in particular, that an old person has just as long an expected future life as a young person, hence the title of this section. The assumption that the probability of dying is independent of age is the key to the tractability of this model.[34]

Because we work in continuous time, the instantaneous probability p can take any value between 0 and infinity.[35] To see what this constant probability assumption implies, note that it can equivalently be stated that the random variable "time until death" has an exponential distribution. Let X be this variable, with its density function given by

$$f_x(t) = p \exp(-pt).$$

Its expected value is given by

$$E(X) = \int_0^\infty tp \exp(-pt) \, dt$$

$$= \left[-t \exp(-pt) \right]_0^\infty + \int_0^\infty \exp(-pt) \, dt = p^{-1}.$$

We can think of p^{-1} as an index of the effective horizon of individuals in the model. As the probability of death decreases, the horizon index increases. In the limit, as p goes to zero, the horizon becomes infinite, and we are back in the Ramsey model.

At every instant of time a new cohort, composed of people with constant probability of death p, is born. Each cohort is large enough so that p is also the rate at which the cohort size decreases through time. Thus although each person is uncertain about the time of his or her death, the size of a cohort declines deterministically through time. A convenient normalization is that the size of a new cohort is also equal to p. Thus a cohort born at time s has a size, as of time t, of $p \exp[-p(t - s)]$. The size of the total population at any time t is equal to

$$\int_{-\infty}^{t} p \exp[-p(t - s)]\, ds = 1.$$

The Availability of Insurance
We assume that individuals maximize expected lifetime utility, with no concern for their heirs or parents. In the absence of insurance, and given the uncertainty about time of death, individuals would die leaving either unintended bequests if their wealth was positive or unintended negative bequests if they died in debt. If dying in debt were prohibited, individuals would have to solve for the best consumption path subject to a nonnegative nonhuman wealth constraint.

Given the assumption that there is individual but no aggregate uncertainty, there is, however, scope for insurance. Suppose that there are insurance companies that offer positive or negative life insurance. The typical individual in our model who has accumulated wealth faces the possibility of dying before he can use it. He would be better off if he could sell the claim on his wealth in the event he dies, in exchange for command over resources while he is alive.

There will thus be a demand for insurance that takes the form of the insurance company making premium payments to the living in exchange for receipt of their estates in the event they die. This is the reverse of the term insurance usually purchased, where the insured makes payments to an insurance company while alive in exchange for a payment to his or her heirs in the event of death.[36]

Given free entry and zero profit in the insurance industry, the insurance premium must be p per unit time: individuals will pay (receive) a rate p to receive (pay) one good contingent on death. In the absence of a bequest motive, and with negative bequests prohibited, individuals will contract to have all of their wealth, v_t, go to the insurance company contingent on their deaths. In exchange the insurance company will pay them a premium of pv_t per unit time.

The insurance company just balances its books: it is receiving payments from those who die, at the rate pv_t, while paying out premia at a rate pv_t. It faces no uncertainty because the proportion dying per unit time, p, is not stochastic.

The other assumptions of the model are conventional, and we will give them as we go along.

Individual and Aggregate Consumption

Individual Consumption

Denote by $c(s, t)$, $y(s, t)$, $v(s, t)$, and $h(s, t)$ consumption, labor income, non-human and human wealth, respectively, of an individual born at time s, as of time t.[37] Individuals born at time s are said to belong to generation s. Since we focus first on individual consumption, we will suppress the s index until we have to discuss aggregation over individuals in different generations. Thus, instead of $c(s, t)$ we write $c(t)$, and so on.

Individuals face a maximization problem under uncertainty. At time t they maximize

$$E\left[\int_t^\infty u(c(z)) \exp[-\theta(z - t)]\, dz \,|\, t\right]. \tag{36}$$

Uncertainty about consumption at any future date, and thus the need to take expectations (as of time t) in (36), comes from the possibility of death. The probability of being alive at time z is given by $\exp[-p(z - t)]$. In case of death, utility is assumed to be zero. If alive, utility is $u(c(z))$; we further assume that $u(\cdot)$ is given by $\log c(z)$. The logarithmic utility assumption, made for convenience, is restrictive, for it imposes unit elasticity of substitution between consumption across different periods.[38] Finally, we assume that there is no other source of uncertainty in the economy so that expectations of $y(z)$, $v(z)$, and $h(z)$, $z \geqslant t$, are held with subjective certainty. We may then write the objective function as

$$\int_t^\infty \log c(z) \exp[-(\theta + p)(z - t)]\, dz. \tag{36'}$$

The effect of the exponential probability of the death assumption is simply to increase the individual's rate of time preference.[39]

If an individual has nonhuman wealth $v(z)$ at time t, he receives $r(z)v(z)$ in interest, where $r(z)$ is the interest rate, and $pv(z)$ is the premium from the insurance company. Thus the individual's dynamic budget constraint, while alive, is

$$\frac{dv(z)}{dz} = [r(z) + p]v(z) + y(z) - c(z). \tag{37}$$

As usual, a no-Ponzi-game condition is needed to prevent individuals from going infinitely into debt and protecting themselves by buying life insurance. We impose a condition that is the extension of that used in the deterministic case. If an individual is still alive at time z, then

$$\lim_{z \to \infty} \exp \left\{ -\int_t^z [r(\mu) + p] \, d\mu \right\} v(z) = 0. \tag{38}$$

An individual cannot accumulate debt forever at a rate higher than the effective rate of interest facing him, the interest rate on debt plus the insurance premium he has to pay when borrowing.

It will be convenient notationally to define the discount factor

$$R(t, z) \equiv \exp \left\{ -\int_t^z [r(\mu) + p] \, d\mu \right\}. \tag{39}$$

Using the NPG condition (38), we can integrate equation (37) forward to obtain the intertemporal budget constraint:

$$\int_t^\infty c(z) R(t, z) \, dz = v(t) + h(t), \tag{40}$$

where

$$h(t) \equiv \int_t^\infty y(z) R(t, z) \, dz.$$

The individual maximizes expected utility (36') subject to the budget constraint (40), or equivalently subject to the accumulation equation (37) and the NPG condition (38). Comparing this maximization problem to that faced by infinitely lived consumers shows that the presence of a positive probability of death affects both the rate at which future utility is discounted ($\theta + p$ instead of θ) and the effective rate of interest faced by the individual ($r + p$ instead of r).

We use the maximum principle, as in chapter 2, to obtain the following first-order condition (in addition to the usual transversality condition):

$$\frac{dc(z)}{dz} = \{[r(z) + p] - (\theta + p)\} c(z) = [r(z) - \theta] c(z). \tag{41}$$

Thus individual consumption rises (falls) if the interest rate exceeds (is less than) the subjective discount rate. We will contrast this to the behavior of aggregate consumption later.

Integrating (41) to express $c(z)$ as a function of $c(t)$ and replacing in the budget constraint (40) gives a solution for $c(t)$:

$$c(t) = (\theta + p)[v(t) + h(t)]. \tag{42}$$

Individual consumption depends on total individual wealth, with propensity to consume $\theta + p$, which is independent of the interest rate because of the assumption of logarithmic utility and independent of the individual's age because of the assumption of a constant probability of death. The factor used to discount labor income is $r + p$, the same as the rate at which nonhuman wealth accumulates.

Aggregate Consumption

Having analyzed the consumption behavior of one generation, we now sum over generations to derive aggregate consumption.[40] Denote aggregate consumption, labor income, nonhuman wealth, and human wealth at time t by $C(t)$, $Y(t)$, $V(t)$, and $H(t)$, respectively. The aggregates are derived by integrating over the generations, where we now restore the double indices to $c(s, t)$, etc., and recalling that the size of a generation born $t - s$ periods ago is $p \exp[-p(t - s)]$. Thus aggregate consumption is given by

$$C(t) = \int_{-\infty}^{t} c(s, t)p \exp[-p(t - s)] \, ds,$$

and similar definitions apply to aggregate income and to aggregate non-human and human wealth. From equation (42), the definitions of $H(t)$ and $W(t)$, and the fact that the propensity to consume is independent of age, aggregate consumption simply follows:

$$C(t) = (p + \theta)[H(t) + W(t)]. \tag{43}$$

The next step is to derive the dynamic behavior of $H(t)$ and $W(t)$. To derive the behavior of *human wealth*, $H(t)$, we must specify the distribution of labor income across people at any point in time. The following assumption roughly captures retirement, that is, the fact that labor income eventually decreases with age:

$$y(s, t) = aY(t) \exp[-\alpha(t - s)], \qquad \alpha \geqslant 0. \tag{44}$$

Here a is a constant to be determined below. Equation (44) implies that the per capita labor income of a member of a given generation is smaller, the older the generation, except for $\alpha = 0$, in which case per capita labor income is independent of age. Thus, if aggregate labor income is constant, individual labor income is exponentially decreasing through time. To determine the value of a, replace $y(s, t)$ in the expression defining aggregate $Y(t)$, use (44) and solve to obtain

$$a = \frac{\alpha + p}{p}.$$ (45)

Accordingly, $a = 1$ when $\alpha = 0$.

Replacing $y(s, t)$ in the expression for $h(s, t)$ gives

$$h(s, t) = \int_t^\infty aY(z) \exp[-\alpha(z - s)]R(t, z)\, dz,$$

or

$$h(s, t) = a\left\{\int_t^\infty Y(z) \exp[-\alpha(z - t)]R(t, z)\, dz\right\} \exp[-\alpha(t - s)],$$

where the term in braces in the second equation is independent of time of birth. Aggregate human wealth is given by

$$H(t) = \int_{-\infty}^t h(s, t)p \exp[-p(t - s)]\, ds$$

$$= \int_{-\infty}^t ap\left[\int_t^\infty Y(z) \exp[-\alpha(z - t)]R(t, z)\, dz\right]$$

$$\times \exp[-\alpha(t - s)] \exp[-p(t - s)]\, ds$$

so that, upon rearranging and using (45), $H(t)$ can be expressed as

$$H(t) = \int_t^\infty Y(z) \exp\left\{-\int_t^z [\alpha + p + r(\mu)]\, d\mu\right\} dz.$$ (46)

Aggregate human wealth is equal to the present discounted value of labor income accruing in the future *to people currrently alive*, discounted at rate r. Equivalently, it is the present discounted value of total future labor income discounted at the rate $r + p + \alpha$. Both interpretations are eminently intuitive.

An alternative characterization of the behavior of $H(t)$, which will be useful below, is obtained by differentiating (46) with respect to time:

$$\frac{dH(t)}{dt} = [r(t) + p + \alpha]H(t) - Y(t),$$

$$\lim_{z \to \infty} H(z) \exp\left\{-\int_t^z [\alpha + p + r(\mu)]\, d\mu\right\} = 0. \tag{46'}$$

Equation (46) and the two equations in (46') are equivalent.

We finally turn to *nonhuman wealth*. $V(t) \cdot V(t)$ is given by

$$V(t) = \int_{-\infty}^t v(s, t)p \exp[-p(t - s)]\, ds.$$

Differentiating $V(t)$ with respect to time gives

$$\frac{dV(t)}{dt} = pv(t, t) - pV(t) + \int_{-\infty}^t \left[\frac{dv(s, t)}{dt}\right] p \exp[-p(t - s)]\, ds. \tag{47}$$

The first term is the nonhuman wealth of a new cohort at birth, which is clearly equal to zero. The second represents the wealth of those who die at t, and the third is the change in the nonhuman wealth of the others. Using $v(t, t) = 0$ and equation (37) gives

$$\frac{dV(t)}{dt} = r(t)V(t) + Y(t) - C(t). \tag{48}$$

Note that although individual nonhuman wealth accumulates at rate $r + p$ if an individual remains alive, aggregate wealth accumulates only at rate r. This is because the amount pV is a transfer, through insurance companies, from those who die to those who remain alive; it is not an addition to aggregate wealth. This result, that there is a difference between the social and private returns on wealth, will be crucial to some of the results to come.

Aggregate Behavior
Collecting equations, and dropping the time index t wherever it is not misleading to do so, we write the aggregate equations of this economy as

$$C = (p + \theta)(H + V), \tag{43}$$

$$\frac{dV}{dt} = rV + Y - C, \tag{48}$$

$$\frac{dH}{dt} = (r + p + \alpha)H - Y, \tag{46}$$

$$\lim_{z \to \infty} H(z) \exp\left\{-\int_t^z [r(\mu) + p + \alpha]\, d\mu\right\} = 0.$$

These simple aggregate equations are the reward for the detailed aggregation procedure that has been followed, which ensures that the aggregate economy is built on explicit microfoundations.

Note that both the propensity to consume and the discount rate for human wealth are increasing functions of the probability of death; the shorter the horizon, the higher is the propensity to consume and the more future labor income is discounted. Similarly, the more rapidly labor income declines over time (the larger is α), the higher is the discount rate on future aggregate labor income.

There is an alternative characterization of aggregate consumption that will be useful. Differentiating (43) and eliminating dV/dt and dH/dt gives

$$\frac{dC}{dt} = (r + \alpha - \theta)C - (p + \alpha)(p + \theta)V, \tag{49}$$

$$\frac{dV}{dt} = rV + Y - C. \tag{48}$$

In the infinite horizon case, in which $p = 0$ and in which α should logically be set at zero,[41] the rate of change of consumption is a function of the difference between r and θ. If p is positive, the rate of change of consumption also depends on the level of nonhuman wealth. [Contrast the behavior of aggregate consumption with that of individual consumption given by (41).]

We are ready to turn to the characterization of general equilibrium. We assume, to begin with, that the labor income of each individual is a constant share of the aggregate, that is, $\alpha = 0$. Then we look at the effects of $\alpha > 0$, of decling relative labor income through life.

Dynamics and Steady State with Constant Relative Labor Income

To close the model and characterize capital accumulation, we need to specify the technology that determines output, labor income, and interest rates. Assume that there are two factors of production, capital, K, and labor. We have already assumed that the size of the labor force is equal to one. Define the net production function as

$$F(K) \equiv \mathbf{F}(K, 1) - \delta K,$$

where $\mathbf{F}(\cdot)$ exhibits constant returns to scale and δ is the depreciation rate. Note that $F'(\cdot)$ may be positive or negative.

The only form of nonhuman wealth is capital. Thus $V = K$. The interest rate is accordingly the marginal product of capital, $r = F'(K)$.

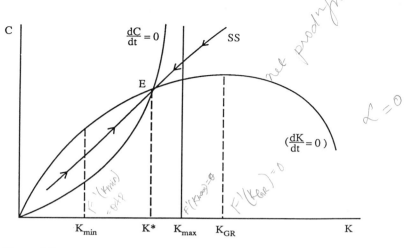

Figure 3.5
Dynamic adjustment with uncertain lifetime

Using equations (48) and (49), and the assumption that $\alpha = 0$, gives the following dynamics:

$$\frac{dC}{dt} = [F'(K) - \theta]C - p(p + \theta)K, \tag{50}$$

$$\frac{dK}{dt} = F(K) - C. \tag{51}$$

Figure 3.5 is the phase diagram for this dynamic system. The $dK/dt = 0$ locus traces out the net production function. We define three different levels of capital. The first, K_{GR}, is such that $F'(K_{GR}) = 0$; since there is no population growth, K_{GR} is the *golden rule* capital stock, the level that maximizes steady state consumption. The others are K_{max}, such that $F'(K_{max}) = \theta$, and K_{min}, such that $F'(K_{min}) = \theta + p$. Note that $K_{min} < K_{max} < K_{GR}$. The $dC/dt = 0$ locus for C positive is upward sloping and convex, goes through the origin and reaches K_{max} asymptotically. The two loci are drawn in figure 3.5.[42]

There are two equilibria, the origin and E. Equilibrium E has a saddle point structure. The saddle point path SS is upward sloping. Any other trajectory can be shown (using an argument similiar to that in section 2.1) to imply a negative level of C or K in finite time, and thus to violate equation (50) or (51) at that time. Thus, given an initial stock of capital K, C is uniquely determined by the requirement that the economy be on the saddle point path.

What are the *characteristics of the steady state*? First, the steady state level of capital K^* is such that

$$\theta < F'(K^*) < (\theta + p). \tag{52}$$

The first inequality, $\theta < F'(K^*)$, follows from equation (50) when $dC/dt = 0$. The second inequality can be proved through contradiction. Suppose that, contrary to the second inequality,

$$F' = \theta + p(1 + \varepsilon), \qquad \varepsilon > 0.$$

Then from (50), with $dC/dt = 0$,

$$(1 + \varepsilon)C = (p + \theta)K^*,$$

or, using (51) with $dK/dt = 0$,

$$(1 + \varepsilon)F(K^*) = (F' - p\varepsilon)K^*.$$

But this last equality is impossible because $F(K^*) > K^*F'(K^*)$ from concavity of $F(\cdot)$. It follows that $F'(K^*) < (\theta + p)$.

Second, K^* is a decreasing function of p. An increase in p shifts the $dC/dt = 0$ locus to the left, decreasing K^*.

We thus have two important results for this model with $\alpha = 0$. If people have finite horizons, the interest rate, r, will be higher than the subjective discount rate θ. Thus in this case, despite the fact that people have finite horizons, the equilibrium is necessarily dynamically efficient (i.e., r is greater than n which is equal to zero here), unlike the case in the Diamond model. Further, the shorter the individual's horizon is, the higher the interest rate and the lower the capital stock.

To understand these results, suppose that r were equal to θ. Then individuals with infinite horizons would, as we saw in chapter 2, choose a flat consumption profile in steady state associated with a level of capital such that the marginal product equals θ. Things are very different when individuals have finite horizons. If $r = \theta$, individuals who are born with no nonhuman wealth would choose a flat consumption path. Because in steady state the life time path of labor income is also flat (by assumption), these individuals would choose a level of consumption equal to labor income. They would neither save nor dissave. As a result there would be no aggregate capital accumulation, and this could not be an equilbrium.

What is needed to generate a positive aggregate level of capital? Individuals must be saving, at least initially in their lives: consumption must initially be low and thus increasing. The interest rate has to exceed θ. It is easy to show that if r is higher than θ, individual nonhuman wealth is increasing through life. There is therefore aggregate capital accumulation.

The higher p is, equivalently, the shorter expected life is, the smaller the average individual wealth and the aggregate capital stock.

Dynamics and Steady State with Declining Relative Labor Income

We now show that the equilibrium may become dynamically inefficient when $\alpha > 0$. The reason is not far to seek. When an individual expects declining labor income, he is likely to want to accumulate more capital to finance consumption late in life when income is low. This increased capital accumulation by individuals who take the path of interest rates as given is likely to drive the interest rate down.

The dynamics are now given by

$$\frac{dC}{dt} = [F'(K) + \alpha - \theta]C - p(p + \theta)K,$$

$$\frac{dK}{dt} = F(K) - C.$$

(49'')

The $dK/dt = 0$ locus is the same as before. Define K_{max} so that $F'(K_{max}) = \theta - \alpha$. The $dC/dt = 0$ locus for C positive is upward sloping, goes through the origin, and reaches K_{max} asymptotically. The steady state capital stock is thus such that the steady state marginal product of capital exceeds $\theta - \alpha$. Because $\theta - \alpha$ can be negative or positive, K may be larger or smaller than the golden rule capital stock K_{GR}. The equilibrium is characterized in figure 3.6. It is again saddle point stable, with saddle point path SS.

An increase in α moves the $dC/dt = 0$ locus down, thereby increasing the steady state capital stock. Since there is no natural upper bound on α, we cannot rule out the possibility that the capital stock is higher than the golden rule level.

To summarize the results of this section, we have constructed an aggregate overlapping generations model in which all behavioral functions are derived from utility maximization. We have shown that the existence of a life cycle has two opposite effects on capital accumulation. The fact that people do not live forever leads to less capital accumulation: the shorter their horizon, the lower the steady state level of capital. But the fact that people retire, that labor income eventually declines, leads to more capital accumulation. The net effect is ambiguous, and if the second effect is strong enough, the economy may be dynamically inefficient. Both effects are

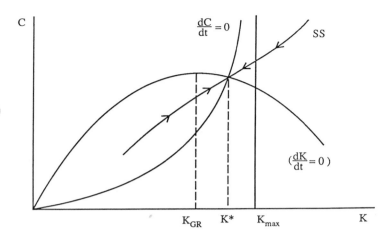

Figure 3.6
Dynamic adjustment with declining labor income

present in the Diamond model studied earlier. Both play an important role in capital accumulation.

3.4 Fiscal Policy: Debt and Deficit Finance

Does it matter whether the government finances its spending by (lump-sum) taxes or borrowing? We saw that the answer in the infinite horizon optimizing model in chapter 2 was no. In that model, capital accumulation and individuals' consumption decisions were totally unaffected by differences in the timing of taxes, which is what deficit finance is.[43] In this section we show that deficit finance does have real effects in the life-cycle model.

The key to the different results in the Ramsey and life-cycle models is that in the life-cycle model taxes levied at different times are levied on different sets of people. If the government finances spending by current taxes, those now alive bear the direct tax burden. If it borrows to finance the spending and later pays off the debt by taxing future generations, those currently alive may not be there when the taxes are raised. Thus, in general, the behavior of people now alive will be affected by the timing of taxes.

We will examine the consequences of deficit finance for capital accumulation and interest rates. We will pay particular attention to the contentious issue of whether an increase in the government budget deficit increases the real interest rate.

The Government Budget Constraint

The government budget constraint is the same whether or not people have finite lives. We have examined it in chapter 2 and briefly repeat the basic points. The government spends G on goods and collects taxes T. To focus on issues of government finance, we assume that G does not affect the marginal utility of private consumption C; thus the level of G has no direct effect on consumption/savings decisions. For similar reasons we assume that taxes are lump sum.

Let B be the level of government debt. The dynamic government budget constraint is

$$\frac{dB(t)}{dt} = r(t)B(t) + G(t) - T(t). \tag{53}$$

Note that the interest rate at which the government can issue debt is $r(t)$, not $r(t) + p$. This will be important below.

Although we saw in the previous section that the interest rate, r, could be positive or negative in equilibrium, here we will limit ourselves to the case where r is positive. Even in this case the government budget constraint does not by itself impose any constraint on the government. Equation (53) is simply an accounting statement that records the implied change in the level of debt whatever deficit the government is running. We therefore impose the NPG condition

$$\lim_{z \to \infty} B(z) \exp \left[- \int_t^z r(\mu) \, d\mu \right] = 0. \tag{54}$$

Integrating (53) forward subject to (54) implies that

$$B(t) = - \int_t^\infty [G(z) - T(z)] \exp \left\{ - \int_t^z [r(\mu) \, d\mu] \, dz \right\}. \tag{55}$$

This is the government's *intertemporal budget constraint*, implied by and implying (53) and (54). It states that *the current level of debt must be equal to the present discounted value of primary surpluses.* If the government is currently a net debtor, it must intend to run primary surpluses at some time in the future.[44] Note what equation (55) does not imply. The equality of current debt and the present value of surpluses does not imply that debt is ultimately repaid or even that debt is ultimately constant. All it implies is equation (54), namely, that the debt ultimately grows less rapidly than the interest rate.

Fiscal Policy and Consumption: Partial Equilibrium

The government affects the total demand for goods (aggregate demand) in three ways. It directly purchases goods in amount G, and it affects private consumption demand both through taxes, current and anticipated, and through debt.

Turning to private aggregate consumption, we must modify equations (43), (46), and (48) (assuming that $\alpha = 0$ for simplicity) to

$$C(t) = (p + \theta)[H(t) + V(t)],$$

$$V(t) = B(t) + K(t),$$

$$\tag{56}$$

$$H(t) = \int_t^\infty [Y(z) - T(z)] \exp\left\{-\int_t^z [r(\mu) + p]\, d\mu\right\} dz, \tag{57}$$

$$\frac{dV(t)}{dt} = r(t)V(t) + Y(t) - C(t) - T(t). \tag{58}$$

Financial wealth, V, now includes both government debt B and other assets, K: government debt is clearly wealth to those who hold it. Human wealth is the present discounted value of noninterest income minus taxes, discounted at rate $r + p$.

Consider an intertemporal reallocation of taxes, keeping the path of government spending constant. More precisely, consider a decrease in taxes at time t associated with an increase at time $t + s$. Given the government budget constraint (55), and given an unchanged path for G, these two changes must satisfy

$$dT(t + s) = \left\{-\exp\left[\int_t^{t+s} r(\mu)\, d\mu\right]\right\} dT(t).$$

The increase in taxes at time $t + s$ must be equal to the initial decrease at time t compounded at the rate of interest.

Because $B(t)$ is unchanged at time t (the increase in the deficit, which is a flow, does not instantaneously change the stock of debt), this reallocation has an effect on aggregate demand at time t only to the extent that it has an effect on consumption, through its effect on human wealth. From equation (57) this effect is

$$dH(t) = -dT(t) - dT(t + s) \exp\left\{\int_t^{t+s} [r(\mu) + p]\, d\mu\right\},$$

or using the government budget constraint,

$$dH(t) = -dT(t)[1 - \exp(-ps)].\tag{59}$$

Since taxes are cut at time t, $dT(t) < 0$, the move to deficit finance increases human wealth for given pre-tax current and future incomes and given interest rates. Accordingly, it raises aggregate consumption.

Note that the longer taxes are deferred (the larger s is), the larger the effect of the tax cut on human wealth. The key point is this: the effect of the reallocation of taxes comes from the different discount rates in the government budget constraint (r) and in the definition of human wealth ($r + p$). This in turn reflects the fact that *taxes are partly shifted to future generations*. Note that $1 - \exp(-ps)$ is simply the probability, for individuals currently alive, of not being around to have to pay the future taxes when the government levies them.[45]

There is an exception. As (59) shows, if p $= 0$, if individuals live forever, the change in the timing of taxes has no impact on current human wealth and consumption and thus no effect on aggregate demand. In this case a decrease in taxes, although it increases current disposable income, leads to increased private saving. Consumption does not change at all, for private saving rises exactly as much as disposable income and therefore by exactly as much as public dissaving (the budget deficit) has risen. Because individuals know that sooner or later they will have to pay for the increase in taxes, they willingly absorb the debt issued by the government at an unchanged interest rate.

Ricardian Equivalence

The proposition that deficit finance is no different from current taxation, because individuals fully take into account the future taxes they will have to pay, has been noted earlier in this chapter and in chapter 2. The proposition was briefly discussed by Ricardo and is often referred to as the Ricardian Equivalence Theorem. The Ricardian Equivalence Theorem holds in the Ramsey model, which is the same as the present model with $p = 0$. When individuals have shorter horizons in the current model ($p > 0$), Ricardian equivalence fails, for the reason discussed above.

We have already seen in section 3.2 that when individuals leave bequests because they are concerned with the utility of their heirs, the overlapping generations model behaves like an infinite horizon model. In that case Ricardian equivalence holds: although the taxes will be levied on future generations, they are generations that matter to those now alive. Suppose that the government switches from a balanced budget to deficit finance. People now alive can precisely offset the future taxes that will be levied on their children by increasing their saving to buy the bonds the government is selling to finance the deficit. They then give the bonds to their children, through a bequest, and the children can pay the taxes the government will levy by giving the bonds back to the government.

The effect of finite horizons is the most obvious reason that Ricardian equivalence may fail. But a host of other arguments has been brought to bear. The most important of these is that individuals may be liquidity constrained, that is, unable to borrow; then, when the government cuts taxes, individuals can increase spending. It is as if the government is borrowing on behalf of the liquidity-constrained individuals. The theoretical arguments supporting and contradicting Ricardian equivalence are discussed in detail in Bernheim (1987).[46] Since there are good arguments suggesting that Ricardian equivalence should fail (some people are childless, some people do not care about their children, many people do not leave bequests, credit markets are imperfect, etc.), it is clear that the issue is essentially empirical, one of determining how important the departures from Ricardian equivalence are.

Fiscal Policy and Interest Rates
We now look at the general equilibrium effects of changes in fiscal policy. In the presence of fiscal policy, equations (51) and (52), derived under the assumption that α is equal to zero, become, dropping time subscripts,

$$\frac{dC}{dt} = (r - \theta)C - p(p + \theta)(B + K), \tag{60}$$

$$\frac{dK}{dt} = F(K) - C - G, \tag{61}$$

$$\frac{dB}{dt} = rB + G - T, \tag{62}$$

$$r = F'(K). \tag{63}$$

Debt is part of wealth and enters the consumption equation. Government purchases of goods affect the capital accumulation equation. Taxes, spending, and debt enter the government debt accumulation equation. The interest rate is equal to the net marginal product of capital. Given paths for G and T that satisfy the intertemporal government budget constraint, we can, in principle, solve for the paths of C and K, given fiscal policy.

This is often technically difficult. We first briefly discuss the properties of the steady states of the economy. Then we simplify by switching to an exchange economy in which output is exogenous and examine the effects of fiscal policy on interest rates.

Steady States

In steady state the following relationships, corresponding to (60) through (62) hold:

$$[F'(K^*) - \theta]C^* = p(p + \theta)(B^* + K^*), \tag{60'}$$

$$F(K^*) = C^* + G, \tag{61'}$$

$$F'(K^*)B^* = T - G. \tag{62'}$$

Here asterisks indicate steady state values. If equation (62') is read as anything other than a steady state condition, it appears to prove that an increase in government spending reduces the national debt. The right interpretation is different. If the government decides on a higher steady state level of spending with the same steady state level of taxes, it must, to balance the steady state budget, reduce the national debt. Thus, to achieve this new steady state, it must temporarily increase taxes or decrease spending.[47]

We assume that in steady state private wealth $(B + K)$ is positive, that if government debt is negative (a rare event historically), it is not too negative. It follows from (60') that $r^* > \theta$. Thus the equilibrium in this model will not be dynamically inefficient. This is the same result as that obtained with $\alpha = 0$ in section 3.3.

Suppose now that the government temporarily cuts taxes, holding its spending constant. This raises the deficit and increases the debt. Then, later, the government raises taxes to bring the budget back to balance and thereafter keeps adjusting taxes to maintain a constant level debt. Thus we are considering a sequence of policy actions that ends up increasing the debt but leaving G unaffected.

Examining (60') and (61'), we ask what effect this increase in B^* has on the steady state capital stock. By substituting (61') into (60'), we obtain

$$\frac{dK^*}{dB^*} = \frac{p(p + \theta)}{F''C^* + (r^* - \theta)r^* - p(p + \theta)}.$$

The equation $C^* = r^*(B + K) + w - T$ and equation (60') imply that

$$\frac{dK^*}{dB^*} = \frac{p(p + \theta)}{F''C^* - (r^* - \theta)(w - T)/(B^* + K^*)} \tag{64}$$

Here w is the wage. Thus a sufficient condition for an increase in the debt to decrease the capital stock is $w < T$, a condition we assume to be satisfied.

We see once again that the stock of government debt matters because it displaces capital from the portfolios of savers. We could similarly examine the effects of an increase in G on the capital stock, holding constant the level of the primary deficit (or surplus) by a corresponding increase in taxes. We would find that an increase in G reduces the steady state capital stock. This again contrasts with the result in the Ramsey model where the steady state capital stock is determined solely by individuals' rate of time preference. In both the Ramsey and the overlapping generations models, an increase in G reduces steady state consumption.

Fiscal Policy and Interest Rates: Dynamic Adjustment

To pursue more systematically the dynamics of adjustment, particularly of interest rates, we simplify by assuming an exchange economy in which output is exogenous and constant and there is no capital. The interest rate is then not linked to the capital stock but must be such that the aggregate demand for goods equals the exogenous supply.

The economy is now described by

$$\frac{dC}{dt} = (r - \theta)C - p(p + \theta)B, \tag{60''}$$

$$Y = C + G, \tag{61''}$$

$$\frac{dB}{dt} = rB + G - T. \tag{62''}$$

If we consider fiscal policies with constant level of spending, $\hat{G}$, equation (61'') with Y constant implies that $dC/dt = 0$. In equilibrium the interest rate in (60'') must always be such as to imply constant consumption. Solving (60'') for $dC/dt = 0$ gives

$$r = \theta + p(p + \theta)\left(\frac{B}{Y - G}\right). \tag{65}$$

Therefore in this simple exchange economy the interest rate increases with both the level of debt and the level of government spending. Deficits at time t have no effect at time t on either $G(t)$ or $B(t)$ and thus no effect on the short-term rate of interest or, more precisely, the instantaneous rate of interest at time t. Deficits do, however, affect the level of debt over time, thus affecting future short-term rates and in turn current long-term rates.

To examine the relation between deficits, debt, and the term structure of interest rates, we now consider a specific example. Consider the sequence of deficits implied by

$$\frac{dB}{dt} = rB + G - T(B, x), \qquad T_B > r + B\left(\frac{dr}{dB}\right), \qquad T_x > 0. \tag{66}$$

Taxes are now assumed to be an increasing function of both the level of debt and a shift parameter x. The exercise we consider is to decrease x, starting from an initially balanced budget; taxes decrease, and the deficit increases. Debt grows over time and so do taxes until a balanced budget is again achieved. The condition on T_B ensures that, as B increases, taxes rise faster than the interest burden.

To examine the effects of such a policy on the term structure of interest rates, we introduce a "long-term rate."[48] We define the long-term rate as the yield on perpetuities paying a constant coupon flow of unity. Let R be their yield and thus $1/R$ be their price.[49] The instantaneous rate of return on perpetuities is then

$$\frac{1 + d(1/R)/dt}{1/R} = R - \frac{dR/dt}{R}.$$

It is the sum of the yield and the expected rate of capital gain, which is negative if yields increase. By arbitrage between short and long bonds

$$R - \frac{dR/dt}{R} = r,$$

or equivalently

$$\frac{dR/dt}{R} = R - r. \tag{67}$$

Eliminating r, using (67) in (65) and (66), gives a dynamic system in R and B. We characterize its dynamics using the phase diagram in figure 3.7. The equilibrium E has a saddle point structure, and the saddle point path SS is upward sloping.

Can we again restrict our attention to the path SS? Consider the other paths. On all other paths, B eventually converges to B^*. Equation (65) implies that r must also converge to r^*. The long-term rate, however, diverges either to infinity or zero. Why is this? Take the case of paths below SS, where R is below r [from (67)] and decreasing. Along these paths the price of perpetuities is higher than on the saddle point path, but the higher purchase price is offset by an anticipated price increase and thus by an expected capital gain. In the previous model we could exclude such paths because they

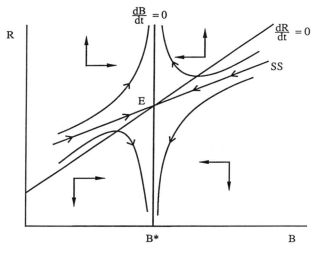

Figure 3.7
Interest rate dynamics

violated either transversality or feasibility conditions. Here it is not clear that we can. We will nevertheless exclude them a priori and return to this issue in depth in chapter 5. For the time being, we will restrict ourselves to the saddle point path.

A decrease in x, that is, a decrease in taxes, shifts the $dB/dt = 0$ locus to the right, to $(dB/dt = 0)'$. Thus, starting from point E in figure 3.8, R jumps to C, and R and B move over time along CE'.

The decrease in x creates a deficit and a consequent increase in debt over time. The effect on short-term rates is initially small, but because debt levels are anticipated to increase, the effect is larger on anticipated future short-term rates. Thus at the time of the change in policy, long-term rates increase in anticipation of high short-term rates later. The term structure of interest is upward sloping. Over time both R and r converge to their new higher level.

This simple example suggests what the effects of deficits would be in a model with capital accumulation. The same sequence of deficits would lead to an increase in long-term rates and a decrease in capital accumulation. A new equilibrium would be reached with a higher level of debt and a lower level of capital, as in our steady state analysis of the previous model summarized in equation (64). Thus, for example, if increased defense spending during a war is deficit financed, the economy at the end of the war

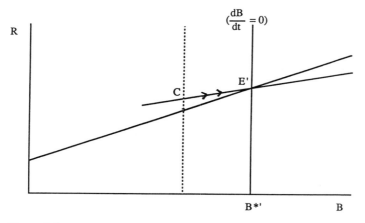

Figure 3.8
The effects of a temporary increase in the deficit

will have lower capital and higher government debt. It is in this sense that deficit finance and higher debt impose a "burden" on the economy: they reduce capital accumulation, and thus the stock of capital available to future generations.

3.5 Aggregate Saving and the Interest Rate

Net saving in the United States has averaged less than 8% of GNP over the past 20 years, while the Japanese net saving rate has been above 20% of GNP and the German close to 15%.[50] Many economists have argued that the low rate of saving in the United States is a primary cause of slow growth and have proposed measures to increase it. Most of the proposals imply an increase in the rate of return on saving, for instance, by exempting from income tax both the initial contributions to savings plans and the interest they earn.

Whether an increase in the rate of return on saving would in fact increase saving, and consequently investment and the capital stock, is the subject of much controversy. Some argue that both theory and empirical evidence suggest that the elasticity of aggregate saving with respect to the interest rate is approximately equal to zero. Others argue that the elasticity is, instead, very large, perhaps even infinite. In this section we examine the issue of the elasticity of saving with respect to its rate of return, using models developed in chapter 2 and earlier in this chapter.

Much of the controversy in the literature arises from a failure to distinguish between two questions. The first is that of the response of the rate of saving at a moment of time to a change in the rate of return; the second is that of the eventual response of aggregate wealth to a change in its rate of return. We may concentrate on the response of either aggregate saving (the rate at which wealth increases) or aggregate wealth (the stock that results from past saving) to the interest rate.

With saving being the rate of change of wealth, there is no fundamental difference between the two questions. For judging long-run responses to changes in the rate of return,[51] the more interesting question is how the stock of wealth responds. In the long run in a stationary economy, net saving will be zero; thus across steady states in a stationary economy, changes in the rate of return do not affect the rate of saving. However, the levels of wealth and of welfare may well differ between the steady states before and after the tax change.

To see this, consider figure 3.9 which plots the (nonhuman) wealth of an individual through life. By assumption, the individual starts and ends his life with no wealth so that his lifelong net saving is equal to zero. When the economy is in steady state and all individuals have the same time profile of wealth, we can interpret figure 3.9 as a cross section of the wealth positions of individuals of different ages. Thus area A represents aggregate wealth and may be affected by the interest rate. Aggregate saving, however, is equal to the sum of individual saving over the individual's lifetime and thus necessarily equal to zero.

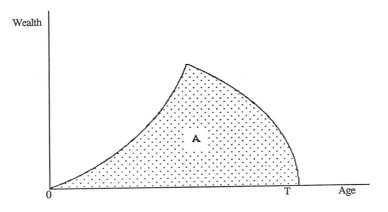

Figure 3.9
Life-cycle profile of nonhuman wealth

If agents have finite horizons, a necessary condition for aggregate saving to be positive is either population or productivity growth. Population growth, for example, implies that the number of young individuals who are likely to be net savers is larger than the number of dissavers, and thus there is aggregate positive saving.[52]

The relation between the interest rate, population, productivity growth, and either the aggregate saving rate or aggregate wealth is generally a complex one. We thus focus on simple cases that serve to show the possible extremes.

The Two-Period Model

We start with the two-period-life, no-bequest, overlapping generations model developed in section 3.1. The supply of capital in this model is equal to the savings of the young and is thus given by their savings function:

$$s = s(w_t, r_{t+1}).$$

Net saving is equal to the saving of the young minus the dissaving of the old.

We saw in section 3.1 that s_r is ambiguous and depends on the relative importance of income and substitution effects. These effects are characterized in figure 3.10. An increase in the interest rate shifts the budget constraint from AB to AB' and the equilibrium from E to E'. The movement from E to E' can be decomposed into a substitution effect from E to E'', along

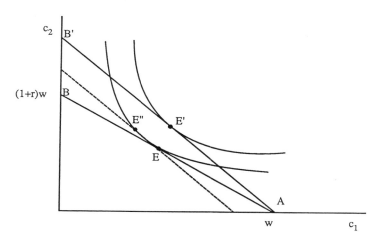

Figure 3.10
Income and substitution effects of a change in the interest rate

the indifference curve, and an income effect from E'' to E. Saving increases when the substitution effect outweighs the income effect. Equivalently, saving increases, remains constant, or decreases depending on whether the elasticity of substitution is greater, equal to, or less than unity; when utility is logarithmic, there is no effect of the interest rate on the supply of savings. It is this result that has led many to conclude that the elasticity of the supply of wealth with respect to the interest rate may well be close to zero.

This model, however, is special in many ways. Individuals live only for two periods, so the stock of capital is determined by the young generation only and the short-run and long-run responses of capital are, given wage income, the same. Individuals receive wage income only in the first period of their lives. Indeed, it can be shown that the ambiguity is significantly reduced if individuals earn also some wage income in the second period of their lives (see problem 4).

The Model of Perpetual Youth

To analyze the issue in a less constrained model, we turn to the finite horizon model of section 3.3 and ask how an increase in the interest rate affects saving. Recall that in that model we assumed a logarithmic utility function in order to derive the behavior of consumption. We will assume here that labor income, w, is constant through time and is received by all in equal proportions (i.e., $\alpha = 0$).[53]

We will assume that both the interest rate, r, and noninterest income, w, are exogenous, and we will examine the effect of a change in r. The analysis can thus be viewed either as a partial equilibrium in nature or as describing the behavior of a small open economy with a given endowment and a given world interest rate. The equations of motion are

$$C = (p + \theta)\left(K + \frac{w}{r + p}\right),$$
(68)

$$\frac{dK}{dt} = S = rK - C + w.$$
(69)

Aggregate consumption is a linear function of wealth. Human wealth is the present discounted value of labor income, which with constant r and w reduces to $w/(r + p)$. Wealth accumulation is equal to aggregate saving.

What are the dynamic effects of a permanent increase in interest rates? We first consider the case where r is less than $\theta + p$ but greater than θ. The dynamics are characterized by the phase diagram of figure 3.11. Consump-

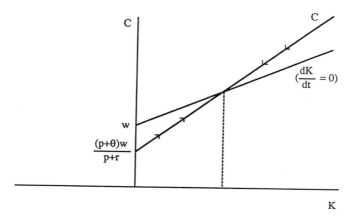

Figure 3.11
Dynamics of consumption ($p + \theta > r > \theta$)

tion, given the level of wealth, satisfies equation (68). Equation (69) determines the movement of wealth. The dynamic system is stable and wealth converges to K^*.

Figure 3.12 characterizes the effects of an increase in r. When r increases, human wealth declines, decreasing consumption. The locus corresponding to equation (68) shifts downward. The higher interest rate increases interest payments given K: the locus corresponding to (69) rotates upward. The new steady state level of wealth, $K^{*\prime}$, is unambiguously higher.

We can solve for K^* algebraically, using (68) and (69) with $dK/dt = 0$ to get

$$K^* = \left[\frac{r - \theta}{(p + \theta - r)(r + p)} \right] w > 0, \qquad \text{if} \quad p + \theta > r > \theta, \tag{70}$$

so that

$$\frac{dK^*}{dr} = \frac{[(r - \theta)^2 + p(\theta + p)]w}{(r + p)^2(p + \theta - r)^2} > 0.$$

The adjustment path to the new steady state is EBE' in figure 3.12. Saving is given by the vertical distance between the two loci so that it initially increases from zero to AB. When the interest rate increases, income increases because of higher interest payments. Consumption decreases because of the decrease in human wealth. Thus saving increases on both counts. As wealth accumulates, consumption increases faster than income. In the new steady state, wealth is higher and saving is again equal to zero.

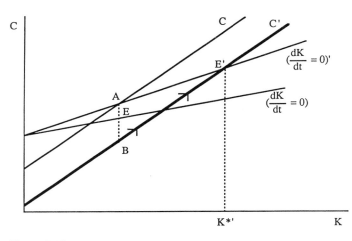

Figure 3.12
The effects of an increase in the interest rate

In this model the effect of the interest rate on steady state wealth can be quite substantial. If, for example, $p = \theta = 4\%$, an increase of r from 5% to 6% increases wealth by a factor of 2.7.

What happens if r is greater than $\theta + p$? This case is characterized in figure 3.13. Although there is an equilibrium with negative wealth, it is unstable. Starting, for example, with zero wealth, saving is positive and increasing, leading to unending capital accumulation. Why is this? The high rate of interest leads individuals to postpone consumption and to choose individual paths on which wealth grows at a rate higher than p. It follows that although the size of each cohort decreases at rate p, cohort wealth, and by implication aggregate wealth, increases forever. Thus, if, for example, the interest rate is increased from a value below to a value above $\theta + p$, the long-run wealth response, at a given interest rate, is infinite. This is of course a partial equilibrium result. Remember that in section 3.3 we showed that the steady state interest rate in a closed economy would be less than $\theta + p$. Once the interest rate is endogenized, measures that increase the return on saving (e.g., a reduction in the tax on interest income) will lead to an increase in saving and capital that reduces the pre-tax interest rate.

This analysis relies on the maintained assumption that utility is logarithmic, that the elasticity of substitution is equal to unity. One may guess that if the elasticity of substitution were lower, the interest rate elasticity of saving and wealth would be smaller, maybe even negative. This possibility has been analyzed by Summers (1981), who concludes that under realistic

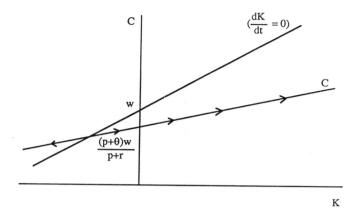

Figure 3.13
Dynamics of consumption $(r > \theta + p)$

assumptions about the path of labor income through life, the interest rate elasticity of aggregate wealth implied by the life-cycle model is likely to remain positive even for very low elasticities of substitution. Simulations have shown, however, that the dynamic effects of the interest rate on saving may be slow: consumption may increase initially in response to the increase in rates, and saving may initially decrease. The higher interest rate, however, implies a higher rate of wealth accumulation, and this effect eventually dominates the first, leading to a positive long-run response of aggregate saving and wealth.

How do we reconcile these results with those of the two-period model? The difference is due mainly to different assumptions about the path of labor income through life. In both models, under the logarithmic assumption, the impact effect of an increased interest rate on consumption, *given wealth*, is equal to zero. This is due to the opposite and canceling "income" and substitution effects. In the first model, however, human wealth is also un-affected by the increase in the interest rate; this is because labor income is received only in the first period of life. In the second model, in which labor income is received throughout life, human wealth falls when the interest rate rate increases. Therefore so does consumption, and the rate of saving increases. As a matter of fact, individuals receive labor income throughout their lives. In this respect at least, the second model is more realistic than the first. The presumption is therefore that the elasticity of the (stock) supply of wealth to the interest rate is likely to be positive and could even be large.

The Infinite Horizon Model

What is the effect on saving of an increase in the interest rate if individuals have infinite horizons, that is, if they care about the utility of their heirs enough to make bequests? Recall from chapter 2 the first-order condition in the Ramsey problem, that dC/dt is of the same sign as $r - \theta$. This implies that individuals will accumulate endlessly if $r > \theta$, will not accumulate at all if $r = \theta$, and will try to dissave if $r < \theta$. Accordingly, the elasticity of supply of capital is infinite, though the elasticity of the flow of saving with respect to the interest rate is finite.

This is simply another way of stating the result derived in chapter 2, namely, that with an infinite horizon the interest received by consumers must, in steady state, be equal to the discount rate (plus, possibly, the rate of growth of population). This same result can be derived using equations (68) and (69), with p set equal to zero.

General Equilibrium

The infinite elasticity of the supply of wealth with respect to the interest rate is of course a partial equilibrium or *ceteris paribus* result that takes the interest rate as given. In a complete model the effect on the steady state capital stock of a policy that changes the rate of return on saving depends also on the response of the interest rate to the increase in the stock of wealth.

Consider, in particular, the Ramsey model, which has the modified golden rule as a steady state condition:

$$f'(k^*) = \theta + n.$$

Now suppose that a subsidy is given to capital, making the return to savers equal to $(1 + \varepsilon) f'(k)$. This implies the steady state condition

$$(1 + \varepsilon) f'(k^*) = \theta + n. \tag{71}$$

What is the effect of an increase in ε on the steady state capital stock? By differentiating (71) and evaluating the derivative at the point where $\varepsilon = 0$, we obtain

$$\frac{dk^*}{d\varepsilon} = -\frac{f'}{f''}.$$

Using the definition of the elasticity of substitution in production,[54] σ, we obtain

$$\frac{dk^*/d\varepsilon}{k^*} = \frac{\sigma f(k^*)}{w}. \tag{72}$$

The subsidy to capital at the initial interest rate stimulates saving that reduces the interest rate. The steady state effects are determined entirely by the characteristics of the production function. The greater the elasticity of substitution and the smaller the share of wages in output, the larger is the effect of the subsidy on interest income. The role of the elasticity of substitution reflects the fact that capital accumulation stops when the aftertax interest rate has risen to its former level, and that requires a greater increase in the capital stock, the more substitutable labor and capital are.

Even in this general equilibrium context subsidies to capital that raise the rate of return can have large effects on the capital stock. Suppose, for example, that the production function is Cobb-Douglas with labor's share equal to 0.75. Suppose then that ε is increased from 0% to 25%, meaning that the rate of return on capital is being subsidized by 25%. The steady state capital stock increases by 33%.

The conclusion from these exercises must be that there is a strong theoretical presumption of a positive elasticity of saving with respect to the interest rate. A very large body of empirical research has not, however, discovered such large saving and wealth elasticities. One potential explanation may be that although the experiments considered above study the effects of a permanent change in the real rate, such permanent changes are rare. More frequent are temporary movements. Because the movements are not expected to last, the human wealth effect may be small. Because the movements do not last, we observe only short-run elasticities of saving that are likely to be smaller than long-run elasticities: when the elasticity of substitution is low, the effect of an increase in interest rates on the saving rate may be initially negative, only to turn positive later on. Alternatively, it may be that the models of saving examined in chapter 2 and here are missing a crucial element of saving behavior and overemphasize the potential effects of interest rates on saving and wealth.

Problems

1. In the simplest two-period life-cycle model, the model of section 3.1, assume that the utility function is nonseparable, and derive explicitly the expressions for s_w and s_r. Explain under what circumstances

(a) $0 < s_w < 1$.
(b) $s_r > 0$.

2. *Growth and the saving rate.*

Consider an overlapping generation economy in which each individual lives for two periods.

Population is constant. The individuals' endowments in each period are exogenous. The first-period endowment of an individual born at time t is equal to e_t, and the second-period endowment of the same individual to $e_t(1 + g)$, where g can be negative. Each individual saves by investing in a constant returns technology, where each unit invested yields $1 + r$ units of output in the following period.

An individual born at time t maximizes

$$U(c_{1t}, c_{2t+1}) = \log(c_{1t}) + (1 + d)^{-1} \log(c_{2t+1}), \qquad d > 0.$$

Finally, the first period endowments grow at rate m so that

$$e_t = (1 + m)e_{t-1}.$$

(a) How does an increase in the growth rate of income expected by one individual, g, affect his saving rate?
(b) How does an increase in m affect aggregate saving?
(c) Assuming that $g = m$ (or $g = m - x$, for a given x), how does an increase in m affect aggregate saving?
(d) In light of these results, assess the theoretical validity of the claim that high growth is responsible for the high Japanese saving rate.
(e) "The reason why the saving rate has gone down in the United States in the 1980s despite the supply side incentives is that growth prospects are much more favorable than in the 1970s." Comment.

3. *Shocks and the current account.*

A small open economy is inhabited by two-period-lived individuals who receive an exogenous endowment, y_t, in the period when they are born and receive no further endowment in the second period of life. Population is constant. Individuals have access to a world capital market with interest rate r. The individual's utility function is

$$U = \frac{(c_{1t})^{1-R}}{1 - R} + \frac{(1 + \theta)^{-1}(c_{2t+1})^{1-R}}{1 - R}, \qquad R > 0.$$

(a) Derive the individual's consumption function, and show how first-period consumption is related to the interest rate.
(b) Compare your results with those stated in section 3.5 where the effects of the interest rate on saving in this model are discussed.
(c) Calculate the current account of the balance of payments (assume that there is only one person per generation for convenience) as a function of y_t and other variables.
(d) Suppose there is a temporary reduction in y_t, from y^* to $y^* - \varepsilon_t$. In the next period y is back at y^*. Show how the current account is affected in period t and subsequently.

(c) Now suppose the decline in endowment is permanent. Show how the current account adjusts.

(d) Compare your results with those at the end of chapter 2 and explain.

4. *The interest elasticity of saving revisited.*

(a) Suppose that an individual receives wages w_1 and w_2 in the two periods of life and has a constant relative risk aversion utility function. Examine the effects of a change in the interest rate on saving, and contrast the results with those in problem 3(a).

(b) Suppose that $w_1 = w_2$. Can the steady state in this model be dynamically inefficient? Why?

5. *Government debt and private wealth accumulation.*

Consider an economy with dynamics characterized by the following equations:

$$C_t = (p + \theta)\left[\left(\frac{Y - T}{r + p}\right) + D + F_t\right],$$

$$\frac{dF_t}{dt} = rF_t + Y_t - C_t - G.$$

Domestic production, Y, is given and constant. The world interest rate, r, at which the country can freely borrow and lend is constant, such that $\theta < r < \theta$. D is government debt, F is net holdings of foreign assets, T is taxes, and G is government spending. Because we are considering paths where D, T, and G are constant, they are not indexed by time.

(a) Explain where the first equation may come from.

(b) Suppose that the economy is initially in steady state with $D = T = G = 0$. Suppose that the government (unexpectedly) distributes government bonds to the people so that D increases from 0 to dD and, to balance the budget the government increases taxes permanently by $dT = rdD$. Characterize the dynamic effects of this change on consumption, the current account, and net holdings of foreign assets. Explain why this policy has real effects.

(c) "Even if we are able to eliminate U.S. fiscal deficits over the next five to ten years, we will be paying the costs of those deficits forever." Discuss this statement in light of the preceding results.

6. *Social security and capital accumulation.*

Assume a Cobb-Douglas production function, with share of labor α, and the simplest two-period-lived overlapping generations model. The population grows at rate n. Individuals supply inelastically one unit of labor in the first period of their lives and have logarithmic utility over consumption:

$$U = \ln c_{1t} + (1 + \theta)^{-1} \ln c_{2t+1}.$$

(a) Solve for the steady state capital stock.

(b) Show how the introduction of pay-as-you-go social security, in which the government collects amount d from each young person and gives $(1 + n)d$ to each old person, affects the steady state capital stock.

7. *The elasticity of substitution and the interest elasticity of wealth.*

Consider a continuous time economy in which one individual is born at each instant. Each individual lives for one unit of time, say, from $t = 0$ to $t = 1$, for example, and retires at age a, $0 < a < 1$. At any point in time the distribution of ages in the population is therefore uniform over [0, 1]. Income while working is a constant, y, and is equal to zero during retirement. There is no uncertainty. The interest rate is given and equal to r.

Individuals have Leontief (zero elasticity of substitution) utility, which can be considered as the limit of the CRRA utility function as the elasticity of substitution goes to zero. Their subjective discount rate is equal to zero.
(a) Derive the optimal consumption for each individual. (Do not try to work directly with a Leontief utility function. Derive the first-order conditions for the general CRRA case, and take the limit as the elasticity goes to zero.)
(b) Derive the path of asset accumulation and saving over life for an individual. Show how this path is affected by an increase in the interest rate.
(c) Derive aggregate consumption. Suppose that $r = 0$ initially. What is the impact effect of an increase in r?
(d) (This is difficult.) Derive aggregate wealth in this economy. What is the effect of an increase in r on aggregate wealth?

Notes

1. We assume additive separability of the utility function for convenience; Diamond (1965) assumes that the utility function takes the more general form $u(c_{1t}, c_{2t+1})$.

2. The interest rate received by savers is equal to the rental rate paid by firms on the assumption that the relative price of capital is constant at one. This is the case so long as capital can be consumed, which we assume, and the economy is never in a situation such that the young wish to consume all their income in the first period.

3. If capital once installed cannot be consumed, then the market equilibrium has to be such that the old cannot consume more than the value of capital they are able to sell to the young. In such a setting it would be necessary to introduce a market price for installed capital, which would differ from one (being below it) whenever at a price of one the demand for capital fell below the supply.

4. We examine the effects of the interest rate on saving in more detail in section 3.5.

5. The correspondence principle, due to Samuelson (1947), states that the comparative static and the dynamic properties of a system are typically closely linked and, specifically, that the assumption that a system is dynamically stable will often make it possible to deduce its comparative static properties. Diamond (1965) uses the correspondence principle extensively.

6. Ramsey considered such discounting of future generations utilities morally indefensible.

7. This follows Samuelson (1968).

8. We will later allow the planner's horizon, T, to go to infinity. We start with a finite horizon so that we can discuss the implications of the central planner placing a greater weight on the utilities of later than earlier generations ($R < 0$), and so that we can, en route, display a turnpike theorem.

9. As we will show later, the economy never reaches that steady state but, for a large T, remains very close to it for a long time.

10. This can be seen by writing the entire function as $G(x)$ and noting that $G(0) > 0$, $G(1) < 0$, $G(1 + R) < 0$, and $G(\infty) > 0$.

11. The turnpike property could equally well have been demonstrated in the Ramsey problem of chapter 2. If consumers choose an optimal path of consumption, subject to both an initial condition for $k(0)$ and an arbitrary terminal condition $k(T)$ for some large T, the level of capital will be close to the modified golden rule capital stock for most of the time. This can be seen as follows: using, for example, the phase diagram of figure 2.2, it is easy to see that the optimal path that satisfies $k(0) = k_0$ and $k(T) = k_T$ will go very close to the steady state if T is large. Close to the steady state, however, the equations of motion imply that both k and c are moving slowly. Thus a path that veers close to a steady state is a path in which the variables stay close to their steady state values for a long time.

12. It is possible in these cases to discuss optimality using the *overtaking criterion*, which essentially states that path A overtakes path B if there exists a finite T^* such that the present value (in utility terms) associated with path A up to time T^* exceeds that associated with path B up to T^*, and that the inequality remains in the same direction for all $T > T^*$. A path is optimal if it overtakes all other paths. See Burmeister (1980, ch. 6).

13. Our analysis has been limited here to steady states. Cass (1972) gives a necessary and sufficient condition for a path $\{k_t\}$ $t = 0, \ldots, \infty$ to be dynamically inefficient. The condition is the following. Define Π_t as

$$\Pi_t = \prod_{s=1}^{t} \frac{1 + f'(k_s)}{1 + n}.$$

Then a necessary and sufficient condition for the path to be dynamically inefficient is that

$$\sum_{t=1}^{\infty} \Pi_t < \infty.$$

14. Suppose that the period is 30 years long, and that n is such that $1 + n = (1.01)^{30}$; δ is such that $(1 - \delta) = (0.95)^{30}$, and $\alpha = 0.25$. Then if θ is given by $(1 + \theta) = (1.03)^{30}$, $r^* = 0.75 > n$; if θ is equal to zero, then $r^* = 0.11 < n$.

15. Abel et al. (1987) discuss this issue. They derive a sufficient condition for dynamic efficiency and conclude that this condition is almost surely satisfied, that the U.S. economy is almost surely dynamically efficient.

16. Kotlikoff and Summers (1981) estimate that at least 70% of wealth in the United States is attributable to bequests rather than life-cycle savings; Modigliani (1988) reverses these proportions.

17. Abel (1985) studies a model in which bequests are accidental.

18. An alternative specification, the "joy-of-giving" bequest motive, would make V_t depend not on V_{t+1} but on the size of the bequest left to the next generation. The formulation is less attractive because it implies that a parent would leave the same amount to the child independent of the child's economic circumstances: it is difficult to believe that the size of the bequest rather than the benefits it will bring is what enters the parent's utility function. The joy-of-giving bequest motive has very different implications for efficiency than the bequest motive studied in the text; they will be noted later.

19. There is a subtle difference, in that in the command optimum we included $u(c_{20})$ in the planner's utility function: the planner was concerned about all those currently alive and yet to be born. The utility of the current old does not appear in (15); instead, it is assumed that the current young are the family decision makers and that the current old are merely consuming the saving they set aside for themselves when they were young. Start-up conditions in the overlapping generations model are somewhat problematic because it is not clear whether one should treat the first period as the first period of creation, in which there are no old (we guess, though, chickens and eggs may have arrived together), or merely as the first period of optimization, in which the old already exist.

20. This follows Weil (1985, ch. 2), who gives a more formal argument.

21. Weil (1987) shows that equilibria may be inefficient when everyone now alive is infinitely lived but new infinitely lived families with no (caring) predecessors are being added to the population.

22. The discussion here draws on Abel (1987b) and Kimball (1987).

23. Recall the discussion at the end of chapter 2. The discrete time equivalent of the exponential discounting needed for time consistency in chapter 2 is geometrically declining discount factors.

24. There is a subtle issue about the assumptions the individual makes when giving a gift to his parent. In equation (27), in differentiating $u(c_{2t})$ with respect to g_t, we assume that he takes the actions of his siblings as given when deciding on his own gift. Alternatively, the children could act cooperatively. In that case, in differentiating $u(c_{2t})$ with respect to g_t, an extra $1 + n$ term would appear on the right-hand side of (27). The difference arises, as Abel (1985) points out, because, although each parent has $1 + n$ children, each child (in this model) has one parent.

25. In the cooperative equilibrium for making gifts, the left-hand term in (29) is multiplied by $1 + n$. This raises the minimal value of r^* but still does not guarantee dynamic efficiency.

26. This follows Samuelson (1975).

27. The intent when the system was set up in 1935 was to have a largely funded system. This was changed in 1939. The U.S. social security system is not entirely on a pay-as-you-go basis: contributions and benefits do not match each year, and there is a small trust fund.

28. This is an example of the use of the correspondence principle. We used condition (5), which characterizes dynamic adjustment, to deduce the impact of the introduction of social security.

29. This can be shown more formally by extending the bequests model of section 3.1 to include social security contributions of d_t per old person and then showing that, provided that bequests are being made, $db_t/dd_t = -1$. The individual's saving decision is unaffected and therefore so is the capital stock.

30. The term "Ricardian equivalence" was coined by Barro (1974), who argued that debt and tax finance are equivalent. We return to this issue in section 3.4. Although the argument that intergenerational transfers could be offset by private behavior was indeed presented by Ricardo, he also expressed doubts as to the empirical relevance of the argument.

31. More generally, social security will affect saving if it provides insurance on terms different from those available in the private market.

32. Social security has real effects in this case because it makes everyone contribute to the system, thereby avoiding the adverse selection problem facing an insurance company that cannot distinguish the strong from the sick.

33. The problem is computational rather than conceptual, which means that the behavior of quite complex overlapping generations models can be simulated on the computer. See, for example, Auerbach and Kotlikoff (1987).

34. This assumption is clearly made for convenience rather than realism.

35. The probability p is a rate per unit time and thus does not need to be bounded between zero and one. The probability that an individual dies within any given discrete time period, say, between $t = 0$ and $t = 1$, is bounded between zero and one.

36. See Yaari (1965) for a discussion of the role of life insurance in the context of uncertain lifetimes.

37. The double time indicators, t and s, are a result of the overlapping generations structure: recall that in section 3.1 we had to distinguish between c_{1t} and c_{2t}, the consumptions of the young and old in period t, and between c_{1t} and c_{2t+1}, the consumptions of a given generation in the two periods of life.

38. The extension to the CRRA class is given in Blanchard (1985).

39. This result is obtained by Cass and Yaari (1967).

40. This step, involving several integrals, is time-consuming but ends up with simple aggregate functions.

41. Recall that we are assuming here no growth in population. If no one dies, then the population is unchanging, and we should assume that each individual receives the same share of income all the time.

42. Comparing figure 3.5 with figure 2.2 which describes dynamics in the Ramsey model, note that the major difference is that the $dC/dt = 0$ locus in the Ramsey model is vertical at the modified golden rule capital stock.

43. Of course, distortionary taxation, such as the taxation of capital, does affect the allocation of resources in any model.

44. Here is one place where the assumption $r > 0$ matters. With $r < 0$, the government could run a deficit forever without the debt exploding. In each period it could issue debt equal in value to the negative interest it pays (i.e., the positive payments it receives from the public that is holding the debt).

45. This simple exercise is extended by Blanchard and Summers (1984), who derive and construct an index of fiscal policy, summarizing the effects of current debt and of current and anticipated taxes and spending on the aggregate demand for goods.

46. A *reductio ad absurdum* approach has been taken by Bernheim and Bagwell (1986). They point out that if people currently alive are linked at some future date through descendants (e.g., their great-grandchildren may marry), then they can and may want through their current actions to offset the effects of any government intertemporal or atemporal reallocations. They develop this argument to show that even the distortions from potentially distortionary taxes may be internalized if everyone is effectively linked through some potential future relationship. And having gone this far, they conclude that it is clear that at least one of their assumptions, which are essentially the same as those needed for Ricardian equivalence, must be wrong.

47. We implicitly hold r constant in this explanation.

48. The long-term rate is a shadow rate in this economy. That is, the government issues only short-term instantaneous bonds. The long-term rate we compute, R, is the rate that would apply to a long-term bond, if we were to introduce one in this economy.

49. Although they are related, R here is not the same as $R(t, z)$ defined earlier.

50. Net saving is equal to the sum of private sector (household and corporate) saving and government saving. It is equal to the sum of net investment and the current account (of the balance of payments) surplus.

51. Obviously, the rate of return on saving is in generally an endogenous variable; we implicitly mean here that some policy action is taken that affects the rate of return on saving at each given level of the capital stock. For instance, interest income may be exempted from taxation.

52. Modigliani (1975) provides an account of the discovery in the mid-1950s by Brumberg and him of the role of population and income growth in determining aggregate savings.

53. The case $\alpha > 0$, which tilts labor income to earlier in life, will generate results closer to those of the simplest two-period model.

54. For the constant returns to scale production function that allows us to write output as $f(k)$, the elasticity of substitution is

$$\sigma = -\frac{f'(k)w}{f''(k)f(k)k}.$$

References

Abel, Andrew (1985). "Precautionary Saving and Accidental Bequests." *American Economic Review* 75, 4 (Sept.), 777–791.

Abel, Andrew (1987a). "Aggregate Savings in the Presence of Private and Social Insurance." In R. Dornbusch et al. (eds.), *Macroeconomics and Finance: Essays in Honor of Franco Modigliani*. Cambridge, MA: MIT Press.

Abel, Andrew (1987b). "Operative Gift and Bequest Motives." NBER Working Paper 2331.

Abel, Andrew, N. Gregory Mankiw, Lawrence H. Summers, and Richard Zeckhauser (1987). "Assessing Dynamic Efficiency: Theory and Evidence." NBER Working Paper 2097.

Allais, Maurice (1947). *Economie et interet*. Paris: Imprimerie Nationale.

Auerbach, Alan, and Laurence Kotlikoff (1987). *Dynamic Fiscal Policy*. Cambridge University Press.

Barro, Robert J. (1974). "Are Government Bonds Net Wealth?" *Journal of Political Economy* 82, 6 (Dec.), 1095–1117.

Bernheim, B. Douglas (1987). "Ricardian Equivalence: An Evaluation of Theory and Evidence." *NBER Macroeconomics Annual* 2, 263–303.

Bernheim, B. Douglas, Andrei Shleifer, and Lawrence H. Summers (1985). "The Strategic Bequest Motive." *Journal of Political Economy* 93, 6 (Dec.), 1045–1076.

Bernheim, B. Douglas, and Kyle Bagwell (1986). "Is Everything Neutral?" Mimeo.

Blanchard, Olivier J. (1985). "Debt, Deficits, and Finite Horizons." *Journal of Political Economy* 93, 2 (April), 223–247.

Blanchard, Olivier J., and Lawrence H. Summers (1984). "Perspectives on High Interest Rates." *Brookings Papers on Economic Activity* 2, 273–334.

Burmeister, Edwin (1980). *Capital Theory and Dynamics*. Cambridge University Press.

Cass, David (1972). "On Capital Overaccumulation in the Aggregate, Neoclassical Model of Economic Growth: A Complete Characterization." *Journal of Economic Theory* 4, 200–223.

Cass, David, and Menahem E. Yaari (1967). "Individual Saving, Aggregate Capital Accumulation, and Efficient Growth." In K. Shell (ed.), *Essays on the Theory of Optimal Economic Growth*. Cambridge, MA: MIT Press.

Diamond, Peter A. (1965). "National Debt in a Neoclassical Growth Model." *American Economic Review* 55, 5 (Dec.), 1126–1150.

Feldstein, Martin S. (1974). "Social Security, Induced Retirement, and Aggregate Capital Accumulation." *Journal of Political Economy* 82, 4 (Oct.), 905–926.

Katona, George S. (1965). *Private Pensions and Individual Savings*. Ann Arbor: University of Michigan Survey Research Center.

Kimball, Miles S. (1987). "Making Sense of Two-Sided Altruism." *Journal of Monetary Economics* 20, 2 (Sept.), 301–326.

Kotlikoff, Laurence J., and Lawrence H. Summers (1981). "The Role of Intergenerational Transfers in Aggregate Capital Accumulation." *Journal of Political Economy* 89, 4 (Aug.) 706–732.

Modigliani, Franco (1975). "The Life-Cycle Hypothesis of Saving Twenty Years Later." In M. Parkin (ed.), *Contemporary Issues in Economics*. Manchester University Press.

Modigliani, Franco (1984). "Measuring the Contribution of Intergenerational Transfers to Total Wealth; Conceptual Issues and Empirical Findings." Mimeo.

Modigliani, Franco (1988). "The Role of Intergenerational Transfers and Life Cycle Saving in the Accumulation of Wealth." *Journal of Economic Perspectives* 2, 2 (Spring), 15–40.

Munnell, Alicia H. (1974). *The Effect of Social Security on Personal Savings*. Cambridge, MA: Ballinger.

Samuelson, Paul A. (1958). "An Exact Consumption-Loan Model of Interest with or without the Social Contrivance of Money." *Journal of Political Economy* 66, 6 (Dec.), 467–482.

Samuelson, Paul A. (1947). *Foundations of Economic Analysis*. Harvard University Press.

Samuelson, Paul A. (1968). "The Two-Part Golden Rule Deduced as the Asymptotic Turnpike of Catenary Motions." *Western Economic Journal* 6, 2 (March), 85–89.

Samuelson, Paul A. (1975). "Optimum Social Security in a Life-cycle Growth Model." *International Economic Review* 16, 3 (Oct.), 539–544.

Summers, Lawrence H. (1981). "Capital Taxation and Accumulation in a Life-Cycle Growth Model." *American Economic Review* 71, 4 (Sept.), 533–544.

Weil, Philippe (1985). "Essays on the Valuation of Unbacked Assets." Ph.D. Dissertation. Department of Economics, Harvard University.

Weil, Philippe (1987). "Permanent Budget Deficits and Inflation." *Journal of Monetary Economics* 20, 2 (Sept.), 393–410.

Wetterstrand, W. H. (1981). "Parametric Models for Life Insurance Mortality Data: Gomperty's Law over Time." *Transactions of the Society of Actuaries* 33, 159–179.

Yaari, Menahem E. (1965). "Uncertain Lifetime, Life Insurance, and the Theory of the Consumer." *Review of Economic Studies* 32 (April), 137–150.

4   Money

Money plays two distinct roles in the economy: money is the medium of exchange, and it is usually also the unit of account. As a medium of exchange, it must be held between exchanges and thus also serves also a store of value. As a store of value, however, it is dominated by many other assets.[1] The unit of account and medium of exchange functions of money are conceptually distinct and have sometimes been distinct in practice, especially during times of high inflation when a foreign money is often used as unit of account while the local money continues to be used as medium of exchange. In this chapter we focus on money as a medium of exchange. Whether it is also the unit of account is of little relevance to the issues at hand. Later in the book, when we study business cycles, we will consider how both roles may combine to generate a potential role of money in business cycle fluctuations.

Early monies took the form of commodities whose value in exchange was equal to their consumption value as commodities.[2] The fact that these commodities were used as money raised their relative price. In contrast, the value of an unbacked, noncommodity money such as modern money derives only from the fact that it can be exchanged. We consider two types of questions in this chapter. The first is why and how unbacked paper money, which is inherently useless, is valued. The second is how the presence of money affects real decisions and the dynamic equilibria we have studied in the previous two chapters.[3] In this chapter we focus on unbacked paper money but drop the adjectives, and we maintain the assumptions of perfect competition and certainty; these assumptions will be relaxed in later chapters.

For money to be valued, it must either facilitate existing trades or allow for new ones. A simple version of the overlapping generations (OLG) model due to Samuelson (1958) satisfies these two conditions and provides a tractable setting in which to study the determinants of the value of money and its effects on the allocation of resources. The OLG model has been extremely influential, and we present it in section 4.1. However, despite several attractive features the model is misleading as a model of money. This is because money is not dominated as a store of value, an assumption that is both counterfactual and the source of some of the striking results in section 4.1. In the rest of the chapter we study the role of money when it is dominated as a store of value.

Building a model that formally explains why money is used in transactions when it is dominated as a store of value has proved to be a difficult task. Consequently, most of the research has taken a shortcut and started with the assumption that money must be used in some transactions; this constraint is known as the Clower, or cash-in-advance, constraint. We briefly review the constraint and its rationale in section 4.2.

In sections 4.3 and 4.4 we develop a model based on a Clower constraint in which money is held for transaction purposes. This is a general equilibrium extension of the early models of money demand by Baumol (1952) and Tobin (1956). Its main contribution is to show how the presence of money affects the consumption-saving decision (which we focused on in chapters 2 and 3) and to establish the determinants of the demand for money. After examining the steady state properties of the model in section 4.3, we consider in section 4.4 a simplified version of the model that makes it possible for us to analyze the dynamic effects of changes in the quantity of money.

Models based explicitly on Clower constraints, such as the one analyzed in sections 4.3 and 4.4, can quickly become analytically cumbersome. Much of the research on the effects of money has taken a different shortcut, that of treating money symmetrically with other goods by putting real money services directly in the utility function. We present such a model in section 4.5 where we also discuss the pros and cons of the practice.

In section 4.6 we broaden the discussion by distinguishing between inside and outside money, the former not being net wealth for the private sector. We discuss the Wicksellian notion of a pure credit economy and the analytic issues that arise in considering the competitive supply of monies.

Finally, in section 4.7 we analyze the interactions among deficits, seigniorage (i.e., government revenues from money creation), money growth, and inflation. We examine, in particular, the potential of deficits to generate inflation and the respective roles of money growth and inflation expectations in hyperinflations.

The models presented in this chapter help us to understand the basic differences between a monetary and a nonmonetary economy. They suggest, however, at most small effects of changes in money on real activity. Put another way, they suggest that in order to explain the apparently large effects of monetary disturbances on economic activity, other elements must be introduced into the analysis, an issue to which we return at length in the rest of the book.

4.1 The Overlapping Generations Model with Money

Samuelson's extraordinarily influential "consumption loans model" (1958) showed how the use of money could overcome the absence of a double coincidence of wants in an explicitly intertemporal context.[4] Its structure is deceptively simple:

Time is discrete, and individuals live for two periods. N_t individuals are born at time t and population grows at rate n, so that by appropriate normalization, $N_t = (1 + n)^t$. An individual born at time t is young at t and old at $t + 1$.

Each individual is endowed with one unit of a consumption good when young but receives no endowment when old. In the most striking version of the model the good received by the young is perishable. Later we will assume that each individual has access to a storage technology, such that each unit saved at time t yields $1 + r$ units at time $t + 1$, and we will allow for productive storage, with $r > 0$. When the good is perishable, $r = -1$.

The utility function of an individual born at time t is given by $u(c_{1t}, c_{2t+1})$.

The Barter Equilibrium

Figure 4.1 shows the consumption possibilities facing society in a given period. If all the goods are given to the young, they can consume only one unit each. If, instead, all the goods were given to the old, they could each consume $1 + n$ units because there are only $1/(1 + n)$ of them per each young person. And since population, and thus the total endowment, is growing steadily, each individual could over his lifetime enjoy the consumption possibilities shown by line AB in figure 4.2. An individual faced with the budget constraint AB would prefer to spread consumption over his lifetime, for example at point C in figure 4.2.

But—and this point is crucial—this allocation is not attainable through bilateral trade. The young would like to exchange goods this period against goods next period. But they can only trade this period with the old who will not be there next period and will therefore not be able to deliver goods next period. Thus no trade can take place, and the decentralized outcome is

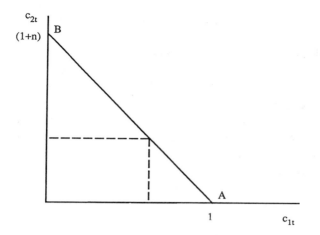

Figure 4.1
Society's consumption possibilities in period t

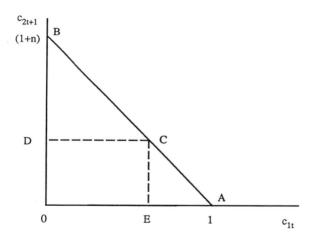

Figure 4.2
Lifetime consumption possibilities for an individual

given by A, with individuals consuming all of their endowment when young and consuming nothing when old.

The decentralized equilibrium is clearly not Pareto optimal. Suppose that in period zero the young give to the old an amount OD per old person, reducing their own first-period consumption to OE. Suppose that thereafter the old receive OD per person from the young. From period zero on, all individuals are better off under this arrangement, in which they consume at point E, than they would have been consuming at A.[5] We will now see that the introduction of money may allow for these trades, which were previously impossible, to take place.

The Introduction of Money

Suppose that at time zero the government gives to the old H completely divisible pieces of paper called money. Suppose that the old and every generation thereafter believe that they will be able to exchange money for goods, at price P_t in period t. P_t will be referred to as the price level. If this is the case, the maximization problem of an individual born at t, $t \geqslant 0$, is now given by

$$\max u(c_{1t}, c_{2t+1}) \tag{1}$$

subject to

$$P_t(1 - c_{1t}) = M_t^d \qquad \text{and} \qquad P_{t+1} c_{2t+1} = M_t^d,$$

where M_t^d is the individual's demand for money.

Individuals can now consume in both periods. To do so, they sell goods to obtain money when young and sell money when old to obtain goods. Because there is no intrinsic uncertainty in this model, it is reasonable to assume perfect foresight, in which case the actual and expected price levels at time $t + 1$ are the same.[6]

The first-order condition for maximization is given by

$$\frac{-u_1(c_{1t}, c_{2t+1})}{P_t} + \frac{u_2(c_{1t}, c_{2t+1})}{P_{t+1}} = 0, \tag{2}$$

which in turn implies a demand for money function

$$\frac{M_t^d}{P_t} = L\left(\frac{P_t}{P_{t+1}}\right). \tag{3}$$

The demand for money is just a saving function. The rate of return on money is given by P_t/P_{t+1} or, if we define the rate of deflation g_t by $(1 + g_t) \equiv$

(P_t/P_{t+1}), by $1 + g_t$. We know from the previous chapter that income and substitution effects lead to an ambiguous effect of g on savings M^d/P so that $L'(\cdot)$ can be positive or negative.

Equilibrium

We now characterize equilibrium in the money market—or equivalently, by Walras' law, in the goods market—at time t. The old supply inelastically the money they have saved, which must be equal to H. The young buy money according to equation (3). This implies the following equilibrium condition:

$$(1 + n)^t M_t^d = H. \tag{4}$$

We will for the time being limit our analysis to steady states, leaving the dynamics for chapter 5. Using (4) and (3) at time t and $t + 1$ gives

$$(1 + g_t)^{-1}(1 + n) = \frac{L(1 + g_t)}{L(1 + g_{t+1})}. \tag{5}$$

In steady state g must be constant so that, from (5), $g = n$. The rate of deflation must be equal to the rate of growth of the population: prices must decrease at a rate such that the real money supply grows at the same rate as the aggregate demand for money, which is itself growing at the rate of population growth, n.

Note that the assumption that the economy goes on forever is a necessary condition for money to be valued in this economy. If the economy ended at some time T, say, by both old and young dying at the end of T, the young at time T would not want to buy money that they could not spend at time $T + 1$. This in turn implies that the young at time $T - 1$ would not want to buy money because they would know that they could not sell it in their old age at time T. Proceeding backward, no one would ever want to buy money, money would not be valued, and the economy would remain at the barter equilibrium.[7]

It is also clear that the condition that the economy goes on forever is a necessary but not a sufficient condition for money to be valued. If at period zero the young do not believe that money will be valued at time 1, they will not buy money, and money will never be valued. Thus the barter equilibrium may remain an equilibrium even after the introduction of the H pieces of paper.

With a rate of deflation equal to n, the budget line for the individual coincides with the frontier AB in figure 4.2 and individuals will choose point C.

We therefore have derived the following set of results: (1) Money can have positive value. (2) If money is valued, the introduction of money allows for new trades. (3) Assuming that the economy reaches steady state (an issue we will defer until chapter 5), the introduction of money can lead to a Pareto optimal allocation of resources across generations. These are striking results, especially the third. Before discussing them, we examine how they are affected when goods are nonperishable and when the stock of nominal money grows over time.

Money in an Economy with Storage

Suppose now that goods can be stored and that the rate of return from storage is $r > -1$. There are two cases to consider depending on whether r is greater or less than n.

If r is negative, or positive but less than n (i.e., if storage is not too productive), the individual can in the absence of money choose any point on AG in figure 4.3 that has slope $-(1 + r)$. But the social possibility frontier is still given by AE, with slope $-(1 + n)$, which lies above AG. By an argument similar to that used earlier, the barter economy equilibrium is still not a Pareto optimum. If a fixed amount of money H is introduced and is valued, it will in steady state have a rate of return of n. Individuals will be able to achieve point C, and the economy will achieve a Pareto optimum. Storage will not be used in the monetary equilibrium. The results are therefore similar to those obtained when goods are perishable.

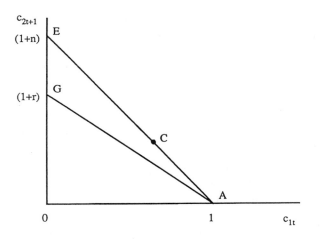

Figure 4.3
Equilibrium with storage

Things are different, however, if r is larger than n. First, the barter equilibrium is a Pareto optimum. And there cannot be a monetary equilibrium with a constant money stock. To see why, suppose that there exists a steady state with constant H in which money is valued. The rate of deflation must be equal to n. But, because the rate of return on money is less than the return to storage, nobody wants to hold money; thus money is not valued, which contradicts our initial assumption. Similarly, we can rule out non-steady-state paths in which the price level is falling at a rate greater than n, for in that case if real balances are initially positive, their value will eventually exceed unity, which implies a value of real balances acquired by the young that exceeds their endowment. Since this is impossible, such paths cannot exist.

We can therefore extend our third result to read: if the barter equilibrium is not a Pareto optimum, there exists a monetary equilibrium that leads to a Pareto optimum; if the barter equilibrium is already a Pareto optimum, there cannot be a monetary equilibrium.

The Effects of Money Growth

So far the stock of nominal money has been held constant. Suppose, however, that the nominal money stock grows at rate σ. Inflation must then be equal to $\sigma - n$ in steady state. The effects of money growth on the allocation of resources depend on how the new money is introduced into the economy. We will consider two cases, one in which new money is introduced through lump-sum transfers to the old, and the other in which money is introduced via interest payments to money holders. We assume in both cases that goods are perishable.

In the first case transfer payments are independent of individual money holdings and, we assume, are made to the old. We denote by ΔM_t the nominal transfer made to each old person at the beginning of period $t + 1$. The maximization problem of an individual born at time t is now given by

$$\max u(u_{1t}, c_{2t+1}) \tag{6}$$

subject to

$$P_t(1 - c_{1t}) = M_t^d \qquad \text{and} \qquad P_{t+1}c_{2t+1} = \Delta M_t + M_t^d.$$

The individual assumes that ΔM_t is not affected by his own actions. The first-order condition is then the same as equation (2). Solving it gives

$$\frac{M_t^d}{P_t} = L\left(\frac{P_t}{P_{t+1}}, \frac{\Delta M_t}{P_{t+1}}\right). \tag{7}$$

The demand for money function now depends on the rate of return and on the second-period money transfer, which is treated by the individual as an exogenous endowment. An increase in the second-period endowment unambiguously decreases savings, implying that L_2 is negative.

The aggregate money stock grows at rate σ so that

$$H_{t+1} = H_t + \Delta H_t = (1 + \sigma)H_t.$$

With the new money being distributed equally among the old, $\Delta H_t = N_t \Delta M_t$. The equilibrium condition in the money (goods) market at time t requires that

$$N_t M_t^d = H_t. \tag{8}$$

In a steady state per capita real balances are constant so that $H_t/P_t N_t$ is constant. It follows that P_t must decrease at rate g, where $1 + g = (1 + n)/(1 + \sigma)$, which for small values of n and σ is approximately equal to $n - \sigma$.

Because it affects the inflation rate, money growth affects the rate of return on money (which is the negative of the inflation rate) and thereby, as we shall see, the allocation of resources. Money is therefore not *superneutral*.[8] Figure 4.4 shows the effects of the combination of transfer payments and change in the inflation rate caused by money transfers. The allocation of goods in the steady state with constant money stock is given by point J on the budget line AE, which has slope $-(1 + n)$. Positive money growth at rate σ moves the initial endowment from A to D as a result of

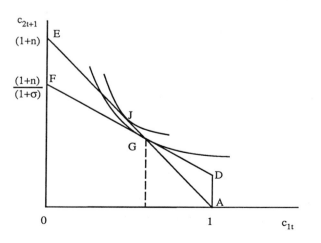

Figure 4.4
Effects of increased money growth (through lump-sum transfer) on welfare

the second-period transfer. The slope of the budget line facing an individual is now given by $-(1 + n)/(1 + \sigma)$. The equilibrium is achieved at G, where utility is maximized and the market for money clears.

The implication of allowing for money growth is that the monetary equilibrium is no longer a Pareto optimum. At point G individuals do not face the marginal rate of transformation implied by society's budget constraint AB. All individuals would be made better off by returning to zero money growth, in which case they would again be at point J.

If we allowed for storage, then the existence of a monetary equilibrium would depend on the rate of inflation. If the rate of return on money were less than the rate of return on storage, there would be no monetary equilibrium. A necessary condition for a monetary equilibrium is therefore that $(1 + n)/(1 + \sigma)$ be greater than or equal to $(1 + r)$. For a monetary equilibrium to exist, money growth cannot be too large.

Results are drastically different if new money is introduced into the economy through interest payments to money holders. The inflation rate increases as before by the amount of the increase in the growth rate of money. But in this case money is superneutral because the interest payment, in the form of transfers to holders of money, precisely compensates them for the additional inflation. This can be shown by changing the second-period budget constraint in (6) to $P_{t+1} c_{2t+1} = M_t^d (1 + \sigma)$ and then proceeding as above.

Money in the Overlapping Generations Model: An Assessment

We have derived strong results on the effects of money in this simple OLG model. They can be summarized by two propositions. There can be a monetary equilibrium only if the barter equilibrium is not a Pareto optimum. Although monetary equilibria are not all Pareto optima, there is a monetary equilibrium that is Pareto optimal.[9]

There is a close relation between these results and those on *dynamic efficiency* in the previous chapter. The results can be restated as follows: if the economy is dynamically inefficient (if r is less than n), the introduction of money can make everybody better off. This is not the case if the economy is dynamically efficient. Money here plays the same role that social security or government debt played previously; the new insight is that money provides a way in which transfers of resources, if they are Pareto improving, can be achieved voluntarily rather than through government programs.

But this equivalence also suggests that the role of money is overstated in the OLG model. Money is valued in this simple OLG model only when it is not dominated in rate of return by any other asset. Thus, if storage yields a higher return than money, money is no longer valued. Existence of a monetary equilibrium is tenuous: money disappears when the rate of inflation is too high, for example. But, in practice, money is dominated in rate of return by many assets and continues to be used even during the most extreme hyperinflations.[10] This suggests that the role of money should be studied in models in which money is indeed dominated in rate of return, and in which many of the dramatic results obtained here are likely to disappear. We now turn to such models.

4.2 Explaining the Use of Money

Why is money used in exchange in preference to other goods or assets? The triangular trade diagram in figure 4.5 provides a simple example that helps us to think about the answer: it shows how money helps an economy to avoid the need for a double coincidence of wants, defined as the requirement that each individual in an exchange acquire a good that he plans to consume or use in production rather than for further exchange.

In figure 4.5 individuals A, B, and C are endowed with one unit of goods 1, 2, and 3, respectively, and want to consume one unit of goods 3, 1, and 2, respectively. No individual wants to consume the good with which he is endowed, but no direct exchange is possible between individuals who each want to consume the other's goods.[11] Nevertheless, indirect exchange is possible: for instance, B can exchange good 2 for good 1 with A, and then

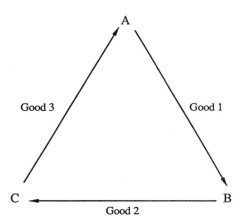

Figure 4.5
Indirect exchange

A can exchange good 2 against good 3 with C. If there are costs of transporting goods, then the good that is cheapest to transport is likely to end up being used in indirect exchange and to serve as a medium of exchange.[12] Alternatively—and here paper money comes in—the optimal allocation is attainable if individuals are willing to exchange their goods against pieces of paper that can later be used to acquire goods. The pieces of paper circulate and goods move only once, from initial owner to final consumer.

The example of figure 4.5 is suggestive, but there are other ways of organizing exchange. One alternative is a credit system in which individuals who purchase goods before selling their own are given credit by a bank or a record-keeping system. What is the comparative advantage of money over such a credit system? Money may be more cumbersome to carry, but a credit system, and its need for record keeping, may be expensive to run. This may lead to the use of money for small transactions and of a credit system for large ones. A credit system requires information as to the ability of those receiving credit to repay; a money system, which in effect requires each individual to have a positive balance at all times, does not require such information.[13] Thus in the presence of uncertainty about endowments or about relative prices (which here have been assumed to be equal to 1 and constant), money may dominate a credit system.

Even if an explanation could be found for the use of money, for example, in terms of requiring less information than credit, there remains the question of why suppliers of money do not pay interest on it. The answer depends on the type of money issued and who its issuer is. A monopoly producer, such as government, may maximize profits by not paying interest: the sheer technical difficulty and the small efficiency gains from doing so prevent the payment of interest on currency. When there are competitive suppliers of money, such as deposit-taking banks, they should be expected to pay interest on money unless regulatory restrictions prevent their doing so. Regulatory restrictions are nearly always present, however.

The Clower Constraint

Explaining why and when money is used instead of credit is difficult. Accordingly, much of the research on the effects of money on macro-economic equilibrium simply assumes explicitly or implicitly that money must be used in all or most transactions and proceeds from there. "Money buys goods, goods buy money, but goods do not buy goods." This assumption is known as the "Clower," or "finance" or "cash-in-advance," constraint.[14] The approach takes monetary arrangements and institutions as given and thus cannot by its very nature explain the evolution of monetary arrangements, such as the increased use of credit cards or the payment of interest on some forms of money. It could also be misleading if the form of these institutions and arrangements is sensitive, for example, to changes in monetary growth and inflation.

A simple version of the Clower constraint is that, in discrete time, purchases of goods must be paid for with money held at the beginning of the period. More formally, consider the following intertemporal utility maximization problem:

$$\max \sum_{t=1}^{\infty} (1 + \theta)^{-t} u(c_{1t}, \ldots, c_{nt})$$

subject to

$$\sum_{i=1}^{n} P_{it} c_{it} + M_{t+1} + B_{t+1} = Y_t + M_t + B_t(1 + \rho_{t-1}),$$

where there are n consumption goods, money M earning no nominal interest, and bonds B earning nominal interest at rate ρ. In the absence of other constraints than this dynamic budget constraint and if the nominal interest rate on bonds is positive, the individual will not hold money. Ruling out negative holdings of money, if no individual wants to hold money, money will not be valued in equilibrium. Now add to the above problem the constraint

$$\sum_{i=1}^{n} P_{it} c_{it} \leqslant M_t,$$

which requires the individual to enter the period with money balances sufficient to finance the purchases of consumer goods.[15] This will certainly generate a demand for money, and under certainty the demand for money will be just equal to planned and actual purchases.

This simple form of the cash-in-advance constraint is very tractable. It is, however, too simple for many purposes because it implies a velocity of money of one per period and, given consumption, no elasticity of the demand for money to the nominal interest rate. It can be generalized in various ways.

One approach, pursued by Lucas and Stokey (1987), is to allow for two types of goods: goods that can be bought on credit and goods that must be bought with cash. Changes in the inflation rate will then affect the relative price of the two types of goods and, in turn, the velocity of money in terms of overall consumption. However, it is unlikely that the distinction between cash and credit goods is itself independent of the inflation rate.

Another approach is to introduce uncertainty: the individual has to determine his money holdings for a given period before the uncertainty relevant to that period is resolved. In the presence of a Clower constraint, having more money gives the consumer more flexibility in choosing consumption. Uncertainty leads to a precautionary demand for money. We now briefly present a model along these lines and show its implications.

The Clower Constraint and the Precautionary Demand for Money

An old theme in monetary theory is that holding money gives more flexibility in spending. The following model shows the main implications of this precautionary motive for velocity and the demand for money.[16]

We consider the behavior of an individual who looks ahead just two periods at the time he makes his portfolio decision (period zero). He has a nominal endowment Y, which he can hold either as money or as bonds. Money earns no interest, but it can be spent in either period one or period two. Bonds earn interest but can only be sold in the second period. The individual will want to spend either in period one or in period two, but not both. There is a probability q that he will want to spend in period one, and $1 - q$ that he will want to spend in period two. Treating the period in which the portfolio decision is made as t, the individual will have utility $u(c_{t+1})$ if he consumes in period $t + 1$ and utility $u(c_{t+2})$ if he consumes in period $t + 2$.

This simple setup captures the notion of the liquidity of money. By having all of their portfolio in currency, individuals can make sure that they will be able to consume as much as they want in period one if they should turn out to want to consume in that period. But if they hold only money, they will forgo the interest they could have received on bonds.

We now characterize the maximization problem faced by an individual at time t. He allocates his initial endowment between M_t and B_t. If he consumes early, consumption at time $t + 1$ is given by M_t/P_{t+1}. If he consumes late, consumption at time $t + 2$ is given by $[M_t + B_t(1 + i)]/P_{t+2}$. He maximizes expected utility, which is given by

$$qu(c_{t+1}) + (1 - q)u(c_{t+2}),$$

or, using the relations above,

$$qu\left(\frac{M_t}{P_{t+1}}\right) + (1 - q)u\left[\frac{M_t + B_t(1 + i)}{P_{t+2}}\right].$$

The first-order condition for utility maximization is

$$\frac{qu'(c_{t+1})}{P_{t+1}} = \frac{(1-q)iu'(c_{t+2})}{P_{t+2}}.$$

The demand for money is obtained by solving this first-order condition. In the special case of a constant relative risk aversion form, with coefficient of risk aversion given by γ, the demand for money is given by

$$\frac{M_t}{Y} = \frac{1+i}{(1+\pi)^{(\gamma-1)/\gamma}[(1-q)i/q]^{1/\gamma}+i}, \tag{9}$$

where π is the inflation rate between periods $t+1$ and $t+2$, and i is the nominal interest rate.

Thus the precautionary motive leads to a demand for money that, if γ is different from one, depends on both the nominal rate of interest (the opportunity cost of holding money) and the inflation rate. For this example, the effect of inflation on the precautionary demand for money depends on the degree of risk aversion, γ. If γ is greater than one (if individuals are sufficiently risk averse), an increase in inflation decreases the demand for money given Y.

The examples we have just studied assume that, within the period, bonds cannot be exchanged for money at any cost. This assumption is counterfactual. At any point of time one can in fact exchange bonds, or other forms of wealth, for money, although at some cost and inconvenience: the choice of when and how often to get money is an important margin of choice for consumers. In the next section we maintain the assumption that all goods must be bought with money but allow individuals to exchange bonds against money, at a cost, as often as they like. More frequent exchanges of bonds against money, or equivalently more frequent trips to the bank, allow individuals to maintain smaller average money balances, though frequent trips may be very costly. This approach is the extension to general equilibrium of the partial equilibrium models of the demand for money developed by Baumol (1952) and Tobin (1956).

4.3 A General Equilibrium Baumol-Tobin Model

We now consider a continuous time overlapping generations model, due to David Romer (1986), in which money and interest-earning bonds coexist.[17] Individuals receive an endowment from which they consume and save, holding either bonds or money that does not yield interest. We impose the Clower constraint condition that purchases of goods can be made only by using money. Individuals can at any point in time exchange bonds against money at a cost. They have to decide how much to consume and how to allocate their wealth over time between money and bonds.

The model serves three main functions. The first is to show how the presence of money affects the *consumption-saving* choice studied in the two previous chapters. The second is to characterize the *demand for money*. The third is to show the *effects of money growth* on the real allocation in general equilibrium.

The model is a continuous time overlapping generation model. At each instant an individual is born. Each individual lives for length of time T, implying that there is a uniform distribution of individuals aged 0 to T in the economy at any point in time. The analysis in this section is limited to steady states; in the next section we shall study the dynamics of a simplified version of the model. We start by characterizing individual behavior.

Individual Behavior

At birth each individual receives an endowment E of goods and a lump-sum transfer of money equal in real terms to S. The total endowment $E + S$ is denoted by Y. There are two ways of storing wealth: as money, which has a real rate of return of $-\pi$ where π is the rate of inflation, or in the form of bonds, which yield a real rate of return r. By assumption, wealth cannot be kept in the form of goods. (The goods may, for example, be perishable.) Bonds are zero coupon bonds whose value rises at rate r. The difference between the rates of return on bonds and money, the nominal interest rate, is denoted by $i = r + \pi$. Thus, if i is positive, holding bonds gives a higher return than holding money. Purchases of consumption goods, however, require the use of money. Bonds can be exchanged against money at any time, at a fixed utility cost of b per transaction, and their cost is independent of the amount exchanged.

The intertemporal utility function of an individual is given by

$$U = \int_0^T \ln(c_t)\, dt - Nb.$$

The first component of utility is the sum of instantaneous utilities, which are assumed to be logarithmic in consumption; there is no subjective discounting.[18] The second component of utility represents the utility cost of transacting, which is linear in N, the number of transactions between money and bonds (equivalently the number of trips to the bank) during life.

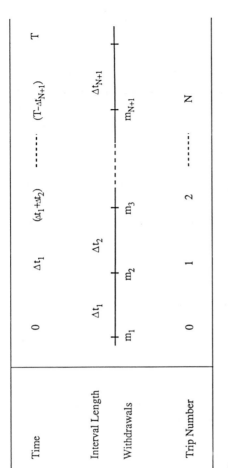

Figure 4.6
Timing and notation in the Romer model

The first transaction in which an individual decides how to allocate Y between money and bonds is costless and not counted in N.

Figure 4.6 gives the (slightly awkward) conventions for numbering real balance withdrawals, trips, and time intervals for somebody born at time zero. At time zero the individual receives the endowment Y out of which she keeps real balances m_1 and buys bonds with the remainder. The first sale of bonds to obtain money (equivalently the trip to the bank to withdraw cash) takes place at time Δt_1 when the individual sells bonds (withdraws cash) of real value m_2. The last, Nth, trip takes place at time $T - \Delta t_{N+1}$, at which time the individual makes her final withdrawal m_{N+1}.

Utility Maximization
Individuals must decide on the number, timing, and size of withdrawals and on their paths of consumption. A detailed derivation of the following results is given in appendix A. We first state them and then discuss their implications.

First, individuals choose to go to the bank at constant intervals of time throughout life. Thus, if an individual makes N trips to the bank, the interval between trips will be equal to $\mu \equiv T/(N + 1)$. The *optimal time between trips*, ignoring the integer constraint as to the number of trips, is given by

$$\mu = \sqrt{\frac{2b}{i}}. \tag{10}$$

The formula is similar to the square root rule derived by Baumol and Tobin, who were taking consumption as given. The optimal interval is a decreasing function of i, the opportunity cost of holding money versus bonds. It is an increasing function of the fixed cost of exchanging bonds for money.

The *amount of real balances withdrawn* during trip j, m_{j+1}, is equal to

$$m_{j+1} = \left(\frac{Y}{N+1}\right) \exp(r\mu j), \qquad \text{for } j = 1, \ldots, N. \tag{11}$$

The formula also applies to the amount of real money balances kept at birth, taking $j = 0$. Thus real withdrawals increase in size through life at rate r. If r is equal to zero, real withdrawals are of constant size through life.

Finally, *consumption* is characterized during each interval between trips to the bank as a function of the real value of the withdrawal. For example, for a withdrawal m_{j+1} at time $j\mu$, consumption is given by

$$c_t = \left(\frac{m_{j+1}}{\mu}\right) \exp[-\pi(t - j\mu)], \tag{12}$$

for t between $j\mu$ and $(j + 1)\mu$ or, combining equations (11) and (12),

$$c_t = \left(\frac{Y}{T}\right) \exp[r\mu j - \pi(t - \mu j)],$$

for t between $j\mu$ and $(j + 1)\mu$. Between trips to the bank, consumption changes at the negative of the rate of inflation. If inflation is equal to zero, consumption is constant between trips. If it is positive, consumption declines between trips.

The level of utility, given optimal choices of m and c, can be expressed as

$$U^* = T \ln\left(\frac{Y}{T}\right) + \frac{rT^2}{2} - \frac{(r + \pi)T^2}{2(N + 1)} - Nb,$$

where $N = (T/\mu) - 1$ and equation (10) gives μ. Utility is an increasing function of the real rate r and a decreasing function of the nominal rate.

These results fully characterize individual behavior. We now draw their implications more explicitly.

The Effects of Money on the Consumption-Saving Decision
How does the Clower constraint affect the consumption-saving choice? Suppose that the economy is not subject to the Clower constraint, so individuals can use bonds to buy goods. Then (assuming that money growth, and thus inflation, was larger than $-r$) individuals will not hold money and as a result money is not valued. Given the form of the utility function in (9) and the zero subjective discount rate, consumption increases at rate r over time. Given the initial endowment Y, consumption is given by

$$c_t = \left(\frac{Y}{T}\right) \exp(rt). \tag{13}$$

Now compare consumption between the monetary and nonmonetary economies.[19] In the monetary economy, equations (11) and (12) imply that consumption, measured at the time of withdrawals μj, is given by

$$c_t = \left(\frac{Y}{T}\right) \exp(r\mu j). \tag{14}$$

But, from (13), this is the same as consumption in the nonmonetary economy, given the same endowment Y. Thus, given Y, individual consumption will be the same at points in time corresponding to times of withdrawal of cash in the monetary economy. There are, however, two complications that account for the relationship between the two paths of consumption shown in figure 4.7. First, given Y, consumption in the two economies will

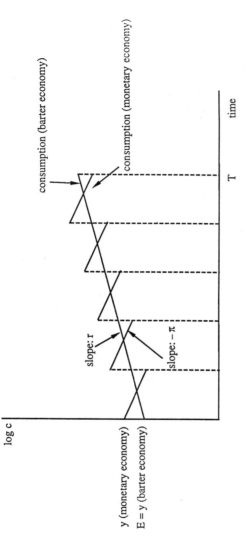

Figure 4.7
Consumption paths in monetary and nonmonetary economies

not be equal except at times of withdrawal. Consumption in the nonmonetary economy grows continuously at rate r. By contrast, in the monetary economy, consumption changes at the negative of the rate of inflation between trips. This produces the sawtooth pattern of consumption in the monetary economy, a result of the fact that two rates of interest are now relevant. *Across trips to the bank, the relevant rate is the rate on bonds. Between trips, however, the relevant rate is the return on money.*

The second complication is that the endowment, Y, will not in fact be equal between the two economies. In the monetary economy the individual receives a cash endowment at the beginning of life. Thus Y is greater than E, the endowment of goods that would be received in a nonmonetary economy. How much greater depends on the value of the monetary endowment that will be determined in general equilibrium later.

We now compare the paths of nonmonetary wealth in the two economies, initially again for a given endowment. Wealth in the nonmonetary economy is given by

$$B_t = Y\left[1 - \left(\frac{t}{T}\right)\right]\exp(rt).$$

Wealth in the form of bonds in the monetary economy is given, except at points of withdrawal, by

$$B_t = Y\left(\frac{N - j + 1}{N + 1}\right)\exp(rt).$$

At the times when the individual withdraws, such as time $j\mu$, wealth in the form of bonds is given by the expression above before withdrawal, and by

$$B_t = Y\left(\frac{N - j}{N + 1}\right)\exp(rt)$$

after withdrawal.

Figure 4.8 compares the paths of nonmonetary wealth in the two economies.[20] *For a given endowment,* nonmonetary wealth is the same in the monetary economy at the points of withdrawal, before withdrawal, as in the nonmonetary economy. But after withdrawal and between trips, nonmonetary wealth is lower in the monetary economy. The endowment, however, is larger in the monetary economy.

How large therefore are the effects of the requirement that money be used in exchange on individual consumption and savings decisions? Figures 4.7 and 4.8 show that this depends on the length of the interval between trips compared to the length of life. If, as is the fact, μ is very small compared

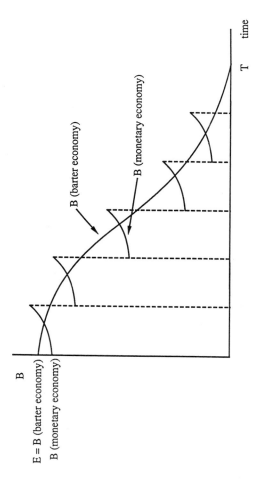

Figure 4.8
Paths of bond holdings in monetary and nonmonetary economies

to T, the sawtooth pattern will be barely visible, and for a given endowment, the path of nonmonetary wealth will nearly coincide with what it would be in an economy in which bonds could be used for making purchases.

This suggests that the requirement that money be used in exchange does not necessarily cause large deviations from the allocation of resources attainable in an idealized frictionless economy. However, since the Clower constraint was simply imposed, we have no explicit model here of the technological possibilities that would exist in a barter economy. We thus cannot evaluate in this model the gains from monetary exchange.

The Demand for Money
The individual demand for money obtained in this model is very similar to traditional specifications. We will for the moment refer to the demand for money as the amount of money withdrawn from the bank during a particular trip. This amount is given by (11). It is not a function of income or consumption as in traditional specifications because both consumption and withdrawals are endogenous variables.

We can nevertheless derive the relation between withdrawal and consumption at time $j\mu$, say, using equations (10) to (12). This gives

$$m_{j+1} = \sqrt{\frac{2b}{\pi + r}}\, c_t, \qquad t = \mu j. \tag{15}$$

The amount withdrawn is a linear function of consumption at the time of the withdrawal and a decreasing function of the nominal interest rate, with elasticity $-1/2$. At the individual level, the model implies a rather conventional demand for money.

We now turn to the general equilibrium properties of this economy. We first derive aggregate demands for goods, bonds, and money.

Aggregate Demands for Consumption, Bonds, and Money

Since we limit ourselves to the analysis of the steady state in which the population is constant, the aggregate demand can be obtained by summing consumption either over the population at a point in time or over an individual's lifetime. We use the second approach.

To derive aggregate consumption, we first calculate the integral of individual consumption over each interval between trips to the bank, and then we sum over the intervals. If we normalize population to be equal to one, aggregate consumption is equal to the integral of an individual's consumption over his lifetime divided by T.

Given trip j at time $j\mu$, consumption at any time t between $j\mu$ and $(j + 1)\mu$ is given, from (11) and (12), by

$$c_t = \left(\frac{Y}{T}\right) \exp(rj\mu) \exp[-\pi(t - j\mu)].$$

Integrating from $j\mu$ to $(j + 1)\mu$ gives

$$\int_{j\mu}^{(j+1)\mu} c_t \, dt = \int_{j\mu}^{(j+1)\mu} \left(\frac{Y}{T}\right) \exp(rj\mu) \exp[-\pi(t - j\mu)] \, dt$$

$$= \left(\frac{Y}{T}\right) \exp(rj\mu) \left[\frac{1 - \exp(-\pi\mu)}{\pi}\right].$$

Summing over intervals and dividing by T gives aggregate consumption C (no time index is needed as aggregate consumption is constant in steady state):

$$C = \left(\frac{1}{T}\right) \sum_{j=0}^{N} \left(\frac{Y}{T}\right) \exp(rj\mu) \left[\frac{1 - \exp(-\pi\mu)}{\pi}\right].$$

Solving for the sum and using $\mu = T/(N + 1)$ gives

$$C = \left(\frac{1}{T}\right)\left(\frac{Y}{T}\right) \left[\frac{\exp(rT) - 1}{\exp(r\mu) - 1}\right]\left[\frac{1 - \exp(-\pi\mu)}{\pi}\right]. \tag{16}$$

Aggregate consumption is, given Y and μ, an increasing function of the real interest rate, and a decreasing function of the rate of inflation.

Similarly, aggregate bond holdings (aggregate nonmonetary wealth) are given by

$$B = \left(\frac{Y}{T}\right)\left(\frac{1}{r}\right)\left\{\frac{(\mu/T)[\exp(rT) - 1]}{[\exp(r\mu) - 1]} - 1\right\}. \tag{17}$$

Aggregate bond holdings are affected by inflation only to the extent that inflation affects either Y or μ.

Finally, aggregate money holdings, m, are given by

$$m = \left(\frac{1}{T}\right)\left(\frac{Y}{T}\right) \left[\frac{\exp(rT) - 1}{\exp(r\mu) - 1}\right]\left[\frac{\exp(-\mu\pi) + \mu\pi - 1}{\pi^2}\right]. \tag{18}$$

Even given Y and μ, inflation directly affects real money balances. This is because the rate of inflation determines, both directly and indirectly through the rate of consumption, the path of real money balances between trips to the bank.

Despite the extreme simplicity of the underlying model, the properties of the demand functions for money and bonds, (17) and (18), are not transparent. Nonetheless, some derivatives can be calculated. For instance, holding Y and r constant, an increase in the nominal interest rate reduces m in (18).

Closing the Model

So far we have derived the aggregate demand for goods, money, and bonds as functions of the inflation rate, π, the real rate of interest, r, and the price level (which affects the real value of monetary transfers, and thus the value of the total endowment Y). These variables, however, are endogenous in the general equilibrium. We now describe the rest of the economy and characterize the equilibrium.

In addition to individuals there are firms, banks, and a government. Firms have access to a constant returns to scale technology—which does not use labor and can therefore be thought of as a productive storage technology—with rate of return r. (The assumption made earlier that individuals cannot hold wealth in the form of goods can be interpreted as saying that they do not have direct access to the storage technology.) This determines the real interest rate in the economy. The firms receive the endowment of the young and put it into productive storage, issuing in exchange bonds that also pay the rate of return r. "Capital," the amount stored at any time by firms, is thus equal to B. Firms sell goods from production to individuals in exchange for money.

Banks exchange bonds for money and money for bonds. Individuals deposit with the banks the bonds they have received from the firms, and exchange those bonds for money when they go to the banks. The firms in turn redeem the bonds from the banks with the money they have received from households by selling goods. Banks thus exchange money for bonds with individuals, and bonds for money with firms.[21]

The government issues money, which it gives to the newborn as transfers, at a constant rate. The real value of these transfers is equal to S, which has to be determined in the general equilibrium of the economy.

Figure 4.9 traces out the flow of transactions between individuals, firms, banks, and the government at any point in time. It shows in particular the *flow of money* at any point in time. Money flows from the government to the newborn, in the form of transfers, and from the banks, against bonds, to those who are making trips to the banks. Money flows from individuals to firms, in exchange for goods. It flows back from firms, which redeem bonds,

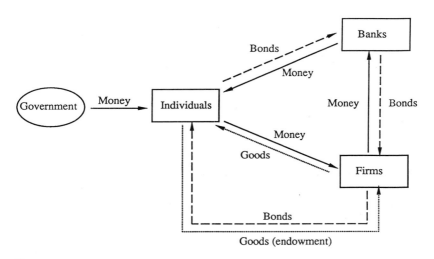

Figure 4.9
Flows of money, bonds, and goods in the Romer model

to banks. This gives a flavor of the complexity of money flows in an actual economy.

We can also look at the distribution of the *stock of money* at any point in time. Only individuals hold money for more than one instant; at any point in time there is a distribution of money holdings across individuals in the economy. Although individual money holdings are continually being de-cumulated and accumulated, this aggregate distribution remains constant over time.

General Equilibrium
There are three variables that are taken as given by individuals but are endogenous in general equilibrium. The first is the rate of return on bonds. Given our assumptions, r is simply equal to the rate of return on storage. The second is the rate of inflation, π. In steady state the real money stock is constant; thus the rate of inflation is equal to the rate of money growth.

The third endogenous variable is the price level, which determines the real value S of revenues from money growth to the government, "seigniorage," and in turn the nominal transfers to the newborn from the government. The real value of S must be such that the demand for goods, which depends on the endowment, equals the supply of goods:

$$C = \frac{E}{T} + rB. \tag{19}$$

Given (16) and (17), and the fact that $Y = E + S$, (19) implicitly defines the real value of S. No simple expression emerges linking C to the inflation rate. The discussion of the effects of money growth on capital accumulation that follows bears directly on this question.

Money Growth and Capital Accumulation

We now analyze how money growth affects capital accumulation and welfare in this economy. Capital is equal to aggregate bond holdings and is thus given by (17). Money growth affects capital accumulation by affecting S, the real value of transfers, and μ, the interval between trips to the bank.

We solve first for the effects of inflation on the real value of transfers. We limit the analysis to the special case where r is equal to zero, where storage is unproductive. In this case equations (16) and (17) become[22]

$$C = \left(\frac{Y}{\mu T}\right)\left[\frac{1 - \exp(-\pi\mu)}{\pi}\right] \tag{16'}$$

and

$$B = \left(\frac{Y}{2T}\right)(T - \mu). \tag{17'}$$

Solving (19) for S gives in this case

$$S = E\left[-1 + \frac{\mu\pi}{1 - \exp(-\mu\pi)}\right]. \tag{19'}$$

Replacing in (17') finally gives the aggregate capital

$$B = E\left(\frac{T - \mu}{2T}\right)\left[\frac{\pi\mu}{1 - \exp(-\pi\mu)}\right]. \tag{20}$$

Differentiating B with respect to π, both directly and through its effects on μ, which we know from (10) is a decreasing function of inflation, yields an ambiguous derivative. First, more rapid money growth leads to more frequent trips to the bank and higher holdings of bonds (capital) relative to money. This is the effect emphasized by Tobin (1965) in one of the first analyses of the relation between inflation and capital accumulation, and thus is known as the Tobin effect. Second, money growth affects the real value of transfers. If money demand is not too elastic with respect to inflation, then an increase in money growth increases the real value of transfers, and in turn savings and capital; this works in the same direction. But if money demand is sufficiently elastic, then seignorage may go down and with it capital; the net effect of money growth may be to decrease capital.[23]

The Optimum Quantity of Money

The next logical step is to derive the rate of inflation that maximizes welfare, taking into account its effects on capital accumulation. Somewhat awkwardly, this question is known as that of the *optimal quantity of money*. Friedman (1969) suggested that given that money was costless to produce, it would be optimal to have the same rate of return on money as on other assets, thus to have a rate of deflation equal to the interest rate. In this way individuals would not economize on the use of money and transactions costs would be reduced or removed.

To study this question, again in the case where r is equal to zero, we can use the equation derived earlier for maximized utility and replace S by its value from (19'). This yields

$$U^* = T \ln\left[\frac{(E/T)(\mu\pi)}{1 - \exp(-\mu\pi)}\right] - \frac{\pi T \mu}{2} - \left(\frac{T - \mu}{\mu}\right)b.$$

Maximizing with respect to π yields $\pi = 0$.

The optimal rate of money growth is equal to zero, which is also the rate of interest. In this case transfers are equal to zero, individuals only save in the form of money, and consumption is not sawtoothed as in figure 4.7 but constant throughout life. Nonmonetary wealth and capital are equal to zero, but given that capital is not productive, this is indeed optimal.

The result, however, is not general. It goes away in this model when r is positive, when capital is productive. In this case it is optimal to have positive capital accumulation, but if the nominal rate of interest is equal to zero (plus epsilon), individuals hold all their wealth in the form of money and the aggregate capital stock will be equal to zero. We will return to the issue of the optimal quantity of money a few more times in this chapter. Note that optimal monetary policy in the OLG model, when r was less than n, was to maintain a constant money stock, generating a deflation rate of n. This too is a case of the optimal quantity of money.

This model has shown how the real models of previous chapters can be extended to accommodate the presence of money and how money growth affects the real allocation. It has also shown that under realistic assumptions, these effects are likely to be quite small in steady state so that ignoring the presence of money may, for many purposes, be acceptable.

4.4 Real Effects of Open Market Operations

In the previous model we examined the steady state effects of changes in money growth. Across steady states a once-and-for-all increase in the *level* of nominal balances would affect only the price level, changing it proportionately while leaving all real variables unchanged. Now we turn to the question of whether changes in the level of nominal money translate into price level changes instantaneously or have transitory effects on real variables.

Some types of changes in the nominal money stock should leave all real variables unchanged. An unanticipated distribution of additional money, in proportion to existing money holdings across the population, is an example of such a change. If prices are fully flexible, equilibrium can be restored by a proportional increase in the price level that leaves all real money balances unchanged. This result is similar to that obtained in the OLG model when new money is introduced in proportion to existing holdings, that is, in the form of interest on money.

But most changes in nominal money are not of that kind. In most cases money is introduced through open market operations (OMO) in which the central bank buys bonds and pays for them with money. In this section we characterize the effects of an increase in the money stock brought about through an open market operation. Although the model of section 4.3 could in principle be used for the purpose, it is not analytically tractable outside of steady state. Thus we consider a simpler model along the same lines that has a more mechanical Clower constraint.[24]

The Model
Time is discrete and starts at $t = 1$. Output is exogenous and is equal to one in each period.

There are two infinitely long-lived individuals in the economy, denoted a and b. Each is entitled to a constant share of the output in each period. Instead of receiving goods directly, however, each receives a claim to half of the output. These claims to output are deposited directly in an interest-yielding account at a bank; the bank also holds whatever amount of government bonds individuals may hold. Individuals must use money to buy goods. Each of them goes to the bank every two periods to withdraw money. Individual a goes to the bank at even times and b at odd times, each of them using the money to buy goods over the two periods following the trip.

The government decreases (increases) the quantity of money by selling (buying) government bonds in exchange for money through open market operations. It raises taxes to pay for the interest on bonds and collects them directly from interest-yielding accounts.

The time sequence and timing conventions are represented in figure 4.10, which shows the transactions of individual a. Individual a has initial nominal money holdings of M_0^a. He goes to the bank for the first time just before the beginning of period two and withdraws M_1^a to pay for consumption

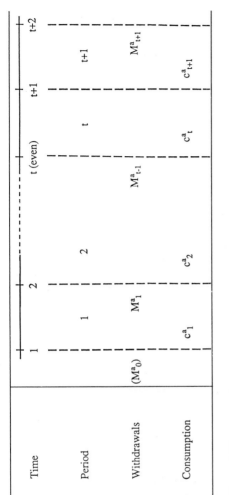

Figure 4.10
Timing of transactions

c_2^a and c_3^a. In general, if t is even, he withdraws M_{t-1}^a just before period t for consumption c_t^a and c_{t+1}^a.

Individual a faces the following intertemporal maximization problem:

$$\max \sum_{t=1}^{\infty} (1 + \theta)^{-(t-1)} \ln(c_t^a),$$

where we are again making the convenient assumption that instantaneous utility is logarithmic. The constraints faced by the individual are of two types: Clower constraints and the traditional intertemporal budget constraints. The Clower constraints are given by

$$P_1 c_1^a \leqslant M_0^a \tag{21}$$

$$P_t c_t^a + P_{t+1} c_{t+1}^a \leqslant M_{t-1}^a, \qquad \text{for } t \text{ even.}$$

The intertemporal budget constraint is most easily written in nominal terms. Let R_t be the nominal discount rate for period t, that is, $1/(1 + i_t)$ where i_t is the nominal interest rate for period t. Let W_0^a be the nominal value of wealth, excluding money balances, at the beginning of period one. Then the constraint is given by

$$P_1 c_1^a + \sum_{\substack{t=2 \\ t \text{ even}}}^{\infty} (R_1 \dots R_{t-1} M_{t-1}^a) \leqslant M_0^a + W_0^a. \tag{22}$$

The present value of cash withdrawals, plus current consumption, must be equal to nominal money balances plus nominal wealth.

Nominal wealth, W_0^a, is in turn given by

$$W_0^a = s^a(P_1 + R_1 P_2 + R_1 R_2 P_3 + \cdots) + B_0^a - \frac{B_0}{2}. \tag{23}$$

s^a is the share of total real income, the latter being equal to 1 in each period. The first term is therefore equal to the present value of nominal income. The second term is equal to the nominal value of government bonds held by a. The third is equal to the nominal present value of taxes. Because the government does not spend and only uses taxes to pay interest on the debt, the present value of taxes is equal to government bonds outstanding, B.[25] Each individual has to pay half of total taxes. Similar expressions hold for individual b, with t odd.

Equilibrium

Market equilibrium conditions are

$$c_t^a + c_t^b = 1, \tag{24}$$

$$M_t^a + M_t^b = M_t. \tag{25}$$

At any point of time the demand for goods must be equal to the supply, which, by assumption is equal to 1. At any point in time the stock demand for money must be equal to the outstanding stock.[26]

These two conditions can be manipulated to yield a more intuitive condition for the equilibrium flow of money. Assuming that t is even, then for individual b,

$$P_t c_t^b = M_{t-1}^b.$$

For individual a,

$$M_t^a = M_{t-1}^a - P_t c_t^a.$$

Combining these equations, and substituting in (24) and (25), gives

$$P_t(c_t^a + c_t^b) + M_t^a = P_t + M_t^a = M_{t-1}^a + M_{t-1}^b = M_{t-1}.$$

Finally, since $M_t^a = M_t - M_t^b$,

$$P_t + \Delta M_t = M_t^b, \tag{26}$$

where ΔM_t is defined as $M_t - M_{t-1}$.

This condition has a simple interpretation. P_t is the nominal value of purchases of goods, and ΔM_t is the injection of new money through open market operations. The left-hand side is therefore the flow of money into banks. The right-hand side is the withdrawal of money from the bank by individual b. Equation (26) states that the flow in and out of banks must be equal. An open market operation that increases ΔM_t must induce changes in prices and nominal rates such that individual b willingly increases his real withdrawal of money, M_t^b/P_t.

Solving for Equilibrium Prices

To solve for the equilibrium, we could follow the same approach as in the previous model: solve for individual behavior given prices and nominal rates, and then determine prices and interest rates from equilibrium conditions. We will, instead, use a shortcut and solve directly for the equilibrium price level. This can be done here because of the simple structure of the model. Having done this, we will solve back for consumption and finally for nominal rates.

We start by solving for the optimal consumption of a at time t and $t + 1$, given money withdrawals M_{t-1}^a. Given a logarithmic utility, the optimal consumption is

$$P_t c_t^a = \left(\frac{1+\theta}{2+\theta}\right) M_{t-1}^a$$

and

$$P_{t+1} c_{t+1}^a = \left(\frac{1}{2+\theta}\right) M_{t-1}^a. \tag{27}$$

Next we return to equation (25), the condition for money stock equilibrium. We replace M_t^b by its value from (26). M_t^a must in turn equal $P_{t+1} c_{t+1}^a$, which from the preceding equation equals $[1/(2+\theta)]M_{t-1}^a$. Finally, we lag (26) once to replace M_{t-1}^a, and rearrange it to obtain

$$P_t = \left(\frac{1+\theta}{2+\theta}\right)[-(1+\theta)^{-1}P_{t-1} + M_{t-1} + (1+\theta)^{-1}M_{t-2}]. \tag{28}$$

This first-order equation determines the dynamic behavior of P. Given P, we can recover c_t^a and c_{t+1}^a from (27) and the equivalent expressions for b. From the values of c, and the first-order conditions of individuals, we could recover the nominal rates of interest that support the consumption paths of consumers.[27]

The Effects of Open Market Operations

For a given value of M, equation (28) is stable, and the price level converges to a steady state. This steady state value is given by

$$P = \left(\frac{2+\theta}{3+\theta}\right) M.$$

Thus money is neutral in steady state. A doubling of the money stock will double prices and leave consumption unchanged. Note that in the steady state individual consumption is constant, but money holdings keep being accumulated and decumulated by each individual; at any point in time the distribution of money holdings across a and b is proportional to $(1, 1/(2+\theta))$, with 1 being the relative money holdings of the individual who just went to the bank.

Starting from the steady state, we derive the dynamic effects of an open market operation that increases the nominal money stock permanently at time t in amount dM. From (28) the initial effects on the price level are given by

$$dP_{t+1} = \left(\frac{1+\theta}{2+\theta}\right) dM$$

$$dP_{t+2} = \left[\frac{3 + 3\theta + \theta^2}{(2 + \theta)^2}\right] dM.$$

From then on, the price level converges to its new steady state level in damped oscillations.

To understand why the price level does not respond one for one instantaneously, consider the goods market equilibrium conditions at time $t + 1$, $t + 2$, and so on. At time $t + 1$,

$$1 = \left(\frac{1 + \theta}{2 + \theta}\right)\left(\frac{P_t + dM}{P_{t+1}}\right) + \left(\frac{1}{2 + \theta}\right)\left(\frac{P_{t-1}}{P_{t+1}}\right).$$

The first term on the right-hand side is the consumption of those who went to the bank at time t and thus must have been induced to hold the additional money; the second term is the consumption of those who went to the bank before the open market operation. It is clear that P_{t+1} must exceed $P_t (= P_{t-1})$. It is also clear that P_{t+1} cannot increase in proportion to the increase in nominal money. This would reduce the first term to its pre-open-market operation value but would decrease the second term, and there would thus be an excess supply of goods.

At time $t + 2$, the goods market equilibrium condition is

$$1 = \left(\frac{1 + \theta}{2 + \theta}\right)\left(\frac{P_{t+1}}{P_{t+2}}\right) + \left(\frac{1}{2 + \theta}\right)\left(\frac{P_t + dM}{P_{t+2}}\right).$$

By the same reasoning, P_{t+2} must exceed P_{t+1}.

At time $t + 3$,

$$1 = \left(\frac{1 + \theta}{2 + \theta}\right)\left(\frac{P_{t+2}}{P_{t+3}}\right) + \left(\frac{1}{2 + \theta}\right)\left(\frac{P_{t+1}}{P_{t+3}}\right).$$

This now implies that P_{t+3} must be less than P_{t+2}.

As these equations make clear, the consumption paths of a and b are also affected by the open market operation. In the case where $s^a = s^b$, so that $c^a = c^b$ in steady state, c^a exceeds c^b at time $t + 1$, c^b exceeds c^a at time $t + 2$, and so on, given that t is odd.

Where do the dynamic effects of open market operations come from in this model? They result from the distribution effects implied by the fact that individuals do not hold the same level of real money balances at any point of time. This must be true of a monetary economy: it is in the nature of such an economy that some are accumulating money balances while others are decumulating. Indeed, there cannot be an equilibrium in which all individuals accumulate and decumulate in unison.

How large are the effects of these open market operations likely to be? As in the previous model, if individuals go to the bank reasonably often, we are led to the conclusion that the effects are likely to be small. This conclusion is reinforced by the fact that open market operations are in practice conducted between specialized buyers, who may act as buffers, and the government.[28] The explanation for the apparently large effects of open market operations on real variables will have to be sought elsewhere than in this class of models. We return to this issue at length in the second half of the book.

4.5 Money in the Utility Function

Tracing the flow of money through the economy and specifying the nature of the Clower constraint for each type of transaction can quickly become cumbersome as well as analytically intractable. This has led to the use of the device of putting money directly into either the production function or the utility function. In this section we develop the well-known model of Sidrauski (1967a), which follows the second route and extends the Ramsey model to allow both consumption and real money balances to enter the utility function. We then discuss the relation between the money in the utility function and Clower constraint approaches. We end by summarizing what we have learned about the relationship among money growth, capital accumulation, and welfare.

The Sidrauski Model

The economy is populated by infinitely lived families, with population growing at rate n. Each household solves the following maximization problem:

$$\max V_s = \int_s^\infty u(c_t, m_t) \exp[-\theta(t-s)]\, dt, \qquad u_c, u_m > 0, u_{cc}, u_{mm} < 0,$$

where c and m are consumption and real money balances per capita. The household can hold its wealth in the form of either money or capital. Its budget constraint is given by (ignoring time indexes)

$$C + \frac{dK}{dt} + \frac{dM/dt}{P} = wN + rK + X,$$

where N, C, K, and M are (household) size, consumption, holdings of capital, and nominal money, respectively; X is government transfers; w and r are the real wage and the rate of interest; and P is the price level. Dividing both sides of the constraint by N, denoting per capita variables by lowercase letters (except for m which denotes *real* rather than nominal money balances per capita), using $(dK/dt)/N = dk/dt + nk$ and $(dM/dt)/PN = dm/dt + \pi m + nm$, where π is the rate of inflation, gives

$$c + \frac{dk}{dt} + nk + \frac{dm}{dt} + \pi m + nm = w + rk + x.$$

It is convenient to define total household wealth, $A = K + M/P$. Letting a be per capita wealth and substituting in the above constraint yields

$$\frac{da}{dt} = [(r - n)a + w + x] - [c + (\pi + r)m]. \tag{29}$$

This equation gives the rate of change of total wealth per capita as the difference between income and consumption, where consumption is now the sum of two terms, c and $(\pi + r)m$. This last term is equal to the interest forgone by holding money instead of capital, equal to the nominal interest rate times real money balances: it therefore measures the implicit consumption of money services. The sum of the two terms is sometimes called full consumption.

In addition we must impose the usual no-Ponzi-game condition:

$$\lim_{t \to \infty} a_t \exp - \left[\int_0^t (r_v - n)\, dv \right] = 0.$$

Let λ_t be the costate variable associated with equation (29) at time t. (Note that a is a state variable, c and m control variables.) The Hamiltonian associated with the maximization problem is

$$H = \{u(c, m) + \lambda[(r - n)a + w + x - c - (\pi + r)m]\} \exp(-\theta t).$$

First-order conditions for maximization are

$$u_c(c, m) = \lambda, \tag{30}$$

$$u_m(c, m) = \lambda(\pi + r), \tag{31}$$

$$\frac{d\lambda}{dt} - \theta\lambda = -(r - n)\lambda, \tag{32}$$

$$\lim_{t \to \infty} a_t \lambda_t \exp(-\theta t) = 0. \tag{33}$$

In examining these conditions, note that as in the Ramsey model, λ is the marginal utility of consumption. It is, however, no longer uniquely related to c because the marginal utility of c depends in general on m. The first two conditions imply that $u_m = u_c(\pi + r)$ so that the marginal rate of substitution between consumption and real money balances is equal to the nominal interest rate, which has therefore the interpretation of a price of money services. The costate variable λ follows the same equation as in the Ramsey model, implying that the Keynes-Ramsey condition holds: the marginal rate of substitution between consumption at two points in time must equal the rate of transformation.

Closing the Model
The model is closed in the same way as the decentralized Ramsey model, by assuming that firms use a constant returns to scale technology and that factor markets are competitive. Accordingly,

$$r = f'(k)$$

and

$$w = f(k) - kf'(k). \tag{34}$$

Finally, the lump-sum transfers are equal to the seigniorage from money issue so that

$$x = \frac{dM/dt}{PN} = \left(\frac{dM}{M}\right)\left(\frac{M}{PN}\right) = \sigma m, \tag{35}$$

where σ is the rate of money growth.

Note that although in equilibrium all households receive transfers proportional to their money holdings (because they are identical), when making decisions, each of them takes the amount it receives as given and independent of its money holdings.

Steady State
We limit our analysis to studying the steady state of this economy.[29] The steady state is shown in appendix B to be locally saddle point stable. We will, however, return to the issue of stability in chapter 5 and show that there might sometimes be paths that satisfy all the above conditions but do not converge to the steady state and are characterized, instead, by hyperinflation or deflation.

In the steady state $da/dt = dm/dt = d\lambda/dt = 0$. The condition $dm/dt = 0$ implies that

$$\pi = \sigma - n. \tag{36}$$

By combining equations (32) and (34), we obtain the steady state interest rate and capital stock

$$f'(k^*) = \theta + n. \tag{37}$$

Substituting equations (29) and (34) to (37) gives the steady state level of consumption

$$c^* = f(k^*) - nk^*. \tag{38}$$

From equations (30), (31), (34), and (37), we obtain the steady state level of real money balances:

$$u_m(c^*, m^*) = (\theta + \sigma)u_c(c^*, m^*). \tag{39}$$

We now interpret these conditions.

Superneutrality
The main result is that the level of the steady state capital stock and of consumption is given by the same conditions as in the nonmonetary Ramsey model. They are both independent of money growth. Money is therefore *superneutral* in steady state.

The level of real money balances is a function of the level of money growth. Differentiating (39) with respect to σ and m gives

$$dm = \left[\frac{u_c}{u_{mm} - (\theta + \sigma)u_{cm}} \right] d\sigma = \left[\frac{u_c}{u_{mm} - (u_m/u_c)u_{cm}} \right] d\sigma.$$

If consumption and real money balances are both normal goods, the term in brackets is negative, and the effect of higher money growth is to decrease real money balances.

The Optimal Quantity of Money
The superneutrality result has direct implications for the optimal rate of money growth. Because money growth does not affect real consumption in the steady state, the steady state utility is maximized by making real balances large enough that their marginal utility equals zero. From equation (31) this implies having a rate of deflation equal to the real rate of interest, or equivalently a rate of money growth equal to $-\theta$. Thus in this model we obtain the Friedman result that it is optimal to satiate individuals with money and that the rate of return on money should be the same as on capital.

These results about the effects of money growth on capital accumulation and welfare differ from those derived in the previous sections. To assess them, we first discuss the relation between models with money in the utility function and models that treat transactions between money and goods explicitly.

Money in the Utility Function

To think about whether putting money in the utility function is appropriate, we can ask the following question: Is it possible to rewrite the maximization problem of an individual who faces an explicit transactions technology, for example, the Baumol-Tobin transactions technology in section 4.3, as a maximization problem with a pseudo-utility function with money and consumption, as we have done here?

In some cases the answer is straightforward. Consider, for example, the simplest Clower constraint in which money must be held at the beginning of the period in order to buy consumption goods. In this case, if m_t denotes real money balances at the beginning of the period and c_t purchases during the period, we can redefine the objective function to be $v(c_t, m_t) = u[\min(c_t, m_t)]$, and rewrite the maximization problem ignoring the Clower constraint but having money in the utility function. This argument has been extended by Feenstra (1986) who has shown that maximization problems subject to a Baumol-Tobin transaction technology can be approximately rewritten as maximization problems with money in the objective function.[30] Thus putting money directly in the utility function may not be misleading.

This approach has two shortcomings, however. The first is that we can lose sight of actual transactions and of the exact role played by money. The second is that we do not know what restrictions to impose on the objective function. For example, should it have u_{mc} positive or negative, or should u_m be positive for all m?

Money, Growth, and Capital Accumulation

Leaving aside the overlapping generations model of section 4.1 with money as the only asset, which we have argued is misleading, we still have conflicting results on the effects of money growth. In the model of section 4.3 money growth affects capital accumulation; in the model of this section it does not. We have just concluded that the difference does not necessarily arise from the fact that the transactions technology is treated explicitly in section 4.3 and only implicitly in this section. So where does the difference come from?

The source of the difference is the assumption that agents are infinitely lived. In the infinite horizon model individuals will keep accumulating capital as long as the effective real interest rate $r - n$ exceeds the rate of time preference θ. This ensures that eventually the steady state capital stock will reach the same level it did in the Ramsey model. When individuals are finitely lived, as in the Romer model, they are likely to accumulate more capital if a higher rate of inflation induces them to hold less money. Although rebating of seignorage in the form of transfers may also affect capital accumulation, the two effects have in general no reason to cancel.

But the assumption that individuals are infinitely long lived is far from sufficient for superneutrality. In the Sidrauski model a change in money growth will in general (unless instantaneous utility is separable) temporarily affect capital accumulation.[31] If the model is modified to allow money to enter the production function, or to allow labor supply to be endogenous, money growth does affect the steady state capital stock. Thus the general conclusion must be that money growth has an effect on capital accumulation.

Calculations suggest, however, that the effects of changes in the inflation rate on capital accumulation in models of the type developed in this chapter are very small. If inflation has systematic effects on capital accumulation (and there is empirically a negative association), it is probably for reasons not included so far. One likely reason is that the tax system is not neutral with respect to inflation.[32]

4.6 Money, Inside and Outside

It has been assumed in the models examined so far that money is a liability of the government that is introduced through transfer payments or asset purchases. Any money that on net is an asset of the private economy is an *outside money*. Under the gold standard, gold coins were outside money; in modern fiat money systems currency and bank reserves, high-powered money or the money base, constitute outside money. However, most money in modern economies is *inside money*, which is simultaneously an asset and liability of the private sector. Inside money takes the form of bank deposits, which are an asset to their holders and a liability of the banks.

The literature has discussed inside money systems in three closely related contexts. The first is the famous Wicksell *pure credit economy*. Wicksell (1907) asked how an economy that ran on pure credit would operate, and particularly how the price level would be determined in such an economy. By a pure credit economy Wicksell meant one in which all transactions were financed by bank loans. It is clear that in such a pure credit economy the price level cannot be determined without some restriction on the nominal quantity of credit.

That raises the question of how the restriction on the nominal quantity of credit could be enforced. If there were a monopoly bank, the constraint could be enforced by fiat. If the banking system were competitive, some way would have to be found for banks to compete for the right to make nominal loans. The right to make loans could be auctioned off; we do not know what the equilibrium price of the right to make a loan would be in such an economy.[33]

Second, there has been discussion of the significance of the difference between inside and outside money, centered on the fact that outside money is net wealth for the private sector whereas inside money is not. The question this raises is whether there is any welfare significance to the difference in wealth between inside and outside money economies. The simple answer is, not necessarily. The value of wealth in an economy can be raised by artificially restricting the supply of some commodity, creating monopoly profits that can be capitalized to increase wealth, but this does not indicate that welfare has been increased.[34]

The third question is that of how a system with private monies would operate. The notion here is that anyone who wished to do so could set up a bank that issued a "money." Hayek (1976) has argued that a stable money would emerge from competition in the issue of monies.

There has been little analytical progress in examining the behavior of a system with competing privately issued monies. There is no difficulty in describing a system with banks competing on the terms at which they offer deposits that are convertible into a dominant medium of exchange. So long as the supply of dominant money is fixed, the price level in a competitive system of this type would be determinate, and it is likely that Hayek's claims for the efficiency of the competitive outcome would hold, if the monetary authority were in turn determining the supply of the dominant money optimally.

The more interesting and more difficult question is whether banks could try to issue their own fiat media of exchange. Because the essence of a medium of exchange is that it is acceptable to others—there is a network externality—it seems unlikely that a competitive equilibrium in which each bank is free to issue an unconvertible currency of its own can exist. The other problem faced by a bank trying to ensure acceptability of its currency is that of dynamic inconsistency: so long as the bank profits by issuing money, it has the temptation to issue more. Indeed, it used to be argued that a competitive fiat money system would inevitably degenerate into a commodity money system. But if it is known that a bank will behave that way, it will not be able to issue the money in the first place. However, the problem of dynamic inconsistency for an issue of a fiat money may not be insuperable; the problem is similar to that faced by a durable goods monopolist, for instance, by an artist who has to avoid flooding the market with his lithographs.

4.7 Seigniorage and Inflation

We have seen how putting money in the utility function can cut through the complexities of the cash-in-advance constraint. Sometimes an even more drastic shortcut is warranted, and one may want to start by directly specifying the demand for money function. A set of issues for which such a shortcut has proved very useful is that of the relation between seigniorage, deficits, and inflation.

Until now we have taken the rate of growth of money as given, noting that it implies a certain amount of government revenue from the creation of money, or *seigniorage*. Seigniorage is one of the sources of government revenue, accounting in low-inflation industrialized economies for about 0.5% of GNP in government revenue and in high inflation economies yielding far more. Indeed, in extreme hyperinflations money printing often becomes virtually the only source of goverment revenue. In this section we focus on two questions. First, how much revenue can a government obtain from money creation? And second, can hyperinflation result from attempts by the government to collect seigniorage to finance too large a budget deficit? Since we want to focus on situations of high inflation, we shall simply assume that real variables move sufficiently slowly compared to the price level that they can as a first approximation be taken as given.

The basic model is composed of two equations, an equation giving the demand for money and an equation describing the formation of expectations. It is due to Cagan (1956). The money demand function is given by

$$m \equiv \frac{M}{P} = c \exp(-a\pi^*),$$

where c is a constant term and π^* is the expected rate of inflation. The higher expected inflation, the lower will be the demand for real money balances. Two important assumptions are implicit in this formulation. The first is that output is given and thus is part of the constant term c. The second is that the real interest rate is constant and thus also included in the constant term—this is why the expected inflation rate, and not the nominal interest rate, appears in (40). The main rationale for this functional form is convenience, though it appears consistent with the data from hyperinflations. In an equilibrium the real money stock must be equal to the money demand, and (40) can be interpreted as an equilibrium equation.

Next we specify how expectations are formed. We depart from our previous practice of assuming perfect foresight and, following Cagan, assume instead *adaptive expectations* about inflation.[35] Under adaptive expectations, expectations of inflation are adjusted according to

$$\frac{d\pi^*}{dt} = b(\pi - \pi^*). \tag{41}$$

If current inflation exceeds expected inflation, expected inflation increases. The coefficient b reflects the speed at which individuals revise their expectations. Note that the expected inflation depends only on past inflation. Equation (41) can be integrated to yield

$$\pi_t^* = b \int_{-\infty}^{t} \pi_s \exp[b(s - t)] \, ds.$$

Given the dynamics of money growth, equations (40) and (41) determine the dynamics of inflation.

Stability under Constant Money Growth

The first question asked by Cagan is the following: When money growth is constant at rate σ, will inflation converge to σ or will it take off on its own toward hyperinflation?

To answer that question, we differentiate equation (40) after taking logarithms. This gives

$$\sigma - \pi = -a\left(\frac{d\pi^*}{dt}\right). \tag{42}$$

Eliminating $d\pi^*/dt$ between (41) and (42) gives a relation between π, π^*, and σ:

$$\sigma - \pi = -ab(\pi - \pi^*). \tag{43}$$

We show (43) in figure 4.11, along with the locus $d\pi^*/dt = 0$, in (π, π^*) space. There are two cases to consider. In figure 4.11a, $ab < 1$ so that $d\pi/d\pi^* < 0$ along (43) and the equilibrium is stable; in figure 4.11b, $ab > 1$ so that $d\pi/d\pi^* > 0$ along (43) and the equilibrium is unstable. In the unstable case, depending on the initial conditions, the economy can have either accelerating inflation or accelerating deflation. Thus whether there can be hyperinflation under constant money growth depends on the parameters a and b, which reflect respectively the elasticity of money demand and the speed of revision of expectations.

Why is the equilibrium unstable if $ab > 1$? If b is large, higher inflation leads money holders to quickly revise upward their expectations of inflation and thus to attempt to reduce their money holdings; given money growth, this leads to further inflation, further revisions, and accelerating inflation. If a is large, an increase in inflation that leads to an upward revision of expected

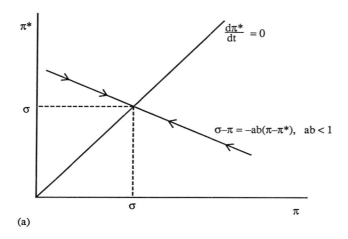

(a)

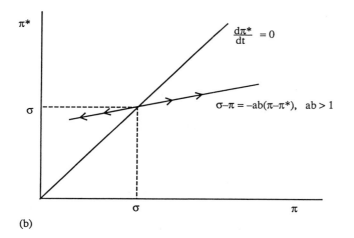

(b)

Figure 4.11
Dynamics of inflation for a given rate of money growth

inflation has a strong negative effect on money demand, leading again to accelerating inflation. Accordingly, if individuals have adaptive expectations, it is possible for hyperinflation to result not from accelerating money growth but rather from a self-generating unstable process.[36]

Seigniorage and Inflation

The second question raised by Cagan is: If the equilibrium is stable, what is the maximum amount of seigniorage that the government can collect? Equivalently, what is the maximum deficit that the government can finance by the creation of money?

Seigniorage is equal to

$$S \equiv \frac{dM/dt}{P} = \left(\frac{dM/dt}{M}\right)\left(\frac{M}{P}\right) = \sigma m. \tag{44}$$

Using equation (40) and the fact that in steady state (without growth) $\pi^* = \sigma$ gives

$$S = \sigma c \exp(-a\sigma).$$

Accordingly, steady state seigniorage is maximized when $\sigma = 1/a$.

Put another way, and noting that the elasticity of money demand with respect to inflation is equal to $-a\sigma$, the condition states that seigniorage is maximized when the elasticity of the tax base m with respect to the tax rate σ is equal to -1. This is a familiar condition from monopoly theory.[37]

The analysis of seigniorage is also called *inflation tax* analysis. The inflation tax is the tax imposed on money holders as a result of inflation. It is related but not necessarily identical to seigniorage. The actual tax that inflation imposes on money holders is the loss in the value of their real balances, $\pi M/P$; seigniorage is $\sigma M/P$. Only when $\pi = \sigma$ are the two equal. That holds in a steady state when there is no output growth, but not generally.

Exogenous Seigniorage

If the government seeks to obtain a given amount of revenue from seigniorage, it may be more realistic to study the dynamics of inflation given S rather than given σ as we have done above. We now do so, again under the assumptions of adaptive expectations.[38] The dynamics are characterized by

$$S = \sigma c \exp(-a\pi^*) \tag{45}$$

and

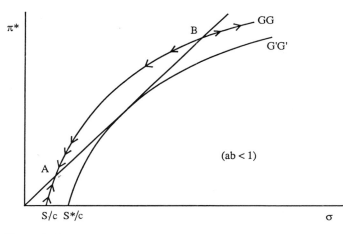

Figure 4.12
Dynamics of inflation given seigniorage

$$\frac{d\pi^*}{dt} = b(\pi - \pi^*), \tag{41}$$

where S is given and σ is now endogenously determined.

In figure 4.12 we show in (π^*, σ) space the combinations of expected inflation and money growth rates that yield a given level of seigniorage S. The locus GG is upward sloping, with slope $d\pi^*/d\sigma = 1/a\sigma$. The intercept of GG with the horizontal axis is equal to S/c.

In the steady state, $\pi^* = \sigma$ so that the steady state value of σ is given by the intersection of GG and the 45-degree line. There may therefore be two steady states, as is the case with GG in figure 4.12, one steady state, or none. There is one steady state shown by $G'G'$ which is tangent to the 45-degree line, which is the case where $a\sigma$ equals 1. This is just the condition we derived earlier for maximum seigniorage, S^*. There is no steady state if S exceeds S^*: there is no way the government can collect more than S^* from the inflation tax in steady state.

Note that the government can collect more seigniorage than S^* if the economy is not in steady state. On any iso-seigniorage locus below $G'G'$ the government revenue exceeds S^*. There cannot be a steady state on such a locus because the expected inflation rate is not equal to the rate of money growth. But if the expected inflation is low enough, the government can, by producing rapid money growth, obtain more revenue than it could in steady state.

If S is less than S^*, there are two equilibria, A and B in figure 4.12. A is a low-inflation equilibrium with large real money balances, and B is a high-inflation equilibrium with small real money balances. Both A and B yield the same amount of seigniorage. This result is quite general and only requires that tax revenues eventually go to zero as the rate of money growth increases.

At what equilibrium will the economy operate? It is clear that A is a better equibrium than B, implying a smaller opportunity cost of holding money for a given amount of government revenue. The outcome, however, depends on the dynamics. Substituting (42) into (41) gives

$$\frac{d\pi^*}{dt} = \left(\frac{b}{1-ab}\right)(\sigma - \pi^*).$$

The dynamics depend again on whether ab is less or greater than 1. Expected inflation and money growth are always on the schedule GG. If $ab < 1$, then expected inflation is rising for all points below the 45-degree line and falling for all points above. This implies that A is the stable steady state and that B is unstable.

In this case, if the economy starts from any point to the left of B, it will converge to the low-inflation equilibrium at A. If it starts from a position to the right of B, the inflation rate will keep increasing, with the government continually increasing the growth rate of money as expectations slowly adapt to increasing inflation. At the end lies hyperinflation.

A one-time unexpected permanent increase in seigniorage from S to S' shifts GG to the right. If S' is less than S^*, there remain two equilibria. This is the case drawn in figure 4.13. If the economy starts at the stable equilib-

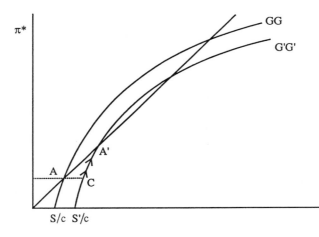

Figure 4.13
Dynamic effects of an increase in seigniorage

rium A, the increase in S implies an instantaneous jump in the growth rate of money (and of the actual inflation rate) from A to C and a gradual further movement of σ and π from C to A' thereafter. If S increases beyond S^*, inflation increases indefinitely, as the government collects seigniorage by accelerating inflation.

The stability-instability properties of A and B are reversed if $ab > 1$, that is, if expectations adjust quickly or if the demand for money is very interest elastic. In the first case, the economy ends up with high inflation and low real money balances. In the second, an increase in seigniorage leads in steady state to lower inflation. In the short run, however, it leads to higher money growth because in the short run, given expected inflation and thus real money balances, this is the only way to increase revenues.[39]

We have shown that there are two steady state rates of inflation that yield the same amount of seigniorage. We have also shown that the economy may end up at the higher rate of inflation and that attempts by the government to increase seigniorage can cause hyperinflation. Quite crucial to the results is the way in which expectations are formed. We will examine issues of expectations formation further in the next chapter, with the Cagan model providing a convenient framework from which to start the discussion. We will also return to the relation between deficits and inflation in chapter 10.

Appendix A: Derivation of Individual Behavior in Section 4.3

We solve for utility maximization in three steps and in reverse order of the results in the text. First, we derive optimal consumption between trips to the bank given their timing and the amount withdrawn. Second, we show that trips to the bank will be equally spaced. Finally, we derive the size and the number of transactions.

The timing conventions are repeated here for convenience:

Time	0	Δt_1	$(\Delta t_1 + \Delta t_2)$	$\cdots$	$(T - \Delta t_{N+1})$	T
Length of interval		Δt_1	Δt_1			Δt_{N+1}
	$--\cdot+------+$	$-------+-----------+-----+$				
Withdrawals	m_1	m_2	m_3		m_{N+1}	
Trip number	0	1	2	$\cdots$	N	

Optimal Consumption between Trips

Given a withdrawal of real money balances m_j at time s, the individual solves the following problem for the interval $[s, s + \Delta t_j]$:

$$\max \int_s^{s+\Delta t_j} \ln c_t \, dt \qquad (A1)$$

subject to

$$\int_s^{s+\Delta t_j} P_t c_t \, dt = m_j P_s.$$

P_t is the price level at time t. Nominal expenditures during the interval must equal the nominal value of the money withdrawals at time s, $m_j P_s$. The joint assumptions that utility is logarithmic and that there is no discounting imply that the individual chooses to have constant nominal expenditures within the period between trips to the bank:

$$P_t c_t = \frac{m_j P_s}{\Delta t_j}$$

so that

$$c_t = \left(\frac{m_j}{\Delta t_j}\right)\left(\frac{P_s}{P_t}\right) = \left(\frac{m_j}{\Delta t_j}\right) \exp[-\pi(t-s)]. \qquad (A2)$$

The interest rate relevant to consumers *between* trips to the bank is the rate of return on money (i.e., the negative of the rate of inflation). Replacing c_t from (A2) in the expression for utility during that interval gives

$$U_j^* = \int_s^{s+\Delta t_j} \left[\ln\left(\frac{m_j}{\Delta t_j}\right) - \pi(t-s)\right] dt = \Delta t_j \ln\left(\frac{m_j}{\Delta t_j}\right) - \left(\frac{\pi}{2}\right)(\Delta t_j)^2. \qquad (A3)$$

Time between Transactions

Total lifetime utility can be rewritten as the sum of utilities over each interval between trips. Given (A3), this implies that

$$U^* = \sum_{j=0}^{N} \left[\Delta t_{j+1} \ln\left(\frac{m_{j+1}}{\Delta t_{j+1}}\right) - \left(\frac{\pi}{2}\right)(\Delta t_{j+1})^2\right] - Nb \qquad (A4)$$

subject to

$$Y = m_1 + m_2 \exp(-r\Delta t_1) + m_3 \exp[-r(\Delta t_1 + \Delta t_2)] + \cdots$$
$$+ m_{N+1} \exp[-r(T - \Delta t_{N+1})].$$

Note the unusual form of the intertemporal budget constraint, which clearly shows the role of the Clower constraint. The endowment is equal to the present value of real money withdrawals, discounted at the real rate of return on bonds, which is the relevant rate *across* trips to the bank.

To solve for optimal spacing, assume first that there is only one trip to the bank during life. We will show that in this case it will take place at $T/2$. With only one trip, equation (A4) becomes

$$U^* = \Delta t_1 \ln\left(\frac{m_1}{\Delta t_1}\right) + (T - \Delta t_1) \ln\left[\frac{m_2}{T - \Delta t_1}\right] - \left(\frac{\pi}{2}\right)[\Delta t_1{}^2 + (T - \Delta t_1)^2]$$

subject to

$$Y = m_1 + m_2 \exp(-r\Delta t_1).$$

Let λ be the Lagrange multiplier on the budget constraint. The first-order conditions are

$$\frac{\Delta t_1}{m_1} = \lambda, \qquad \frac{T - \Delta t_1}{m_2} = \lambda \exp(-r\Delta t_1),$$

and

$$\ln\left(\frac{m_1}{\Delta t_1}\right) - \ln\left[\frac{m_2}{T - \Delta t_1}\right] - \pi\Delta t_1 + \pi(T - \Delta t_1) - \lambda r m_2 \exp(-r\Delta t_1) = 0.$$

By substituting the first two equations in the third we show that $\Delta t_1 = T/2$. A similar proof applies over any subperiod in which there is one transaction to be made between two others. All transactions will be equally spaced. Optimal Δt_j is thus given by

$$\Delta t_j = \Delta t = \frac{T}{N + 1}. \tag{A5}$$

Trips will be equally spaced through life.

The Size of Transactions and the Level of Consumption

Replacing Δt_j by its expression from (A5) in (A4) gives the following value for U^* and the budget constraint:

$$U^{**} = \sum_{j=1}^{N+1} \left\{\left(\frac{T}{N + 1}\right) \ln\left[\frac{m_j(N + 1)}{T}\right] - \left(\frac{\pi}{2}\right)\left(\frac{T}{N + 1}\right)^2\right\} - Nb \tag{A6}$$

subject to

$$Y = m_1 + \cdots + m_{N+1} \exp\left[-r\left(\frac{NT}{N + 1}\right)\right].$$

Solving for optimal withdrawals, given N, implies that

$$m_{j+1} = \left(\frac{Y}{N + 1}\right) \exp\left(\frac{rjT}{N + 1}\right). \tag{A7}$$

Finally, we solve for the optimal number of trips, N. To do so, we once again replace the value of optimal m_{j+1} from (A7) in (A6) to get, after some manipulation,

$$U^{***} = T \ln\left(\frac{Y}{T}\right) + \frac{rT^2}{2} - \frac{(r + \pi)T^2}{2(N + 1)} - Nb. \tag{A8}$$

Ignoring integer constraints, we solve for N and obtain

$$\mu \equiv \frac{T}{N+1} = \sqrt{\frac{2b}{r+\pi}}. \tag{A9}$$

Equation (A9) is equation (10) in the text. Equation (A7) is equation (11) in the text. Equations (A2) and (A5) give (12) in the text.

Appendix B: Derivation of Local Dynamics and Stability in the Sidrauski Model

The adjustment path is described by three differential equations: (B1) gives the evolution of λ, the marginal utility of consumption; (B2) gives the dynamics of capital accumulation; (B3) gives the dynamics of real money balances.

$$\frac{d\lambda/dt}{\lambda} = n + \theta - f'(k), \tag{B1}$$

$$\frac{dk}{dt} = f(k) - nk - c(\lambda, k, \pi), \qquad c_1 < 0, \quad c_2 > 0, \quad c_3 < 0, \tag{B2}$$

$$\frac{dm/dt}{m} = \sigma - n - \pi(\lambda, k, m), \qquad \pi_1 < 0, \quad \pi_2 > 0, \quad \pi_3 < 0. \tag{B3}$$

Equation (B3) is derived by differentiating the definition $m = M/PN$ and using (31) to express π as a function of λ, k, and m. The function $c(\lambda, k, \pi)$ is obtained by solving equations (30) and (31) for c and m as functions of λ, π, and k.

The properties of $c(\cdot)$ and $\pi(\cdot)$ are obtained by total differentiation of (30) and (31). For example, $c_1 = [u_{mm} - (r + \pi)u_{cm}]/(u_{mm}u_{cc} - u_{cm}^2)$. By equations (30) and (31) this is equal to $[u_{mm} - (u_m/u_c)u_{cm}]/(u_{mm}u_{cc} - u_{cm}^2)$. If real money and consumption are normal goods, then $c_1 < 0$.

Linearizing this system around its steady state, and evaluating all derivatives at the steady state, gives[40]

$$\begin{bmatrix} \dfrac{d\lambda/dt}{\lambda} \\[2ex] \dfrac{dk}{dt} \\[2ex] \dfrac{dm/dt}{m} \end{bmatrix} = \begin{bmatrix} 0 & -f''(k^*) & 0 \\ -c_1 - c_3\pi_1 & \delta & -c_3\pi_3 \\ -\pi_1 & -\pi_2 & -\pi_3 \end{bmatrix} \begin{bmatrix} \lambda - \lambda^* \\ k - k^* \\ m - m^* \end{bmatrix}$$

While the capital stock is given at any point in time, both the price level (and therefore m) and λ can jump at any point in time. Thus for the system to have (locally) a unique stable path, it must have two positive roots (or a pair of complex roots with positive real part) and one negative real root. (If, for example, it had three negative roots, then starting with any value of m and λ, the system would—locally—converge. There would be nothing to tie down the price level or the level of λ.)

To verify this, we look at the determinant of the preceding matrix. The determinant given by $f''\pi_3 c_1 < 0$ is equal to the product of the roots, and its trace, $\pi_3 + \delta > 0$, is equal to the sum of the roots. Since the sum of the roots is positive, there must be at least one positive root. But for the determinant to be negative, there must be either zero or two positive roots. Thus, combining the two conditions, we see that there are two positive roots to the system and that the determinant is locally saddle point stable.

Problems

1. *The Baumol-Tobin model. (This follows Baumol 1952 and Tobin 1956.)*

An individual receives income Y which he consumes at a constant rate over a period whose length is unity. Income, which is received at the beginning of the period, is deposited directly into an interest-yielding account. The individual can then hold his wealth either in this interest-yielding account or in the form of money. The interest on the interest-yielding account is paid at the end of the period on the average balance during the period. However, money is needed for transactions. To get money, the individual must go to the bank to exchange money for bonds; he incurs a fixed cost of b for any such trip.

The individual chooses the number of trips so as to maximize interest payments, net of the cost of trips to the bank.

(a) Assume for simplicity that trips to the bank are equally spaced. What is the average money balance of an individual who goes to the bank N times? (*Note:* He has to go to the bank at the beginning if he is to consume at all.) What is the average balance in his interest-yielding account?

(b) Write down the maximization problem faced by the individual. Solve for the optimal number of trips, ignoring the integer constraint.

(c) Using (a) and (b), derive the average money balance held by the individual. Compute the interest elasticity of money demand.

(d) Assuming that most individuals are paid monthly, we may think of the period as being a month. Using your best guesses of numerical values for the relevant parameters, derive the optimal number of trips made by a representative individual. Derive the aggregate average money holdings. How does it compare to actual numbers for U.S. money demand?

(e) Compare the setup and results of this model with those of the Romer model.

2. Is money superneutral in the model of section 4.4?

3. Suppose that the instantaneous utility function is

$$U(c, m) = \frac{(c^a m^{1-a})^{1-\gamma}}{1 - \gamma}, \qquad 0 < a < 1, \gamma > 0,$$

and that the production function is Cobb-Douglas.

(a) Calculate the steady state capital stock in this economy when the rate of time preference is θ and the growth rate of money σ.

(b) What is the optimal steady state growth rate of money σ^*? Explain.

4. *The Tobin effect: inflation and capital accumulation. (This is adapted from Tobin 1965.)*

Consider the following economy:

$$\frac{dk}{dt} = f(k) - c - nk, \qquad f' > 0, f'' < 0,$$

$$m = k\phi(r + \pi^*), \qquad \phi' < 0,$$

$$c = c(a), \qquad c' > 0,$$

$$a = m + k,$$

$$r = f'(k).$$

All symbols are as in the text. In particular, m is real money balances per capita.
(a) Explain briefly where these equations may come from.
(b) Assuming rational expectations (i.e., $\pi^* = \pi$) and using the fact that $dm/dt = (\sigma - \pi - n)m$, where σ is the rate of growth of nominal money, reduce this system of equations to a dynamic system in m and k.
(c) Characterize the conditions under which this system is locally saddle point stable. Why is saddle point stability a desirable property of the equilibrium?
(d) Assuming local saddle point stability, characterize the effects of the rate of growth of nominal money on capital accumulation and consumption. Explain your results, and contrast them with those obtained in the Sidrauski model.

5. *Money as a factor of production. (This is adapted from Dornbusch and Frenkel 1973.)*

Consider the Sidrauski model presented in section 4.5. Assume, however, that money services are also an input in production. A simple formalization is that production is given by $[1 - v(m)]f(k)$, where $v'(\cdot) < 0$, $v''(\cdot) > 0$, $v(0) = 1$, and v tends to zero as m goes to infinity. Assume for simplicity that $n = 0$. Characterize the steady state, and contrast the effects of money growth with those obtained in the original Sidrauski model.

6. *Seigniorage, inflation, and growth.*

In the model of section 4.7 reintroduce income as an argument in the demand function for money. Assume unitary income elasticity. Assume that income is growing at rate g in steady state. What is the maximum seigniorage revenue the government can obtain as a percentage of GNP?

7. For the model of section 4.7, assume that the government wants to raise a given amount of seigniorage and that there exist two equilibria. Discuss the stability of the two equilibria when expectations are rational. (This question is tricky and deals with issues discussed in the next chapter, as well as in chapter 10.)

Notes

1. The classical explanation for the existence of money, at least since Aristotle, has been in terms of its functions. Jevons (1875) states that money has four functions, as a medium of exchange, a store of value, a unit of account, and a standard of deferred payments.

2. Under a liberal interpretation of what constitutes a medium of exchange, money has been used in virtually all economies. See Einzig (1966).

3. That monetary disturbances appear to have strongly affected economic activity in the United States is the theme of Friedman and Schwartz (1963).

4. We will later critize the Samuelson model as a model of money, but as the first and simplest OLG model, it has proved incredibly useful to analyze a host of issues. It is the father of the Diamond (1965) model, which we used at length in the previous chapter.

5. This argument, just as the argument made in the previous chapter that a dynamically inefficient steady state in the Diamond model was not a Pareto optimum, relies on the economy lasting forever. If there is a last generation, that generation will be worse off.

6. We will see in the next chapter, however, that even in this case there may exist equilibria with extrinsic uncertainty. Then perfect foresight must be replaced by rational expectations.

7. We will see in chapter 5 that under uncertainty money may be valued even if there is some probability that the economy may come to an end in each period, so long as there is no period beyond which it is certain that the economy will have ended. If money is not intrinsically useless (i.e., yields direct utility even if not used in exchange), it may be valued even if the economy comes to an end with certainty at some future date.

It is often convenient to work with models of n period economies. A standard approach is to impose a condition that guarantees a positive value in the final period. This can be done, for example, by having the government require that taxes be paid in money in the final period.

8. Money is said to be neutral if changes in the level of nominal money have no effect on the real equilibrium. It is said to be superneutral if changes in money growth have no effect on the real equilibrium.

9. These results are extended to more complex OLG models by Cass, Okuno, and Zilcha (1980). They show in particular that neither proposition survives in pure form when there are differences in tastes and endowments across agents.

10. These and other criticisms are made by Tobin (1980) and McCallum (1983). Our assessment of the weaknesses of the model is not universally shared. Wallace (1981) has argued that the OLG model is the only model we have in which there is a clear rationale for the use of money and thus should be, for lack of a better model, the model used to study, for example, the effects of open market operations.

11. Note the analogy between this atemporal example and the intertemporal model examined in the previous section. In both cases individual A wants to trade with individual B, B with C, and so on. The analogy, emphasized by Cass and Yaari (1966), is nevertheless partly misleading: in the intertemporal model with a terminal condition (a finite number of generations), there is no set of trades that can make

everybody better off. To make everybody better off, a direct trade would be required between the first and the last generation, a physical impossibility.

12. Niehans (1978, ch. 6) develops an analysis of the medium of exchange that focuses on transportation costs. For an alternative approach, see Jones (1976). For a recent treatment, based on storage costs, see Kiyotaki and Wright (1988).

13. See Ostroy (1973).

14. See Clower (1967) for the argument that such a constraint provides a good basis for differentiating a monetary from a barter economy. Kohn (1981) defends the constraint; Svensson (1985) reviews earlier papers that have used it.

15. Note that the constraint could be instead that purchases of goods and bonds require cash-in-advance. Then the constraint would become, under the assumption that bonds have a one-period maturity,

$$\sum_{i=1}^{n} P_{it} c_{it} + B_{t+1} \leqslant M_t.$$

16. Whalen (1966) and Goldman (1974) present early partial equilibrium precautionary demand models. Krugman, Persson, and Svensson (1985) develop a general equilibrium version of a precautionary demand model. Svensson (1985) studies asset pricing in such a context. The model presented here is a simplified, partial equilibrium version of Woodford (1984), which is in turn closely related to Diamond and Dybvig (1984). Diamond and Dybvig use their model to study bank runs and deposit insurance.

17. A closely related model has been developed by Jovanovic (1982).

18. These two assumptions (logarithmic utility and no discounting) are both essential for tractability.

19. We will refer to the economy in which bonds can be used to make purchases as "nonmonetary." We do not thereby imply, however, that the allocation of resources attainable in this case would be attainable in a true barter economy, as presumably some other resources would have to be expended in trade.

20. The path of bonds is drawn as downward sloping in the figure. This may not be the case: if $1 - rT$ is positive, bonds increase before decreasing to zero.

21. Note that the treatment of transaction costs for firms and individuals is asymmetric. Individuals incur a cost b for each transaction with banks, whereas firms incur none. This is done only for simplicity.

22. Since both numerator and denominator go to zero with r in (16) and (17), one must use L'Hospital's rule, which says that $\lim f(\cdot)/g(\cdot)$, as both f and g go to zero is equal to $f'(0)/g'(0)$.

23. Romer (1986) considers alternative schemes in which transfers are given at the end of life, in which seigniorage revenue is not rebated but used to buy goods, or in which seigniorage is initially maximized so that any change in money growth decreases seigniorage.

24. The simpler model we will use here is due to Grossman and Weiss (1983). A more general model, with capital, is developed by Rotemberg (1984).

25. See chapters 2 and 3 for a derivation of the intertemporal budget constraint of the government. Because the individuals are infinitely long lived, the economy is subject to Ricardian equivalence of debt and taxes.

26. We do not specify the institutions or the flow of transactions in the economy. Goods can be thought of as being sold by a warehouse firm which sells goods to individuals against money and turns the money back to the bank to extinguish claims on output. The reader should, as in the Romer model, attempt to trace the flow of money between individuals, the bank, the warehouse, and the government in each time period.

27. See Grossman and Weiss (1983) for details concerning this analysis.

28. Romer (1987) explores the issue of the effects of endogenizing the timing of transactions. He finds that the effects of open market operations may actually be more persistent in that case.

29. Fischer (1979) and Cohen (1985) characterize the dynamics of the economy in response to a change in money growth.

30. The related question of when it is appropriate to put money in the production function has been examined by Fischer (1974).

31. See Fischer (1979) and Cohen (1985).

32. See, for example, Feldstein (1980).

33. See McCallum (1985).

34. This issue is discussed in Fischer (1972).

35. We return to the dynamics of this model under rational expectations in the next chapter.

36. Cagan estimated a and b and concluded that the stability condition was satisfied for most hyperinflations, implying that hyperinflation was due to unstable money growth rather than any inherent instability of the private economy.

37. The condition was also stated by Bailey (1956).

38. See Bruno and Fischer (1987) who also study the dynamics under rational expectations.

39. Note that, in the short run, while money growth increases, inflation and then expected inflation decrease. This raises the question of the plausibility of the assumption of adaptive expectations in this case. It is at least plausible that when individuals see higher money growth, they will increase rather than decrease their expectations of inflation.

40. It can be shown that $c_2 + c_3\pi_2 = 0$, so that the middle element of the diagonal is just equal to δ, and that $\pi_2 = -f''$.

References

Bailey, Martin (1956). "The Welfare Cost of Inflationary Finance." *Journal of Political Economy*, 64–93.

Baumol, William (1952). "The Transactions Demand for Cash." *Quarterly Journal of Economics* 67, 4 (Nov.), 545–556.

Bruno, Michael, and Stanley Fischer (1987). "Seigniorage, Operating Rules, and the High Inflation Trap." NBER Working Paper 2413. October.

Cagan, Phillip (1956). "The Monetary Dynamics of Hyperinflation." In Milton Friedman (ed.), *Studies in the Quantity Theory of Money* University of Chicago Press.

Cass, David, Masahiro Okuno, and Itzhak Zilcha (1980). "The Role of Money in Supporting the Pareto Optimality of Competitive Equilibrium in Consumption-Loans Models." In John Kareken and Neil Wallace (eds.), *Models of Monetary Economies*. Federal Reserve Bank of Minneapolis.

Cass, David, and Menahem Yaari (1966). "A Re-examination of the Pure Consumption Loans Model." *Journal of Political Economy* 74, 353–367.

Clower, Robert (1967). "A Reconsideration of the Microeconomic Foundations of Monetary Theory." *Western Economic Journal* 6 (Dec.), 1–8.

Cohen, Daniel (1985). "Inflation, Wealth and Interest Rates in an Intertemporal Optimizing Model." *Journal of Monetary Economics* 16, 73–85.

Diamond, Peter (1965). "National Debt in a Neo-Classical Growth Model." *American Economic Review* 55 (Dec.), 1126–1150.

Diamond, Douglas, and Philip Dybvig (1983). "Bank Runs, Deposit Insurance and Liquidity." *Journal of Political Economy* 91, 3 (June), 401–419.

Dornbusch, Rudiger, and Jacob Frenkel (1973). "Inflation and Growth: Alternative Approaches." *Journal of Money, Credit and Banking* 50, 1 (Feb.), 141–156.

Einzig, Paul (1966). *Primitive Money in its Ethnological, Historical and Economic Aspects*. New York: Pergamon Press.

Feenstra, Robert (1986). "Functional Equivalence between Liquidity Costs and the Utility of Money." *Journal of Monetary Economics* 17, 271–291.

Feldstein, Martin (1980). "Fiscal Policies, Inflation and Capital Formation." *American Economic Review* 70, 636–650.

Fischer, Stanley (1972). "Money, Income and Welfare." *Journal of Economic Theory* (April), 289–311.

Fischer, Stanley (1974). "Money in the Production Function." *Economic Inquiry* 12, 4 (Nov.), 518–533.

Fischer, Stanley (1979). "Capital Accumulation on the Transition Path in a Monetary Optimizing Model." *Econometrica* 47, 1433–1439.

Friedman, Milton (1969). *The Optimum Quantity of Money and Other Essays*. Chicago: Aldine.

Friedman, Milton (1971). "Government Revenue from Inflation." *Journal of Political Economy* 79, 4 (July–Aug.), 846–856.

Friedman, Milton, and Anna J. Schwartz (1963). *A Monetary History of the United States*. Princeton University Press.

Goldman, Steven (1974). "Flexibility and the Demand for Money." *Journal of Economic Theory* 9, 203–222.

Grossman, Sanford, and Laurence Weiss (1983). "A Transactions-Based Model of the Monetary Transmission Mechanism." *American Economic Review* 73, 5 (Dec.), 871–880.

Hayek, Friedrich von (1976). *Denationalization of Money*. London: Institute of Economic Affairs.

Jones, Robert A. (1976). "The Origin and Development of Media of Exchange." *Journal of Political Economy* 84, 4 (Aug.), 757–776.

Jevons, W. Stanley (1875). *Money and the Mechanism of Exchange*. London: Routledge and Kegan Paul.

Jovanovic, Boyan (1982). "Inflation and Welfare in the Steady State." *Journal of Political Economy* 90, 3 (June), 561–577.

Kareken, John, and Neil Wallace (1981). "On the Indeterminacy of Equilibrium Exchange Rates." *Quarterly Journal of Economics* 96, 2 (May), 207–222.

Kiyotaki, Nobuhiro, and Randall Wright (1988). "On Money as a Medium of Exchange." CARESS working paper, University of Pennsylvania. January.

Kohn, Meir (1981). "In Defense of the Finance Constraint." *Economic Inquiry* 29 (April), 177–195.

Krugman, Paul, Torsten Persson, and Lars Svensson (1985). "Inflation, Interest Rates and Welfare." *Quarterly Journal of Economics* 100, 3 (Aug.), 677–696.

Lucas, Robert E., Jr., and Nancy L. Stokey (1987). "Money and Interest in a Cash-in-advance Economy." *Econometrica* 55, 3 (May), 491–514.

McCallum, Bennett (1983). "The Role of Overlapping Generations Models in Monetary Economics." *Carnegie Rochester Conference Volume*, 18.

McCallum, Bennett (1985). "Bank Deregulation, Accounting Systems and the Unit of Account: A Critical Review." In Karl Brunner and Alan Meltzer (eds.), *Carnegie Rochester Conferences on Public Policy*, 23, Autumn.

Niehans, Jurg (1978). *The Theory of Money*. Johns Hopkins Press.

Ostroy, Joseph (1973). "The Informational Efficiency of Monetary Exchange." *American Economic Review* 63, 597–610.

Romer, David (1986). "A Simple General Equilibrium Version of the Baumol-Tobin Model." *Quarterly Journal of Economics* 101, 4 (Nov.), 663–686.

Romer, David (1987). "The Monetary Transmission Mechanism in a General Equilibrium Version of the Baumol-Tobin Model." *Journal of Monetary Economics* 20, 105–122.

Rotemberg, Julio (1984). "A Monetary Equilibrium Model with Transactions Costs." *Journal of Political Economy* 92, 2 (Feb.), 40–58.

Samuelson, Paul A. (1958). "An Exact Consumption Loan Model of Interest with or without the Social Contrivance of Money." *Journal of Political Economy* 66, 1002–1011.

Sidrauski, Miguel (1967a). "Rational Choice and Patterns of Growth in a Monetary Economy." *American Economic Review* 57, 2 (May), 534–544.

Sidrauski, Miguel (1967b). "Inflation and Economic Growth." *Journal of Political Economy* 75 (Dec.), 798–810.

Svensson, Lars E.O. (1985). "Money and Asset Prices in a Cash-in-Advance Economy." *Journal of Political Economy* 93, 5 (Oct.), 919–944.

Tobin, James (1956). "The Interest Elasticity of the Transactions Demand for Cash." *Review of Economics and Statistics* 38 (Aug.), 241–247.

Tobin, James (1965). "Money and Economic Growth." *Econometrica* 32 (Oct.), 671–684.

Tobin, James (1980). "Discussion." In J. Kareken and N. Wallace (eds.), *Models of Monetary Economies*. Federal Reserve Bank of Minneapolis, 83–90.

Wallace, Neil (1981). "A Modigliani-Miller Theorem for Open Market Operations." *American Economic Review* 71, 3 (June), 267–274.

Whalen, E.L. (1966). "A Rationalization of the Precautionary Demand for Cash." *Review of Economic and Statistics* 38 (Aug.), 241–247.

Wicksell, Knut (1907). *Lectures on Political Economy*. Vol. 2. Reprinted 1935. London: Routledge and Kegan Paul.

Woodford, Michael (1984). "Transaction Costs, Liquidity and Optimal Inflation." MIT. Mimeo.

5

Multiple Equilibria, Bubbles, and Stability

We have skipped some difficult issues at various points in the last four chapters. Confronted with saddle point equilibria, we proceeded to focus on the behavior of the economy along the convergent path; in some cases restricting our attention to that path was indeed warranted, but in many others no formal argument was given to rule out other paths. In other places we studied the properties of steady states without checking whether they were stable. We now examine these issues in more detail. The outcome turns out to be more than just a cleaning up of untidy detail. Rather, the chapter opens up broad and fascinating issues, from multiple equilibria to speculative bubbles and chaos.

In section 5.1 we start by analyzing the solution to a simple linear difference equation under rational expectations. This difference equation has various interpretations: it may arise, for example, from an arbitrage relation, from a linearized version of the OLG model with money analyzed in chapter 4, or from the Cagan model also analyzed in chapter 4. The solution to this simple equation is remarkably rich. For some parameter values, the solution may exhibit bubbles, components that explode in expected value over time. For other parameter values, there is an embarrassing wealth of stable solutions, in some of which variables matter just because individuals believe they do. The rest of the chapter is spent analyzing these issues in a general equilibrium context.

In section 5.2 we focus on the question of whether there can be bubbles on real assets in general equilibrium. Bubbles are ruled out when individuals have infinite horizons. However, when individuals have finite horizons, there are circumstances under which bubbles may exist and even be beneficial. To analyze the conditions under which bubbles exist, we use the Diamond overlapping generations model introduced in chapter 3. We conclude the section with a brief discussion of how econometric methods can be used to detect the presence of bubbles in asset markets.

From the purely real models of section 5.2 we turn in section 5.3 to the question of whether there can be price level bubbles in monetary models. The main issue is whether general equilibrium considerations allow us to rule out self-generating hyperinflations or deflations. We conclude, using a model in which money provides direct utility services, that there are cases in which self-generating hyperinflations cannot be ruled out.

The most remarkable set of results appears in section 5.4, where we examine general equilibrium models in which there is an infinity of stable equilibria. For convenience, we use the OLG model. We show how and when the equilibrium may have cycles, may exhibit chaos, may exhibit sunspots, and be affected by extrinsic uncertainty. We also discuss whether configurations of parameters that allow for such strange phenomena are likely to occur.

In section 5.5 we study the role and implications of learning. The explicit introduction of learning can help to narrow the range of probable solutions. We conclude in section 5.6 with an assessment of the relevance of the various types of multiplicity of equilibria presented in the chapter.

One word of clarification: this is not the only chapter in the book in which the possibility of multiple equilibria is discussed. We have already in the analysis of seigniorage in chapter 4 examined one case of multiple equilibria. We discuss other examples, consistent with the Keynesian notion that self-justifying "animal spirits" may cause output expansions and contractions, in chapter 8.

5.1 Solutions to a Simple Equation

In this section we characterize the behavior of a variable y that obeys the following expectational difference equation:

$$y_t = aE[y_{t+1}|t] + cx_t, \tag{1}$$

where $E[y_{t+1}|t]$ denotes the expectation of y_{t+1} held at time t so that y depends on the current expectation of its value next period as well as on the variable x.

To solve for the behavior of y, one must specify how individuals form expectations. We will assume in this chapter that individuals have *rational expectations*, that is, expectations equal to the mathematical expectation of y_{t+1} based on information available at time t.[1]

We make two further assumptions in defining this rational expectation. The first is that individuals know the model, namely, equation (1) and the parameters a and c. In most real world situations this will obviously not be the case; individuals will also be learning, and most likely disagreeing, about the model at the same time as they are forming expectations. We return to the issue of learning later in this chapter.

The second assumption is that all individuals have the same information set at time t so that we can indeed talk about "the" mathematical expectation based on "the" information set. However, different individuals often have different information sets, each with a piece of information that the others do not have. We will see examples of such models in the next chapter.[2]

We define $E[y_{t+1}|t]$ by

$$E[y_{t+1}|t] = E[y_{t+1}|I_t], \tag{2}$$

where

$$I_t = \{y_{t-i}, x_{t-i}, z_{t-i}, i = 0, \ldots, \infty\}.$$

$E[y_{t+1}|t]$ is equal to the mathematical expectation of y_{t+1} based on the information set I_t. The information set contains current and lagged values of y and x; it may also include current and past values of other variables in a vector z_t that, though not present in equation (1), may help predict future values of x and y. Note that this definition of the information set implies no loss of memory, as anything known at time t is still known at time $t + 1$.

Before characterizing solutions to (1) and (2), we give three economic interpretations of this model.

Three Examples

Arbitrage
The first interpretation of (1) is as an arbitrage equation, for example, between stocks and a riskless asset. Let p_t be the price of a stock, d_t be the dividend, and r be the rate of return on the riskless asset, assumed constant over time. Then, if risk neutral individuals arbitrage between stocks and the riskless asset, the expected rate of return on the stock, which is equal to the expected rate of capital gain plus the dividend–price ratio, must equal the riskless rate:

$$\frac{E[p_{t+1}|I_t] - p_t}{p_t} + \frac{d_t}{p_t} = r,$$

or by reorganizing,

$$p_t = aE[p_{t+1}|I_t] + ad_t,$$

where

$$a \equiv \frac{1}{1 + r} < 1.$$

This is of the same form as (1). The coefficient a in this case is equal to the one-period discount factor and is less than one so long as the interest rate is positive. The price today depends on the expected price tomorrow but by less than one for one.

The Cagan Model
The second interpretation of (1) is as the equilibrium condition in the Cagan model, presented at the end of the previous chapter and analyzed there under the assumption of adaptive expectations. The Cagan money demand function makes the demand for real balances an exponential function of the negative of the expected rate of inflation. In equilibrium money demand must be equal to the real money stock. In discrete time, equation (40) of the previous chapter becomes

$$\frac{M_t}{P_t} = \exp\left[-\alpha \left(\frac{E[P_{t+1}|I_t] - P_t}{P_t} \right) \right],$$

where we have set c in equation (40) of chapter 4 equal to unity and replaced the a in (40) by α.

Taking logarithms on both sides, denoting logarithms by lowercase letters, and using the approximation $E[p_{t+1}|I_t] - p_t = (E[P_{t+1}|I_t] - P_t)/P_t$, we get

$$m_t - p_t = -\alpha(E[p_{t+1}|I_t] - p_t).$$

Reorganizing gives

$$p_t = aE[p_{t+1}|I_t] + (1 - a)m_t,$$

where

$$a \equiv \frac{\alpha}{1 + \alpha}.$$

This is in the same form as (1). The price level depends on the price level expected for next period and on the current nominal money stock. Since in this model the demand for money is necessarily a decreasing function of the expected rate of inflation, α is necessarily positive so that a is between zero and one. The elasticity of the price level today with respect to its expected value tomorrow is less than one.

The OLG Model with Money

The third interpretation is as a loglinear approximation to the OLG model with money, also examined in the previous chapter. In that model money is demanded by the young who buy it so as to exchange it against goods when old. Extending equation (3) in the previous chapter to allow for uncertainty, we have

$$\frac{M_t}{P_t} = L\left(\frac{E[P_{t+1}|I_t] - P_t}{P_t}\right).$$

The left-hand side is the real supply of money, supplied inelastically by the old. The right-hand side is the demand for money by the young, which is a function of the expected rate of inflation (the negative of the rate of return on money). Taking a loglinear approximation, denoting logarithms by lowercase letters, using as before the approximation $E[p_{t+1}|I_t] - p_t = (E[P_{t+1}|I_t] - P_t)/P_t$, and ignoring an unimportant constant term, we get

$$m_t - p_t = -\alpha(E[p_{t+1}|I_t] - p_t).$$

Reorganizing implies that

$$p_t = aE[p_{t+1}|I_t] + (1 - a)m_t,$$

where

$$a \equiv \frac{\alpha}{1 + \alpha}.$$

This is similar to the equation derived for the Cagan model, with one important difference: $L(\cdot)$ is now a savings function and its elasticity with respect to the rate of return is, as we saw in chapter 3, ambiguous in sign. If the substitution effect dominates, the effect of an increase in expected inflation is to decrease saving, so that α is positive and a is between zero and one as in the Cagan model. However, if the income effect dominates, α can be negative. If α is not only negative but also less than minus one half, a is greater than one in absolute value. Thus, we cannot exclude a priori the possibility that, in this model, the elasticity of the price level with respect to its expected value is greater than one in absolute value.

In the first two examples a is less then one in absolute value. In the third, a may be greater than one in absolute value. We will see shortly that solutions are very different depending on whether a is greater or less than one in absolute value. We examine first the case $|a| < 1$ and then later the case $|a| > 1$.

Solutions When $|a| < 1$: Fundamentals and Bubbles

The "Fundamental" Solution
Various methods available to solve linear equations with rational expectations are described in appendix A. The most convenient method in the
simplest cases, such as (1), is repeated substitution.

All the methods of solution rely on the following statistical fact, known
as *the law of iterated expectations*:[3] let Ω be an information set and ω be a
subset of this information set. Then for any variable x,

$$E[E[x|\Omega]|\omega] = E[x|\omega].$$

Or, heuristically, if one has rational expectations and is asked how she would
revise her expectation were she given more information, the answer must
be that she is as likely to revise it up or down so that on average the revision
will be equal to zero. Applied to the information set I_t, this implies, in
particular, that[4]

$$E[E[x|I_{t+1}]|I_t] = E[x|I_t].$$

Today's expectation of next period's expectation of the variable x is the
same as today's expectation of x.

We now write equation (1) at time $t + 1$ and take expectations of both
sides conditional on information at time t:

$$E[y_{t+1}|I_t] = aE[E[y_{t+2}|I_{t+1}]|I_t] + cE[x_{t+1}|I_t].$$

Using the law of iterated expectations,

$$E[y_{t+1}|I_t] = aE[y_{t+2}|I_t] + cE[x_{t+1}|I_t].$$

Replacing in (1) gives

$$y_t = a^2 E[y_{t+2}|I_t] + acE[x_{t+1}|I_t] + cx_t.$$

Solving recursively up to time T,

$$y_t = c\sum_{i=0}^{T} a^i E[x_{t+i}|I_t] + a^{T+1}E[y_{t+T+1}|I_t].$$

For the first term to converge as T tends to infinity, the expectation of x
must not increase too fast. If the expectation of x grows at a rate no
faster than exponential, the condition for this sum to converge is that the
expectation of x grow at rate no larger than $(1/a) - 1$. In the case where (1)
has the interpretation of an arbitrage relation, this requires dividends not to
grow faster than the interest rate. In the case where (1) has the interpretation

of money market equilibrium condition, such as in the last two examples, this requires that the logarithm of money not increase faster than at the rate $(1/a) - 1$. Note that any constant exponential growth rate of the level of money, which implies that the logarithm increases linearly, will satisfy this condition. We shall therefore assume in what follows that the first sum converges. Then, if

$$\lim_{T \to \infty} a^{T+1} E[y_{t+T+1}|I_t] = 0, \tag{3}$$

the following is a solution:

$$y_t = c \sum_{i=0}^{\infty} a^i E[x_{t+i}|I_t]. \tag{4}$$

Note that equation (4) satisfies condition (3), so it is indeed a solution to equation (1). It gives y as the discounted sum of future expected x's. In our first example this implies that the price of a stock is the present discounted value of expected future dividends. In the other two examples it implies that the price level depends on the whole sequence of future expected money stocks, with decreasing weights.

If we are willing to specify an expected path for x, we can solve (4) explicitly for y. Equivalently, if we specify a process for x, we can solve for the process for y. We present two examples. The first is that of an increase in x from x_0 to x_T, announced at time t_0 to take place at time $T > t_0$. The path of y is then given by

$$y_t = (1 - a)^{-1} c x_0, \qquad\qquad\qquad \text{for } t < t_0,$$
$$\quad = (1 - a)^{-1} c x_0 + a^{T-t}(1 - a)^{-1} c(x_T - x_0), \qquad \text{for } t_0 \leqslant t < T,$$
$$\quad = (1 - a)^{-1} c x_T, \qquad\qquad\qquad \text{for } t \geqslant T.$$

Consider the interpretation of this equation as deriving from the Cagan model. The path of the nominal money stock, the price level, and real money balances are drawn in figure 5.1.[5] The equation shows that the announcement of a future increase in the money stock itself increases the price level today. Real money balances decrease, and the price level slowly increases to its new higher level over time. Inflation therefore takes place in advance of the increase in the money stock. This is because individuals look forward. They know that in the period before the money stock is increased, people will anticipate inflation and attempt to reduce their real money balances. In so doing, they will cause the price level to go up before the

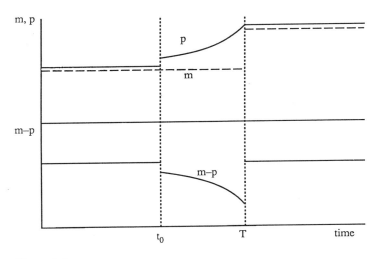

Figure 5.1
Effects of an anticipated increase in nominal money

money stock increases. Working this logic back to the present, current money holders attempt to reduce current real balances, therefore driving up the current price level.

Suppose that x instead follows the first-order stochastic process:

$$x_t - \bar{x} = \rho(x_{t-1} - \bar{x}) + e_t,$$

where e_t belongs to I_t and $E[e_t|I_{t-1}] = 0$. Then by using iterated expectations,

$$E[x_{t+i}|I_t] = \bar{x} + \rho^i(x_t - \bar{x}),$$

so that if ρ is less than $(1/a)$,

$$y_t - \bar{y} = \left(\frac{c}{1 - a\rho}\right)(x_t - \bar{x}),$$

with

$$\bar{y} = \left(\frac{c}{1 - a}\right)\bar{x}.$$

In the arbitrage example this implies that the price of the stock will be a function of current dividends only. It will, however, vary proportionally less than dividends as long as ρ, the degree of persistence, is less than unity. This is because the stock price is the present discounted value of future dividends, and dividends are expected to return to their normal value at rate $(1 - \rho)$. In the money examples, if ρ is less than one, this solution implies that real money balances will be high when the money stock is high and low when the money stock is low.

In the case of arbitrage it is natural to call the solution that gives the price as the present discounted value of dividends the "fundamental" solution. This terminology has now become standard, even in contexts other than arbitrage. But, as we now show, the fundamental solution is far from being the only solution to equation (1).

The Set of Solutions: Bubbles

Although equation (4) is a solution to (1), it is not the only solution. We derived it by imposing condition (3), that the expectation not explode too fast. When we relax this arbitrary condition, equation (1) admits many other solutions.

Let y_t^* denote the solution given by (4), and let us write any other solution as

$$y_t = y_t^* + b_t.$$

We now examine the restrictions that have to be imposed on b_t in order for y_t to be also a solution to (1).

If $y_t = y_t^* + b_t$, then $E[y_{t+1}|I_t] = E[y_{t+1}^*|t] + E[b_{t+1}|I_t]$. Replacing y_t and $E[y_{t+1}|I_t]$ in (1) implies that

$$y_t^* + b_t = aE[y_{t+1}^*|I_t] + aE[b_{t+1}|I_t] + cx_t.$$

By the definition of y_t^* in (4), this reduces to

$$b_t = aE[b_{t+1}|I_t], \tag{5}$$

or equivalently,

$$E[b_{t+1}|I_t] = a^{-1}b_t.$$

Thus, for any b_t that satisfies (5), $y_t = y_t^* + b_t$ is also a solution to (1). Note that since a is less than one, b_t explodes in expected value:

$$\lim_{i \to \infty} E[b_{t+i}|I_t] = a^{-i}b_t = \begin{cases} +\infty, & \text{if } b_t > 0, \\ -\infty, & \text{if } b_t < 0. \end{cases} \tag{6}$$

The following examples of b_t processes show that b_t embodies quite well the popular notion of speculative bubbles. For that reason, while y_t^* is called the fundamental solution, b_t is called a bubble.

An Ever-Expanding Bubble

In the first example b simply follows a time trend:

$$b_t = b_0 a^{-t}, \qquad \text{for arbitrary } b_0.$$

Consider the interpretation of equation (1) as an arbitrage equation and assume for simplicity that dividends, and thus p^*, are constant. If b_t is a time trend, and b_0 is positive, the price of the stock will increase exponentially, though the dividends are constant. What happens is that individuals are ready to pay a higher price for the stock than the price corresponding to the present value of the dividends because they anticipate the price will rise further, resulting in capital gains that precisely offset the low dividend price ratio. This anticipation of ever-increasing prices is self-fulfilling and satisfies the arbitrage condition.

A Bursting Bubble

The ever-expanding bubble has to go on forever, so that it will eventually become very large. In the next example the bubble has a probability of bursting each period. Consider the following process for b_t:

$$b_{t+1} = (aq)^{-1} b_t + e_{t+1}, \qquad \text{with probability } q,$$

$$= e_{t+1}, \qquad \text{with probability } 1 - q,$$

and

$$E[e_{t+1} | I_t] = 0.$$

This process satisfies (5). The bubble bursts with probability $1 - q$ each period and continues with probability q. If it bursts, it returns in expected value to zero. To compensate for the probability of a crash, the expected return, if it does not crash, is higher than in the previous example. The disturbance e allows bubbles to have additional noise and permits new bubbles to form after a bubble has crashed.

Note that e_t can be correlated with unexpected movements in any variable and still satisfy the condition that its conditional expectation be zero. Thus, if the market believes that unexpected sunspots affect the price, they will indeed do so.[6] The example can be further refined to allow q to be stochastic and for q to be affected by other variables. These modifications provide good accounts of the suggestive informal descriptions of speculative bubbles.[7]

Eliminating Bubbles

An issue that arises is whether, in deriving these solutions, we have not ignored conditions other than (1) that must also be satisfied by a solution.

For instance, in the case of the ever-expanding bubble perhaps the value of the bubble becomes too large to be consistent with the finiteness of the economy. There is, as we shall see in this chapter, no general conclusion that bubbles can always be ruled out, but often there are conditions that make it possible to rule out some of the solutions.[8]

Consider, for example, the case where equation (1) is derived from arbitrage and y gives the price of an asset. If the asset can be freely disposed of, then its price cannot be negative. This in turn implies that there cannot be negative bubbles. If b was negative, then, by (6), the expectation of b in the far future would go to minus infinity. Thus the expectation of the price would also go to minus infinity, which is impossible.[9] Thus b cannot be negative.

However, no such simple argument allows us to eliminate positive bubbles. But other conditions may be present that rule out positive bubbles. If y is the price of a physical asset and if a substitute is available in infinitely elastic supply, possibly at a very high price (think of oil and solar energy), then there cannot be positive bubbles. If b is positive, then the expected price goes to infinity and consequently exceeds the price at which the substitute is available, which is impossible. Thus with free disposal and the existence of a perfect substitute in infinitely elastic supply at some price, there cannot be any bubbles at all.[10]

If y is the price of a share, the question arises of whether firms will issue more shares when there is a bubble on share prices. If issuing more shares does not affect the bubble, for example, does not make the bubble crash, it is in the interests of the initial shareholders to issue more shares and invest the proceeds. However, it seems unlikely that the markets would absorb an ever-increasing supply of an asset at an unchanging price. This decreases the likelihood of a bubble on an easily reproducible asset.[11]

Thus one would generally expect bubbles when fundamentals are difficult to ascertain, such as in the gold, art, or foreign exchange markets, rather than on assets whose fundamentals are clearly defined, such as blue chip stocks.

If y is subject to a terminal condition at some future time, then since y must be equal to this value at the terminal time, b must then be equal to zero. Working backward in time, b must be equal to zero always, and there cannot be bubbles. There therefore cannot be bubbles on bonds, except on perpetuities (or "consols").

We have listed here only partial equilibrium arguments that can be used to eliminate the possibility of bubbles. In sections 5.2 and 5.3 we will examine whether and when general equilibrium considerations also lead to the elimination of bubbles.

Solutions When $|a| > 1$: Indeterminacies

We have until now considered the case where $|a|$ was less than one and concluded that there was an infinity of solutions. If, however, we were ready to impose a nonexplosion condition, we would be left with only one solution—the fundamental solution. We turn now to the case $|a| > 1$, which, as we showed earlier, could be consistent with equation (1) interpreted as the equilibrium condition of an OLG model with money when the income effect is sufficiently strong.

This radically changes the nature of the results. Now the fundamental solution is no longer well defined. More precisely, the sum in (4) is unlikely to converge in general. And there is an infinity of bubbles, which are now stable rather than exploding. For example, suppose x is identically equal to one for all t. Then the set of solutions is given by

$$y_t = (1 - a)^{-1}c + b_t,$$

where

$$b_t = a^{-1}b_{t-1} + e_t, \qquad E[e_t|I_{t-1}] = 0. \tag{7}$$

This implies, in particular, that if we make e identically equal to zero, then y will converge to $(1 - a)^{-1}c$ for any initial value of y_0. Without a more detailed specification, it is difficult to think of reasons why the economy will (or economists analyzing the model should) choose one solution over another. Various criteria have been offered to choose among solutions, but none of them is very convincing.[12] The multiplicity of solutions is definitely more perplexing in this case. We will return to this, as well as to related issues, in section 5.4.

Extensions

Higher-Dimensional Systems
The behavior of y in (1) depends on whether $|a|$ is less or greater than one. The more likely case is that in which $|a|$ is less than one. We now examine how this condition extends to higher-dimensional systems and whether it is likely to be satisfied.

Returning to equation (1), ignoring uncertainty and expectations, the condition $|a| < 1$ can be stated as the condition that the difference equation that gives y_{t+1} as a function of y_t should be *unstable* or have a root $1/a$ that is strictly greater than one in absolute value. In this case, for a given sequence of x, there is a unique value of y^* for which y does not explode.

This condition generalizes if the economy is characterized by a difference equation system.[13] Suppose there are n predetermined, state, variables at time t, and m variables (sometimes called "jumping" variables, or by analogy with optimal control problems, "costate" variables) that are not predetermined. Then the system must have exactly m roots outside the unit circle in order to have a unique nonexploding solution. For example, if we consider a model of money and capital in which there is one predetermined variable, capital, and one jumping variable, the price level, the system must have one root between -1 and $+1$ and one root outside that range. Equivalently, it must have the saddle point property.[14]

All the dynamic systems examined in the previous chapters had the saddle point property. When we assumed that the economy chose the saddle point path, we were in effect choosing the fundamental solution. On any other path the value of the variables could have been expressed as the sum of the fundamental solution and a bubble growing at the rate determined by the positive root of the system.

The fact that all the systems we have looked at in this chapter were saddle point stable and thus satisfied the extension of the condition $|a| < 1$ is an indication that this condition is often likely to be satisfied. We will return to this point in the conclusion of this chapter.

Nonlinear Dynamics
We end this section with a caveat. Thus far we have limited ourselves to linear systems. Indeed, most of what we know is limited to such systems, at least under uncertainty. The following example, from Azariadis (1981), shows that even if a nonlinear system satisfies locally the condition $|a| < 1$ around a steady state, it may have more than one nonexploding solution.

The expectations difference equation is

$$y_t^2 = \left(\frac{1}{2}\right) E[y_{t+1}|y_t], \qquad y_t \in [0, 1].$$

The value $y = 1/2$ is a solution to the equation. If we linearize the system around $y = 1/2$, then $dy_t/dE[y_{t+1}|y_t] = 1/2$ so that, if the system were linear, $y = 1/2$ would be the only nonexploding solution. Note, however, that the following is also a solution:

$$y_{t+1} = y_t^2, \qquad \text{with probability } q_t = \frac{1 - 4y_t^2}{1 - 2y_t^2},$$

$$= \frac{1}{2}, \qquad \text{with probability } 1 - q_t.$$

By construction, q_t is always between zero and one. So the system has at least two nonexploding solutions. The first is $y = 1/2$. In the second, y follows stochastic cycles, although there is no intrinsic uncertainty. We will return to issues related to nonlinearity in section 5.4.

5.2 Bubbles on Assets in General Equilibrium

Whether there can be bubbles on real assets in general equilibrium depends on whether individuals have finite or infinite horizons and, if they have finite horizons, on whether the economy is dynamically efficient. After showing the conditions under which bubbles on real assets can exist, we draw parallels between results derived here and various results obtained in chapters 2 and 3. We end the section by discussing the empirical evidence on the presence or absence of bubbles.

The Case of Infinite Horizons

Bubbles are not unlike Ponzi games; assets are bought only on the anticipation that they can be resold at a higher price to somebody else who will buy them for the same reason. It is therefore not surprising that bubbles cannot arise when there is a finite number of individuals who have infinite horizons.

The proof of this very general proposition was given by Tirole (1982). The logic is as follows. Suppose that there is a finite number of infinitely lived individuals. The asset yields dividends or services every period. If it yields services, they can be rented out to the person who values them most that period. This implies that the fundamental value, p_t^*, is the same for all individuals at all times. Finally, the services or dividends do not depend on the price. This excludes money, whose services depend on the price level.

Suppose that, under these assumptions, there is a negative bubble, with $p_t < p_t^*$. Then all individuals will want to buy and keep the asset forever. Purchasing the asset costs p_t, holding the asset forever, and renting it out every period yields p_t^* in present value. There would therefore be excess demand for the asset, and $p_t < p_t^*$ cannot be an equilibrium.

Suppose, alternatively, that there is a positive bubble so that $p_t > p_t^*$. If short selling is allowed, an argument symmetrical to the preceding one implies excess supply and rules out positive bubbles. But it is possible to exclude positive bubbles even without short selling. If p exceeds p^*, an individual who buys the asset must do so with the anticipation of eventually realizing his capital gain by selling the asset in the future. Let t_i be the date by which individual i intends to resell, and let T be the maximum of t_i over i. By T all individuals plan to have resold the asset. But this implies that nobody plans to be holding the asset after T, and this cannot be an equilibrium.

This argument allows us to rule out bubbles on real assets in economies in which individuals have infinite horizons. It tells us that if bubbles can exist in a general equilibrium, it must be because new players come into the game over time. We therefore turn to overlapping generation models in which a new generation is born every period.

Finite Horizons

The following argument is sometimes given to show that there cannot be bubbles in general equilibrium. A bubble must grow at the rate of interest. This suggests that at some stage the value of the bubble will be too large relative to the economy, and this appears to rule out bubbles. But the argument is not quite right because the economy itself is growing. If the interest rate is less than the growth rate (if the economy is dynamically inefficient), the economy will grow faster than the bubble, so it is not clear that the above argument does go through. In what follows we formalize and extend this intuitive counterargument. In doing so, we closely follow Tirole (1985) and Weil (1987), both of whom use the Diamond model presented in chapter 3.

Recall that in the Diamond model agents live for two periods, working, consuming, and saving in the form of capital in the first period and consuming their savings in the second. Capital yields a rate of return r equal to its marginal product. In the absence of bubbles, the dynamics of capital accumulation are given by equation (4') in chapter 3:

$$k_{t+1} = (1 + n)^{-1}\{s[w(k_t), r(k_{t+1})]\}.$$

Or by expressing savings directly as a function of k_t and k_{t+1}, we get

$$k_{t+1} = (1 + n)^{-1}s(k_t, k_{t+1}), \qquad s_1 > 0, s_2 \gtrless 0. \tag{8}$$

The capital stock at time $t + 1$ is equal to the savings of the young at time t, which depend on their labor income w and on the rate of return on savings r. Since w_t depends on k_t, and r_{t+1} on k_{t+1}, savings can be rewritten directly as a function of k_t and k_{t+1}. We assume that the condition that guarantees that the equilibrium in the Diamond economy is stable and nonoscillating, namely, that $s_1/(1 + n - s_2) \in [0, 1]$ is satisfied.

We now introduce bubbles, starting with bubbles on intrinsically useless assets and then allowing for bubbles on intrinsically useful assets, assets that yield services or dividends every period. In each case we ask under what conditions these bubbles may be valued and, if they are, what their effects are on real activity.

Bubbles on Intrinsically Useless Assets
Suppose now that M intrinsically useless pieces of paper are introduced into the economy. We examine the conditions under which these pieces of paper may have positive value and characterize their effects on the allocation of resources. We start by describing the equilibrium conditions on the assumption that they are indeed valued.

Individuals can now save by holding either capital or bubbles (the intrinsically useless assets). If they hold capital at time t, they earn a gross rate of return of $1 + f'(k_{t+1})$. If bubbles sell at price p_t in terms of goods, the gross rate of return on bubbles is equal to p_{t+1}/p_t. Arbitrage between the two assets implies that

$$1 + f'(k_{t+1}) = \frac{p_{t+1}}{p_t}. \tag{9}$$

Let B_t be the aggregate value of the bubble so that $B_t = Mp_t$. From (9),

$$B_{t+1} = B_t[1 + f'(k_{t+1})],$$

or in per capita terms

$$b_{t+1} = \frac{b_t[1 + f'(k_{t+1})]}{1 + n}. \tag{10}$$

The bubble will grow in per capita terms if $f'(k)$ exceeds n.

The goods market equilibrium condition in the presence of bubbles is given by

$$K_{t+1} = (1 + n)^t s(k_t, k_{t+1}) - B_t.$$

Since part of saving goes to buy the bubble asset, capital accumulation is reduced. In per capita terms

$$k_{t+1} = (1 + n)^{-1}[s(k_t, k_{t+1}) - b_t]. \tag{11}$$

Equations (10) and (11) give the dynamics of the system in k and b. There are two further constraints on k and b: $k_t \geqslant 0$ and, if bubbles can be freely disposed of, $b_t \geqslant 0$.

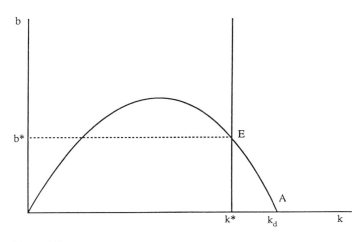

Figure 5.2
Steady state of the Diamond model with bubbles

In figure 5.2, we show steady state combinations of b and k that satisfy (10), (11), and the nonnegativity constraints. If b is constant, and different from zero, (10) implies that $f'(k) = n$. If b is equal to zero, any point on the horizontal axis satisfies (10). If k is constant in (11), b obeys

$$b = s(k, k) - (1 + n)k. \tag{12}$$

The value of the bubble is equal to net savings. Under standard assumptions the net steady state savings, $s(k, k) - (1 + n)k$, is first an increasing and then a decreasing function of k. Point A in figure 5.2 is the point where $b = 0$ and is the Diamond steady state, the steady state that the economy would reach in the absence of bubbles. We denote the associated level of capital by k^d. From figure 5.2 it is clear that whether there exists a steady state with positively valued bubble depends on whether the line $f'(k) = n$ crosses (12) in the positive orthant; equivalently, such a steady state exists if $f'(k^d)$ is less than n.

If the Diamond economy is dynamically efficient, if $f'(k^d)$ exceeds n, there cannot be a steady state with a positively valued bubble. The intuition for this result was given at the beginning of this section. In the absence of a bubble the interest rate already exceeds the growth rate. If there was a bubble, it would decrease the part of savings that went into capital, further increasing the interest rate. The bubble would grow at the rate of interest, faster than the economy. But this is impossible because the bubble would eventually become larger than the income of the young.

If the Diamond economy is dynamically inefficient, there is a steady state with a positively valued bubble at point E. The interest rate is then equal to n, so the bubble removes the inefficiency and the economy is at the golden rule. The bubble grows at the rate of population growth, at the same rate as the economy. There is still, however, another steady state, the Diamond equilibrium at point A in which the bubble is not valued and the economy remains inefficient.

Dynamics

To gain understanding of when the economy will go to one equilibrium rather than the other, we turn to the dynamics of the system. Rewrite (11) as

$$k_{t+1} - k_t = g(k_t, b_t).$$ (13)

In figure 5.3, we draw the locus where $k_{t+1} - k_t$ equals zero as KK; it is obviously the same as OA in figure 5.2.

Replacing k_{t+1} from (13) in (10) gives

$$b_{t+1} - b_t = \frac{b_t \{ f'[k_t + g(k_t, b_t)] - n \}}{1 + n}.$$ (14)

We draw the locus where $b_{t+1} - b_t = 0$, or equivalently $f'[k_t + g(k_t, b_t)] = n$ as BB. Given the assumption that saving is an increasing function of income, BB is upward sloping and crosses KK at the steady state point E.[15]

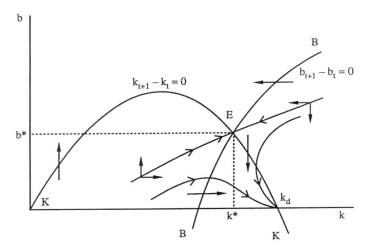

Figure 5.3
Dynamics of the Diamond model with bubbles

The dynamics of k and b are as follows. If, starting on a point on $g(k_t, b_t) = 0$, we increase b_t, we decrease savings in the form of capital, and capital decreases. The capital stock is therefore decreasing at all points above KK. Starting from a point on BB, if we decrease k, we increase the marginal product of capital and the rate at which the value of the bubble is required to increase. The bubble per capita is therefore increasing at all points to the left of BB and decreasing at all points to the right. The equilibrium with a positively valued bubble in steady state is saddle point stable. The Diamond 'bubbleless' equilibrium is stable.[16]

In figure 5.4 we assume that the economy has initial capital k_0 and look at possible trajectories. Consider first a point above the stable arm, say, C. At that point the bubble is large and increasing. As it increases, capital accumulation decreases, until eventually the capital stock starts decreasing. All along, the interest rate increases, making the value of the bubble grow even faster. At some point the bubble becomes so large that capital decumulation exceeds the existing capital stock. Of course this is impossible, and this rules out any bubble above the stable arm. Bubbles cannot be that large.

Consider now a point below the stable arm, say, D. At D the bubble is such that though it reduces capital accumulation, it leaves the steady state interest rate below the rate of population growth. Thus the bubble increases at rate r, but the bubble per capita eventually decreases: the bubble becomes

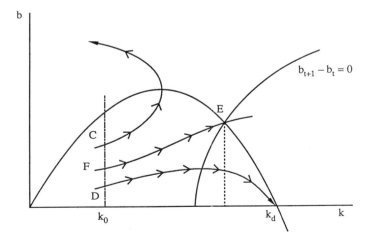

Figure 5.4
Alternative bubble paths in the Diamond model

small compared to the economy. Asymptotically, the bubble per capita becomes so small that the economy converges to the Diamond equilibrium. Although there is a bubble, it makes no difference to the steady state. More generally, bubbles smaller than that on the saddle point path (for a given value of the capital stock) can exist in that economy, but they make no difference to the steady state equilibrium of the economy. Of course they do affect the dynamic approach to the steady state and therefore are not neutral with respect to the allocation of resources.

The knife-edge case where the bubble is just such that the economy is on the saddle point path, though unlikely, is interesting. In this case the bubble is just such as to make the interest rate asymptotically equal to n. Thus not only does the bubble per capita remain large compared to the economy, but the bubble solves the dynamic inefficiency problem by driving the steady state interest rate to the value n!

Up to this point we have shown that bubbles on intrinsically useless assets cannot exist if the economy without bubbles is already dynamically efficient. If the economy is dynamically inefficient, bubbles can exist as long as they are not too large. Except in a knife edge case, they do not affect the steady state, though they do affect the dynamic approach to the steady state. We next extend the analysis to the more interesting case where the bubble is on an intrinsically useful asset.

Bubbles on Intrinsically Useful Assets
Consider another asset, in addition to capital, say, a tree that yields one unit of the good every period. Let P_t^* denote its fundamental value, P_t its price, and B_t the bubble on the asset so that $P_t = P_t^* + B_t$.

Arbitrage requires that P_t^* and B_t satisfy

$$P_t^* = [1 + f'(k_{t+1})]^{-1} P_{t+1}^* + 1$$

and

$$B_t = [1 + f'(k_{t+1})]^{-1} B_{t+1}.$$

Integrating the first equation forward and using the transversality condition gives P^* as the present discounted value of a stream of one good every period. The second equation says that the bubble component must grow at the rate of interest. This implies that the ratio of P_t^* to B_t must eventually go to zero or, equivalently, that the price is asymptotically equal to the bubble component. Asymptotically therefore, whether the bubble is on an intrinsically useful or intrinsically useless asset does not in this case matter, and the previous analysis applies. If the economy is dynamically inefficient, there can be bubbles on intrinsically useful assets, such as the tree of our example, a painting, or a share, a title to the stream of marginal products on a unit of capital. Note, however, that bubbles cannot exist on assets that pay dividends that grow at the same rate as the economy. The existence of such assets implies in the first place that the economy cannot be dynamically inefficient and thus rules out bubbles.

Stochastic Bubbles

Our analysis has focused only on deterministic bubbles, which grow forever at the rate of interest. Weil (1987) has shown that simple stochastic bubbles, namely the bursting bubbles described in the previous section (with the noise term e identically equal to zero), can also exist in a general equilibrium. However, the condition for their existence is more stringent in that the economy must, in the absence of bubbles, be sufficiently dynamically inefficient. There are not yet results on the feasibility of more general stochastic bubbles in general equilibrium.

Bubbles, Money, and Dynamic Efficiency

There are several places in this section where déjà vu sets in. There are indeed parallels between this analysis of bubbles in a general equilibrium and some results derived in the previous chapters.

A necessary condition for bubbles to exist is that the economy be dynamically inefficient. When this is the case, not only can bubbles exist, but they can be beneficial by temporarily or permanently reducing capital accumulation. If the bubble is of the right size, the economy may even become asymptotically efficient.

The analogy between these results and those obtained for money in OLG models in which money does not yield transaction services is obvious. In chapter 4 we saw that money would be valued in such a model only if the economy were dynamically inefficient. If this were the case, money could also remove the dynamic inefficiency. We could reinterpret the analysis of this chapter as an analysis of the role of money in an OLG model that also includes capital.

The analogy with the role of government debt in the Diamond model in chapter 3 is also clear. We saw there that when the economy was dynamically inefficient, government debt could remove the inefficiency. We also saw that when the interest rate was less than or equal to the rate of growth, new debt could be issued to pay interest payments while leaving the debt income ratio constant. Equivalently, the government could lead the economy to the golden rule just by rolling over its debt. The results of this section suggest that we can reinterpret government debt in that case as a public bubble.

One should not see too much in these analogies and conclude that money, bubbles, and government debt are always one and the same. Bubbles are likely to be small and have additional distortionary effects by changing the relative prices of assets: for example, a bubble on housing may lead to too large a stock of housing compared to other forms of capital. We have argued that OLG models in which money does not yield transaction services give an inaccurate description of the role of money.

What all these analyses have in common is the fact that if people save less, or hold a larger proportion of their portfolio in the form of money, bonds, or bubbles, there will be less capital accumulation. If the economy is dynamically inefficient, reducing capital accumulation is likely to be a good thing. As we indicated in chapter 3, tackling the question of whether the actual economy is dynamically inefficient requires a more explicit treatment of uncertainty than we have given until now, and this will have to wait until the next chapter.

Looking for Bubbles: Volatility Tests

Well before the theoretical analysis presented in this section was formalized, tests for the excess volatility of asset prices were developed and implemented. These tests were motivated in part by convincing accounts of historical bubbles, but more from the suspicion generated by observation of asset markets that fluctuations in asset prices are too large to be explained purely by changing views of fundamentals. We review here recent attempts to look at the evidence on the excess volatility of asset prices. We conclude by discussing the relation between tests of excess volatility and the presence of bubbles.

Returning to the example of arbitrage between stocks and a riskless asset, we have seen that in the absence of bubbles, and given a constant real interest rate, the price would be given by

$$p_t = E\left(\sum_{i=0}^{\infty} a^{i+1} d_{t+i} | I_t \right),$$ (15)

where

$$a = \frac{1}{1+r}.$$

One seemingly obvious way of proceeding would be to compute the right-hand side and compare it to the price. But this is impossible, as expectations are inherently unobservable. Pursuing the same logic, one could specify the information set and construct estimates of the expectations, and thus of the right-hand side, and test whether it is significantly different from the actual price. But this requires specifying the information set, and it is unrealistic to assume that we can specify fully the information used by market participants to price assets in speculative markets. What is needed is therefore a test that does not require a full specification of the information set.

Such tests were first proposed by Shiller (1981) and LeRoy and Porter (1981). Subsequent tests have extended the approach to take care of statistical problems to which the early tests were subject, but they rely on the same general and simple logic. The argument is that if prices have a bubble component in addition to the fundamentals given by (15), they are likely to move even when fundamentals do not change much, and thus are likely to move too much. The tests are therefore tests of excess volatility in asset prices.

The Shiller Test

We start with the Shiller (1981) test. Let p_t' be the *ex post* price of an asset, that is, the price that an asset would have had at time t if future dividends had been known with perfect foresight at time t. The ex post price p_t' is therefore given by

$$p_t' = \sum_{i=0}^{\infty} a^{i+1} d_{t+i},$$ (16)

where

$$a = \frac{1}{1+r}.$$

From the definition of p_t', it follows that

$$p_t' = p_t + u_t,$$

where

$$E(u_t|p_t) = 0.$$

This is the key rational expectations insight, the basis of the Shiller test. The difference between the ex post and the actual price should be uncorrelated with the current price.

By assuming that the variances of p'_t and p_t exist (an assumption to which we return below), and taking variances in the previous equation, we obtain

$$V(p') = V(p) + V(u),$$

which implies that

$$V(p') \geqslant V(p). \tag{17}$$

Equation (17) is the inequality initially tested by Shiller. It says that the variance of the ex post price should exceed the variance of the actual price. The intuition is that since p is a forecast of p', it should move less than p'.

To compute variances in (17), Shiller proceeded as follows: First, to compute p' which is given by an infinite sum in (16), he noted that (16) could be rewritten as

$$p'_t = \sum_{i=0}^{T-t-1} a^{i+1} d_{t+i} + a^{T-t} p'_T,$$

where T was the last observation in the sample. By approximating p'_T by the sample mean of p_t, he constructed, using the above relation, an estimate of p'_t for $t < T$. He then constructed deviations from a deterministic trend for both p and p' and computed sample variances for those deviations from trend. He found, using many data sets, for example, the Standard and Poor stock price index extending back to 1871, that the variance inequality was dramatically violated, namely, that the estimated ratio $V(p)/V(p')$ was often in excess of 5. This finding triggered both strong reactions and subsequent research. Much of the research involves complex statistical issues, and we will only review it informally.

Distributional Assumptions
The first line of attack on the Shiller results has questioned the distributional assumptions of the test and the distributional properties of his estimates (Flavin 1983; Marsh and Merton 1986). Marsh and Merton have questioned the assumption of stationarity of dividends and prices. Without stationarity, the unconditional variances of p and p' do not exist. Marsh and Merton have shown that the sample variances may in this case violate the inequality even if (15) is true.

To see this, we return to equation (15). Although equation (15) is true and gives a relation between the price and expected dividends, the firm can also choose the timing of payment for those dividends and thus decide to make dividends a function of the price as long as this dividend policy satisfies (15). Suppose that the firm decides to pay dividends each year equal to the annuity value of p_t, rp_t. Returning to the arbitrage equation and using the above assumption for dividends yields

$$p_t = ad_t + aE(p_{t+1}|I_t) = arp_t + aE(p_{t+1}|I_t),$$

which in turn implies that

$$E(p_{t+1}|I_t) = p_t.$$

Given this dividend policy, the price follows a random walk, and so does the dividend. Thus the assumption of stationarity underlying the use of sample variances in the Shiller test is no longer satisfied. Marsh and Merton then show that if one computes sample variances for p and p', one finds that $V(p) > V(p')$, although (15) holds.[17] The reason is a simple one: under this dividend policy the ex post price satisfies

$$p'_t = r \sum_{i=0}^{\infty} a^{i+1} p_{t+i}, \tag{16'}$$

where

$$a = \frac{1}{1+r}.$$

The ex post price is a weighted average of the current and future values of the actual price. This implies that its sample variance will always be less than the sample variance of the actual price. This is certainly a serious criticism of the initial tests. However, a new generation of tests has been developed that does not require stationarity of p_t and also suggests that there is too much volatility (Blanchard and Watson 1982; West 1988; Mankiw, Romer, and Shapiro 1985; Campbell and Shiller 1987). The rejections are, however, not as strong as in the initial Shiller tests.

Auxiliary Assumptions
The second line of attack points out that the hypothesis being tested is a joint hypothesis and that it is not clear exactly what is rejected and thus what the rejection points to.

The hypothesis has three main components. The first is that of arbitrage by risk neutral individuals who can borrow at a constant real rate of interest. The second is that these individuals have rational expectations. The third is that there are no rational bubbles.

Variance tests cannot distinguish among the three sources of rejection. We know that the first component of the joint hypothesis cannot be literally true: short rates are not constant, and investors are not risk neutral. The

second component may also fail; individuals may not have rational expectations. For instance, fads may play an important role in pricing.[18] The joint
hypothesis may well fail therefore because of a failure of rational arbitrage
and not because of the presence of rational bubbles.

There appears to be a way out because the joint hypothesis of arbitrage
and rational expectations can be tested independently of the third, the
absence of bubbles. This is indeed what the "efficient market" tests have
done for many years.[19] Consider again the arbitrage equation:

$$\frac{E(p_{t+1}|I_t) - p_t}{p_t} + \frac{d_t}{p_t} = r,$$

which implies in turn that

$$p_{t+1} - (1 + r)p_t + d_t = u_{t+1}, \tag{18}$$

where

$$E(u_{t+1}|I_t) = 0.$$

Equation (18) can be tested by regressing the left-hand side of (18) on
any element in the information set. If variables in I_t consistently help predict
the actual excess return as defined on the left-hand side of (18), the arbitrage
relation is rejected. Unfortunately, the power of this test is quite low.
Although there is substantial evidence that (18) is rejected, it is not clear
whether this can explain the rejection implied by volatility tests.

Bubbles and Excess Volatility
To summarize the main arguments of this section, partial and general
equilibrium arguments often but not always permit us to rule out bubbles.
When they do, they often rely on an extreme form of rationality and are
not, for this reason, altogether convincing. Often bubbles are ruled out
because they imply, with a very small probability and very far in the future,
some violation of rationality, such as nonnegativity of prices or the bubble
becoming larger than the economy. It is conceivable that the probability
may be so small, or the future so distant, that it is simply ignored by market
participants.

One may therefore think of the existence of bubbles as an empirical
question to be settled by the data. Tests for excess volatility strongly
suggest that asset prices are affected by more than fundamentals. This is
consistent with the presence of rational bubbles. It is also consistent,
however, with the presence of fads or other failures of arbitrage or rational
expectations. On this point the evidence is not very strong.

5.3 Price Level Bubbles, Hyperinflations, and Hyperdeflations

We now turn to the question of whether there can be bubbles in the price of money when money yields transaction services. The two examples given in section 5.1 cannot give a full answer to that question. The first, the Cagan model, is not derived explicitly from maximizing behavior. In the second, the OLG model with money, we used a loglinear approximation, thus preventing ourselves from studying behavior far away from the equilibrium, which is where bubbles may take the economy. Nor can we use the general result presented at the beginning of the second section to rule out bubbles on real assets when individuals are infinitely long lived: money differs from other assets in that its services depend on its price. We therefore study the question anew, using for this purpose a simplified version of the Sidrauski model with infinitely long-lived individuals presented in the previous chapter. We will show that we cannot always rule out self-generating hyperinflations or hyperdeflations in that model.[20]

Bubbles in the Sidrauski Model

We simplify the Sidrauski model by making money, which enters the utility function, the only asset.[21] This simplification is made for convenience; as we will demonstrate below, it is not essential.

The economy is populated by a given number of infinitely lived families. There is no population growth. Money is the only asset, and there is an exogenous flow of perishable output at constant rate y per capita. Each household solves the following maximization problem:

$$\max V_s = \int_s^\infty u(c_t, m_t) \exp[-\theta(t - s)] \, dt, \tag{19}$$

subject to

$$c + \frac{dm}{dt} = y - \pi m + x, \tag{20}$$

where π is the actual and (because of the assumption of perfect foresight) also the expected rate of inflation, and x is the real value of transfer payments to the family.

Since money is the only asset, and money holdings cannot be negative, we also have $m_t \geq 0$, for all t. There is no need in this case for an additional no-Ponzi-game condition.

Let λ_t be the costate variable associated with (20) at time t. The first-order conditions for maximization are

$$u_c(c, m) = \lambda, \tag{21}$$

$$\frac{d\lambda/dt}{\lambda} = \theta + \pi - \frac{u_m(c, m)}{\lambda}, \tag{22}$$

$$\lim_{t \to \infty} \lambda_t \exp(-\theta t) m_t = 0. \tag{23}$$

Note that these are optimizing conditions for the individual family. Each family believes that it can save by consuming less than income, though the economy as a whole clearly cannot. Equilibrium with identical families implies that $c_t = y$ for all families. The transversality condition rules out overaccumulation of wealth: if the limit in (23) were positive, a family would be accumulating too much wealth for too long and could make itself better off by reducing money holdings and increasing consumption.

We assume to begin with that the instantaneous utility function is separable in consumption and real money balances. In this case, given that c in equilibrium must be equal to y which is constant, (21) implies that λ, the marginal utility of consumption, is constant. By an appropriate choice of units, we can set λ to equal unity. Equation (22) then implies

$$u_m(m) = \theta + \pi. \tag{24}$$

This equation can be interpreted as a demand for money equation. Note also that if σ is the rate of growth of nominal money,

$$\frac{dm/dt}{m} = \sigma - \pi. \tag{25}$$

It follows from (24) and (25) that

$$\frac{dm}{dt} = (\theta + \sigma)m - u_m(m)m. \tag{26}$$

We now have a differential equation as a necessary condition for optimality and, in equilibrium, as an equation describing the behavior of real money balances. Figure 5.5 plots dm/dt as a function of m. There is a unique steady state with $m > 0$ shown as m^* at the point where $u_m(m) = \theta + \sigma$. Further, since $u_{mm}(m) < 0$, dm/dt is positive to the right of m^* and negative to the left. Thus the equilibrium associated with m^* is unstable: if the economy does not start at m^*, it does not converge to m^*. This is, as we have now seen many times, a familiar and desirable property of such an equilibrium,

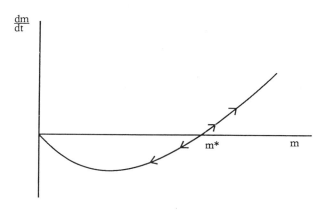

Figure 5.5
Dynamics of real money balances

for if we require that the economy converge to m^*, this property uniquely determines the price level.

The question we now examine is whether the model allows us to exclude all the divergent paths. We start by considering paths where real money increases through time. Suppose first that $m_0 > m^*$ so that the real money stock is to the right of m^* and keeps growing. Is this consistent with the transversality condition (23)? Given that λ is constant, the transversality condition requires m to grow less rapidly than at rate θ. This is the familiar condition that with infinitely long-lived individuals, the interest rate not exceed the subjective discount rate. If

$$\lim_{m \to \infty} u_m(m) = 0 \qquad \text{and} \qquad \sigma > 0,$$

then

$$\lim_{m \to \infty} \frac{(dm/dt)}{m} = \theta + \sigma > \theta$$

so that the transversality condition is violated. Faced with such interest rates, families would want to consume increasing amounts over time, and this cannot be an equilibrium. Therefore, under those assumptions, there cannot be explosive real money paths, or, equivalently, hyperdeflation.[22]

We examine next paths on which real money balances decrease, paths that start to the left of m^*. There are two possibilities which we illustrate in figures 5.6 and 5.7. In figure 5.6,

$$\lim_{m \to 0} m u_m(m) > 0,$$

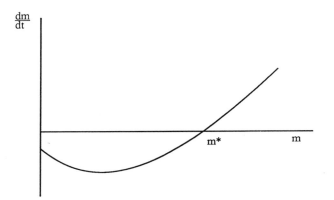

Figure 5.6

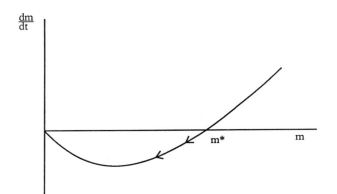

Figure 5.7

whereas in figure 5.7,

$$\lim_{m \to 0} m u_m(m) = 0. \tag{27}$$

In figure 5.7, dm/dt is equal to zero when m is equal to zero, and accordingly, there is an equilibrium without money at the origin. Paths starting to the left of m^* can be ruled out as competitive equilibria in figure 5.6 [equation (26) must be violated when m reaches zero and dm/dt is strictly negative] but cannot in figure 5.7. The question therefore becomes a question about the essentiality of money. For hyperinflation to be ruled out, money has to be essential in the sense that the marginal utility of money must increase faster than the rate at which real money goes to zero.[23] This is obviously a stronger condition than

$$\lim_{m \to 0} u_m(m) = \infty.$$

If condition (27) holds, then the economy may develop a perfect foresight hyperinflation path that is fully consistent with individual optimization. On such paths everyone is worse off than they would have been on the path starting, and ending, at m^*.

Generalizations and Discussion

We conclude by discussing briefly four issues relating to the analysis of hyperinflation in the Sidrauski model. The first two have to do with the generality of the above results and concern the roles of the assumption of nonseparability and of the absence of other assets than money. The next is whether the government can prevent such hyperinflations. The last is the relation of the hyperinflations studied here to actual hyperinflations.

The separability assumption is of no great significance: hyperinflations can arise even when u_{cm} is different from zero. The same is true of the absence of other assets. Obstfeld and Rogoff (1983) show that the existence of a nonproduced asset (land) does not remove the possibility of hyperinflation. Nor, if the utility function is separable, does the presence of capital, for the real economy proceeds in this case independently of the behavior of money.

Does the government have any way of avoiding hyperinflations? One institutional provision is "backing" of the currency. If the government provides a promise that one unit of currency can be exchanged at positive real value for goods (if goods are perishable, for a stream of goods), there cannot be hyperinflation. The reason is that under hyperinflation the price of money would eventually be low enough that individuals would exchange their money against goods with the government. From then on, the price of money could not decrease further. But if there cannot be hyperinflation from that time on, there cannot be hyperinflation before that time either.

Another possibility is for the government to promise to follow a feedback rule, the anticipation of which prevents it from being used. In the context of the simple model we use above, the following rule for money growth would prevent hyperinflation:

$$\sigma = u_m(m) - \frac{a}{m}.$$

This implies that

$$\frac{dm}{dt} = \theta m - a.$$

Under this policy the government announces that it will reduce the growth rate of nominal money if real balances ever become very low and that it will do so at a very rapid rate as real balances approach zero. This rule in effect turns figure 5.7 into figure 5.6: the economy will not have hyperinflation, and the policy need never be used. What is interesting here is not the specific form of the rule but the fact that the government can prevent the emergence of hyperinflation by announcing a stabilizing feedback rule.

Finally, we consider the relationship between the hyperinflation of this section and the real world. In this section we have studied the possibility of hyperinflation, given constant money growth. The main conclusion is that we cannot rule out such hyperinflation even in models with infinitely long-lived, utility-maximizing agents. Actual hyperinflations certainly do not have constant money growth, but rather accelerating money growth. The relevant issue is then whether hyperinflations can be entirely explained by actual and anticipated accelerating money growth or whether there is a component of the hyperinflation that is, like the paths we have analyzed here, self-fulfilling.

This question was initially studied by Cagan, who assumed adaptive expectations. As we saw at the end of chapter 4, the answer in that context depended on the elasticity of the demand for money and the speed at which expectations were revised. Cagan found that the stability condition was not violated in the hyperinflations he studied.

The question has been reexamined by Flood and Garber (1980) who assume rational expectations in the context of the German hyperinflation. They look for a deterministic bubble and find little econometric evidence in support of the presence of such a bubble. Finding a bubble in a hyperinflation is, however, a difficult task because of the difficulty of ascertaining the value of fundamentals during such a period. In the absence of bubbles and under rational expectations, the price level should depend on expectations of future money growth, which is usually changing in complex ways during a hyperinflation, especially during the last stages, when a price bubble is most likely to arise.

5.4 Multiple Equilibria, Sunspots, and Cycles

We have in the last two sections focused on economies that have a saddle point equilibrium (or, in the case of systems with only one dimension, a strictly unstable equilibrium) and thus a unique convergent path. We then asked whether we could rule out the divergent—bubble—paths. We now consider the possibility that the economy does not satisfy the appropriate saddle point condition and has instead many convergent paths. We examine both the conditions under which this may happen and the consequences. In addition to examining the case of multiple convergent paths, we examine when there may be sunspot equilibria and deterministic cycles. As we shall see, the conditions under which these various phenomena occur are related but not identical.

The first examples of models that did not satisfy the saddle point property appeared in the research on growth models with many capital goods by Hahn (1968) and Burmeister et al. (1973). Later examples were given by Black (1974) and Taylor (1977), among others. But these examples did not include optimization by individuals, and it was not clear whether such properties would disappear if one started from explicit utility and value maximization. The analysis of the dynamics of overlapping generations models has made clear that utility maximization does not rule out such cases, as we will show in this section.

We will analyze in detail the dynamics of the OLG model with money.[24] Although we have argued earlier that it is not an appropriate model in which to study the role of money, it is the simplest dynamic general equilibrium model available and thus the most convenient one with which to study these issues. Most of the results we derive will also hold in more attractive but more complex models and in models without money. We will indicate how results extend as we go along.

The Offer Curve

Throughout this section we use a simple extension of the Samuelson OLG model with money.[25] Time is discrete, and individuals live for two periods. The same number of individuals, normalized to one, is born every period. An individual born at time t is young at time t, and old at time $t + 1$, and has utility $u(c_{1t}, c_{2t+1})$.

Each individual receives an endowment of e_1 when young and e_2 when old.[26] The endowment is perishable, and the only way to save is to hold money. Let P_t be the price level at time t. The maximization problem of an individual born at time t is

$$\max u(c_{1t}, c_{2t+1})$$

subject to

$$c_{1t} + \frac{M_t}{P_t} = e_1$$

and

$$c_{2t+1} = e_2 + \frac{M_t}{P_{t+1}}, \qquad M_t \geq 0.$$

The solution is characterized by the first-order condition

$$u_1(c_{1t}, c_{2t+1}) = \left(\frac{P_t}{P_{t+1}}\right) u_2(c_{1t}, c_{2t+1}).$$

To study the dynamics, we will make extensive use of the offer curve, following Cass, Okuno, and Zilcha (1979). Figure 5.8 traces out the offer curve, which is the set of first-period and second-period consumptions chosen as the rate of return (P_t/P_{t+1}) increases. For a sufficiently low rate of return, individuals will want just to consume their endowment and neither save nor dissave. As the rate of return increases, the slope of the budget line going through the endowment point increases, and we trace out the offer curve from the tangencies between the budget line and indifference curves.

It will be convenient to work with the offer curve in a different space. If we define

$$m_t \equiv \frac{M_t}{P_t} = e_1 - c_{1t}$$

and

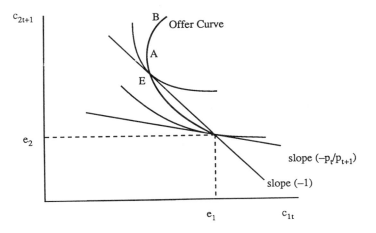

Figure 5.8
The offer curve in the (c_1, c_2) space

$$z_t \equiv \frac{M_t}{P_{t+1}} = c_{2t+1} - e_2,$$

which are, respectively, the excess supply of goods when young and the excess demand for goods when old, we can redraw the offer curve in (m_t, z_t) space. This is done in figure 5.9. Points E, A, and B in figure 5.9 correspond to Points E, A, and B in figure 5.8.

What are the properties of this offer curve? Obviously, m_t, which is savings of the young at time t, cannot exceed e_1, the endowment of the young. As $z_t/m_t = (M_t/P_{t+1})/(M_t/P_t) = P_t/P_{t+1}$, the slope of the line from the origin to any point on the offer curve is equal to P_t/P_{t+1}. In particular, the slope of the tangent at the origin gives the rate of return at which individuals are willing to consume exactly their endowment in each period. Since the budget line cannot be tangent to two indifference curves in figure 5.8, a line through the origin in figure 5.9 cannot cross the offer curve twice.

The property that will turn out to be very important later is the degree to which the offer curve can be backward bending. It is clear that the offer curve can be backward bending because an increase in the rate of return (P_t/P_{t+1}) has both income and substitution effects and thus may either increase or decrease savings, m_t. (It always increases z_t if consumption is a normal good in both periods.) To get insights into what determines the slope of the offer curve as well as to pave the way for later analysis, we assume that utility is separable in consumption in the two periods and of the form

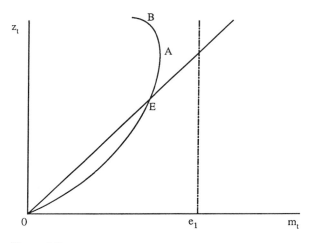

Figure 5.9
The offer curve in the (m, z) space

$$u(c_{1t}, c_{2t+1}) = u(c_{1t}) + v(c_{2t+1}).$$

By defining the gross rate of return $R_t = P_t/P_{t+1}$, and given the definitions of m_t and z_t, we can express the maximization problem as

$$\max u(e_1 - m_t) + v(m_t R_t + e_2).$$

The first-order condition implicitly defines m_t as a function of R_t:

$$-u'(e_1 - m_t) + R_t v'(m_t R_t + e_2) = 0.$$

Differentiating this first-order condition with respect to m_t and R_t gives

$$dm_t = \left\{ \frac{-[R_t m_t v''(\cdot) + v'(\cdot)]}{\Delta} \right\} dR_t, \tag{28}$$

where

$$\Delta \equiv [u''(\cdot) + R_t^2 v''(\cdot)] < 0,$$

and using $z_t = m_t R_t$,

$$dz_t = \left\{ \frac{[m_t u''(\cdot) - v'(\cdot)R_t]}{\Delta} \right\} dR_t. \tag{29}$$

Whether the offer curve is backward bending depends on the sign of dm_t/dR_t, as $dz_t/dR_t \geq 0$. Equation (28) shows this sign to be ambiguous and to depend on the curvature of $v(\cdot)$. To go further, we can introduce the coefficient of relative risk aversion associated with $v(\cdot)$, which is given by $\gamma(c_{2t+1}) \equiv [-c_{2t+1} v''(\cdot)/v'(\cdot)]$. The numerator of (28) becomes

$$\left[\left(\frac{z_t}{c_{2t+1}}\right)\gamma - 1\right]v'(\cdot).$$

Since z_t/c_{2t+1} is less than or equal to one, a necessary condition for the offer curve to be backward bending is that γ be greater than one. Thus if, for example, second-period utility is logarithmic, the offer curve is never backward bending. If the second-period endowment is relatively large so that z_t/c_{2t+1} is small, substantial risk aversion is needed to generate a backward-bending offer curve.

In an equilibrium the dissavings of the old—the supply of money—must in each period be equal to the savings of the young—the demand for money. Thus $z_t = m_{t+1}$. Replacing z_t by m_{t+1}, the offer curve gives us a dynamic relation between m_{t+1} and m_t. We now explore those dynamics.

Existence of a Monetary Steady State

The steady states of the economy will be at the intersection of the offer curve, which now gives m_{t+1} as a function of m_t and of the 45-degree line on which $m_{t+1} = m_t$.[27] In figure 5.9, for example, there are two steady states, one nonmonetary at the origin, and one where real money is positive at point E.

Whether there is a monetary equilibrium depends therefore on the slope of the offer curve at the origin. If the slope exceeds 45 degrees, the offer curve lies above the 45-degree line, and there is no monetary equilibrium. The slope of the offer curve at the origin gives the rate of return consistent with individuals just consuming their endowment in each period. If this slope exceeds one, this implies that at the rate of return consistent with a monetary steady state, namely, one, individuals would be dissaving in the first period. But this is inconsistent with the existence of a monetary equilibrium, since they cannot have negative holdings of money. This is the same result as in the OLG models with money in chapter 4. There exists a monetary equilibrium only if, at the rate of return consistent with a monetary steady state, there is positive savings in the form of money.

This condition on the offer curve depends in a simple way on utility and endowments. Under the assumption that utility is separable, it requires that

$$u'(e_1) < v'(e_2).$$

If consumption can be transferred from one period to the other at a rate of one for one, the marginal utility of consumption when old must exceed the marginal utility of consumption when young. Only in that case will individuals be willing to save.

We now assume that a monetary steady state exists and consider the dynamics of the economy. We do so first in the case where the monetary steady state is unstable and then in the case where it is stable.

Dynamics with an Unstable Monetary Equilibrium

Consider first the case where the offer curve is either upward sloping or backward bending, but with its slope greater than one in absolute value when it crosses the diagonal. That is, we assume that $|dm_t/dm_{t+1}| < 1$ at the monetary equilibrium—the same condition as $|a| < 1$ in section 5.1.

Figure 5.10 presents the dynamics for an upward-sloping offer curve. Starting from any initial level of real balances, m_0, for example, the offer curve implies a level m_1 next period, m_2 the period after, and so on. The monetary equilibrium in figure 5.10 is unstable. Paths starting to the right of m^* increase until eventually m becomes larger than e_1, which is impossible. This rules out such paths. Paths starting to the left have steadily decreasing real money balances, and all converge asymptotically to the nonmonetary steady state. The rate of inflation increases and tends asymptotically to the inverse of the slope of the offer curve at the origin minus one. The paths do not violate any physical or individual optimality conditions and cannot be excluded.

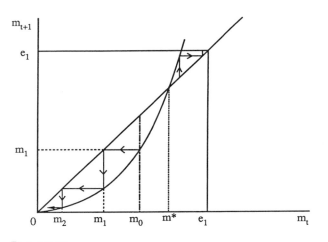

Figure 5.10
Dynamics with an unstable monetary equilibrium

The results are therefore fairly familiar. There is a unique monetary equilibrium. The model does not imply a nonexplosion condition, but if such a condition is nevertheless imposed, the price level is uniquely determined.

Dynamics with a Stable Monetary Equilibrium

The more interesting case in this section occurs when the offer curve is not only backward bending but sufficiently so that it crosses the 45-degree line with a slope less than one in absolute value. Then $|dm_t/dm_{t+1}| > 1$ and the monetary equilibrium is locally stable. This is drawn in figure 5.11.

In this case the economy eventually converges to the monetary steady state, starting from any price level in some region around m^*. There is no condition in this model that allows us to exclude any of these paths. Furthermore even imposing an additional nonexplosion restriction is of no help here, for there is no exploding price level. This is worrisome, the more so when one realizes that there are many solutions other than these deterministic converging paths, as we will show below.

Before becoming too worried, we should ask how likely such a case is to emerge. Even apart from its implications, it is rather strange. It requires income effects to be sufficiently strong that savings is a strongly decreasing function of the rate of return and a strongly increasing function of the rate of inflation. Or, in terms of the price level, it requires that the price level today depend on the expected price level tomorrow, not only negatively but also more than one for one. It is clear, however, that utility maximization

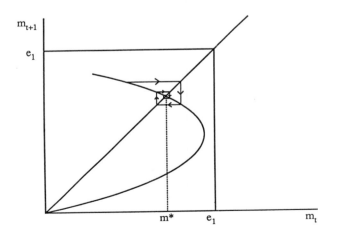

Figure 5.11
Dynamics with a stable monetary equilibrium

per se is consistent with any slope for the offer curve when it crosses the 45-degree line. To see the restrictions on the utility function needed to obtain such a backward-bending offer curve, we return to the separable utility function.

With a separable utility function the slope of the offer curve evaluated at the steady state, at which $R = 1$, is, from equations (28) and (29),

$$\frac{dm_{t+1}}{dm_t} = \frac{v'(\cdot) - mu''(\cdot)}{v'(\cdot) + mv''(\cdot)}. \tag{30}$$

Suppose first that the utility function is the same in both periods, up to discounting: $v(\cdot) = (1 + \theta)^{-1} u(\cdot)$. Then the slope is

$$\frac{dm_{t+1}}{dm_t} = \frac{[(1 + \theta)^{-1} u'/mu''(\cdot)] - 1}{[(1 + \theta)^{-1} u'/mu''] + (1 + \theta)^{-1}}.$$

The most backward-bending offer curve is obtained if $u''(\cdot) = -\infty$, if utility is Leontief. In this case the slope of the offer curve at the intersection with the 45-degree line is equal to $-(1 + \theta)$. Thus, as long as individuals discount the future ($\theta > 0$), we cannot obtain the condition needed for the steady state equilibrium to be stable. What is needed is a preference for the future, for θ to be negative. This in effect reinforces the income effect.

Another way to make the offer curve very flat at the monetary steady state, followed by Grandmont (1983), is to allow $u(\cdot)$ and $v(\cdot)$ to have different curvature. Equation (30) makes it clear that if the coefficient of risk aversion is higher in the second period than in the first, the condition for stability of the equilibrium is more likely to be met. This will also reinforce income effects. [Draw, for example, the offer curve for $u(c_1, c_2) = c_1 + \min(c_2, c^*_2)$.]

Stable equilibria such as this one can be obtained even in models without money. Geanakopolos and Polemarchakis (1983) have shown that a version of the Diamond model extended to allow for endogenous labor supply could also have a multiplicity of convergent solutions. The condition in that model is that income effects be strong enough to generate a sharply backward-bending supply of labor.

Some general results on the conditions for multiplicity in overlapping generations models (Kehoe and Levine 1983, 1985, in particular) are available. They confirm that multiplicity cannot be ruled out by standard assumptions on utility and technology and that it requires strong income effects. Kehoe and Levine show that in exchange models with n goods and money, the dimension of indeterminacy can be equal to $n - 1$: *all* relative prices may be indeterminate. Although the indeterminacy goes away when all agents are infinitely long lived, Woodford (1984) shows that the presence of some infinitely long-lived agents does not remove the indeterminacy, as long as they are not too large compared to the economy.

Cycles and Chaos

Under the condition that the monetary steady state is stable, not only do we have a multiplicity of convergent solutions, we also have cyclical solutions. To see this, we return to the configuration of figure 5.11. In figure 5.12 we draw the offer curve from figure 5.11 and its mirror image around the 45-degree line.[28] The two curves intersect at the steady state on the diagonal. Given that the slope of the offer curve at the steady state is less than one in absolute value, they also intersect at two other points, A and B.

This implies that the economy may have a two-period cycle. Suppose that real balances are equal to m_a in period 1. Corresponding to m_a in period 1, the offer curve shows that m_b is the equilibrium level of real balances in period 2. But then starting at m_b, the economy comes back to m_a in the next period. It follows that the economy has a cycle of period 2.

The first issue that arises is whether there are other cycles. This has been studied by Grandmont (1985). Note that because the offer curve is backward bending, there is not always a unique value of m_{t+1} given m_t. There is, however, a unique value of m_t given m_{t+1}. For that reason, although our interest is obviously in the dynamics of the system running forward in

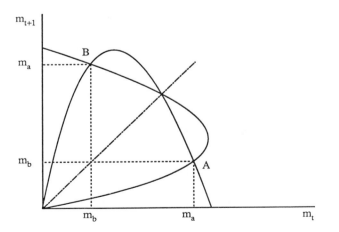

Figure 5.12
Cycle of period 2

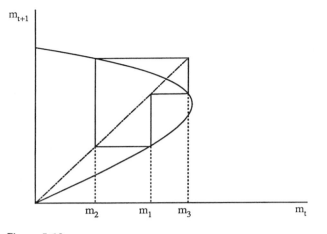

Figure 5.13
Cycle of period 3

time, we must first study the properties of the backward dynamic relation $m_t = \varphi(m_{t+1})$, which is defined implicitly by the offer curve. Grandmont first studies whether this function $\varphi(\cdot)$ can generate cycles of periodicity higher than 2 and shows that it can. If the degree of relative curvature of second-period utility is sufficiently high, there is a cycle of period 3. A cycle of period 3 is drawn in figure 5.13. The existence of a cycle of period 3 is important because it implies the existence of cycles of all periodicities![29] It may also have aperiodic (or chaotic) trajectories; such trajectories, though deterministic, will not exhibit any periodicities and appear similar to stochastic processes. Cycles running backward in time clearly imply cycles running forward in time. Thus the model may generate a large number of cycles, or even chaotic behavior.[30]

Grandmont then examines the conditions under which these various cycles are stable. Again, the study of stability must be done by looking at the properties of the backward relation, by running time backward. A cycle is said to be stable in backward dynamics if, when the economy does not start with exactly the correct initial conditions, it nevertheless settles into that cycle. Under additional restrictions on the offer curve, there will be at most one such stable cycle. Running time forward, this implies that there is at most one unstable cycle. This may be considered good news: if, by analogy with the cases studied in the previous sections in which we chose the unstable equilibrium, we choose the unstable cycle, we get rid of the indeterminacy. Reasons for choosing the unstable cycle are less compelling here than the reason for choosing the unstable (or saddle point) equilibrium in the previous sections. However, Grandmont shows this unstable cycle to be the one to which the economy will converge under simple learning rules (we will return to the role of learning in the next section). If there is no such unstable cycle, then the multiplicity remains.

The other issue is that of the relation between multiplicity and cycles. In our example, multiplicity is a sufficient but not a necessary condition for the existence of cycles. We easily confirm this by drawing an offer curve that has slope greater than one in absolute value when it crosses the 45-degree line but still intersects its mirror image. There appears generally to be no simple relation between the two phenomena.[31]

Sunspots

The condition that the monetary equilibrium is stable also implies the possibility of *sunspot equilibria*, that is, equilibria that depend on extraneous uncertainty only because agents believe it to be so. We have already seen sunspot equilibria in the previous sections. But these equilibria implied explosive, bubble, paths. Sunspots here are consistent with nonexplosive paths.

Denote by m^* the steady state in figure 5.11. To find a sunspot equilibrium, we must find m_a and m_b and associated transition probabilities such that if individuals are expected utility maximizers, m_a and m_b are equilibria. Denote by q_a the probability that the economy will be in state a next period given that it is in state a today. Similarly, let q_b denote the probability that the economy will be in state b next period given that it is now in state b. The probabilities q_a and q_b can come from anywhere, sunspots or brainstorms.

We again assume that utility is separable, of the form $u(c_{1t}) + Ev(c_{2t+1})$ where we now have to use expected utility in period 2 because of the presence of uncertainty. Let P_a and P_b denote the price level in states a and b. If the economy is in state a, the first-order condition for maximization is

$$\frac{u'(e_1 - M/P_a)}{P_a} = q_a \left[\frac{v'(e_2 + M/P_a)}{P_a} \right] + (1 - q_a) \left[\frac{v'(e_2 + M/P_b)}{P_b} \right].$$

By multiplying through by M and solving for q_a, we get

$$\frac{q_a}{1 - q_a} = \frac{m_a u'(e_1 - m_a) - m_b v'(e_2 + m_b)}{m_a v'(e_2 + m_a) - m_a u'(e_1 - m_a)}. \tag{31}$$

Similarly, for q_b,

$$\frac{q_b}{1 - q_b} = \frac{m_b u'(e_1 - m_b) - m_a v'(e_2 + m_a)}{m_b v'(e_2 + m_b) - m_b u'(e_1 - m_b)}. \tag{32}$$

For any given m_a and m_b, the conditions for there to be a stochastic sunspot equilibrium is that the solutions for q_a and q_b in (31) and (32) lie between zero and one, or equivalently that the right-hand side of each of equations (31) and (32) be positive. We now show that these conditions are satisfied if the equilibrium is stable.[32]

Let m^* be the value of money at the steady state equilibrium, and let $m_a = m^* - a\varepsilon$ and $m_b = m^* + b\varepsilon$. Taking limits as ε goes to zero in (31) and using L'Hospital's rule as both numerator and denominator go to zero gives

$$\frac{q_a}{1 - q_a} = \frac{au' - amu'' + bv' + bmv''}{av' + mav'' - au' + amu''},$$

where all derivatives are evaluated at the steady state equilibrium. From (30) the slope of the offer curve, when it crosses the steady state locus, is equal to $S = (v' - mu'')/(v' + mv'')$. Using the fact that because of utility maximization, $u' = v'$ and that at the equilibrium $R = 1$, we can rewrite S as $(u' - mu'')/(v' + mv'')$. This in turn implies that

$$\frac{q_a}{1 - q_a} = \frac{(b/a) + S}{1 - S}. \tag{33}$$

Similarly, we obtain

$$\frac{q_b}{1 - q_b} = \frac{(a/b) + S}{1 - S}. \tag{34}$$

One can find a, b positive such that (33) and (34) are both positive if and only if S is between -1 and $+1$, that is, if and only if the steady state equilibrium is stable. There is therefore in this context a close relation between multiplicity and sunspots. Although we have limited ourselves to binary sunspot equilibria, we can show by the same argument that there are sunspot equilibria that can take any of n values, $n \geqslant 2$.

The conditions for multiplicity and sunspots are, however, not the same. Although the stability of the equilibrium is a necessary and sufficient condition for the existence of sunspots close to the equilibrium, it is not a necessary condition for the existence of sunspots farther away from the equilibrium. There appears to be a closer connection between cycles and sunspots. Azariadis and Guesnerie (1984) show that, in a class of OLG models, binary sunspots exist if and only if there exist cycles of period 2.

5.5 Learning

In studying the dynamics of the economy under rational expectations, we have assumed so far that individuals know the model. A weaker assumption is that individuals, although they do not know the model, know enough to form optimal forecasts of the variables they need to predict. This weaker assumption is sufficient to obtain many of the results of this chapter. However, it becomes problematic when there is a change in policy that changes the time series properties of endogenous variables.

In practice, though, individuals know neither the structural model in which they operate nor the reduced form needed to make optimal forecasts. Most of the time they are learning about both structure and reduced form while they are forming forecasts. It is therefore important to study the dynamics of the economy under learning. The interaction of learning and dynamics is interesting in itself. It is also interesting in the context of this chapter, since it may reduce the multiplicity of equilibria: it may be that if individuals use optimal or at least plausible learning mechanisms, the economy tends to converge to a particular one of the many possible steady states.

We present here a simple model of learning.[33] Although it just scratches the surface of the issue, it does show some of the insights that are obtained by modeling learning explicitly. We start from a simplified version of equation (1):

$$y_t = k + aE[y_{t+1}|t] + v_t, \tag{35}$$

where v_t is white noise. We assume to begin with that $|a| < 1$, and later we briefly discuss the implications of the alternative assumption, $|a| > 1$.

Suppose first that individuals know the model, namely, equation (35), and have rational expectations. We also assume that the information set at time t, on which expectations of y_{t+1} are based, includes past but not current values of y_t or v_t.[34] If we limit ourselves to the class of solutions that expresses y_t as a linear function of past y's and current and past v's, it is easy to show that the class of such linear functions is given by

$$y_t = \xi_0 + \xi_1 y_{t-1} + v_t + \xi_2 v_{t-1}, \tag{36}$$

where either of the two following sets of conditions hold:

(A) $\xi_0 = (1 - a)^{-1}k,$ $\xi_1 = \xi_2 = 0;$

(B) $\xi_0 = -a^{-1}k,$ $\xi_1 = a^{-1},$ ξ_2 free.

The solution that satisfies (A) is, using the terminology introduced in section 5.1, the fundamental solution. The solutions that satisfy (B) can be rewritten as the fundamental solution plus a bubble. Note, however, that (B) does not include all bubbles. For example, it does not allow for other variables than past y and current and past v to affect current y.

Assume next that individuals no longer know the model. They form expectations based on the belief that y_t is a linear function of past y's and current and past v's. At time t they believe that y_t follows the stochastic process:

$$y_t = \delta_n + \alpha_n y_{t-1} + \beta_n v_t + \psi_n v_{t-1}. \tag{37}$$

The reason for indexing the coefficients by n will be clear below. Allowing for a longer distributed lag on y and v would complicate the derivation but not change the final result.

If individuals believe (37), their expectation of y_{t+1} based on information available at time t will be given by

$$E[y_{t+1}|t] = \delta_n(1 + \alpha_n) + \alpha_n^2 y_{t-1} + \alpha_n \psi_n v_{t-1}. \tag{38}$$

If we substitute in (35), this in turn implies that y_t follows:

$$y_t = [a\delta_n(1 + \alpha_n) + k] + (a\alpha_n^2)y_{t-1} + v_t + (a\alpha_n \psi_n)v_{t-1}. \tag{39}$$

The expectations held by individuals affect the process followed by y_t. But unless we are already at a rational expectation equilibrium, (39) will not be the same as (37). It is likely that individuals will realize over time that (37) does not produce optimal forecasts and revise it accordingly. One simple way to formalize this revision process is to assume that individuals act using (37) long enough, say, T, periods to generate enough observations on (39) and learn (approximately) the parameters in (39). They then believe (39) for another T periods, generate a new reduced form, and so on. This is the assumption made, among others, by DeCanio (1979) and Evans (1985) and the assumption that we will make here. A more attractive but less tractable assumption is that agents reestimate the model every period by least squares and form optimal forecasts given these estimates; this is the approach followed by Friedman (1979) in a partial equilibrium context and by Bray (1982) and Marcet and Sargent (1986, 1987). Yet another approach is to assume that agents use Bayesian learning (Taylor 1975; Townsend 1978; Bray and Savin 1986).

Given our assumption, and given (37) and (39), the parameters α_n, β_n, ψ_n, and δ_n, will follow

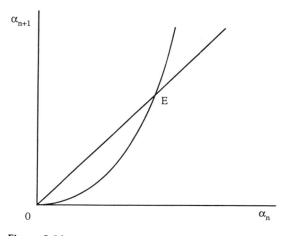

Figure 5.14
Dynamics of α_n

$$\alpha_{n+1} = a\alpha_n^2, \tag{40}$$

$$\beta_{n+1} = 1,$$

$$\psi_{n+1} = a\alpha_n\psi_n,$$

$$\delta_{n+1} = a(1 + \alpha_n)\delta_n + k.$$

Consider first the equation that gives the dynamics of α_n. These dynamics are plotted in figure 5.14. There are two equilibria, E and O. E is unstable whereas O is stable. As long as individuals start with α_0 less than $\sqrt{1/a}$, α_n will converge to zero. If they start with α_0 greater than $\sqrt{1/a}$, α_n will increase forever.

The equation for β_n shows that it converges to one in one step. If α_n converges to zero, so does ψ_n. Finally, as long as $|a| < 1$, and if α_n converges to zero, δ_n converges to $(1 - a)^{-1}k$.

We therefore have a few interesting results. The first is that $|a| < 1$ is necessary and sufficient for the economy to converge to rational expectations, as long as initial beliefs about α_0 are not too large. The second is that the economy converges to the *fundamental* solution, and not to a bubble solution. This gives some justification for choosing the fundamental solution.[35]

If $|a| > 1$, equation (36) still gives the set of rational expectation solutions that express y as a function of current v and past v and y. But the last equation in (40) shows that the economy never converges to any of these solutions. Not only do we have a multiplicity of stable solutions, but learning does not lead the economy to converge to any of these solutions.

There are no general results about learning as of yet. But the preceding results are representative of those obtained in the literature. Where the condition $|a| < 1$ or its extension holds, the fundamental solution appears to be the only stable one under various alternative learning schemes. We know very little about learning in nonlinear models. One result, obtained by Grandmont, is that in the nonlinear model presented in the previous section, the unstable cycle, if it exists, is also stable under a simple learning process. (For a futher discussion of learning when there are sunspot equilibria, see Woodford 1987.)

5.6 Conclusions

What is the economic significance of the multiplicity of solutions studied in this chapter? We have in effect identified two very different types of multiplicity, and the answer is quite different depending on which one prevails.

The first is the multiplicity studied in sections 5.2 and 5.3; it arises when the equilibrium is unstable, or saddle point stable in systems of higher dimension. Here there is a unique nonexplosive solution, the fundamental solution, and a multiplicity of divergent solutions, the bubbles. These divergent solutions can sometimes be ruled out by partial or general equilibrium arguments, although the arguments often rely on a degree of rationality and foresight that is unlikely to be present in practice. Our brief study of the implications of learning also suggests that the fundamental solution is more likely to be reached than the bubbles.

In this context it appears reasonable to adopt the following research strategy. Unless the focus is specifically on bubbles, assume that the economy chooses the saddle point path, which is the fundamental solution. This is what we have done in chapters 3 and 4 and will do in the rest of the book. In parallel, research can proceed on bubbles, aimed both at finding evidence of their presence and at understanding their implications.

The second type of multiplicity, the multiplicity of stable equilibria studied in section 5.4, is more unsettling. It has led to different reactions. One has been nihilistic, arguing that there is simply little that can be said by economists about economic dynamics under such conditions.

Other approaches have been more positive. One has been to explore the implications of chaotic trajectories, which may appear together with the multiplicity of stable equilibria—although, as we have seen, the conditions for each to arise are not identical. It has been argued that chaos offers an alternative to the now prevalent formalization of business cycles as resulting from the dynamic effects of stochastic shocks through propagation mechanisms (a view we will develop at length in the rest of the book). It has been argued that chaos, which can be generated by simple deterministic systems, offers a less ad hoc explanation of fluctuations than one based on unexplained shocks. Some work has examined empirically whether the behavior of economic variables is better explained by chaotic or linear stochastic processes (see Brock 1986), but without clear conclusions as of yet.

Another reaction, associated with Grandmont, has been to concentrate on cycles and reduce the dimension of indeterminacy. As we noted earlier, Grandmont has shown that under some additional assumptions there may exist a unique unstable cycle that is stable under simple learning rules. Grandmont argues that such deterministic cycles provide an alternative to the linear stochastic process view of cycles. If he is correct, policy can have very drastic effects on the dynamics of the economy by changing the specific form of the nonlinearity.

We are not at this stage convinced by either of these last two approaches. Although the nonlinearity needed to obtain multiple stable equilibria, sunspots, cycles, or chaos is consistent with optimizing behavior, the conditions for such equilibria still appear unlikely. In the models considered in this chapter, for example, they require implausibly large income effects.[36] Thus, for the time being, though we find the phenomena analyzed in this chapter both interesting and disturbing, we are willing to proceed on the working assumption that the conditions needed to generate stable multiplicities of equilibria are not met in practice.

Appendix: A Tool Kit of Solutions to Linear Expectational Difference Equations

In section 5.1 we solved a difference equation with rational expectations by using the method of repeated substitution. That method is convenient in simple cases but rapidly becomes unwieldy. In this appendix we present the two methods that are most often used to solve such difference equations analytically. We make no attempt at generality or rigor. Surveys by Taylor (1985) on methods of solution in small models and by Blanchard (1985) on analytical and numerical methods of solution in large models give both a more exhaustive presentation and further references.

We will solve the following equation:

$$p_t = a_0 E[p_{t+1}|t] + a_1 p_{t-1} + a_2 E[p_t|t-1] + a_3 m_t + e_t. \tag{A1}$$

We use the notation $E[p_{t+i}|t - j]$ to denote the rational expectation of p_{t+i} based on information available at time $t - j$. The information set is assumed to include at least current and lagged values of m, e, and p. The variable p is endogenous, the variable m is exogenous, and e is a stochastic disturbance. For the moment we do not need to specify the processes followed by either m or e.

Such an equation, in which a variable depends both on itself lagged and on past expectations of current values and current expectations of future values of itself, is fairly typical. One interpretation is that p is the logarithm of the price level and m the logarithm of the nominal money stock. In this case one may want to impose the additional homogeneity restriction $a_0 + a_1 + a_2 + a_3 = 1$.

It is convenient to define

$$x_t \equiv a_3 m_t + e_t \tag{A2}$$

so that

$$p_t = a_0 E[p_{t+1}|t] + a_1 p_{t-1} + a_2 E[p_t|t - 1] + x_t. \tag{A1'}$$

The Method of Undetermined Coefficients

The method of undetermined coefficients consists of guessing the form of the solution and then solving for the coefficients. The guess may come from experience or from attempts at repeated substitution. An educated guess here is that p will depend on itself lagged once, and on current and once-lagged expectations of once-lagged current and future values of x:

$$p_t = \lambda p_{t-1} + \sum_{i=0}^{\infty} c_i E[x_{t+i}|t] + \sum_{i=0}^{\infty} d_i E[x_{t+i-1}|t - 1]. \tag{A3}$$

The method is to find values of λ, c_i, and d_i such that (A3) is a solution to (A1'). The first step is to derive $E[p_t|t - 1]$ and $E[p_{t+1}|t]$ implied by (A3). By taking expectations of both sides of (A3), both at time t and $t + 1$, and using the law of iterated expectations, we get

$$E[p_t|t - 1] = \lambda p_{t-1} + \sum_{i=0}^{\infty} c_i E[x_{t+i}|t - 1] + \sum_{i=0}^{\infty} d_i E[x_{t+i-1}|t - 1], \tag{A4}$$

$$E[p_{t+1}|t] = \lambda p_t + \sum_{i=0}^{\infty} c_i E[x_{t+i+1}|t] + \sum_{i=0}^{\infty} d_i E[x_{t+i}|t]. \tag{A5}$$

Now, by substituting (A4) and (A5) into (A1'), we get

$$p_t = a_0 \left(\lambda p_t + \sum_{i=0}^{\infty} c_i E[x_{t+i+1}|t] + \sum_{i=0}^{\infty} d_i E[x_{t+i}|t] \right) + a_1 p_{t-1}$$

$$+ a_2 \left(\lambda p_{t-1} + \sum_{i=0}^{\infty} c_i E[x_{t+i}|t - 1] + \sum_{i=0}^{\infty} d_i E[x_{t+i-1}|t - 1] \right) + x_t, \tag{A6}$$

or

$$p_t = (1 - a_0\lambda)^{-1} \left\{ a_0 \left(\sum_{i=0}^{\infty} c_i E[x_{t+i+1}|t] + \sum_{i=0}^{\infty} d_i E[x_{t+i}|t] \right) + (a_1 + a_2\lambda)p_{t-1} \right.$$

$$\left. + a_2 \left(\sum_{i=0}^{\infty} c_i E[x_{t+i}|t-1] + \sum_{i=0}^{\infty} d_i E[x_{t+i-1}|t-1] \right) + x_t \right\}. \qquad (A6')$$

For (A3) to be a solution to (A1), (A6') and (A3) must be identical. Thus we equate the coefficients for each variable. Starting with the coefficient on p_{t-1},

$$\lambda = (1 - a_0\lambda)^{-1}(a_1 + a_2\lambda)$$

or, equivalently,

$$a_0\lambda^2 + (a_2 - 1)\lambda + a_1 = 0. \qquad (A7)$$

There will generally be two solutions for λ in (A7). If the model we are dealing with satisfies the extension of the condition $|a| < 1$ in section 5.1, one of the roots will be smaller than one in absolute value and the other larger than one. It will have the saddle point property.[37] By choosing the smaller of the roots as the coefficient on p_{t-1}, we are in effect choosing the stable, nonexploding solution.

Suppose for example that the equation gives the price level as a function of money and that a_0, a_1, a_2, and a_3 are all positive and sum to one, so that $a_0 + a_1 + a_2 < 1$. Then from the definition

$$\Psi(\lambda) = a_0\lambda^2 + (a_2 - 1)\lambda + a_1,$$

it follows that $\Psi(0) > 0$, $\Psi(1) < 0$, and $\Psi(\infty) > 0$ so that one root is between zero and one and the other is larger than one.

We will assume that the condition for the existence of a unique stable solution is satisfied and proceed. Let λ_1 be the root that is less than one in absolute value, and let λ_2 be the other. Note, for later use, that $\lambda_1\lambda_2 = a_1/a_0$ and that $\lambda_1 + \lambda_2 = (1 - a_2)/a_0$. We now solve for c_i and d_i, using the assumption that λ in the equations for these coefficients is λ_1, the root that implies the stable solution. We have

x_t: $\qquad\qquad c_0 = (1 - a_0\lambda_1)^{-1}[1 + a_0d_0],$

$E[x_{t+1}|t]$: $\qquad c_1 = (1 - a_0\lambda_1)^{-1}[a_0(c_0 + d_1)],$

$E[x_{t+i}|t]$: $\qquad c_i = (1 - a_0\lambda_1)^{-1}[a_0(c_{i-1} + d_i)],$

x_{t-1}: $\qquad\qquad d_0 = (1 - a_0\lambda_1)^{-1}[a_2d_0],$

$E[x_t|t-1]$: $\qquad d_1 = (1 - a_0\lambda_1)^{-1}[a_2(c_0 + d_1)],$

$E[x_{t+i}|t-1]$: $\quad d_{i+1} = (1 - a_0\lambda_1)^{-1}[a_2(c_i + d_{i+1})].$

Noting that $d_0 = 0$, and with some manipulation, we get

$$c_0 = (1 - a_0\lambda_1)^{-1},$$

$$c_i = \left(\frac{\lambda_1 a_0}{a_1}\right)c_{i-1} = \lambda_2^{-1}c_{i-1}, \qquad \text{for } i = 1, \ldots,$$

$$d_i = \left(\frac{a_2}{a_0}\right) c_i, \qquad \text{for } i = 1, \dots.$$

Thus, if λ_2 is larger than one, the sequences c_i and d_i converge to zero as i gets large.

We have solved for p_t as a function of lagged p_t and past and current expectations of current and future x. Sometimes the process for x is specified. Then we would want to solve directly for p as a function of observable variables. There are two procedures. One is to derive the solution for p as a function of expectations of x as we have just done, and then to solve for expectations of x as a function of observable variables in (A3). The other is to use the method of undetermined coefficients to solve directly for p_t as a function of observable variables.

Suppose, for example, that e is identically equal to zero and that m (and therefore x) follows

$$m_t = \rho m_{t-1} + v_t,$$

where v_t is white noise. We would then guess that the solution is of the form

$$p_t = \lambda p_{t-1} + c m_t + d m_{t-1} \qquad \text{(A3')}$$

and solve for λ, c, and d as above.

Despite its widespread use the method of undetermined coefficients suffers from a few handicaps. First, the initial guess may fail to include a solution or may inadvertently discard other solutions. Second, the method reveals only indirectly whether the model has the desirable saddle point property. Third, like repeated substitution, it can become somewhat unwieldy.

Factorization

The method of factorization was introduced to economics by Sargent (see Sargent 1979 for a detailed presentation). It is best seen as a convenient shortcut to the method of z-transforms (see Whiteman 1983).

The method proceeds in three steps.

The *first* [which is needed only if the equation includes both current and lagged expectations, if a_2 is different from zero in equation (A1')] is to take expectations on both sides of (A1') conditional on the farthest lagged information set in (A1). In (A1') we take expectations based on information at time $t - 1$. This implies

$$E[p_t|t - 1] = a_0 E[p_{t+1}|t - 1] + a_1 p_{t-1} + a_2 E[p_t|t - 1] + E[x_t|t - 1], \qquad \text{(A1'')}$$

or

$$(1 - a_2) E[p_t|t - 1] = a_0 E[p_{t+1}|t - 1] + a_1 p_{t-1} + E[x_t|t - 1].$$

In the *second* step we factor equation (A1'') to express $E[p_t|t - 1]$ as a lagged function of itself, and of expectations of current and future values of x, $E[x_{t+i}|t - 1]$, $i \geq 0$. To do so, we introduce the lag operator, L, which operates on the time subscript of a variable (not on the time at which the expectation of that variable is held):

$LE[p_{t+i}|t - 1] = E[p_{t+i-1}|t - 1],$

so that, in particular,

$LE[p_{t+1}|t] = E[p_t|t] = p_t.$

For convenience, we also introduce the forward operator, $F = L^{-1}$. Thus

$FE[p_{t+i}|t - 1] = E[p_{t+i+1}|t].$

Using the definitions of F and L, we can rewrite (A1") as

$$[-a_0 F + (1 - a_2) - a_1 L]E[p_t|t - 1] = E[x_t|t - 1]. \tag{A8}$$

The next step is to factor the polynomial in parentheses. To do so, we rewrite (A8) as

$$\left[F^2 - \left(\frac{1 - a_2}{a_0}\right)F + \left(\frac{a_1}{a_0}\right)\right]LE[p_t|t - 1] = \left(\frac{-1}{a_0}\right)E[x_t|t - 1]. \tag{A9}$$

We can factor the polynomial $\{F^2 - [(1 - a_2)/a_0]F + (a_1/a_0)\}$ as $(F - \lambda_1) \times (F - \lambda_2)$, where

$$\lambda_1 + \lambda_2 = \frac{1 - a_2}{a_0} \quad \text{and} \quad \lambda_1\lambda_2 = \frac{a_1}{a_0}. \tag{A10}$$

Note that λ_1 and λ_2 are the same as λ_1 and λ_2 derived in the method of undetermined coefficients. Thus the same discussion applies, and we assume that λ_1 is less than one in absolute value and that λ_2 is larger than one in absolute value.

We can rewrite (A9) as

$$(F - \lambda_1)(F - \lambda_2)LE[p_t|t - 1] = \left(\frac{-1}{a_0}\right)E[x_t|t - 1],$$

or

$$(1 - \lambda_1 L)E[p_t|t - 1] = \left(\frac{1}{a_0\lambda_2}\right)(1 - \lambda_2^{-1}F)^{-1}E[x_t|t - 1]. \tag{A11}$$

Since $|\lambda_2^{-1}| < 1$, we can expand $(1 - \lambda_2^{-1}F)^{-1}$ as $\sum_{i=0}^{\infty}\lambda_2^{-i}F^i$ to get

$$E[p_t|t - 1] = \lambda_1 p_{t-1} + \left(\frac{1}{a_0\lambda_2}\right)\sum_{i=0}^{\infty}\lambda_2^{-i}E[x_{t+i}|t - 1]. \tag{A12}$$

Equation (A12) gives the expectation of p_t as of $t - 1$. The last step is to derive p_t itself. [Note again that if a_2 were equal to zero, we would not have gone through the first step, so (A12) would give p_t as a function of p_{t-1} as well as current expectations of current and future x. This would be the solution, and there would be no need for the third step.]

The *third* step is to derive the solution for p_t. To do so, we use (A12) to get an expression for $E[p_{t+1}|t]$ and replace both $E[p_{t+1}|t]$ and $E[p_t|t - 1]$ in (A1'). This gives

$$p_t = a_0 \lambda_1 p_t + \left(\frac{1}{\lambda_2}\right) \sum_{i=0}^{\infty} \lambda_2^{-i} E[x_{t+i+1}|t] + (a_1 + a_2\lambda_1)p_{t-1}$$

$$+ \left(\frac{a_2}{a_0\lambda_2}\right) \sum_{i=0}^{\infty} \lambda_2^{-i} E[x_{t+i}|t - 1] + x_t.$$

Reorganizing, and using the fact that, from the definition of λ_1, $(a_1 + a_2\lambda_1)/(1 - a_0\lambda_1) = \lambda_1$, gives

$$p_t = \lambda_1 p_{t-1} + \left(\frac{1}{1 - a_0\lambda_1}\right) \sum_{i=0}^{\infty} \lambda_2^{-i} E[x_{t+i}|t]$$

$$+ \left(\frac{1}{1 - a_0\lambda_1}\right)\left(\frac{a_2}{a_0}\right) \sum_{i=0}^{\infty} \lambda_2^{-i-1} E[x_{t+i}|t - 1]. \tag{A13}$$

This solution is the same as that obtained by the method of undetermined coefficients.

Problems

1. Assume that the simple linear difference equation of section 5.1 is derived from an arbitrage equation between stocks and bonds and that the real interest rate is constant. Assume that dividends follow the stochastic process

$$d_t = (1 - \rho)d_0 + \rho d_{t-1} + v_t, \qquad d_0 > 0, 0 < \rho < 1,$$

where v_t is white noise. The variance of v_t is σ^2.

(a) Solve for the current price of the stock as a function of current and past dividends. Explain.
(b) Calculate the unconditional variance of the stock price as a function of σ^2 and other relevant parameters.
(c) How does the variance of the stock price change as ρ increases?

2. In section 5.2 we showed that if the money stock follows a first-order autoregressive process with $c < 1$, then in the Cagan model real balances will be high when the money stock is high and low when the money stock is low.

(a) Give the economic intuition behind this result.
(b) Suppose that the *growth rate* of money follows a stable first-order autoregressive process. Solve for the process for the price level.
(c) Does the same characterization hold with the addition of the words "relative to trend" following high and low?

3. *Land and bubbles.*

In an overlapping generations model in which people live for two periods, with the population growing at rate n and no production (all goods come from the exogenous endowment of the young), there is a given amount of land. The land has no productive use.

(a) Can there be a bubble on land in this economy? Discuss the relationship between your answer and the efficiency of equilibrium in the real world in view of the fact that land is valued in the real world.

(b) Suppose now that the economy becomes a production economy, that individuals' only endowment is one unit of labor in the first period of life and that the production function is Cobb-Douglas, with constant returns to scale in terms of land, labor, and capital. Can there be a steady state?

(c) Can there be a bubble on land in this economy in which land is a productive asset?

4. (a) Return to problem 1. On the assumption that $\rho < 1$, show that the variance of the "ex post" price of the stock (defined in section 5.2) exceeds the variance of the actual price.

(b) Suppose now that $\rho = 1$, with the dividend following a random walk. What happens to the unconditional variance of the price of the stock?

5. Suppose that, in the model of section 5.3, the representative family has an instantaneous utility function

$U(c, m) = a \ln(c) + b \ln(m).$

(a) Could a self-generating hyperinflation develop in an economy populated by such families?

(b) In evaluating this possibility, and the problem of multiple equilibria, what weight should be attached to the fact that there is no known hyperinflation in which money growth did not become extremely high?

6. A learning problem in which individuals do not know the current state of the economy is solved in section 5.5. Using that model, assume that individuals have information on current values of Y and v, and solve for the dynamics of the model. Answer, in particular, the question of whether the economy converges to the fundamentals equilibrium.

Notes

1. Muth (1961) was the first to use this assumption and the term "rational expectation." Until his article, and also for a long time after, researchers used plausible but arbitrary expectation formation mechanisms, the most popular being that of adaptive expectations (of which we saw an example in the last chapter). In another important paper (1960) Muth found the conditions under which adaptive expectations about a variable y would indeed be rational.

2. In the classic rational expectations macroeconomic article by Lucas (1973), individuals do not all have the same information set. Lucas showed in this article why policymakers may not be able to use the Phillips curve trade-off and also how prices convey information to market participants. We present this model in the next chapter.

3. The importance of this law for economics and finance was demonstrated by Samuelson (1965), who used it to show that future prices would follow a martingale.

4. Note that we are using here the assumption of no memory loss. The result does not go through without it.

5. The solution to the Cagan model under rational expectations was first obtained by Sargent and Wallace (1973).

6. Sunspots have become the generic example of a variable that affects the equilibrium only because individuals believe it does. We will see later other examples of extrinsic uncertainty potentially affecting the equilibrium. However, Jevons (1884) who introduced sunspots into economics believed that they mattered because they affected agricultural output.

7. Among the most famous historical episodes are the Dutch tulip mania (1634–1636) and the South Sea Bubble (1720). See Charles MacKay (1841) and Charles Kindleberger (1978) for accounts of these and other fascinating episodes.

8. These issues are discussed at greater length in Blanchard and Watson (1982) and in Fischer and Merton (1984).

9. Note that if the bubble is stochastic, the probability that the price will become negative may be very small. There is some evidence that individuals systematically ignore very small probabilities. This weakens the argument made here for eliminating bubbles as well as some of the arguments made later in the chapter.

10. The remark of the previous note applies here as well.

11. This is similar to the conclusion for a physical asset available in infinitely elastic supply.

12. Taylor (1977) proposed one such criterion.

13. Precise statements are given in Blanchard and Kahn (1981) and in Whiteman (1983).

14. There are corresponding conditions in differential equation systems. The general condition becomes that the system must have exactly m roots with positive real parts (see Buiter 1984). In the example given here the differential system in prices and capital should have one positive and one negative root.

15. In figure 5.2, all we needed to do was to plot the combinations of constant (b, k) which satisfied (10) and (11). Here, because we want to characterize the dynamics, we must first derive the loci of (k_t, b_t) along which $b_{t+1} = b_t$ and $k_{t+1} = k_t$ respectively. Hence the derivation of (13) and (14).

16. Care must be taken in using a phase diagram to analyze the dynamics of a *difference* equation system. The economy will not, as in the case of a differential equation system, move continuously along one of the trajectories, but rather it will jump from point to point on that trajectory. An equilibrium that appears stable on the phase diagram may be in fact unstable. The economy, though staying on the

path that converges to the equilibrium, may oscillate back and forth in oscillations of increasing size. Thus we must check in this case whether the system is indeed saddle point stable around E and stable around A by computing the roots of the sytem linearized around each of the two equilibria. This check is left to the reader.

17. What is important in the Marsh-Merton example is not that the dividend depends on the price but that the particular dividend policy implies nonstationarity of prices (here, a random walk).

18. Shiller (1984) and Summers (1986) have pointed out that fads, if they lead to long overvaluations or undervaluations of the stock, may look very much like rational bubbles.

19. See Merton (1987) for a review of the evidence. West (1987) has constructed a two-step volatility test that first tests the arbitrage relation and then the variance inequality. He concludes that the rejection does not come from a failure of arbitrage.

20. The analysis in this section is based on Brock (1975), Calvo (1978), Gray (1982), Obstfeld (1984), and Obstfeld and Rogoff (1983).

21. Despite the fact that money is the only asset, the model has none of the pathological properties of the OLG model with money. This is because money enters the utility function and is used both (implicitly) for transaction services and as a vehicle for saving.

22. The case where σ is negative and hyperdeflation cannot be ruled out by the transversality condition is discussed by Brock (1975).

23. Obstfeld and Rogoff (1983) discuss this condition at greater length. If $u(m)$ is of the form

$$u(m) = \frac{m^{1-\gamma}}{1-\gamma};$$

this condition is satisfied if $\gamma > 1$.

24. Note that we saw in the third example of section 5.1 that a loglinear version of the model can have a multiplicity of convergent paths, when $\alpha < -1$. We now look at the dynamics of the model without linearization.

25. The model is a simplified version of the model used by Grandmont (1985). Grandmont allows for endogenous labor supply, but we take the endowments as given. We also draw in what follows on the survey by Woodford (1984).

26. In chapter 4 we considered the case where e_2 was equal to zero.

27. If there were population growth at rate n, the steady state equilibrium would occur where the offer curve intersects the line $m_{t+1} = (1 + n)m_t$, that is, the line where prices are falling at rate $1 + n$.

28. This construction is due to Azariadis and Guesnerie (1984).

29. This is an implication of Sarkovskii's theorem, presented by Grandmont (1983).

30. For a relatively simple presentation of the theory of periodic and aperiodic behavior of one-dimensional dynamic systems, see Grandmont (1983). The possibility of chaos in deterministic systems has been explored by various authors; see, for example, Day (1982, 1983).

31. See Guesnerie (1986).

32. The example comes from Azariadis (1981). The proof follows Woodford (1987).

33. The model is a simplified and slightly modified version of Evans (1985).

34. This assumption, which differs from that of section 5.1, makes the problem more interesting. The case where the information set includes current values of y and v is easier and is left to the reader.

35. Marcet and Sargent (1987) show, in the context of the Cagan hyperinflation model with two equilibria (studied at the end of chapter 4), that with least squares learning the economy converges to the low-inflation equilibrium.

36. Multiple stable equilibria may also emerge in a different class of models, models that allow for increasing returns and/or externalities in labor and goods markets. Multiplicity in those models does not rely on the presence of income effects. We present and discuss such models, and the likelihood of multiple equilibria, in chapter 8.

37. The intuition for this is as follows: Suppose that individuals have perfect foresight, so that equation (A1) is simply a difference equation in p_{t-1}, p_t, p_{t+1}, and x_t. Given p_{t-1} at time t, for p_t to be uniquely determined by the condition that the equation does not explode, the equation must have one root smaller and one root greater than 1 in absolute value. If both roots were, for example, smaller than one in absolute value, the difference equation would converge for any value of p_t. The system would have the type of multiplicity studied in section 5.4. [The specific condition for saddle point stability in systems such as (A1) is given by Blanchard 1985.] The roots of equation (A7) turn out to be the inverses of the roots of the difference equation obtained by assuming perfect foresight in (A1). Thus, for saddle point stability, they must also be such that one is smaller and one larger than 1 in absolute value.

References

Azariadis, Costas (1981). "Self-Fulfilling Prophecies." *Journal of Economic Theory* 25, 3 (Dec.), 380–396.

Azariadis, Costas, and Roger Guesnerie (1984). "Sunspots and Cycles." CARESS Working Paper 83-22R. University of Pennsylvania. March.

Black, Fischer (1974). "Uniqueness of the Price Level in Monetary Growth Models with Rational Expectations." *Journal of Economic Theory* 7, 1 (Jan.), 53–65.

Blanchard, Olivier, and Mark Watson (1982). "Bubbles, Rational Expectations and Financial Markets." In P. Wachtel (ed.), *Crises in the Economic and Financial Structure*. Lexington, MA.: Lexington Books.

Blanchard, Olivier (1985). "Methods of Solution for Dynamic Rational Expectations Models: A Survey." *Mathematical Programming Study* 23, 210–225.

Blanchard, Olivier, and Charles Kahn (1981). "The Solution of Linear Difference Models under Rational Expectations." *Econometrica* 48 (July), 1305–1311.

Bray, Margaret (1982). "Learning, Estimation and the Stability of Rational Expectations Models." *Journal of Economic Theory* 26, 318–339.

Bray, Margaret, and N. Savin (1986). "Rational Expectations Equilibria, Learning and Model Specification." *Econometrica* 54, 5 (Sept.), 1129–1160.

Brock, William (1975). "A Simple Perfect Foresight Monetary Model." *Journal of Monetary Economics* 1, 2 (April), 133–150.

Brock, William (1986). "Distinguishing Random and Deterministic Systems: An Expanded Version." Mimeo. University of Wisconsin.

Buiter, Willem (1984). "Saddlepoint Problems in Continuous Time Rational Expectations Models: A General Method and Some Macroeconomic Examples." *Econometrica* 52, 3 (May), 665–680.

Burmeister, Edwin, Christopher Caton, A. Rodney Dobell, and Stephen Ross (1973). "The 'Saddlepoint Property'" and the Structure of Dynamic Heterogeneous Capital Good Models." *Econometrica* 41, 1 (Jan.), 79–95.

Burmeister, Edwin, Robert Flood, and Peter Garber (1982). "On the Equivalence of Solutions in Rational Expectations Models." *Economic Letters*.

Calvo, Guillermo (1978). "On the Indeterminacy of Interest Rates and Wages with Perfect Foresight." *Journal of Economic Theory* 19 (Dec.), 321–337.

Campbell, John, and Robert Shiller (1987). "Cointegration and Tests of the Present Value Relation." *Journal of Political Economy* 95, 1062–1088.

Cass, David, M. Okuno, and I. Zilcha (1979). "The Role of Money in Supporting the Pareto Optimality of Competitive Equilibrium in Consumption-Loan Type Models." *Journal of Economic Theory* 20, 41–80.

Day, Richard (1982). "Irregular Growth Cycles." *American Economic Review* 72, 406–414.

Day, Richard (1983). "The Emergence of Chaos from Classical Economic Growth." *Quarterly Journal of Economics* 98, 201–213.

DeCanio, Stephen (1979). "Rational Expectations and Learning from Experience." *Quarterly Journal of Economics* 93, 1 (Feb.), 47–58.

Evans, George (1985). "Expectational Stability and the Multiple Equilibria Problem in Linear Rational Expectations Models." *Quarterly Journal of Economics* 100, 4 (Dec.), 1217–1233.

Fischer, Stanley, and Robert Merton (1984). "Macroeconomics and Finance: The Role of the Stock Market." *Carnegie Rochester Conference Series. Vol. 21. Essays on Macroeconomic Implications of Financial and Labor Markets and Political Processes.* Autumn, 57–108.

Flavin, Marjorie (1983). "Excess Volatility in the Financial Markets: A Reassessment of the Empirical Evidence." *Journal of Political Economy* 91, 6 (Dec.), 929–956.

Flood, Robert, and Peter Garber (1980). "Market Fundamentals versus Price Level Bubbles: The First Tests." *Journal of Political Economy* 88, 747–770.

Friedman, Benjamin (1979). "Optimal Expectations and the Extreme Information Assumptions of 'Rational Expectations' Macromodels." *Journal of Monetary Economics* (Jan.), 23–41.

Geanakopolos, John, and Herakles Polemarchakis (1983). "Walrasian Indeterminacy and Dynamic Macroeconomic Equilibrium: The Case of Certainty." Mimeo. August.

Grandmont, Jean Michel (1983). "Periodic and Aperiodic Behavior in Discrete Dynamical Systems." CEPREMAP Working Paper 8317. September.

Grandmont, Jean Michel (1985). "On Endogenous Business Cycles." *Econometrica* 53, 5 (Sept.), 995–1045.

Gray, JoAnna (1982). "Dynamic Instability in Rational Expectations Models: An Attempt to Clarify." International Finance Discussion Paper 197. Federal Reserve Board. January.

Guesnerie, Roger (1986). "Stationary Sunspot Equilibria in an *n* Commodity World." Mimeo. Presented at the Conference on Non-Linear Economic Dynamics. Paris. June 1985.

Hahn, Frank (1968). "On Warranted Growth Paths." *Review of Economic Studies* 35, 175–184.

Jevons, W. Stanley (1884). *Investigations in Currency and Finance*. London: Macmillan.

Kehoe, Timothy, and David Levine (1983). "Indeterminacy of Relative Prices in Overlapping Generations Models." MIT Working Paper 313. April.

Kehoe, Timothy, and David Levine (1985). "Comparative Statics and Perfect Foresight in Infinite Horizon Economies." *Econometrica* 53, 433–453.

Kindleberger, Charles (1978). *Manias, Panics and Crashes*. New York: Basic Books.

LeRoy, Stephen, and Richard Porter (1981). "The Present Value Relation: Tests Based on Variance Bounds." *Econometrica* 49, 3 (May), 555–574.

Lucas, Robert (1973). "Some International Evidence on Output-Inflation Trade-offs." *American Economic Review* 63, 3 (June), 326–334.

MacKay, Charles (1841). *Extraordinary Popular Delusions and the Madness of Crowds.* Reprinted by Farrar, Strauss and Giroux, 1932.

Mankiw, N. Gregory, David Romer, and Matthew Shapiro (1985). "An Unbiased Reexamination of Stock Market Volatility." *Journal of Finance* 40 (July), 677–687.

Marcet, Albert, and Thomas J. Sargent (1986). "Convergence of Least Square Learning Mechanisms in Self Referential Linear Stochastic Models." Mimeo. October.

Marcet, Albert, and Thomas J. Sargent (1987). "Least Squares Learning and the Dynamics of Hyperinflation." Mimeo. June.

Marsh, Terry, and Robert Merton (1986). "Dividend Variability and Variance Bounds Tests for the Rationality of Stock Market Prices." *American Economic Review* 76, 3 (June), 483–498.

Merton, Robert (1987). "On the Current State of the Stock Market Rationality Hypothesis." In Rudiger Dornbusch et al. (eds.), *Macroeconomics and Finance: Essays in Honor of Franco Modigliani.* Cambridge, MA: MIT Press.

Muth, John (1960). "Optimal Properties of Exponentially Weighted Forecasts." *Journal of the American Statistical Association* 55, 290–306.

Muth, John (1961). "Rational Expectations and the Theory of Price Movements." *Econometrica* 39, 315–334.

Obstfeld, Maurice (1984). "Multiple Stable Equilibria in an Optimizing Perfect Foresight Model." *Econometrica* 52, 1 (Jan.), 223–228.

Obstfeld, Maurice, and Kenneth Rogoff (1983). "Speculative Hyperinflations in Macroeconomic Models: Can We Rule Them Out?" *Journal of Political Economy* 91, 4 (Aug.), 675–687.

Samuelson, Paul (1965). "Proof that Properly Anticipated Prices Fluctuate Randomly." *Industrial Management Review* 6 (Spring), 41–49.

Sargent, Thomas, and Neil Wallace (1973). "The Stability of Models of Money and Growth." *Econometrica* 41, (Nov.), 1043–1048.

Sargent Thomas (1979). *Macroeconomic Theory.* New York: Academic Press.

Shiller, Robert (1981). "Do Stock Prices Move Too Much to Be Justified by Subsequent Changes in Dividends?" *American Economic Review* 71, 3 (June), 421–436.

Shiller, Robert (1984). "Stock Prices and Social Dynamics." *Brookings Papers on Economic Activity* 2, 457–510.

Summers, Lawrence (1986). "Do Market Prices Accurately Reflect Fundamental Values?" *Journal of Finance* 41, 3 (July), 591–601.

Taylor, John (1975). "Monetary Policy During a Transition to Rational Expectations." *Journal of Political Economy* 83, 5, 1009—1021.

Taylor, John B. (1977). "Conditions for Unique Solutions in Stochastic Macroeconomic Models with Rational Expectations." *Econometrica* 33, (Oct.), 671—684.

Taylor, John B. (1985). "New Econometric Techniques for Macroeconomic Policy
Evaluation." In Zvi Griliches and Michael D. Intriligator (eds.), *Handbook of Econometrics*. Vol. 3. Amsterdam: North-Holland.

Tirole, Jean (1982). "On the Possibility of Speculation under Rational Expectations."
Econometrica 50 (Sept.), 1163—1181.

Tirole, Jean (1985). "Asset Bubbles and Overlapping Generations." *Econometrica* 53,
6 (Dec.), 1499—1528.

Townsend, Robert (1978). "Market Anticipations, Rational Expectations and
Bayesian Analysis." *International Economic Review* 19 (June), 481—494.

Weil, Philippe (1987). "Confidence and the Real Value of Money in Overlapping
Generation Models." *Quarterly Journal of Economics* 102, 1 (Feb.), 1—22.

West, Kenneth (1988). "Dividend Innovations and Stock Price Volatility." *Econometrica* 56, 1 (Jan.), 37—61.

West, Kenneth (1987). "A Specification Test for Speculative Bubbles." *Quarterly
Journal of Economics* 102, 553—580.

Whiteman, Charles (1983). *Linear Rational Expectations Models: A User's Guide.*
Minneapolis: University of Minnesota Press.

Woodford, Michael (1984). "Indeterminacy of Equilibrium in the Overlapping
Generations Model: A Survey." Mimeo. Columbia. May.

Woodford, Michael (1987), "Learning to Believe in Sunspots." Mimeo. Graduate
School of Business, Chicago.

6

Optimal Consumption, Investment, and Inventory Behavior

The next four chapters are aimed at explaining the recurrent, economywide fluctuations in output, employment, and prices that were described in chapter 1. This chapter sets some foundations by extending the analysis of optimal decisions by firms and individuals carried out in previous chapters to the case of uncertainty. The next three develop alternative explanations of aggregate fluctuations. To motivate the organization of those chapters, we start with a brief overview of the history of business cycle theory and of the current state of economic discourse.[1]

The wealth of business cycle explanations that had been developed in the pre-Keynesian period is most apparent in Haberler's *Prosperity and Depression*,[2] first published in 1937, which summarized the theories prevalent in the economics literature up to that time. Among the topics listed in the table of contents are The Purely Monetary Theory, The Over-investment Theories, Changes in Cost, Horizontal Maladjustments and Over-indebtedness, Under-consumption Theories, Psychological Theories, and Harvest Theories.

Although abounding in conflicting theories, the discussions were not purely theoretical, for early authors often had a keen eye for facts. It had long been noted, for example, that the output of capital goods was much more cyclical than that of consumption goods, and many early theorists invoked the accelerator mechanism to explain the greater variability of the output of investment goods.[3] The most systematic collection of business cycle facts was assembled in a series of National Bureau of Economic Research sponsored projects, carried out by Wesley C. Mitchell, whose first book on cycles was published in 1913, by Simon Kuznets and others. In 1946 Arthur Burns and Mitchell published their massive volume *Measuring Business Cycles*. Using a reference chronology of business cycles, their book documented the existence of regular cycles and characterized the behavior of a large number of price and quantity series relative to the stages of the cycle.

Both the empirical work of Burns and Mitchell and the informal theoretical approach summarized in Haberler were, however, swept aside by the rapidly advancing Keynesian revolution and the work of the Cowles Commission. The Keynesian approach proposed a unified explanation of aggregate fluctuations, together with the promise that such fluctuations could be reduced or eliminated by the appropriate use of policy. The emphasis was shifted from the study of cycles to the study of macroeconomic policies needed to reduce fluctuations. The Cowles Commission advocated the use of formal modeling and testing, and branded the work of Burns and Mitchell as a dangerous example of measurement without theory.[4] Given the existence of the emerging Keynesian framework, a preferable alternative was at hand: work was to be directed towards the construction of structural models and was to go beyond the collection of stylized facts à la Burns-Mitchell.

The Keynesian program dominated most of the following 30 years. The wealth of alternative explanations of the cycle gave way to the development of a broadly accepted framework, the "neoclassical synthesis." Theoretical and econometric work, rather than being aimed at explaining business cycles directly, turned to the specification and estimation of the various blocks of the general model: consumption, investment, the demand for money, the price wage block, and so on.[5] The strategy was that by studying and estimating these components separately, one would obtain a general equilibrium model that would, when shocked by disturbances to the different equations, closely replicate aggregate fluctuations. That aggregate Keynesian models, when shocked by disturbances, could generate cyclical behavior was indeed shown by Adelman and Adelman (1959). The validation of these models, however, and the focus of econometric research were more on individual equations and their empirical fit than on the stochastic properties of the models themselves or their ability to explain business cycles.

By the mid-1970s, three sets of events combined to lead to a major crisis in this research program and in macroeconomics in general. The first was the reaction of developed economies to the increases in oil shocks, the slowdown in productivity, and the poor performance of Keynesian models in explaining the events of the 1970s. The second was the forceful attack of Lucas and others on the theoretical flaws of the Keynesian approach. The third was the attack by Sims and others on the abuses of the Cowles Commission program to the estimation of structural models. Although the assessment of damages differed among researchers, it was generally agreed that the Keynesian program had proceeded too fast and that a reassessment was needed. This is what has happened over the last ten years. Although there is again a wealth of alternative and conflicting theories, they share many common elements. One of them is the return to small, explicitly stochastic, general equilibrium models, with the goal of explaining the main characteristics of business cycles.[6] Technological progress makes it now much easier to study such general equilibrium models under uncertainty than was the case earlier. In parallel, econometric work has largely moved away from estimation of individual equations to more agnostic, less structural, modes of investigation, which are direct descendents—in spirit rather than in method—of Burns and Mitchell. We are not, however, back to where we were in 1946; we now review current approaches.

6.1 The State of Play

Early business cycle theorists were unclear as to what generated recurrent, though not regular, fluctuations that did not explode over time. Most descriptive theories were cast in terms of self-sustaining cycles, with each boom containing the seeds of the subsequent slump and each slump containing in turn the seeds of the following boom. Formally, Kaldor's (1940) model was, for example, a nonlinear deterministic system that produced a limit cycle.

This approach has largely disappeared.[7] Thanks to the early work of Frisch (1933) and Slutsky (1937), and to the development of the theory of time series, most macroeconomists now share the same general analytical approach, that based on the distinction between *impulse* and *propagation* mechanisms. In this approach serially uncorrelated shocks (or impulses) affect output through distributed lag relations (the propagation mechanism) leading to serially correlated fluctuations in output. As was shown by Frisch and Slutsky, even simple linear propagation mechanisms appear to have the ability of explaining the stochastic behavior of economic variables. Because such linear propagation mechanisms are easy to estimate empirically and relatively easy to analyze, their use has led to a much better integration of theory and empirical work than was the case earlier.[8]

However, beyond this shared general framework there is little agreement as to the main sources of disturbances—monetary or real, and if real from changes in tastes or in technology, from the private sector, or from the government—and the precise nature of the propagation mechanisms. Part of the diversity arises from the nature of the research effort: in order to analyze the implications of a particular type of shock or propagation mechanism, it is necessary to ignore other shocks and propagation mechanisms, at least initially. But part of the diversity goes beyond the dynamics of research. There are two main directions of research at this stage.

The first and more recent, known as real business cycle theory, explores the idea that macroeconomic fluctuations can for the most part be accounted for by the dynamic effects of technological shocks in a competitive economy. The initial impetus for this approach came from Lucas (1972, 1973) who was trying to explain the role of monetary disturbances in a competitive economy with imperfect information. Because of both its mixed empirical success and the internal dynamics of the research program launched by Lucas, the analysis now emphasizes real shocks, with monetary shocks assumed to play either little or no role in fluctuations.[9] The real business cycle approach builds in many ways on previous research: the propagation mechanisms, as well as the dynamics of consumption, savings, and investment in response to shocks, had been studied at length by macroeconomists in the Keynesian tradition. But it breaks with that tradition in two important ways, by its insistence on perfect competition as a maintained "as if" assumption and by its focus on technological shocks. For most of the postwar period until the 1970s, technological shocks had been subsumed in a smooth, often deterministic, trend term and had been assumed to play little role in fluctuations.

The second approach has its roots in the Keynesian tradition. It sees aggregate demand shocks as playing an important role in fluctuations, a role more important than seems to be consistent with the competitive market assumption.[10] Where previous Keynesian models had largely started from the assumption that prices and wages adjusted slowly in response to movements in demand, research has now focused on what market imperfections can account for this systematic effect of aggregate demand on output in the short and the medium run.

The next four chapters develop these alternative business cycle approaches. This chapter sets the foundations by analyzing aspects of firms' and individuals' optimal behavior under uncertainty. Its focus is on the implications of optimal behavior for the dynamic characteristics of consumption and fixed and inventory investment. These elements are an integral part of any theory of fluctuations. The next three chapters turn to the study of general equilibrium. Chapter 7 provides the logical starting point: it introduces shocks into the dynamic equilibrium models that we analyzed in earlier chapters and characterizes their dynamic effects. We examine whether we can in such models generate the fluctuations in output and its components, as well as the fluctuations in employment, that are observed in reality. Finding this class of real business cycle models lacking in some important directions, we turn in the following two chapters to models in which aggregate demand plays a more important role.

This chapter has four sections. Sections 6.2 and 6.3 extend our analyses of consumption/saving and investment choices to the case where individuals and firms face uncertainty. Section 6.4 studies inventory decisions by firms, a decision factor that plays an important role in fluctuations, though we have not considered it until this point. Throughout our purpose is not to give a general treatment of dynamic behavior under uncertainty but to study how consumers and firms react to shocks in an uncertain environment. These are the central elements of the propagation mechanisms that we will study in later chapters.

6.2 The Consumption/Saving Choice under Uncertainty

In chapters 2 and 3 we studied individual consumption behavior under certainty. We showed that individuals would, at any point in time, choose the slope of their consumption path according to the Keynes-Ramsey rule. Given this slope, they would then choose the highest level of consumption consistent with their intertemporal budget constraint. We now introduce uncertainty and ask how we should modify this characterization of optimal decisions. Throughout this section one of the facts that motivates our analysis, and has motivated much of the work on consumption, is the strong correlation between income and consumption movements documented in chapter 1.

A word of warning before we start. One cannot study the consumption-saving choice in the abstract, that is, independently of the structure of markets. Thus the treatment we give here must be tailored to each case and to each economy. We do not formalize the labor supply decision and take labor income as given. This makes our treatment consistent with most formalizations of the labor market; we return to the labor supply decision at length in chapter 7. We implicitly assume that individuals can buy as many goods as they want so that there is no rationing in the goods market. We assume the existence of a riskless asset and that individuals can borrow and lend freely at the riskless rate, therefore excluding potential credit market imperfections; we return to those issues in chapter 9. We consider alternative assumptions as to the set of assets available to individuals, including the very relevant case where labor income risk is not fully diversifiable.

The Maximization Problem

The problem of how people should choose between consumption and saving under uncertainty was analyzed by Samuelson and by Merton in 1969. We follow Samuelson here.[11]

Consider a consumer who maximizes as of time zero,

$$E\left[\sum_{t=0}^{T-1} (1 + \theta)^{-t}U(C_t)|0\right]. \tag{1}$$

The notation $E(\cdot|t)$ denotes an expectation conditional on information at time t; it stands for $E(\cdot|I_t)$, where I_t is the information set at t. As is usual, θ is the individual's rate of time preference. Thus the consumer maximizes the present discounted value of expected utility, conditional on information at time zero.

This is a straightforward extension of the objective function used to characterize behavior under certainty. The utility function $U(\cdot)$ now does double duty, however. Not only does it characterize the degree of substitution between consumption in different periods as before, but being a von Neumann-Morgenstern utility function, it also reflects now the attitude of the consumer toward risk.[12]

The consumer is assumed to be uncertain about both future labor income and the returns on assets.[13] His budget constraint is given by

$$A_{t+1} = (A_t + Y_t - C_t)[(1 + r_t)\omega_t + (1 + z_t)(1 - \omega_t)],$$

$$Y_t \in I_t, \quad A_\tau \geqslant 0. \tag{2}$$

A_t is financial wealth at the beginning of the period. Y_t is labor income, which is random but known as of time t. Given consumption C_t, the consumer has gross savings of $(A_t + Y_t - C_t)$. He has the choice between two assets, one riskless and the other risky. The riskless asset has rate of return r_t, which is a deterministic function of time.[14] The risky asset earns a rate of return z_t which is random and not known as of time t. The portfolio decision is characterized by the share of the portfolio invested in the riskless asset, ω_t. The expression in brackets therefore gives the realized rate of return on the portfolio.

The consumer must choose a consumption and portfolio plan at time 0, knowing that he will be able to choose a new plan at time 1, and so on, until time $T - 1$. The most convenient method to solve such dynamic decision problems under uncertainty is that of stochastic dynamic programming, which is the method we now use.[15]

Dynamic programming reduces multiperiod problems to a sequence of simpler two-period decision problems. The first step is to introduce a *value function* $V_t(A_t)$, which is defined as

$$V_t(A_t) = \max E\left[\sum_{s=t}^{T-1} (1 + \theta)^{-(s-t)}U(C_s)|t\right] \qquad \text{subject to (2).} \tag{3}$$

The value function at time t is the present discounted value of expected utility evaluated along the optimal program. This value clearly depends on financial wealth at the beginning of period t, A_t. It also depends on the conditional joint distribution of future labor income and rates of return and on the length of time between t and T. This dependence is allowed for by the time index on V, which indicates that the form of the function is likely to change over time.[16]

From (3) the value function satisfies the following recursive equation, known as the Bellman equation:

$$V_t(A_t) = \max_{\{C_t, \omega_t\}} \{U(C_t) + (1 + \theta)^{-1} E[V_{t+1}(A_{t+1})|t]\}. \tag{4}$$

The value function at time t is equal to the utility of consumption at time t plus the expected value of the discounted value function at time $t + 1$.

First-Order Conditions

Suppose for the moment that we know the form of the function $V(\cdot)$. Then the problem of the consumer in period t is reduced to a two-period problem, that of trading off consumption at time t for more financial wealth at time $t + 1$, that of maximizing the right-hand side of (4) subject to the budget constraint (2). Using equation (2) to eliminate A_{t+1}, the first-order conditions are

C_t: $U'(C_t) = E[(1 + \theta)^{-1}((1 + r_t)\omega_t + (1 + z_t)(1 - \omega_t)) V'_{t+1}(A_{t+1})|t]$,

ω_t: $E[V'_{t+1}(A_{t+1})(r_t - z_t)|t] = 0$.

In the second equation, we have used the fact that $(1 + \theta)^{-1}(A_t + Y_t - C_t)$ is known as of time t.

Given that the functional form of the value function is not known, those first-order conditions do not appear very useful. There is, however, a simple *envelope* relation between the value of $V'_t(A_t)$ and $U'(C_t)$ along the optimal path. To see that, consider the effect of a small change in A_t on both sides of (4). By the envelope theorem, we can use the budget constraint (2) to get

$$V'(A_t) = E[(1 + \theta)^{-1}((1 + r_t)\omega_t + (1 + z_t)(1 - \omega_t)) V'_{t+1}(A_{t+1})|t],$$

$$= U'(C_t),$$

where the second equality follows from the first of the first-order conditions given above. The marginal value of financial wealth along the optimal path must be equal to the marginal utility of consumption. Using this relation to eliminate $V'(A_{t+1})$ from the first-order conditions gives

$$U'(C_t) = E[(1 + \theta)^{-1}((1 + r_t)\omega_t + (1 + z_t)(1 - \omega_t))U'(C_{t+1})|t], \tag{5}$$

$$E[U'(C_{t+1})(1 + r_t)|t] = E[U'(C_{t+1})(1 + z_t)|t]. \tag{6}$$

Equivalently, we can substitute (6) into (5), and the two conditions become

$$U'(C_t) = (1 + \theta)^{-1}(1 + r_t)E[U'(C_{t+1})|t] \tag{5'}$$

and

$$U'(C_t) = (1 + \theta)^{-1}E[(1 + z_t)U'(C_{t+1})|t]. \tag{5''}$$

Both equations (5') and (5'') have simple interpretations as generalizations of the Keynes-Ramsey condition under certainty that the marginal rate of substitution between consumption in two periods must be equal to the marginal rate of transformation. In the case of (5'), suppose that the consumer decreases consumption by dC_t at time t, invests dC_t in the riskless asset and consumes the proceeds at time $t + 1$. The decrease in utility at time t is $U'(C_t)$. The increase in expected utility at time $t + 1$, viewed as of time t, is equal to $(1 + \theta)^{-1}(1 + r_t)E[U'(C_{t+1})|t]$. Along the optimal path this small reallocation should not change the value of the program, so (5') must hold. Equation (5'') has a similar interpretation but corresponds to the case where the consumer saves at the margin in the risky rather than the riskless asset. What matters here is the return of the risky asset in each state multiplied by marginal utility in that state. Thus what appears in (5'') is the expectation of the product of the random rate of return and the marginal utility of consumption over states of nature.[17]

Like the Keynes-Ramsey rule, equations (5') and (5'') give only the first-order conditions but not the full solution to the problem. Even so, they put strong restrictions on the dynamic behavior of consumption. Equation (5') implies that

$$(1 + r_t)(1 + \theta)^{-1}U'(C_{t+1}) = U'(C_t) + \overline{e}_{t+1}, \qquad E(\overline{e}_{t+1}|t) = 0. \tag{7}$$

This says that given $U'(C_t)$, no additional information available at time t should help predict the left-hand side of (7). Under further assumptions equation (7) may take an even simpler form. For instance, suppose that $U(\cdot)$ is quadratic so that $U'(\cdot)$ is linear in C, and that the riskless rate, r_t, is constant through time and equal to the subjective discount rate θ. Then (7) becomes

$$C_{t+1} = C_t + e_{t+1}, \qquad E(e_{t+1}|t) = 0, \tag{8}$$

where e is equal to a constant times $\overline{e}$ defined in (7). Consumption follows a martingale: given C_t, no other variable known at time t should help predict consumption at time $t + 1$, C_{t+1}.[18] This striking implication was first emphasized and tested by Hall (1978)[19] and has been the subject of extensive theoretical and empirical investigation since.[20]

Can we go from these first-order conditions to derive an explicit solution for consumption and saving? In general, we cannot, but for specific utility functions and assumptions about asset returns and labor income, we can. There are two main cases in which an explicit solution can be derived. The first is that of diversifiable income risk and the second that of quadratic utility. Both are useful benchmarks, and we present them in turn; both, however, exclude important aspects of reality. We conclude the section with what is known in the general case.[21]

Diversifiable Labor Income, Consumption, and Saving

The first case where an explicit solution can be derived is when labor income risk is diversifiable. This assumption is slightly less implausible than it first appears. Even though there is no market in human capital, individuals may be able to diversify part of their labor income risk by holding a portfolio of financial assets whose returns are negatively correlated with labor income. Life insurance also offers protection against one type of labor income risk. But the assumption that all labor income risk can be diversified is surely not satisfied in practice. The solutions to the consumption-saving problem we are about to present are therefore of limited empirical relevance. They constitute nonetheless a useful benchmark from which to explore the implications of nondiversifiable risk later on.

If labor income is fully diversifiable, we can, without loss of generality, focus on the case where there is no labor income and all income is derived from tradable wealth.[22] In that case explicit solutions for the consumption-savings problem of the consumer can be derived for a large class of utility functions, the "HARA class."[23] The HARA class includes the isoelastic (or constant relative risk aversion, CRRA), the exponential (or constant absolute risk aversion, CARA), and the quadratic utility functions.

A convenient method for finding the solution is to use Bellman's optimality principle, which states that, for any given value of the state variable(s) in a given period, the solution from that point on must be optimal. Using this principle and the value function introduced earlier, the solution is found by backward induction. Thus in period $T - 2$, for any given value of wealth A_{T-2}, the individual faces a two-period optimization problem. Solving that problem, the individual obtains a consumption function, which gives consumption as a function of wealth, and a portfolio share rule, from which the the expectation of utility from period $T - 2$ on (i.e., for periods $T - 2$ and $T - 1$), and thus the value function for period $T - 2$, can be derived. Equipped with that value function, the consumer faces a two-period problem in period $T - 3$, which gives the value function for period $T - 3$, and so on, proceeding backward. The reason the HARA utility functions are tractable is that the value function belongs to the same family as the underlying utility function, in which case all that remain to be found to characterize the value function are its parameters.

The solution for an infinite horizon problem can usually be obtained by taking the limit of the solution to the T period problem as T becomes large. Alternatively, it may be possible to solve directly for the infinite horizon solution.[24] For example, suppose that the consumer has an infinite horizon, that the riskless rate is constant and equal to r, and that z_t is i.i.d. with density function $f(z_t)$. For any given A_t, the problem faced by the consumer is then the same at any point in time, and it is reasonable to expect the value function to be the same over time, that is, $V_t(A_t)$ to be of the form $V(A_t)$.[25] We may then guess the form of $V(\cdot)$, derive implied consumption, and check whether our guess is correct.

Consider the simple case where $U(C_t) = \ln(C_t)$.[26] Using Merton's result that the value function is of the same functional form as the utility function for the HARA utility functions, we guess that the value function is of the form

$$V(A_t) = a \ln(A_t) + b,$$

where a and b are constants to be determined. That guess allows us to formulate the maximization problem at time t:

$$\max \ln(C_t) + (1 + \theta)^{-1} E[a \ln(A_{t+1}) + b | t]$$

subject to

$$A_{t+1} = (A_t - C_t)[(1 + r)\omega_t + (1 + z_t)(1 - \omega_t)].$$

Solving for consumption, C_t, and the portfolio share, ω_t, gives

$$C_t = [1 + a(1 + \theta)^{-1}]^{-1} A_t$$

and

$$E[(r - z_t)[(1 + r)\omega + (1 + z_t)(1 - \omega)]^{-1} | t] = 0. \tag{9}$$

The first equation gives consumption as a linear function of wealth. The second equation implicitly defines the optimal ω, which is the optimal share of the safe asset in the portfolio. Under the assumption that z_t is i.i.d, this value is constant over time and thus independent of the level of wealth.

These equations, however, depend on a, which we do not know yet. Thus the last step is to derive the implied value function for time t, obtained by replacing C_t and ω by their values from equation (9) in the above objective function. This both provides a check on whether the initial guess was correct and, by providing the solution for the parameter a, makes it possible to obtain an explicit solution for the consumption function. This computation shows the guess to be indeed correct and a to be equal to $(1 + \theta)/\theta$ (b is a complicated and unimportant constant). Replacing a in (9) gives

$$C_t = \left(\frac{\theta}{1 + \theta}\right) A_t. \tag{10}$$

Thus, under the assumptions that labor income risk is diversifiable and that utility is logarithmic, we obtain a characterization of consumption that is identically the same as under certainty. Consumption is a linear function of wealth. The marginal propensity to consume out of wealth is approximately equal to the subjective discount rate[27] so that the saving/consumption decision is a function only of the rate of time preference and not of financial variables. Changes in future income (dividends) or in interest rates affect consumption through their effect on wealth.

When more general utility functions within the HARA class are considered, under the maintained assumption that labor income is diversifiable, the results still closely resemble the results obtained under certainty. If, for example, utility is of the CRRA form, the marginal propensity to consume out of wealth depends on the expected rate of return on the portfolio in the same way as in chapter 2. The sign of the effect of changes in the expected rate of return depends on whether the degree of risk aversion is less or greater than one, or equivalently on whether the elasticity of substitution is greater or less than one. Thus the results up to this point are quite consistent with our earlier characterization of consumption under certainty.

Quadratic Utility and Certainty Equivalence

We now turn to the second case in which an explicit solution can be obtained for consumption. In this case the restrictions are not on labor income but on the form of the utility function. Assume that there is only one, riskless, asset and that utility is quadratic. Then the maximization problem becomes

$$\max E\left[\sum_{t=0}^{T-1} (1 + \theta)^{-t}(aC_t - bC_t^2)|0\right]$$

subject to

$$A_{t+1} = (1 + r_t)(A_t + Y_t - C_t), \qquad A_T \geqslant 0. \qquad (2')$$

This is now a standard linear quadratic problem for which an explicit solution is easily derived. Linear quadratic problems are problems in which either a quadratic objective function is being maximized subject to a linear constraint or a linear objective function is being maximized subject to a quadratic constraint.[28] Suppose further—and only for convenience since a solution can be derived without this further assumption—that r_t is constant and equal to θ. In this case the first-order condition for consumption implies that

$$E[C_{t+1}|t] = C_t,$$

which implies that $E[C_t|0] = C_0$ for $t = 0, \ldots, T- 1$. The optimal path of consumption is such that consumption is expected to be constant over the remainder of the program. Turning to the budget constraint, we integrate it forward in time from 0 to T to get

$$A_T = A_0(1 + r)^T + \sum_{t=0}^{T-1} (Y_t - C_t)(1 + r)^{T-t}.$$

Because the individual does not derive utility from A_T, his consumption in the last period will be such that $A_T = 0$—as long as his marginal utility is positive, a condition we assume to be satisfied.[29] Using this assumption, and discounting to time 0 gives

$$\sum_{t=0}^{T-1} (1 + r)^{-t}C_t = \sum_{t=0}^{T-1} (1 + r)^{-t}Y_t + A_0.$$

This is, however, only the *realized* budget constraint. As of time zero, future values of Y are not known, and thus this constraint cannot be used. However, taking expectations of both sides as of time zero gives an *expected value* budget constraint (note that the realized budget constraint implies the expected value constraint but not the reverse):

$$E\left[\sum_{t=0}^{T-1} (1 + r)^{-t}C_t|0\right] = E\left[\sum_{t=0}^{T-1} (1 + r)^{-t}Y_t|0\right] + A_0.$$

Using the first-order condition to express expectations of C_t as a function of C_0 gives the solution for C_0. For example, in the case where T goes to infinity, C_0 is given by

$$C_0 = \left(\frac{r}{1 + r}\right)\left[E\left[\sum_{t=0}^{\infty} (1 + r)^{-t}Y_t|0\right] + A_0\right].$$

As in all linear quadratic problems the solution exhibits the certainty equivalence property. The solution is the same as that which would obtain if there was no uncertainty, or if equivalently the individual held expectations of labor income with subjective certainty. Consumption is a linear function of total wealth, which is the sum of financial wealth and the present discounted value of expected labor income. The marginal propensity to consume out of wealth is equal (approximately) to the interest rate, which is in turn equal to the rate of time preference.

Within this context we can study how changes in income affect consumption as well as the conditions under which consumption smooths or amplifies movements in income. The marginal propensity to consume out of labor income clearly depends on the persistence of the process for labor income. To see this, note that the preceding equation implies that

$$C_t - C_{t-1} = \left(\frac{r}{1+r}\right) \sum_{i=0}^{\infty} (1+r)^{-i}(E[Y_{t+i}|t] - E[Y_{t+i}|t-1]).$$

The change in consumption depends on the present value of revisions in future labor income. Note that this is consistent with equation (8) derived earlier. It tells us how the innovation in consumption is determined by revisions of expectations about future labor income. Now assume that labor income follows an autoregressive process of order k:

$$Y_t = \sum_{i=1}^{k} \psi_i Y_{t-i} + \varepsilon_t,$$

$$\sum_{i=1}^{k} \psi_i \leqslant 1.$$

Then the change in consumption is given by[30]

$$C_t - C_{t-1} = \left[\frac{r/(1+r)}{1 - \sum_{i=1}^{k} (1+r)^{-i}\psi_i} \right] \varepsilon_t.$$

If labor income follows, for example, a stationary first-order process, with coefficient ρ, or follows a first-order process around a deterministic trend, then the marginal propensity to consume out of income, measured as the change in consumption in response to an unexpected change in income, is given by $r/(1 + r - \rho)$, which is less than one. This is the result emphasized by both Friedman (1956) in the "permanent income hypothesis" and by Modigliani (1986) in the "life cycle" theory that consumption smooths transitory changes in income.

As ρ approaches one, and labor income approaches a random walk, the propensity to consume out of income approaches unity. Consumption may actually respond more than one for one to unexpected changes in income if labor income follows a nonstationary process. For example, suppose that the first difference in labor income follows a first-order process with coefficient ρ so that $\psi_1 = 1 + \rho$ and $\psi_2 = -\rho$. In that case the marginal propensity to consume is equal to $(1 + r)/(1 + r - \rho)$, which, if ρ is positive, is greater than one. In this case unexpected movements in income have, given interest rates, more than a one for one effect on consumption. This takes us back to issues discussed in chapter 1. The evidence appears to be that GNP, and by implication labor income, are subject to both shocks with permanent and shocks with transitory effects. On the basis of the above result (given interest rates, a quadratic function, etc.), we would expect consumption to smooth shocks with transitory effects but possibly to respond strongly to those with permanent effects on income. The fact that consumption appears to smooth such income fluctuations is in this light an empirical puzzle.[31]

The linear quadratic case and its simple characterization of consumption behavior has played a central role in recent empirical research. But the assumption of quadratic utility is as unappealing as the assumption of diversifiable labor income made earlier. Quadratic utility is an unattractive description of behavior toward risk: it implies increasing absolute risk aversion, that is, a willingness to pay more to avoid a given bet as wealth increases. We now look at what happens in the general case where income is not diversifiable and utility is not quadratic.

The General Case: Precautionary Saving

When labor income is not diversifiable and utility is not quadratic, the presence of uncertainty generally affects consumption, leading consumers to be more prudent. We now consider the implications of this precautionary effect of uncertainty, concentrating on the effects of labor income uncertainty.

Assume, for simplicity, that the riskless rate is constant and equal to the subjective discount rate so that the first-order condition (5') becomes

$$E[U'(C_{t+1})|t] = U'(C_t). \tag{5'}$$

This expression allows us to characterize the effects of uncertainty on consumption. So long as consumers are risk averse (so long as $U'' < 0$), increased uncertainty, say, in the form of an increase in the variance of consumption, decreases expected utility. But the effect of uncertainty on behavior depends on whether it affects consumers' expected marginal utility, that is, the first-order condition (5').

If utility is quadratic, marginal utility is linear ($U''' = 0$) in consumption: an increase in the variance of consumption has no effect on expected marginal utility, and thus no effect on optimal behavior. This is the certainty equivalence result derived in the case we studied above. But most plausible utility functions, that is utility functions that imply plausible behavior toward risk, are such that $U''' > 0$. This means that marginal utility is convex in consumption, and an increase in uncertainty raises the expected marginal utility. To maintain equality in (5'), the expected future consumption must increase compared to current consumption. Uncertainty leads consumers to defer consumption, to be more *prudent*. The role of the condition $U''' > 0$ in generating more prudent behavior in the face of uncertainty was first derived by Leland (1968) and further analyzed by Sandmo (1970) and Dreze and Modigliani (1972).

It is, however, analytically difficult, and in some instances even impossible, to solve for optimal consumption in the presence of prudent behavior. A case that can be solved is that of constant absolute risk aversion (Caballero 1987a; Kimball and Mankiw 1987). We consider this case in a simple example that shows clearly the effects of labor income uncertainty on the level of consumption.

Assume that the consumer maximizes

$$\max E\left[\sum_{t=0}^{T-1}\left(-\frac{1}{\alpha}\right)\exp(-\alpha C_t)|0\right]$$

subject to

$$A_{t+1} = (A_t + Y_t - C_t)$$

and

$$Y_t = Y_{t-1} + e_t, \qquad e_t \sim N(0, \sigma^2).$$

The consumer has constant absolute risk aversion, with coefficient α and lives for T periods. The subjective discount rate, is equal to the riskless interest rate, and they are both equal to zero. Labor income follows a random walk, with normally distributed innovations. The important assumption is that of constant absolute risk aversion. The assumptions that the discount rate and the riskless rate are both equal, and equal to zero, that income follows a random walk, and that income innovations are normally distributed are made for simplicity (see Caballero 1987a).

It is then easy to verify that optimal consumption satisfies

$$C_{t+1} = C_t + \frac{\alpha\sigma^2}{2} + e_t$$

and that the level of consumption is given by

$$C_t = \left(\frac{1}{T-t}\right)A_t + Y_t - \frac{\alpha(T-t-1)\sigma^2}{4}.$$

In deriving the first equation, we use the first-order condition and make use of the fact that if x is normally distributed with mean $E[x]$ and variance σ_x^2, $E[\exp(x)] = \exp(E[x] + \sigma_x^2/2)$. We then use that equation and the intertemporal budget constraint to solve for the level of consumption. Check that the equation satisfies the intertemporal budget constraint for any sequence of realizations of labor income.

The first equation shows the effect of income uncertainty on the slope of the consumption path. Higher income uncertainty and higher risk aversion lead to a steeper slope, to more prudent behavior. The second equation gives the level of consumption as a function of wealth, income, and uncertainty. Under certainty equivalence the solution would be given by the first two terms only. Prudence is reflected in the third term: the higher the uncertainty, the lower will be the level of consumption, given income and wealth.

This simple example shows how uncertainty may affect the level of consumption. But the constant absolute risk aversion case still has the unattractive property that the marginal utility of consumption is finite at zero consumption, which means that consumption could be negative along the optimal path. Constant relative risk aversion, on the other hand, would rule out negative consumption. Clearly, consumers who want to avoid zero consumption when labor income is nondiversifiable will want to exercise extreme prudence and build wealth as a precaution. In this case, however, it is not possible to obtain a closed form solution. From the few analytical results we have by Kimball (1987) and from simulations by Zeldes (1984), for example, we know the following: The clear dichotomy between the effects of expected income and the effects of uncertainty exhibited in the example above disappears. On the one hand, the impact of uncertainty depends on the level of wealth, and thus it becomes less important as wealth increases. But, because uncertainty affects the marginal propensity to consume, a large increase in expected income may decrease the need for precautionary saving and lead to a large increase in consumption.

To summarize, consumption under uncertainty naturally depends on the same variables as consumption under certainty: current and anticipated rates of return and labor income, and wealth. In both cases consumption tends to smooth transitory fluctuations in labor income. But uncertainty about (undiversifiable) labor income generally creates an additional precautionary motive for saving.[32]

So far in our discussion on how consumers react to shocks, on consumption behavior as part of the propagation mechanism, we have not explored the effect of shocks on consumption as a potential source of fluctuations. Such shocks consist of aggregate movements in consumption that cannot be attributed to news about interest rates or income. They are most easily thought of as "taste shocks," although they may reflect aggregation or other effects that influence the relation between aggregate consumption and other aggregate variables. Extending the analysis of this section to allow for random shocks to marginal utility is relatively straightforward. Recent work exploring the empirical importance of these shocks has reached mixed conclusions, however (see Hall 1986; Caballero 1987b).

6.3 Investment under Uncertainty

In chapter 2 (section 4 and appendix) we characterized optimal investment by firms under certainty as the result of value maximization, subject to convex costs of adjustment for capital. This led to a characterization of optimal investment known as the q theory. Investment is a function of q, the shadow price of an additional unit of capital. q in turn is the present discounted value of marginal profits. Movements in demand, interest rates, or taxes affect investment through their effect on q.

We now extend this analysis to allow for uncertainty. The first question we ask is what the appropriate objective function of firms is in this case. Then we turn to the question of the optimal investment. As we deal with these questions, the fact that motivates our analysis is once more the strong procyclical movement of fixed investment, which we described in chapter 1.

As in the previous section, a word of warning is required. We cannot develop a theory of investment independently of the market structure in which the firm operates. Our analysis of the appropriate definition of the objective function of the firm shows the importance of the structure of financial markets and discusses its implications. Our analysis of investment initially proceeds with a general profit function, which is consistent with either competitive or noncompetitive labor and goods markets. Some of our examples will pertain to perfect competition when the profit function is assumed to be linear in capital; others will pertain to imperfect competition when the firm is assumed to take a demand curve or even the level of demand as given.

The Value of the Firm

Just as under certainty, the firm maximizes its value to its owners, and that value in turn is the present value of the cash flows it generates. But at what rate should firms discount future cash flows? The answer follows from the first-order conditions of consumers which we derived earlier. Let V_t be the value of the firm, and let π_t be its cash flow, its profits net of investment expenditures.[33] Then the rate of return from holding the firm for one period, $1 + z_t$, is equal to $(V_{t+1} + \pi_{t+1})/V_t$. Thus, from equation (5"), V and π must satisfy

$$U'(C_t) = E\left[(1 + \theta)^{-1} \left(\frac{V_{t+1} + \pi_{t+1}}{V_t} \right) U'(C_{t+1}) | t \right]. \tag{11}$$

Equation (11) makes the basic point that the returns generated by the firm in each state of nature in period $t + 1$ are weighted by the marginal utility of consumption in that state.

Consider, for instance, two firms with the same level of expected returns. One has returns positively correlated with $U'(C_{t+1})$ (i.e., its $V_{t+1} + \pi_{t+1}$ are high when consumption is low), and the other's returns are negatively correlated with $U'(C_{t+1})$ (i.e., its returns are high when consumption is high). The first firm will be worth more because it enables its owners to hedge against low consumption. This relationship underlies the capital asset-pricing model (CAPM) which states that the higher the correlation of a firm's returns with returns on the market, the higher the equilibrium yield on that stock has to be.[34]

By multiplying by V_t on both sides of (11), solving recursively forward, and assuming away bubbles, we get

$$V_t = E\left[\sum_{i=1}^{\infty} \left(\frac{(1 + \theta)^{-i} U'(C_{t+i})}{U'(C_t)} \right) \pi_{t+i} | t \right]. \tag{12}$$

This shows that the value of the firm is equal to the present discounted value of expected cash flows. The discount rate for each time and for each state is the marginal rate of substitution between consumption at time t and consumption at that time and in that state. Thus, to reiterate, the higher the correlation between a firm's cash flows and consumption, the higher will be the discount factor applied to high cash flows, and thus the lower will be the value of the firm. Equivalently, a firm that has procyclical profits is a risky firm, so it must pay a higher expected rate of return.

Heterogeneous Consumers and the Value of the Firm
Equations (11) and (12) suggest that consumers are identical in their spending habits, for otherwise their marginal utilities would differ across states of nature. If, however, there are enough securities, (if existing securities span the different states of nature), the marginal rates of substitution for different individuals [the ratios $U'(C_{t+i})/U'(C_t)$ across different states of nature] will be the same for all individuals. It is convenient at this stage to introduce "prices" that represent the value in term of current (period t) goods of one (real) unit of goods in a given future state of nature. Thus $p_{j,t+i}$ is the price, measured in terms of period t goods, of one unit of goods in state of nature j in period $t + i$. These prices are equated by consumers to their marginal rates of substitution, and therefore

$$p_{j,t+i} = \frac{(1 + \theta)^{-i} q_{j,t+i} U'(C_{j,t+i})}{U'(C_t)},$$

where $C_{j,t+i}$ is consumption in state of nature j in period $t + i$, $j = 1, \ldots, J$, and where $q_{j,t+i}$ is the probability of state j in period $t + i$.

Using these state contingent prices, we can rewrite (12) as

$$V_t = \sum_{i=1}^{\infty} \sum_{j=1}^{J} [p_{j,t+i} \pi_{j,t+i} | t], \tag{12'}$$

where $\pi_{j,t+i}$ is profits in state j in period $t + i$, and we retain the $[\ldots|t]$ notation to indicate that the probabilities and prices are those that apply from the perspective of period t.

What if there were fewer securities than states? A general treatment here would take us too far afield, and we limit ourselves to a few remarks. If existing securities do not span the states of nature, then the above prices of the state contingent claims are not uniquely defined. Any set of prices for state contingent claims that is consistent with the prices of existing securities can be used in (12') to give the same value. But under what conditions can a firm use the expression given by (12') to evaluate the effects of new projects on the value of the firm? The answer is a simple one. As long as the firm is evaluating projects or securities that are in the space spanned by existing securities, it can use (12'). We will see shortly examples in which this condition is satisfied. If, however, the firm is evaluating new projects or securities that are not spanned by existing securities, it cannot use (12').

A simple example may help to explain this further. Suppose that there are n contingent claims in the economy. Each of them pays one unit of good in state j, $j = 1, \ldots, n$. The number of securities, n, is less than J, the total number of states of nature. As long as a firm is evaluating the value of a project with positive return only in states 1 to n, or evaluating the value of a new security whose payoff is spanned by existing securities, it can use the set of prices of the existing n contingent claims and make use of (12'). It cannot, however, assess the value of a project with positive return in any of the $J - n$ remaining states.

When Is the Use of a Constant Discount Rate Appropriate?
In practice, it is often assumed that firms maximize the present discounted value of profits by using a deterministic discount rate. For firms opting to do this, (12) becomes

$$V_t = E\left[\sum_{i=1}^{\infty} \left(\prod_{j=1}^{i} (1 + r_{t+j})^{-1} \right) \pi_{t+i} | t \right]. \tag{12''}$$

The value of the firm is then equal to the present value of expected cash flows, which is discounted at a deterministic rate. That is, at each date the same rate is used to evaluate returns in different states. But, the above analysis suggests that this is generally inappropriate. It also suggests that there are two alternative sets of conditions under which this may be acceptable. Again, the argument here is informal.

The first is that consumers are risk neutral, so their utility is linear and their $U'(C)$ is constant. In the risk neutral case r_t is not only deterministic but also constant and equal to θ, the subjective discount rate of individuals. Thus equation (12'') simplifies further to

$$V_t = E\left[\sum_{i=1}^{\infty} (1 + \theta)^{-i} \pi_{t+i} | t \right]. \tag{12'''}$$

The other is that the firm is evaluating decisions that do not affect the relative distribution of returns across states, though they change its scale. In this case the firm may use the riskless rate of interest adjusted for a risk premium that reflects the specific risk associated with the firm's activities. A firm that has highly procyclical cash flows may use a high risk premium adjustment, whereas a firm with countercyclical cash flows may use a negative premium instead.

Neither of these conditions is likely to hold exactly for any firm. But they may be acceptable approximations, and because of their convenience, equations (12″) or (12‴) are often used to analyze the firm's behavior under uncertainty when considerations of risk aversion are not central to the issue at hand.

The Irrelevance of Finance and the Modigliani-Miller Theorem
From equation (12′) we can derive the famous Modigliani-Miller theorem (Modigliani and Miller 1958, 1963) that the total value of a firm is independent of the structure of ownership claims, for instance, between debt and equity. The proposition holds under reasonably general conditions and is striking because it implies[35] that corporate finance, at least as it relates to the structure of corporate liabilities, is irrelevant.

The argument can be presented by supposing that the firm divides its cash flows arbitrarily into two streams so that $\pi_{j,t} = \pi_{1,j,t} + \pi_{2,j,t}$, and it issues titles to each stream. Using the prices defined in (12′), the value of the title to each part of the profit stream is given by

$$V_{s,t} = \sum_{i=1}^{\infty} \sum_{j=1}^{J} [p_{j,t+i} \pi_{s,j,t+i} | t], \qquad s = 1, 2.$$

Each unit of cash flow in each state of nature is valued at the same price as when the cash flows are bundled together. Therefore adding the values of the two assets gives $V_{1t} + V_{2t}$ as the present discounted value of π_t so that $V_{1t} + V_{2t} = V_t$. The total value of the firm is invariant to the way profits are distributed between different claims. In particular, the above result implies that the value of the firm is invariant to whether the firm finances itself through bonds or equities.[36]

This result does not, of course, imply that the required rate of return on both bonds and equities must be the same. Bonds and equities will have different stochastic characteristics, as measured by the covariation of their rate of return with the marginal rate of substitution, and bonds may well have a lower required rate of return than equities. The result is simply that a shift from equity finance to bond finance will not change the average rate of return that the firm has to pay to consumers who buy the claims on it. If it substitutes cheaper debt for equity, it has to pay a correspondingly higher return on equity, which has become more risky as a result of the firm's enhanced leverage.

The result holds only if the division of π between π_1 and π_2 does not affect the size of π. There are several reasons why this may not be true. The first is the fact that only dividends are taxed at the corporate level.[37] A shift to bond finance therefore reduces the tax burden and increases π. The second is that there may be bankruptcy costs, so a shift to bond finance that increases the risk of bankruptcy may decrease π. For both reasons, the above result may not hold. In the rest of this chapter, however, we will implicitly assume that it does hold and ignore the form of finance by firms.[38]

Optimal Capital without Costs of Adjustment

It is instructive to start with the case of no cost of adjustment. In this case the investment decision of the firm is simple. In each period the firm chooses the optimal amount of capital for that period:

Let $\Psi(K_t, X_t)$ be the profit function of the firm, given optimal use of all factors other than capital, with X representing the effects of those factors on profits. Thus, for a firm that takes prices of inputs and outputs as given, X will include all factor prices. If a firm has monopoly power in the goods market, X will include all the factors that shift the demand facing the firm. Let p_k be the price of capital goods in terms of output, and let δ be the rate of exponential depreciation.

Assume that capital accumulation is given by

$$K_{t+1} = (1 - \delta)K_t + I_t,$$

so that I_t, investment at time t, becomes productive at time $t + 1$.

Then, if the value of the firm is given by (12'), the first-order condition characterizing the optimal choice of K_t is given by

$$p_{kt} = \sum_{j=1}^{J} p_{j,t+1}[\Psi_K(K_{t+1}, X_{j,t+1}) + (1 - \delta)p_{k,j,t+1}], \qquad (13)$$

where both X_{t+1} and p_{kt+1} are uncertain as of time t and thus indexed by the state j. The left-hand side is the marginal cost of buying a unit of capital in period t. The right-hand side gives the expected marginal gain from using that additional unit in production and selling the remaining capital (after depreciation) at time $t + 1$. Equation (13) is simply a generalization of the condition for optimal investment that would be obtained under certainty: the generalization is that there is more than one state of nature in period $t + 1$, and it is therefore necessary to consider the outcome in each state on the right-hand side of the equation.

Under additional assumptions, (13) can be simplified. If we assume risk neutrality, then $p_{j,t+1}$ is equal to $(1 + \theta)^{-1}q_{j,t+1}$. In this case

$$E[\Psi_K(K_{t+1}, X_{t+1})|t] = p_{kt}(1 + \theta) - E[p_{kt+1}|t](1 - \delta)$$

$$= p_{kt}\left\{\theta + \delta - (1 - \delta)\left(\frac{E[p_{kt+1}|t] - p_{kt}}{p_{kt}}\right)\right\}. \qquad (13')$$

Expected marginal profit must be equal to the user cost, which is equal to the price of capital times the interest rate plus the depreciation rate minus the expected rate of change of the relative price of capital goods. This implicitly determines the optimal capital stock at time $t + 1$ and thus investment at time t.

Optimal Investment with Costs of Adjustment

Firms, however, cannot costlessly and instantaneously adjust capital. They face building lags, delivery lags, and costs of installation or disinstallation.

There are two main formalizations of the costs of adjusting the capital stock. The first is the *time-to-build* approach[39] which assumes that it takes time to change the capital stock. The preceding example was one simple case of time to build: it took one period for investment to come on line. More generally, an investment project initiated in period t may require inputs in periods $t, t + 1$, etc., and only come on line after a lengthy building process (which in the case of nuclear power plants may exceed a decade).

Provided the firm can freely buy and sell capital goods at any stage of production or building, no new issues are introduced by the assumption of a time-to-build investment technology. The first-order condition for optimal investment for the firm will still be that marginal cost must be equal to marginal return, with the difference being that the costs may occur over several periods rather than just in the first period, as assumed in deriving equation (13).

However, the problem becomes substantially more complicated when there are no markets for capital in process and for used capital. For instance, if the firm cannot sell its capital in process, it has to consider, when starting the project, the likelihood that conditions will change in the meantime and cause it to want to stop the project. Although this introduces considerations that are surely relevant in many investment projects, it greatly complicates the analysis of investment behavior and makes the time-to-build approach much less tractable.

The second formalization of the costs of adjustment is chapter 2's q theory, which is based on convex costs of adjustment. We now extend it to account for uncertainty. Like the time-to-build formalization, the q theory is based on the premise that there are markets for new and used capital. But, instead of delivery or time-to-build lags, it assumes that it is costly to the firm to install or remove capital, with the marginal cost being an increasing function of the rate at which (gross or net) investment takes place. As in the consumption/savings problem there are only a few cases in which an explicit solution can be derived. We consider two. The first is when profit is linear in capital. The second is when we can approximate the maximization problem by a linear quadratic problem.

An explicit solution can be obtained when profit is linear in K_t, as it is for a firm that operates under constant returns to scale in competitive markets. In this case profits can be written as $K_t \varphi(X_t)$, where X_t is a vector of factor input prices. Assume that the total cost of purchasing and installing I_t, where I_t is gross investment, are given by $p_{kt}[I_t + D(I_t)]$, where D is nonnegative, convex in I_t, and $D(0) = 0$.[40] Assume that investment at time t becomes productive at time $t + 1$. Assume, finally, that the value of the firm is given by (12'). Then optimal investment is given by

$$p_{kt}[1 + D'(I_t)] = q_t \equiv \sum_{i=1}^{\infty} \sum_{j=1}^{J} [p_{j,t+i}(1 - \delta)^{-i}\varphi(X_{j,t+i})|t], \tag{14}$$

where $p_{j,t+i}$ is the (state contingent) present value of a unit of output in state j and period $t + i$.

To understand this condition, consider an increase in gross investment at time t of dI_t, with no further change in gross investment in the future. The left-hand side gives the marginal cost of doing so, and the right-hand side the present discounted value of marginal benefits. Under the assumption that profit is linear in K, the right-hand side is independent of future capital accumulation.

The variable q is the shadow value of capital. By observing the left-hand side of (14), we see that q_t is also a sufficient statistic for investment, which is determined by driving I_t to the point where the first equality in (14) holds. However, q is by no means a simple expression, as it depends on the expectation of a sum of products of random variables. Under additional restrictions q can be further simplified. If, for example, consumers are risk neutral, $p_{j,t+i} = (1 + \theta)^{-i}q_{j,t+1}$ and q is the present discounted value of expected future marginal profits, with a constant discount rate θ. Given a specification of $\varphi(\cdot)$, $D(\cdot)$ and of the stochastic behavior of the elements of X_t, such as real wages or productivity shocks, we can solve for investment as an explicit function of these determinants.[41]

When profit is not linear in K—for instance, if firms have monopoly power or face decreasing returns to scale—equation (14) still holds, but marginal profit is given by $\Psi_K(K_t, X_t)$. Future marginal profits depend on future capital, which in turn depends on current and future investment. The first equality in equation (14) no longer suffices to determine the rate of investment because q depends on future capital stocks, which themselves depend on current investment. In such a case the solution to the investment problem can still be obtained in closed form if we set up the problem as linear quadratic, with profit and installation costs quadratic in K and other variables X, and assume constant interest rates and price of capital. We now give such an example.

Consider a firm owned by risk neutral individuals that maximizes

$$V_t = E\left[\sum_{i=1}^{\infty} (1 + \theta)^{-i}\pi_{t+i}|t\right].$$

(12''')

The firm takes output Y_t as given. This assumption is made for convenience, but it can be extended to allow for a downward-sloping demand curve and joint determination of prices and investment. Its cost in period t is given by

$$C_t = \left(\frac{1}{2}\right)(aY_t - K_t)^2 + \left(\frac{b}{2}\right)(I_t)^2, \qquad a, b > 0.$$

The first term reflects the cost of producing Y_t, given that the firm has capital K_t. It is clearly only a quadratic approximation to the appropriate cost function. All other factors affecting cost are left out for simplicity. Changes in productivity would easily be accommodated by allowing for a random productivity term in the first term and replacing $(aY_t - K_t)$ by $(aY_t - K_t + u_t)$, with u capturing productivity. The second term reflects quadratic costs of adjustment: the marginal cost of installation is a linear increasing function of the level of gross investment. Finally, capital accumulation is given by

$$K_t = (1 - \delta)K_{t-1} + I_t.$$

Investment becomes productive instantaneously.[42]

Given output, the value maximization is equivalent here to the minimization of the present value of costs, subject to the capital accumulation equation. Introducing q_t as the Lagrange multiplier associated with the capital accumulation constraint at time t, we get the following two first-order conditions:

$$I_t = \left(\frac{1}{b}\right)q_t,$$

$$q_t = \left(\frac{1 - \delta}{1 + \theta}\right)E[q_{t+1}|t] + (aY_t - K_t).$$

These conditions are familiar. The first states that investment is an increasing function of the shadow value of capital, q_t. Solving the second recursively forward gives q_t as the present discounted value of expected marginal profit. This system, however, gives q_t as a function of future expected capital stocks, which themselves depend on past investment and thus on q_t. To solve for I_t as a function of current and expected Y, we first eliminate q_t and $E[q_{t+1}|t]$ between the two equations and use the capital accumulation equation to obtain

$$-E[K_{t+1}|t] + \left[\frac{(b+1)(1+\theta)}{b(1-\delta)} + 1 - \delta\right] K_t - (1+\theta)K_{t-1} = \left(\frac{a(1+\theta)}{b(1-\delta)}\right) Y_t.$$

This gives capital at time t as a function of lagged capital, of expected capital at time $t + 1$, and of current output. By using the method of factorization developed in the appendix of chapter 5, we solve for K_t:

$$K_t = \lambda K_{t-1} + \left(\frac{a\lambda}{b(1-\delta)}\right) \sum_{i=0}^{\infty} \left(\frac{\lambda}{1+\theta}\right)^i E[Y_{t+i}|t],$$

where λ is the smallest root of

$$\lambda^2 - \left[\frac{(b+1)(1+\theta)}{b(1-\delta)} + 1 - \delta\right]\lambda + (1+\theta) = 0, \qquad 0 < \lambda < 1.$$

Capital is a function of itself lagged and of current and expected future output. As adjustment costs become more convex, as b increases, the coefficient on past capital increases and so does the discount rate $\lambda/(1 + \theta)$, implying that the firm puts more weight on the distant future. This model delivers the familiar *accelerator* relation between investment and output. If, for example, output follows a stationary first-order autoregressive process, an unexpected increase in output leads to a temporary increase in capital and an initial increase in investment followed later by a decrease, as both capital and output return to normal. If b is not too large, if a is larger than one, and if output movements are sufficiently correlated, it is quite possible for investment to respond more than one for one to an unexpected increase in output. This is the traditional accelerator explanation of the relation between investment and output movements documented in chapter 1. This is, as we will see, not the only explanation of the comovements between investment and output. Another is that both investment and output respond to underlying productivity shocks, and this makes it attractive for firms both to produce more and to invest more.

Although we have focused in this example on the relation between output and investment, we could have used a linear quadratic framework to study the effects of wages, or changes in productivity, on output and investment. The linear quadratic case allows for the derivation of an explicit solution, but its underlying assumptions are definitely unappealing. Apart from the approximations it requires, the nature of the linear quadratic problem in this context prevents us from looking at the effects of changes in the required rate of return. More important—and this is probably even more important here than in the case of the consumption problem—the linear quadratic problem may understate the importance of uncertainty for investment behavior. Irreversibility must be an essential element in many capital accumulation decisions. Recently, some progress has been made in this direction that suggests the potential importance of uncertainty and of changes in uncertainty on investment dynamics when investment decisions are largely irreversible (Bernanke 1983; Bertola 1987).

In sum, we have shown how the investment decision depends on current and expected required rates of return, and on current and expected demand and cost conditions. In few cases, however, were we able to obtain explicit solutions.

After a decade of work spurred by Jorgenson and his collaborators (e.g., see Jorgenson and Hall 1967), empirical work on investment has slowed down (in sharp constrast with empirical work on consumption, which we described earlier). This is not because empirical characteristics of investment are well understood. Indeed, there is still considerable uncertainty as to the effects of the user cost on investment, or on how much of the relation between investment and output is due to demand shocks or to joint responses to productivity developments (see Pindyck and Rotemberg 1983, and Shapiro 1986 for more recent work on this problem).

6.4 Inventory Behavior under Uncertainty

We have thus far considered firms' fixed investment decisions and altogether ignored inventory investment. We now turn to investigate inventory investment, and since our focus is on fluctuations, we concentrate on short-run fluctuations in inventory investment, which as we saw in chapter 1 are large and procyclical. One matter to think about in this regard is that although inventory investment on average amounts to only about 1% of GNP, declines in inventory investment often account for 50% of the fall in output in recessions.

The motive most often emphasized for why firms hold inventories is their desire to smooth production during fluctuations in demand. Much recent research on inventories has been motivated, however, by the fact that at the aggregate level as well as for most sectors in the economy, the variance of production exceeds the variance of sales. Models based on production smoothing suggest that production should be less variable than sales; it is accordingly clear that some reason beyond production smoothing plays a role in accounting for the actual behavior of inventories. That motive may be to avoid stock-outs, and thus lost sales, when production decisions must be made before demand is fully known. We start by presenting a model that emphasizes this second motive[43] and then turn to a model in which both motives play a role.

Stock-outs, Inventories, Sales, and Production

Consider a firm that takes the process generating its demand, D_t, as given. While we will assume that the firm faces a given level of demand and does not use price to ration demand, Kahn (1987) considers also the case where the firm makes price as well as production and sales decisions. The analysis is more involved but the qualitative results are similar.

Quantity demanded follows the stochastic process:

$$D_t = d + \rho D_{t-1} + v_t \tag{15}$$

where $|\rho| \leq 1$ and v_t is a white noise normal random variable, with mean zero and standard deviation σ^2. The firm must decide about production, Y_t, before v_t is known. It cannot adjust its current level of output to meet current demand; rather it has to meet demand D_t out of the stocks carried over from the previous period and the level of production Y_t in this period which is completed before demand is revealed. It can carry inventories at no cost. Inventories carried over from the previous period are denoted I_{t-1}. Thus sales, S_t, are given by

$$S_t = \min(I_{t-1} + Y_t, D_t). \tag{16}$$

It is assumed that the firm satisfies demand if it can. If it cannot satisfy part of demand this period, that demand is lost.[44] In practice, demand can sometimes be backlogged, which implies that the penalty for being out of inventories is lower than that implied by condition (16). The inclusion of backlogging would complicate the analysis but not change the qualitative results, except in the extreme and implausible case when demand can be backlogged with no adverse consequences for the present value of sales.

The price of output, p, is assumed to be constant through time. Marginal cost, c, is independent of the level of production and also constant through time so that there is no production smoothing in the model.[45] The firm is assumed to be risk neutral and therefore maximizes

$$E\left[\sum_{i=0}^{\infty}(1+\theta)^{-i}(pS_{t+i}-cY_{t+i})|t\right], \qquad I_t=\{v_{t-1},v_{t-2},\ldots\}.$$

I_t is the information set at time t.

In this model the firm carries inventories as a result of its inability to predict demand perfectly. It has to have goods available if it is to sell them. When it predicts sales incorrectly, it either runs out or has goods left over. These are carried as inventories to the next period.

Define A_t as $I_{t-1}+Y_t-E[D_t|t]$. A_t is the amount of inventories at the end of period t if demand is equal to its expected value. Define the cumulative standard normal distribution function as $\Phi(\cdot)$. Then the first-order condition for the problem is given by

$$-c+\text{Prob}(D_t<I_{t-1}+Y_t)c(1+\theta)^{-1}+\text{Prob}(D_t>I_{t-1}+Y_t)p=0,$$

or, using the definitions of A_t and $\Phi(\cdot)$,

$$-c+(1+\theta)^{-1}\Phi\left(\frac{A_t}{\sigma}\right)c+\left[1-\Phi\left(\frac{A_t}{\sigma}\right)\right]p=0. \tag{17}$$

The marginal cost of producing an additional unit is c. If there is no stock-out, an event that has probability $\Phi(A_t/\sigma)$, the marginal unit produced is carried to the next period, and it reduces marginal cost by c.[46] This reduction, discounted to time t, is the second term in (17). If there is a stock-out, an event that has probability $1-\Phi(A_t/\sigma)$, the marginal unit yields an additional sale at price p; this is the third term in (17). Along the optimal path the marginal cost of production must equal the expected marginal revenue.

Equation (17) thus implies that A_t must be constant. It follows that the firm must plan to have inventories after production equal to expected demand plus a constant k, which depends on the parameters p, c, θ, and σ.[47] More specifically, A is given by the implicit relation

$$\Phi\left(\frac{A}{\sigma}\right)=\frac{p-c}{p-(1+\theta)^{-1}c}.$$

Thus

$$Y_t=-I_{t-1}+E[D_t|t]+k$$

and

$I_t = \max(I_{t-1} + Y_t - D_t, 0) = \max(k - v_t, 0)$.

This in turn implies that

$Y_t = d + \rho D_{t-1} + \min(v_{t-1}, k)$

and

$S_t = d + \rho D_{t-1} + \min(v_t, k)$.

Suppose for the moment that k is large enough so that the disturbance terms in the two preceding equations are always equal to v, that is, inventories are large enough so that there is never a stock-out. Then, using (15), we see that both Y_t and S_t follow ARMA processes given by

$Y_t = d + \rho Y_{t-1} + (1 + \rho)v_{t-1} - \rho v_{t-2}$,

$S_t = d + \rho S_{t-1} + v_t$.

By computing the unconditional variances in Y and S, we get

$$\sigma_Y^2 = \left[\left(\frac{1}{1 - \rho^2}\right) + 2\rho\right]\sigma^2 = \sigma_S^2 + 2\rho\sigma^2.$$

This last result is interesting because the variance of output is likely to exceed the variance in sales. All that is needed is for ρ to be positive, that is, for demand to be positively serially correlated. The intuition for the result is simple: production responds to an increase in sales in the previous period more than one for one, both to replenish inventories and to satisfy expected demand, which is higher if ρ is positive. The first effect would make production as variable as sales; the second leads to the inequality.

The assumption that k is so large as to avoid stock-outs is, however, inconsistent with the first-order condition. A more general proof of the variance inequality defines $v'_t \equiv \min(v_t, k)$. Then it follows that

$\sigma_Y^2 = \sigma_S^2 + 2\rho \, \text{cov}(v'_t, v_t)$,

which yields the same result if ρ is positive.

The desire to avoid stock-outs therefore leads to larger variance in production than in sales; this is consistent with the empirical evidence. Note, however, that the model also implies that an unexpected increase in sales is perfectly negatively correlated with inventory investment. This is clearly inconsistent with the positive correlation between innovations in GNP and innovations in inventory investment presented in chapter 1. One possible partial reconciliation is that the period of estimation used in chapter 1 is longer than the period for which production is fixed. Over periods longer than the period of the model, the correlation may become positive. Whether time aggregation can explain the empirical correlation is an open issue at this stage.

Although the desire to avoid stock-outs may well be important, production smoothing is still probably relevant as the evidence suggests that marginal cost is indeed increasing with the level of production.[48] We now turn to a model that accommodates both motives and study their joint implications.

Production Smoothing and Stock-outs

The model just developed is highly nonlinear and does not easily accommodate more general assumptions about technology. The more common approach, pioneered by Holt et al. (1960), has been to formalize the decision of the firm as a linear quadratic problem. We present here a related formalization that both captures the essence of the stock-out model and allows for production smoothing.

Let Y_t and S_t denote production and sales at time t, and let I_{t-1} denote inventories at the beginning of period t. Assume that the firm takes the process for sales as given and thus minimizes the present discounted value of costs given by[48]

$$E\left[\sum_{i=0}^{\infty}(1+\theta)^{-i}\left\{\left(\frac{a}{2}\right)(Y_{t+i}-u_{t+i})^2+\left(\frac{b}{2}\right)(Y_{t+i}+I_{t+i-1}-I_{t+i}^*)^2\right\}\Big| t\right],$$

$$I_t^* = E[S_t|t] + k,$$

$$I_t = I_{t-1} + Y_t - S_t,$$

$$\Omega_t = \{S_{t-1}, S_{t-2}, \ldots, u_t, u_{t-1}, \ldots\}.$$

The firm is assumed to be risk neutral, with discount rate θ. Cost at time t is the sum of two terms. The first term reflects the convexity of the cost of production and allows for a productivity shock, u, that affects marginal cost. Under constant marginal cost a would be equal to zero.[50] The second term reflects the costs of having inventories after production depart from a target level, I_t^*. Since the target level would, in a complete model, be based on costs of stocking out and costs of carrying inventories, the second term implicitly reflects those costs. To define I^* (target inventories), we build on the results of the previous model and assume that the firm would like to have inventories after production equal to expected demand plus a constant k and that there is a quadratic cost of deviating from that target.[51]

The third equation is the inventory accumulation identity. We ignore the nonnegativity constraint for inventories; implicitly, k and b are assumed to be large enough that this constraint is not binding. Finally, the last equation defines the information set and says that, in the spirit of the previous model, production must be chosen before current sales are known. The current productivity shock, however, is known when the production decision is taken.

In this model the firm carries inventories both to meet expected sales, and to reduce production costs. With increasing marginal cost of production, it pays to shift production across periods to smooth out expected fluctuations in sales. Note that models of this type in which no nonnegativity constraint is imposed on inventories have to include some form of target inventory behavior. Otherwise, because future costs are discounted, the model has the tendency to produce solutions in which production is put off as long as possible in order to reduce expected costs—and that is achieved by generating negative inventories.

The simplest method of solution here is to eliminate Y_t from the objective function by using the accumulation equation and to differentiate the objective function with respect to I_{t+i}, $i = 0, \ldots, \infty$. The first-order condition for I_t is given by

$$E\left[-I_{t-1} + \left[1 + (1+\theta)^{-1} + \left(\frac{b}{a}\right) \right] I_t - (1+\theta)^{-1} I_{t+1} \right.$$

$$\left. + (S_t - u_t) - (1+\theta)^{-1}(S_{t+1} - u_{t+1}) | t \right] - \frac{bk}{a} = 0,$$

and a similar relation holds for all $i \geq 0$.

This equation can be solved by factorization to give

$$E[I_t | t] = \alpha + \lambda I_{t-1} + \sum_{i=0}^{\infty} [\lambda(1+\theta)^{-1}]^{i+1} E[\Psi_{t+i} | t],$$

where $\Psi_t \equiv -(1+\theta)(S_t - u_t) + (S_{t+1} - u_{t+1})$, α is an unimportant constant and where λ is the smallest root of

$$\lambda^2 - \left[2 + \theta + (1+\theta)\left(\frac{b}{a}\right) \right] \lambda + (1+\theta) = 0,$$

which implies that $\lambda < 1$.

Taking expectations in the inventory identity implies the level of production:

$$Y_t = E[I_t | t] - I_{t-1} + E[S_t | t].$$

Rearranging, the expression for expected end-of-period inventories can be rewritten as

$$E[I_t|t] = \alpha + \lambda I_{t-1} - \lambda E[S_t - u_t|t]$$

$$+ (1 - \lambda) \sum_{i=0}^{\infty} [\lambda(1 + \theta)^{-1}]^i E[S_{t+i} - u_{t+i}|t].$$

Expected inventories for the end of period t (the firm does not know S_t and thus cannot control I_t exactly) depend on inventories at the end-of-period $t - 1$ and on the expected sequence of sales. If marginal cost is constant, then λ is equal to zero and planned inventories are constant, just as in the previous model. However, if marginal cost is increasing in output, production smoothing comes into play: the firm takes into account its initial inventory position and also compares current to expected future sales. Higher temporary sales are satisfied partly out of inventory, leading to lower inventories for a while.

To better understand the implied dynamics of production in response to shocks in both demand and in productivity, consider two special cases: The first focuses on shocks to *demand*. Assume that there are no productivity shocks and that sales follow a first-order autoregressive process:

$$S_t = \rho S_{t-1} + v_t.$$

Then production is given by

$$Y_t = \alpha + (\lambda - 1)I_{t-1} + \left[\frac{\rho(1 + \theta)(1 - \lambda)}{1 + \theta - \lambda\rho}\right] S_{t-1}.$$

The more persistent the sales process (the larger ρ is), the larger is the reaction of production to sales. By assumption, in the current period, production cannot respond to current sales. But in the period following the increase, production increases both to increase stocks and to satisfy current and expected future demand. Table 6.1 shows the response of inventories and output to a sales shock—an unexpected positive realization in v—in period zero, along with the implication of that shock for future sales: In this case output fluctuates more than sales.

The second example focuses, instead, on the dynamic effects of shocks to *productivity*. Suppose now that demand is constant and that productivity follows an AR(1) process:

$$u_t = \rho u_{t-1} + \varepsilon_t$$

Then production is given by

Table 6.1
Impact of a sales shock on inventories and production (derivations from no-shock path)

Time	0	1	2	3
dS	1.00	0.90	0.81	0.73
dI	-1.00	-0.58	-0.36	-0.25
dY	0	1.32	1.03	0.85

Parameter values
$\rho = 0.9$
$\theta = 0$
$\lambda = 0.5$

$$Y_t = \alpha + (\lambda - 1)I_{t-1} + \left[\frac{\lambda(1 - \rho + \theta)}{1 + \theta - \lambda\rho}\right]u_t,$$

where α is a constant of no further significance.

Production depends negatively on inventories and positively on productivity shocks (recall that sales are constant). A favorable productivity shock leads the firm to increase production, building up inventories to sell them later. It therefore generates a positive correlation between production and inventory innovations. The firm reduces costs and increases profits by substituting production today for production in future. The more temporary the shock (the lower ρ is), the stronger is the effect on current production. The presence of inventories thus leads to stronger but less persistent effects of productivity shocks on production.[52]

Recent empirical research by Blanchard (1983), Blinder (1986), and Ramey (1987) has explored the relative importance of stock-out versus production smoothing. Research by West (1986) has focused on the relative importance of cost versus demand shocks. No consensus has yet been reached. Finally, there is also some ongoing research on the effects of interest rates on inventory investment, an issue we have not discussed here; the evidence in favor of such effects appears, at this stage, to be weak or nonexistent.

Having examined the behavior of consumption, investment, production, and sales in a partial equilibrium framework, we are now ready to turn, in the next chapter, to the effects of shocks in general equilibrium.

Problems

1. Taking C_t to be aggregate consumption, is equation (8) consistent with the estimated process for consumption and the cross correlations between GNP and consumption innovations reported in table 1.1? Why or why not?

2. Risk aversion and precautionary saving.

Assuming that utility exhibits constant relative risk aversion and that the conditional distribution of C_{t+1} is lognormal, use equation (5′) to derive the relation between expected consumption next period and consumption this period. Show how it depends on the riskless interest rate, the subjective discount rate, and the variance of next period's consumption. Explain.

3. Consumption under constant relative risk aversion. (This is adapted from Samuelson 1969.)

(a) Derive the portfolio balance relation and the consumption function under the assumptions made in deriving (9), but assume, instead, that the utility function is of CRRA form.

(b) Show precisely the sense in which the consumption decision depends on the portfolio balance decision.

4. Consumption expenditures and durables.

In the text we assumed that there was no difference between consumption services and consumption expenditures. This is not the case if consumption goods are durable. This problem explores the implications of durability. (See Mankiw 1985 for further treatment and empirical evidence.)

A consumer maximizes

$$E\left[\sum_{t=0}^{\infty}(1+\theta)^t U(K_t)|0\right]$$

where

$$K_t = (1-\delta)K_{t-1} + X_t$$

and

$$A_{t+1} = (1+r_t)(A_t + Y_t - X_t).$$

All symbols are standard. K_t is the stock of durables; consumption services are proportional to the stock. K_t depreciates at rate δ. X_t is expenditures (the purchases or sales of durables).

(a) Derive the first-order conditions.

(b) Assume that r is constant and equal to θ, and that δ is equal to zero. Assume further that the utility function is quadratic. Show that though consumption follows a random walk, consumption expenditures follow a white noise process. Explain.

(c) Expenditures on durables appear to follow a process close to a random walk. Can you reconcile this fact with the above results?

5. Taste shocks and consumption.

A consumer maximizes

$$E\left[\sum_{t=0}^{\infty}(1+\theta)^t((a+e_t)C_t - bC_t^2))|0\right]$$

subject to

$$A_{t+1} = (1 + \theta)(A_t + Y_t - C_t).$$

The disturbance term e_t captures taste shocks, shocks to marginal utility. For simplicity, the interest rate is equal to the subjective discount rate.

(a) Derive the first-order conditions.

(c) Assume that e_t follows a first-order autoregressive process. Characterize the consumption process.

(d) What is the process followed by consumption when e_t follows a random walk? Why?

6. *Investment and the real wage.*

Consider a firm with a Cobb-Douglas production technology, $Y_t = AK_t^a L_t^{1-a}$, depreciation at rate δ and quadratic costs of adjustment of capital bI_t^2, $K_t = (1 - \delta)K_{t-1} + I_t$. The price of new capital goods in terms of output is equal to one. The firm operates in competitive goods and labor markets and takes the real wage, w_t, as given. Wages are the only source of uncertainty. The firm is owned by risk neutral owners, with subjective discount rate θ.

(a) Assuming that the firm chooses employment freely in each period, solve for profit at time t given K_t and w_t.

(b) Show how optimal investment depends on current and future expectations of wages.

(c) Assume that the wage follows a Markov process. It can take one of two values, w_1 and w_2. The transition probabilities are given by

$$\text{Prob}(w_{t+1} = w_1 | w_t = w_1) = p$$

and

$$\text{Prob}(w_{t+1} = w_2 | w_t = w_2) = q.$$

Derive the process followed by optimal investment. Characterize the effects of p and q on investment. Explain.

(d) What is the steady state distribution of capital? (Be careful.)

7. *The variance of sales and the variance of production.*

In section 6.3, we presented an example of inventory behavior for a linear quadratic case where there are no cost shocks and demand follows a first-order process; for that case calculate the unconditional variance of production, and compare it with the unconditional variance of sales. (Use the equation for output presented in the text, combined with the inventory identity, to obtain a difference equation for output as a function of sales.) What determines whether output fluctuates more than sales?

Notes

1. For a review of the interaction of events and ideas in macroeconomics over the postwar period, see Gordon (1980).

Following tradition, we use the word "business cycle" to denote aggregate fluctuations in output and employment. But, as we said in chapter 1, we are not wedded to the idea, sometimes implicit in the use of the word "cycle," that all fluctuations in output are temporary deviations from a deterministic trend.

2. See also Zarnowitz (1985).

3. See Haberler (1937, p. 87).

4. See Koopmans (1947).

5. A prime example of this strategy is the MPS (MIT-Penn-SSRC) macroeconometric model, which was developed and estimated by Modigliani and many collaborators. The MPS model is still being used by the Federal Reserve to study the effects of alternative monetary policies on economic aggregates.

This summary does not do justice to early work in the Keynesian tradition that considered the effects of business cycles. For example, Samuelson (1939) and Metzler (1941) showed that the multiplier-accelerator mechanism and inventory behavior could generate cycles; Hicks (1950) developed a complete nonlinear trade cycle model.

6. Lucas had a profound influence on this general research strategy. His 1977 paper sets out the basic themes of his approach.

7. As we saw in chapter 5, there has been a recent revival of nonlinear deterministic models. For the time being, most of dynamic macroeconomic theory is still cast within the Frisch-Slutsky approach.

8. Although the Frisch-Slutsky approach suggests that linear models can generate rich dynamics, theoretical models often suggest the presence of some nonlinearities. These nonlinearities are sometimes present in the models that we will discuss in this chapter, but they usually do not play a crucial role in the propagation mechanism of shocks.

9. Originally the Lucas approach was known as the "rational expectations approach." Once it was realized that the distinctive conclusions reached by Lucas came more from the assumption that markets cleared continuously than from rational expectations, the name changed to the "equilibrium business cycle approach." "Real business cycle theory" is a subset of equilibrium business cycle theory that emphasizes real shocks and deemphasizes monetary shocks. In light of the imperfect competition approaches to macroeconomics presented in chapters 8 and 9, the most accurate name for the current line of research sparked by Lucas is the "competitive equilibrium business cycle approach."

10. By this definition, monetarism has its roots in the Keynesian tradition, which agrees with our view. This statement is less shocking from the perspective of the 1980s than it would have been two decades earlier.

11. Samuelson used a discrete time approach, and Merton a continuous time approach. The continuous time approach often allows for sharper results, but it requires a heavier initial technical investment. For that reason, we limit ourselves

to the discrete time treatment here. Merton (1971) extends the results in Merton (1969). A very general treatment of the optimization problem is given in Karatzas et al. (1986).

12. Indeed, under additive separability the two are closely related: the degree of relative risk aversion is equal to the inverse of the elasticity of substitution. Some recent work has explored more general specifications that allow for attitudes to risk and intertemporal substitution to be independent; see, for example, Weil (1987), Epstein and Zin (1987), and Hall (1987a). This work relaxes the assumption of additive separability.

13. Note that we take labor income as given and do not formalize the labor supply decision. We return to the labor supply decision at length in the next chapter.

14. The assumption that there is an asset with a known real rate of return is unlikely to be satisfied in practice, except (and then in practice not perfectly) in economies in which governments issue indexed bonds.

15. What follows can be understood without specific knowledge of stochastic dynamic programming. A good introduction to stochastic dynamic programming is given by Sargent (1987). A more general treatment is presented in Stokey, Lucas, and Prescott (1988).

16. The reason for treating A_t explicitly and other variables implicitly, through the time index for V, is that A_t is the only state variable under the control of the consumer.

17. Note that equation (6) can be seen as an asset-pricing relation, giving the equilibrium rate of return on any asset given consumption. As we concentrate on consumption here, we do not explore this direction further in this chapter. In chapter 10, however, we will return to this issue and will present a model of asset pricing along those lines.

18. This result is sometimes known as the "random walk" result, but individual consumption does not always follow a random walk. We show later in this chapter that e_t reflects news about future labor income and rates of return on assets. If labor income follows a stationary process and there is no retirement, the importance of news on consumption will increase as the consumer gets nearer to T even if the variance of labor income is constant. This is because the consumer has fewer periods over which to smooth the income shock. Thus the variance of e_t will increase through time.

19. This condition holds for one individual and one must be careful as to how it extends to aggregate consumption (Blanchard 1981, Deaton 1986). For a review of the research spurred by Hall (1978), see Hall (1987b).

20. Hall's insight has had a profound impact on macroeconometrics. Most inter-temporal decision problems have relatively simple first-order conditions but rarely have an explicit solution. Hall's insight is that in testing a theory, one does not need to derive an explicit solution. All one needs is to test the first-order conditions. If

they fail the test, the theory can be rejected. The econometric methods appropriate for tests of first-order conditions have been largely developed by Hansen; see, for example, Hansen (1982).

21. The failure to obtain an explicit solution does not mean, of course, that no solution exists—the existence of a solution can be proved under quite general conditions, as discussed in Lucas, Stokey, and Prescott (1988)—nor that it is impossible to derive some properties of the solution either from the first-order conditions or by numerical methods.

22. In the presence of diversifiable labor income risk, we can think of the individual as selling shares to his human wealth, so the problem can be recast in terms of portfolio choice, with no labor income.

23. HARA stands for hyperbolic absolute risk aversion; see Merton (1971).

24. One benefit of deriving the solution to the infinite horizon problem as the limit of a finite horizon problem is that the procedure implicitly imposes a transversality condition, that $\lim A_T$ is equal to zero as T goes to infinity.

25. The assumption that z_t is i.i.d. is clearly important here. If z_t followed, for example, a first-order autoregressive process, one might expect the value function to be of the form $V(A_t, z_{t-1})$, that is, to depend on both state variables, A_t and z_{t-1}.

26. The case of constant relative risk aversion (of which this is a special case, for the coefficient of relative risk aversion is equal to one) is treated in problem 3 of the chapter.

27. When the horizon is finite, the value function takes the form $V_t(A_t) = a_t + b_t \ln(A_t)$, where a and b are now functions of time.

28. Such problems may arise, for example, when a linear profit function is being maximized subject to quadratic costs of adjusting inputs. We will see such an example later in this chapter.

29. This condition has to be assumed because, for high enough levels of consumption, marginal utility is negative for the quadratic utility function.

30. See, for example, Flavin (1981).

31. For further discussion and empirical evidence, see Deaton (1986), and Campbell and Deaton (1987).

32. For lack of space we have not dealt with the implications of imperfections in credit markets, that is, of "liquidity constraints," for consumption. See Hayashi (1985) for a recent survey. We also return to closely related issues in chapter 9.

33. Although we use the notation V to denote the value of the firm, which is also a value function, $V(\ )$ in this section is not the same as the value function of the consumer that went under the same notation.

34. Equivalently, the higher "beta" is, the higher will be the equilibrium yield on the firm. The "consumption CAPM" recognizes that the rates of return derive from

correlations with the level of consumption rather than with the market. See, for instance, Breeden (1979).

35. Franco Modigliani always adds "to a first approximation."

36. The logic of the argument makes it clear that it does not require that consumers be the same or that markets be complete in the sense we mentioned earlier: the result holds for any set of prices for contingent claims, whether or not there is a unique set of prices consistent with the prices of existing securities.

37. This is the source of the well-known "dividend puzzle," which is why firms continue to pay dividends (and finance themselves through equity) when bond finance receives a more favorable tax treatment.

38. We return to this issue in chapter 9, when we study imperfections in credit markets.

39. Kydland and Prescott (1982) emphasize the time-to-build aspect of investment; Taylor (1982) uses and solves a model of investment in which he assumes that it takes several periods to build the investment project.

40. Note that this specification implies that profit net of installation expenditures is *not* homogeneous of degree one in K and I. This contrasts with the assumption in chapter 2 that the cost of installation per unit of investment is a function of the investment to capital ratio. This implies that the Hayashi (1982) result of equality between marginal q, and average q (the value of the firm divided by the capital stock) does not hold for this case.

41. See, for example, Abel (1983).

42. Note that the timing—investment becomes productive in the period in which it is installed—is different from that used earlier. This makes the derivations slightly easier.

43. This follows Kahn (1987).

44. This period's unsatisfied demand is lost, but to the extent that demand is positively serially correlated, high demand in this period (whether satisfied or not) implies higher expected demand in the next period.

45. Production smoothing occurs when the firm moves production between periods in order to reduce costs. This is a strategy a firm uses when marginal cost increases with the level of production: the firm can then decrease costs if it meets temporarily high demand by smoothing production over several periods.

46. It is assumed here that production takes place in every period.

47. It is here that the constant marginal cost assumption clearly plays a key role: the firm is willing to move production up one for one with expected sales because this has no adverse cost consequences.

48. See Bils (1987), for example. We return to this issue in chapter 9.

49. Taking sales as given is again a shortcut that allows for a simple analytical treatment. Results allowing the firm to choose price, production, and sales are not qualitatively different. We study the general equilibrium extension of this model in chapter 7.

50. Linear terms are ignored for notational convenience. They affect only the constant term in the solution.

51. We simplify this model by assuming that target inventories are equal to expected sales plus a constant. This is not likely to be the case when the marginal cost of production is not constant.

52. Again, we have taken sales as exogenous; we endogenize them in the next chapter.

References

Abel, Andrew (1983). "Optimal Investment under Uncertainty." *American Economic Review* 73, 2 (March), 228–233.

Adelman, Irma, and Frank Adelman (1959). "The Dynamic Properties of the Klein-Goldberger Model." *Econometrica* 27, 4 (Oct.), 596–625.

Altonji, Joseph (1982). "The Intertemporal Substitution Model of Labor Market Fluctuations: An Empirical Analysis." *Review of Economic Studies* 47, 783–824.

Bernanke, Ben (1983). "Irreversibility, Uncertainty and Cyclical Investment." *Quarterly Journal of Economics* 98, 1 (Feb.), 85–106.

Bertola, Giuseppe (1987). "Dynamic Programming, Option Pricing and Irreversible Investment." Mimeo. MIT. July.

Bils, Mark (1987). "The Cyclical Behavior of Price and Marginal Cost." *American Economic Review* 77, 5 (Dec.), 838–855.

Blanchard, Olivier (1981). "What is Left of the Multiplier-Accelerator?" *American Economic Review* (May), 150–154.

Blanchard, Olivier (1983). "The Production and Inventory Behavior of the American Automobile Industry." *Journal of Political Economy* 91 (June), 365–400.

Blinder, Alan, and Stanley Fischer (1981). "Inventories, Rational Expectations and the Business Cycle." *Journal of Monetary Economics* 8, 3 (Nov.), 277–304.

Blinder, Alan (1986). "Can the Production Smoothing Model of Inventory Behavior be Saved?" *Quarterly Journal of Economics* 101, 3 (Aug.), 431–453.

Breeden, Douglas (1979). "An Intertemporal Asset Pricing Model with Stochastic Consumption and Investment Opportunities." *Journal of Financial Economics* 7, 265–296.

Burns, Arthur, and Wesley C. Mitchell (1946). *Measuring Business Cycles*. New York: National Bureau of Economic Research.

Caballero, Ricardo (1987a). "Consumption and Precautionary Savings: Empirical Implications." Mimeo. MIT.

Caballero, Ricardo (1987b). "The Role of Taste Shocks in Consumption Fluctuations." Mimeo. MIT.

Campbell, John, and Angus Deaton (1987). "Is Consumption Too Smooth?" NBER Working Paper 2134.

Deaton, Angus (1986). "Life Cycle Models of Consumption: Is the Evidence Consistent with the Theory?" NBER Working Paper 1910.

Dreze, Jacques, and Franco Modigliani (1972). "Consumption Decisions Under Uncertainty." *Journal of Economic Theory* 5, 308–335.

Epstein, Larry, and Stanley Zin (1987). "Substitution, Risk Aversion and the Temporal Behavior of Consumption and Asset Returns II: An Empirical Analysis." Mimeo. Toronto. September.

Flavin, Marjorie (1981). "The Adjustment of Consumption to Changing Expectations about Future Income." *Journal of Political Economy* 89, 5 (Oct.), 974–1009.

Friedman, Milton (1956). *Studies in the Quantity Theory of Money*. Chicago: University of Chicage Press.

Frisch, Ragnar (1933) "Propagation and Impulse Problems in Dynamic Economics." In *Economic Essays in Honor of Gustav Cassel*, 171–205.

Gordon, Robert G. (1980). "Postwar Macroeconomics: The Evolution of Events and Ideas." In Martin Feldstein (ed.), *The American Economy in Transition*. NBER and University of Chicago Press, 101–162.

Haberler, Gottfried (1946). *Prosperity and Depression*. United Nations. (Second edition, League of Nations, 1946.)

Hall, Robert, and Dale Jorgenson (1967). "Tax Policy and Investment Behavior." *American Economic Review* 57 (June), 391–414.

Hall, Robert (1978). "Stochastic Implications of the Life Cycle Permanent Income Hypothesis: Theory and Evidence." *Journal of Political Economy* 86, 5 (Oct.), 971–987.

Hall, Robert (1986). "The Role of Consumption in Economic Fluctuations." In Robert Gordon (ed.), *The American Business Cycle; Continuity and Change*. NBER and University of Chicago Press, 237–266.

Hall, Robert (1987a). "Intertemporal Substitution in Consumption." *Journal of Political Economy*, forthcoming.

Hall, Robert (1987b). "Consumption." NBER Working Paper 2265.

Hansen, Lars (1982). "Large Sample Properties of Generalized Method of Moments Estimators." *Econometrica* 50, 1029–1054.

Hansen, Lars, and Thomas Sargent (1980). "Formulating and Estimating Dynamic Linear Rational Expectations Models." *Journal of Economic Dynamics and Control* 2, 7–46.

Hayashi, Fumio (1982). "Tobin's Marginal q and Average q: A Neoclassical Interpretation." *Econometrica* 50 (Jan.), 213–224.

Hayashi, Fumio (1985). "Tests for Liquidity Constraints: A Critical Survey." NBER Working Paper 1720.

Hicks, J. R. (1950). *A Contribution to the Theory of the Trade Cycle.* Oxford University Press.

Holt, Charles, Franco Modigliani, John Muth, and Herbert Simon (1960). *Planning Production, Inventories and Work Force.* Englewood Cliffs, NJ: Prentice-Hall.

Ioannides, Yannis, and Bart Taub (1987). "Time to Build and Aggregate Fluctuations: A Note." Mimeo. Virginia Polytechnic Institute. June.

Kaldor, Nicholas (1940). "A Model of the Trade Cycle." *Economic Journal* 50, p. 78.

Kahn, James (1987). "Inventories and the Volatility of Production." *American Economic Review* 77, 4 (Sept.), 667–679.

Karatzas, Ioannis, John Lehoczky, Suresh Sehti, and Steven Shreve (1986). "Explicit Solution of a General Consumption/Investment Problem." *Mathematics of Operations Research* 11, 2 (May), 261–294.

Kimball, Miles (1987). "Essays on Intertemporal Household Choice." Ph.D. dissertation. Harvard University.

Kimball, Miles, and N. Gregory Mankiw (1987). "Precautionary Saving and the Timing of Taxes." Mimeo. Harvard University.

Koopmans, Tjalling (1947). "Measurement without Theory." *Review of Economics and Statistics* 29, 3, 161–172.

Kydland, Finn, and Edward C. Prescott (1982). "Time to Build and Aggregate Fluctuations." *Econometrica* 50, 6 (Nov.), 1345–1370.

Leland, Hayne (1968). "Saving and Uncertainty: The Precautionary Demand for Saving." *Quarterly Journal of Economics* 82 (Aug.), 465–473.

Lucas, Robert E. (1972). "Expectations and the Neutrality of Money." *Journal of Economic Theory* 4, (April), 103–124.

Lucas, Robert E. (1973). "Some International Evidence on Output-Inflation Trade-offs." *American Economic Review* 63 (June), 326–334.

Lucas, Robert E. (1977). "Understanding Business Cycles." In Karl Brunner and Allan Meltzer (eds.), *Stabilization of the Domestic and International Economy*, 7–29.

Mankiw, Gregory, N. (1985). "Consumer Durables and the Real Interest Rate." *Review of Economics and Statistics* 67, 3 (Aug.), 353–362.

Merton, Robert C. (1969). "Lifetime Portfolio Selection under Uncertainty: The Continuous Time Case." *Review of Economics and Statistics* 51, 247–257.

Merton, Robert C. (1971). "Optimum Consumption and Portfolio Rules in a Continuous Time Model." *Journal of Economic Theory* 3, 373–413, and erratum, *Journal of Economic Theory* 6 (1973), 213–214.

Metzler, Lloyd A. (1941). "The Nature and Stability of Inventory Cycles." *Review of Economic Statistics* 23 (Aug.), 113–129.

Modigliani, Franco, and Merton Miller (1958). "The Cost of Capital, Corporation Finance and the Theory of Investment." *American Economic Review* 48 (June), 261–297.

Modigliani, Franco, and Merton Miller (1963). "Corporate Income Taxes and the Cost of Capital: A Correction." *American Economic Review* 53 (June), 433–443.

Modigliani, Franco (1986). "Life Cycle, Individual Thrift and the Wealth of Nations." *American Economic Review* 76, 3 (June), 297–313.

Pindyck, Robert, and Julio Rotemberg (1983). "Dynamic Factor Demand Functions Under Rational Expectations." *Scandinavian Journal of Economics*, 223–238

Prescott, Edward (1986). "Theory Ahead of Business Cycle Measurement." Federal Reserve Bank of Minneapolis, *Quarterly Review* (Fall), 9–22.

Ramey, Valerie (1987). "NonConvex Costs and the Behavior of Inventories." Mimeo. San Diego, December.

Samuelson, Paul A. (1939). "Interactions between the Multiplier Analysis and the Principle of Acceleration." *Review of Economic Statistics* 21 (May), 75–78.

Samuelson, Paul A. (1969). "Lifetime Portfolio Selection by Dynamic Stochastic Programming." *Review of Economics and Statistics* 51 (Aug.), 239–246.

Sandmo, Agnar (1970). "The Effect of Uncertainty on Saving Decisions." *Review of Economic Studies* 37 (July), 353–360.

Sargent, Thomas (1979). *Macroeconomic Theory*. New York: Academic Press.

Sargent, Thomas (1987). *Dynamic Macroeconomic Theory*, Cambridge, MA: Harvard University Press.

Shapiro, Matthew (1986). "The Dynamic Demand for Capital and Labor." *Quarterly Journal of Economics* 101, 3 (Aug.), 513–542.

Slutsky, Eugen (1937). "The Summation of Random Causes as the Source of Cyclic Processes." *Econometrica*, 312–330.

Stokey, Nancy, Robert E. Lucas, and Edward Prescott (1988). *Recursive Methods in Economic Dynamics*. Cambridge, MA: Harvard University Press.

Summers, Lawrence (1986). "Some Skeptical Observations on Real Business Cycle Theory." Federal Reserve Bank of Minneapolis, *Quarterly Review* (Fall).

Taylor, John (1982). "The Swedish Investment Funds System as a Stabilization Rule." *Brookings Papers on Economic Activity* 1, 57–99.

Weil, Philippe (1987). "Non-Expected Utility in Macroeconomics." Mimeo. Harvard University, September

West, Kenneth (1986). "A Variance Bounds Test for the Linear Quadratic Inventory Model." *Journal of Political Economy* 43, 374–401.

Zarnowitz, Victor (1985). "Recent Work on Business Cycles in Historical Perspective: A Review of Theories and Evidence." *Journal of Economic Literature* 23, 2 (June), 523–580.

Zeldes, Steve (1984). "Optimal Consumption with Stochastic Income." Ph.D. dissertation. MIT.

7   Competitive Equilibrium Business Cycles

In this chapter we explore the idea that macroeconomic fluctuations can for the most part be explained by the dynamic effects of shocks in a competitive economy. This line of inquiry is recent.[1] For most of the twentieth century, especially since the Great Depression, most macroeconomists have looked upon the sharp fluctuations in output and unemployment as prima facie evidence of major market imperfections and explored what these imperfections may be. In the last 15 years, however, some have argued that this is a misguided research strategy, since macroeconomic fluctuations can be explained without invoking imperfections. The first statement, that fluctuations can be explained as the realization through time of the set of transactions agreed upon in a complete market Arrow-Debreu economy, was presented by Black (1982). In a series of papers Prescott (1986, for example) has explored this idea further, by examining the dynamic effects of productivity shocks on the competitive equilibrium allocation, to conclude: "Economists have long been puzzled by the observations that, during peacetime, industrial market economies display recurrent, large fluctuations in output and employment over relatively short time periods. . . . These observations should not be puzzling, for they are what standard economic theory predicts."

As will become clear, we do not believe that the line of research that we present in this first chapter on aggregate fluctuations is likely to provide a satisfactory explanation of fluctuations. Nevertheless, this chapter is important for two reasons. The first is that it is a logical starting point to the study of fluctuations. To see why one may want to explore the role of imperfections in fluctuations, it is essential to understand what the dynamic effects of shocks would be in a competitive economy. The second is that productivity shocks, even if they do not account for all or even for most fluctuations, may nevertheless play a more important role in fluctuations than has been emphasized until now.

The chapter has three sections. In section 7.1 we extend the representative agent dynamic models of chapters 2 and 3 to allow for productivity shocks and uncertainty. Our emphasis in this section is on the dynamics of output and its components when productivity is random. We do not strive for generality, preferring where possible to obtain closed-form solutions that illustrate both the approach and the basic dynamic mechanisms at work.

In section 7.2 we relax the assumption of constant employment and examine the mechanisms that may be capable of generating the comovements in output and employment that characterize actual fluctuations. The challenge is to explain how technological shocks can generate persistent movements not only in output but also in employment. We indicate why we do not think that the challenge is met or is likely to be met by that approach to business cycles.

In the final section we explore the implications of decentralized markets for the dynamic effects of shocks on the economy. We analyze first a simple model of search to show how the heterogeneity of workers and jobs in the labor market modifies the effects of productivity shocks on employment, wages, and output. We then extend the model to allow for imperfect information about the realizations of current shocks and for two different types of shocks, real and monetary, an approach to fluctuations first explored by Lucas. Imperfect information modifies the dynamic effects of real shocks. It also implies a potential effect of monetary shocks which would not be present under perfect information. We conclude with an assessment of the competitive equilibrium approach.[2]

7.1 Productivity Shocks, Consumption, and Capital Accumulation

When studying the dynamics of capital accumulation in the models of chapters 2 and 3, we made counterfactual assumptions of certainty and perfect foresight. This was a necessary first step, but we now recognize the presence of uncertainty. The economy is constantly affected by the introduction of new technologies, by changes in tastes for specific goods, by changes in government policy, and so on. Most of these changes are neither perfectly predictable nor perfectly predicted by individuals and firms. The presence of uncertainty affects the behavior of agents. The shocks themselves lead them to constantly revise their optimal plans.

In this section we focus mostly on the dynamic effects of one type of shock, shocks to productivity. We concentrate on two main issues. First, we examine whether the propagation mechanism tends to amplify or to dampen the effects of shocks on aggregate output and whether productivity shocks can plausibly explain the pattern of serial correlation of output characterized in chapter 1. Second, we examine whether productivity shocks can explain the comovements of output and its components, also characterized in chapter 1. Finally, we take a brief detour and return to an issue that was central to many of our discussions in earlier chapters, that of the form of the golden rule under uncertainty.

We start by introducing shocks in both the Diamond and the Ramsey models—more specifically, in versions of those models for which explicit solutions can be obtained: this is a fairly substantial restriction.[3] We then turn to the additional dynamics introduced by inventory behavior.

Multiplicative Shocks in the Diamond and Ramsey Models

Productivity Shocks in the Diamond Model
Productivity shocks that affect output in the current period are likely to lead to increased consumption as well as to increased saving, and thus to increased capital accumulation. Because increased capital accumulation leads to higher output later, productivity shocks lead to a serially correlated response of output. This point can be made straightforwardly in a simple stochastic version of the Diamond overlapping generations model with capital.

Population is assumed to be constant. People live for two periods, each person supplying one unit of labor inelastically in the first period. For convenience, the size of each generation is normalized to one. The production function is assumed to be Cobb-Douglas, with production given by

$$Y_t = U_t K_t^a N_t^{1-a} = U_t K_t^a, \tag{1}$$

where U_t is the level of productivity (a random variable with properties to be defined later), K_t is capital, and L_t is labor. The second equality results from the normalization of the labor force. Y_t is gross output, that is, output that includes the capital stock left after production. Equivalently, Y_t is net output, and capital depreciates fully after one period.[4]

An individual born at time t supplies one unit of labor and earns a wage ω_t. She then chooses consumption at time t to maximize her expected utility:

$$\ln C_{1t} + (1 + \theta)^{-1} E[\ln(C_{2t+1})|t]$$

subject to the budget constraint

$$C_{2t+1} = (1 + r_t)(\omega_t - C_{1t}).$$

The assumption of logarithmic utility yields a simple solution to the maximization problem. First-period consumption and savings are proportional to wage income and independent of the interest rate. The independence of savings from the interest rate, which is stochastic here, is what makes the model so tractable. Letting S_t denote the savings of the young, and noting that $S_t = \omega_t - C_{1t}$,

$$S_t = \frac{\omega_t}{2 + \theta}.$$

Thus, by using the fact that $\omega_t = (1 - a)U_t K_t^a$, and that $K_{t+1} = S_t$, we obtain a stochastic difference equation for the capital stock:

$$K_{t+1} = \frac{(1 - a)U_t K_t^a}{2 + \theta}. \tag{2}$$

The capital stock today determines labor income, which in turn determines saving and the capital stock in the next period.[5]

Equation (2) is linear in logarithms. We denote logarithms by lowercase letters:

$$k_{t+1} = b + ak_t + u_t, \tag{3}$$

where

$$b \equiv \ln\left(\frac{1 - a}{2 + \theta}\right).$$

By taking logarithms in (1) and replacing capital by its expression from (3), we obtain a dynamic equation for output:

$$y_t = ab + ay_{t-1} + u_t. \tag{4}$$

The logarithm of output follows a first-order difference equation, with forcing term u_t; the first-order autoregressive coefficient a is equal to the share of capital in output. This shows the contribution of capital accumulation to the persistence of the effects of technological shocks on output. We now explore this contribution further.

Suppose first—and counterfactually—that u_t is a white noise random variable so that the logarithm of productivity is equal to a constant plus white noise. In this case output follows a first-order autoregressive process, with a serial correlation coefficient equal to a: a positive productivity shock leads to an increase in consumption and savings and to higher levels of capital and output. Over time, capital and output return to their initial levels.

The empirical counterpart of a is difficult to determine, since this is a gross production function for a model with a unit period of about 30 years. But consideration of the economics of the mechanism specified here suggests it can account for relatively little serial correlation. Suppose that a shock raises GNP this year by 1% and that saving increases by as much as 0.5% of GNP—a very high saving response. With the real return on capital equal to about 10%, the extra saving would increase GNP in the following year by 0.05%. Capital accumulation clearly cannot account for much of the serial correlation in output.

The assumption of white noise productivity, or even of white noise productivity around a deterministic trend, is, however, not particularly appealing. New techniques, once introduced, should be available forever. Suppose that innovations in productivity have permanent effects on the level of productivity, that is, the process for productivity has a unit root.[6] A stochastic process that may more accurately describe productivity growth is

$$u_t = g + u_{t-1} + \varepsilon_t$$

where ε_t is white noise. Productivity follows a random walk with drift g so that it grows on average at rate g.[7] Put another way, productivity growth is a white noise process. Given this process for productivity, we replace it in (4), and output becomes

$$\Delta y_t = g + a \Delta y_{t-1} + \varepsilon_t. \tag{5}$$

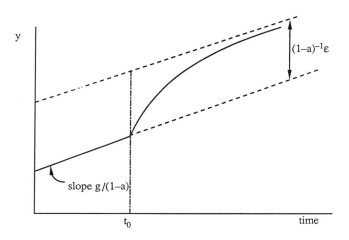

Figure 7.1
Effects of an increase in ε at t_0 on output

As a result of capital accumulation, *output growth* is serially correlated, with serial correlation coefficient a. The effects of a positive productivity shock, an increase in ε, on the level of y are given in figure 7.1. Output increases above its initial growth path at time zero, and increases further through time at a rate faster than g. Eventually, the rate of growth returns to g, but the level of output is higher than it would otherwise have been.

As we noted earlier, the coefficient a is, in practice, likely to be small, and therefore capital accumulation does not amplify the dynamics of productivity shocks significantly *through this particular mechanism*.[8] Also virtually any stochastic process that is desired for output can be obtained by appropriately specifying the corresponding stochastic process for the productivity shock. Thus independent information on the stochastic process for productivity shocks is needed to assess their role in economic fluctuations.

Productivity Shocks in the Ramsey Model
Very similar results obtain in the corresponding version of the Ramsey model with infinitely long-lived individuals. Consider the following modification of the model of chapter 2; in it we again rely on logarithmic specifications of utility and production functions to obtain explicit solutions.

There is no population growth, and the population size is normalized to one. Individuals live forever, supplying one unit of labor in each period and maximizing at time t:

$$\sum_{i=0}^{\infty} (1 + \theta)^{-i} E[\ln C_{t+i}|t]$$

subject to

$$K_{t+i+1} + C_{t+i} = Y_{t+i} \equiv U_{t+i} K_{t+i}^a.$$

As before, U, a random variable, is the level of productivity, and the production function represents gross output. From the first-order conditions we obtain[9]

$$\left(\frac{1}{C_t}\right) = (1 + \theta)^{-1} E\left[\frac{aU_{t+1} K_{t+1}^{a-1}}{C_{t+1}}\bigg| t\right].$$

An educated guess at the solution to this difference equation is that $C_t = \beta U_t K_t^a$ for a value of β to be determined. If we replace it in the above expression and use the budget constraint, the guess proves to be right and the appropriate value of β to be $1 - [a/(1 + \theta)]$.

The logarithmic assumptions therefore deliver the very strong result that consumption and saving are proportional to income, independent of the stochastic properties of U.[10] The implied process for capital is

$$K_{t+1} = S_t = \left(\frac{a}{1+\theta}\right) U_t K_t^a, \tag{6}$$

or, using logarithms,

$$k_{t+1} = b + ak_t + u_t, \tag{7}$$

where

$$b \equiv \ln\left(\frac{a}{1+\theta}\right).$$

The results are therefore similar to those of the Diamond model. The only difference is in the constant term, which determines the average level of capital in the economy.

Multisector Extension
Long and Plosser (1983) have developed a multisector extension of the Ramsey model. Each sector is affected by its own productivity shock and uses as inputs both labor and the outputs of other sectors, with a one-period production lag. The dynamics of the system are richer because the deterministic part of the system now has as many roots as the number of sectors, in constrast to the dynamic system given by equation (7) which has only one root.[11] Using an aggregate empirical input-output table to calibrate their model, they show that even under the assumption that productivity shocks are independent both across time and across sectors, the outputs of individual sectors may exhibit both serial and cross correlations. The average pairwise cross correlation across sectors is around 20%, and the average first-order serial correlation (for annual data) around 30%.

A Detour: The Modified Golden Rule under Uncertainty

Having introduced uncertainty in the Ramsey model, we can return to the form of the modified golden rule, this time under uncertainty. What is the relation between the *marginal product of capital* and the *discount rate* in this stochastic extension of the Ramsey model?

Assume, for simplicity, that the stochastic process for productivity is either stationary or has a unit root and zero drift [i.e., if productivity follows the process given by equation (5), g is equal to zero]. Then under certainty the modified golden rule in this economy, without population or productivity growth, would be that the gross marginal product of capital, which would also be equal to the gross interest rate, is equal to one plus the subjective discount rate. This can be seen, for instance, by setting U in (6) equal to a constant and solving for the real interest rate with $K_{t+1} = K_t$, which is the steady state condition.

To see what holds here, consider the logarithm of the marginal product of capital (MPK), which is given by

$$\ln(\text{MPK}_t) = \ln a + u_t + (a - 1)k_t. \tag{8}$$

By solving for k_{t+1} as a function of past u's in (7), replacing k_t in (8), and rearranging, we get

$$\ln(\text{MPK}_t) = \ln(1 + \theta) + (1 - aL)^{-1}(u_t - u_{t-1}), \tag{9}$$

where L is the lag operator. Thus, by taking unconditional expectations on both sides,[12] we get

$$E[\ln(\text{MPK})] = \ln(1 + \theta).$$

In this version of the Ramsey model with uncertainty, the modified golden rule is that the expectation of the logarithm of the marginal product is equal to the logarithm of one plus the discount rate. By Jensen's inequality, this implies that under uncertainty the expectation of the marginal product exceeds one plus the discount rate.

If we are ready to specify the process for productivity, we can go further and get an explicit solution for the expected value of the marginal product. If, for example, productivity growth is white noise, with innovations e_t normally distributed with variance σ^2, we have from equation (9),

$$E[\ln(\text{MPK})] = \ln(1 + \theta)$$

and

$$V[\ln(\text{MPK})] = \left(\frac{1}{1 - a^2}\right)\sigma^2.$$

Thus

$$E[\text{MPK}] = (1 + \theta) \exp\left[\frac{\sigma^2}{2(1 - a^2)}\right].$$

We can also derive the relation between the *riskless rate* and the discount rate. Although there is no riskless asset in this economy, we can find out what its equilibrium rate of return would be, were we to introduce one at the margin. The rate of return on the riskless asset in period t, R_t, would have to satisfy the first-order conditions of consumers, namely,

$$\frac{1}{C_t} = R_t(1 + \theta)^{-1}E\left[\left(\frac{1}{C_{t+1}}\right)\Big| t\right],$$

or, upon rearranging,

$$\ln(R_t) = \ln(1 + \theta) - \ln\left(E\left[\frac{C_t}{C_{t+1}}\Big| t\right]\right).$$

If we assume that productivity growth is white noise, with innovations e_t normally distributed with variance σ^2, the logarithm of consumption follows

$$c_{t+1} - c_t = a(c_t - c_{t-1}) + e_t$$

so that

$$\ln(R_t) = \ln(1 + \theta) + a(c_t - c_{t-1}) - \left(\frac{\sigma^2}{2}\right).$$

The riskless rate is therefore not constant. At time t it depends on the past change in consumption. Because changes in consumption are positively correlated, an increase in consumption in period t implies an expected increase in consumption from t to $t + 1$ and thus a higher riskless rate. The riskless rate is a decreasing function of the uncertainty associated with changes in consumption. An intuitive explanation, based on our analysis of precautionary saving in the previous chapter, is as follows: an increase in uncertainty makes people more prudent, so that, at the same real rate, they would consume less today and more tomorrow. To reestablish equilibrium, the real rate must decrease, leading to an offsetting increase in consumption today and a decrease tomorrow.

The last step is to compute the unconditional expected value of the riskless rate. From above,

$$E[\ln(R_t)] = \ln(1 + \theta) - \left(\frac{\sigma^2}{2}\right),$$

$$V[\ln(R_t)] = \frac{a^2\sigma^2}{(1 - a^2)}.$$

The variance in the logarithm of the riskless rate depends on the variance in the expected rate of change of consumption. From the above equations we get

$$E[R] = (1 + \theta)\exp\left\{\left(\frac{\sigma^2}{2}\right)\left[\frac{a^2}{1 - a^2} - 1\right]\right\}.$$

The effect of uncertainty is ambiguous. The riskless rate may be greater or smaller than the subjective discount rate. The closer consumption growth is to white noise, the more likely it is that the real rate is less than the subjective discount rate.[13]

We have shown that in a dynamically efficient economy such as the Ramsey economy, there is, once we allow for uncertainty, no simple relation between the marginal product of capital, the riskless rate, and the subjective discount rate. The reason for deriving those results was, however, our interest in a different but closely related question, that of dynamic efficiency in an arbitrary economy. In an economy where people have finite horizons and where there is uncertainty, what rate should we look at to tell if the economy is dynamically efficient? Empirically, the average real rate of interest on (relatively) safe Treasury bills has averaged less than 1% over the past 60 years, while the return on stocks has exceeded the rate of growth. Which is the relevant rate of return to compare with the rate of growth in assessing whether the economy has overaccumulated capital? The preceding example suggests that neither of the two rates is likely to be appropriate and that there may not be a simple answer to that question. The question of how to assess empirically whether an economy is dynamically efficient is still quite open. Abel et al. (1986) derive a sufficient condition for efficiency,[14] that the level of investment must be less in every year than the share of profits. (Under certainty the dynamic efficiency can be stated as the condition that investment must be less or equal to the share of profits. This was first shown by Phelps 1961.) They show that this condition has been satisfied in every year since 1929 and therefore, they reason, the U.S. economy is very likely to be dynamically efficient.

Additive Shocks in a Linear Ramsey Model

The assumptions made thus far in this section imply that the saving rate is constant and independent of the process followed by productivity. To obtain some insight into dynamics when the saving rate can vary, we develop another simplified case. We continue to use the Ramsey model but assume that productivity shocks are additive rather than multiplicative and that the real interest rate is constant. As we shall see, this affects not only the short-run but also the long-run effects of productivity shocks.

Consider an economy with a constant population whose size is normalized at one. Individuals are infinitely long lived and maximize at time t:

$$\sum_{i=0}^{\infty} (1 + \theta)^{-i} E[C_{t+i} - bC_{t+i}^2 | t], \qquad b > 0$$

subject to

$$K_{t+i+1} + C_{t+i} = Y_{t+i} \equiv (1 + r)K_{t+i} + U_{t+i}.$$

Instantaneous utility is quadratic. Production requires only capital and takes place under constant returns to scale, with r being the net marginal product of capital. (An alternative interpretation, similar to a model developed in chapter 2, is that this is a small economy that can borrow and lend at the world interest rate r.) U_t is now additive and therefore does not affect the marginal product of capital.[15] It is best thought of as an exogenous endowment each period, as manna from heaven, that follows a given stochastic process. We will refer to it as the endowment. Together these assumptions yield certainty equivalence.

Recalling the results of chapter 2, an economy with infinitely long lived individuals will, if r is different from θ, be either accumulating or decumulating capital forever. Thus, to obtain a well-behaved stochastic steady state, we assume in what follows that θ is equal to r, that is, the discount rate is equal to the marginal product of capital. Given this assumption, the first-order conditions imply that

$$C_t = E[C_{t+i}|t], \qquad \text{for all } i > 0.$$

Consumers choose to have constant expected consumption. The highest feasible expected level of consumption that satisfies the intertemporal budget constraint is given by[16]

$$C_t = r\left\{ K_t + (1 + r)^{-1} \sum_{i=0}^{\infty} (1 + r)^{-i} E[U_{t+i}|t] \right\}. \tag{10}$$

The basic feature of this economy can be understood by examining the coefficient associated with U_t in equation (10). That coefficient is $r/(1 + r)$. This means that the consumer treats U_t as an annuity, from which he draws down the interest for consumption each period. Thus, if movements in U_t are transitory, there is consumption smoothing in this version of the Ramsey model. Consumption depends on the current capital stock and the expected present discounted value of endowments.

Replacing this expression for consumption in the budget constraint gives the behavior of capital and thus also (from the production function) that of output:

$$K_{t+1} = K_t + \left\{ U_t - r(1 + r)^{-1} \sum_{i=0}^{\infty} (1 + r)^{-i} E[U_{t+i}|t] \right\}. \tag{11}$$

The change in the capital stock is equal to the difference between the current endowment and the expected present discounted value of current and future endowments.

We can obtain further insight by solving for a specific endowment process. For a change we consider the following IMA(1, 1) process:

$$U_t = U_{t-1} + e_t - ae_{t-1}, \qquad |a| < 1.$$

This is the simplest process that allows for both permanent and transitory effects of shocks on endowments. The long-run effect of a shock e on U is equal to $1 - a$. Thus, if $a = 1$, the process reduces to white noise, with shocks having purely transitory effects. For a between 0 and 1, shocks have a permanent effect, though smaller than their initial effect. If a is equal to 0, the process reduces to a random walk. For a between 0 and -1, the permanent effect exceeds the initial effect.

By solving for expectations in (11), we find the impact of a given shock e_t on the change in the capital stock:

$$K_{t+1} - K_t = \left(\frac{a}{1 + r}\right)e_t. \qquad (12)$$

Thus a shock, e, increases capital accumulation only to the extent that its effect on productivity is *transitory*. If its effect is permanent, if productivity follows a random walk, the increase in output is matched by an equal increase in consumption, resulting in an unchanged capital stock. If, however, its effect is partly transitory (a between 0 and 1), consumption increases less than one for one with output, resulting in an increase in capital accumulation. This ensures that the effects of the productivity increase on consumption are spread over time.

In this case, in contrast to the previous examples, even purely transitory shocks ($a = 1$) have a permanent effect on capital accumulation and output. This occurs because the model, by assuming that the interest rate is constant and independent of the level of capital, implicitly assumes constant returns to scale given labor, an assumption we have made for convenience of argument and without explicit justification.[17]

The first two examples emphasized the fact that positive technological shocks generally lead to more capital accumulation, which then amplifies the initial effect of these shocks. This example, by contrast, emphasizes the potential role of consumption smoothing in determining the serial correlation of output.[18]

Inventories, Taste, and Technology Shocks

We finally turn to the role of inventories in the propagation mechanism of shocks on activity. To do so, we extend to a general equilibrium setting the model of inventory behavior studied in the previous chapter.[19] The model is again a variation on the Ramsey model, with quadratic utility and production and with additive shocks. However, we ignore capital accumulation and look instead at inventory behavior.[20] This time, to relate the results of our model to the literature, we allow for both taste and productivity shocks.

The Objective Function
The infinitely lived consumer-producers in the economy maximize

$$E\left[\sum_{i=0}^{\infty}(1+\theta)^{-i}\left\{-\left(\frac{d}{2}\right)(C_{t+i}-V_{t+i})^2-\left(\frac{a}{2}\right)(Y_{t+i}-U_{t+i})^2\right.\right.$$
$$\left.\left.-\left(\frac{b}{2}\right)(I_{t+i})^2\right\}\bigg|\omega_t\right]$$

subject to

$$I_{t+i}=I_{t+i-1}+Y_{t+i}-C_{t+i}, \qquad a, b, d \geqslant 0$$

where C_t denotes consumption, Y_t production and I_t end-of-period t inventories. Consumption no longer needs to coincide with production but can be met out of inventory decumulation.

Consumers maximize the expected present discounted value of the consumer surplus, which is the sum of three terms, reflecting respectively the utility of consumption, the cost of production and the cost of deviating from target inventory:

The first term reflects the decreasing marginal utility of consumption, which, other things being equal, leads to *consumption smoothing*.[21] V is a taste shock that affects the marginal utility of consumption; a positive realization of V increases marginal utility.

The other two terms in the sum capture the two aspects of production and inventory behavior studied in the previous chapter. The first, $(-a/2)(Y-U)^2$, implies an increasing marginal cost of production and leads, other things being equal, to *production smoothing*. Since no distinction is made between employment and production, this can be thought of as an increasing marginal disutility of work. U is a favorable technological shock; a positive realization of U decreases marginal cost. The second term,

$(-b/2)(I)^2$, reflects the benefits and costs of having inventories on hand. We showed in chapter 6 how this term approximately captures the stock-out motive, the desire of firms not to lose sales because of insufficient inventories on hand.

The *information structure* is important here. For the stock-out motive to be relevant, production decisions must be taken before sales are known. In our present model this implies that Y must be decided before the current realization of V, the taste shock, is known. Thus we assume the following structure: Production decisions at time t are taken based on knowledge of the current value of U. Once the production decision is made, consumption and therefore end-of-period inventory decisions are made based on knowledge of current values of both V and U. It is convenient to introduce two information sets for time t, $\omega_t = \{U_t, U_{t-1}, V_{t-1}, \ldots\}$ on which production decisions are based and $\Omega_t = \{U_t, V_t, U_{t-1}, V_{t-1}, \ldots\}$ on which consumption decisions are based. Note that $\Omega_{t-1} \subset \omega_t \subset \Omega_t \subset \cdots$. Finally, and again for simplicity, we assume that both V and U are i.i.d., with zero mean, and mutually independent.[22]

First-Order Conditions
Replacing C by its value from the inventory accumulation equation, and maximizing with respect to I and Y, gives a set of first-order conditions. For time t these are

$$Y_t: \quad -a(Y_t - U_t) - d(-E[I_t|\omega_t] + I_{t-1} + Y_t) = 0,$$

$$I_t: \quad d(-I_t + I_{t-1} + Y_t - V_t) - bI_t - (1+\theta)^{-1}d(-E[I_{t+1}|\Omega_t] + I_t$$

$$+ E[Y_{t+1}|\Omega_t]) = 0.$$

The first condition states that the marginal cost of production must be equal to the expected marginal utility of consumption. The second states that the increase in marginal utility from consuming one more unit today instead of tomorrow must equal the marginal cost of deviating from target inventory. The different information sets reflect the different timings of production and consumption decisions.

Solving the first equation for the level of production gives

$$Y_t = \left(\frac{d}{a+d}\right)(E[I_t|\omega_t] - I_{t-1}) + \left(\frac{a}{a+d}\right)U_t. \tag{13}$$

Production depends on the expected change in inventories as well as on the current technology shock. Replacing Y_t and $E[Y_{t+1}|\Omega_t]$ by their value implied by (13) in the second first-order condition gives a dynamic equation in I_t:

$$d\{-(a+d)I_t + dE[I_t|\omega_t] + aI_{t-1} + aU_t - (a+d)V_t\}$$

$$-b(a+d)(I_t) + (1+\theta)^{-1}ad(E[I_{t+1}|\Omega_t] - I_t) = 0. \tag{14}$$

The Solution

To solve equation (14), we follow the method developed in the appendix to chapter 5. We proceed in two steps, solving first for $E[I_t|\omega_t]$ and then for I_t.

By taking expectations conditional on ω_t on both sides of (14), and reorganizing, we get

$$E[I_t|\omega_t] = (1+\theta)zI_{t-1} + zE[I_{t+1}|\omega_t] + (1+\theta)zU_t, \tag{15}$$

where

$$z \equiv \frac{ad}{ad(2+\theta) + b(1+\theta)(a+d)}.$$

Expected inventories depend on lagged and expected future inventories, as well as on the current technological shock. We use factorization techniques to solve (15):

$$E[I_t|\omega_t] = \lambda I_{t-1} + \lambda U_t, \tag{16}$$

where λ is the smallest root of the equation

$$\lambda^2 - z^{-1}\lambda + (1+\theta) = 0.$$

From the definition of z, λ is between zero and one. Expected inventories depend on themselves lagged, as well as on the current technological shock. (Remember that under the assumption that shocks are white noise, expected future shocks are equal to zero.)

From equation (13), we can solve for production at time t:

$$Y_t = (a+d)^{-1}[d(\lambda - 1)I_{t-1} + (d\lambda + a)U_t]. \tag{17}$$

Production depends negatively on lagged inventories and positively on this period's technology shock.

The final step is to solve for I_t and C_t. A simple way of doing this is to guess, based on (16), that I_t is given by

$$I_t = \lambda I_{t-1} + \lambda U_t - \alpha V_t, \tag{18}$$

with α to be determined. To solve for α, we take expectations of (14) conditional on ω_t and subtract them from (14). Equation (18) implies that $I_t - E[I_t|\omega_t] = -\alpha V_t$ and that $E[I_{t+1}|\Omega_t] - E[I_{t+1}|\omega_t] = -\alpha\lambda V_t$. By putting these results together, we obtain

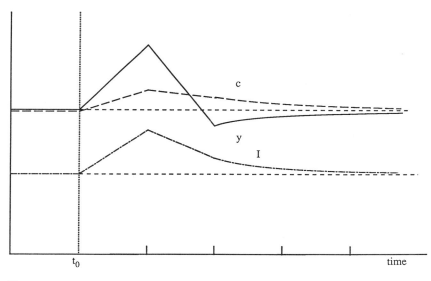

Figure 7.2
Effects of a technological shock on output, consumption, and inventories

$$\alpha = \frac{d(a + d)}{(a + d)(d + b) + (1 + \theta)^{-1}ad(1 - \lambda)} \geq 0.$$

Using the inventory accumulation equation, we can solve for C_t:

$$C_t = (a + d)^{-1}[a(1 - \lambda)I_{t-1} + a(1 - \lambda)U_t] + \alpha V_t. \tag{19}$$

This fully characterizes the solution. We are now in a position to examine the dynamic effects of shocks on inventories and output. The effects of technological and taste shocks on production, consumption, and inventories are presented in figures 7.2 and 7.3 respectively.

A favorable technology shock ($U > 0$) initially increases production and inventories. The lower marginal cost this period leads producers to intertemporally substitute and to increase production this period. Consumption also increases but by less, leading to inventory accumulation. Over time, lower production and higher consumption imply a return of inventories to their initial level. Serially uncorrelated technological shocks lead to negative serial correlation in output and a positive serial correlation in consumption.

A positive taste shock ($V > 0$) initially increases consumption and decreases inventories. The higher marginal utility in this period leads consumers to intertemporally substitute, to consume more in the current period. Because production is predetermined, the increase in consumption

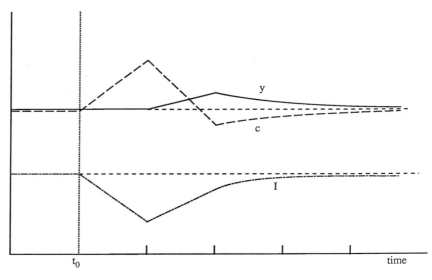

Figure 7.3
Effects of a taste shock on output, consumption, and inventories

is met by inventory decumulation.[23] Over time, inventories are replenished at rate λ, and production remains higher and consumption lower until inventories are back to their initial level. Serially uncorrelated taste shocks therefore lead to positive serial correlation in output and negative serial correlation in consumption.

To summarize, compared to the case where no inventories are held, optimal inventory behavior is likely to increase the serial correlation of output with respect to taste shocks but to decrease it with respect to technological shocks.

What should we conclude from the sequence of models presented in this section? Positive productivity shocks are likely to lead, through capital accumulation, to more serial correlation in output than in productivity. They are likely to lead to increases in consumption and in fixed and inventory investment, thus fitting the procyclical behavior of these three components of output, which was documented in chapter 1. At that level of abstraction, productivity shocks in an equilibrium model appear to be able to explain the basic features of the joint movements of GNP and its components that are observed in practice.[24] Although we have not explored their effect systematically, taste shocks appear less able, at least by themselves, to fit the basic facts. Taste shocks lead, in this equilibrium framework, to large fluctuations in consumption relative to output and do not generate the procyclical movement in inventory and investment that is observed in the data.

One obvious question at this stage is whether shocks in aggregate productivity are sufficiently large to explain short-run fluctuations in output. If these shocks are truly productivity shocks, we might expect new technologies to be introduced only slowly and smoothly through time. Moreover, true productivity shocks are likely to be only weakly correlated across sectors, thus leading, by the law of large numbers, to aggregate shocks with relatively small variance.[25] Suppose that there are, for example, one hundred sectors in the economy of the same size and that in each of them the innovation in the rate of yearly productivity growth has a standard deviation of 3%. If the shocks are uncorrelated, the standard deviation of the innovation for aggregate productivity growth will be equal to 0.3%. This standard deviation, however, increases rapidly with the degree of correlation. If the pairwise correlation across sectors is equal to 0.2, the standard deviation of aggregate productivity innovations increases to 1.4%.[26] Whether there is enough variance in sectoral productivity or enough correlation across sectors to explain substantial aggregate fluctuations is at this stage an open issue.

The other question is whether productivity shocks can explain movements in employment, which we have until now assumed to be constant. This is the question we explore in the next section.

7.2 Output and Employment Fluctuations

So far we have looked at output fluctuations, given a constant labor force. But, as we saw in chapter 1, although productivity is procyclical, output and employment generally move together. Over the long term much of this comovement is due to the demographic evolution of the labor force, which leads to increases in both employment and output over time. But there is clearly more to that relation: fluctuations in output are associated with systematic movements in the number of hours worked by those who remain employed, in the number of persons employed, and in the number of people participating in the labor force. Lilien and Hall (1986) give, for the postwar United States, the decomposition of the change in total hours worked between the change in the number of persons employed and the change in the number of hours worked by those who remain employed. They conclude that changes in employment account for approximately 75 to 80% of cyclical changes in total hours worked.[27] Further, these movements in employment are, as we also saw in chapter 1, associated with only small movements in the real wage.

These facts need to be explained by any theory of fluctuations, and they present a difficult challenge for equilibrium cycle theories. We start at the obvious place by introducing leisure into the utility function, thereby allowing the labor supply decision to become endogenous. We characterize the implied comovements of employment, real wages, and consumption and show why they are difficult to reconcile with the facts.

Intertemporal Substitution and Employment Fluctuations

To explain the positive covariance in output and employment associated with only small movements in the real wage, Lucas and Rapping (1969) argued that small temporary movements in the real wage would elicit a response in the labor supply, with workers willingly substituting leisure for labor from periods in which it was expensive to periods in which it was cheap. This forms the basis of the *intertemporal substitution of leisure* explanation for the joint behavior of employment and wages over the cycle.

Rather than introduce leisure as a choice variable in the dynamic models developed above, we illustrate the general characteristics of the problem with a special case, a two-period maximization problem under certainty.[28] Consider a person who consumes and works in two periods and has the utility function

$$U(c_1, c_2, x_1, x_2) = \sum_{i=1,2} (1 + \theta)^{-i-1} \left[\ln c_i - \left(\frac{\gamma \sigma}{\sigma + 1} \right) x_i^{(\sigma+1)/\sigma} \right], \quad \sigma > 0,$$

where c_i is consumption and x_i is labor. Utility is additively separable over time. The important coefficient for our purposes is σ, which is the elasticity of substitution of labor across periods. The smaller σ is, the greater is the curvature of the disutility of labor function and the less willing are individuals to substitute labor intertemporally. As σ tends to infinity, the marginal disutility of labor becomes approximately constant.

Letting λ be the Lagrange multiplier associated with the budget constraint $c_1 + c_2/(1 + r) = w_1 x_1 + w_2 x_2/(1 + r)$, we derive the first-order conditions:

$$c_1 = \left(\frac{1}{\lambda} \right),$$

$$c_2 = \left(\frac{1}{\lambda}\right)\left[\frac{1+r}{1+\theta}\right],$$

$$x_1 = \left(\frac{\lambda w_1}{\gamma}\right)^\sigma,$$

$$x_2 = \left\{\left(\frac{\lambda w_2}{\gamma}\right)\left[\frac{1+\theta}{1+r}\right]\right\}^\sigma.$$

We may think of these first-order conditions as giving the supply of labor and the demand for goods given the marginal utility of wealth, λ. From the two first-order conditions on labor supply, we get

$$\frac{x_1}{x_2} = \left[\frac{w_1}{w_2(1+\theta)/(1+r)}\right]^\sigma. \tag{20}$$

Relative labor supply depends on the relative wage across periods, with elasticity σ.

Finally, we solve for λ, the marginal utility of wealth. Using the budget constraint, we obtain

$$\lambda = (\text{constant})[w_1^z + (\text{constant})w_2^z]^{-1/z}$$

where the two unimportant constants depend on θ, r, and β and $z \equiv \sigma + 1$.

We can now characterize the effects of wages on labor supply. Consider first a multiplicative increase in the wage in both periods, such as would result, for example, from a permanent technological shock to the marginal product of labor or a permanent change in labor income tax rates. From equation (20) it is clear that such a permanent change has no effect on relative labor supply across periods. The first-order conditions, together with the equation for the marginal utility of wealth, imply a stronger result: a permanent wage change has no effect on labor supply in either period. What is at work here is the familiar conflict between income and the substitution effects of a wage change. The assumption that the wage change is permanent implies a strong income effect that, given the specification we have chosen, exactly cancels the substitution effect.

This result points to the type of wage change that *will* have an effect on labor supply. Consider a temporary increase in wages, an increase in w_1 with no change in w_2. From equation (20) this will lead individuals to substitute leisure intertemporally, to supply relatively more labor in the period in which the wage is high.[29] The smaller the curvature of the disutility of labor (the larger σ), the stronger the effect. This is a result about *relative* labor supply; solving for levels shows the effect of the wage change to be positive on x_1 and negative—but smaller in absolute value—on x_2. The income effect is in this case weaker than in the case of a permanent change.

This remains the basic result of more general models of labor supply: labor supply will respond to *temporary* movements in the real wage, even though it may not respond to *permanent* changes in the real wage. In response to transitory wage fluctuations, intertemporal substitution can generate large fluctuations in labor supply. Permanent wage movements are likely to have little or no effect on labor supply.

Intertemporal substitution leads workers to shift labor supply away from times when the wage is relatively low toward times when the wage is relatively high. Other things being equal, it generates a negatively serially correlated response of labor supply and employment to wage shocks: increases in labor supply today reflect expected decreases in the labor supply later. The question therefore arises of whether models with endogenous labor supply and intertemporal substitution can explain both the strong response of employment to shocks and the high positive serial correlation in employment observed in the data.

This question has been examined by Sargent (1979) who characterizes the dynamics of wages and employment in a labor market in which workers intertemporally substitute and in which firms face convex costs of adjustment in employment.[30] The answer is that with costs of adjustment of employment for firms, even temporary technological shocks can potentially explain both the response of employment to shocks and the serial correlation in employment. In response to a positive shock, firms increase labor demand, although by less than they would in the absence of costs of adjustment, and this leads to an increase in the wage and an increase in the labor supply. In the following periods, although the technological shock is no longer present, labor demand, which depends in part on past employment, remains relatively high. Wages return slowly to equilibrium, and so does the labor supply. Thus, with costs of adjustment, white noise technological shocks lead to positive serial correlation in both wages and employment. This is a fortiori true of serially correlated technological shocks, although the higher serial correlation decreases the incentive for intertemporal substitution and thus further reduces the initial effect of shocks on employment. Thus it is possible to construct models based on intertemporal substitution that generate serially correlated movements in employment together with small procyclical movements in the wage. Does this make intertemporal substitution a likely channel of transmission of shocks to employment? We now look at that question more closely.

Intertemporal Substitution: An Assessment

For intertemporal substitution to explain fluctuations in employment in the above framework, two conditions are needed: the elasticity of substitution between leisure in different periods must be high, and aggregate real wage movements must be largely transitory. Empirical evidence suggests that neither condition is satisfied.

Panel data evidence on the *elasticity of substitution*, σ in the earlier example, suggests that it is small. In his survey of research on the labor supply of men, Pencavel (1986) shows most estimates to be between 0 and 0.45. In their parallel survey of research on the labor supply of women, Killingsworth and Heckman (1986) present a wide range of estimates, from -0.3 to 14.00; they do not venture a guess as to which is correct but conclude that the elasticity is probably somewhat higher for women than for men.

More important, there is *no evidence of important transitory components in aggregate real wages*. As we saw in chapter 1, aggregate real wages follow univariate processes that have little or no transitory component: for the two consumption wages considered in that chapter, an unexpected increase in real wages leads to expected further increases in real wages later. An unexpected increase in the manufacturing wage of 1 at time t leads to an increase of 1.49 in the expected wage four quarters ahead. If anything, this should lead workers to defer labor supply, not to increase it at time t. Not surprisingly therefore, formal estimation of the first-order conditions for labor supply, using panel or aggregate data, along the lines of (20) but extended to allow for uncertainty, has resulted in failure.[31]

Can the intertemporal substitution hypothesis be rescued? Three directions have been explored. The first has examined the role of interest rates, which we have neglected until now. The second has studied the implications of more general specifications of utility. The third has explored the implications of insurance, under which the real wage may include an insurance component and thus may not equal the marginal product of labor.

Interest Rates, Wages, Consumption, and Employment
If we return to equation (20) of the two-period example developed earlier, relative labor supplies depend not only on relative wages but also on the real interest rate. Workers compare the wage today to the discounted value of future wages. An increase in the interest rate decreases the discounted value of those wages and makes it more attractive to work today. Thus, even if productivity shocks did not affect wages, they could in principle

affect employment by affecting the marginal product of capital and interest rates.[32] Employment fluctuations could come from variations in the interest rate.

Apart from the strong feeling of implausibility this potential explanation generates, it suffers from two serious problems. The first is that estimation of the first-order condition corresponding to equation (20) under uncertainty, and allowing for interest rate as well as wage effects, has been just as unsuccessful as estimation ignoring interest rates. The second is that models in which technological shocks affect employment through channels other than current wages have, under standard assumptions about utility, a clear counterfactual implication. This implication, which has been emphasized by Barro and King (1984), is the following: Suppose that utility is additively separable in time, and that each period utility is given by $U(c, x)$, where x is work. Then one of the necessary first-order conditions for maximization is that for any period t,

$$w_t U_c(c_t, x_t) = -U_x(c_t, x_t).$$

The marginal rate of substitution between work and consumption must be equal to the wage. Thus, if the wage does not change in period t, this first-order condition implies a fixed relation between consumption and work. If neither consumption nor leisure is an inferior good, increases in consumption of goods—say, in response to changes in interest rates or in wealth—must be associated with increases in leisure, or equivalently with decreases in labor supply.

To return to the question at hand, this implies that to the extent that shocks affect labor supply decisions mainly through interest rates, we would expect fluctuations to be characterized by a *negative* covariation of consumption and employment. But, as we well know, fluctuations are characterized by a positive covariation of employment and consumption, not the reverse. Mankiw, Rotemberg, and Summers (1985) have examined whether the comovements of wages, interest rates, employment, and consumption are consistent with the set of first-order conditions of a representative worker-consumer who maximizes the expected present discounted value of utility, with utility being additively separable in time and in each period a function of leisure and consumption.[33] Their results formally confirm the conclusions drawn above that the aggregate data are simply not consistent with that set of first-order conditions: in particular, consumption and leisure move in opposite directions, without the required movement in the real wage.

More General Specifications of Utility

The assumption of additive separability of utility in time does not have particularly convincing justifications beyond analytical convenience. Surely, the marginal disutility of work today depends not only on consumption today but also on work yesterday or in the previous week. Some studies have explored whether relaxing the assumption of additive separability can reconcile facts and theory. Kydland and Prescott (1982) have examined the implications of a utility function of the form

$$U[c_i, a(L)(\bar{x} - x_i)],$$

where

$$a(L) = \sum_{i=0}^{n} a_i L^i,$$

so that utility at time i depends on both the current consumption and a distributed lag of leisure, $\bar{x} - x_i$, where $\bar{x}$ is the total time available and x_i is the time spent working. If the elements of $a(L)$ are positive, low leisure in the past implies high marginal utility of leisure today: this captures the idea of fatigue. If, instead, the elements of $a(L)$ are negative, low leisure in the past implies low marginal utility of leisure today: this captures the idea of habit formation.

It is clear that this utility function is more general than the additively separable version. It is also clear why, when the elements of $a(L)$ are positive and close to one, this specification is likely to generate stronger movements in employment in response to changes in wages. If, for example, the coefficients a_i are all equal to one, leisure in periods t to $t + n$ are all perfect substitutes from the point of view of utility at time t; small movements in relative wages may therefore lead the worker to concentrate labor supply in the period in which the wage is high.[34] But estimation of the first-order conditions of a representative worker-consumer with Kydland-Prescott preferences by Eichenbaum, Hansen, and Singleton (1987) has shown that this generalization does not help in explaining the comovements of employment, consumption, and real wages. This direction does not seem particularly promising.

A related direction has been explored by Rogerson (1985), Hansen (1985), and Hall (1987).[35] It recognizes that the labor supply decision has two dimensions. The first is the decision that one faces each day whether to work or not. The second is how many hours to work if one works. In addition there is a fixed cost of working, which is independent of how many hours are worked and captures commuting and setup costs.

Absent this fixed cost, and assuming that the disutility of hours worked is convex, workers prefer, other things being equal, to work every day and to work the same number of hours per day.[36] In the presence of fixed costs, however, this may not be optimal if it results in short workdays. The optimal labor supply decision is then as follows: so long as the wage is high enough, workers work every day, and the variation in labor supply comes from variations in hours. The elasticity of labor supply then depends on the convexity of the disutility of hours and may therefore be low. As the wage decreases, it reaches a critical value at which workers are indifferent between coming to work on a given day or not. At that wage, labor supply is completely elastic, and the number of days is determined by labor demand. At a lower wage, labor supply is equal to zero.

Can we conclude from the fact that most workers do not work every day that they are operating on the flat portion of their labor supply? Clearly not.[37] It is clear that the disutility of working is in fact convex in the number of days worked during the year and that workers are not indifferent as to the number of days they work. We must conclude that the assumption that the daily utility function is additively separable—an assumption that underlies the above argument—is not appropriate, and that the number of days worked in the past affects the current marginal utility of leisure. This line of research may be useful to explain vacations and weekends. It seems, however, of little relevance when the goal is to explain the effects of changes in wages on employment in the business cycle.

A third direction focuses on heterogeneity among workers. Under that interpretation employment fluctuations are accounted for mainly by movements in and out of employment by workers with different reservation wages, in response to movements in their real wage. In that view the slope of the aggregate labor supply curve has little to do with intertemporal substitution but rather with the distribution of reservation wages across workers.[38]

This approach can potentially explain employment fluctuations in response to technological shocks. However, in its simplest form it has one clear counterfactual implication: if the distribution of reservation wages remains unchanged through time and if technological progress is on average positive, the argument implies that participation rates should steadily increase over time in line with technological progress. Although participation rates vary over time, they do not, however, appear to do so in a way directly related to the level of productivity.[39] One obvious way of extending the simplest version is to allow reservation wages to change over time, perhaps in response to unemployment benefits or other factors that may themselves depend, directly or indirectly, on current and lagged wages, not to mention social changes. This extended version suggests a much more complex dynamic response of employment to technology shocks.

Does the heterogeneity of workers explain the main characteristics of fluctuations in real wages and employment across the cycle? It could a priori do so, since small increases in the real wage could tip many people over the edge of their reservation wage into employment. There has been, to our knowledge, no systematic empirical investigation by macroeconomists of the power of this hypothesis. There is indeed some evidence that real wages of women vary more with output and that, as we have noted, the elasticity of labor supply may be larger for women. Heterogeneity may therefore explain some of the fluctuations in female, or more specifically secondary earner, employment. Whether it accounts for more than a negligible portion of movements in male (primary earner) employment is very much in doubt.

Real Wages, Technological Shocks, and Intertemporal Substitution
Until now we have assumed that real wages are equal to the marginal product of labor, perhaps appropriately adjusted to take account of costs of adjustment of employment. But this may not be the case: an extensive literature, which we will analyze in detail in chapter 9, has explored the possibility that firms may partially insure workers against income fluctuations, leading to wages that vary less than the corresponding marginal product. The assumption in those models is that firms are less risk averse than workers. The scope for insurance is clearly more limited within the strict confines of the representative agent model, where the firms' owners and workers are one and the same and thus have the same degree of risk aversion. But these confines may be too strict.

Some of the puzzles about the comovement of real wages and employment, or about the comovements of real wages, employment, and consumption, can be dismissed as irrelevant if real wages include an insurance component that causes them not to vary with the underlying marginal product of labor. If for insurance or other reasons the real wage is not equal to the marginal product of labor, but competitive equilibrium ensures that resources are allocated efficiently, then workers will intertemporally substitute leisure in response to shifts in the marginal product of labor even without wage movements. This is the approach taken, for example, by Prescott (1986) who explores whether technological shocks can generate observed fluctuations in quantities while ignoring altogether the issue of whether movements in quantities are consistent with the observed behavior of real wages.

That real wages are not equal at all times to the underlying marginal product of labor is indeed very likely. There are two elements to consider in judging whether this rescues the intertemporal substitution hypothesis. The first is whether the presence of insurance can reconcile the behavior of observed real wages and employment. We defer this question to chapter 9, where it is explored at length. The second and more important question is whether the necessary ingredients for intertemporal substitution are present in the economy. The first is the presence of temporary productivity shocks: if technological shocks are for the most part permanent, there is no scope for intertemporal substitution by workers. At this stage there is little evidence of such transitory components, or of components perceived as such by workers. The second ingredient is the desire of workers to intertemporally substitute over periods of years. As we saw above, the relevant elasticity of substitution seems to be too small to generate large employment movements, at least for men.

Although some believe that the verdict is still out, it appears that the view of employment and output fluctuations as being roughly consistent with the representative agent–competitive market–technology shock model is difficult to hold. This class of models must be extended in some fundamental way if it is to explain the basic characteristics of aggregate fluctuations in output and employment.

7.3 Unemployment, Heterogeneity, Shocks, and Imperfect Information

All the models we have reviewed until now implicitly assume that workers are either in the labor force and working, or are out of the labor force. They cannot account for unemployed workers, if unemployed workers are defined as workers without a job and looking for one. To account for unemployment in an equilibrium framework requires introducing heterogeneity of workers and/or jobs, and as a result, search.

The notion of labor markets as decentralized markets characterized by search on the part of workers and firms not only goes in the direction of increased realism but also implies dynamic effects of shocks which can be quite different from those derived earlier. We start this section by presenting a simple model of search, due to Howitt (1988), that allows us both to present a theory of the equilibrium rate of unemployment and to examine the dynamics of unemployment and wages in response to productivity shocks.[40] We then discuss how sector-specific productivity shocks can, in the context of search, generate fluctuations in aggregate employment.

Finally, we consider a model with decentralized markets and imperfect information, due to Lucas (1973). We show how imperfect information not only modifies the effects of real shocks but also allows for effects of monetary shocks, which would not be present under perfect information.

Search, Unemployment, and Productivity Shocks

The following model captures the basic implications of search behavior for aggregate fluctuations:

The economy is composed of F competitive firms, and N identical workers.[41] Time is discrete. In each period a fraction δ of the employed is laid off and joins the unemployment pool.[42] At the same time firms are hiring workers from the pool of unemployed. It is not possible for firms to hire employed workers directly from other firms.

The *marginal cost of hiring* for each firm is an increasing function of its level of hiring and a decreasing function of unemployment, which is taken as given by the firm. More specifically, the cost of hiring h workers in period t is given by

$$C(h_t) = \left(\frac{G}{2}\right)\left(\frac{h_t^2}{U_{t-1}}\right), \tag{21}$$

where G is a constant, U_{t-1} is unemployment at the end of period $t-1$ (equivalently at the beginning of period t) and h_t is the number of hires by the firm in period t. The marginal cost of hiring is increasing in the rate of hiring: this captures the idea that a high rate of hiring may force firms to increase their search intensity or, in a more general model with hetero- geneous workers, to accept poorer matches between workers and jobs. The marginal cost is a decreasing function of aggregate unemployment: this captures the idea that high aggregate unemployment makes it easier and cheaper for the firm to find willing and competent workers. This specification is central to the results. We will return to it later.

Each firm chooses the rate of hiring, h_t, by equating the marginal cost of hiring to the *net marginal benefit of hiring*, λ_t:

$$\frac{Gh_t}{U_{t-1}} = \lambda_t.$$

We now turn to the determination of λ_t. At any point in time the value of the marginal product of each worker is equal to μ_t, which reflects the level of technology and follows a stationary first-order autoregressive process, with mean equal to f:

$$(\mu_t - f) = \rho(\mu_{t-1} - f) + v_t, \tag{22}$$

where v_t is white noise. The implicit assumption here is that there are constant returns to labor in production.

Assuming the firm to be risk neutral, the marginal value to the firm of a worker hired in this period is the expected present value of his marginal product so long as he works with the firm:

$$q_t = E\left[\sum_{i=0}^{\infty} \beta^i (1 - \delta)^i \mu_{t+i} | t\right]. \tag{23}$$

Future marginal products are discounted by the factor β^i to take account of time and by $(1 - \delta)^i$ to take account of the probability that a given worker will have left the job by time $t + i$.

The net marginal benefit of hiring is equal to this marginal value minus the present discounted value of wages to be paid to the worker who is newly hired. One theme of search theories of unemployment is that because job matches require an explicit search process, there is no "labor" market in which the wage is set and wage setting is likely to involve some element of bilateral monopoly (e.g., Mortensen 1982). Here, we simply assume that the wage is set in a bargain that divides the surplus from the job between the worker and the firm. In the present model the worker is assumed to experience neither costs nor benefits from unemployment, so the total surplus from the job is just the marginal value given in equation (23).[43] It is assumed that the worker obtains a share ξ of the surplus and the firm $(1 - \xi)$, with the size of ξ reflecting bargaining power. Thus

$$\lambda_t = (1 - \xi)q_t.$$

Given these assumptions, we can solve for λ_t and h_t for each firm:

$$\lambda_t = (1 - \xi)\left[\frac{f}{1 - \beta(1 - \delta)} + \frac{\mu_t - f}{1 - \beta\rho(1 - \delta)}\right], \tag{24}$$

$$h_t = \left(\frac{1}{G}\right)(U_{t-1}\lambda_t).$$

Let employment in a firm be denoted by n_t so that n_t follows[44]

$$n_t = (1 - \delta)n_{t-1} + h_t.$$

Finally, let the unemployment rate U_t/N be denoted by u_t so that, assuming all firms to be the same, $u_t = 1 - (F/N)n_t$. Putting all these equations together, we get an equation characterizing the *dynamics of the unemployment rate:*

$$u_t = \delta + \left(1 - \delta - \frac{F}{G}\lambda_t\right)u_{t-1}, \tag{25}$$

where λ_t is given by (24).

The unemployment rate depends on itself lagged, with the coefficient on lagged unemployment depending, through λ_t, on the state of technology, μ_t. We will first characterize the equilibrium level of unemployment and then turn to the dynamics.

The Natural Rate of Unemployment

Since equation (25) is nonlinear in u_t, u_{t-1}, and μ_t (through λ_t), the average, or *natural*, rate of unemployment in the economy depends on the properties of the process followed by λ_t and, in particular, on the variance in the innovation v_t. We do not investigate this dependence but shortcut the issue by evaluating the equilibrium rate when μ_t has zero variance, when $\mu_t = f$. In this case the natural rate u^* is given by

$$u^* = \frac{\delta}{\delta + (F/G)\lambda},$$

where

$$\lambda = \frac{(1 - \xi)f}{1 - \beta(1 - \delta)} \tag{26}$$

This gives the dependence of u^* on the structural parameters. In particular, the larger the separation rate, δ (both directly and indirectly through λ), and the larger the parameter G, which reflects the difficulty of locating workers and the efficiency of search, the higher is unemployment.

We do not analyze the optimality properties of the equilibrium. But it is clear that there are two reasons in this model why the natural rate is unlikely to be optimal. The first is that the marginal cost of hiring is a decreasing function of aggregate unemployment. Thus, by hiring an extra worker and decreasing the unemployment rate, a firm increases the marginal cost of hiring to other firms, an effect it does not take into account. This effect leads to too much hiring compared to what is socially optimal and thus to too low an equilibrium rate of unemployment. The other effect is that though the social marginal benefit to hiring is given by q_t, the private marginal benefit to the firm is given by $\lambda_t = (1 - \xi)q_t$. This leads, if ξ is positive, to too little hiring and thus to too high an equilibrium rate of unemployment. The net effect is ambiguous.

Dynamics of Unemployment and Productivity Shocks
We turn next to the dynamics. Even when productivity is serially uncorrelated, the model still implies serial correlation of unemployment: a temporary adverse shock in productivity decreases hiring and increases unemployment. While productivity and the net marginal value of labor return to their initial level, the unemployment rate only slowly returns to normal through increased hiring. If productivity is serially correlated, unemployment may have a hump-shaped response to innovations in productivity: an adverse productivity shock leads initially to lower hiring and higher unemployment. As the adverse shock fades over time, hiring increases again, but possibly not fast enough to prevent an increase in unemployment for a while. Finally, note again that the dynamic equation is nonlinear and that a productivity shock has a greater effect on the unemployment rate when it is high than when it is low: this is because it is cheaper for the firm to hire when there are more unemployed.

How successful is this model in terms of the initial objective of explaining the joint behavior of employment, output, and real wages? The model shows that the presence of search can generate employment fluctuations in response to technology shocks. In an economy with firms with the same technology and workers with the same (zero) reservation wage, but with a centralized labor market and no impediments to mobility of labor, productivity shocks would have no effect on employment: all workers would always be employed, and the wage would clear the labor market. With search and an increasing marginal cost of hiring, it does not pay for firms to always hire workers so as to maintain full employment (even if they appropriate all of the surplus, if $\xi = 0$).

The model may also explain why fluctuations in employment are associated with only small fluctuations in real wages. Since, by assumption, workers and firms share the surplus from their match in constant proportion, real wages vary here with productivity, both current and anticipated. High rates of hiring are associated with high real wages. The model indicates, however, that if ξ is small, variations in real wages may be small. More generally, to the extent that search introduces an element of bilateral monopoly, the relation between marginal product and the real wage will be much less tight than was suggested by the centralized labor market models analyzed earlier.

Extensions
The crucial equation above is equation (21). It is also where we have taken a substantial shortcut. Equation (21) should itself be derived from a specifi-

cation of the search technology used by workers and firms, of the matching process of workers and jobs, and from optimal behavior by firms and workers. This has been the focus of much of the research on equilibrium with search.[45] Pissarides (1985), for example, studies a closely related model, starting from such first principles. His approach has the advantage of showing explicitly how the rate of hiring depends on the characteristics of labor markets. It also helps in thinking about what may determine ξ in the bargaining process between workers and firms. Pissarides shows how the bargaining power of firms and workers resides in the option they have of turning down the match and looking for another match.

In general, models of equilibrium with search imply that shocks to the economy lead to a serially correlated response of employment: the reason is that high rates of matching of workers and firms are likely to be costly. Also the equilibrium rate of unemployment is unlikely to be socially optimal.[46] Two effects are usually at work. The first is the difference between private and social marginal benefits from a match that arises from bargaining (whereby ξ is different from zero in the above model). The second is the presence of externalities. One, also present above, is the "congestion" externality, whereby hiring by one firm decreases the unemployment pool and increases the cost of hiring for others. Another, which is absent from the above model, is a "thin market" externality. In this instance, a search effort by either side decreases the cost of search to the other side. Higher levels of recruiting effort by firms make it cheaper for workers to find jobs. Greater search effort by workers makes it cheaper for firms to hire. This effect has been emphasized in particular by Diamond (1982b): if greater search effort by one side not only decreases the cost of search by the other side but also leads the other side to increase its own search effort, then there may occur multiple equilibria, an issue that we leave aside for the moment but to which we will return in chapter 9.[47]

Sectoral Shifts and Unemployment

Once we allow for the fact that the economy is composed of different sectors, of decentralized markets, not only does this affect, as we have just seen, the dynamic effects of aggregate shocks, but it opens up the possibility that sectoral shocks have aggregate effects on output and unemployment. The effect of sectoral shocks—be it changes in the relative demand for goods or in relative productivity—on aggregate unemployment when labor cannot instantaneously and costlessly be reallocated across sectors is emphasized by Lilien (1982). It can be shown in two simple examples.[48]

Consider first an economy with two sectors. Labor is immobile within periods but fully mobile across sectors across periods. Workers in each sector have a reservation wage w_R and supply one unit of labor inelastically if the wage exceeds w_R. Suppose that the initial equilibrium is as shown in figure 7.4, with wages equal in each sector to w. Consider then a shift in relative labor demands, with labor demand shifting down in sector 1 and up in sector 2. Within the period wages decrease to w_1' in sector 1 and increase to w_2' in sector 2. If the shift is large enough that sector 1 operates on the flat portion of labor supply, total employment declines, and the aggregate wage increases. The sectoral shift increases unemployment in the current period. It also increases the aggregate wage. In the following period labor reallocates itself, and aggregate employment returns to normal.

The second example leads to a slightly different timing of the effects of sectoral shifts. Labor is still immobile within periods, and it now takes one period of unemployment for workers to move from one sector to the other. Suppose that the initial equilibrium is as shown in figure 7.5 and that, after the shift in relative demand, equilibrium wages are equal to w_1' in sector 1 and w_2' in sector 2. In the case drawn in the figure, there is no effect on employment or on the aggregate wage within the period. In the following period, however, some workers move from sector 1 to sector 2 in response to the wage differential. Employment in sector 2 remains constant, while employment in sector 1 decreases to $N_1(+1)$. Aggregate employment is lower, but the aggregate wage higher. In the next period the equality of wages is restored, and aggregate employment is back to normal.

Lilien constructed the time series of the standard deviation of rates of change in employment across eleven sectors for the U.S. economy and showed that this time series was highly positively correlated with unemployment for the postwar United States. This work was extended by Davis (1987) with similar conclusions. Times of high unemployment appear to be times of high dispersion in employment growth rates.

These findings and their interpretation have been the subject of substantial controversy. Abraham and Katz (1986) have suggested that one should also look at vacancies, interpreted as a measure of search by firms. The sectoral shifts hypothesis suggests that times of high unemployment should be times of high dispersion in employment rates as well as times of intensive search by firms. Vacancies, however, are highly procyclical, being low when unemployment is high. Abraham and Katz therefore interpret the result of Lilien as a case of reverse causality, with movements in aggregate demand generating high employment growth dispersion because of different income

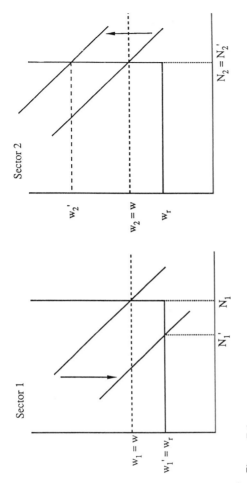

Figure 7.4
Sectoral shifts, employment and wages

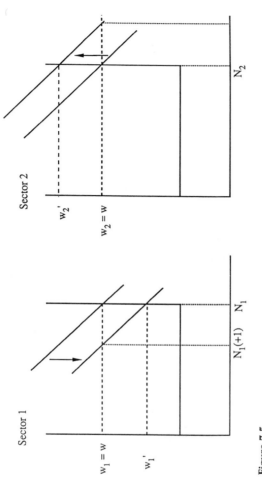

Figure 7.5
Sectoral shifts, employment and wages

elasticities of sectoral demands and different growth rates of employment across sectors.

Measures of employment growth dispersion are clearly only proxies for measures of labor reallocation. Recent work has examined the relation between labor reallocation and cyclical conditions using panel data on individuals. The evidence, at this stage, seems also to contradict the sectoral shifts hypothesis, at least in its original formulation: movements of workers across sectors seem to decrease as unemployment increases (Murphy and Topel 1987; see, however, Lilien 1988). Thus, although sectoral shifts may well play a role in unemployment fluctuations, they do not appear to be one of the main determinants of such fluctuations.

Money, Demand Shocks, and Output

Until now we have for the most part concentrated on the effects of technological shocks. But within the models we studied we could have examined, instead, the effects of taste or fiscal policy shocks. We could also have extended the models to allow for the existence of money, and thus observed the effects of changes in the nominal money stock on output. The results would have been disappointing. The effects of taste shocks on employment would have been small unless the shocks induced intertemporal substitution. Further, as was apparent in the models of chapter 4, the real effects of changes in the nominal money stock would have been small or nonexistent.

How then do we explain the correlations between nominal money and real output described in chapter 1? Researchers working within the equilibrium approach have followed two strategies. The first has been to explain the money-output relation as a case of reverse causality. The second has been to extend the initial class of models to allow for imperfect information and thus potential confusion between shocks, in particular, between nominal and real shocks.[49] We review each direction in turn.

Money, Output, and Reverse Causality

Money may be endogenous in the business cycle either because central banks pursue accommodating policies or because most of the money stock is inside money, whose real volume adjusts to the level of economic activity. Tobin (1970) emphasized the first possibility, showing how, in a model in which money did not affect output, endogenous monetary policy could cause movements in money to lead movements in output.

The analysis has been extended by King and Plosser (1984) to show how similar results can hold in a world with inside money. They model transaction services as a factor of production and assume that banks produce transaction services using labor, capital, and outside money as factors of production. If production takes time, a positive productivity shock may increase the demand for transaction services and other inputs today, and production next period. Assuming that the supply of transaction services is positively related to the real stock of bank deposits (inside money), the real money stock will appear to Granger-cause output. This theory, however, does not explain the behavior of the price level, which in such models would be driven ultimately by the nominal stock of outside money. Thus correlations between nominal money and output would have to be explained in part by the behavior of the outside money stock.

The endogenous-money approach provides a warning that the correlation between money and output is likely to reflect in part causality from output to money. In addition, depending on the technology linking inside money (or its counterpart on the other side of the balance sheet, bank credit) and outside money, the approach may imply that the real volume of inside money is more closely linked to the cycle than the volume of outside money. This indeed seems to be the case empirically (Stephen King 1983).

But the endogenous money approach does not dispose of all the evidence. As we discussed in chapter 1, recent disinflation episodes are strongly suggestive of real effects of money. Indeed, it was to provide an explanation of why money could affect output that Lucas developed his imperfect information model. We now review that direction of research.

Imperfect Information, Nominal Money, and Output

Phelps (1970) developed the idea that if markets were decentralized and participants in each market had only limited information about other markets, they could misinterpret price signals and respond to shocks they would not have responded to, had they had complete information. A macroeconomic model formalizing this idea was built by Lucas in an important paper in 1973.[50] The model is well worth presenting, for it has implications that go far beyond providing an explanation for the money-output relation.

The Lucas Model

The economy is composed of many separate competitive markets, or to use Phelps's expression, many islands. Demand in each market is affected by two shocks. One is an aggregate shock, a shock to nominal money. The second is a sector-specific shock. Suppliers would like to respond differently to each type, namely, not to respond to the first but to respond to the second. They do not, however, have enough information to distinguish between them.

This leads both types of shocks, thus including nominal shocks, to have an effect on output.

More specifically, the *supply curve* in each market $i = 1, \ldots, n$ is given by

$$y_t^i = b(p_t^i - E[p_t|I_t^i]), \tag{27}$$

where y_t^i and p_t^i are the logarithms of output and the nominal price of output in market i in period t and where I_t^i is the information available in market i at t, consisting of full information about the economy up to and including $t - 1$ and of the price p_t^i.[51] No distinction is made between workers and firms: suppliers should be thought of as worker-producers or yeomen-farmers. Equation (27) is postulated rather than derived from first principles. It embodies the idea that suppliers increase supply only in response to what they perceive to be relative price movements.[52]

Suppliers do not observe the price level directly. In deciding how much to supply, they must form an estimate of it. Before they enter the market, they have a prior distribution for p_t that is normal with mean $E[p_t|I_t]$ and variance σ_p^2, where I_t is therefore the information set consisting of full information about the economy up to and including $t - 1$ but not including p_t^i. They then observe p_t^i, and they know that p_t^i follows

$$p_t^i = p_t + z_t^i, \tag{28}$$

where z_t^i is a market specific shock so that the sum of z_t^i's over i is equal to zero. The relative disturbance z_t^i is white noise, normally distributed, and has variance σ_z^2.

The price in market i, p_t^i, can therefore be thought of as a realization from a distribution with mean p_t so that, by Bayes' rule, suppliers form a posterior mean for p_t:

$$E[p_t|I_t^i] = (1 - \theta)E[p_t|I_t] + \theta p_t^i, \tag{29}$$

where

$$\theta = \frac{\sigma_p^2}{\sigma_p^2 + \sigma_z^2}.$$

The posterior mean is a weighted average of the prior mean and the price observed in market i. The weight depends on the relative variances of the prior distribution and of z. If, for example, σ_z^2 is small, an increase in p_t^i is taken to be largely a signal that p_t has increased, and it leads to a small increase in the estimate of the relative price. Substituting (29) and (28) into (27) gives

$$y_t^i = b(1 - \theta)(p_t^i - E[p_t|I_t])$$

$$= \beta(p_t^i - E[p_t|I_t]), \tag{30}$$

where

$$\beta \equiv \frac{b\sigma_z^2}{\sigma_p^2 + \sigma_z^2}.$$

Defining y_t as the sum of y_t^i over i and aggregating (30) over i gives[53]

$$y_t = \beta(p_t - E[p_t|I_t]). \tag{31}$$

Equation (31) is the famous *Lucas supply function* which shows output as an increasing function of the price surprise, the unanticipated increase in the aggregate price level. This is also Lucas's explanation of the Phillips curve. Whereas Phillips (1958) had rationalized that relation as an expression of the response of wages to labor market disequilibrium, the Lucas supply function assumes that supply is equal to demand in each market. It is thus an equilibrium explanation of the relationship between unexpected inflation and output and, as we shall see shortly, of the relationship between monetary shocks and output.

We now specify *aggregate demand* in order to solve for the market equilibrium, the rationally expected price level $E[p_t|I_t]$, and the value σ_p^2. A standard and simple way of specifying a relation between output, the price level, and nominal money is to start from the quantity equation in logarithms:

$$m_t + v_t = p_t + y_t, \tag{32}$$

where v_t is (the log of) velocity.

Without a specification of velocity, this is simply an identity. If we postulate the behavior of velocity, for example, that v is constant and equal to zero (recall that this is a logarithm, so that putting it equal to zero is an innocuous normalization), it becomes an aggregate demand equation, giving the demand for output as a function of real money balances. In view of our treatment of the dynamics of consumption and investment above, as well as in previous chapters, this is a drastic simplification of the treatment of the demand side. But it is a shortcut that we will use frequently in what follows. Its justification is to give a simple relation between nominal money, the price level, and the demand for goods, which may be appropriate when the focus is, as it is here, on the decision of suppliers. We return to the adequacy of this shortcut in chapter 10.

Using (32) together with $v_t = 0$ to eliminate y_t from (31) and solving for $E[p_t|I_t]$ gives $E[p_t|I_t] = E[m_t|t]$. Substitution into (31) and (32) gives output and the price level as functions of actual and anticipated money:

$$y_t = \left(\frac{\beta}{1+\beta}\right)(m_t - E[m_t|I_t]), \tag{33}$$

$$p_t = (1+\beta)^{-1}(\beta\, E[m_t|I_t] + m_t). \tag{34}$$

Output responds to unanticipated changes in nominal money, with an elasticity of $\beta/(1+\beta)$. Surprise developments in aggregate demand thus affect the level of output, accounting for the correlation between monetary disturbances and output. The extent to which any given demand disturbance affects output depends (positively) on β, the elasticity of the Lucas supply function, which is in turn a function of σ_p^2. The last step is therefore to solve for σ_p^2.

Let e_t be the innovation in money, $m_t - E[m_t|I_t]$. Let e_t be normally distributed with variance σ_e^2. Then from (34),

$$\sigma_p^2 = (1+\beta)^{-2}\sigma_e^2. \tag{35}$$

Equation (35) implicitly determines σ_p^2 as a function of σ_e^2 and σ_z^2 [through $\beta \equiv b\sigma_z^2/(\sigma_p^2 + \sigma_z^2)$].

Implications and Extensions
The Lucas model shows how equilibrium models with decentralized markets and imperfect information can account for the effects of nominal as well as real shocks on output.[54] The original model, however, suffers from two shortcomings. As a theoretical model it postulates the central equation (27) rather than deriving it from explicit maximization.[55] Models in which supply is explicitly derived from intertemporal substitution were subsequently worked out, in particular, by Barro (1976) and (1981).

Second, as a description of the economy, the model has no dynamics: unanticipated money affects output for one period only. Subsequent research therefore has also concentrated on finding the reasons why demand shocks have lasting effects on output. We have analyzed several such channels in this chapter in our discussion of the mechanisms through which temporary productivity shocks could have persistent effects on output. They include capital accumulation (Lucas 1975), inventory behavior (Blinder and Fischer 1981), costs of adjustment (Sargent 1979), and search in the labor market. Howitt (1988), for example, shows how in a multisector economy, in which each sector is similar to the economy described in the search model of this chapter, confusion between real and nominal shocks leads to long-lasting effects of nominal shocks on output and employment. Another channel arises here if, even ex post, suppliers cannot for a long time fully identify the origin of the shocks they have experienced. In this case nominal shocks can have persistent effects on output (Taylor 1975; Lucas 1975)

Decentralized Markets and Fluctuations: An Assessment

Do the extensions studied in this section rescue the equilibrium hypothesis?

That markets are decentralized obviously affects the dynamic effects of shocks. The process of job-worker matching in labor markets is likely to lead to longer lasting effects of shifts in the determinants of labor supply and labor demand. Yet, despite the obvious importance of search to an understanding of labor market dynamics, the explanation of unemployment fluctuations as the result of optimal search in an equilibrium model is not convincing. It conflicts with too many characteristics of labor markets. Workers often lose their jobs involuntarily. Finding a new job is apparently easier for the already employed than for the unemployed, while many of the latter seem in any case not to be searching. It is also hardly plausible that sustained movements in aggregate unemployment over periods of years can be attributed to the difficulty of matching workers and jobs.

Further, the issues of information and coordination raised by the presence of decentralized markets are clearly important. It is, however, unclear how one should interpret imperfect information equilibrium models. Is Lucas's model to be taken more or less literally, or is it merely an example of a type of coordination problem faced by large decentralized economies? Taken literally, the basic assumptions do not seem very sensible. How can agents suffer from a lack of information about other prices, or about money, when this information is available publicly within weeks and could be made available faster at relatively low cost?[56] Nonetheless, and somewhat surprisingly, a large body of empirical research did, for almost a decade, test the implications of the Lucas model quite literally interpreted. Initial empirical results by Barro (1977) strengthened the case for this approach. But results by Boschen and Grossman (1982), which showed that output appeared to be affected by the currently perceived money stock, and related results by Barro and Hercowitz (1980), coming as they did from proponents of the approach, were significant nails in the coffin. To the extent that the Lucas setup is an example of coordination problems in a decentralized economy, alternative interpretations have not been explored by the proponents of the equilibrium approach. Two opposite directions of research have been followed since.

The first has dismissed the idea that aggregate demand movements have an important effect on output by explaining the comovements in money and output in terms of reverse causality, and dismissing the rest of the evidence on the effects of demand shocks as weak or unconvincing. This is the "real business cycle" approach reviewed in this chapter. We have assessed it at length in this chapter.

The second direction of research has focused on issues of coordination, returning to earlier Keynesian themes and exploring more rigorously the idea that imperfections can lead to strong effects of aggregate demand on output. This is the direction we analyze in the next two chapters.

Problems

1. *Stochastic population growth and fluctuations.*

Consider a Diamond model with stochastic population growth. Production is of the form $Y_t = K_t^a N_t^{1-a}$. Population growth is given by $N_{t+1} = N_t V_{t+1}$. V is lognormal, i.i.d., with $E[\ln V] = g$, and $\text{Var}[\ln V] = \sigma^2$. Preferences are of the Cobb-Douglas form $\ln(C_{1t}) + (1 + \theta)^{-1} E[\ln(C_{2t+1})|t]$.

(a) Derive the equations of motion for capital and for output per capita.
(b) Characterize the dynamic effects on output of a large increase in population at time t and a large value of V_t. Explain.

2. *Taste shocks in the additive Ramsey model.*

Consider an economy with infinitely lived individuals. There is no population growth, and the population size is normalized to one. Individuals live forever and maximize at time t:

$$\sum_{i=0}^{\infty} (1 + \theta)^{-i} E[C_{t+i} - b(C_{t+i} + V_{t+i})^2 | t]$$

subject to

$$K_{t+i+1} + C_{t+i} = Y_{t+i} \equiv (1 + \theta) K_{t+i}.$$

Output is produced under constant returns to scale using only capital. The only source of uncertainty is uncertainty about future tastes. V_t is white noise, with $E[V_t] = 0$.

(a) Characterize and interpret the first-order conditions.
(b) Characterize the dynamic effects on consumption and output of a positive taste shock at time t.
(c) "Temporary consumption binges are paid for by lower consumption forever." Discuss this statement.

3. *Fatigue, adjustment costs, and the dynamic effects of productivity shocks.*
(This is adapted from Sargent 1979.)

Consider a competitive labor market with many firms and many workers. Each worker maximizes the present discounted value of utility:

$$\sum_{i=0}^{\infty} (1 + \theta)^{-i} E[C_{t+i} - a(N_{t+i} - V_{t+i})^2 - b(N_{t+i} + N_{t+i-1})^2 | t], \qquad a, b > 0,$$

subject to

$$C_{t+i} = W_{t+i} N_{t+i},$$

where V_t is white noise, C and N are consumption and work, and V is a taste disturbance. The third term captures the idea of fatigue.

Each firm maximizes the present discounted value of profits

$$\sum_{i=0}^{\infty} (1 + \theta)^{-i} E[N_{t+i} - c(N_{t+i} - U_{t+i})^2 - d(N_{t+i} - N_{t+i-1})^2 - W_{t+i} N_{t+i} | t], \quad c > 0,$$

where U is a productivity disturbance, also assumed to be white noise. The third term in the sum captures costs of adjustment for employment.

(a) Derive the first-order condition for the representative worker. Solve for labor supply as a function of itself lagged, of current and expected future wages, and of the current value of the taste shock. Explain.

(b) Derive the first-order condition for the representative firm. Solve for labor demand as a function of itself lagged, of current and expected future wages, and of the current value of the productivity shock. Explain.

(c) Normalizing, for convenience, the number of workers and firms to be one, eliminate the wage between the two first-order conditions. Solve for equilibrium employment as a function of itself lagged and of current taste and productivity disturbances.

(d) Characterize the dynamic effects of taste and productivity disturbances on employment.

Notes

1. Unless one includes explanations of macroeconomic fluctuations based on agricultural cycles. These disappeared with the declining importance of agriculture in the economy.

2. The order of presentation in this chapter reverses the course of intellectual history. The imperfect information approach came first, introduced by Lucas. The real business cycle approach, which focuses on productivity shocks rather than monetary shocks and abandons imperfect information, came later.

3. A general analysis of the stochastic growth model was given by Brock and Mirman (1972) for white noise disturbances and later extended by Donaldson and Mehra (1983).

4. Both assumptions, that the gross production function is Cobb-Douglas, and that capital depreciates fully in one period, are empirically unattractive. The trade-off is

that by making gross output multiplicative in the level of productivity, they allow for the derivation of an explicit solution later.

5. If utility were isoelastic rather than logarithmic, the difference equation characterizing capital accumulation would still be first order but nonlinear in K, or in its logarithm.

6. By definition, the stock of genuine knowledge must always be increasing. Mistakes can be made, however, in choosing technologies. Did the Keynesian revolution represent technical progress, and if so, was the counterrevolution also technical progress? Or, was the use of DDT, or its subsequent ban, technical progress? Furthermore, not all supply shocks are increases in knowledge. The weather, for example, affects agricultural production and is better formalized, in its role as an economic variable, as a stationary process.

7. It is possible to impose a constraint that productivity never decreases by specifying the support of the distribution of ε such that ε always exceeds $-g$. For a discussion of whether such a constraint would be warranted, however, see note 6.

8. Note also that productivity growth is assumed to proceed independently of capital accumulation. It is clear, however, that part of productivity growth occurs because of the installation of new capital. It is furthermore quite possible that part of productivity growth may result from increasing returns.

9. Note that we solve directly for the central planning problem. We are exploiting the equivalence between the central planning allocation and that achieved by the decentralized economy.

10. Why doesn't consumption smooth the path of income in this model?

11. Long and Plosser also allow for endogenous labor supply. But with their logarithmic specification, income and substitution effects lead to constant labor supply over time. We will return to the issue of movements in employment at length in the next section.

12. These are well defined under our assumptions for the productivity process.

13. Note, however, that for realistic values of σ and a, the differences between the average riskless rate, the marginal product, and the discount rate are likely to be small, much smaller than their empirical counterparts appear to be. This raises the issue of whether this type of model can explain the different rates of return on assets. Following this line of inquiry would take us too far here afield; for a discussion, see, for example, Mehra and Prescott (1985). We return to a related set of issues in chapter 10.

14. See also Zilcha (1987) for a characterization of dynamic inefficiency in overlapping generation models.

15. It is easy to characterize the effects of taste shocks in this model. Taste shocks can be introduced by replacing the instantaneous utility by $E(C_{t+i} - b(C_{t+i} + V_{t+i})^2|t)$, where V_t is a random variable. This case is left to problem set 2.

16. Because of different timing conventions, this formula differs slightly from those derived in the previous section. In particular, the marginal propensity to consume out of wealth is equal to r, not $r/(1 + r)$.

17. Lucas (1985) and Rebelo (1987) discuss the dynamic effects of shocks in growth models with a similar constant returns property. They also discuss whether and when this assumption of constant returns may be justified.

18. None of these three examples incorporates either costs of adjustment or time-to-build considerations. These concepts are difficult to incorporate while maintaining analytical tractability. A study of the dynamics of a Ramsey model with time-to-build restrictions (under certainty) is given by Ioannides and Taub (1987)

19. See Blinder and Fischer (1981) for an analysis of the role of inventories in fluctuations.

20. Of course, in practice, fixed capital and inventory accumulation jointly affect the dynamic behavior of the economy. We model them seriatim for the sake of tractability. Any serious empirical model of economic fluctuations would have to include both, in addition to other mechanisms studied in this and the following chapters.

21. The objective function can also be interpreted as a quadratic utility function with the linear term in consumption (and other variables) omitted; the linear terms affect only constants in the solutions and are omitted for notational convenience.

22. For reasons explained in the previous section, this eliminates the possibility that in the absence of technological shocks, the variance in production exceeds the variance in sales or, in this case, consumption. If we instead allow U to be positively serially correlated, this model can generate a higher variance in production than in consumption.

23. Even if production was not predetermined, part of the increase in consumption would come from a decrease in inventories.

24. Models with more appealing descriptions of either utility or technology, which can be solved numerically but not analytically, have been developed by Kydland and Prescott (1982), Prescott (1986), Christiano (1987), among others. Those models allow also for variations in employment, an issue we examine in the next section.

25. This remark applies with less force to taste shocks, for example. A shift in preferences toward current consumption may well be highly correlated across individuals.

26. If σ is the standard deviation of individual productivity innovations, n the number of sectors, and ρ their pairwise correlation, the standard deviation of aggregate productivity is equal to $\sigma[\sqrt{(1 + (n - 1)\rho)}]/\sqrt{n}$. Thus, for large n, it is approximately equal to $\sigma\sqrt{\rho}$. For a further discussion, see McCallum (1988).

27. The relation between output, employment, hours and unemployment was examined by Okun (1962) and summarized in what has come to be known as

"Okun's law." This "law" holds, roughly, that an increase of 3% in output over its normal growth rate over a year leads to an increase of 2% in employment and a decrease of 1% in the unemployment rate.

28. For a more general treatment of labor supply in a dynamic context, see for example, MacCurdy (1981).

29. This is the direction first explored by Lucas and Rapping (1969).

30. For tractability, the specification used by Sargent for the optimization problem of workers is an ad hoc approximation to the standard maximization problem. It embodies, however, the idea that workers are willing to substitute leisure over time in response to changes in real wages. See problem 3.

31. See, for example, Altonji (1982)

32. See Hall (1980) for a discussion of the role of interest rates on labor supply.

33. Mankiw, Rotemberg, and Summers use the following utility function:

$$U(c_i, x_i) = \left(\frac{1}{1-g}\right)\left[\left(\frac{1}{1-a}\right)(c_i^{1-a} - 1) + d\left(\frac{1}{1-b}\right)(x_i^{1-b} - 1)\right]^{1-g}.$$

This allows for different elasticities of intertemporal substitution for consumption and leisure. When $g = 0$, when utility is additively separable, these are given by $1/a$ and $1/b$, respectively.

34. We do not doubt that leisure is highly substitutable over very short periods; the behavior of authors who have deadlines to meet provides strong support for this view.

35. Hall (1987) presents and assesses that direction of research. Our discussion follows his.

36. We are here implicitly keeping the wage constant.

37. Kevin Murphy has pointed out that the same argument can be used to show that the demand for Chinese food is completely elastic: although the price is constant, we do not eat Chinese food every day.

38. See, for example, Heckman (1984).

39. Participation rates for men in the United States have decreased from 87% in 1890 to 77% in 1982 (Pencavel 1986). On the other hand, U.S. participation rates for women have increased dramatically, from 19% in 1890 to 50% in 1980 (Killingsworth and Heckman 1986), while the increase in other countries was smaller. But it is hard to believe that this increase has been entirely the result of labor demand shifting along an unchanged distribution of reservation wages.

40. The emphasis on the importance of search in decentralized markets was the theme of an early and influential book edited by Phelps (1970), which contains some of the first formal models. Lucas and Prescott presented in 1974 a general equilibrium model of unemployment generated by stochastic sectoral shocks and

a one-period lag by workers in moving between sectors. More recently, Diamond (1981, 1982a) and Pissarides (1985) have developed and worked with several continuous time general equilibrium models of search. Recent reviews are given in Mortensen (1986) and Sargent (1987).

41. The model developed by Howitt actually has J sectors, each with F competitive firms and N workers attached to the sector. This allows him to consider the effects of both sector-specific and aggregate shocks, both when firms can distinguish between the two and when they cannot. We return to the implications of such potential confusion between different types of shocks later in this chapter.

42. The reason for these separations is not made explicit but could be found in deteriorating job-worker matches, the need for some workers to follow their spouses, the need for some firms to relocate, and so on. The model is set up so that there is no expected benefit to workers quitting to look for better jobs.

43 In a model in which leisure is valued, or in which there are unemployment benefits, the surplus would be the difference between the marginal value product and the worker's best alternative use of time.

44. Separations only affect the existing labor force, n_{t-1}, not the newly hired.

45. See references listed in note 40.

46 An exception is Lucas and Prescott (1974).

47. We present the Diamond model in chapter 9.

48. Most of the work here has been empirical. See, however, Rogerson (1987) and Lilien (1988) for models of sectoral reallocation.

49. The second approach was historically first. Lucas' goal in constructing his 1973 model, which we will review shortly, was to provide an equilibrium explanation for the effects of demand (money) shocks. It is partly because Lucas' approach has proved unconvincing that research in the equilibrium tradition has concentrated on the effects of real shocks and deemphasized the importance of demand shocks.

50. Lucas (1972) is a less transparent but more micro-based forerunner of the 1973 model.

51. The spirit of loglinear approximations is very much alive in (45), where suppliers respond to the ratio of the logarithm of the price to the expectation of that logarithm.

52. Barro (1981) has provided an intertemporal substitution justification for such behavior.

53. This is another instance in which the use of logarithms creates problems. Output is implicitly defined as the product of individual outputs rather than their sum.

54. The Lucas model was also influential in establishing two other results. The first is *policy ineffectiveness*, whereby, for policies that would have no effect under perfect

information, only unexpected policy movements matter. We return to that issue in chapter 11.

The second result is the *econometric policy evaluation critique*, of which the model provides an example and which Lucas further developed in his (1976) article. The critique asserts that because apparently structural parameters may change when policy changes, existing econometric models cannot be used to study alternative policy regimes. It applies at two levels. On the first level, estimated distributed lags may be convolutions of expectational and other lags so that a change in policy changes the way expectations are formed, and thus the distributed lag itself. On the second, even if the first problem is eliminated, for example because expectations are observable, the coefficients themselves may be functions of policy. Equation (31) provides an example. Even if $E(p_t|I_t)$ is observable, β is a function of policy (through its dependence on σ_e^2). Much econometric work has been devoted to solving the first problem by separating expectational from other sources of lags (e.g., Hansen and Sargent 1980), and the critique has had a major impact on macroeconometrics. Little has been done to address the second.

55. As noted earlier, a theoretically much tighter but more difficult model, with optimizing agents, decentralized markets, and imperfect information was, however, developed by Lucas (1972).

56. A possible lead was given by Lucas in "Understanding Business Cycles" (1977). His informal argument was that if idiosyncratic shocks were the dominant factor for individual fortunes and if collecting information about aggregates involved even a small cost, then individuals could rationally decide to ignore aggregate variables. The private cost to them would be small, but the aggregate result could be fluctuations in response to demand shocks. This idea has not been formalized further within this framework. But a similar idea is central to the menu cost approach studied in the next chapter.

References

Abel, Andrew, N. Gregory Mankiw, Lawrence Summers, and Richard Zeckhauser (1986). "Assessing Dynamic Efficiency: Theory and Evidence." NBER Working Paper 2097.

Abraham, Katherine, and Lawrence Katz (1986). "Cyclical Unemployment: Sectoral Shifts or Aggregate Disturbances." *Journal of Political Economy* 94 (Nov.), 507–522.

Altonji, Joseph (1982). "The Intertemporal Substitution Model of Labor Market Fluctuations: An Empirical Analysis." *Review of Economic Studies* 47, 783–824.

Barro, Robert (1976). "Rational Expectations and The Role of Monetary Policy." *Journal of Monetary Economics*, 1–32.

Barro, Robert (1977). "Unanticipated Money Growth and Unemployment in the United States." *American Economic Review* 67, 1 (March), 101–115.

Barro, Robert (1981). "The Equilibrium Approach to Business Cycles." In *Money, Expectations and Business Cycles*. New York: Academic Press.

Barro, Robert, and Zvi Hercowitz (1980). "Money Stock Revisions and Unanticipated Money Growth." *Journal of Monetary Economics* 6 (April), 257–267.

Barro, Robert, and Robert King (1984). "Time Separable Preferences and Intertemporal Substitution Models of the Business Cycle." *Quarterly Journal of Economics* 99, 4 (Nov.), 817–840.

Black, Fischer (1982). "General Equilibrium and Business Cycles." NBER Working Paper 950.

Blinder, Alan, and Stanley Fischer (1981). "Inventories, Rational Expectations and the Business Cycle." *Journal of Monetary Economics* 8, 3 (Nov.), 277–304.

Boschen, John, and Herschel I. Grossman (1982). "Tests of Equilibrium Macroeconomics Using Contemporaneous Monetary Data." *Journal of Monetary Economics* 10 (Nov.), 309–333.

Brock, William, and Leonard Mirman (1972). "Optimal Economic Growth and Uncertainty: The Discounted Case." *Journal of Economic Theory* 4 (April), 479–515.

Christiano, Lawrence (1987). "Is Consumption Insufficiently Sensitive to Innovations in Income?" *American Economic Review* 77, 2 (May), 337–341.

Davis, Steve (1987). "Allocative Disturbances and Specific Capital in Real Business Cycles." *American Economic Review* 77, 2 (May), 333–336.

Diamond, Peter A. (1981). "Mobility Costs, Frictional Unemployment, and Efficiency." *Journal of Political Economy* 89, 4 (Aug.), 798–812.

Diamond, Peter A. (1982a). "Wage Determination and Efficiency in Search Equilibrium." *Review of Economic Studies* 49, 217–227.

Diamond, Peter A. (1982b). "Aggregate Demand Management in Search Equilibrium." *Journal of Political Economy* 90, 5 (Oct.), 881–894.

Donaldson, John, and Rajnish Mehra (1983). "Stochastic Growth with Correlated Production Shocks." *Journal of Economic Theory* 29, 282–312.

Eichenbaum, Martin, Lars Hansen, and Kenneth Singleton (1988). "A Time Series Analysis of Representative Agent Models of Consumption and Leisure." *Quarterly Journal of Economics*, forthcoming.

Hall, Robert (1980). "Labor Supply and Aggregate Fluctuations." In Karl Brunner and Allan Meltzer (eds.), *On the State of Macroeconomics*. Carnegie-Rochester Conference Series on Public Policy. Amsterdam: North-Holland.

Hall, Robert (1987). "The Volatility of Employment with Fixed Costs of Going to Work." Mimeo. Stanford. June.

Hansen, Gary (1985). "Indivisible Labor and the Business Cycle." *Journal of Monetary Economics* 16, 3 (Nov.), 309–328.

Hansen, Lars, and Thomas Sargent (1980). "Formulating and Estimating Dynamic Linear Rational Expectations Models." *Journal of Economic Dynamics and Control* 2, 7–46.

Heckman, James (1984). "Comments on the Ashenfelter and Kydland Papers." In Karl Brunner and Allan Meltzer (eds.), Carnegie-Rochester Conference Series on Public Policy. Amsterdam: North-Holland.

Howitt, Peter (1988). "Business Cycles with Costly Search and Recruiting." *Quarterly Journal of Economics* 103, 1 (Feb.), 147–166.

Ioannides, Yannis, and Bart Taub (1987). "Time to Build and Aggregate Fluctuations: A Note." Mimeo. VPI&SU. June.

Killingsworth, Mark, and James Heckman (1986). "Female Labor Supply." In O. Ashenfelter and R. Layard (eds.), *Handbook of Labor Economics*. Vol. 1. Amsterdam: North-Holland, 103–204.

King, Robert, and Charles Plosser (1984). "Money, Credit and Prices in a Real Business Cycle." *American Economic Review* 74, 3 (June), 363–380.

King, Stephen (1983). "Macroeconomic Activity and the Rate of Interest." Ph.D. dissertation. Northwestern University.

Kydland, Finn, and Edward C. Prescott (1982). "Time to Build and Aggregate Fluctuations." *Econometrica* 50, 6 (Nov.), 1345–1370.

Lilien, David (1982). "Sectoral Shifts and Cyclical Unemployment." *Journal of Political Economy* (Aug.), 777–792.

Lilien, David, and Robert Hall (1986). "Cyclical Fluctuations in the Labor Market." In Orley Ashenfelter and Richard Layard (eds.), *Handbook of Labor Economics*. Vol. 2. Amsterdam: North-Holland, 1001–1038.

Lilien, David (1988). "Frictional and Structural Unemployment in Equilibrium." Mimeo. University of California, Irvine. June.

Long, John, and Charles Plosser (1983). "Real Business Cycles." *Journal of Political Economy* 91, 1 (Feb.), 39–69.

Lucas, Robert E., and Leonard Rapping (1969). "Real Wages, Employment and Inflation." *Journal of Political Economy* 77 (Sept.–Oct.), 721–754.

Lucas, Robert E. (1972). "Expectations and the Neutrality of Money." *Journal of Economic Theory* 4 (April), 103–124.

Lucas, Robert E. (1973). "Some International Evidence on Output-Inflation Trade-offs." *American Economic Review* 63 (June), 326–334.

Lucas, Robert E. (1975). "An Equilibrium Model of the Business Cycle." *Journal of Political Economy* 83, 6 (Dec.), 1113–1144.

Lucas, Robert E. (1976). "Econometric Policy Evaluation: A Critique." In Karl Brunner and Allan Meltzer (eds.), *The Phillips Curve and Labor Markets*, Carnegie-Rochester Conference Series, Vol. 1. Amsterdam: North-Holland, 19–46.

Lucas, Robert E. (1977). "Understanding Business Cycles." In Karl Brunner and Allan Meltzer (eds.), *Stabilization of the Domestic and International Economy*. Amsterdam: North-Holland, 7–29.

Lucas, Robert E. (1985). "On the Mechanics of Economic Development." Marshall Lectures. Unpublished manuscript.

Lucas, Robert E., and Edward Prescott (1974). "Equilibrium Search and Unemployment." *Journal of Economic Theory* 7 (Feb.), 188–209.

MacCurdy, Thomas (1981). "An Empirical Model of Labor Supply in a Life Cycle Setting." *Journal of Political Economy* 89 (Dec.), 1059–1085.

Mankiw, Gregory, Julio Rotemberg, and Lawrence Summers (1985). "Intertemporal Substitution in Macroeconomics." *Quarterly Journal of Economics* 100, 1 (Feb.), 225–253.

McCallum, Bennett (1988). "Real Business Cycle Models." NBER Working Paper 2480. January.

Mehra, Rajnish, and Edward Prescott (1985). "The Equity Premium: A Puzzle." *Journal of Monetary Economics* 15, 1 (Jan.), 145–161.

Mortensen, Dale (1970). "A Theory of Wage and Employment Dynamics." In Edmund Phelps (ed.), *Microeconomic Foundations of Employment and Inflation Theory*. New York: Norton.

Mortensen, Dale (1982). "The Matching Process as a Noncooperative Bargaining Game." In J. J. McCall (ed.), *The Economics of Information and Uncertainty*. University of Chicago Press.

Mortensen, Dale (1986). "Job Search and Labor Market Analysis." In Orley Ashenfelter and Richard Layard (eds.), *Handbook of Labor Economics*. Vol. 2. North-Holland: Amsterdam, 849–920.

Murphy, Kevin, and Robert Topel (1987). "The Evolution of Unemployment in the United States." *NBER Macroeconomics Annual*. Cambridge, MA: MIT Press, 11–57.

Okun, Arthur (1962). "Potential GNP: Its Measurement and Significance." Reprinted in Joseph Pechman (ed.), *Economics for Policy Making*. Cambridge, MA: MIT Press, 1983.

Pencavel, John (1986). "Labor Supply of Men: A Survey." In Orley Ashenfelter and Richard Layard (eds.), *Handbook of Labor Economics*. Vol. 1. Amsterdam: North-Holland, 3–102.

Phelps, Edmund (1961). "The Golden Rule of Accumulation: A Fable for Growthmen." *American Economic Review* 51 (Sept.), 638–643.

Phelps, Edmund (1970). *Microeconomic Foundations of Employment and Inflation Theory*. New York: Norton.

Phillips, A. W. (1958). "The Relation between Unemployment and the Rate of Change of Money Wages in the United Kingdom 1861–1957." *Economica* 25, 283–299.

Pissarides, Christopher (1985). "Short-Run Equilibrium Dynamics of Unemployment, Vacancies, and Real Wages." *American Economic Review* 75, 4 (Sept.), 676–690.

Prescott, Edward (1986). "Theory Ahead of Business Cycle Measurement." Federal Reserve Bank of Minneapolis, *Quarterly Review* (Fall), 9–22.

Rebelo, Sergio (1987). "Long Run Policy Analysis and Long Run Growth." Working Paper. Rochester. November.

Rogerson, Richard (1985). "Indivisible Labor, Lotteries, and Equilibrium." Unpublished manuscript. University of Rochester.

Rogerson, Richard (1987). "An Equilibrium Model of Sectoral Labor Reallocation." *Journal of Political Economy* 95, 4 (Aug.), 824–834.

Samuelson, Paul (1969). "Lifetime Portfolio Selection by Dynamic Stochastic Programming." *Review of Economics and Statistics* 51 (Aug.), 239–246.

Sargent, Thomas (1979). *Macroeconomic Theory*. New York: Academic Press.

Sargent, Thomas (1987). *Dynamic Macroeconomic Theory*. Cambridge, MA: Harvard University Press.

Sargent, Thomas, and Neil Wallace (1975). "'Rational Expectations,' the Optimal Monetary Instrument and the Optimal Money Supply Rule." *Journal of Political Economy* 83, 2 (April), 241–254.

Summers, Lawrence (1986). "Some Skeptical Observations on Real Business Cycle Theory." Federal Reserve Bank of Minneapolis, *Quarterly Review* (Fall) 1986.

Taylor, John (1975). "Monetary Policy during a Transition to Rational Expectations." *Journal of Political Economy* 83 (Oct.), 1009–1022.

Tobin, James (1970). "Post Hoc Ergo Propter Hoc." *Quarterly Journal of Economics* 84 (May), 310–317.

Zilcha, Itzhak (1987). "Dynamic Efficiency in Overlapping Generations Models with Stochastic Production." Mimeo. Foerder Institute. Tel-Aviv. September.

8

Nominal Rigidities and
Economic Fluctuations

We ended the previous chapter by concluding that the equilibrium approach does not provide satisfactory explanations of either the comovements of real wages, employment, and output or the effects of aggregate demand changes on employment and output.

The main alternative, the Keynesian approach, attempts to explain both sets of facts. A key assumption of the Keynesian approach is that wages and prices are sticky. This assumption, or observation, is by no means confined to Keynesians; it can be found in the writings of most analysts of the aggregate economy, certainly in Hume (1752) whose account of the effects of an increase in the money stock on output relies on slow price adjustment, and more recently in Irving Fisher and Milton Friedman.

Nevertheless, the sticky wage and price assumption is now identified mainly with Keynesians. The argument is simple. Individual wages and prices respond slowly to an increase in aggregate demand, and so too, therefore, does the aggregate price level. During the process of adjustment, output is affected by the change in demand. Both wages and prices adjust slowly, and there is not necessarily a pattern to the ratio of the two, the real wage. There is therefore no reason to expect any particular covariation between wages and employment in response to demand shocks.[1]

The implications of sticky prices and wages in general equilibrium were systematically explored in the 1970s in the so-called "disequilibrium" or "fixed price equilibrium" macroeconomics.[2] The general strategy was to take the vector of prices and wages as given, to specify rationing rules in each market, and then to examine the characteristics of the resulting macro-economic equilibrium. The main insight was that the economy would respond differently to a given shock, depending on how the price vector differed from the equilibrium vector. The economy could be in different regimes, corresponding to situations of excess supply or demand in different markets, and shocks could have different propagation mechanisms, depending on the particular regime.

The disequilibrium approach proved useful in analyzing the role of the price of oil, real wages, and demand in the European economies in the period after the 1973 oil shock (Bruno and Sachs 1985). By the end of the 1970s, however, it had become clear to many that the approach had reached a dead end: the assumption of given prices, which had appeared initially to be a useful shortcut, turned out to be a misleading one. Futher, in the absence of microfoundations that accounted for the price stickiness, it was difficult to make progress on several ambiguities that emerged from the framework. For example, results on the effects of particular shocks depended on how rationing rules were specified: whether suppliers satisfied demand even if it exceeded their desired supply or whether, instead, the minimum rule (quantity is the minimum of supply and demand at the given price) applied, in which case the outcome was determined by the short side of the market. But how could one choose among such rationing rules in the absence of well-specified reasons for the price not being at the equilibrium level? More fundamentally, there was no real justification for the asymmetry between the treatment (or lack of treatment) of price decisions and the sophisticated treatment of other decisions, such as investment or consumption.

These problems led, in the 1980s, to a change in research strategy.[3] Recent research has started from explicitly specified market imperfections and attempted to derive price or wage stickiness and other macroeconomic implications by examining optimal behavior under such imperfections. A wealth of imperfections, and thus of different and potentially conflicting explanations, have been explored and the current state of affairs is still one of exploration rather than synthesis.

Two general themes have emerged. The first is that price stickiness is in part the result of coordination problems. Price-setters in imperfectly competitive markets may find that, given other prices, not changing their own prices or changing them only infrequently, may cost them relatively little. But the macroeconomic implication may be slow changes in the price level, large effects of aggregate demand on output, and large output fluctuations. This problem of coordination among price-setters and thus of *nominal rigidities* is an old, though often vague, theme in the Keynesian literature;[4] recent work has shown more precisely its structure as well as its limitations.

However, this first theme of nominal rigidities can only go so far. To take an example, if fluctuations in demand lead to unemployment and if being unemployed is much worse than being employed, it is hard to see why individual workers do not take a cut in their wages to gain employment. The second general theme is therefore that labor and goods markets differ in important ways from the competitive paradigm. In particular, they appear to be such that shifts in demand lead to less variation in prices and more variation in quantities than would be predicted by the competitive paradigm. In the labor market, shifts in the demand for labor lead to small changes in the real wage and large changes in employment. In the goods markets, shifts in the demand for goods are accommodated mostly by changes in output rather than by changes in markups. We will refer to this as *real rigidities*. Recent research aims to explain such rigidities and their macroeconomic implications.

The body of research discussed in this chapter and the next can be called the *new Keynesian approach*. Most of the models of fluctuations developed within this approach have built on both themes. But there are sharp differences of emphasis. The relative roles of nominal and real rigidities are one area of difference. At one end of the spectrum, some economists, following the textbook version of Keynes, have introduced nominal wage rigidity as the only explicit deviation from the standard neoclassical model. At the other end, recent work has developed models in which nominal rigidity plays little or no role.[5] The specific nature of imperfections in the goods, labor and credit markets is another area of difference. In the labor market, for example, some have emphasized the importance of bargaining or of interpersonal comparisons of utility, whereas others have insisted on the role of imperfect information about workers' characteristics or behavior. The purpose of the next two chapters is to present these approaches, to clarify their interrelationships, and to show their implications for the study of economic fluctuations.

This chapter focuses on the reasons for nominal rigidities and their role in the transmission mechanism of aggregate demand movements on output. Further imperfections in the goods, labor, and credit markets, and their implications for the transmission mechanism, either alone or in combination with nominal rigidities, are the subject of the next chapter. Dealing first with nominal and then with real rigidities makes sense only if the issues discussed in this chapter are likely to be relevant in the models studied in the next, and if the issues of nominal and real rigidities are independent. As we shall see by the end of chapter 9, this is probably largely but not entirely true. These issues can be more fruitfully discussed after the approaches are presented and analyzed.

Outline

For issues of price setting to be of interest, price-setters must have some monopoly power. Thus we must replace the assumption of perfect competition by one of imperfect competition. Therefore in section 8.1 we construct a model of an economy in which monopolistic competitors set the prices of the goods they produce. Monopoly power on the part of producers leads of course to an inefficient equilibrium; nevertheless, fluctuations in aggregate demand, which we take to be fluctuations in nominal money, are still neutral just as they would be under perfect competition. When there are costs of changing prices, however, price-setters may decide not to adjust their prices in response to small shifts in demand, and movements in nominal money may accordingly lead to movements in output. More interestingly, the welfare effects of the implied output movements are likely to be much larger than the costs of changing prices. This provides some basis for the idea that, while each individual price-setter may not lose much from not adjusting her own price, the aggregate effects of price level inertia can be large. The model is, however, static and in the rest of the chapter we consider how the results extend to the dynamic context.

In a dynamic context, costs of changing prices lead price-setters to change them at discrete intervals of time. If the costs of changing prices come mostly from collecting information, it may be optimal for price-setters to change their prices at fixed intervals of time, to use "time-dependent" price rules. If, instead, the costs of changing prices are physical, "menu costs," it may then be optimal to change prices as a function of the state, to use "state-dependent rules." The macroeconomic implications of both types of rules are quite different, and we examine them separately in sections 8.2 and 8.3.

We conclude the chapter with a discussion of the limitations and implications of the analysis so far. We show why nominal rigidities can only be part of the overall story, thereby providing a transition to the study of real rigidities in the next chapter.

Before we start, a word of warning. In this chapter, to better isolate the implications of nominal rigidities, we remove all the sources of dynamics we have so painstakingly analyzed in the previous chapter. This formalization strategy, though appropriate, creates too sharp a contrast between the two chapters. In practice, nominal rigidities interact with the other sources of persistence in the economy. Producing fully specified analytic models that encompass all these mechanisms is difficult, though such models can be solved on the computer.[6]

8.1 Price Setting under Monopolistic Competition

A Model of Monopolistic Competition.[7]

We consider an economy with n goods, all being imperfect substitutes, and money. Each good is produced by one producer who acts as a monopolistic competitor, choosing the nominal price and the level of production of the good given the demand function she faces.[8] Each producer is also a consumer, who therefore derives utility from the consumption of all goods and of the services of real money balances. This leads to a set of demand functions for goods that depend on relative prices as well as on initial real money balances.

Our interest is in the effects of shifts in aggregate demand on output in that economy. We focus on the effects of a change in the nominal stock of money; our reason for choosing to study this rather than the effects of a change in tastes, for example, is that such a change in nominal money would have no real effects in our model under perfectly competitive behavior. Thus whatever effects it has derive from departures from perfectly competitive behavior.[9]

More formally, let n be the number of producer-consumers (producers for short) in what follows. Producer i has the following utility function:

$$U_i = \left(\frac{C_i}{g}\right)^g \left(\frac{M_i/P}{1-g}\right)^{1-g} - \left(\frac{d}{\beta}\right) Y_i^{\beta}, \qquad 1 > g > 0, d > 0, \beta \geqslant 1, \qquad (1)$$

where

$$C_i = n^{1/(1-\theta)} \left(\sum_{j=1}^{n} C_{ji}^{(\theta-1)/\theta}\right)^{\theta/(\theta-1)}$$

and

$$P = \left(\frac{1}{n}\sum_{i=1}^{n} P_i^{1-\theta}\right)^{1/(1-\theta)}$$

Producer i's utility, U_i, depends positively on consumption C_i and on real money balances M_i/P, and negatively on the level of production of good i, Y_i.

Consumption, C_i, is a function of the level of consumption of each good j, C_{ji}. All goods enter the utility function symmetrically. The specific functional form implies a constant elasticity of substitution between goods, equal to θ; θ is an important parameter in what follows. If θ is large, goods are close substitutes. It will turn out that to guarantee the existence of an equilibrium, θ has to be larger than one: otherwise, as we shall see, the demand facing each producer would have elasticity less than one and the producer would want to choose an infinite price. The constant term in C_i is introduced for convenience and simplifies derivations later.

Real money balances are assumed to affect utility directly. This is clearly a shortcut, which yields below the implication that an increase in real money balances increases the demand for goods. A full treatment of the role of money would, as we have discussed in chapter 4, require a dynamic model, something we do not want to do here.[10] Because money is implicitly used to buy goods, the appropriate price deflator is the nominal price index associated with C_i. It is given by P, the price level. The price level is homogeneous of degree one in all nominal prices, P_i, $i = 1, \ldots, n$.

Output of good i, Y_i, affects utility negatively. This is because production of good i requires work as an input and thus reduces leisure. The expression $\beta - 1$ gives the elasticity of marginal disutility with respect to output, which is the most important coefficient in what follows. It is implicitly the product of two factors: the elasticity of marginal disutility with respect to work and the elasticity of work with respect to output, the inverse of the degree of returns to labor in production. If the marginal disutility of work is constant and there are constant returns to labor in production, $\beta - 1$ is equal to zero. If, however, marginal disutility increases with the amount worked or if there are decreasing returns to labor in production, $\beta - 1$ will be positive.

The utility function is clearly special. In particular, it is homogeneous of degree one in consumption and real money balances, as well as separable in consumption and real money, on the one hand, and leisure, on the other. This has, as we shall see, the convenient implication that the marginal utility of wealth is constant, which in turn facilitates welfare evaluations. The introduction of constants, such as the division of C_i by g is done only to simplify notation later and is of no consequence.

Individual i faces the budget constraint

$$\sum_{j=1}^{n} P_j C_{ji} + M_i = P_i Y_i + \overline{M}_i \equiv I_i. \tag{2}$$

Nominal consumption expenditures plus the demand for nominal money balances must be equal to nominal income from the sale of the produced good plus the individual's initial holdings of money balances. It is convenient for later use to define "wealth" I_i as the sum of income and initial balances.

Our first task is to characterize the equilibrium of the economy characterized by equations (1) and (2). To do so, we proceed in three steps. First, taking wealth as given, we solve for the allocation of wealth between purchases of goods and money. Second, using these individual conditional demand functions, we derive the demand function facing each producer. Finally, we solve the producer's maximization problem and derive equilibrium prices and quantities.

Individual Demand Functions
We first derive the demand for goods and money of a given individual i. Given wealth I_i, maximization of utility with respect to $C_{ji}, j = 1, \ldots, n$, and M_i/P implies that

$$C_{ji} = \left(\frac{P_j}{P}\right)^{-\theta}\left(\frac{gI_i}{nP}\right), \qquad j = 1, \ldots, n,$$

and

$M_i = (1 - g)I_i.$
The demand for each good is linear in wealth and a function of the relative price of the good, with elasticity $-\theta$. The demand for real money balances is also linear in wealth. Given these choices, we can derive for future use an indirect utility function by replacing C_{ji} and M_i/P in equation (1) by their optimal values given wealth, $P_iY_i + \overline{M_i}$. This gives

$$U_i = \left(\frac{P_i}{P}\right)Y_i - \left(\frac{d}{\beta}\right)Y_i^\beta + \frac{\overline{M_i}}{P}. \tag{3}$$

The Demand Facing a Given Producer
Second, we derive the demand function facing producer i. Define $\overline{M}$ as the sum of money balances in the economy, $\sum \overline{M_i}$, and M as the sum of money demands, $\sum M_i$. Further, define aggregate demand Y as the sum of consumption demands over goods and consumers:

$$Y \equiv \sum_{i=1}^{n}\sum_{j=1}^{n}\frac{P_iC_{ji}}{P} = g\left(\sum_{j=1}^{n}\frac{I_j}{P}\right).$$

Note that in equilibrium (when aggregate demand is equal to output) $\sum(I_j/P)$ is equal to $Y + \overline{M}/P$. Replacing and solving for Y implies that

$$Y = \left(\frac{g}{1 - g}\right)\left(\frac{\overline{M}}{P}\right). \tag{4}$$

There is thus a simple quantity-theory-like relation among nominal money, the price level, and aggregate demand.

The *demand facing producer i* is then given by

$$Y_i = \sum_{j=1}^{n} C_{ji} = \left(\frac{P_i}{P}\right)^{-\theta}\left(\frac{Y}{n}\right) = \left(\frac{P_i}{P}\right)^{-\theta}\left(\frac{g}{(1-g)n}\right)\left(\frac{M}{P}\right).$$

The demand facing each producer is proportional to aggregate demand and a decreasing function of the relative price with elasticity $-\theta$. To save on notation, it is convenient to define M' as $[g/(1-g)n]\overline{M}$. (M' has the interpretation of nominal income per capita; we will refer to it simply as money.) This yields for the demand function facing producer i,

$$Y_i = \left(\frac{P_i}{P}\right)^{-\theta}\left(\frac{M'}{P}\right). \tag{5}$$

Producer i's Output and Price Decisions
Third, we solve for the price and output chosen by producer i, who maximizes the indirect utility function (3) subject to the demand function given by equation (5). Equation (3) looks exactly like a conventional profit function, except for the last term which is, however, given to the producer. From that maximization we derive[11]

$$\frac{P_i}{P} = \left[\left(\frac{d\theta}{\theta-1}\right)\left(\frac{M'}{P}\right)^{\beta-1}\right]^{1/[1+\theta(\beta-1)]}. \tag{6}$$

This is an important equation, as it gives the nominal price P_i as a function of the aggregate price P and money M'. Under our assumptions the relative price chosen by producer i is a nondecreasing function of real money balances, which shift the demand curve that the producer faces. If the marginal cost of production is constant (i.e., if β is equal to one), the producer reacts to shifts in demand by changing output while leaving the relative price constant.[12] If, however, because of either decreasing returns or increasing marginal disutility of work, or both, β is greater than one, the response to an increase in demand is to increase both the relative price and the level of output.

General Equilibrium
Equation (6) gives the relative price chosen by each producer as a function of real money balances. But in equilibrium the average relative price, appropriately defined, must be equal to one. Here, since there is complete symmetry across producers, relative prices must all be equal to one.

In equation (6) there is a unique level of real money balances such that each producer chooses a relative price equal to one. If the real money stock were higher, all producers would want to choose a nominal price higher than the others, and this is impossible. Thus equation (6), together with the equilibrium requirement $P_i/P = 1$ for all i, determines the equilibrium level of real money balances and, given nominal money, the price level.

From equation (5) we then get the equilibrium level of output produced by each producer. Equilibrium price and output are

$$P = \left(\frac{\theta - 1}{\theta d}\right)^{1/(1-\beta)} M'$$

and   (7)

$$Y_i = \left(\frac{\theta - 1}{\theta d}\right)^{1/(\beta-1)} \qquad i = 1, \ldots, n.$$

Figure 8.1 gives a graphical characterization of the equilibrium. It draws for a given level of real money balances M'/P, the demand function, the marginal revenue function, and the marginal cost function faced by a producer. The profit-maximizing level of output is at the intersection of marginal revenue and marginal cost, with the associated relative price given by point A of the demand curve.

The requirement that in symmetric equilibrium all relative prices must be equal to one determines in turn the position of the demand curve facing each producer and also the level of real money balances and the price level consistent with equilibrium.

To introduce the issues that we study below, it is helpful to describe informally the process of adjustment through which equilibrium may be reached. In response to, say, an increase in money, each producer observes, at existing prices, an increase in its demand. Each producer attempts to increase her relative price, but this only leads to an increase of all nominal prices and an increase in the price level. Pressure on the price level continues until demand is back to normal, and relative prices are again equal to unity. This happens when the price level has increased in proportion to the increase in money.

Monopolistic versus Competitive Equilibrium

How does the monopolistically competitive equilibrium differ from a competitive equilibrium? If each producer acted competitively, the equilibrium would be at the intersection of the marginal cost and demand curves. In symmetric equilibrium, P_i/P would again be equal to one, implying that the

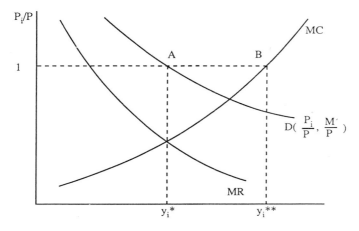

Figure 8.1
Equilibrium under monopolistic competition

equilibrium would be at point *B* in figure 8.1 instead of at *A*. This in turn implies that since the demand curve must go through *B*, equilibrium real money balances would be higher under perfect competition: output would be higher and the price level lower.

Note that because all producers have the same degree of monopoly power, monopoly power has no effect on the relative price of produced goods. Monopolistic competition affects, instead, the relative price of goods in terms of money, the price level, which is higher than under competition. Welfare, measured by consumer and producer surplus,[13] is higher under perfect competition.

Up to this point we have gained few macroeconomic insights by moving from competition to monopolistic competition. The response of both economies to aggregate demand shifts is likely to be similar. In particular, equation (7) makes it clear that money is neutral under monopolistic competition just as it is under perfect competition.[14] We therefore need to go further. We now ask what happens if price-setters face costs of changing prices.

Costs of Changing Prices and Real Effects of Nominal Money

Before we turn to the costs of changing prices, it will be useful to recast the inefficiency of the monopolistically competitive economy as the result of a pecuniary—or "aggregate demand"—externality.

This externality arises because a decrease in an individual producer's nominal price has two effects. First, it increases the demand for that producer's good; second, by decreasing (slightly) the price level, it increases real money balances, and thus increases demand and output for all other producers. In equilibrium prices are such that the first effect on profit is equal to zero to a first order: each producer has no incentive to change her price. But, because output is initially below its socially optimal level under monopolistic competition, the second effect leads to an increase in welfare.

Put another way—which will be convenient below—a small proportional decrease in all nominal prices, that is, a decrease in the price level, would increase aggregate demand and output and have a first-order positive effect on welfare. But no individual producer has an incentive to decrease her own price given other prices, since she would experience a second-order loss in profit.

Although this externality leads to too low an equilibrium level of output, it does not imply that money is nonneutral in the absence of costs of changing prices. Suppose, however, that producers face costs of changing prices. The costs may be small, as is emphasized by calling them "menu costs." They may, however, include more than just the physical costs of printing new menus or changing labels, and we will return to consider their nature later.

More precisely, assume that each producer faces second-order costs of changing prices. Now, instead of a small decrease in the price level given nominal money, consider a small increase in nominal money given the price level. Output and welfare increase to a first order, but each producer has only a second-order incentive to increase her price. Absent menu costs, the economy would return to the initial level of output with higher prices. But second-order menu costs, as long as they are larger than the second-order loss in profit associated with not changing the price, will prevent this adjustment. This is the key point: if small menu costs make it optimal for producers not to change prices when demand changes, nominal prices will not adjust, and the change in nominal money will affect output and have first-order effects on welfare.

This argument takes as given that producers who do not adjust prices will accommodate the higher level of demand so that output will increase. But for small changes in nominal money, this must indeed be true: price initially exceeds marginal cost so that producers will willingly increase output even if they do not adjust prices. In figure 8.1 producers will be willing to increase output up to point B at unchanged prices.

The trivial part of the above result is that in the presence of costs of changing prices, prices may not adjust, and nominal money may affect output. The interesting part is that costs of changing prices that are sufficient to prevent such adjustment may be far smaller than the welfare effects—positive or negative, depending on the sign of the change in nominal money—that follow from nonadjustment of prices. This point was first made by Akerlof and Yellen (1985a, b) who emphasized its generality: in any economy with distortions the decision by one individual to react or not to react to a change in his environment entails only a second-order private loss; the presence of distortions, however, makes it likely that the effects on welfare will be of first order.[15]

The argument indeed yields an embarrassment of riches (technically, *embarras de richesses*). In particular, why should we focus on its implications for prices and not for other variables under the control of the firm, such as output? This is a serious issue to which we will return shortly.

Small versus Large Changes in Demand
For larger changes in the nominal money stock, the private opportunity costs of not adjusting are no longer negligible and depend on the parameters of the model. We now investigate this dependence. From the profit function of each producer, we can compute the loss in profit that comes from not adjusting her price in response to a proportional change in nominal money of dM/M, given that other prices do not adjust. Expressed as a ratio of initial revenues, this loss is given to a second-order by[16]

$$L = \frac{(1/2)(\beta - 1)^2 (\theta - 1)}{[1 + \theta(\beta - 1)]} \left(\frac{dM}{M}\right)^2. \tag{8}$$

The loss is an increasing function of $\beta - 1$, the elasticity of marginal disutility with respect to output.

The case where β is equal to one, though admittedly very special, is interesting. If β is equal to one, the condition for an equilibrium (other than output equal to zero or infinity) to exist is that $P_i/P = d\theta/(\theta - 1) = 1$. If this condition on the parameters d and θ is satisfied, any level of output is an equilibrium, and welfare is increasing in the level of output. In that case, starting from an arbitrary equilibrium, consider an increase in nominal money. The private loss to not adjusting the relative price is equal to zero since it is indeed privately optimal not to adjust the relative price in response to a change in demand in that case. Since relative prices do not change, nominal prices and the price level do not change either, and the increase in nominal money increases real money, output, and welfare. In this case we do not need menu costs to get real effects of nominal money, but it is admittedly a very special case.

The loss is an increasing function of the elasticity of substitution. The higher the elasticity of substitution, the higher the opportunity cost of not adjusting prices—although the desired adjustment will be smaller (this point will be relevant in the next section). To summarize the main point of the argument, the flatter the marginal cost curve, the smaller are the costs of changing prices needed to obtain effects of money on output and on welfare.

Interactions among Price-Setters: Multiple Equilibria

We have examined the question of how costly it is for one producer not to adjust her nominal price in response to a change in nominal money, given that the other producers do not change their nominal prices. A related but different question that arises when nominal demand changes is whether price adjustment by other producers makes it more or less likely that an individual producer will want to adjust her price too.[17]

To answer this question, let us assume that in response to a change in nominal money, the price level adjusts by a fraction k of that change. (The parameter k is not exactly the proportion of price-setters who adjust, except for $k = 0$ or 1, since those who adjust will not usually increase their prices in the same proportion as the change in money.) Formally, let

$$\frac{dP}{P} = k\frac{dM}{M}.$$

If $k = 0$, no producer adjusts her price, and we are back to the case just studied. If $k = 1$, all producers adjust their price, and the real money stock and demand do not change. We now ask what the private loss is to a given producer from not adjusting her price when money changes and the price level adjusts by $k\%$ of the change in money. The private loss, expressed as a ratio to initial revenues, is now given by

$$L(k) = \frac{(\frac{1}{2})(\theta - 1)\{k[1 + (\beta - 1)(\theta - 1)] + (\beta - 1)\}^2}{1 + \theta(\beta - 1)}\left(\frac{dM}{M}\right)^2.$$

This expression is more complicated than before, since it depends not only on β and θ but also on k. Differentiating L with respect to k, we find that

$$\text{sign}\left(\frac{dL}{dk}\right) = \text{sign}[1 + (\beta - 1)(\theta - 1)] > 0.$$

An increase in k unambiguously increases the opportunity cost of not adjusting prices for an individual producer.

Put another way, the smaller the number of producers who adjust, the less costly it is for others not to adjust as well. This is an important result that will reappear later in various guises. The intuition for it can be obtained by returning to the price rule for each producer, equation (6), which gives the price that producer i would choose in the absence of menu costs, and rewriting it as

$$P_i = (\text{constant}) P \left(\frac{M}{P}\right)^{(\beta-1)/[1+\theta(\beta-1)]}$$

$$= (\text{constant}) P^a M^{1-a}, \tag{9}$$

where $a \equiv [1 + (\beta - 1)(\theta - 1)]/[1 + \theta(\beta - 1)]$ and the constant depends on structural parameters and is of no importance here.

An increase in P has two effects on P_i. The first is that as producer i sets a relative price, an increase in P, with no change in the demand function facing the producer, leads to a proportional increase in P_i. The second is that an increase in P leads to a decrease in real money balances, thus to a decrease in aggregate demand, a shift in the demand facing the producer, and a desired decrease in the relative price. The net effect is given by the coefficient a, whose sign depends again on $1 + (\beta - 1)(\theta - 1)$ and is thus unambiguously positive.

An increase in the aggregate price level makes each producer want to increase her nominal price, although less than one for one. Thus, the larger the increase in the price level in response to money, the higher is the cost for any producer from not adjusting her price.

This result, unlike those derived earlier, is not a general feature of monopolistic competition. It could be reversed if, for example, the elasticity of aggregate demand with respect to real money, which is one in our model, were much greater than one. The aggregate demand effect could then dominate the relative price effect and a could be negative.

This result implies that there may well be *multiple equilibria* in the presence of menu costs. To see this, consider figure 8.2 which gives the opportunity cost $L(k)$ as an increasing function of k and for a given value of $(dM/M)^2$. Let A and B be the values of L for $k = 1$ and $k = 0$, respectively. Producers will adjust prices if and only if L exceeds the menu cost, c.

If c is large, namely, greater than A, then the equilibrium is such that no price is adjusted. If c is small, namely smaller than B, then the equilibrium is such that all prices are adjusted. But if c is between A and B, there are two stable equilibria, one in which all prices are adjusted and one in which no price is adjusted.

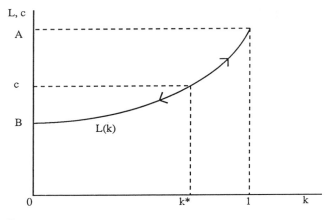

Figure 8.2
Multiple equilibria in price setting

To see why, consider a value of c between A and B. If the proportion of producers who adjust is just such that $L(k) = c$, then no producer has an incentive to shift from adjusting to not adjusting. This is clearly an equilibrium, but it is unstable in the following sense. Suppose that initially $L(k)$ is slightly greater than c. Then, for all producers who are not adjusting prices, the opportunity cost of not adjusting, $L(k)$, exceeds the cost of adjusting, c; thus producers will start adjusting prices, and this will go on until the economy reaches A, at which point all producers adjust prices and money is neutral.[18] By a symmetrical argument, if $L(k)$ is slightly smaller than c initially, the economy reaches B, at which point no producer adjusts prices and money strongly affects output. There is nothing in the model that allows us to decide which of these two equilibria will prevail.

The Issues
We have shown that small costs of changing prices could lead price-setters to keep relative prices constant in response to changes in aggregate demand. In so doing, they create nominal price rigidity, and thereby potentially large output and welfare effects from movements in demand. We have shown also that, under plausible assumptions, price rigidity on the part of some price-setters makes price rigidity more likely for the others.

These are attractive results for the view that nominal rigidities play an important role in the transmission mechanism. However, they raise several important issues.

The first was raised earlier. Why should "doing nothing" mean not adjusting prices rather than not adjusting quantities? Equivalently, why is there a discrete cost of changing price but not of changing output? If producers decide not to adjust quantities and to allow their output price to change, output would remain at its initial equilibrium value, and nominal money would be neutral. The answer, if any, must be that producers find it more convenient to post prices, change them at discrete intervals of time, and let demand determine quantities during those intervals. While one can think of reasons why this might be so, those reasons are not explicitly in the model; introducing them could change some of the conclusions.

The second problem is that the model, by design, has no dynamics. This makes it possible to focus on the effects of price setting, but the lack of an explicit time dimension makes some of the results quite misleading. Here are three examples:

1. Suppose that equilibrium is characterized in each period by the model developed above. We must then compare menu costs, not to the current opportunity cost of not changing prices, but to the present value of these opportunity costs, which may be quite large. This suggests at the least that prices are more likely to be adjusted when changes in nominal money are perceived as permanent than when they are perceived as transitory.

2. Suppose that there is an underlying trend in nominal money growth and inflation. If producers quote fixed nominal prices, they must then readjust their price regularly to maintain their relative price. But if this is true, then even in the presence of menu costs, a step increase in nominal money does not have a permanent effect on output. If the cost of adjusting prices is invariant to the size of the adjustment, producers are likely, when they choose a new nominal price, to adjust not only for trend growth in money but also for the step increase in nominal money. This raises the issue of how long the effects of changes in nominal money on output will last.

3. The model has assumed that all prices were initially equal and set optimally. In a dynamic economy and in the presence of menu costs, such a degenerate distribution is unlikely. But if prices are not all equal or optimal to start with, it is no longer obvious that even a small change in money will leave all prices unaffected. It is accordingly no longer obvious that money will have large effects on output.

We will deal with this set of issues in the next two sections.

The third issue concerns the interaction of the real wage and the level of output. We can think of the relative price charged by each producer as a real wage, the ratio of the price of the good she produces and sells with her labor to the price of the basket of goods she consumes. It thus appears that menu costs can explain why fluctuations in employment can take place without movements in the real wage.

But of course matters are not so simple. For small menu costs to explain large fluctuations in output, it must not be too costly for price-setters to keep prices unchanged and to let demand determine output and work. Going back to equation (8), the opportunity cost of not adjusting prices, L, increases quickly with the parameter $\beta - 1$; for the opportunity cost not to be too large, $\beta - 1$ must be small.

What does that condition mean? If, instead of producing for themselves, individuals with the utility function described in (1) supply labor competitively in the labor market, the elasticity of labor supply with respect to the real wage would be given by $1/(\beta - 1)$. Thus the condition that $\beta - 1$ be small can be interpreted as a condition that (implicit) labor supply be very elastic. But as we have discussed at length in the previous chapter, without strong intertemporal substitution effects, we would not expect labor supply to be very elastic.

The menu cost argument thus runs into the same problems as the models based on imperfect information studied in the previous chapter. It requires the equivalent of an elastic labor supply in order to generate large fluctuations in output and employment from small menu costs. We will ignore the issue in the rest of this chapter and assume that $\beta - 1$ is indeed small. But a good portion of the next chapter is devoted to this issue.

8.2 Time-Dependent Rules, Staggering, and the Effects of Money

In dynamic models the issue is no longer whether prices will adjust in the presence of menu costs and whether or not money will have real effects but rather how often prices will be readjusted, and how long the real effects of money will last. It turns out that the answer depends very much on the specific form of the price rules adopted by price-setters. Two distinctions are important in this context.

The first is between *time- and state-dependent price rules*. Under time-dependent rules, the price is changed as a function of time. Under state-dependent rules, it is changed as a function of the state. This section studies time-dependent rules, and the next one state-dependent rules. We can easily point to examples of both types of rules. Contract wages are changed at fixed intervals of time, when contracts expire. The length of time between changes for most list prices appears to be largely random and presumably a function of the state.[19] After analyzing their respective effects, we return to the issue of why price-setters may choose one or the other, or hybrids of the two.

The second distinction, within the class of time-dependent rules, is between those rules that predetermine the path of prices and the simpler rules that fix nominal prices for given lengths of time. A nominal price is *predetermined* for a given length of time, say, t to $t + i$, if its path from t to $t + i$ is predetermined as of time t. A nominal price is *fixed* for a given length of time if it is not only predetermined but also constant during that length of time. We can again point to examples of both. Most list prices are clearly fixed, not predetermined between reassessments. Perhaps the clearest example of predetermined prices are wages fixed by contracts that pre-specify different wage rates for different periods covered by the contract. For example, a contract may specify a new base wage for the first year of the contract and then increases of specified percentages or amounts for the second and (perhaps) third years. In this section we study the implications of both predetermined and fixed price rules, and then we take up the question of why price- or wage-setters would choose one rather than the other.

Throughout, we assume that (apart from the mechanics of price setting) the economy is characterized in each period by the model presented in section 8.1. This is clearly a drastic simplification, that eliminates all the sources of dynamics studied in the previous chapter.[20] The only dynamics left are the dynamics introduced by price setting. This is appropriate given our focus, but it must be kept in mind in judging whether these models successfully replicate the dynamics of the actual economy.

Before looking at the implications of alternative price-setting rules, we summarize the structure of the model in the absence of constraints on price setting. There are n producer–price-setters, each setting a nominal price for her product. From profit maximization each chooses a relative price that is an increasing function of real money balances. This is because an increase in real money balances increases aggregate demand, shifting out the demand faced by the producer and leading her, unless the marginal disutility of production is constant, to increase her relative price. From equation (9), by taking logarithms, denoting them by lowercase letters, and ignoring the (unimportant) constant, we obtain the equation giving the relative price chosen by producer i:

$$p_i - p = (1 - a)(m - p), \qquad 0 < a \leqslant 1, \tag{9'}$$

or equivalently

$$p_i = ap + (1 - a)m.$$

The other important equation gives aggregate demand and output as a function of real money balances. By taking logarithms and again ignoring the constant, we transform equation (4) into

$$y = m - p. \tag{4'}$$

In equilibrium all prices are the same. Thus from (9'), $p = m$. From (4'), $y = 0$ (given our exclusion of constant terms) and is independent of nominal money. We are now ready to turn to the implications of alternative price-setting rules.

Predetermined Prices and The Effects of Money[21]

We start by considering the simplest possible case, the case where prices are set every period for one period. We then consider the case where prices are predetermined for two periods. Each period, half of the price-setters predetermine their prices for the next two periods.

One-Period Predetermination of Prices
The economy proceeds through time, which is discrete. In each period the economy has, except for price setting, the same structure as that described above. The nominal money stock is now random, however.

At the beginning of each period t, each producer chooses a nominal price for that period, based on full knowledge of history but without knowing the realization of the money stock for period t. Let us denote the expectation of a variable x conditional on such an information set at time t simply as Ex. In view of equation (9') we assume that prices at time t are chosen according to[22]

$$p_i = aEp + (1 - a)Em. \tag{10}$$

(The time index is not needed and thus is omitted for the time being.)

Aggregate demand and output depend on actual real money balances. Thus from (4'),

$$y = m - p. \tag{11}$$

Equations (10) and (11) characterize the behavior of the economy. We can easily solve for the equilibrium. Because all price decisions are based on the same information, the price level can be computed by price-setters and is therefore known as of the beginning of period t. Thus by replacing Ep by p in (10) and realizing that all prices will be the same, solving for p, and substituting in (11), we obtain

$$p = Em$$
$$y = m - Em.$$
(12)

These equations fully characterize the equilibrium. Price-setters all set prices equal to expected nominal money. To the extent that movements in nominal money are unexpected, they affect aggregate demand and output one for one in percentage terms.

Equations (12) implicitly assume that movements in aggregate demand are satisfied, even if output is above its equilibrium (flexible price) value. This is an issue we have analyzed in the previous section, and we simply restate the earlier conclusion: for small increases in output, producers willingly accommodate the higher level of demand. For larger increases, the question is whether marginal cost at the quantity demanded exceeds price. If marginal cost exceeds price, suppliers may want not to satisfy demand.

This first model implies that movements in money can indeed affect output. But it is only unanticipated nominal money that matters, and its effects last only so long as each price remains fixed. This leads us to consider a second model, in which prices are now predetermined for two periods.

Two-Period Predetermination of Prices and Staggering
Prices are predetermined for two periods but are still fixed for only one period. That is, a producer at time t specifies a nominal price for period t and another for period $t + 1$. For symmetry, we assume that half of the producers take decisions at time t for two periods and half at time $t + 1$, also for two periods: thus price decisions are equally staggered over time.

Let p_1 and p_2 denote the prices associated with the two sets of producers at any given time (producers choosing their price at the same time will obviously choose the same price). We approximate the price level by[23]

$$p = \frac{1}{2}(p_1 + p_2).$$
(13)

Ignoring for a moment issues of predetermination, substituting (13) in (9'), and reorganizing gives

$$p_1 = bp_2 + (1 - b)m,$$

$$b \equiv \frac{a}{2 - a} \qquad \text{so that } 0 < b \leqslant 1,$$
(14)

and a similar equation holds for p_2. The price set by each half of the price-setters, say, p_2, affects the price set by the other half, p_1; this is because p_2 affects both the relative demand for goods with price p_1 and aggregate demand through the aggregate price level.

We are now ready to examine the effects of predetermination of prices in this two-period case. To do so, we introduce some notation. Let $p_{t,t+i}$ denote the nominal price chosen at time t for period $t + i$. Let $E[\cdot|t - i]$ denote the expectation of a variable held as of time $t - i$, which is based on information up to but excluding period $t - i$. Consider the prices chosen by those who set at time t their prices for t and $t + 1$. In view of equation (14) we assume that

$$p_{t,t} = (1 - b)E[m_t|t] + bp_{t-1,t}$$

and

$$(15)$$

$$p_{t,t+1} = (1 - b)E[m_{t+1}|t] + bE[p_{t+1,t+1}|t].$$

The nominal price chosen at time t for period t depends on money expected for time t and on the other nominal price, which was chosen at time $t - 1$ for t. The nominal price chosen at time t for period $t + 1$ depends on money expected at time $t + 1$ and on the nominal price which is expected to be chosen at time $t + 1$ by the other half of the firms for period $t + 1$. Similar equations hold for all t. The level of output is in turn given by

$$y_t = m_t - \frac{1}{2}(p_{t,t} + p_{t-1,t}).$$

$$(16)$$

Equations (15) and (16) characterize the behavior of the economy given the behavior of the money stock. We now solve for the equilibrium.

Equilibrium in the Two-Period Model
The first step is to solve for $p_{t,t}$. Using the second equation of (15) lagged once to get $p_{t-1,t}$ and substituting in the first equation in (15) gives

$$p_{t,t} = (1 - b)E[m_t|t] + b(1 - b)E[m_t|t - 1] + b^2E[p_{t,t}|t - 1].$$

Taking expectations of both sides and rearranging gives

$$E[p_{t,t}|t - 1] = E[m_t|t - 1].$$

Replacing back into the expression for $p_{t,t}$ gives

$$p_{t,t} = (1 - b)E[m_t|t] + bE[m_t|t - 1].$$

The nominal price chosen at time t for period t depends on both the expectation at time t and the expectation at time $t - 1$ of nominal money for time t. The reason for the presence of lagged expectations is that $p_{t,t}$ depends on $p_{t-1,t}$, which itself was determined at $t - 1$ based on expectations, as of then, of the price level and money for period t.

Solving for $p_{t-1,t}$ in similar fashion gives

$$p_{t-1,t} = E[m_t|t - 1].$$

As the price level $p_t = (1/2)(p_{t,t} + p_{t-1,t})$, this finally gives the equilibrium values of p_t and y_t:

$$p_t = \frac{1}{2}(1 - b)E[m_t|t] + \frac{1}{2}(1 + b)E[m_t|t - 1],$$

$$(17)$$

$$y_t = \frac{1}{2}(1 - b)(m_t - E[m_t|t]) + \frac{1}{2}(1 + b)(m_t - E[m_t|t - 1]).$$

Output depends on the current money stock relative to the stock that was expected at the beginning of the current period and that expected at the beginning of the previous period. To see what this implies, assume, for example, that nominal money follows a random walk:

$$m_t = m_{t-1} + \varepsilon_t.$$

Then output is given by

$$y_t = \varepsilon_t + \frac{1}{2}(1 + b)\varepsilon_{t-1}.$$

More generally, aggregate demand can affect output for a period as long as the length of time for which each price is predetermined. In addition there is, as we now show, a role for policy to stabilize output.

Policy and Output Stabilization
To examine the role of stabilization policy, we extend the model to provide a potentially useful role for active policy. To this end we modify the aggregate demand equation to

$$y_t = m_t - p_t + v_t,$$

where v_t stands for velocity or nonpolicy shocks to aggregate demand.[24]
The derivation of the behavior of output is the same as above, with $m_t + v_t$ replacing m_t so that output is given by

$$y_t = \frac{1}{2}(1 - b)(m_t + v_t - E[m_t + v_t|t])$$

$$+ \frac{1}{2}(1 + b)(m_t + v_t - E[m_t + v_t|t - 1]).$$

To take a specific example, suppose that v_t follows a random walk, with $v_t = v_{t-1} + \varepsilon_t$, and consider the following class of monetary feedback rules:

$$m_t = a_1 \varepsilon_{t-1} + a_2 \varepsilon_{t-2} + \cdots + a_n \varepsilon_{t-n} + \cdots .$$

Thus the nominal money stock at time t is allowed to depend on all demand shocks up to $t - 1$. In other words, the monetary authority has no more information at any time t than individual price-setters. Solving for output implies that

$$y_t = \varepsilon_t + \frac{1}{2}(1 + b)(1 + a_1)\varepsilon_{t-1}.$$

If the aim of monetary policy is to minimize the variance of output, the optimal monetary rule is to set $a_1 = -1$. All other coefficients are irrelevant to the behavior of output. The intuition for this result is straightforward. The optimal rule is one that sets money each period so as to offset the anticipated nonpolicy shock next period. The other coefficients are irrelevant because movements in aggregate demand (whether in nonpolicy shocks or in money) that are anticipated more than two periods in advance have no effect on output.

The money rule that minimizes the variance in output implies that output deviations are white, despite the existence of two-period predetermination of prices. Put another way, the monetary authority can, in principle, offset the additional variability of output due to more than one-period predetermination of prices on output. This result would remain if we were to consider predetermination of prices for n periods as well as more general processes for the nonpolicy shock, v_t. In general, monetary policy that is based on an information set larger than that available to individuals when they set prices can be used to affect the pattern of output. For example, if the monetary authority could set the money stock each period after the velocity shock becomes known, it could prevent all divergences of output from a given constant level.[25]

One characteristic of this class of models is that in the absence of other sources of persistence, the effect of aggregate demand on output lasts only for a period equal to the period for which prices are predetermined. We now turn to models in which prices are not only predetermined but also fixed and show how this result is modified.

The Effects of Fixed Prices and Staggering[26]

Our starting point is the model developed above in which prices are predetermined for two periods, with half of the price-setters choosing prices each period for two periods. However, instead of assuming that the prices chosen for the first and second periods can be different, we assume that the same price is chosen for both periods.

In terms of the notation developed above, we assume that

$$p_{t,t} = p_{t,t+1} \equiv x_t.$$

Here x_t is the price set in period t by the firms that set prices in that period for both periods t and $t + 1$.

In view of equation (15) we assume that x_t is given by

$$x_t = \frac{1}{2}\{bx_{t-1} + (1 - b)E[m_t|t]\} + \frac{1}{2}\{bE[x_{t+1}|t] + (1 - b)E[m_{t+1}|t]\}. \quad (18)$$

The nominal price chosen at time t is a weighted average, with equal weights, of the optimal price for period t and the expected optimal price for period $t + 1$. The optimal price for period t depends on the nominal price paid to the other half of the producers at time t, x_{t-1}, and expected nominal money. The expected optimal price for period $t + 1$ depends on the nominal price expected to be chosen the next period by the other half of the producers, $E[x_{t+1}|t]$, and on expected nominal money for $t + 1$.[27]

Using the methods developed in the appendix to chapter 5, we can derive the stable solution to equation (18). It is given by

$$x_t = \lambda x_{t-1} + \left[\frac{\lambda(1 - b)}{b}\right] \sum_{i=0}^{\infty} \lambda^i \{(E[m_{t+i}|t] + E[m_{t+i+1}|t]\}, \quad (19)$$

where

$$\lambda \equiv \frac{1 - \sqrt{(1 - b^2)}}{b}, \quad \text{so that } 0 < \lambda < 1.$$

Thus the nominal price chosen at time t for t and $t + 1$ depends on the nominal price chosen at time $t - 1$ for $t - 1$ and t as well as on the expectations of nominal money from t to infinity. The price level and output are given in turn by

$$p_t = \frac{1}{2}(x_t + x_{t-1}), \tag{20}$$

$$y_t = m_t - p_t = m_t - \frac{1}{2}(x_t + x_{t-1}). \tag{21}$$

These equations fully characterize the equilibrium for any process for money. To better understand its characteristics, we now consider the implications of a specific process for nominal money.

The Dynamic Adjustment to Demand Shocks
Consider the case where nominal money follows a random walk:

$$m_t = m_{t-1} + \varepsilon_t.$$

In this case all expectations of future money are equal to the most recent value of money in the information set so that

$$E[m_{t+i}|t] = m_{t-1}, \qquad \text{for all } i \geqslant 0.$$

Replacing in (19), (20), and (21), and noting that from the definition of λ, $2\lambda(1 - b)/b(1 - \lambda) = (1 - \lambda)$, we obtain

$$x_t = \lambda x_{t-1} + (1 - \lambda)m_{t-1}, \tag{22}$$

$$p_t = \lambda p_{t-1} + \frac{1}{2}(1 - \lambda)(m_{t-1} + m_{t-2}), \tag{23}$$

$$y_t = \lambda y_{t-1} + [m_t - \frac{1}{2}(1 + \lambda)m_{t-1} - \frac{1}{2}(1 - \lambda)m_{t-2}]. \tag{24}$$

The effects of an innovation ε_t on x_{t+i}, p_{t+i}, and y_{t+i} are characterized in table 8.1. Both the wages and price levels adjust slowly to a permanent

Table 8.1
Dynamic effects of a unit shock, with two-period fixed prices

Effects of $\varepsilon_t = 1$ on:	x	p	y
at time t	0	0	1
$t + 1$	$1 - \lambda$	$1 - (1/2)(1 + \lambda)$	$(1/2)(1 + \lambda)$
$t + 2$	$1 - \lambda^2$	$1 - (1/2)(1 + \lambda)\lambda$	$(1/2)(1 + \lambda)\lambda$
$\cdots$			
$t + i$	$1 - \lambda^i$	$1 - (1/2)(1 + \lambda)\lambda^{i-1}$	$(1/2)(1 + \lambda)\lambda^{i-1}$
$\cdots$			

increase in money, ε_t. As a result the effects of a nominal disturbance on output are long lived, dying exponentially at rate λ. If λ is close to one, the effects of money on output are large for periods of time much longer than the length of time during which each price is predetermined. This is an important result: under time-dependent rules, fixed prices and staggering, nominal money can have long-lasting effects on output.

Why is the effect long lived? This is because of the interdependence between price decisions, the implications of which were already explored in the previous section. In response to an increase in nominal money, price-setters whose turn it is to change prices will not, if λ is close to one, want to increase their relative price very much. Thus, given that half of the price-setters cannot adjust their prices in that period, those who can adjust will not increase their nominal price very much; over time nominal prices will increase slowly until output is back to normal.[28]

From (24) it is clear that the important parameter in determining dynamic adjustment is λ, which can be called the *degree of inertia* of nominal prices. Recalling the definition of λ, and of b earlier, we can express λ as a function of the structural parameters θ and β. After some simplification, we get

$$\lambda = \frac{\beta + \theta(\beta - 1) - 2\sqrt{[(\beta - 1)(1 + \theta(\beta - 1))]}}{1 + (\beta - 1)(\theta - 1)}.$$

Thus λ is a decreasing function of $\beta - 1$. When $\beta - 1 = 0$, λ is equal to one, and changes in the nominal money stock have permanent effects on output. This is by now a familiar result. If the marginal disutility of production is constant, price-setters are only concerned about their relative price: they want to maintain their relative price constant independently of the level of aggregate demand, of aggregate real money balances. In response to a change in nominal money, no price-setter wants to change her relative price, but this means that nominal prices and the price level do not adjust. We saw in the previous section that small values of $\beta - 1$ were required to explain why prices would not be adjusted in response to shifts in demand; we see here that small values of $\beta - 1$ are required to get a slow adjustment of nominal prices to money.

It can also be seen that λ is an increasing function of θ, the elasticity of substitution between goods. As θ tends to infinity, λ tends to one. This appears to imply that the more competitive are the goods markets, the less price-setters will want to change relative prices and the slower will be the adjustment of nominal prices! Although there is technically nothing wrong with this statement, taking as given the length of time during which prices are not changed, we know from the previous section that the opportunity cost, of keeping prices fixed is an increasing function of the elasticity of substitution. Thus, if we were to endogenize the length of time during which prices are fixed, an increase in θ would lead to a decrease in the time between price decisions and thus, most likely, to a faster adjustment of prices to money.[29]

To summarize, staggered price decisions can generate long-lasting effects of money on output. Both anticipated and unanticipated money matter, and in the presence of nonpolicy shocks, policy can decrease the amplitude of output fluctuations. The role of policy in this context has been examined, for example, by Taylor (1980).

Other Staggering Structures

We have concentrated on the effects of staggering in an economy composed only of price-setters. But a large body of research has examined the effects of staggering in economies with both wages and prices, and staggering of wages only, of prices only, or of both.

Taylor (1979) examines the effects of wage staggering in an economy with flexible prices. His specification for the behavior of wages is in effect identical to equation (18) and, although Taylor does not do it, could be derived, for example, from optimal wage setting by unions which are imperfect substitutes in the labor market. Firms operate under constant returns to scale so that the price level is a fixed markup over the average wage. In that model, fluctuations in money affect output, with slow adjustment of nominal wages and prices and a constant real wage (which follows directly from the assumption of constant markup of the price level over the wage).

Blanchard (1986) examines, instead, the effect of staggering of wage and price decisions. Assuming that both prices and wages are fixed for some period of time and that price and wage decisions are not all taken at the same time, he derives the dynamic effects of nominal money on output. After an increase in the nominal money stock which, given the price level, increases aggregate demand, output, and employment, workers want a higher real wage, which means a higher nominal wage given the price level; firms want to increase or at least to maintain their markup, that is, to increase or at least maintain their price given the nominal wage. This leads to an upward adjustment of nominal prices and wages until output returns to normal. During the adjustment process there is again no correlation between the real wage and output.

Blanchard (1987) explores, both theoretically and empirically, the idea that as goods are produced through a chain of production and pricing, final goods prices may move slowly even if each individual price along the chain is set for a short period of time. He examines the implications of a production structure in which production takes place in n steps, each of them associated with a sale from one producer to the next, and in which price decisions along the chain are staggered. The conclusion is that the degree of price level inertia is indeed an increasing function of the number of steps and that this may well generate substantial price level inertia.

Finally, Calvo (1982) has developed an alternative formalization of staggering. In his model there is a constant probability that a given price-setter will change his price at any instant. This, together with the assumption that there is a large number of price-setters who act independently, implies that there is a constant proportion of prices being changed at any instant. Although not particularly realistic, this set of assumptions leads to a very simple continuous time version of the models presented in this section. Quite surprisingly, the economy exhibits dynamics similar to one in which price-setters face quadratic costs of adjustment for prices, an approach explored by Rotemberg (1982, 1983). We develop the Calvo model in chapter 10.

Why Is There Staggering?

We have until now taken as given both the length of time between price decisions by an individual price-setter and its timing with respect to decisions by other price-setters. Both are clearly decision variables of price-setters. We will not examine in detail what determines the first, as the structure of that decision is straightforward: the length of time will be such that the marginal cost of decreasing the interval (of taking price decisions more often) is equal to the marginal benefit of doing so. The first factor will depend on the costs of adjusting prices, and the second on the opportunity cost of not adjusting prices, which we have analyzed at length in the previous section.[30]

We will examine the second decision at greater length. The results we have obtained have made clear the importance of staggering for the dynamic effects of money: under synchronization—"bunching"—and in the absence of other propagation mechanisms, the real effects of nominal money would not last for a period longer than that of the length of time for which prices are fixed; under staggering, they do. This contrast forcefully raises the issue of why there is staggering. Is it privately optimal for price-setters to stagger, even if their doing so may have adverse macroeconomic effects? A first step is to ask whether staggering can be an equilibrium in the two models with staggering that we have analyzed in this section if we allow price-setters to choose the timing of their decision.

The answer is that staggering is unlikely to be an equilibrium in such models. The informal argument is the following: In the first section of this chapter we examined the question of whether an increase in the proportion of price-setters who changed their price made it more attractive for each price-setter to change her own price. For that model, the answer was that the higher the proportion of price-setters who adjust, the higher is the opportunity cost of not adjusting for any price-setter. We also indicated that the result could be reversed in more general models but that the assumptions needed to obtain the opposite result were less plausible. That answer is directly relevant here.

Suppose that a proportion k of the price-setters change their prices at even times, and a proportion $1 - k$ at odd times. Given k, each price-setter has the option of moving at even times, together with a proportion k of price-setters, or at odd times, with a proportion $1 - k$; which timing should she choose? If k is greater than $1/2$, each price-setter will want to move at even times. If she moved at odd times, her price would be fixed in even periods, in periods when the majority of price-setters change prices and thus when the opportunity cost of not adjusting is high. By moving at even times, she ensures that her price is fixed when a majority of other prices are fixed, hence when the opportunity cost is low. But if this is true of one price-setter, it must be true of all. Thus, the only equilibrium, if k is greater than $1/2$, is k equal to 1, with all price decisions bunched at even times. By a symmetric argument, for k less than $1/2$, the only equilibrium is k equal to 0.

If k is equal to $1/2$, in which case there is symmetric staggering, no price-setter has any incentive to change her timing because the stochastic environment she faces is the same whether she changes at even or odd times.[31] Thus k equal to $1/2$ is also an equilibrium, but it is an unstable one: unless the economy starts with symmetric staggering, it will end with bunching of price decisions in even or in odd periods.

However, this argument is only informal. A formal argument is more difficult to derive. The shortcuts we have used to derive the macroeconomic models of this section (the approximations to the optimal price rule and to the definition of the price level) cannot be used, since the welfare of the price-setters under alternative timing must be evaluated using the optimal rules in each case. Various papers have made progress by using approximations or linearizations: these include Parkin (1986), Ball (1986), and Ball and Romer (1987b).[32] Their results are consistent with the argument sketched above.

Do extensions of the model make it more likely that one can derive stable staggering? The introduction of stochastic idiosyncratic shocks does not make staggering more likely. With respect to idiosyncratic shocks, choosing odd or even timing is irrelevant. Thus each individual price-setter ordinarily still has an incentive to move with the majority of price-setters, and this again leads to bunching of price decisions. If idiosyncratic shocks have a deterministic "seasonal" component, if, for example, some firms experience shocks mostly at even times, some mostly at odd times, then staggering may be a stable equilibrium, with each firm choosing its natural timing habitat. This line has been explored by Ball and Romer (1987b). However, the empirical importance of such shocks seems limited, and is surely insufficient to provide a general explanation of staggering.

Another possibility, explored by Ball and Cecchetti (1987), is that in the presence of imperfect information, prices carry information. It may then be optimal for a price-setter to wait for that information before deciding on her own price. There is, however, a question whether an equilibrium will exist in such a context. If each price-setter prefers to take decisions just after the others, it is not clear that an equilibrium exists, at least not an equilibrium with fixed timing of price decisions. Yet another possibility, explored by Maskin and Tirole (1986), is that staggering may change the nature of the game played by price-setters and allow price-setters to achieve a more collusive sustainable outcome. These last two approaches have implications that go far beyond providing an explanation of staggering. Imperfect information reintroduces some of the channels studied in chapter 6.[33] Maskin and Tirole show that games with staggered decisions may generate outcomes that resemble, for example, those obtained with kinked demand curves so that the price rules we have used would be inappropriate. We return to this issue in the next chapter when we look at goods markets.

It may well be that in most cases trying to generate staggering, given fixed timing of individual price changes, is the wrong strategy. After all, it is plausible that if price-setters experience different histories of shocks, they will naturally change prices at different times. Staggering may not be strategic but rather unavoidable. This, however, points to state- rather than time-dependent rules, rules in which the decision to change prices is a function of the state. We now examine the aggregate implications of such rules.

8.3 State-Dependent Rules and the Effects of Money

In the previous section we assumed that costs of adjusting prices lead price-setters to change prices at fixed intervals, and to change them by an amount that depends on the change in nominal money and the price level since the previous change. An alternative rule is for price-setters to change prices whenever they deviate too much from their desired value. In that case the time between price decisions becomes random, and at least in simple rules, the amount of the price change becomes nonrandom. In this section we examine the effects of such state-dependent price-setting rules. We should note, though, that relatively few results have yet been obtained in this area.

We start by examining a partial equilibrium model of a price-setting monopolist, and we derive the optimal state-dependent price-setting rule in that context. We then examine the macroeconomic implications of the use of such rules. The task of aggregating over individual price-setters is generally intractable. As we will show in this section, the problem can be solved in one special case that leads to results that are dramatically different from those derived in the previous section: despite the presence of infrequent individual price adjustment and of equilibrium staggering, nominal money has no effect on output. We end the section by discussing why this result does not extend, at least in pure form, to more general cases.

An Optimal Ss Rule for a Price-Setting Monopolist[34]

Consider a monopolist who faces the following linear demand and quadratic cost functions:

$$Y = \alpha - \beta P + u, \qquad \alpha, \beta > 0, \tag{25}$$

$$C = a + bY + cY^2, \qquad b, c > 0, \tag{26}$$

where Y is output, P is the real price, C is cost, and u is a demand disturbance. The only source of uncertainty is u,[35] which is assumed to follow a symmetric random walk with unit steps each period:

$$u = u(-1) + \varepsilon,$$

where $\varepsilon = +1$ or -1, in each case with probability $1/2$.

The firm maximizes profit so that if it were free to set a price at no cost, it would choose

$$P^*(u) = \frac{\alpha + \beta(b + 2c\alpha) + (1 + 2\beta c)u}{2\beta(1 + c\beta)}. \tag{27}$$

There is, however, a cost to changing prices, which is assumed to be constant independent of the magnitude of the change, and equal to γ in real terms. In determining its optimal rule, the firm must therefore balance the opportunity cost of having a "wrong" price and the cost of changing it.

Suppose that the price is set so as to be optimal for some value of u, and suppose that u changes. The opportunity cost is given by the difference in profit if the firm adjusts its price optimally and the level of profit if the firm keeps the initial price unchanged. Denote by $Q(\Delta u)$ the opportunity cost of keeping prices unchanged in the face of a change in u of Δu, assuming prices to be set optimally for the initial value of u. Straightforward computation gives

$$Q(\Delta u) = \theta \Delta u^2,$$

where

$$\theta \equiv \frac{(1 + 2c\beta)^2}{4\beta(1 + c\beta)} > 0.$$

Note that this opportunity cost is of second order in Δu: this is the same result as that obtained earlier in the chapter. Note also that it does not depend on the initial value of u but only on the deviation from it. It is an increasing function of the degree of convexity of costs, c.[36]

Given that the opportunity cost of not changing prices depends on Δu, the change in u since the time the price was last set, but not on the initial value of u itself, we would expect the rule as to when the price is changed to depend on Δu only. Given that the current value of u summarizes all past history relevant to predicting the future behavior of u, we would expect the price after readjustment to be a function of the current level of u only.

Indeed, the optimal policy in this case takes the following form: when Δu, the change in u since the last adjustment, either exceeds an upper bound $S > 0$ or becomes less than a lower bound $s < 0$, the price is changed so that Δu is set equal to zero.[37] Because of its form such a policy is known as an *Ss rule*.

Given the symmetry of the random walk for u and therefore the symmetry of the process for Δu, the two bounds S and s are given by h and $-h$, for some number h to be determined. Figure 8.3 shows a sample path corresponding to this $(-h, h)$ rule. Adjustment takes place at time t_0 and t_1. In each case the price is reset optimally.[38]

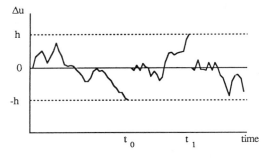

Figure 8.3
Sample path with symmetric Ss rule

What remains is to determine the optimal value of h. A small value of h implies frequent readjustments, small values of Δu on average, and small opportunity costs but high costs of price changes. A large value of h implies large opportunity costs and small costs of price changes. We assume that the monopolist is risk neutral so that she minimizes the expected present discounted value of costs, and that the discount rate is zero. Thus she minimizes the expected cost per unit time, which is equal to the expected number of changes per unit time (i.e., the inverse of the expected time between price adjustments, D) plus the expected opportunity cost:

$$\gamma\left(\frac{1}{D}\right) + \theta E(\Delta u^2).$$

Both D and $E(\Delta u^2)$ depend on the distribution of Δu.

Given the rule described above and the process followed by u_t, the transition probabilities for Δu are given by

$$P(\Delta u_{t+1} = \Delta u_t + 1) = P(\Delta u_{t+1} = \Delta u_t - 1) = \frac{1}{2},$$

$$\text{for } h - 1 > \Delta u_t > -(h - 1),$$

$$P(\Delta u_{t+1} = 0) = P(\Delta u_{t+1} = \Delta u_t - 1) = \frac{1}{2}, \qquad \text{for } \Delta u_t = h - 1,$$

$$P(\Delta u_{t+1} = 0) = P(\Delta u_{t+1} = \Delta u_t + 1) = \frac{1}{2}, \qquad \text{for } \Delta u_t = -(h - 1).$$

These transition probabilities imply in turn that the expected time between price changes is given by[39]

$$D = h^2.$$

The transition probabilities can also be used to derive the unconditional or "steady state," distribution for Δu. Let $f(\Delta u)$ denote the steady state probabilities. They are given by

$$f(\Delta u) = \frac{1 - (\Delta u/h)}{h}, \qquad \text{for } 0 \leqslant \Delta u < h,$$

$$= \frac{1 + (\Delta u/h)}{h}, \qquad \text{for } -h < \Delta u \leqslant 0.$$

The steady state density function is triangular, with maximum value for $\Delta u = 0$. This implies in turn that the steady state variance $E(\Delta u^2)$, which is the average value of Δu^2 when a $(-h, h)$ rule is used, is given by

$$E(\Delta u^2) = \frac{h^2}{6}.$$

Replacing D and $E(\Delta u^2)$ in the expression for expected cost per unit time and minimizing with respect to h, ignoring integer constraints, gives

$$h^* = \left(\frac{6\gamma}{\theta}\right)^{1/4},$$

where h is a decreasing function of θ, with elasticity $-1/4$, and an increasing function of γ, with elasticity $1/4$.[40] This completely characterizes the behavior of the price in the case of stochastic demand.

Ss Price-Setting Rules: Extensions
The preceding results are based on many assumptions. Unfortunately, nearly all of them matter in the sense that relaxing any of them is likely to lead either to an intractable maximization problem or to rules that, though being of the Ss type, are substantially more complicated than the rule just derived.

Changes in functional forms of demand or cost, or the introduction of discounting, quickly lead to problems for which no explicit solution has been derived. If, for example, we were to use constant elasticity schedules and multiplicative shocks as in the first section of the chapter, the opportunity cost would depend on the initial level of output, and a constant Ss rule would clearly not be optimal. In many cases, however, a simple Ss rule may still be a good approximation to the optimal rule.[41]

Two deviations from the previous model, which are both important in what follows, do lead to optimal rules that are substantially different from the rule characterized above:

1. In the above model, u follows a random walk so that future values of Δu are by assumption uncorrelated with the current value of u. Thus, after a large value of u that triggers adjustment, the price-setter has no reason to expect either a high or a low realization of Δu in the next period. But, if u follows a more general stochastic process, the expected movement of Δu will generally depend on current and past values of u. When changing the price, the price-setter will want to take into account the expected movement in Δu. Put another way, the S and s bounds, rather than being constant as they were above, will usually depend on current and lagged realizations of u. There exists, however, at this stage no derivation of optimal rules for that class of extensions.

2. In the above model, u follows a symmetric random walk. But in many cases we would expect u to exhibit drift, either positive or negative. Demand may be expected to increase over time. When we allow for price level uncertainty and let firms choose a nominal price, the price level is also likely to be on average increasing over time, leading to an increase in the nominal individual price. Allowing for a random walk with drift, however, complicates the solution substantially.[42]

We give only a general characterization of the solution as a function of drift, concentrating on the features that will be relevant later. When there is no drift (the case studied above), the Ss rule implies a return of Δu to 0, to the currently optimal price, from symmetric upper and lower bounds. The steady state distribution is triangular, with high probabilities around the return point as it is reached both from the upper and lower bounds. The size of the adjustment is equal to half the size of the Ss band.

When there is positive drift, the return point for Δu is negative. Returning to $\Delta u = 0$, to the currently optimal price, would imply that the actual price would be on average lower than the optimal price, which is increasing over time, and the more so the larger the drift; this is unlikely to be optimal. What happens to the bounds S and s is difficult to characterize. Because of the drift, Δu is more likely to be above the return point than below it, and thus the steady state distribution is skewed, with larger probabilities above the return point than below the return point (see Tsiddon 1987a). Finally, because of the drift the return is more likely to be from the upper bound than from the lower bound; the average size of the adjustment is larger than half the size of the band.[43]

When the drift is sufficiently large that u becomes nondecreasing in time so that Δu is necessarily nonnegative, things become much easier again. The optimal Ss rule is easy to derive and can be shown to be the best rule (Scarf

1959). In that case the lower bound s becomes irrelevant because it is never reached. The Ss rule implies a return of Δu, whenever an upper bound S is reached, to a return point s. We will refer to that type of Ss policy in which there is return only from the upper bound as *one sided*, and we will refer to those in which return can take place from either bound as *two sided*. For one-sided rules, if one has no information on the past history of the realizations of Δu, it is clear that any point within the band is as likely as any other: thus, not surprisingly, the unconditional (or steady state) distribution of Δu is uniform. Finally, the size of the adjustment, when it takes place, is equal to the size of the Ss band.

Ss Price-Setting Rules and Inflation

The model we have analyzed concentrates on the effects of demand movements but implicitly assumes a constant price level. Other papers have examined, instead, the effects of price level movements, keeping the demand function constant. When the price level is allowed to change over time, it is empirically reasonable to allow for inflation, that is, a positive drift in the price level. In general, if the price level has drift, but can still either increase or decrease, the Ss rule becomes very complicated.

If the drift is sufficiently large that the price level cannot decrease, the Ss rule becomes a much simpler one-sided rule. This is the assumption that has been made in all papers dealing with inflation. Sheshinski and Weiss (1977) consider the problem of a monopolistic price-setter who faces a constant rate of inflation and no uncertainty in demand. They show that, under their assumptions, a one-sided Ss policy is indeed optimal: the optimal policy is to keep the same nominal price until the real price has decreased to a lower bound s. The nominal price is then readjusted to a level such that the real price is equal to its upper bound S. They derive the values of s and S as a function of the underlying parameters and show, interestingly, that faster inflation does not necessarily lead to more frequent price adjustments.

Sheshinski and Weiss (1983) and Caplin and Sheshinski (1987) extend the analysis to the case of stochastic inflation; for the very specific inflation processes that they consider, an Ss rule similar to that derived in the case of uncertainty is again optimal.[44] These papers assume that the goods sold by the monopolist are nonstorable; Benabou (1986a) considers the case of constant inflation but with storable goods. It is clear that the Ss rule derived by Sheshinski and Weiss can no longer be optimal: if price changes were nonrandom, consumers would buy in advance of the price increase, leaving the firm to sell little or nothing after the price change. Attempts by the firm to increase prices earlier would only lead consumers to buy earlier, and so on. Benabou shows that the optimal price-change strategy in this case is generally to randomize price changes; this is an interesting result as it shows that even in the absence of uncertainty about demand or inflation, optimal price setting may still be stochastic.

Aggregation of Ss Rules

The two central questions about aggregation in this chapter are: Given that shocks affecting price-setters are likely to be cross correlated, should we expect uniform staggering or, instead, bunching of price decisions? In response to an aggregate shock, say, a change in nominal money, should we expect the nominal price level to adjust slowly over time in a manner comparable to that obtained under staggering and time-dependent rules, or is the adjustment likely to be qualitatively different, with bunching of price changes at the time of the aggregate shock, for example? Our knowledge of the answers to these questions is limited. Only in the case of one-sided rules does aggregation seem tractable, and we start with that case.

Consider an economy in which there are n price-setters, indexed by $i = 1, \ldots, n$, and assume that in the absence of costs of adjusting prices, each of them would choose[45]

$$p_i^* = m, \tag{27}$$

where p_i^* is the logarithm of the nominal price i and m is the logarithm of nominal money. In view of equation (9'), which gave optimal individual prices as a function of nominal money and the price level, this would seem to be a drastic simplification, one that avoids one of the main issues, that of the interaction among prices set by different firms. We will, however, relax it below and show that it does not affect the results.

Time is continuous. We assume that m follows a stochastic process and is nondecreasing in time: $t_1 > t_2$ implies that $m(t_1) \geq m(t_2)$. This assumption implies that the Ss rule will be one sided. Money is also assumed to change continuously: this rules out jumps in money and thereby makes simple aggregation possible, as we will see below.[46]

Aggregate output is given by

$$y = m - p, \tag{28}$$

where p is the logarithm of the price level, and y is the logarithm of output.[47]

Each price-setter faces fixed costs of changing prices and uses the following Ss rule: when the deviation between the optimal and the actual nominal

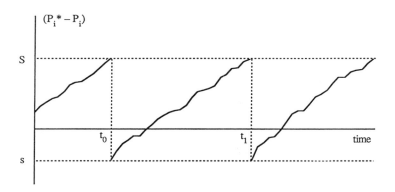

Figure 8.4
Sample path for a one-sided *Ss* rule

price, $p_i^* - p_i$, reaches an upper bound S, the nominal price p_i is readjusted upward so that $p_i^* - p_i$ is equal to a lower bound s. In general, for an arbitrary process for m, an Ss rule with constant bounds is unlikely to be optimal; this issue is bypassed, and it is simply assumed here that the rule chosen by price-setters is of this form. A sample path for $p_i^* - p_i$ is given in figure 8.4. The lower bound is likely to be negative: as the optimal price is expected to increase over time, the nominal price, when it is changed, will be set at a level higher than the current optimal price. There is no reason, however, to expect the Ss interval to be centered around zero (see Sheshinski and Weiss 1983). As indicated above, under such a rule, the unconditional (or steady state) distribution of the price deviation $p_i^* - p_i$ is uniformly distributed between S and s.

Turning to aggregation, we have to make an assumption as to the initial distribution of price deviations across price-setters at, say, t_0. We assume that at t_0 the deviations $p_i^* - p_i$ are uniformly distributed between S and s. This is in effect an assumption of uniform staggering, and in the light of our difficulties in generating staggering under time-dependent rules, it requires some justification. Within the model as defined here, without idiosyncratic shocks, there is nothing to determine the time structure of price decisions: if all price decisions are bunched to start with, they will always remain bunched thereafter. However, Caplin (1985) has shown that if firms face both idiosyncratic and aggregate shocks and use one-sided Ss rules, price deviations will be independent across firms, even if the variance in the idiosyncratic shocks is arbitrarily small (but not zero): knowing the price deviation of one firm will be of no help in predicting the price deviation of

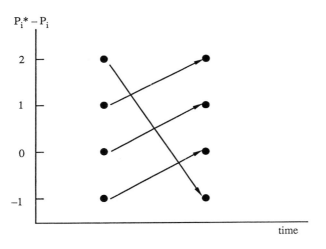

Figure 8.5
Effects of an increase in nominal money

another. This is an important result as it implies that under one-sided rules, staggering is the natural outcome.[48]

Such an economy therefore exhibits discrete individual price changes and staggering. Does this imply that the price level adjusts slowly to an increase in nominal money? The answer is, surprisingly, no. To understand why, consider, for example, the effects of an increase of unity in nominal money, assuming that there are four prices in the economy and that price deviations are initially uniformly distributed on the interval $(-1, +2)$.

The initial distribution as well as the distribution after the increase in nominal money and implied price adjustments are given in figure 8.5. The remarkable fact is that they are identical. Although only one price adjusts, it adjusts by a large amount, namely, 4. The distribution of nominal prices is still uniform, but with its support shifted up by 1. Thus the price level increases in the same proportion as nominal money. The proof for the general case is simply a formalization of this argument (see Caplin and Spulber 1986).

It is clear that everything we have said would have applied if, instead of equation (27), we had assumed an equation such as equation (9'), namely,

$$p_i^* = ap + (1 - a)m.$$

Suppose that in this case price-setters believed that p moved one for one with m. The equation would reduce to (27), and price-setters would behave as they do above. But we have seen that if they do, the price level moves indeed like nominal money, validating their initial beliefs. Money is neutral in that case as well.

Thus the surprising conclusion is that aggregation of one-sided Ss rules does not lead to price level inertia and does not imply real effects of nominal money. This is an important counterexample to the results obtained in the previous section in which price changes were time rather than state dependent.[49]

Extensions

The striking conclusion of the previous model is that money is neutral despite the presence of fixed costs of changing prices. Is this conclusion likely to hold across models with more general state-dependent rules? Unfortunately, aggregation is hard if not impossible in most models with state-dependent rules, so we do not know the answer. From the few examples we have, however, it appears that the neutrality result is not robust.

We present such an example based on individual two-sided rules.[50] Suppose that the money stock, instead of being nondecreasing through time, follows a symmetric random walk. In that case a symmetric two-sided rule may be optimal, and we assume that price-setters use such a rule.

What is then the effect of a change in the nominal money stock on prices and output? A natural starting point is to derive the unconditional distribution of price deviations across price-setters and to examine the effects of a change in the nominal money stock. But it is extremely difficult to derive the steady state distribution[51] under both common and idiosyncratic shocks. It is likely, however, that this distribution will have higher probability at the return point than close to the bounds. Assume, for example, that the initial distribution is triangular, between $S = +2$ and $s = -2$, as in figure 8.6. Figure 8.6 gives the distribution before the change in the nominal money stock, and the distribution after the change and the price adjustments. The price level increases in this case only by half of the increase in nominal money and, in the absence of further shocks, remains at this lower level forever. The example is suggestive—though no more than suggestive—of lasting real effects of nominal money.

Why is money neutral under one-sided Ss rules and not under other, state- or time-dependent rules? One-sided Ss rules have two relevant characteristics here. The first, which they share with other Ss rules but not with time-dependent rules, is that the price-setters who adjust are those who are furthest away from their desired price; this is clearly an attractive feature of Ss rules. The second, which other Ss rules do not share, is that the adjustment

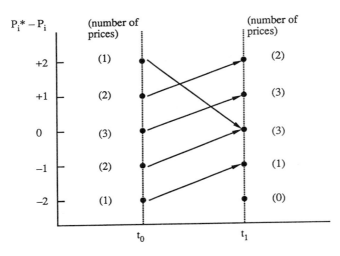

Figure 8.6
Effects of an increase in nominal money

that takes place is equal to the Ss band, the band in which price deviations are not adjusted. The adjustment of prices under symmetric two-sided rules is, instead, equal to half of the Ss band and is thus smaller. The rule that price-setters actually use must depend on the underlying rate of inflation: the higher the rate of inflation, the closer they must be to using one-sided rules. This has an interesting implication for the relation between money and inflation under Ss pricing: the higher the inflation rate, the more likely it is for money to be neutral.[52]

Time- versus State-Dependent Rules

Given the different implications of alternative price rules, we end this section with two questions. First, what is the form of observed wage and price rules? Second, under what conditions would we expect a price- or wage-setter to use one or the other?

We have direct evidence on contract wages, which, however, apply to less than 20% of the labor force in the United States. Contract negotiations are usually time dependent. Although the contracts often include reopening clauses, they are rarely invoked. In such contracts nominal wages are not fixed but predetermined, with deferred increases over the life of the contract. Many contracts include indexation clauses, the provision of which is often itself state dependent; that is, indexation provisions are put into effect only if inflation is within some range.

We also have some evidence on individual prices. Carlton (1986) has examined the behavior of contract prices within manufacturing, finding substantial nominal rigidity in the form of long intervals of time between price changes. There are also a few studies of final goods prices. Cecchetti (1986), for example, has looked at the price of newspapers. He finds that the average time between price changes is not constant, and is a decreasing function of inflation. This is consistent with some state dependence, or with time dependence where the time between decisions is a function of the underlying relevant parameters, such as the inflation rate and its variance. Kashyap (1988) has looked at catalog prices and concludes that neither simple Ss or time-dependent rules capture the basic aspects of price setting.[53] Most wage- and price-setting rules do not seem to fit either of the two extremes—of time and state dependency—that we have examined above but rather seem to be combinations of these two.

We turn next to the second question: What determines the form of the rule chosen by a price- or wage-setter? There are in fact two costs of changing prices, the first being the cost of learning the state (or agreeing on the state in the case of prices or wages set by bargaining) and the second being the cost of actually changing the price and printing new catalogs or new menus. If only the first cost is present, the rule cannot be simply state contingent since the state is not observable without cost; the optimal rule is then time dependent, and the length of time between changes depends on the underlying moments of the variables characterizing the state. If only the second, "menu," cost is present, a state-dependent rule such as an Ss rule may well be optimal.

If both costs are present, the optimal rule is likely to be more complex. It may imply collecting information at fixed intervals but deciding to change the price only if the deviation of the price from the optimal price is large enough: this leads to a rule that is both time and state dependent. It suggests, for example, that wages, for which the first cost is large, are more likely to follow time-dependent rules and that final goods prices, for which the second cost may be more relevant, are more likely to follow state-dependent rules.

8.4 Conclusion

This chapter has shown that if individual price-setters do not lose much from not adjusting their own price, small private costs of changing prices may induce substantial aggregate nominal price rigidity and long-lasting effects of changes in aggregate demand on output. These effects may be accompanied by relatively small changes in the real wage, whose direction will depend on the timing of price and wage changes.

The models used are special, and the results depend in part on whether price adjustments are time or state dependent. If price setting is time dependent, monetary shocks generally have real effects. If price setting is state dependent, the question whether money has real effects is more delicate. In the only worked-out example, money is neutral even though prices are sticky. This result appears to be a polar rather than a typical case, but it has to be recognized that nonpolar cases have not been worked out yet.

This summary makes clear both the contribution and the limits of the research explored in this chapter. It formalizes an old and important idea that if price-setters do not want to change relative prices in response to demand, there will result nominal inertia and fluctuations from aggregate demand movements.

A necessary ingredient is, however, that price-setters do not want to change relative prices very much in the first place. In the case of the labor market this means the opportunity cost of not adjusting wages is not very large. But the chapter provides no explanation for a key issue: Why would the wage-setters, be they individual workers, or workers and firms establishing wages through bargaining, accept large variations in employment with little change in the real wage? In this respect a theory based only on nominal rigidities encounters exactly the same problems as those we examined in the previous chapter.

In chapter 9 we will turn to labor and other markets in order to see if we can provide such an explanation.

Problems

1. Calculate the utility of a producer-consumer in the model of section 8.1, assuming

(a) monopolistic competition,
(b) perfect competition.

2. *Duopoly and menu costs. (This is adapted from Caminal 1987.)*

Consider two firms producing imperfect substitutes. Both firms can produce at zero marginal cost. The demand for the good produced by firm i is given by

$$y_i = a - bp_i + cp_j, \qquad i, j = 1, 2.$$

(a) Show that, in the absence of menu costs, the (Bertrand-Nash) equilibrium is given by $p_1 = p_2 = a/(2b - c)$. Note that given the price quoted by the other firm, each firm's profit function is perfectly symmetric with respect to its own price.

Now suppose that both firms enter the period with price p^*, which is the Nash equilibrium price for some value of a, a^*. They know b and c. They each observe the value of a for the period, and each firm must independently quote a price for the period. If it wants to quote a price different from p^*, it must pay a cost k. Otherwise, it pays nothing. Once prices are quoted, demand is allocated, demand determines production, and profits are realized.

(b) Compute the set of values of a (around a^*) for which not to adjust prices is a Nash equilibrium.

(c) Compute the set of values of a (around a^*) for which to adjust prices is a Nash equilibrium.

(d) Check that all equilibria are symmetric and therefore that there are no other equilibria than the ones computed above.

(e) If only Pareto optimal equilibria (in the sense of equilibria for which no other equilibrium exists with profits higher for one firm and not lower for the other) are observed, discuss the following statement: "Duopolistic prices are more sensitive to positive shocks than to negative shocks of the same magnitude."

3. *The Fischer model of staggered labor contracts.*

Consider an economy in which, in every period, half of the labor force presets its nominal wages for two periods, the current and the next. Each nominal wage is set so as to achieve a constant expected real wage in each of the two periods. The following equations describe the economy:

$$y_t = (m_t - p_t) + v_t,$$

$$y_t = -a\left[\frac{1}{2}(w_t + w_{t-1}) - p_t\right],$$

$$w_t = E[p_t|I_t], \quad w_{t-1} = E[p_t|I_{t-1}],$$

$$I_t = \{m_{t-1}, v_{t-1}, m_{t-2}, v_{t-2}, \ldots\}.$$

The first equation is an aggregate demand equation, where v is velocity. Both velocity and nominal money are random variables, following arbitrary linear stochastic processes. The second equation is the labor demand of firms, which face decreasing returns to scale and pay an average wage equal to $(w_t + w_{t-1})/2$. The third line formalizes wage setting. The last line defines the information set. Neither current m nor current v is known when wages are chosen at time t.

(a) Solve for output as a function of current and past shocks to velocity and to nominal money.

(b) Assume that v follows a random walk, $v_t = v_{t-1} + e_t$, where e is white noise. Solve for the monetary policy that minimizes the variance of output, assuming that money cannot respond to the current realization of v. Explain your results.

(c) Compare your results with those obtained in the two-period predetermined price model of monopolistic competition analyzed in the text.

(d) What is the correlation of real wages and output in this model?

4. Using the two-period predetermined price model of section 8.2, show whether money has a greater real effect on output when price setting is staggered or synchronized.

5 (a) In the two-period predetermined price model in which velocity follows a random walk, find the monetary policy that minimizes the variance of the price level. [Note: You will have to amend the first equation in (17) to take account of variable velocity in order to answer this question.]
(b) Is there any conflict in this model between the goals of price and output stabilization?

6. From table 8.1, which shows the effects of an increase in ε_t on output and the price level, calculate the mean lag in the effect of ε_t on output, and then explain why the parameters that affect the mean lag matter in the way they do.
[If for two variables z and x, $z = \sum_{i=0}^{\infty} a_i x(-i)$, then the mean lag of z on x is given by $(\sum_{i=0}^{\infty} a_i i)/(\sum_{i=0}^{\infty} a_i)$.]

7. *The Taylor model of staggered labor contracts. (This is adapted from Taylor 1979.)*

Consider an economy where, in every period, half of the labor force chooses its nominal wage for two periods. The following equations characterize the economy:

$$y_t = m_t - p_t,$$

$$p_t = \frac{1}{2}(w_t + w_{t-1}) + u_t,$$

$$w_t = \frac{1}{2}(w_{t-1} + E[w_{t+1}|I_t])a(y_t + E[y_{t+1}|I_t]), \qquad a > 0,$$

$$I_t = \{m_{t-1}, u_{t-1}, m_{t-2}, u_{t-2}, \ldots\}.$$

The first equation gives aggregate demand. There is no velocity disturbance. The second gives prices as a function of the average wage, $(w_t + w_{t-1})/2$, and the level of productivity u_t. Since the level of output does not enter into this equation, it implicitly assumes constant returns to scale. The third equation gives w_t, the wage chosen at time t by half of the labor force for time t and $t + 1$. w_t is assumed to depend on the wage paid to the other half of the labor force at time t, on the expected wage paid to the other half of the labor force at time $t + 1$, and on the level of activity at time t and expected for time $t + 1$. The sources of uncertainty are m and u. Current values of m and u are not in the information set of workers at time t.

(a) Assuming m and u to be white noise, solve for output and prices under rational expectations. Characterize and explain the dynamic effects of productivity and monetary shocks on output.

(b) Compare these results to those obtained in the monopolistic competition model with staggered fixed prices developed in the text. What substantive differences are there between the two models?
(c) Assume u to be white noise. Assume that money now follows the feedback

rule $m_t = \beta y_t$, $0 \leqslant \beta < 1$. The coefficient β can be thought of as the degree of accommodation of monetary policy. Solve for output and prices. Characterize the dynamic effects of a productivity shock on output and on prices as a function of β. What happens as β goes to one? Why?

8. *Quadratic costs of adjusting prices and effects of money. (This is adapted from Rotemberg 1982.)*

Consider a firm i that minimizes at time t:

$$E\left[\sum_{j=0}^{\infty} (1 + \theta)^{-j}((p_{it+j} - p^*_{it+j})^2 + c(p_{it+j} - p_{it+j-1})^2|t], \qquad c > 0.\right.$$

p_{it+j} is the logarithm of the nominal price of firm i in period $t + j$. p^*_{it+j} is the logarithm of the nominal price that the firm would choose in period $t + j$ in the absence of costs of changing prices. Costs of changing nominal prices are captured by the second term in the objective function. The information set at time t includes current and lagged p^*_{it} and p_{it}.

(a) Are quadratic costs of adjustment—compared to, say, the fixed cost case studied in the text—in any way plausible?
(b) Derive the first-order condition of the above minimization problem, giving the price p_i as a function of itself lagged, of itself expected, and of the optimal price. Solve by factorization.
(c) Assume that, as in the model developed in the text, p^*_i is given by

$$p^*_{it} = ap^*_t + (1 - a)m_t, \qquad 0 < a < 1,$$

where p is the logarithm of the price level and m is the logarithm of nominal money. The current value of m_t is in the information set at time t. Replacing p^*_{it} in the first-order condition above and assuming symmetry, solve for the price level as a function of itself lagged and of current and expected values of nominal money.
(d) Assume that m_t follows a random walk, $m_t = m_{t-1} + \varepsilon_t$, where ε_t is white noise. Solve for p_t as a function of p_{t-1} and m_t. Assume further that $y_t = m_t - p_t$, and solve for the dynamic effects of ε_t on y_t. Explain.

Notes

1. Early Keynesian models, including Keynes', emphasized wage rather than price rigidity. Versions of those models, still often found in textbooks, imply that under decreasing returns to labor the real wage should fall as output rises in response to demand shocks. There is little evidence, however, to support this implication, and many Keynesian models therefore emphasize the presence of both wage and price rigidity.

2. The basic reference is Barro and Grossman (1976). Early contributions were made by Patinkin (1965) and Clower (1967). Important contributions are by Benassy (1982), Malinvaud (1977), and Negishi (1979). Research, both theoretical and empirical, is still active, especially in Europe. For a bibliography, see Quandt (1987).

3. To be fair, those working on fixed price models were well aware of the need to endogenize price behavior and did make progress in this direction. See, for example, Hahn (1978), Negishi (1979), and the survey by Drazen (1980). Work by Benassy (1987), for example, on monopolistic competition is closely related to some of the models developed later in this chapter.

4. The notion is clear in the *General Theory* (pp. 267–268) where Keynes discusses the desirability of adjusting to shocks by changing wages, on the one hand, or the money stock, on the other.

5. This may be the case, for example, if the economy exhibits multiple equilibria. In this case movements in aggregate demand may shift the economy from one equilibrium to the other without nominal rigidities. This may also occur if movements in the price level, together with credit market imperfections, have major effects on activity. We will give examples of both cases in the next chapter.

6. Some of the models we will present in chapter 10 integrate the dynamic effects from both chapters. The dynamics in those models derive from the dynamics of both aggregate demand (consumption, investment) and price adjustment.

7. The model presented here builds on Kiyotaki (1985) and is a simplified version of that presented in Blanchard and Kiyotaki (1987).

8. Our model is a direct macroeconomic extension of the partial equilibrium models of monopolistic competition developed by Spence (1976) and Dixit and Stiglitz (1977). The characteristic feature of those formalizations of Chamberlinian monopolistic competition is that it leads to price elasticities of demand that are both constant and independent of the number of products available in the economy. The constant price elasticity feature is very convenient here; it also eliminates potential differences between imperfect and perfect competition, to which we will return in chapter 9.

9. This is one reason why new Keynesian economists often focus on the effects of nominal money rather than on the effects of other demand shocks, even if they believe that changes in nominal money play only a small role in economic fluctuations or that monetary policy actually decreases the amplitude of fluctuations.

10. Rotemberg (1987) provides such a dynamic model, introducing money through a cash-in-advance constraint.

11. This assumes that n is large enough that each producer takes the price level as given when choosing her price.

12. This is a basic result in monopoly theory. Under constant marginal cost and isoelastic demand, multiplicative shifts in demand leave price unaffected.

13. Because the marginal utility of wealth is constant, the sum of the consumer and producer surplus for a given producer is indeed the appropriate measure of welfare. In this case welfare can be calculated exactly, using (3); we ask the reader to do this in a problem set.

14. Depending on the extent of their impact on the elasticity of demand facing producers, other aggregate demand shifts, such as changes in tastes, can have different effects under monopolistic than under perfect competition.

15. The application to price setting under monopolistic competition was made simultaneously by Akerlof and Yellen (1985b) and Mankiw (1985).

16. To obtain (8), we take a second-order expansion of the welfare function around the initial equilibrium. Then we calculate the difference in welfare, assuming either no adjustment or optimal adjustment of the price. Note the absence of a first-order term: this is the result described earlier.

17. The conceptual difference is the following: The externality we considered earlier depends on how the price decision of producer i affects the utility of other producers. The effect we consider now depends on how the price decision of producer i affects the price decisions of other producers. This distinction is emphasized by Cooper and John (1988), who refer to interactions between decisions as strategic complementarities or substitutabilities and show the potential macroeconomic implications of such complementarities. The question of price interactions in the context of the model we present here has been studied by Rotemberg (1987) and Ball and Romer (1987a).

18. We do not include formal dynamics here although this could easily be done. The process of adjustment described in the text could happen either over time or instantaneously, with the economy instantaneously reaching A or B.

19. See Cecchetti (1986) and Kashyap (1987). We will return to discuss the evidence at the end of the next section.

20. In particular, this means that we maintain the assumption that individuals maximize one-period utility functions subject to one-period budget constraints. Models of price setting with nominal rigidities in which individuals maximize the present discounted value of utility subject to an intertemporal budget constraint have been provided by Rotemberg (1987) and Svensson (1986).

21. This is a liberal adaptation of Fischer (1977) to the model of monopolistic competition developed in section 8.1. The original model, which is presented in problem 3, has explicit goods and labor markets and distinguishes between wages and prices. Wages are predetermined, but prices are flexible.

22. This price rule can be derived exactly from expected profit maximization by producers under uncertainty provided that P_i and M are jointly lognormal, which itself will follow in equilibrium from the assumption that M is lognormal.

   The first-order conditions for maximization of expected utility, allowing for the possibility that neither P nor M is known as of the time when P_i is chosen, give

$$P_i^{1+\theta\beta-\theta} = -\left(\frac{\theta d}{1-\theta}\right)\frac{E[P^{\beta(\theta-1)}\overline{M}^\beta]}{E[P^{\theta-2}\overline{M}]}.$$

Assume that $p = \log P$ and $m = \log \overline{M}$ are conditionally (conditional on the information set) normally distributed, with means Ep and Em, variances s_p^2 and s_m^2

and covariance s_{pm}. Then this formula reduces to

$$p_i = \text{constant} + aEp + (1 - a)Em,$$

where the constant term is given by

$$\left[\frac{1}{1 + \theta\beta - \theta}\right]\left[\log\left(\frac{\theta d}{1 - \theta}\right)\right] + \left[\frac{1}{2(1 + \theta\beta - \theta)}\right]\{(\beta^2(\theta - 1)^2$$
$$- (\theta - 2)^2)s_p^2 + (\beta^2 - 1)s_m^2 + [2\beta^2(\theta - 1) - 2(\theta - 2)]s_{pm}\}.$$

The second term gives the effect of uncertainty on pricing. When, as in the first model, p is known when p_i is chosen, s_p^2 and s_{pm} are equal to zero, and the formula simplifies accordingly. To the extent that this second term is not equal to zero, the economy will not operate at the same average level of output under uncertainty than under certainty. By ignoring constant terms, we ignore this effect in the text.

23. This is a shortcut. The reason it is only an approximation is that the price level is, as we have seen, a constant elasticity of substitution function of individual prices, with elasticity $(1/\theta)$ which is less than one. The approximation in the text assumes that this elasticity is equal to one. Again, the purpose is to preserve loglinearity.

24. We could formally derive such an equation from the model of the previous section by allowing for the presence of taste shocks that do not affect the marginal utility of leisure. (Otherwise, v would also appear in the price rule.)

25. Monetary policy can clearly affect the behavior of the price level whether or not the monetary authority has better information than individuals. Thus a monetary authority that wants to stabilize the price level may run an active monetary policy to offset velocity shocks whether or not it can thereby also affect the behavior of output.

26. The model that follows is an adaptation of Taylor (1979, 1980) to the monopolistic competition model developed earlier. In the Taylor model different groups of workers set nominal wages. Firms then operate by setting prices as markups over wages. Wages, which are predetermined in the Taylor model, play the same role as predetermined prices here. The Taylor model is presented in problem 7.

27. This equation is definitely a shortcut. Even under lognormality of money and the price level (actually, even under certainty) the optimal rule is not (18). For example, the subjective discount rate of price-setters should enter the optimal rule. Helpman and Leiderman (1987) have examined, under certainty, the implications of the theoretically correct price rule.

28. Taylor (1979) looks, instead, at the dynamic effects of supply shocks, which here would be shocks to the utility of leisure, and at the role of feedback rules for money in that case. Such shocks, if permanent, would have once-and-for-all effects in an economy without nominal rigidities; they have dynamic effects here.

29. This points to the dangers of looking at the effects of changes in the coefficients of the model while taking as given the length of time between price decisions as well as the structure of staggering.

30. The closely related problem of the optimal length of contracts with indexing is analyzed by JoAnna Gray (1978).

31. This assumes that money does not behave systematically differently in odd and even periods. If there were some systematic difference, symmetric staggering would probably not be an equilibrium. It also assumes that each price-setter is small compared to the economy, so that the change in her timing does not affect the behavior of output and the price level. If price-setters were large, shifting one price-setter from even to odd timing would lead to more price movement in odd periods, and staggering would again not be an equilibrium. (This point is made by Fethke and Policano 1986.)

32. The three models differ in various ways. The first two assume that prices are predetermined but not fixed between price decisions. While this makes the analysis easier, it also makes the case less interesting since, as we have seen, staggering does not then lead to long-lasting between-price decisions. Parkin allows money to follow a feedback rule, whereas the two other papers take money as exogenous.

33. Nishimura (1986) studies the implications of imperfect competition and imperfect information in this context.

34. This closely follows Barro (1972). As will be clear, the assumptions of this model as to functional forms are different from those underlying the model used in sections 8.1 and 8.2.

35. Note the differences between this formalization of the firm's problem and that used in the first section of the chapter. First, we use linear demand and quadratic cost rather than constant elasticity formulations. Using constant elasticity specifications would make the analysis less tractable here, but more important, it would change the form of the optimal rule. Second, the only source of uncertainty is an additive shock to demand. This formally rules out movements in the price level, since they would change the real price charged by the firm for a given nominal price. We will return to these issues later.

36. This result uses the second-order condition for profit maximization, which implies that $c\beta > -1$. Note that in the constant elasticity case with multiplicative shocks (as in the model of section 8.1). $c = 0$ implies a constant optimal price and thus no opportunity cost from holding it fixed. This is not the case here.

37. The policy can be stated equivalently in terms of P: let X be defined as $(1 + 2c\beta S)/2\beta(1 + c\beta)$, and let x be defined as $(1 + 2c\beta s)/2\beta(1 + c\beta)$. Then, when $P^* - P$, the difference between the current optimal price and the actual price, exceeds X, the price is adjusted upward so that $P^* - P = 0$. When $P^* - P$ becomes negative and less than x, the price is adjusted downward so that $P^* - P = 0$.

38. For a proof that an Ss rule is optimal in this context, see Orr (1970, ch. 3, app.).

39. What follows uses results from the theory of random walks with reflecting barriers. See Feller (1968).

40. Because we have assumed unit steps for u, we cannot consider the effects of changing the variance of the process for u. This can be done, however, by allowing u to take more than one step per period. When this is done, h^2 is a function of the standard deviation of the process for u. See Barro (1972).

41. It is interesting to note in this context that the early work on Ss rules by Arrow, Harris, and Marschak (1951) viewed them as plausible rules only. Optimality was proved much later.

42. See Miller and Orr (1968) who study the structure of the maximization problem for money demand in the related case where the probabilities of positive and negative innovations may differ. Frenkel and Jovanovic (1980) derive, for a restricted class of Ss rules, a solution in the case of a random walk with drift. Bar-Ilan (1987) extends Frenkel and Jovanovic's analysis.

43. We know, however, of no proof for the last statement.

44. See also Danziger (1983).

45. This follows Caplin and Spulber (1987).

46. This assumption implies that two price-setters who have different prices initially will not change prices at the same instant. Thus we avoid potential bunching of price changes, which would make aggregation too difficult.

47. In the models of the previous section, we needed, for tractability, to approximate the price level as a geometric average of prices. This approximation is not needed here, and the price level can be the true price index as defined in section 8.1.

48. Caplin examines the problem of the distribution of inventory levels when firms use one-sided Ss rules. The problem is, however, formally the same as for prices, and his analysis can be applied to this problem directly. The result by Benabou (1986a), described earlier, that firms that sell storable goods will randomize price changes even in the absence of uncertainty suggests another reason for staggering to be the outcome.

49. Another general equilibrium model with Ss rules has been developed by Benabou (1986b). In his model, Ss prices are optimal given the demand curves faced by price-setters, which are generated from search by customers. In turn, search by customers is optimal given the price distribution implied by the Ss rules. In that model, money is also neutral. The model makes it possible to look at many other issues, such as the effects of search and costs of changing prices on the equilibrium distribution of prices.

50. Another example, based on one-sided rules, but with variable Ss bounds, is given by Tsiddon (1987b). He shows that a decrease in expected money growth leads to an increase in the price level at the time of the change in expectations, thus causing a contraction in output.

51. This statement refers to the steady state distribution of price deviations across price-setters, and not of price deviations for a given price-setter, which is triangular, as we saw earlier.

52. Compare this proposition with the proposition implied by the Lucas model described in the previous section, that the higher the variance in the inflation rate, the smaller the real effects of money. The dependence of the real effects of money on both the level of and the variance in the inflation rate is examined in Ball, Mankiw, and Romer (1988).

53. Kashyap also finds some evidence in favor of the hypothesis that prices tend to stay longer at "focus" points, such as prices that end with 99 cents, a type of nominal rigidity quite different from those studied in this chapter.

References

Akerlof, George, and Janet Yellen (1985a). "Can Small Deviations from Rationality Make Significant Differences to Economic Equilibria?" *American Economic Review* 75 (Sept.), 708–721.

Akerlof, George, and Janet Yellen (1985b). "A Near-Rational Model of the Business Cycle with Wage and Price Inertia." *Quarterly Journal of Economics*, supplement 100, 823–838.

Arrow, Kenneth, Thomas Harris, and Jacob Marschak (1951). "Optimal Inventory Policy." *Econometrica* 19, 250–272.

Ball, Laurence (1986). "Externalities from Contract Length." Mimeo. New York University. March.

Ball, Laurence, and David Romer (1987b). "The Equilibrium and Optimal Timing of Price Changes." NBER Working Paper 2412. October.

Ball, Laurence, and David Romer (1987a). "Sticky Prices as Coordination Failures." Mimeo. New York University. March.

Ball, Laurence, and Stephen Cecchetti (1987). "Imperfect Information and Staggered Price Setting." NBER Working Paper 2201. April.

Ball, Laurence, N. Gregory Mankiw, and David Romer (1988). "The New Keynesian Economics and the Output-Inflation Tradeoff." *Brookings Papers on Economic Activity*, forthcoming.

Bar Ilan, Avner (1987). "Stochastic Analysis of Money Demand Using Impulse Control." Mimeo.

Barro, Robert (1972). "A Theory of Monopolistic Price Adjustment." *Review of Economic Studies* 34, 1 (Jan.), 17–26.

Barro, Robert, and Herschel Grossman (1976). *Money, Employment and Inflation.* Cambridge: Cambridge University Press.

Benabou, Roland (1986a). "Optimal Price Dynamics and Speculation with a Storable Good." Chapter 1. Ph.D. dissertation. MIT. February.

Benabou, Roland (1986b). "Searchers, Price-setters, and Inflation." Chapter 2. Ph.D. dissertation. MIT. February.

Benassy, Jean-Pascal (1982). *The Economics of Market Disequilibrium.* New York: Academic Press.

Benassy, Jean-Pascal (1987). "Imperfect Competition, Unemployment and Policy." *European Economic Review* 31, 1/2, 417–426.

Blanchard, Olivier (1986). "The Wage Price Spiral." *Quarterly Journal of Economics* 101 (Aug.), 543–565.

Blanchard, Olivier (1987). "Individual and Aggregate Price Adjustment." *Brookings Papers on Economic Activity* 1, 57–122.

Blanchard, Olivier, and Nobu Kiyotaki (1987). "Monopolistic Competition and the Effects of Aggregate Demand." *American Economic Review* 77, 4 (Sept.), 647–666.

Bruno, Michael, and Jeffrey Sachs (1985). *Economics of Worldwide Stagflation.* Cambridge, MA: Harvard University Press.

Calvo, Guillermo (1982). "On the Microfoundations of Staggered Nominal Contracts: a First Approximation." Mimeo. Columbia University. January.

Caminal, Ramon (1987). "Three Essays on the Theory of Price Adjustment in Models of Imperfect Competition." Ph.D. dissertation. Harvard University. June.

Caplin, Andrew (1985). "The Variability of Aggregate Demand with (S,s) Inventory Policies." *Econometrica* 53 (Nov.), 1395–1410.

Caplin, Andrew, and Daniel Spulber (1987). "Menu Costs and the Neutrality of Money." *Quarterly Journal of Economics* 102, 4, 703–726.

Caplin, Andrew, and Eytan Sheshinski (1987). "Optimality of (S,s) Pricing Policies." Mimeo. Hebrew University of Jerusalem. May.

Carlton, Dennis (1986). "The Rigidity of Prices." *American Economic Review* 76, 4 (Sept.), 637–658.

Cecchetti, Steven (1986). "The Frequency of Price Adjustment: A Study of the Newsstand Prices of Magazines, 1953 to 1979." *Journal of Econometrics* 31, 255–274.

Clower, Robert (1967). "A Reconsideration of the Microfoundations of Monetary Theory." *Western Economic Journal* 6, 1–9. Reprinted in R. W. Clower (ed.), *Monetary Theory.* Penguin Books.

Cooper, Russell, and Andrew John (1988). "Coordinating Coordination Failures in Keynesian Models." *Quarterly Journal of Economics,* forthcoming.

Danziger, Leif (1983). "Price Adjustments with Stochastic Inflation." *International Economic Review* 24, 3 (Oct.), 699–707.

Dixit, Avinash, and Joseph Stiglitz (1977). "Monopolistic Competition and Optimum Product Diversity." *American Economic Review* 67, 3 (June), 297–308.

Drazen, Allan (1980). "Recent Developments in Macroeconomic Disequilibrium Theory." *Econometrica* 48, 2 (March), 283–306.

Feller, W. (1968). "An Introduction to Probability Theory and Its Applications." Vol. 1, 3d ed. New York: Wiley.

Fethke, Gary, and Andrew Policano (1986). "Will Wage Setters Ever Stagger Decisions?" *Quarterly Journal of Economics* 101 (Nov.), 867–877.

Fischer, Stanley (1977). "Long Term Contracts, Rational Expectations, and the Optimal Money Supply Rule." *Journal of Political Economy* 85 (Feb.), 163–190.

Frenkel, Jacob, and Boyan Jovanovic (1980). "On Transactions and Precautionary Demand for Money." *Quarterly Journal of Economics* 95, 1 (Aug.), 25–44.

Gray, JoAnna (1978). "On Indexation and Contract Length." *Journal of Political Economy* 86, 1 (Feb.), 1–18.

Hahn, Frank (1978). "On nonWalrasian Equilibria." *Review of Economic Studies* 45, 1–17.

Helpman, Elhanan, and Leo Leiderman (1987). "The Wage Price Spiral and Inflationary Inertia." Mimeo. Tel Aviv University. April.

Hume, David (1752). "Of Money." In his *Essays*. London: George Routledge and Sons.

Kashyap, Anil (1988). "Sticky Prices: New Evidence from Retail Catalogs." Mimeo. MIT. October.

Keynes, John Maynard (1935). *The General Theory of Employment, Interest and Money*. Reprinted Harbinger, Harcourt Brace and World, 1964.

Kiyotaki, Nobuhiro (1985). "Macroeconomics of Monopolistic Competition." Ph.D. dissertation. Harvard University. May.

Malinvaud, Edmond (1977). *The Theory of Unemployment Reconsidered*. New York: Halsted Press.

Mankiw, Gregory (1985). "Small Menu Costs and Large Business Cycles: A Macroeconomic Model of Monopoly." *Quarterly Journal of Economics* 100, 2 (May), 529–539.

Maskin, Eric, and Jean Tirole (1986). "Dynamics of Oligopoly, Part III: Price Competition." Mimeo. MIT.

Miller, Merton, and Daniel Orr (1966). "A Model of the Demand for Money by Firms." *Quarterly Journal of Economics* 80, 413–435.

Negishi, Takashi (1979). *Microeconomic Foundations of Keynesian Macroeconomics*. New York: North-Holland.

Nishimura, Kiyohiko (1986). "A Simple Rigid-Price Macroeconomic Model under Incomplete Information and Imperfect Competition." Mimeo. University of Tokyo. October.

Orr, Daniel (1970). "Cash Management and the Demand for Money." New York: Praeger.

Parkin, Michael (1986). "The Output-Inflation Trade off When Prices Are Costly to Change." *Journal of Political Economy* 94, 1, 200–224.

Patinkin, Don (1965). *Money, Interest, and Prices.* New York: Harper and Row.

Quandt, Richard (1987). "Bibliography on Disequilibrium." Mimeo. Princeton University.

Rotemberg, Julio (1982). "Monopolistic Price Adjustment and Aggregate Output." *Review of Economic Studies* 44, 517–531.

Rotemberg, Julio (1983). "Aggregate Consequences of Fixed Costs of Price Adjustment." *American Economic Review* (June), 343–346.

Rotemberg, Julio (1987). "The New Keynesian Microeconomic Foundations." *NBER Macroeconomics Annual,* 69–114.

Scarf, Herbert (1959). "The Optimality of (s,S) Policies in the Dynamic Inventory Method." In K. Arrow, S. Karlin, and P. Suppes (eds.), *Mathematical Methods in the Social Sciences.* Stanford University Press, ch. 13.

Sheshinski, Eytan, and Yoram Weiss (1977). "Inflation and Costs of Price Adjustment." *Review of Economic Studies* 44, 2 (June), 287–303.

Sheshinski, Eytan, and Yoram Weiss (1983). "Optimum Pricing Policy under Stochastic Inflation." *Review of Economic Studies* 50, 513–529.

Spence, Michael (1976). "Product Selection, Fixed Costs and Monopolistic Competition." *Review of Economic Studies* 43, 2 (June), 217–235.

Svensson, Lars (1986). "Sticky Goods Prices, Flexible Asset Prices, Monopolistic Competition, and Monetary Policy." *Review of Economic Studies* 53, 385–405.

Taylor, John (1979). "Staggered Price Setting in a Macro Model." *American Economic Review* 69, 2 (May), 108–113.

Taylor, John (1980). "Aggregate Dynamics and Staggered Contracts." *Journal of Political Economy* 88, 1–24.

Tsiddon, Daniel (1987a). "A Derivation of the Distribution of Prices under Asymmetric Two Sided Ss Rules." Mimeo. Jerusalem.

Tsiddon, Daniel (1987b). "On the Stubbornness of Sticky Prices." Mimeo. Columbia University.

9

Goods, Labor, and
Credit Markets

Our conclusions to the two previous chapters were similar in an important way. In chapter 7 we concluded that equilibrium business cycle models do not provide a convincing explanation of why labor and output supply functions would be sufficiently flat to account for the effects of aggregate demand shocks on output. In chapter 8 we argued that if labor supply and output supply (or their counterparts in an imperfectly competitive context) are sufficiently flat, small costs of adjusting prices and wages could generate large output effects of aggregate demand movements. But we concluded that these models, too, require labor and output supply functions to be relatively flat, and did not provide an explanation for why that would be.

This leads us, in this chapter, to further explore pricing and output behavior in the labor and goods markets. In both cases our basic question is the same: Why are shifts in demand largely accommodated by changes in quantities rather than by changes in relative prices?

In the case of labor markets the question is why shifts in the marginal revenue product of labor[1] lead mostly to movements in employment rather than in wages, given prices. We consider various ways in which labor markets deviate from spot competitive markets. In each case our emphasis is on potential macroeconomic implications of those deviations, on whether they can help explain the main characteristics of aggregate fluctuations.

In the case of goods markets the question is why shifts in the demand for goods lead mostly to movements in output rather than movements in prices given wages. This leads us to explore the role and effects of imperfect competition in the goods markets. Again, our focus is not on imperfect competition per se but on how imperfect competition may help explain aggregate fluctuations, alone or in combination with nominal rigidities. In particular, we show that imperfect competition may by itself lead to multiple equilibria.

In the final section of the chapter we introduce and analyze aspects of the operation of credit markets. Credit markets were not explicitly discussed in chapters 7 and 8, where in order to focus on the decisions of suppliers, we simply postulated a direct effect of money on aggregate demand. However, the mechanism by which money affects aggregate demand is also a central aspect of any theory of fluctuations; here again, facts are difficult to reconcile with standard competitive treatments of credit and asset markets. In particular, part of the effect of money seems to take place through direct credit allocation rather than through interest rate movements. In this last section we review why credit markets may operate in this way, and the macroeconomic implications thereof.

9.1 Labor Markets: Introduction

In the first three sections of this chapter we study aspects of labor markets. We take it as the fact to be explained throughout that shifts in the marginal product of labor lead to large employment variations with small variations in real wages. We also take it as given that the explanation probably cannot be found in flat individual labor supply curves, coming from intertemporal substitution, or in a flat aggregate labor supply curve, coming from smooth changes in the reservation wage of marginal workers as employment changes (see chapter 7).

We explore therefore whether allowing for the special characteristics of the labor market (i.e., the numerous deviations from the simplest competitive spot labor market model with homogeneous labor and complete information) can shed light on the macroeconomic facts at hand.

We explore three directions, each of which holds some promise of contributing to the answers. The first, which falls under the general heading of "implicit contracts," builds on the assumption that firms are able to supply workers with insurance against income uncertainty, thereby producing a relatively stable real wage. The second, which falls under the heading of "unions" or "insider-outsider" models, examines the implications of the fact that unions, or more generally, employed workers, may have some bargaining power that leads to a different pattern of real wages and employment than would be observed under competition. The third, which falls under the heading "efficiency wages," explores the implications of the fact that the quality of labor may be related to the real wage.

We now develop these three approaches. In each case we present one or two basic models in detail, and then discuss extensions. In each case also we point out their macroeconomic implications, both alone and in combination with the nominal rigidities discussed in the previous chapter.

9.2 Contracts, Insurance, Real Wages, and Employment

If workers are both more risk averse than firms and have limited access to financial markets, firms may be in a position to partly insure them against income fluctuations. One way for the firms to provide this insurance is by stabilizing the real wage. To the extent that they do so, output can fluctuate while the real wage remains relatively stable—thereby explaining real wage rigidity in the face of employment fluctuations. This basic insight, first formalized by Azariadis (1975), Baily (1974), and Gordon (1974), underlies the "implicit contract" theory of real wages and employment.

We first examine the effects of insurance on employment and real wages when states of nature are observable to both firms and workers; we then turn to the case of asymmetric information.

Contracts with Symmetric Information[2]

A Simple Contract
Suppose that workers are risk averse but do not have access to the capital markets and are therefore unable to insure themselves against income uncertainty, either through direct income insurance or by self-insurance through the accumulation of savings. Firms, by contrast, are assumed to be effectively risk neutral, either because the owner of the firm is risk neutral or because it has access to the capital markets. Under these conditions the firm may provide insurance to the worker through the labor contract.

We start by characterizing the optimal labor contract between one firm and one worker. The worker maximizes expected utility:

$$E[V(C - K(L))], \qquad V' > 0, \quad V'' < 0, \quad K' > 0, \quad K'' \geqslant 0,$$

subject to

$$C = wL,$$

where C is consumption, L is work, and w is the real wage. The budget constraint states that labor income is the only source of income. The firm is risk neutral and thus maximizes expected profit.

The production function is given by

$$Y = sF(L), \qquad F' > 0, \quad F'' < 0,$$

where Y is output. Production takes place under decreasing returns to labor; s is a random variable, which can be thought of as a productivity shock. Each value of s characterizes a "state."

These assumptions capture the essence of the problem. Uncertainty comes from a technological shock, which implies that, without insurance, both wages and employment will vary. But, because workers are risk averse while firms are risk neutral, there is scope for insurance. The question is how this affects wages and employment.

The form of the utility function is chosen to ensure that there is no income effect on labor supply. Insurance has the effect of changing income across states and therefore, in the presence of income effects, affects the marginal rate of substitution between leisure and consumption across states. We want, at least initially, to eliminate this effect, but will return to it below.

What would the equilibrium look like if the labor market operated as a *spot competitive market*, clearing in each state? From the first-order conditions of the worker, labor supply would be given by

$$K'(L) = w.$$

For each s, labor demand would be given by

$$sF'(L) = w.$$

Thus labor market equilibrium would be given by

$$K'(L) = sF'(L).$$

An increase in s would increase wages and employment along the labor supply curve. Thus both the wage and employment would vary across states in the spot market.

Since the firm is risk neutral, it can offer a contract that transfers income across states and increases expected utility given expected profit. We now characterize this contract. Instead of defining a contract in terms of w and L for each s, it is more convenient to define it equivalently in terms of $C\,(= wL)$ and L.

Thus an optimal contract is defined as a set of values of C and L for each s, $\{C(s), L(s)\}$, that maximizes

$$E[sF(L(s)) - C(s)] + \lambda EV[C(s) - K(L(s))].$$

By varying λ, we describe the set of optimal contracts. Which one is chosen depends on the bargaining power of the worker and the firm. If the worker has, for example, the choice between entering a contract or going to another identical spot market, the firm will maximize expected profits subject to expected utility being at least equal to that in a spot market. However, for our purposes, we do not need to specify a value of λ.

Given that the contract specifies C and L for each state, we can maximize with respect to L and C in each state. The first-order conditions for each state are

$$-1 + \lambda V'[C(s) - K(L(s))] = 0, \qquad \text{maximizing with respect to } C(s),$$

which implies that

$$C(s) - K(L(s)) = \text{constant}. \tag{1}$$

In addition, maximizing with respect to $L(s)$,

$$K'(L(s)) = sF'(L(s)). \tag{2}$$

The first condition shows the effects of insurance. The risk neutral firm redistributes income across states until the marginal utility of consumption is equal across states. For our particular utility function, this implies that utility itself is equal in all states.[3] Note that insurance implies constancy of marginal utility, not constancy of real wages.

What happens to real wages depends on $K(\cdot)$. For example, suppose that the marginal disutility of work is constant until full-time work, L^*, is reached, and higher thereafter. The spot market wage would be constant for L less than L^*, and increasing thereafter. The contract wage, w is equal to C/L, which from (1) is given by

$$K + \frac{\text{constant}}{L}$$

which, by contrast, is decreasing in L.

The second condition is more important for our purposes. It shows that employment is exactly the same under the contract as in the spot market in each state. The reason is simple: (2) is an efficiency condition that has to hold with or without insurance. Without income effects of insurance, the condition is the same under the contract as under the spot market.

The conclusion is that in this simplest implicit contract model, the pattern of output is exactly the same as it would be if there were a competitive spot labor market, while the "real wage" (defined as C/L) differs from what it would be in a spot labor market.

Two Extensions

Suppose that the firm contracts instead with N workers, each with the same utility function as above but supplying either one or zero units of labor.

Following the same steps as above, it is easy to show that (1) the number of workers hired is the same as it would be in a spot market and (2) the real wage is constant across states and the unemployed are paid an unemployment benefit such that their level of utility is the same as that of the employed. The contract therefore leads not only to real wage rigidity but also leads again to the same employment fluctuations as in the spot market.

If we allow for a more general utility function, one that implies the presence of income effects, the results change in a potentially interesting way. To the extent that insurance redistributes income from high employment states to low employment states, income tends to be relatively higher (compared to the spot market) in bad states. The marginal utility of leisure is higher and employment is lower.[4] Put another way, one of the reasons why spot labor supply is thought to be rather inelastic to changes in wages is the presence of opposing income and substitution effects; optimal contracts decrease the income effect on labor supply. Thus, if income effects on labor supply are important, the presence of optimal contracts gives more plausibility to the intertemporal substitution mechanism explored in chapter 7.[5] At the same time, however, income effects imply that the unemployed will be better off than the employed, an implication that is definitely counterfactual.

Macroeconomic Implications
To summarize, the simple partial equilibrium model of insurance may explain real wage rigidity and therefore account for the appearance of an elastic output supply function. However, the presence of labor contracts does not per se imply more employment fluctuations than would occur in a spot market. Absent income effects, employment fluctuations are the same as they would be in a spot market (and the unemployed have the same level of utility as the employed); in the presence of income effects insurance may indeed generate larger fluctuations in employment than spot markets.

These results raise the possibility that what appear to be "excessive" fluctuations in output and labor input could really be optimal. To some extent the view that fluctuations are excessive derives from the fact that they occur without much movement in the real wage. Thus some would argue that there is no good reason to think that the labor markets work badly at times. Direct evidence against this latter view consists of the Great Depression and some of the very high unemployment rates during recessions.

What happens when optimal labor contracts with insurance are combined with the nominal rigidities studied in the previous chapter? If contracts between firms and workers choose to have, say, a constant real wage, can't this lead, in the presence of small costs of changing prices and wages, to substantially more nominal rigidity and real effects of aggregate demand? The answer is negative, and it is instructive to see why.

Building on the models developed above and in the previous chapter, suppose that there are n monopolistically competitive firms in the goods market, with the demand facing firm i given by

$$Y_i = \left(\frac{P_i}{P}\right)^{-\sigma}\left(\frac{M}{P}\right), \qquad (3)$$

where all notation is now standard. Each firm operates under constant returns to labor, so that $Y_i = L_i$. It employs one worker, whose utility function is given by

$$V_i = EV\left[\left(\frac{W_i}{P}\right)L_i - KL_i^\theta\right], \qquad \theta > 1. \qquad (4)$$

Each firm i takes both M/P and P as given and determines P_i and W_i. Assuming first that each labor market is organized as a spot competitive market, the equilibrium conditions for market i are

$$\frac{P_i}{P} = \left(\frac{\sigma}{1 - \sigma}\right)\left(\frac{W_i}{P}\right), \qquad (5)$$

$$\frac{W_i}{P} = K\theta L_i^{\theta-1}. \qquad (6)$$

The first equation is derived from the condition that the marginal revenue product is equal to the wage. The second condition states that the marginal disutility of labor be equal to the wage and gives labor supply. Labor market equilibrium requires that the marginal revenue product and the marginal disutility of labor be equal:

$$\frac{P_i}{P} = \left(\frac{\sigma}{\sigma - 1}\right)K\theta L_i^{\theta-1}. \qquad (7)$$

In the absence of costs of changing prices and wages, money is neutral: symmetry implies that all P_i are equal, and thus equal to P. From (7) this determines employment, and thus output, because employment equals output. Equation (3) in turn determines the price level. Fluctuations in M are reflected entirely in fluctuations in P.

We now apply the argument of the previous chapter to this model. At given prices and wages, consider an increase in M that increases demand, output, and employment. Given (6), firms will want to increase P_i only if W_i increases. If the opportunity cost of not adjusting W_i given P is small, small costs of changing wages will prevent wage adjustment, thus preventing price adjustment and leading to real effects of money. As we argued, however, small opportunity costs require a small value of $\theta - 1$, that is, a small elasticity of the marginal utility of leisure with respect to fluctuations in employment. Because we found that assumption implausible, we were led to search for alternative models of the labor market in this section.

With this background, consider now the effects of allowing for insurance contracts in each labor market, assuming each firm to be risk neutral.[6] Following the same steps as in the derivation of the optimal contract earlier, the equations characterizing the wage and the price in contract i are

$$\frac{W_i}{P} = KL_i^{\theta-1} + (\text{constant})L_i^{-1}, \tag{8}$$

$$\frac{P_i}{P} = \left(\frac{\sigma}{1-\sigma}\right)K\theta L_i^{\theta-1}. \tag{9}$$

Equation (8) is the insurance condition implied by the equality of marginal utility across states. The real wage may now be increasing or decreasing in L_i. The second condition is the efficiency condition,[7] which states that the marginal revenue product must equal the marginal disutility of labor. Absent costs of changing prices or wages, the presence of contracts does not affect equilibrium output and employment, and money is still obviously neutral.

What happens if there are small costs of changing prices and wages, and nominal money increases at given prices and wages, increasing demand, output, and employment? Now, from (8), there may be, at a given P, very little pressure on nominal wages to increase (nominal wages may even decrease). But equation (9) shows that the pressure is now on prices. The price set by firm i does not depend on W_i but reflects, instead, the efficiency condition. Thus, if $\theta - 1$ is large, the opportunity cost of not adjusting prices will be large. The difficulty of explaining *nominal wage rigidity* in the economy with spot labor markets has become one of explaining *nominal price rigidity* here. Unless costs of adjusting prices are large, prices will adjust and money will be neutral. The presence of contracts does not change the basic conclusion.

In view of these results contracts with insurance and symmetric information do not appear able to explain large fluctuations in employment, especially fluctuations in which the employed are no better off than the unemployed. The natural next step is to ask whether putting plausible restrictions on these contracts can substantially affect their form and get us closer to where we want to go. Among the various avenues that have been explored, we now pursue the question of what happens when the states are not perfectly observable.

Contracts with Asymmetric Information

A plausible departure from the above assumptions is that firms know more about the state than workers and may therefore be able to lie about the true value of s. Suppose, to make things simple, that in the contract described above, the worker cannot observe the state s at all. How does this affect the optimal contract? There are two alternative ways of thinking about the optimal contract in that context.

The contract can still be thought of as a state-contingent contract, but one that must now satisfy an additional set of constraints. It must be such that the firm has no incentive to lie about the state that has occurred.[8] Let s and s' be two arbitrary states. It must therefore be true that

$$sF(L(s)) - C(s) \geqslant sF(L(s')) - C(s'), \qquad \text{for all } s, s'. \tag{10}$$

The left-hand side of the inequality gives the profit in state s if the firm announces s; the right-hand side gives the profit in state s if the firm announces s' instead. The inequality states that the firm has an incentive to tell the truth. These inequalities are known as incentive compatibility (IC) constraints.

Alternatively, because workers cannot observe s but can observe employment, we can think of the contract as defining the wage as a function of employment rather than the state. The optimal contract then defines a noncontingent wage employment schedule on which the firm freely chooses employment ex post (see Green and Kahn 1983, for example). This second approach may be more appealing, as it appears to correspond more closely to actual contracts, but the two approaches turn out to be equivalent. Depending on the context, one approach is analytically easier to use than the other (see Hart 1983). Here we use the first.

The set of inequalities in (10) makes solving for the optimal contract generally difficult. A first step is to see whether the optimal contract characterized earlier violates these IC conditions. To do so, we use a diagrammatic exposition. Suppose that there are only two states, say, s and s', $s' > s$. We can plot the two points corresponding to the two $(C, F(L))$ pairs characterizing the optimal contract. This is done in figure 9.1, with the

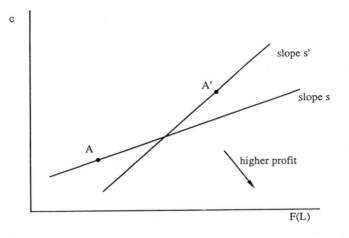

Figure 9.1
An incentive compatible contract

two points denoted A and A'. We can then draw for each state the isoprofit line corresponding to that state and going through the point corresponding to that state. From the definition of profit in (10) above, an isoprofit line in state s has slope s. For a given state, the lower the isoprofit line, the higher the level of profit.

Consider now figure 9.1. In state s, if the firm announces s, it makes the level of profit associated with A; if it lies and announces s', it makes the level of profit associated with A', which is lower than at A. It has therefore no incentive to lie. The same goes for state s': the firm also has no incentive to lie in that state. The optimal contract is incentive compatible. How likely is such a case? Interestingly, the optimal contract for the model we used earlier is indeed incentive compatible. To see this, replace (1) in (10). The IC conditions become

$$sF(L(s)) - K(L(s)) \geqslant sF(L(s')) - K(L(s')), \qquad \text{for all } s, s'. \tag{11}$$

But equation (2) says that L maximizes $sF(L) - K(L)$ over all L. Thus it implies that the inequality in (11) is always satisfied. Thus, in this case, the optimal contract is incentive compatible; workers do not need to observe the state to get full insurance. Employment is the still the same as in the spot market.

This result is by no means robust, and in general it goes away if we allow for income effects. Suppose, for example, that utility is given instead by $V(C) - K(L)$. In the optimal contract, ignoring IC constraints, equality of

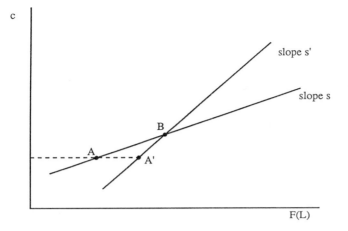

Figure 9.2
A nonincentive compatible contract

marginal utility of consumption across states implies that C is constant across states s and s'. Efficiency implies that employment is higher in good states. Thus, instead of figure 9.1, we now have figure 9.2. It is clear that the optimal contract is not incentive compatible. The firm always has an incentive to claim that the state is s' so as to get more employment at an unchanged wage bill.

Consider now a contract that gives A and B instead of A and A'. It is incentive compatible:[9] it exhibits the same level of employment as the spot market in the bad state but higher employment, "overemployment," in the good state. The intuition is that to force the firm not to claim that a state is good, the contract forces it to have a high level of employment if it so announces. High employment is costly to the firm if the state is truly bad, and this removes the incentive for the firm to lie. This overemployment result turns out to be quite general. It holds as long as leisure is a normal good.

The result also goes away when we allow firms to be risk averse. In this case, if there are no income effects, that is, if the worker's utility function is of the form $V[C - K(L)]$, the optimal IC contract may, instead, exhibit underemployment, which means less employment in the bad state than would be the case under symmetric information.[10]

To the extent that researchers were looking for an explanation for involuntary unemployment, the fact that these contracts can easily deliver overemployment rather than underemployment was disappointing. It is not clear that that reaction is warranted. These models may generate larger fluctuations in employment than spot markets. They provide one explanation for why workers and firms do not sign a contingent contract but rather agree on a wage employment schedule and let the firm choose employment. And the assumption that information is asymmetric must be largely right and relevant.[11]

9.3 Unions, Insiders, Real Wages, and Employment

If wages are set by bargaining between workers and firms, is this likely to lead to smaller fluctuations in real wages and larger fluctuations in employment than one would observe in competitive markets? We pursue this question in five steps. We first develop a framework in which to analyze the issues. We then examine the implications of two alternative structures of bargaining, one in which the union and the firm bargain simultaneously over employment and the wage and one in which the union and the firm bargain over the wage and the firm then chooses employment. Both of these models are static; we therefore extend the analysis to allow for dynamics, showing how this may affect the results. Finally, we discuss macroeconomic implications.[12]

Bargaining between a Union and a Firm: Preliminaries

In formalizing the bargaining between a union and a firm, the first critical assumption concerns the form of the *objective function of the union*. It is clear that we could generate any result we wanted if we allowed it to be unrelated to the utility of the individual members—but we would then have the problem of explaining how the utility function is derived.

We make the reasonable assumption that the union maximizes the expected utility of its representative member.[13] More specifically, we assume that all $\bar{L}$ members are treated symmetrically by the union, which therefore maximizes

$$U = \left(\frac{L}{\bar{L}}\right) U(w) + \left(1 - \frac{L}{\bar{L}}\right) U(R), \qquad \text{if } L \leqslant \bar{L},$$

$$= U(w), \qquad \text{if } L \geqslant \bar{L}. \qquad (12)$$

Each member either works, supplying one unit of labor, or does not work. $U(w)$ is the utility derived from the real wage, net of the disutility of work. $U(R)$ is the utility derived from not working. L is employment. Assuming random allocation of work among members, $L/\bar{L}$, if it less than or equal to one, is the probability of work. Increases in L beyond $\bar{L}$ do not increase the utility of the representative union member because all members are already fully employed. This feature is captured in the second line of (12). Given L, (12) is therefore the expected utility of a member.

We formalize the firm's problem in a conventional way. The firm operates in a competitive goods market and maximizes profit:

$$\pi = \theta F(L) - wL, \qquad F'(\cdot) > 0, \quad F''(\cdot) \leqslant 0, \quad \theta_{max} \geqslant \theta \geqslant \theta_{min}.$$

There are decreasing returns to labor, and θ is a technological shock, with upper and lower bounds θ_{max} and θ_{min}. The firm treats all union members symmetrically.

Let N be the number of workers in the labor market. There is no reason for $\bar{L}$ to be equal to N. This raises two sets of questions. The first concerns what determines $\bar{L}$; for the time being, we will take $\bar{L}$ as given. The second concerns what influence the $(N - \bar{L})$ nonunion members have on bargaining between the union and the firm. We will start with the very strong assumption that they have no influence on bargaining. More specifically, we will assume that the firm can only hire union members and cannot hire more than $\bar{L}$ workers. Thus we stipulate that $L \leqslant \bar{L}$. We will relax these assumptions later.

If there were no union and the labor market operated as a competitive spot market, labor supply would be horizontal at R, the reservation wage, until N is reached, and vertical thereafter, as shown in figure 9.3. Labor demand would be given by profit maximization and would vary between DD_{min} and DD_{max}, corresponding to realizations of θ_{min} and θ_{max}, respectively. The real wage would therefore vary between R and w_{max}. If only union members were allowed to work, but the union supplied labor competitively, the supply curve would, instead, become vertical at $\bar{L}$, and the real wage would vary between R and w'_{max}.

What is the outcome given bargaining? Actual labor contracts appear only to set a wage and to leave the employment decision to the firm. Thus the traditional approach has been to assume that first the firm and the union bargain over the wage, and then employment is freely chosen by the firm so as to maximize profit. Equivalently, the firm and the union *choose a point on the labor demand curve*. This is referred to as the "right-to-manage" approach.[14] An extreme version of it, the "monopoly union," simply assumes that the union unilaterally chooses the wage and that the firm then chooses employment.

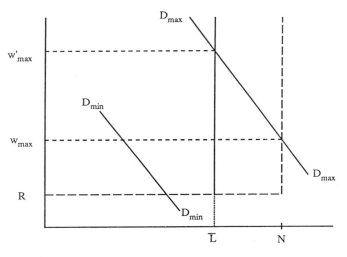

Figure 9.3
Labor supply and demand

But, and this was first pointed out by Leontief (1946), such contracts are not efficient. To see this, we rely on the diagram that he introduced.[15] We can draw, in the (w, L) space, loci along which expected utility is constant (indifference curves) and loci along which profit is constant ("isoprofit loci"). The slope of an indifference curve at any point is given by

$$\frac{dw}{dL} = -\frac{U(w) - U(R)}{LU'(w)}, \qquad \text{if } L \leqslant \bar{L},$$

$$= 0, \qquad \text{if } L \geqslant \bar{L}.$$

The slope of an isoprofit locus is given by

$$\frac{dw}{dL} = \frac{\theta F'(L) - w}{L}.$$

Thus indifference curves are downward sloping, for $L \leqslant \bar{L}$, as long as $w > R$. They are horizontal for $L \geqslant \bar{L}$. Isoprofit loci are first increasing, reaching a maximum when they cross the demand for labor curve—where $\theta F'(L) = w$—and then decreasing. Indifference curves and isoprofit loci are shown in figure 9.4 for a given value of θ.

Now consider the outcome of a right-to-manage bargain. The union and the firm agree on a wage, say w_a. Given w_a, the firm then maximizes profit by choosing L_a on its labor demand schedule. At point A, however, the indifference curve and isoprofit locus going through A are not tangent.

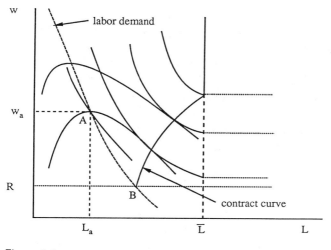

Figure 9.4
Employment and wages in efficient and inefficient contracts

This implies that points just to the southeast of A are associated with both higher profit and higher utility. This inefficiency applies to all points on the labor demand curve (except one: at the competitive equilibrium, point B, the isoprofit locus and the indifference curve both have zero slope so that B is efficient). Thus right-to-manage contracts are inefficient.

This inefficiency suggests that actual contracts are perhaps not well described by the right-to-manage model. Suppose, instead, that even if employment is not explicitly specified in contracts, it is implicitly agreed that the firm will choose an efficient level of employment rather than the point on labor demand. What is then the set of efficient contracts? For a contract to be efficient, the contract must be at a point of tangency between an indifference curve and an isoprofit locus (or if the $\bar{L}$ constraint is binding, that the appropriate inequality holds). Thus, using the above equations, the following condition must be satisfied:

$$\theta F'(L) - w = -\frac{U(w) - U(R)}{U'(w)}, \qquad \text{if } L \leqslant \bar{L},$$

$$\theta F'(L) - w \geqslant -\frac{U(w) - U(R)}{U'(w)}, \qquad \text{if } L = \bar{L}. \tag{13}$$

The set of such points is called the *contract curve*. It starts at the competitive equilibrium and, under our assumptions, is upward sloping. It is drawn in figure 9.4.[16] Thus, if the contract is efficient, the union and the firm *choose a point on the contract curve*. Which point is chosen then depends on the relative bargaining power of the firm and of the union.

We leave aside for the moment the issue of whether actual contracts are more like "right-to-manage" or like "efficient" contracts and start by considering the implications of each. In each case we consider contracts that are signed *after* θ is known, thus eliminating the scope for insurance, which was studied in the previous section. We also do not allow for redistribution of income from the employed to the unemployed within the union.[17]

Efficient Contracts[18]

The first condition that must be satisfied by an efficient contract is therefore that, given θ, w and L be on the contract curve. Where on the contract curve they are presumably depends on the bargaining power of the union and the firm. If the union is relatively weak, the outcome may be close to the competitive equilibrium; if the union is relatively powerful, it may be close to the zero profit point for the firm.

A convenient way to formalize this idea is to use the concept of a *Nash bargain*. Let π be the level of profit, and let U be the level of utility that the firm and the union, respectively, achieve if they sign a contract, and π_n and U_n if they do not. The Nash bargain then maximizes the product $(U - U_n)$ $(\pi - \pi_n)$ over w and L.[19] Under our assumptions it is reasonable to suppose that if no contract is signed, the firm gets zero profit and each member of the union gets $U(R)$, his reservation level of utility. An important aspect of this assumption, and one that may be unappealing when we look at aggregate fluctuations, is that neither π_n nor U_n depends on θ.[20]

Given these assumptions, the Nash bargain maximizes over w and L:

$$L[U(w) - U(R)][\theta F(L) - wL] + \lambda(\bar{L} - L),$$

where λ is the Lagrange multiplier associated with the contraint that L not exceed $\bar{L}$. The first-order conditions with respect to w, L, and λ, respectively, are

$$U'(w)[\theta F(L) - wL] - L[U(w) - U(R)] = 0, \qquad (14)$$

$$[U(w) - U(R)][\theta F(L) - wL] + [\theta F'(L) - w]L[U(w) - U(R)] - \lambda = 0, \qquad (15)$$

$$\lambda(\bar{L} - L) = 0.$$

Assume first that the solution is such that $L < \bar{L}$, so that $\lambda = 0$. Then, by manipulating the first-order conditions, we can derive two conditions. The first is that w and L be on the contract curve, which we rewrite for convenience:

$$\theta F'(L) - w = -\frac{U(w) - U(R)}{U'(w)}. \tag{13}$$

The second is that

$$w = \frac{1}{2}\left[\frac{\theta F(L)}{L} + \theta F'(L)\right]. \tag{16}$$

The wage must be equal to the arithmetic mean of the marginal and the average products of labor; this is the simple form taken by the rent-sharing condition in that case.

What is then the effect of movements in Θ on w and L? A convenient benchmark is the quasi-Cobb-Douglas case where the elasticity of output with respect to employment is constant: $F(L) = L^a$, $a < 1$. Then $F(L)/L = (1/a)F'(L)$ so that from (16),

$$\theta F'(L) = \left(\frac{2a}{a + 1}\right)w. \tag{17}$$

Replacing $\theta F'(L)$ in (13) gives

$$\left(\frac{a - 1}{a + 1}\right)wU'(w) = -[U(w) - U(R)]. \tag{18}$$

Thus the *real wage is constant* at some level w^*.[21] For each value of θ, employment is given by the value of employment on the contract curve for $w = w^*$, or equivalently by its value from (17).

Differentiating (17) with respect to θ and L given w^* implies that employment increases with θ. If the constraint that L be no greater than $\bar{L}$ is binding, λ is different from zero. The wage is then equal to the value implied by (14) for $L = \bar{L}$.

We can now give a complete characterization of the solution, under the constant elasticity assumption. Let w^* be defined by (18). Let θ^* be such that the value of L given by (17) for $w = w^*$ is equal to $\bar{L}$. Then

if $\theta \leqslant \theta^*$, $w = w^*$ and L is given by (17);

if $\theta \geqslant \theta^*$, $L = \bar{L}$ and w is given by (14).[22]

Finally, and as a way of introducing the discussion of the macroeconomic implications, consider the special case where utility is such that there are no income effects on labor supply, the case where $U(\cdot)$ is linear: $U(w) = bw$.

The solution is then the following: Let θ^* be such that $\theta^* F'(\bar{L}) = R$. Then

if $\theta \leq \theta^*$, $w = \left(\dfrac{a+1}{2a}\right) R$ and L is such that $\theta F'(L) = R$;

if $\theta \geq \theta^*$, $L = \bar{L}$ and w is given by $w = \dfrac{aR + \theta F'(\bar{L})}{2a}$.

In this case the real wage is constant until θ exceeds θ^*. The level of employment is the *same*, for each θ, as it would be if union members supplied labor competitively.

Macroeconomic Implications
This last set of results makes clear the close relation between these efficient firm-union contracts and the insurance contracts studied in the previous section. Real wage rigidity derives here not from insurance but from bargaining, and its form is different: the real wage is strictly constant until some critical value of θ, at which point it increases with θ. But, just as in the case of insurance contracts, focusing on the behavior of the real wage would be misleading, for real wage rigidity has no implications for employment fluctuations. Indeed, as in the case of insurance contracts, without income effects employment is the same as it would be if union members supplied labor competitively. Thus the conclusions derived above apply here.

There is, however, one important difference between the two contracts. While insurance contracts are presumably between the firm and all N workers, the contract here is between the firm and the $\bar{L}$ members of the union. To the extent that $\bar{L}$ differs from N and varies over time, the contracts will have different implications for employment. We return to this point below.

The Monopoly Model

Instead of examining general right-to-manage contracts, we focus on the simpler "monopoly union" case, where, for each value of θ, the union unilaterally chooses w, and the firm then maximizes profit given w. Equivalently, the union chooses w so as to maximize (12) given the profit-maximizing labor-demand function by the firm. Let $L(\theta, w)$ be that labor demand function, and let λ be the Lagrange multiplier associated with the constraint $L \leq \bar{L}$. The union maximization problem can be written as

$$\max_{w} L(\theta, w)[U(w) - U(R)] + \lambda[\bar{L} - L(\theta, w)].$$

The first-order conditions give

$$L_w(\theta, w)[U(w) - U(R) - \lambda] + L(\theta, w)U'(w) = 0,$$

$$\lambda(\overline{L} - L) = 0. \tag{19}$$

In the first line the first term gives the marginal cost in terms of employment of increasing the real wage. The second gives the marginal benefit, namely, the increase in the wage for those who remain employed.

Assume first that the solution is such that $L < \overline{L}$, so that $\lambda = 0$. The first-order condition then gives a relation between the wage and θ. A useful benchmark is again the case where the elasticity of output with respect to labor is constant. In that case the elasticity of labor demand with respect to the wage is also constant. Denoting this last elasticity by σ, we have that $-L_w(\theta, w)w/L(\theta, w) = \sigma$. Substituting in (19) and simplifying gives

$$-\sigma\left[\frac{U(w) - U(R)}{w}\right] + U'(w) = 0. \tag{20}$$

Thus in this case the real wage chosen by the union, call it w^*, is invariant to θ. Movements in θ affect only employment. Because $U'(w)$ is positive, $U(w) - U(R)$ must also be positive: the wage must exceed the reservation wage. Given w^*, employment is determined by labor demand, $L(\theta, w^*)$.

If, however, $L = \overline{L}$, the wage is no longer given by w^* but by w such that $L(\theta, w) = \overline{L}$.

A full characterization of the solution, under constant elasticity of labor demand, is therefore as follows: Let w^* be defined by (20) above, and let θ^* be such that $L(\theta^*, w^*) = \overline{L}$. Then

if $\theta \leqslant \theta^*$, $w = w^*$ and $L = L(\theta, w^*)$;

if $\theta \geqslant \theta^*$, $L = \overline{L}$ and w is such that $L(\theta, w) = \overline{L}$. $\tag{21}$

The wage schedule (the implicit supply of labor) chosen by the union is represented in figure 9.5 by $S'S'S'$.

Macroeconomic Implications
So long as θ is below some critical value, the real wage is rigid. Not all union members are employed, and those who are not have lower utility than those who are. In this case real wage rigidity is not a side show: employment is determined by labor demand. This is the result emphasized by McDonald and Solow (1981).

Taken at face value, the result is indeed important. It can explain why technological shocks have large effects on employment. Together with small

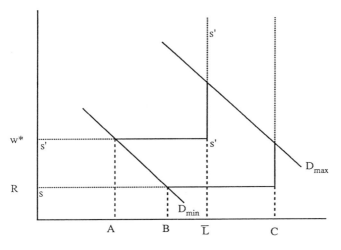

Figure 9.5
Employment with a monopoly union

costs of changing prices, it can also explain why aggregate demand shocks will have long-lasting effects on employment. Let us briefly sketch the argument again in this context. Consider the now familiar economy with monopolistic competition in the goods market. Assume that each firm operates under slightly decreasing returns to labor and faces a union. Bargaining between each firm and each union takes place according to the monopoly union model. Consider now a decrease in nominal money that, at constant nominal prices and wages, decreases demand, output, and employment. Given the price level, nominal wages do not change. Because of decreasing returns each price-setter wants to decrease his price given the wage. But, if the returns to labor are not too decreasing, small costs of changing prices lead price-setters not to change their price. Thus money has real effects and leads to movements in the number of workers involuntarily unemployed.

Despite the obvious appeal of the results, this real wage rigidity result must be qualified, for several reasons. First, the real wage rigidity result is far from robust. In the monopoly model the union acts as a monopolist facing a demand curve. We know that if a monopolist faces an isoelastic demand curve and has constant marginal cost, she will accommodate multiplicative shifts in demand at no change in price. This is exactly what happens here. The role of the constant elasticity of demand was made clear in the derivation. The role of the constant "marginal cost" assumption must also be emphasized. Between 0 and $\bar{L}$ the "marginal cost" is equal to the reservation wage, which is constant. If the labor market were competitive, there would also be "real wage rigidity" so long as L is less than $\bar{L}$: the real wage would be equal to R. In the monopoly case the real wage is also constant, but at a level higher than R, reflecting the monopoly power of the union. This is clearly shown in figure 9.5. Put in this light, the result of real wage rigidity is less surprising. If the competitive labor supply curve were an increasing function of the wage between 0 and $\bar{L}$, there would not be real wage rigidity in the monopoly model either.

Second, although the unemployed are in this model worse off than the employed, all union members are the same ex ante, and knowingly take the risk of being unemployed in exchange for a higher wage.[23]

Finally, it is not clear that employment fluctuations are larger in the presence of the union. This is shown in figure 9.5. Again let D_{max} and D_{min} be the two labor demand functions corresponding to θ_{min} and θ_{max}. Then employment fluctuates between A and $\bar{L}$. The fluctuations are larger than if the union behaved competitively, in which case employment would vary between B and $\bar{L}$. But they are not necessarily larger than they would be if the labor market were competitive, in which case employment would vary between B and C.

Whether employment fluctuations are larger in the presence of the union thus depends very much on the value of $\bar{L}$. It is to the determinants of $\bar{L}$ and to dynamics, in general, that we now turn.

Dynamics of Employment and Wages under Bargaining

The firm and the union are likely to be in a long-term relationship in which they bargain repeatedly over time. This has some important implications. It leads to more scope for insurance, along the lines we explored earlier. It also implies that maximizing short-run profit may no longer be optimal for the firm. Finally, the union membership is likely to evolve over time, and to evolve partly in response to past employment decisions. As we shall see, all these aspects modify the previous results in important ways.

Reputation and Efficient Contracts

The fact that the union and the firm are involved in repeated bargaining makes it more likely that employment will be on the contract curve rather than on the labor demand function, even if the contract states only the wage. The argument has been developed by Espinosa and Rhee (1987).[24]

Suppose that in a given period the union agrees to set the wage on the firm's promise that it will choose the efficient rather than the profit-maximizing level of employment. It also announces that if the firm cheats and chooses a point on the labor demand function, it will never trust the firm again and will choose wages in the future on the assumption that the firm is maximizing short-run profit in each period.

Will the firm keep its promise and choose an efficient level of employment? By cheating, it increases current profit, but because this will lead to inefficient contracts in the future, it will lose profit in all future periods. If the discount rate is sufficiently low, the firm will find it optimal not to cheat, and the efficient contract can be sustained. Even if the efficient contract cannot be sustained, a contract in which the firm chooses a level of employment between the labor demand function and the contract curve—which makes the temptation to cheat smaller—may be sustainable.[25]

What this suggests is that the contrast drawn above between the "right-to-manage" and the "efficient contract" models may be too strong, and that the firm may often give up short-run profit for better contracts in the future.[26]

Membership and Employment
Let us now consider what determines $\bar{L}$, the membership of the union. We have in mind the group of workers that the union actually represents in bargaining, rather than the formal membership of the union, which may be determined in large part by law and by other institutions. The currently employed are likely to have more weight in bargaining than the currently unemployed, even if the latter are members of the union. If this is the case, we would expect the result of real wage rigidity that we obtained earlier to be affected.

Suppose, for example, that membership is equal to last-period employment. Current members are then likely to take the dynamic implications into account: higher employment this period means higher membership, and therefore dilution of monopoly power, in the next period. Lower employment, on the other hand, increases the probability of losing membership in the union, possibly forever. This suggests that current members may aim more at employment stability rather than at real wage rigidity. It also suggests a new channel for persistence in employment movements: low employment today may lead, through membership, to low employment next period.

We now develop the example of the preceding paragraph, using the same monopoly union model as before (for the issues of this section, whether one

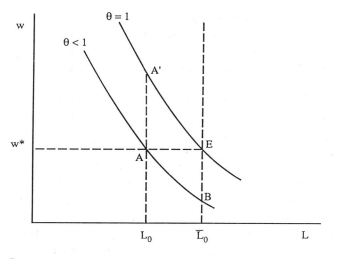

Figure 9.6
Membership effects and employment

assumes an efficient or a right-to-manage contract is relatively unimportant). We assume, however, that $\bar{L}$ is now equal to $L(-1)$, which represents employment in the previous period.

Suppose first that θ is expected to be constant, say, at some value less than one (for notational convenience below) in the current and all future periods. Under this assumption, if unions act myopically, ignoring the implications of their choice for membership, wages, and employment in future periods, the outcome is that represented in figure 9.6. In the first period the membership $\bar{L}_0$, chooses w^* and L_0. In the second period, membership $\bar{L}_1$ is equal to L_0. It chooses the same wage w^*, and the union stays at point A forever. In the present case where productivity is constant, this myopic behavior turns out not to change the solution: the membership at time 1, $\bar{L}_1$, chooses the same point, A, as would have been chosen had the decision been taken at time 1 by the initial membership $\bar{L}_0$.

Myopic behavior, however, is not usually appropriate. Today's members have to take into account the fact that in each period decisions are taken by the then current members, and not by today's members. Suppose that the union, with membership $\bar{L}_0$, and the firm are initially at point E in figure 9.6. Assume that it is known that for one period, θ will be less than one and will then permanently be equal to one in future periods. What should the union do? From the point of view of the current members, the preferred outcome is A in this period and E thereafter. But this outcome is not feasible.

If the union chooses point A, the next period membership is equal to $\bar{L}_0$, and the then members have no incentive to increase employment beyond $\bar{L}_0$; they choose A', not E. Under our assumptions this is actually true of any point between A and B: if employment today is less than $\bar{L}_0$, employment tomorrow is equal to employment today.

What outcome should union members choose? This particular structure makes it easy to derive the solution. Given any wage w that determines today's employment and next period's membership, we know that employment next period will be equal to that period's membership; next period's labor demand in turn determines next period's wage. Let labor demand be given by $L = \theta w^{-s}$, where θ is less than one this period and equal to one thereafter. Then, if the union chooses a wage w today, this implies that the wage tomorrow will be equal to $w\theta^{-1/s}$. Let β be the discount factor applied to future utility, and assume, for convenience, that utility is linear. Finally, assume that workers who lose membership never join the union again and receive their reservation wage forever.

The current members then maximize over w:

$$\left(\frac{L}{\bar{L}_0}\right)\left[(w - R) + \left(\frac{\beta}{1 - \beta}\right)(w\theta^{-1/s} - R)\right]$$

subject to

$$L = \theta w^{-s}.$$

Here $L/\bar{L}_0$ is the probability of being employed this period; further, since from period 1 on, union members choose a wage such that all will be employed, it is also the probability, as of this period, of being employed in all future periods. The benefit to being employed in this period is equal to $w - R$; the benefit to being employed in future periods is equal to $w\theta^{-1/s} - R$.

Maximizing with respect to w gives

$$w^* = \left(\frac{s}{s - 1}\right)\left[\frac{1}{(1 + \beta(\theta^{-1/s} - 1))}\right]R.$$

If β is equal to zero, current members behave myopically, and there is real wage rigidity. But if β is less than one, the threat of being unemployed next period leads current members to accept real wage cuts. As β goes to one, the wage tends to the value needed to maintain employment for current members; in figure 9.6 the outcome tends to point B.

This example suggests that membership considerations lead to more real wage flexibility than the static model implies. Solving the general dynamic problem when θ is random is much harder, and this monopoly union model—in which employment can never exceed membership and thus must be a nonincreasing function of time—is not the best with which to study the issue. Three models working out the implications of the relationship of membership to employment have been developed. The first, by Gottfries and Horn (1986), develops a two-period model of a union that chooses the wage in each period before θ is known. Another, by Blanchard and Summers (1986), develops an intertemporal model in which the union also chooses the wage in each period before θ is known; however, they do not use a representative member expected utility approach. In their framework the expected level of employment implied by the wage chosen by the union is equal to the current membership plus a constant (which may be positive or negative). As a result an increase in employment leads to higher membership and a permanent increase in expected employment in the future. The third, by Drazen and Gottfries (1987), examines the dynamic implications of seniority rules in this context.

Related work has studied the dynamics of unions using, instead, the median voter approach. A myopic median voter in a monopoly union model would choose a wage this period such that he is the marginal worker employed; over time the union would price itself out of existence. But when the median voter recognizes that he is not likely to be the median voter next time, the union need not shrink any longer. Oswald (1987) discusses informally the dynamics of a median voter union; he suggests that if keeping real wages rigid in the face of an adverse shock leaves the probability of being fired for the current median voter strictly equal to zero in all future periods, the dynamics of membership may still be consistent with some wage rigidity.

It would be desirable to extend the above framework in many other ways, particularly by allowing for more general membership rules, by allowing the firm to take into account the future implications of current employment decisions, and by studying the effects of attrition. One important element that we have left out so far is the effect of external constraints on bargaining, to which we now turn.

External Constraints and Dynamics
Where does the union get its bargaining power? Put another way, is the presence of a formal union needed to obtain the results derived earlier?

Unions derive some of their bargaining power from the laws and institutions which they have often helped create. Closed shops, legislation preventing unfair dismissal, and automatic extensions of collective agreements to all firms in an industry, all make it more difficult for a firm to replace—or to threaten to replace—union workers by nonunion workers, or for a new firm to employ nonunion labor. To the extent that these institutions exist, they explain why the union has bargaining power and justify models such as those analyzed above.

But in some economies, such as that of the United States, these legal or institutional protections are of limited importance. The question then arises whether the employed workers have any bargaining power. If the employed workers and the unemployed have the same skills, why isn't the firm able, by threatening to hire the unemployed, to pay the employed their reservation wage?

Consider the following assumptions. Suppose that there is firm-specific knowledge that can be given costlessly and instantaneously by an existing worker to a new worker. Replacing all existing workers may then be very costly to the firm because there is then no one to pass on the knowledge to the new hirees. Replacing a fraction of the existing workers may also be difficult: if existing workers decide to cooperate on behalf of the dismissed workers, and not to communicate their knowledge to new workers, the productivity of new workers will be low, possibly low enough to make it unattractive for the firm to hire them. The effects of firm-specific knowledge have been analyzed from different angles by Lindbeck and Snower (1986) and by Dickens (1986). Lindbeck and Snower focus on the implications of cooperation with, or harassment of, new workers by existing workers. Dickens looks at the closely related question of the wage that the firm must pay if it wants to avoid existing workers cooperating against new hires— behavior that it takes to be the creation of a union and that it assumes to be costly. In both cases the result is the payment to existing workers of a wage higher than their reservation wage.

How are external constraints likely to affect the choice of employment and real wages? In the simple static monopoly model the answer is a simple one: if at some critical wage, w^*, the firm is better off employing new hirees, this will be the limit on what the union is able to extract. Thus a union with a very small membership may no longer be able to restrict employment but will instead get the highest feasible wage, w_u, consistent with their employment. There exists at this stage no formal dynamic model that takes into account both membership effects and explicit external constraints.[27] One would expect that so long as the wage needed to maintain employment of the current membership is less than w_u, membership effects would be strong. But if membership is small, the union will be unable to set a wage high enough to prevent employment of additional workers; one would therefore expect that as membership decreases and the number of nonmembers increases, membership effects become weaker. Other effects may work in the opposite direction. For example, in the context of prolonged high unemployment, such as the current unemployment situation in Europe or the Great Depression, one such effect is the attitude of the long-term unemployed, who may give up looking for employment and thus stop exerting indirect pressure on wage bargaining. Such effects have been emphasized, in particular, by Minford (1985) and Layard and Nickell (1987).[28]

Macroeconomic Implications

At the end of this section our main conclusion is the following: in contrast to the initial simple static models, we would expect the presence of bargaining between unions and firms, or insiders and firms, to lead to less employment fluctuation and more real wage flexibility than in competitive labor markets. There are few formal results at this stage, but the intuition is a simple one: if belonging to a union gives access to rent sharing with the firm, one would expect union members both to want to stay in the union, and thus to stay employed, and not to want to share those rents with new workers. External constraints will attenuate these effects but are unlikely to eliminate them.

Given our goals of explaining employment fluctuations with small variations in real wages, this conclusion is clearly a mixed blessing. The fact that the union cares more about employment stability makes it more difficult to understand why it may set a nominal wage for some period of time and then leave the employment decision to the firm: the opportunity cost of doing so may be quite high.[29] But if it does, then shocks may have long-lasting effects on employment through membership changes.[30]

These persistence effects are formalized in the following macroeconomic model.[31] There are n monopolistically competitive firms in the goods market, with the demand facing each firm given in logarithms by

$$y_i = -s(p_i - p) + (m - p). \tag{22}$$

Each firm operates under constant returns to labor so that, ignoring constants here and below, $l_i = y_i$.[32] From profit maximization under these assumptions, each firm chooses $p_i = w_i$ so that $p = w$, where w is the aggregate wage. Substituting in (22) gives the demand for labor by each firm i:

$$l_i = -s(w_i - w) + (m - w). \tag{23}$$

Labor demand depends on the relative wage and real money in wage units. Each firm operates in a separate labor market; each market is composed of l^* workers, and l^* is assumed fixed. In each market the wage for each period is set, in nominal terms, by a union with $\overline{l}_i$ members so as to achieve in expected value

$$E[l_i] = a\overline{l}_i + (1 - a)l^*, \qquad 0 \leqslant a \leqslant 1. \tag{24}$$

The expectation is based on past values of all variables, including money. The information set does not include current money, which is the only source of uncertainty in the model.

This assumption embodies the spirit of the results derived above.[33] If a is equal to one, employment is equal to membership in expected value. If a is less than one, some weight is also given to nonunion members, reflecting the effects of external constraints on bargaining. Finally, the assumption that w is fixed in nominal terms for one period introduces some nominal rigidity.

Membership is equal to employment last period:

$$\overline{l}_i = l_i(-1).$$

We can now solve for the equilibrium. Taking expectations in (23), replacing $E[l_i]$ from (24), and imposing symmetry gives (dropping the i index as all unions will choose the same wage, and dropping the bracket for the expectation):

$$w = Em - al(-1) - (1 - a)l^*. \tag{25}$$

The nominal wage depends positively on expected nominal money and negatively on last-period employment and the labor force. If a is different from zero, higher employment last period implies higher membership this period and lower nominal wage demands. Substituting in (23) and reorganizing gives the equation describing the dynamics of employment:

$$l - l^* = a[l(-1) - l^*] + (m - Em). \tag{26}$$

Nominal money shocks lead to a first-order process for unemployment. If a is close to one, if membership effects are strong, the effects can be quite persistent. Short-lived (one-period) nominal rigidities, combined with membership effects, lead to long-lasting effects of aggregate demand. Indeed, in the extreme case where the unemployed play no role, unemployment follows a random walk and the effects of nominal shocks are permanent. The persistence comes neither from costs of adjustment of employment, as in chapter 7, nor from staggering of wage decisions, as in chapter 8, but from the fact that the employed have more weight in wage bargaining than the unemployed. Membership effects also have important implications for the dynamic effects of technological shocks on employment; demonstrating this is left to the reader.

9.4 Efficiency Wages

Labor is not a homogeneous commodity. Workers differ in their abilities, and the productivity of a given worker can vary considerably depending on the amount of effort that he devotes to his work. Neither ability nor effort is easy for the firm to assess or monitor. Efficiency wage theories all start from the assumption that productivity may be affected by the wage the firm pays, though the precise mechanism through which the wage affects productivity varies from theory to theory. When workers' efficiency is affected by the wage, a reduction in the wage may in the end increase rather than decrease cost. The wage may accordingly be sticky because it is costly for firms to cut it. We now explore some of the implications of efficiency wage theories, with a focus on their macroeconomic implications.[34]

We start by looking at the implications of the dependence of worker productivity on wages, without yet going into why this might be so. We then examine various channels through which productivity may depend on wages. We end by drawing the macroeconomic implications of those alternative explanations.

A Basic Model of Efficiency Wages

Consider the following model of a firm, due to Solow (1979). The firm's production function is given by

$$Y = sF(e(w)L), \tag{27}$$

where L is the number of workers and e is effort, which is assumed to depend on the wage paid by the firm. The effort function is assumed to satisfy $e(w) = 0$ for $w = R > 0$, $e'(\cdot) > 0$, and $e''(\cdot) < 0$. $F(\cdot)$ satisfies $F'(\cdot) > 0$ and $F''(\cdot) < 0$; s reflects shifts in either technology or in the relative price of the firm (in which case Y has the interpretation of revenue rather than production).

The firm maximizes profit, $sF(e(w)L) - wL$, over w and L. The first-order conditions are

$$\frac{e'(w^*)w^*}{e(w^*)} = 1,$$

$$e(w^*)sF'(e(w^*)L) = w^*. \tag{28}$$

Given our assumptions, the second-order conditions, which require that the elasticity of effort be decreasing in effort at the solution, are satisfied.

The model gives a set of very strong results: the wage is independent of s and entirely determined by the first equation in (28), which says that effort should be such that the elasticity of effort with respect to the wage is equal to one. Given the wage, the second equation determines the level of employment, which must be such that the marginal product of an additional worker is equal to the wage. There is no reason why this level of employment should be equal to the number of workers who want to work. Unemployment can thus be accounted for by the real wage inflexibility resulting from firms' rational resistance to wage flexibility.

Given our goal of understanding why real wages may be rigid, leading to large employment fluctuations in response to shocks, these results are very promising. But they depend crucially on the effort function, which at this stage is postulated rather than derived. We now turn to models in which such a relation can be derived explicitly.

The Relation between Wages and Productivity

The initial motivation for efficiency wages came from research on development, which highlighted the relation between the real wage, the level of nutrition, and productivity. The explanation is, however, marginally relevant at best for developed countries. Other explanations have been offered, ranging from neoclassical imperfect information explanations to sociological explanations based on fairness. We present one explanation in detail and will discuss the others later.

Monitoring, Shirking, and Efficiency Wages

Models in which the payment of high wages lead workers to work hard to keep their jobs have been developed by Calvo (1979), Salop (1979), Shapiro and Stiglitz (1984), and others. We present the Shapiro-Stiglitz model, which motivates the notion of efficiency wages by assuming that firms cannot perfectly observe workers' effort.

Consider an economy with many firms, each of them employing many workers. Firms employ workers who decide whether or not to shirk. In each period, if some workers are shirking, some of them are caught and fired. In addition some workers leave for other reasons. Firms make up for these layoffs and quits by hiring new workers from the unemployment pool. Thus the cost to a worker of being fired is to lose his job and go through unemployment until he is hired by another firm. The question we examine is that of the optimal wage and employment policy of each firm and of the general equilibrium implications of such behavior.

There are N workers in the economy. Each worker is risk neutral, with utility function $U(w, e) = w - e$, where w is the wage, or equivalently consumption, and e is effort. The level of effort, e, can take only two values, 0 if no effort is supplied (i.e., if the worker shirks) or $e > 0$ if the worker does not shirk. Thus, if he is employed and shirks, utility is w; if he is employed and does not shirk, utility is $w - e$. If he is unemployed, his utility is equal to zero. Each worker maximizes the expected present value of utility, V. He has a subjective discount rate equal to r, which is also the interest rate.

There are M firms, indexed by i. Each firm has a production function given by $sF(L_i)$, where L_i is the number of workers employed and not shirking. The output of a worker who shirks is zero. The variable s represents shocks to technology. The firm can only imperfectly monitor workers, though the monitoring technology is not made explicit. It is simply assumed that the probability of being caught, if shirking, is equal to q.

All workers who are caught shirking are fired. In addition there are natural separations. The separation rate—defined as the ratio of separations, for reasons other than shirking, to the number of workers employed—is equal to b and is the same for all firms. Shirking aside, this determines the flow into unemployment. The flow out of unemployment is determined by new hires. The accession rate, defined as the ratio of new hires to the number of unemployed, is denoted by a.

Characterizing the dynamic general equilibrium of the economy when s is a random variable is difficult. Thus we only characterize the steady state of the economy for a given value of s. In this case we can ignore time indexes since all variables are constant through time.

We start with the *problem of firm i*, which takes as given the aggregate wage w and has to decide about its wage, w_i, and its employment, L_i. Recall that workers who shirk produce zero output. If the firm is going to pay a positive wage, it should be such that it induces workers not to shirk.

To calculate the wage at which a worker is induced not to shirk, we examine the decision problem of a worker in firm i. He can either shirk or not shirk. Let V_{ESi}, V_{ENi} denote the expected present value of utility in each of the two cases. Let V_U denote the expected present value of utility if unemployed. We now derive the relation among the three, and the condition under which V_{ENi} will exceed V_{ESi}, making it optimal for a worker not to shirk. In the steady state V_{ESi} and V_{ENi} must satisfy the following equations:

$$V_{ESi} = w_i + (1 + r)^{-1}\{(b + q)V_U + [1 - (b + q)]V_{ESi}\}, \tag{29}$$

$$V_{ENi} = w_i - e + (1 + r)^{-1}[bV_U + (1 - b)V_{ENi}]. \tag{30}$$

If a worker is a shirker—and in the steady state, once a shirker, always a shirker, since the problem he faces is the same each period—he gets w_i in this period. He then becomes unemployed with probability $b + q$ or remains employed with probability $1 - (b + q)$.[35] In the steady state V_{ESi} is the same next period as it is this period. This gives equation (29).[36] A similar argument gives equation (30).

Given (29) and (30), we can compute the wage at which it will not be worthwhile for the worker to shirk. That wage must be such that $V_{ENi} \geqslant V_{ESi}$. Solving out for w_i gives

$$w_i \geqslant \left(\frac{r}{1 + r}\right)V_U + \left[1 + \frac{r + b}{q}\right]e.$$

Given V_U, the wage is an increasing function of r and b but a decreasing function of q. The higher the discount rate or the turnover rate, the higher the wage needed to induce no shirking. The higher the probability of being caught, the lower the wage needed to induce no shirking.

There is no reason for the firm to pay more than necessary to prevent shirking. Thus the above equation holds with equality, and no worker shirks. In this case V_{ESi} and V_{ENi} are equal and can be denoted by V_{Ei}.

V_U is in turn given by

$$V_U = (1 + r)^{-1}[aV_E + (1 - a)V_U],$$

$$V_E = w - e + (1 + r)^{-1}[bV_U + (1 - b)V_E],$$

where V_E is the expected present discounted value of utility of a worker being employed in a representative firm in the economy and w is the wage in the representative firm (all firms are the same in equilibrium). If a worker is unemployed, he becomes employed with probability a in the next period or remains unemployed with probability $1 - a$. In turn, if he is employed, he does not shirk, getting therefore $w - e$ in utility, and becomes unemployed with probability b or remains employed with probability $1 - b$. Solving for V_U gives

$$V_U = \left(\frac{1 + r}{r}\right)\left(\frac{a}{a + b + r}\right)(w - e).$$

Substituting this in the expression for w_i finally gives

$$w_i = \left(\frac{a}{a+b+r}\right)(w - e) + \left[1 + \frac{r+b}{q}\right]e. \tag{31}$$

Equation (31) gives the wage chosen by the firm as an increasing function of the aggregate wage and of the accession rate a. Given w_i, the firm chooses employment such that

$$sF'(L_i) = w_i. \tag{32}$$

General Equilibrium
We next characterize the general equilibrium. Since all firms are the same, $w_i = w$ for all i. In equilibrium firms cannot prevent shirking by paying a wage higher than the average of other firms. Thus, from equation (31), we get

$$w = e + \frac{e(a+b+r)}{q}.$$

In steady state the accession rate must be such that the flow out of unemployment is equal to the flow into unemployment:

$$bL = a(N - L),$$

where L is aggregate employment. Thus $a = bL/(N - L)$. Replacing this in the above wage equation gives

$$w = e + \frac{e\{[bL/(N-L)] + b + r\}}{q}. \tag{33}$$

Equation (33), which links the level of employment and the equilibrium wage, is called by Shapiro and Siglitz, the "no shirking constraint" (NSC). It says that the higher the level of employment, and thus the smaller the expected time spent in unemployment if fired, the less costly it is to be fired and the more tempting it is to shirk. To avoid this, firms must pay a higher wage. The NSC is drawn in figure 9.7, together with the labor supply curve that would be observed if monitoring were costless. In this case the reservation wage of each worker would be e, and the supply curve would be given by SSS.

Finally, aggregate employment is given by the condition that

$$sF'\left(\frac{L}{M}\right) = w, \tag{34}$$

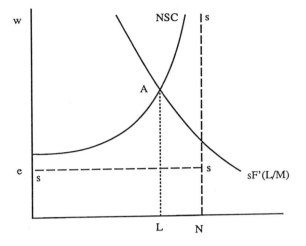

Figure 9.7
Equilibrium unemployment under efficiency wages

where M is the number of firms. The labor demand curve is drawn for a given value of s in figure 9.7. The equilibrium is given by A.

The model has two important implications for our purposes. First, the equilibrium is necessarily associated with unemployment. If there were no unemployment, there would be no cost to a worker of shirking and being fired, since he would be immediately hired by another firm. Second, the unemployment is involuntary: workers who are unemployed would rather work at the prevailing wage.

To see the implications of efficiency wages, consider fluctuations in s. In a competitive market with perfect monitoring, a change in s leads to a change in the wage and not in employment (provided the marginal product of the Nth worker always exceeds his reservation wage). Such fluctuations in s lead here to fluctuations in employment and thus in involuntary unemployment.[37] The real wage is not constant, however, as it was in the simple initial model, but is increasing with employment.

What would happen if we were to introduce small costs of changing wages into the model? This is not a question that we can answer formally, since we have limited ourselves to an analysis of steady states. But we can make some progress.

Suppose that at given wages and prices, there is a change in the nominal money stock that leads to a change in output, employment, and unemployment. How costly is it, then, for a firm not to adjust the wage it pays its workers, given that other wages are not adjusted? The answer clearly depends on the sign of the change. To see this, we rewrite the wage equation for a firm, equation (31), substituting $b(1 - u)/u$ for a, whe e u is the unemployment rate, and then rearrange:

$$w_i = \left[\frac{b(1 - u)}{b + ur}\right](w - e) + \left[1 + \frac{r + b}{q}\right]e. \tag{35}$$

The wage depends on the aggregate wage and on the unemployment rate. Recall that this equation gives the minimum wage consistent with no shirking. Thus, if unemployment decreases, the cost of not changing w_i is very large: all workers start shirking, and the output of the firm drops to zero. If unemployment increases, instead, all the firm is doing is overpaying its workers, and this may indeed not be very costly.

This last result is extreme and depends crucially on the assumption that effort can only take two values. One can think of many reasons why, if the model was extended to allow, for example, for heterogeneity of workers or a continuous value for effort, a decrease in unemployment at a constant wage would only lead to a small decrease in effort and would not be very costly for the firm. But as it is, the result sounds an important warning. Efficiency wages, or the fact that wages depend on other wages, do not necessarily imply that small costs of changing wages will lead to large nominal rigidities. The argument has to be made case by case, and it does not hold in the version of the model we have just described.

Other Rationalizations of Efficiency Wages
Many other channels that generate a relation between wages and productivity have been explored. Some, as in the Shapiro-Stiglitz model, have relied on imperfect information by firms. If, for example, workers' reservation wages and abilities are positively correlated, and if ability is not observable, offering a higher wage will lead to a pool of applicants of better average quality (Stiglitz 1976) and may increase profit. If turnover costs are high, firms may also be able to decrease the quit rate through high wages, along lines similar to the model studied earlier (Salop 1979).

Many of these theories have been criticized on the grounds that more elaborate pay schemes could avoid the market failures they imply. In the case of imperfect monitoring, workers could pay a bond, which they would forfeit if they were found shirking. Workers could then be paid their reservation wage, leading to the efficient outcome. Similarly, it is likely that firms can better assess the ability of a worker after having some time to observe the worker's performance. In this case, firms could ask workers to post performance bonds. Whether some of the characteristics of actual contracts, such as nonvested pension benefits or rising wage profiles, are in fact proxies for such bonding schemes is still very much an open issue.[38]

Others have explored more sociological models, such as the idea that a reduction in wages by one firm may be considered unfair by workers, leading them to supply less effort (Akerlof 1984; Akerlof and Yellen 1987). These models easily lead to real wage rigidity and, in the presence of small costs of changing wages, to nominal wage rigidity as well. Although the notion of fairness clearly plays an important role in labor markets, taking fairness as a primitive assumption is unsatisfactory. Why is it fair for some workers to stay employed at the same wage while others are in consequence laid off? For example, workers may insist on the same wage as workers in other firms because they think of the average wage of similar workers outside the firm as a good proxy for their own market value. But theories that seek to explain "fairness," instead of simply assuming it, may well lead to useful insights.

Macroeconomic Implications

We have already pointed out the potential implications of the Shapiro-Stiglitz model, as well as its potential limitations in explaining why small costs of changing wages may cause shifts in aggregate demand to affect output. If "efficiency wages" imply that firms prefer (or at least find it nearly costless) to keep wages in line with others when the unemployment rate changes, efficiency wages can, in combination with small costs of changing wages and prices, lead to effects of aggregate demand. This was shown by Akerlof and Yellen (1985).

The Akerlof-Yellen model assumes monopolistic competition, among n firms. The demand facing each is given by

$$Y_i = \left(\frac{P_i}{P}\right)^{-\sigma} \left(\frac{M}{P}\right). \tag{36}$$

Each firm operates under decreasing returns to labor. Let $a > 1$ be the inverse of the degree of returns to scale. Solving for the optimal price chosen by each firm given the nominal wage it pays its workers, W_i, yields, using logarithms and ignoring constants,

$$P_i = w_i + (a - 1)(m - p), \qquad \text{for all } i. \tag{37}$$

Each firm operates in its own labor market. Because of efficiency wage considerations (e.g., nutrition), each firm sets a fixed real consumption wage,

$W_i/P = b$, for all i. In logarithms, ignoring the constant,

$$w_i = p. \tag{38}$$

Solving for (37) and (38) under symmetry implies that $w = p = m$. Money is neutral.

Now suppose that there are small costs of changing prices and that a is close to one. It is not very costly, in response to a change in money, for firms not to adjust given wages. However, wages from (38) will not adjust if prices do not adjust. Thus these small costs lead to real effects of nominal money and large output effects.[39]

What should we therefore conclude? Efficiency wage theories clearly can explain both involuntary unemployment and movements in unemployment. They may help to explain why aggregate demand matters, although, as we have seen, this is not necessarily the case. Whether the channels through which wages affect productivity have been adequately identified is subject to debate. But efficiency wage theory is surely one of the most promising directions of research at this stage.

9.5 Goods Markets

From the labor markets we turn to the goods markets, with one major question in mind: Why do shifts in demand facing firms lead largely to adjustments in output rather than in prices, given wages? Or put another way, why is the output supply function so flat?[40] The motivation for this question was made clear in chapter 8: a flat output supply function is a necessary condition for demand shocks to have potentially large effects on output.

Research can be classified under two main headings. The first, both theoretical and empirical, examines the behavior of marginal cost and price under imperfect competition. It focuses on the simple question of whether the small response of prices to shifts in demand is due to a flat marginal cost function or, instead, to a decrease in the markup of prices over marginal cost as output increases. This direction of research is exploring many leads, theoretical and empirical, but has not so far reached consensus.

The second pursues further the general equilibrium implications of constant or even declining marginal costs. It explores the possibility that if costs are declining in the level of activity, the economy may have high and low level activity equilibria. Multiple equilibria of this type have the potential to generate fluctuations even in the absence of any nominal rigidity. They may also combine with nominal rigidities to generate richer dynamic re-

sponses to shocks than those obtained in chapters 7 and 8. We review two
models that exhibit multiple equilibria, one due to Diamond (1982) which
emphasizes positive externalities associated with high activity and one due
to Murphy, Shleifer, and Vishny (1987) which focuses on increasing returns
in production.

Marginal Cost and Prices

There is substantial evidence that firms, given wages, react to shifts in
demand mostly by increasing quantities rather than by increasing prices. In
the 1970s the consensus view had become that prices of produced goods
were set as essentially fixed markups over standard unit labor costs, with
shifts in demand having little effect on the markup. Various measures of
"demand pressure," such as the degree of capacity utilization and the capital
output ratio, were tried in price equations but with little or no success.[41]
The interpretation of these equations has since been questioned, as has the
sensitivity of the results to simultaneity: if productivity shocks as well as
demand shocks are present, an upward-sloping output-supply function is
clearly consistent with little or no empirical correlation between output and
prices.

No evidence has been presented, however, at the aggregate or disaggregated level in favor of a strong effect of demand shifts on prices, given
wages. Thus for the time being this remains a stylized fact. The simplest
potential explanation is obviously that marginal cost is flat, so that firms
have no reason to increase prices in response to demand. Another is that,
though marginal cost is upward sloping, the markup of prices over marginal
cost decreases with the level of output. We review both in turn.

The Slope of the Marginal Cost Curve

By affecting firms' decisions as to capital accumulation and the choice of
inputs, the presence of imperfect competition may potentially affect the
slope of the marginal cost curve. For example, to the extent that firms use
excess capacity as an entry deterrent (e.g., as in Fudenberg and Tirole 1983),
this excess capacity is likely to imply a flatter marginal cost at average levels
of output. (See also Hall 1986, 1987.) However, there has been little
systematic theoretical investigation of the relation between imperfect competition and the slope of the marginal cost curve.

Much of the work has been empirical. Until recently, there was wide
agreement that firms operated at roughly constant marginal cost at average
levels of output. This was based largely on the short-run relation between

employment and output, which is part of Okun's law: in the short run firms are able to supply more output with less than proportional increases in employment.[42] This fact suggests the presence of chronic labor hoarding and thus of low (and possibly constant) marginal cost until firms begin using their labor force fully.

A recent empirical study by Bils (1987) suggests, however, that things may not be that simple. Bils starts from the observation that to satisfy an increase in sales, firms have a choice among various margins. They may satisfy sales out of inventories or they may increase production. If they increase production, they have a choice between increasing either the number of workers or the number of hours per worker. Because the cost-minimizing firm will equalize the marginal cost at all margins, one can look at *any* of these decisions to infer the slope of the marginal cost curve. Bils focuses on the choice of hours and notes that the amount of overtime hours is a smooth increasing function of the level of output and that overtime work is substantially more costly to firms.[43] Using disaggregated data from U.S. manufacturing, he concludes that marginal cost is increasing in output, though this is not reflected in price-marginal cost margins. His study casts doubt on the characterization of firms as having chronic labor hoarding. With this exception, most empirical studies are consistent with the notion that marginal costs are roughly constant or perhaps even declining.[44]

Declining Markups and Output Movements
If marginal cost is increasing in output, another potential explanation for demand shifts having no effect on prices is that imperfectly competitive firms choose countercyclical markups. This is an old idea, dating back at least to Pigou (1927). There are at least four potential categories of explanation of this possibility.

1. *Implicit contracts.* The first parallels the implicit contract argument reviewed in the previous section on labor markets. In effect, it holds that observed prices are not spot market prices but part of a more general contract between buyers and sellers. Transactions may, for example, have two dimensions, time to delivery and price, and the market may clear mostly by variations in time to delivery. Or, in the case of a long-term relationship between buyer and seller, the price may have an insurance component and little bearing on the allocation of the good. This line of argument is clearly relevant in some markets, in particular, the markets for intermediate manufacturing products examined by Stigler and Kindahl (1970) and more recently by Carlton (1986) (see Carlton 1987 for a discussion). Delivery

lags are strongly procyclical in manufacturing.[45] Like its labor market counterpart, this line of argument would lead one to dismiss the rigidity of observed prices as an important fact for macroeconomics, if it were shown that the market prices of most goods had this implicit contractlike feature. Also, like its counterpart, it leaves us searching for an explanation of why demand shocks would affect output.

2. *Procyclical elasticity of demand.* The second explores the possibility that the elasticity of demand facing an industry is procyclical. Faced with a procyclical elasticity of demand, during a boom a monopolist will decrease his markup of price over marginal cost, leading to less variation in price than in marginal cost. But the case of constant elasticity of demand (e.g., which we used, in the basic model of chapter 8) is only a convenient benchmark; there is no strong argument in favor of either systematically procyclical or countercyclical elasticities. Weitzman (1982) has suggested that if increases in demand lead to the production of a larger number of products, these products are likely to be closer substitutes and thus lead to higher elasticity of demand.[46] The argument appears to be most relevant in the medium and the long run. Another approach has explored the possibility that given customers who develop an attachment to particular firms, the incentive for firms to recruit new customers may be higher in booms, leading firms to decrease prices in booms (Bils 1985). One does not get the sense that this line of explanation will be able to explain the general behavior of prices across sectors.

3. *Countercyclical degree of collusion.* The third approach argues that even if the elasticity of demand to the industry remains constant, the degree of collusion between firms in any industry may be countercyclical.

One argument for why this may occur has been formalized by Rotemberg and Saloner (1986). Consider n firms in an industry, producing an identical good at constant marginal cost. Suppose that these firms collude during each period to set a price between the competitive and the monopoly price. Can they sustain this equilibrium? A firm that deviates from the common price can, by undercutting other firms, get the whole market demand for one period and make large profits. It may, however, lose in future periods if other firms decide to punish firms that deviate from the common price. The largest credible punishment is for all firms to return to competitive pricing from the next period on, implying zero profits to all firms forever. Thus each firm has to weigh the benefits versus the costs of deviating from the industry price. The incentive to deviate is stronger, the larger is current compared to expected future demand. Put another way, the sustainable price, the price at which no firm has an incentive to deviate, is lower when demand is high: the markup is countercyclical. This explanation suggests that one should find markups behaving differently depending on market structure. The evidence is somewhat mixed (see Rotemberg and Saloner 1986; Bils 1987; Carlton 1987).

4. *Kinked demand curves.* The fourth approach, which has a long and controversial history, is that firms face kinked demand curves, with the demand for their product decreasing sharply if they increase their price and increasing very little if they decrease it. The traditional explanation is that if a firm decreases its price, its competitors follow, whereas if the firm increases its price, it is not followed by others. This explanation has been shown to be difficult to justify using formal game theory (see, however, Maskin and Tirole 1986 for a related game-theoretic derivation).

A justification based on imperfect information by customers has been sketched by Stiglitz (1979). Stiglitz considers a market in which customers search across firms for the lowest price and examines the equilibrium in which all firms charge the same price. In that equilibrium a firm will attract few customers if it lowers its price, because search is expensive and few potential customers will learn of the price cut. If, on the other hand, a firm increases its price, it may lose a large number of customers who believe rationally that they will find a cheaper product elsewhere. Thus the demand curve faced by a firm has a kink at the existing price. This makes it likely that this price will be the optimal price for the firm. Given such an equilibrium price, small shifts in demand may lead a firm not to change its price, generating countercyclical markups. This theory also has problems, at least as a general theory of price rigidity. First, the model exists only as a sketch, not as a complete formal model. Second, it has sharp implications for price changes as a function of industry structure; in particular, it implies that monopolistic industries should, ceteris paribus, have more flexible prices than oligopolistic industries. Price changes appear, however, to be less frequent under monopoly than under oligopoly (Rotemberg and Saloner 1987).

Thus this direction of research suffers from, if anything, an embarrassment of riches. To the extent that many of those theories have different cross-sectional implications, empirical work may and probably will narrow down the list of plausible explanations. However, many of the explanations have similar macroeconomic implications. As an example, we now show how the presence of a kinked demand curve can lead to large real effects of changes in the nominal money stock.

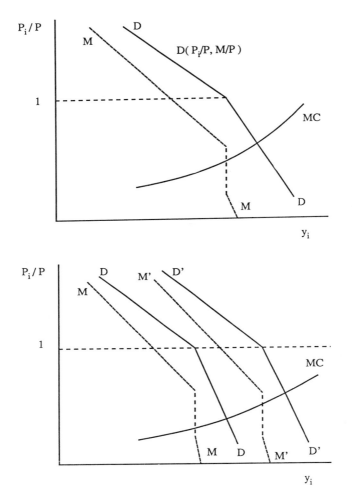

Figure 9.8
Macroeconomic implications of kinked demand curves

The Kinked Demand Curve and the Effects of Nominal Money[47]

Consider the same economy as in chapter 8, with n price-setters, each potentially facing a demand function that depends on a relative price P_i/P and aggregate real money balances M/P and each producing under increasing marginal cost. We modify the model of chapter 8, however, to assume that the demand facing each firm is kinked at $P_i/P = 1$. The motivation is that given by Stiglitz but is not explicitly incorporated into the model.

Figure 9.8 shows the demand, *DD*, the marginal revenue, *MM*, and the marginal cost curves for an individual price-setter. Given this demand curve, the optimal price for the firm is indeed unity, so the figure also describes the general (Nash) equilibrium, with all prices equal across firms, and the level of output produced by each price-setter equal to Y.

Consider now an increase in the nominal money stock, and suppose for the moment that the price level remains the same so that real money balances and aggregate demand increase. The demand curve facing each price-setter shifts to the right, say, to $D'D'$, in figure 9.8. It remains kinked at $P_i/P = 1$ so that marginal revenue shifts to $M'M'$. It is clear that if the increase in money is not too large, $P_i/P = 1$ is still the optimal price for any firm. Thus, given the price level, no price-setter will change his own price, but if no price changes, the price level will not change, validating the initial assumption. The increase in the nominal money stock leads to an increase in output, even in the presence of increasing marginal cost.

Note that the argument in this case does not depend on the presence of menu costs. But note also that the equilibrium with unchanged prices is only one of many. If all nominal prices increased in proportion to nominal money, leaving output unchanged, this would also be an equilibrium. Do we then gain something by introducing menu costs? The answer is mixed and raises issues already discussed in chapter 8. When there are costs of changing prices, price-setters will save menu costs by leaving all nominal prices unchanged. However, this does not imply that the equilibrium with unchanged nominal prices is the only Nash equilibrium:[48] given that other firms change their prices, the fact that demand is kinked makes it now very costly for any firm not to follow suit. Thus, even in the presence of menu costs, there is likely to be a multiplicity of equilibria for nominal prices. The model does not tell us which one to choose.

Thin Markets and Multiple Equilibria

An ebullient economy leads to optimism and to new business opportunities; a depressed economy leads to pessimism, sclerosis, and a lack of entrepreneurial spirit. The idea that ebullience and depression may as a result be largely self-sustaining is an appealing, old, and somewhat vague idea.

A formal model that indeed generates multiple—high and low level activity—equilibria was developed by Diamond (1982). The model is based on trading externalities: the higher the level of activity, the easier it is to trade and the higher the optimal level of production for each producer. Thus the model clearly has the potential to generate multiple equilibria, one in which producers produce little, with little trading and thus little incentive to produce, and another in which there is a high level of production, a high level of trading, and strong incentives to produce.

More specifically, the economy is decentralized, composed of a large number of individuals, all of them alike. To consume, each individual must first produce a good (which he is assumed not to consume) and then exchange it against another good which he can consume. This prohibition against eating one's own production gives rise to the need to trade and captures the implications of the division of labor in actual economies.[49] Production opportunities arrive according to a Poisson process; they all yield one good but at a cost that varies across opportunities. The individual must choose whether to produce or wait for the next opportunity. If he produces, he must then wait to trade this good for another one; trading opportunities also arrive according to a Poisson process. Once trading has taken place, the producer consumes the good, and the process of production and trading starts anew.

The instantaneous utility of the individual is

$$U = y - c,$$

where y is consumption and c is the effort involved in production.[50] Utility is therefore linear in consumption and effort. The intertemporal utility function is given by

$$V = \sum_{i=1}^{\infty} \exp(-rt_i) U(t_i),$$

where, given the linear form of utility and that consumption and production are instantaneous, we just need to add utility at the dates, t_i, when either production or consumption takes place. The subjective discount rate is r.

Production opportunities become available according to a Poisson process, with rate of arrival a. They all yield y but differ in their cost. The cost is a random variable, with cumulative distribution $G(c)$ and support $c \geq \bar{c} > 0$. At any point in time each individual has to decide on a cutoff cost, c^*, such that he produces if $c \leq c^*$ and lets the opportunity pass if $c > c^*$.

We will derive the optimal c^* below. Producers are not allowed to hold more than one unit of the good at a time. Thus, once production has taken place, individuals embark on the search for a trading partner.

Trading opportunities also become available according to a Poisson process, with rate of arrival b. This rate of arrival is taken as given by any trader but depends on the number of individuals searching. Let e be the proportion of people who have produced a good and are therefore searching. For convenience, we follow Diamond in calling e employment and $1 - e$ unemployment, although the use of words is slightly misleading. Then b is assumed to be an increasing function of e and $b(0) = 0$; the specifics of the search-trading technology are not made explicit. If, for example, search is by a random drawing so that the probability of finding another searcher is e in each drawing, then b would be linear in e. Once trade takes place, consumption follows immediately.[51]

Equilibrium

To characterize equilibrium, we first derive e as a function of c^*, and then optimal c^* as a function of e. For a given c^*, the equations of motion of employment are given by

$$\frac{de}{dt} = a(1 - e)G(c^*) - eb(e). \tag{39}$$

The first term gives the flow into employment, the proportion of individuals who are unemployed and who both find and take a production opportunity. The second gives the flow out of employment, the proportion of individuals who are employed and find a trade.

The net flow into employment decreases with employment. The higher the employment rate, the lower will be unemployment, the smaller the flow into employment, and the larger the flow out of employment. The net flow into employment increases with c^*. The higher the cutoff point, the more production opportunities are taken up, and the higher is the flow into employment. In steady state $de/dt = 0$ so that (39) gives us a relation between e and c^*. This relation is shown in figure 9.9. It rises along the vertical axis for $c^* \leqslant \bar{c}$; then e becomes an increasing function of c^*, with e tending to unity as c^* increases further.

The other relation between c^* and e comes from the optimal choice of c^* by producers. The choice of c^* is in effect an optimal stopping problem, familiar in the search literature. Let V_U be the value of intertemporal utility if currently unemployed, and let V_E the value if currently employed. Note that given the structure of the model, V_U and V_E depend on time only

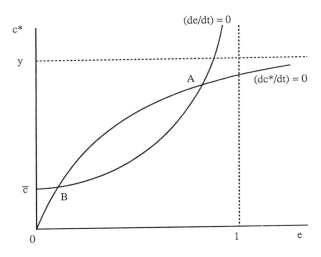

Figure 9.9
Equilibrium employment in the search model

through their dependence on e, which affects b. As in the model of efficiency wages seen in the previous section, both V_U and V_E, being expected present discounted values, follow arbitragelike equations:

$$\left(\frac{dV_U}{de}\right)\left(\frac{de}{dt}\right) + a \int_0^{c^*} (V_E - V_U - c)\, dG(c) = rV_U,$$

$$\left(\frac{dV_E}{de}\right)\left(\frac{de}{dt}\right) + b(y - V_E + V_U) = rV_E.$$

The first term in the first equation gives the expected "capital gain," the expected change in V_U. The second gives the "expected dividend." Either a production opportunity arrives and the cost is below the cutoff point (in which case the individual spends c and produces, changing status from unemployed to employed) or a production opportunity arrives with cost above c^*, or no production opportunity arrives, in which case there is no "dividend." The expected capital gain plus the expected dividend must be equal to the discount rate times the value of being unemployed. A similar interpretation applies to the second equation.

For the program to be optimal, c^* must be such that $V_E = V_U + c^*$, so that the individual is indifferent as to whether he takes the production opportunity and begins to search for a trading partner, or waits for the next opportunity.

By taking the difference between the two equations above, and noting that $(dV_E/de)(de/dt) - (dV_U/dt)(de/dt) = dc^*/dt$,[52] we obtain the equation of motion for c^*:

$$b(e)(y - c^*) - a \int_0^{c^*} (c^* - c) \, dG(c) + \frac{dc^*}{dt} = rc^*. \qquad (40)$$

In the steady state $dc^*/dt = 0$ so that the last equation gives c^* as a function of e. It is easy to show that an increase in e, which increases trading opportunities, increases the cutoff point, or equivalently increases the proportion of production opportunities taken up by individuals. Also, when $e = 0$ so that there is nobody to trade with, there is no incentive to produce: $c^* = 0$. Furthermore c^* never increases above y, the return to production. A locus that satisfies these restrictions is drawn in figure 9.9.

As we have drawn it, and given the various restrictions on $dc^*/dt = 0$ and $de/dt = 0$, figure 9.9 has three equilibria: A, B, and O. Without further restrictions on $G(\cdot)$, there may be more than those three equilibria. These equilibria capture the initial idea that high and low activity may both be self-sustaining, that the economy may be stuck at too low a level of activity.

Two Sets of Issues
This basic multiple equilibrium result raises at least two sets of issues. The first is about dynamics. If the steady states are as in figure 9.9, where is the economy likely to end up? The equations of motion from any point can be derived from equations (39) and (40). Two of the equilibria, A and O, are saddle point equilibria. The intermediate equilibrium is either stable or unstable, depending on parameter values. This opens up various possibilities. The first is that the economy converges either to O, the "pessimistic" equilibrium, or to A, the "optimistic" equilibrium. It may well be, even in this case, that for the given value of e, there are two values of c^*, each of them on one of the saddle point paths. Which value of c^* is chosen is not determined within the model. The second possibility, analyzed by Diamond and Fudenberg (1987), which arises only for specific parameter values, however, is that the economy exhibits deterministic cycles. In a closely related model Howitt and McAfee (1988) show that there may be, just as in chapter 5, sunspot or animal spirits equilibria in which the economy rationally oscillates between the pessimistic and the optimistic equilibrium. The relation between the issues raised for dynamics by these multiple equilibria and the issues raised in chapter 5 is a topic of current research.

The second set of questions concerns the empirical interpretation of the thin market externality formalized by Diamond. The model is at a level of abstraction where it does not lend itself to empirical verification. Howitt and McAfee (1987) have given a labor market interpretation in which higher recruiting by firms induces more search effort by workers. Although the effect is surely present, it appears unlikely that at high unemployment the cost of finding workers is what prevents firms from hiring. Another potential interpretation is given by Blanchard and Summers (1988), based on the presence of firing costs. High unemployment leads to an inactive labor market and decreases quits. A very low quit rate decreases employment flexibility for firms, increasing their cost and in turn reducing the optimal level of employment. Work by Bentolila and Bertola (1987) suggests, however, that this effect is too weak to generate multiple equilibria. Thus what macroeconomic phenomena are captured by models of thin markets is still an open question.

Increasing Returns and Multiple Equilibria

The other oft-mentioned reason why costs may be lower at high levels of activity is the presence of large fixed costs in production. This line of argument has been explored most recently by Murphy, Shleifer, and Vishny (1987). They ask whether an economy may have two equilibria, one in which markets are large enough for firms to use increasing return technologies and the other in which markets are too small to justify the use of those technologies.[53] We now describe their basic model.

Tastes
The economy is composed of one representative consumer and a continuum of produced goods, x, defined over [0, 1]. Utility is given by

$$V = \int_0^1 \log(c(x))\, dx. \tag{41}$$

This utility function implies that spending on each good will be a constant share of income. Given income Y, and given that goods are distributed over [0, 1], spending on each good will also be equal to Y.

Income is equal to labor income plus profit income. Labor, L, is supplied inelastically. Using labor as the numeraire, income is thus given by

$$Y = L + \Pi,$$

where Π is aggregate profit.

Technology and Market Structure

Each good can be produced using one of two technologies. The first is a constant returns to scale technology (CRTS) in which one unit of labor produces one unit of output. This technology is freely available. The second is an increasing returns technology (IRTS) which is only available to a monopolist. It requires a fixed number of units of labor, F; it can then be operated at constant returns, with one unit of labor producing α units of the good, $\alpha > 1$.

Consider a monopolist's decision whether to operate its IRTS technology. The demand for the good is unit elastic, but at any price higher than one, the competitive fringe produces an infinite amount. Thus the profit-maximizing price for the monopolist, if he operates, is unity,[54] with his profit given by

$$\pi = Y - \left(\frac{1}{\alpha}\right) Y - F = aY - F, \qquad \text{with } a = 1 - \left(\frac{1}{\alpha}\right) < 1.$$

Thus π is clearly an increasing function of the size of the market, of aggregate income. If π is positive, the IRTS technology is used.

Equilibrium

We examine whether the economy can have two equilibria: a "low-level activity" equilibrium in which all sectors use the CRTS technology, markets are small, and the IRTS technology is not profitable, and a high-level activity equilibrium in which sectors use the IRTS technology, markets are large, and the IRTS technology is profitable.

We first derive the restrictions on technology such that output is higher when the IRTS technology is used. Let n be the proportion of sectors in which the IRTS technology is used, and let $Y(n)$ be the associated level of output.

If $n = 0$, all sectors use the CRTS technology, profits are equal to zero, and $Y(0) = L$. If, instead, $n = 1$, output is such that

$$\Pi(1) = aY(1) - F$$

and

$$Y(1) = \Pi(1) + L,$$

or solving for $Y(1)$,

$$Y(1) = \frac{L - F}{1 - a} = \alpha(L - F).$$

Output is equal to the productivity of labor times that part of the labor force not used as a fixed cost. For $Y(1)$ to exceed $Y(0)$, the fixed cost must not be too large, or α must be small enough. Using the expressions for $Y(1)$ and $Y(0)$ gives

$$Y(1) > Y(0) \Leftrightarrow F < aL.$$

We assume this condition to be satisfied.[55] Thus output and welfare are higher when the IRTS technology is used in all sectors.

To derive the equilibrium, we proceed in three steps. We first obtain $Y(n)$ and then $\pi(n)$, the profit made by a monopolist using the IRTS technology when a proportion n of the sectors is already using the IRTS technology. We then examine whether $n = 0$ and $n = 1$ can both be equilibria, that is, whether we can have both $\pi(0) < 0$ and $\pi(1) > 0$.

Given n, aggregate profit and output are given by

$$\Pi(n) = n[aY(n) - F]$$

and

$$Y(n) = \Pi(n) + L,$$

so that

$$Y(n) = \frac{L - nF}{1 - an}, \tag{42}$$

$$\frac{dY(n)}{dn} = \frac{aY(n) - F}{1 - an} = \frac{\pi(n)}{1 - an}. \tag{43}$$

An increase in the number of sectors using the IRTS technology increases output (given our assumption that $F < aL$). There are two, equivalent, ways of thinking about why this is so. The first is in terms of aggregate demand. If a sector shifts to an IRTS technology, it makes positive profits. These profits increase income, demand, and demand to the other sectors. To the extent that the other sectors are using an IRTS technology, they in turn increase their profits, which further increases demand, and so on. Thus the multiplier effect is increasing in n, the proportion of sectors using the IRTS technology. The alternative way of thinking about it is in terms of aggregate supply. Note that profit is equal to the amount of labor released from production in the sector. Thus a shift to IRTS releases labor for other sectors; the higher the proportion of sectors using the IRTS technology and the more productive this labor is, the larger is the induced effect on output.[56]

Given n, we obtain from (42) the profit to a monopolist of using the IRTS technology:

$$\pi(n) = aY(n) - F = \frac{a(L - nF)}{1 - an} - F = \frac{aL - F}{1 - an}. \qquad (44)$$

Profit is increasing in n.

Equations (43) and (44) capture the informal story sketched at the beginning of this subsection. A shift to IRTS increases output. In turn higher output implies higher demand and a stronger incentive for each producer to shift to an IRTS technology. Those equations also imply, however, that the interaction, though present, is not strong enough to generate multiple equilibria. Evaluating $\pi(n)$ at zero and at one gives

$$\pi(0) = aL - F > 0,$$

$$\pi(1) = \frac{aL - F}{1 - a}. \qquad (45)$$

Thus, under our assumption that the equilibrium with IRTS yields more output, profit indeed increases with n, yet is positive even if $n = 0$. Thus, even if other firms have not adopted the IRTS technology, it is profitable for a monopolist to do so. There is only one equilibrium, that at which all sectors use IRTS.

The Scope for Multiple Equilibria

This model can be extended so as to reinforce the interaction between decisions and generate multiple equilibria. Assume that the setting up of an IRTS technology requires, in addition to the fixed cost in labor, a nonlabor cost of G in utility terms. Then, given (45), there is a set of values for G such that $\pi(0) - G < 0$ and $\pi(1) - G > 0$. In this case both the low and high output equilibria are indeed equilibria: when $n = 0$, no producer has an incentive to shift to the IRTS technology; when $n = 1$, no producer has an incentive to shift back to CRTS.

Other extensions, which imply multiple equilibria, are given by Murphy, Shleifer, and Vishny. They consider one of particular interest here: a dynamic version of the model in which there is investment. In effect, firms have to pay the fixed cost in the current period to operate the low-cost technology in the next period. The contribution of firms choosing to invest in the IRTS technology this period to aggregate demand next period is no longer just profit but their whole output. This effect can be sufficiently strong to generate multiple equilibria in the level of investment and in output.[57]

In related work Shleifer (1986) has also shown how, if new products lead to temporary rents, firms may want to introduce them at times of high demand, leading to bunching in the introduction of new products and implementation cycles. These cycles emerge even though the rate at which new products are discovered is constant.

Like the Diamond model, the model presented above captures an interaction between firms that is surely part of reality. Whether such interactions are quantitatively sufficient to create multiple equilibria is open to question. However, even if they do not generate multiple equilibria, these models all suggest reasons why an economy in a recession or depression may not easily return to high levels of activity. In terms of the models of chapter 8 which emphasize the role of price and wage decisions in the adjustment process, they all suggest reasons why firms may see their costs increase as output decreases and may not want to cut prices given wages. One of the goals of current research is to assess the relative empirical importance of the many mechanisms presented in this section.

9.6 Financial Markets and Credit Rationing

Thus far in this chapter we have concentrated on behavior in the goods and labor markets, seeking to account for and to appraise the apparent rigidity of the real wage and other relative prices. A related set of issues arises in the capital markets, where monetary policy actions that have only small effects on interest rates appear to have significant impacts on the economy. We shift our attention now to financial markets and to credit rationing.

Despite the complexity and sophistication of the financial markets, they are typically represented in macroeconomic models by only two variables: the money stock and an interest rate. In this respect the financial markets are treated no differently than other complex markets such as the labor market. But there is a recurrent theme in the literature and among market participants that the interest rate alone does not adequately reflect the links between financial markets and the rest of the economy. Rather, it is argued, the availability of credit and the quality of balance sheets are important determinants of the rate of investment.

Further it is often argued that the money stock is not a key quantity in the determination of the price level and output, in part because it is endogenous and in part because the financial system is sufficiently flexible to generate as much inside money as might be needed to finance any given level of activity.

These views were emphasized by Gurley and Shaw (1960) and the Radcliffe Committee (1959). They have recently been revived by, among others, Bernanke and Gertler (1987), Blinder and Stiglitz (1983), and Greenwald and Stiglitz (1988), who emphasize the role of credit in the business cycle, and particularly in the transmission of monetary policy to the economy.[58]

The recent literature builds on the theory of imperfect information. The basic argument is that the capital markets not only intermediate in a mechanical way between savers and investors but in addition deal with a variety of problems that arise from asymmetric information about investment projects between borrower and lender. These informational problems both shape capital market institutions and debt instruments and affect the way in which policy actions are transmitted to the goods markets.

In this section we examine recent theories of the relationship between financial variables and economic activity, starting from the topic of *credit rationing*.[59] If credit is rationed, then it is possible that the interest rate is not a reliable indicator of the impact of financial variables on aggregate demand. It is quite likely in that case that quantity variables, such as the amount of credit, have to be looked at in appraising monetary and financial policy.

There are several definitions of credit rationing, all arising from the view and experience of capital market participants that borrowers cannot borrow as much as they would like to even when the markets appear to be operating well. *Type 1 credit rationing* occurs when an individual cannot borrow as much as he or she wants at the going interest rate. *Type 2 credit rationing* occurs when, among identical borrowers, some who wish to borrow are able to do so, while others cannot (Keeton 1979). Note that this notion is very close to definitions of involuntary unemployment.

Credit rationing is easy to understand when there are interest rate ceilings, for instance, usury laws. Although usury laws are not uncommon, we will not concentrate on them here.[60] Rather, we develop a theory of credit rationing that depends on asymmetric information between borrowers and lenders.

Two main reasons have been advanced for lenders to ration credit rather than raise interest rates to clear markets:

1. *Moral hazard.* When the contract between lender and borrower is a debt contract that allows for bankruptcy, the lender increases the incentive of the borrower to undertake risky investments by raising the interest rate. The increased risk of bankruptcy may actually reduce the lender's expected return when the interest rate rises. This would not be a problem if the lender could observe and control the type of project undertaken by the borrower.

2. *Adverse selection.* Similarly, again assuming that the contract between lender and borrower is a debt contract, lenders may prefer to ration credit rather than to raise the interest rate because more risk averse individuals drop out of the borrowing pool as the interest rate rises. The less risk averse the borrower, the more likely is the borrower to choose risky projects that increase the chance of bankruptcy. This problem would not occur if the lender had full information about the type of project to be undertaken by the borrower.

We now develop a simple model of credit rationing, due to Keeton (1979) and Stiglitz and Weiss (1981).[61] The model raises several major questions, among them whether the phenomenon of credit rationing is an artifact of the restricted form of contract studied, whether credit rationing implies some form of market failure, and whether the existence of credit rationing implies that interest rates are unreliable indicators of the effects of monetary policy actions on the economy. We turn to those and related questions after developing the model.

A Model of Credit Rationing

There is a continuum of entrepreneurs, each of whom has a project that requires an initial investment of K and is indivisible. Each entrepreneur has an endowment of $W < K$ and therefore has to borrow to invest.

All projects yield the same expected return, R, but they differ in risk. For simplicity suppose that projects either succeed, yielding R_i^s, where i is the index of the project, or fail, yielding the common value R^f, which could be zero. The probability of success is p_i. The relation between p_i and R_i^s implied by the assumption that the expected return is the same across projects is therefore

$$p_i R_i^s + (1 - p_i)R^f = R, \qquad \text{for all } i. \tag{46}$$

The distribution of p_i across entrepreneurs is characterized by a density function $g(p_i)$.

Financial institutions, banks for short, make loans to entrepreneurs. Entrepreneurs use their own wealth for self-finance to the maximum extent possible and need to borrow the amount $K - W = B$ in order to undertake a project. The loans are of a standard debt form, on which the borrower pays the specified amount $(1 + r)B$ if he is able to, but in the event of bankruptcy, which is assumed to occur if the project fails, he pays only the actual available return R^f. It is assumed that

$$R_i^s > (1 + r)B > R^f, \qquad \text{for all } i. \tag{47}$$

The key asymmetry of information is that though the entrepreneur knows his probability of success, the bank does not. Further, in the absence of mechanisms to sort individuals into probability classes, the bank potentially makes loans to all who are willing to borrow at the posted rate. If it should decide to ration credit, it cannot do so in a way that discriminates high-risk from low-risk borrowers among those willing to borrow.

Assume that both the bank and the entrepreneur are risk neutral. The expected return to the investor is

$$E(\pi_i) = p_i[R_i^s - (1 + r)B]. \tag{48}$$

The expected payoff to the bank that makes the loan is

$$E(\pi_b) = (1 + r)B \int_0^p p_i g(p_i)\, dp_i + R^f \int_0^p (1 - p_i) g(p_i)\, dp_i, \tag{49}$$

where p is the cutoff probability at which customers come to the bank for loans, to be determined below.

Now consider an entrepreneur deciding whether to borrow. A key feature of the payoff to the investor is that it is decreasing in the probability of success, p_i. (Remember that R is the same across projects so that a lower p_i implies a higher R_i^s.) To see this, substitute from (46) into (48) to obtain

$$E(\pi_i) = R - R^f - p_i[(1 + r)B - R^f],$$

which from (47) is decreasing in p_i. Thus high-risk investors are willing to pay more for a loan. This is the basic source of the credit-rationing result. It clearly depends on the fact that the contract between the borrower and the bank is a debt contract, and we return below to the reasons why the contract may take that form.

Assume that investors have the alternative of holding their wealth, W, in a safe asset that yields a rate of return ρ. They will therefore want to borrow so long as

$$E(\pi_i) \geqslant (1 + \rho)W. \tag{50}$$

Given (50) and the definition of $E(\pi_i)$ above, the higher the interest rate, r, the riskier is the marginal project, that project for which the entrepreneur is indifferent between undertaking the investment project and putting his wealth into the safe asset. This implies that $dp/dr < 0$; that is, the probability of success of the marginal project declines as the interest rate increases.

Now consider the impact of an increase in the loan interest rate on the expected return of any bank that is making loans. Differentiating (49) with respect to r, we obtain

$$\frac{dE(\pi_b)}{dr} = B \int_0^p p_i g(p_i) \, dp_i + \left(\frac{dp}{dr}\right)[(1+r)Bpg(p) + R^f(1-p)g(p)]. \quad (51)$$

The first term on the right-hand side reflects the higher repayments by those who repay. The second term reflects the deterioration in the quality of the pool of applicants. This second term is negative, and it is accordingly possible that an increase in the interest rate charged by the bank reduces its expected profits. Whether this happens depends on the properties of the density function. The bank's profits are maximized at the interest rate at which $dE(\pi_b)/dr = 0$.

In the fourth quadrant of figure 9.10, we show one possible relationship between the rate of interest charged to lenders, r, and the expected return to an individual bank, denoted ρ_b, equal to $E(\pi_b)/B$. Examples of density functions that produce such a relationship between the expected return of the bank and the interest rate to lenders are given in Stiglitz and Weiss (1981) and English (1986); the key to producing a negative relationship is that a small increase in the interest rate drives a large number of relatively safe borrowers out of the market.

The remainder of the diagram shows how credit rationing may arise.[62] The demand for credit is shown by the downward-sloping L_d curve in the first quadrant. The demand for credit is simply

$$B \int_0^p g(p_i) \, dp_i.$$

Its negative slope results from the fact that $dp/dr < 0$. In the third quadrant we show the supply of funds to the bank as a function of ρ_b, assumed here to be increasing. We also assume a direct relationship between the bank's rate of return and the rate it pays on deposits. In the absence of reserve holdings and operating costs, and with a competitive banking system, ρ_b would be equal to the rate of return offered on deposits. If banks hold reserves and have other operating expenses, the rate of return on deposits would be below ρ_b but, in general, an increasing function of ρ_b. The analysis would not change if the elasticity of supply of funds to the bank were infinite.[63]

We can draw the implied "supply" curve in the first quadrant. In the fourth quadrant a given value of r implies a given expected rate of return to the bank, ρ_b. The third quadrant gives the supply of deposits at rate ρ_b. The

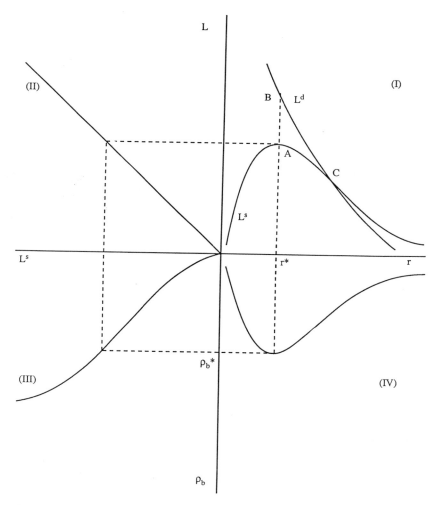

Figure 9.10
Equilibrium credit rationing

45-degree line in the second quadrant allows us to derive the supply of loans in the first quadrant. In the case shown, there is a credit-rationing equilibrium at point A, at the interest rate r^* that maximizes the bank's profits. The demand for loans at that interest rate, shown by point B, exceeds the amount supplied. Credit is therefore rationed. This is type 2 rationing, whereby, among identical projects, some receive financing and others do not—a result of projects having a given minimum size.

There appears to be a standard nonrationed equilibrium at point C. Any bank operating at that point, however, could earn higher profits by cutting its interest rate and returning to point A. It might seem that credit rationing could not persist because banks are earning profits at point A. But nothing in the analysis is inconsistent with the assumption that at point A all expected profits have been competed away; thus point A could be a point of industry equilibrium, implying the possible existence of credit rationing in equilibrium in the setup shown in figure 9.10.

It is also possible to generate credit rationing in a setup in which each investor has several different types of projects. Then, by an analysis similar to that above, we can show the possible existence of a credit-rationing equilibrium in which each investor obtains less financing than he wants at the prevailing interest rate.

Note that in these cases it is not easy to distinguish whether credit rationing results from moral hazard or adverse selection. In both examples there is adverse selection of projects, the selection of riskier projects being responsible for credit rationing. Likewise, in each case credit rationing may be described as arising from moral hazard because it is only the possibility of bankruptcy—willingly entertained by the borrower because of limited liability—that causes rationing.

The Form of Contract

The use of a very restricted form of debt contract in the above model raises the issue of the robustness of the credit-rationing result. One obvious possibility is that the borrower puts up collateral that he forfeits in the event of bankruptcy. If each individual has collateral equal to B, then there is no risk to the lender and no credit rationing. But in this case there would be no need to borrow either.

Could the use of a collateral—interest rate schedule induce borrowers to reveal their type? Stiglitz and Weiss (1981) show that this is not generally the case in a model in which banks set the collateral level. Their proof turns on the assumption that at some point individuals come up against the constraint of their existing wealth, and therefore the above analysis applies again.

Hart (1986) raises the question of why it is possible for the lender to ascertain the amount earned by the borrower in one state of nature (when the payoff is R^f) but not another (R^s). Some progress has been made in answering this question by Gale and Hellwig (1985). They assume that it is costly to monitor the state of nature[64] and then show that in such a case optimal contracts between borrower and lender take the form of debt. By having the borrower make a fixed payment independent of the state of nature for good outcomes, the contract saves on expected monitoring costs. By monitoring when the borrower declares an inability to meet the fixed payment, the contract ensures that the borrower cannot declare an inability to meet the stated payments at will.[65]

Optimality of Credit Rationing

The term rationing automatically creates the impression of nonoptimality. De Meza and Webb (1987) show that if, in the Stiglitz-Weiss model, the supply of funds to the bank is nondecreasing in the rate of return, there is too little investment at the credit-rationed equilibrium. The argument is that since both banks and entrepreneurs are risk neutral, all projects with expected return greater than or equal to the safe interest rate ρ should be undertaken. Thus at the social optimum all projects for which

$$p_i R_i^s + (1 - p_i)R^f \geq (1 + \rho)K \tag{52}$$

should be undertaken.

Investors finance through the bank if

$$p_i[R_i^s - (1 + r)B] \geq (1 + r)W. \tag{53}$$

Consider now the marginal project for which (53) holds with equality. On any project that it finances, the bank's expected return is

$$E(\pi) = p_i(1 + r)B + (1 - p_i)R^f - (1 + \rho)B.$$

On the marginal project the bank's expected return is

$$E(\pi) = p_i R_i^s + (1 - p_i)R_f - (1 + \rho)K.$$

Suppose now that this is also the socially marginal project, for which (52) holds with equality. Then the bank expects to break even on this project but nevertheless will lose money on all other projects as a result, because they are riskier. Since in an equilibrium the bank expects to make zero or positive profits, it cannot at the margin be financing the marginal socially optimal investment. Therefore investments that should be undertaken are not undertaken.

De Meza and Webb (1987) show that in this model an interest subsidy can restore the first-best allocation. They also show that with a backward-bending supply of funds to the banking system, there will be overinvestment at the credit-rationed equilibrium.

However, the nonoptimality of equilibria in the presence of credit rationing is not general: there are examples in which the allocation with credit rationing is that which would be produced by a central planner with the same information as is available to market participants. Thus the allocation in a credit-rationed equilibrium is optimal in the model setup by Williamson (1986); similarly, Keeton (1979) shows in a model with type 1 credit rationing that the allocation is efficient. The point in all of these cases is that credit rationing is an efficient method of preventing overinvestment in risky projects that would otherwise take place because of the lack of information by the lender.

An interesting model in which the allocation of credit is nonoptimal in the absence of credit rationing is presented by Mankiw (1986). The nonoptimality arises from the use of debt contracts, which imply that at equilibrium (where supply equals demand) some safe borrowers who should invest do not do so and some borrowers who should not invest are doing so. Mankiw shows that an increase in the interest rate may destroy the market equilibrium (this is the financial collapse). Because this leads to a nonoptimal allocation of investment, government intervention to prevent market collapse may be socially justified.

The Transmission of Monetary Policy

Interest in credit rationing in the 1950s was motivated by the question whether monetary policy could have powerful effects on the economy if interest rates did not move substantially. At that time monetary policy was constrained by the fear that large interest rate increases would significantly increase the interest burden on the budget. It was accordingly hoped that monetary policy could affect aggregate demand even without having a large impact on interest rates.

The "availability doctrine" argued that because of interest rate ceilings, changes in the quantity of financial assets would affect economic activity even without changes in the interest rate. The question that therefore arises is whether the existence of equilibrium credit rationing implies that monetary policy can have significant impacts on aggregate demand without changing interest rates.

Using figure 9.10, assume that an easing of monetary policy increases the supply of loans to the banks at each deposit interest rate, shifting the locus in the third quadrant to the left. If it does not move the locus in the fourth quadrant, the increase in the supply of funds will shift the L_s curve in the first quadrant up, increasing the quantity of loans offered at each interest rate. The cost of bank loans would be unchanged, and the amount of loans and of investment increased.

If we measured the interest rate by the cost of bank loans, this would show monetary policy affecting the economy without changing the interest rate. The question remains, however, to find the mechanism through which the loan supply curve in the third quadrant moved. English (1986) shows, in a model with a safe asset and credit rationing, that although credit rationing removes a close link between the quantity of bank loans and interest rates charged by banks, the rate of return on the safe asset remains a good indicator of the impact of monetary policy on borrowing.

Stiglitz and Weiss (1981) expand the model developed above to include a variable level of collateral: loan contracts then specify both the level of collateral and an interest rate. The loan interest rate may move either pro- or countercyclically. By including two types of projects, relatively safe and relatively risky, and by allowing productivity shocks to affect the probabilities of success of these projects differentially, they are able to produce a countercyclical pattern in the interest rate paid to bank depositors. The model, however, does not fully specify the links between monetary policy and the availability of funds (in real terms) to the banks.

Bernanke and Gertler (1986) develop a general equilibrium real business cycle model in which collateral plays an important role, thereby opening up a channel through which the quality of balance sheets affects investment and output. In their model investment projects are too large for an individual saver to finance alone. There are nevertheless agency costs associated with external finance so that the more collateral (equivalently one may think of firms' internal financing) that is needed, the greater the deadweight loss associated with the recourse to external finance.[66] Under a general assumption of risk neutrality, the expected return on investment net of agency costs has to be equal to the safe rate of interest, which is itself endogenous. Bernanke and Gertler show, in an overlapping generations model (of the Diamond type studied in chapter 3), that positive productivity shocks that increase output and saving lead to more efficient investment (because collateral is greater), thereby accentuating the effects of the productivity shock relative to a full information economy.

A favorable productivity shock reduces the gap between the safe interest rate and the gross of agency cost expected return on investment; in recessions the safe interest rate may fall while the gross expected return on investment rises. This is a result that is consistent with earlier work by Bernanke (1983), claiming that one of the major propagating mechanisms in the Great Depression was the collapse of financial intermediation that opened the gap between safe and risky rates of interest.

Bernanke and Gertler use their model in addition to discuss the famous Irving Fisher notion of a "debt deflation." Fisher's argument was that deflation increases debt burdens and bankruptcies and therefore reduces investment. If the debt deflation is interpreted as reducing the amount of collateral, the Bernanke-Gertler model can be used to demonstrate the Fisher hypothesis.

Summary

There are now several models in which investment can change without significant movements in interest rates and in which financial variables other than the interest rate affect the rate of investment. In this sense the interest rate may be an inadequate indicator of the thrust of monetary policy.

But these models have not yet reached the point where monetary policy effects themselves are endogenized; at the present state of development they all rely implicitly on some form of nominal rigidity, either on price rigidity so that changes in nominal money affect real money balances and credit or on the existence of nominal bonds, whose value is affected by unexpected inflation or deflation. Once these real effects allow a monetary change to provide an impulse to the system, it is clear that the details of the financial system affect the propagation or transmission mechanism.

9.7 Conclusions

The contrast between the unwieldy and inconclusive presentation of the material in this chapter and the clarity and sense of direction in chapters 2 and 3 is quite obvious. Such is the difference between material which is in large part about 20 years old, thoroughly absorbed and understood, and current research, whose implications and ultimate payoffs cannot yet be fully grasped.

In this and the previous two chapters we have been attempting to provide satisfactory theories to account for the macroeconomic facts outlined in chapter 1—particularly the joint behavior of output and prices, employment and wages, money and output, and aggregate demand and output. Although we have presented many different approaches, they have in common the desire to account for macroeconomic phenomena in a framework in which the motivation and environments of the economic agents and institutions in the model are fully specified. In other words, the new models go beyond the notion common in the 1970s and 1960s of providing a "microeconomic foundation for macroeconomics" and seek rather to provide complete macroeconomic models that are not only analytically coherent but also empirically relevant.

At this stage we cannot discern which model or combination of models will 20 years hence be regarded as absolutely essential to serious macroeconomic theory, as the Ramsey-Sidrauski model and the overlapping generations model are now. However, we can give educated guesses. In the labor markets, notions of efficiency wages have a definite ring of truth. So does monopolistic competition, as a stand-in for imperfect competition, in the goods markets. We believe that the recent work attempting to account for certain features of the financial markets from the viewpoint of asymmetric information is extremely important and that it will be increasingly integrated in complete macroeconomic models. Finally, we are quite sure that nominal rigidities are an important part of any account of macroeconomic fluctuations and that staggering of price and wage decisions is an important element of any complete story.

How those theories must be combined, and whether some unifying principle can be found in the dizzying diversity of explanations, remains to be seen. No doubt some theories that now look promising will turn out to be dead ends, and some that now look moribund or already dead will turn out to be important. How does the process work? To some extent the theories that win are those that are more appealing to our professional standards and prejudices. To a greater extent, they will be the theories that succeed in accounting for the macroeconomic facts as well as the microeconomic evidence.

Problems

1. Labor supply and efficient contracts.

Consider a labor market with one firm and one worker. The firm is risk neutral. It operates under constant returns to labor and is subject to multiplicative technological shocks s_i. Thus, if it uses l_i hours of labor, its output is $s_i l_i$. The worker has utility $E[\ln(l_i w_i) - l_i^b]$, where l is hours of labor, w is the hourly wage, and b is larger than one. l_i can take any nonnegative value.

(a) Characterize the competitive spot market equilibrium graphically and algebraically.

(b) Suppose that an econometrician can observe w_i and l_i in that market. Can he estimate b? Why or why not?

(c) Assume that s_i can be observed by both sides so that contracts can be made contingent on s_i. Characterize the equilibrium under a symmetric information contract.

(d) Suppose that an econometrician can observe w_i and l_i in that market. Can he estimate b? Why or why not? If you were the econometrician, what additional information would you try to obtain in order to estimate b?

2. *Contracts with bilateral private information. (This is adapted from Hall and Lazear 1984.)*

Consider a contract between one worker and one firm. The worker can work or not work; his reservation wage is A, which is random. The marginal product of the worker, if he works in the firm, is M, also a random variable.

The firm and the worker sign a contract before A and M are realized. A and M are private information to the worker and the firm, respectively, so that a contract cannot be made contingent on them. Both the worker and the firm are risk neutral. Thus, letting X be one if work takes place, and zero if not, the contract maximizes $E[XM + (1 - X)A]$.

We consider the properties of three simple contracts:

Contract 1 (the predetermined wage contract) sets the wage, W, at the time of contracting. Based on the realization of M, the firm decides either to employ the worker or to lay him off. Based on the realization of A, the worker decides to work or to quit. Work takes place if there is neither a layoff nor a quit.

In contract 2 the firm is allowed to choose the wage, W, unilaterally after having observed M (but not A). Given W and the realization of A, the worker decides to work or to quit.

In contract 3 the worker is allowed to choose the wage, W, unilaterally after having observed A (but not M). Given W and the realization of M, the firm decides to hire him or to lay him off.

(a) Properties of contract 1: Characterize in the (A, M) space the efficient outcome (work or not work). Then characterize the outcome if a contract of type 1 is used. Characterize the regions where the outcome is inefficient quits and where the outcome is inefficient layoffs. For what joint distributions of (A, M) is a contract of type 1 likely to perform well?

(b) Assume that A and M are independent and uniformly distributed on $[0, 1]$ Characterize the wages chosen in contracts 1, 2, and 3, respectively. Characterize each of the contracts graphically in the (A, M) space. Which of the three contracts performs best? Why don't contracts 2 and 3, which at least use some information, perform better?

(c) It is reasonable to assume that the worker has job-specific skills. Thus assume that A and M are independent, that A is uniform on $[0, 1]$, and M uniform on $[1, 2]$. Derive the form of contracts 1, 2, and 3. Which contract performs better? Why?

(d) If A represents the wage elsewhere in the economy, it is reasonable to assume that it is positively correlated with M. Consider the extreme case where A and M

are perfectly correlated and uniform on [0, 1]. Derive the form of contracts 1, 2, and 3. Which contract performs better? Why?

(e) Can this analysis shed light on the form of the contracts we observe in the real world? Can the analysis shed light on real wage rigidity and large employment fluctuations?

3. *Unions, bargaining, and unemployment. (This is adapted from Jackman, Layard, and Nickell 1988.)*

Consider a firm and a union which bargain over wages and employment. Wages are chosen so as to maximize $N(w - A)[R(N) - wN]$ subject to the "right to manage" constraint, $R'(N) = w$. N is employment, $R(N)$ is the revenue function, and A is the expected level of income if not employed by the firm.

(a) Derive the wage level resulting from the Nash bargain as a function of the "labor income to profits" ratio, θ, the wage elasticity of labor demand, η, and A.

(b) Let A be given by $\bar{w}(1 - u) + Bu$, where u is the rate of unemployment, $\bar{w}$ the wage if employed elsewhere, and B the income if unemployed. Derive the rate of unemployment consistent with a symmetric equilibrium, assuming for convenience that $B/\bar{w}$ is constant and denoted by ρ.

(c) Consider a monopolistically competitive setup with firm i facing a demand curve given by $Y_i = (P_i/P)^{-a}(M/P)$, $a > 1$, and the production function $Y_i = N_i$. Each firm bargains with a union along the lines described above. Determine the (symmetric) equilibrium levels of the real wage and unemployment as a function of a and ρ.

4. *Efficiency wages and effort. (This follows Solow 1979.)*

A sales-constrained firm can sell output q at price 1 and is therefore minimizing costs. Labor, n, is the only input. The wage affects productivity so that the production function is given by $q = f(n, w)$. Let the partial inverse of f, $n = n(q, w)$ exist, with $n_1 = 0$ and $n_2 < 0$.

(a) Write the first-order conditions for cost minimization in terms of the function n and its derivatives.

(b) The sensitivity of the wage to cyclic demand variations in q is measured by dw/dq. We say that the wage is completely sticky if $dw/dq = 0$. Write down the partial differential equation that must be satisfied by the function n for the wage to be completely sticky.

(c) Show that the general solution to the partial differential equation found in (b) satisfies $\ln(n) = A(q) + B(w)$, $A' > 0$, $B' < 0$.

(d) Using the relation derived in (c), show that the wage is completely sticky only if the production function is of the form $q = g[e(w)n]$, $g' > 0$, $e' > 0$.

(e) Show that if the production function is as in (d), then the wage is completely sticky (This completes the proof of an if and only if proposition.)

(f) Interpreting e to be effort, show that the firm's optimal policy is to offer a wage satisfying the condition that the elasticity of effort with respect to the wage is equal to unity.

5. *Increasing returns and efficiency wages.*

There are two goods A and B and half of income is spent on each. The economy is endowed with N units of labor. The production of one unit of either good in the competitive sector requires one unit of labor. There are also two special economic agents. One can produce unlimited quantities of good A by hiring F units of labor and then producing each unit of output with $a < 1$ units of labor. The other can produce good B, in similar fashion, by hiring F units of labor and then producing each unit of output with $a < 1$ units of labor. Let the decision by the two special agents on whether to set up shop be simultaneous.

(a) Describe the set of equilibria as a function of F and a. Show that for given values of F and a, the equilibrium is unique.

(b) Describe the set of equilibria if workers insist on getting paid $(1 + x)$, $x > 0$ times the wage they would earn in the competitive industries when they work for the special agents.

(c) Provide one story for these efficiency wages, and make sure that this story does not lead to a contradiction with the results of your formal analysis in (b).

(d) Rederive your answer to (b) if the two special agents must choose whether to set up shop in sequence. On the basis of the assumptions and results, which case is more plausible?

(e) Assume again that the important decision is simultaneous. Now, however, before setting up shop, the two special agents can make offers to each other. Discuss what offers might be relevant and how they affect the set of equilibria.

6. *Price rigidity, collusion, and booms. (This follows Rotemberg and Saloner 1986.)*

Suppose that a sector, with N firms, faces the demand function, $p = e - bq$, where e is i.i.d. and uniform on $[0, 1]$. The marginal cost of production is equal to zero.

(a) Suppose that the N firms collude to achieve the monopoly outcome. Determine the monopoly price and quantity (assuming that prices are set after e is realized).

(b) Determine the profit of each firm if the sector behaves as a monopolist.

(c) What is the relation between e and the incentive to cheat, that is, the incentive for any of the N firms to post a price ε lower than the others?

(d) Suppose that there is a fixed punishment K for firms that do not cooperate. Write down e^*, the value of the shock such that firms are indifferent between colluding and cheating. Derive the price charged by the sector as a function of e. What is the highest sustainable price when e exceeds e^*?

(e) Suppose that the punishment is that if a firm charges a price lower than other firms in the current period, the market reverts to competitive pricing in all future periods. Is this punishment credible? Assuming that firms discount the future at rate δ, derive K as a function of δ and N.

(f) "This model explains why markups of prices over marginal costs are counter-cyclical." Discuss this statement.

(f) Suppose that firms, instead of having zero marginal cost, have zero marginal cost up to some capacity level, at which point marginal cost becomes vertical. How would this affect the conclusions derived above?

7. *Credit markets and rationing.*

There are many entrepreneurs. Each entrepreneur has access to two projects. Each project requires one unit of input, and entrepreneurs have no wealth. The certain project yields output R^c with probability 1. The uncertain project yields output R^w with probability p, and no output with probability $1 - p$. An entrepreneur can invest in only one of the two projects (he can also choose to invest in neither). Entrepreneurs and lenders are risk neutral, but negative consumption by an entrepreneur is not feasible. The output of the project is publicly observable.

For simplicity, set $R^c = 3$, $R^w = 4$, and $p = 1/2$.

(a) Suppose the entrepreneur borrows at gross rate of return r (i.e., the payment to the lender is the minimum of r and the output of the project). What is the entrepreneur's choice of project as a function of r? What is the expected rate of return to the lender as a function of r?

(b) Let ρ be the safe rate of return (so that there is a perfectly elastic supply of funds to the lender at ρ). Derive r and the choice of project as functions of ρ? How does a change in ρ affect investment?

(c) Is the equilibrium first-best efficient? That is, is the set of projects undertaken the same as the set that the social planner would like to have undertaken? Is the outcome constrained efficient? That is, if the social planner could not dictate the set of projects undertaken but could set r, would she choose a value of r different from the equilibrium value?

(d) If lender and borrowers could write contracts more complicated than debt contracts, would they choose to do so?

(e) How would the results in (a) change if the entrepreneur begins with positive wealth w, $0 < w < 1$? You may want to use a diagram.

Notes

1. We use "marginal product of labor" rather than the simpler "labor demand" because in many of the models we consider later, firms do not operate on their competitive labor demand functions.

2. This is well-traveled ground, with many good surveys. See, for example, Azariadis (1979) for contracts under symmetric information and Hart (1983) and Stiglitz (1986) for contracts under asymmetric information and other extensions. For this reason we make no attempt at generality, referring the reader to these papers for more details.

3. This is not true of more general utility functions; marginal utility of income is always equalized, but this does not imply that utility itself is.

4. Suppose, for example, that the worker has utility $\log(C) + \log(L^* - L)$. In a spot market labor supply is inelastic, so there are no variations in employment. Under the optimal contract labor supply is an increasing function of the wage, so there are employment variations in response to changes in s.

5. Note that transitory shocks are both those that create scope for intertemporal substitution and those that firms, if they have better access than workers to credit markets, can best insure workers against.

6. This glosses over an important issue, which would appear clearly if we derived this version of the monopolistic competition model explicitly, namely, why firms

are less risk averse than the workers. In the model of chapter 8 the owners of the firms and the workers are one and the same. That firms would be able to diversify more easily with respect to idiosyncratic shocks is plausible, but this explanation cannot be used in the case of aggregate fluctuations.

7. This characterizes efficiency from the point of view of the firm and the worker in the contract. Because the firm has monopoly power in the goods market, however, what is best for the contract is not best socially.

8. This is known as the "revelation principle" in the contract literature.

9. We have not shown, however, that this is the optimal incentive-compatible contract, which is harder to derive.

10. This is a standard result in principal-agent problems, of which this is one case. See Hart and Holmstrom (1987).

11. Two models have combined asymmetric information contracts with imperfect information à la Lucas to obtain real effects of nominal money (Grossman, Hart, and Maskin 1983; Canzoneri-Gray 1984).

12. Farber (1987), Oswald (1985), and Pencavel (1985), in their respective surveys, analyze many of the issues discussed in this section and give extensive bibliographies.

13. The question of what unions maximize is an old favorite among labor economists, starting with Dunlop (1944) and Ross (1948). See Pencavel (1985) for a criticism of the assumption used in the text.
   This formalization assumes implicitly that all members are treated equally by both the union and the firm; otherwise, the concept of "representative member" is not well defined. An alternative approach is to recognize that workers differ in terms of seniority—which has implications, in particular, for the order in which layoffs take place—and that the union maximizes the expected utility of the median voter (see Farber 1978; Oswald 1985). A third approach has been to assume that senior workers control the union; its implications are qualitatively similar to the second. We will point out the differing implications of these alternative approaches as we proceed.

14. The expression is from Nickell (1982).

15. This diagram is useful in many other contexts, such as credit rationing.

16. Remember that we are assuming that the firm cannot hire more than $\bar{L}$ workers. If the firm were, instead, allowed to hire nonunion workers at the prevailing wage after union members were already employed, the contract curve could extend beyond $\bar{L}$. If $\theta F'(\bar{L})$ is greater than R, the contract curve for $L > \bar{L}$ will be the labor demand curve. The coincidence of the contract curve and the labor demand curve in such a case has been emphasized by Oswald (1986).

17. See Pencavel (1985) for a discussion.

18. This and the next subsection follow McDonald and Solow (1981).

19. Bishop (1964) was the first to advocate the use of the Nash bargain in this context. Apart from its intuitive appeal, the Nash bargaining solution can also be derived from axiomatic considerations (Nash 1953) or from game theoretic considerations (Binmore, Rubinstein, and Wolinsky 1986).

20. If we think of R as the utility of leisure, it may indeed be approximately constant. If we think of R as the wage available elsewhere, it is implausible to think that it is unaffected by aggregate fluctuations.

21. McDonald and Solow (1981) show that if instead of using a Nash bargain, the union and the firm agree on a "fair share" rule, $wL = k\theta F(L)$, for some k between 0 and 1, and if the elasticity of output with respect to labor is constant, the contract wage will again be constant.

22. If the firm was allowed to hire in excess of $\bar{L}$ at the union wage, the solution would be slightly different, and in an interesting way. For values of θ below some θ^*, the wage would be constant at w^*, the same value as appears in the text. For θ between θ^* and some θ^{**}, increases in θ would lead to increases in the wage, with $L = \bar{L}$. For θ greater than θ^{**}, the wage would, however, remain constant at some value w^{**}, and movements in θ would again translate into movements in employment along the labor demand curve. The intuition for this last segment is that, for very high values of θ, though increases in employment are of no value to union members, they are of great value to the firm. Under the Nash bargain the interests of the firm are sufficiently strong to lead to higher employment.

23. It is true that $N - \bar{L}$ are involuntarily unemployed. But given the exogeneity of $\bar{L}$ and our other assumptions, this is true by assumption.

24. An argument with the same structure, but applied to the behavior of oligopolies in the goods market, will be given later in the chapter.

25. Espinosa and Rhee show how such a model can explain rises in wages in dying industries where the horizon becomes short.

26. See Bils (1988) for a recent empirical attempt to see whether contracts are efficient. Bils concludes that the behavior of employment is not consistent with fully efficient contracts: new contracts appear to undo the unexpected and undesired consequences of previous contracts.

27. Lindbeck and Snower (1987) make progress along those lines. They do not, however, formalize the decision problem of the insiders as an explicitly dynamic one.

28. In relation to European unemployment, Blanchard and Summers discuss other reasons why membership effects may become stronger as membership decreases.

29. Even if the union fixes the nominal wage, one wonders why it does not find ways of constraining hiring by the firm or of organizing the union bylaws such that, for example, the current members maintain control of the union even if they lose their jobs.

30. The analogy between membership effects and some of the channels of persistence studied in chapter 7 should be clear. Both membership effects and, for example, costs of adjustment of employment for firms, make it difficult to understand why employment would vary much with shocks. But if it does, then both imply that the effects will last.

31. This follows Blanchard and Summers (1986).

32. The assumption of constant returns is chosen only for convenience. It implies that the real wage is constant, although employment fluctuates, because firms choose constant markups of prices over wages.

33. However, no such form was derived formally from any of the models presented or discussed earlier.

34. Yellen (1984), Stiglitz (1986), and Katz (1986) give excellent surveys. Katz also reviews the relevant facts. Bulow and Summers (1986) show how the efficiency wage hypothesis can shed light on a large number of issues in labor and macroeconomics.

35. We are assuming that the period is short enough that we can ignore terms that are products of b and q.

36. The assumption is that the worker is paid a wage and then fired or not fired. Shapiro and Stiglitz work with continuous time, which is more elegant, and derive slightly different conditions.

37. This is a comparative statics statement, since we have limited ourselves to an analysis of steady states. Note that we are implicitly comparing the decentralized outcome to the allocation that would be chosen by a central planner were he able to perfectly monitor effort. Another interesting comparison is with the allocation that would be chosen by a central planner having access to the same monitoring technology and thus having to satisfy the NSC. This is done by Shapiro and Stiglitz who show that the allocation would not be the same as that in the decentralized economy.

38. See Katz (1986) for a discussion.

39. If, instead of (38), we had assumed that firms pay the same wage as other firms, $W_i = W$ for all i, the equilibrium, even without menu costs, would be indeterminate. As output changed, and the markup required by firms also changed, workers would still supply labor as long as all wages were the same. This extreme case may well contain a grain of truth, since in high income economies, efficiency wage theories are more easily motivated by the assumption that workers are concerned about the wage they receive relative to wages elsewhere in the economy than by the real wage they receive relative to some absolute standard.

40. Although this way of putting the issue is simpler, it is also slightly misleading, since there is usually no "output supply" locus in imperfectly competitive markets. Shifts in the demand for goods trace out, however, a locus of price and quantity decisions, which can be thought of as "output supply."

41. See, for example, Tobin (1972) and Eckstein and Wyss (1972).

42. See Gordon (1979) for details and qualifications.

43. Bils notes that in the presence of implicit contracts, the overtime wage may not reflect the true marginal cost of labor to firms but rather an installment payment, paid for some reason, in periods of high hours. He uses two alternative methods to estimate marginal cost, one that treats the overtime wage as the true marginal cost of labor and one that does not.

44. Estimating a structural model of output and inventory decisions by firms, at the two-digit industry level, Ramey (1987) finds declining marginal costs of production. How these conclusions can be reconciled with Bils's results remains an open research question.

45. Note that this fact is difficult to reconcile with the results of Ramey, described earlier.

46. This is the natural outcome of Hotelling models of monopolistic competition in which increases in the number of products decrease the distance between products and increase demand elasticities. By contrast, the Dixit-Stiglitz formulation used in chapter 8 implies elasticities that are independent of the number of products.

47. This follows Woglom (1982).

48. This argument is made by Rotemberg (1987).

49. Weitzman (1982) has emphasized the importance for explaining aggregate fluctuations of the fact that individuals cannot produce what they need to consume. This led him to introduce fixed costs in production, making small scale production, for example, too costly to be used by the unemployed.

50. The potentially confusing notation arises because it will turn out that consumption is equal to an individual's output (hence y denotes consumption) and because effort represents the cost of production, c.

51. Note that the fact that both traders have only one unit of the good to trade implies that they will trade one good for the other. Put another way, the relative price of all goods is always one. The fact that relative prices are fixed in this model is one of the features that gives it its tractability. But this also makes it difficult to integrate with models of pricing discussed in the previous chapter.

52. This can be shown by differentiating the equality above with respect to time.

53. The focus of their paper is on the mechanics of development, and not on cycles.

54. As in the Diamond model, this set of assumptions fixes relative prices. This is one of the reasons why the model is so tractable. At the same time it also makes this model harder to integrate with those of the previous chapter.

55. In the present context this seems to be the more interesting case. The basic result, the lack of multiplicity, goes through in the other case as well.

56. Note that the traditional Keynesian multiplier story is similar, but with labor being implicitly available at zero opportunity cost.

57. A model of investment with increasing returns and with similar properties is developed by Kiyotaki (1987). His model is based on Dixit-Stiglitz monopolistic competition and is closely related to that presented in chapter 8.

58. Benjamin Friedman's empirical work (1983) supported the renewed emphasis on credit, though the relationship between credit and GNP appeared to shift subsequently. See Gertler (1987) for a useful review of the literature on financial structure and the macroeconomy.

59. Among earlier contributions are Jaffee and Modigliani (1969) and Jaffee and Russell (1976).

60. It turns out, though, that the type of theory of credit rationing we expound later implies that interest rate controls may increase rather than reduce the volume of lending. For a sophisticated analysis of interest rate controls in the context of modern theories of credit rationing, see Keeton (1979).

61. Many different versions of the basic setup can be found in the literature, for instance, in de Meza and Webb (1987) and English (1986). We draw below on de Meza and Webb.

62. This diagram is taken from Stiglitz and Weiss (1981).

63. In this case the supply "function" in the first quadrant would consist of two points.

64. Townsend (1979) pioneered in this area.

65. A very similar setup has been used by Williamson (1986) to generate both endogenous financial intermediaries and equilibrium credit rationing. Individual lending is dominated by the existence of a financial intermediary because the minimum scale of project is large and financial intermediaries are assumed to be efficient monitors. Debt rather than equity contracts are used to keep the expected costs of monitoring down.

66. The assumption is that the costs of control of the organization are increasing in the number of outside investors; the size of the investing coalition is determined endogenously, and it changes over the cycle.

References

Akerlof, George (1984). "Gift Exchange and Efficiency Wages: Four Views." *American Economic Review* 74 (May), 79–83.

Akerlof, George, and Janet Yellen (1985). "A Near-Rational Model of the Business Cycle, with Wage and Price Inertia." *Quarterly Journal of Economics* 100, supplement, 823–838.

Akerlof, George, and Janet Yellen (1987). "The Fair Wage-Effort Hypothesis and Unemployment." Mimeo. University of California, Berkeley. August.

Azariadis, Costas (1975). "Implicit Contracts and Underemployment Equilibria." *Journal of Political Economy* 83, 1183–1202.

Azariadis, Costas (1979). "Implicit Contracts and Related Topics: A Survey." In Z. Ernstein et al. (eds.), *The Economics of the Labour Market*. London: HMSO.

Baily, Martin (1974). "Wages and Employment under Uncertain Demand." *Review of Economic Studies* 41, 37–50.

Bentolila, Samuel, and Giuseppe Bertola (1987). "Firing Costs and Labor Demand in Europe: How Bad Is Eurosclerosis?" Mimeo. MIT.

Bernanke, Ben (1983). "Nonmonetary Effects of the Financial Crisis in the Propagation of the Great Depression." *American Economic Review* 73, 3 (June), 257–276.

Bernanke, Ben, and Mark Gertler (1986). "Agency Costs, Collateral, and Business Fluctuations." NBER Working Paper 2015.

Bernanke, Ben (1987). "Financial Fragility and Economic Performance." NBER Working Paper 2318.

Bils, Mark (1985). "Essays on the Cyclical Behavior of Price and Marginal Cost." Ph.D. dissertation. MIT.

Bils, Mark (1987). "The Cyclical Behavior of Marginal Cost and Price." *American Economic Review* 77, 5 (Dec.), 838–855.

Bils, Mark (1988). "Testing for Contracting Effects on Employment." Mimeo. University of Rochester. February.

Binmore, Ken, Ariel Rubinstein, and Asher Wolinsky (1986). "The Nash Bargaining Solution in Economic Modelling." *Rand Journal* 17, 176–188.

Blanchard, Olivier, and Lawrence Summers (1986). "Hysteresis and the European Unemployment Problem." *NBER Macroeconomics Annual*, 15–77.

Blanchard, Olivier, and Lawrence Summers (1988). "Beyond the Natural Rate Hypothesis." *American Economic Review* 78, 2 (May), 182–187.

Blinder, Alan S., and Joseph E. Stiglitz (1983). "Money, Credit Constraints, and Economic Activity." *American Economic Review*, Papers and Proceedings, 73, 2 (May), 297–302.

Bulow, Jeremy, and Lawrence Summers (1986). "A Theory of Dual Labor Markets with Application to Industrial Policy, Discrimination and Keynesian Unemployment." *Journal of Labor Economics* 4, 376–414.

Calvo, Guillermo (1979). "Quasi Walrasian Theories of Unemployment." *American Economic Review* 69 (May), 102–107.

Carlton, Dennis (1986). "The Rigidity of Prices." *American Economic Review* 76, 4 (Sept.), 637–658.

Carlton, Dennis (1987). "The Theory and the Facts of How Markets Clear: Is Industrial Organization Valuable for Understanding Macroeconomics?" In R. Schmalensee and R. Willig (eds.), *Handbook of Industrial Organization*, forthcoming.

De Meza, David, and David C. Webb (1987). "Too Much Investment: A Problem of Asymmetric Information." *Quarterly Journal of Economics* 102, 2 (May), 281–292.

Diamond, Peter (1982). "Aggregate Demand Management in a Search Equilibrium." *Journal of Political Economy* (Oct.), 881–894.

Diamond, Peter, and Drew Fudenberg (1987). "Rational Expectations Business Cycles in Search Equilibria." MIT Working Paper 465. October.

Dickens, William (1986). "Wages, Employment and the Threat of Collective Action by Workers." Mimeo. Berkeley.

Drazen, Allan, and Nils Gottfries (1987). "Seniority Rules and the Persistence of Unemployment in a Dynamic Optimizing Model." Mimeo. Tel Aviv. August.

Dunlop, John (1944). *Wage Determination under Trade Unions*. New York: Macmillan.

Eckstein, O., and David Wyss (1972). "Industry Price Equations." In O. Eckstein (ed.), *The Econometrics of Price Determination*. Washington, D.C.: Federal Reserve Board, 133–165.

English, William B. (1986). "Credit Rationing in General Equilibrium." University of Pennsylvania, Center for Analytic Research in Economics and the Social Sciences. Working Paper 86–20.

Espinosa, Maria, and Chang Yong Rhee (1987). "Efficient Wage Bargaining as a Repeated Game." Mimeo. Harvard University.

Farber, Henry (1978). "Individual Preferences and Union Wage Determination: The Case of the United Mine Workers." *Journal of Political Economy* 68, 923–942.

Farber, Henry (1987). "The Analysis of Union Behavior." In O. Ashenfelter and R. Layard (eds.), *Handbook of Labour Economics*. Amsterdam: North-Holland.

Friedman, Benjamin M. (1983). "The Roles of Money and Credit in Macroeconomic Analysis." In J. Tobin (ed.), *Macroeconomics, Prices and Quantities*. Washington D.C.: Brookings Institution.

Fudenberg, Drew, and Jean Tirole (1983). "Capital as a Commitment: Strategic Investment to Deter Mobility." *Journal of Economic Theory* 31 (Dec.), 227–250.

Gale, Douglas, and Martin Hellwig (1985). "Incentive-Compatible Debt Contracts I: The One-Period Problem." *Review of Economic Studies* 52 (Oct.), 647–664.

Gertler, Mark (1987). "Financial Structure and Aggregate Economic Activity: An Overview." Mimeo. University of Wisconsin.

Gordon, David (1974). "A Neoclassical Theory of Keynesian Unemployment." *Economic Inquiry* 12, 431–459.

Gordon, Robert (1979). " 'The End of Expansion' Phenomenon in Short Run Productivity Behavior." *Brookings Papers on Economic Activity* 2, 447–462.

Gottfries, Nils, and Henrick Horn (1987). "Wage Formation and the Persistence of Unemployment." *Economic Journal* 97 (Dec.), 877–886.

Gray, JoAnna, and Matthew Canzoneri (1984). "The Macroeconomic Implications of Labor Contracting with Asymmetric Information." Mimeo. Washington, D.C.: Federal Reserve Board.

Green, Jerry, and Charles Kahn (1983). "Wage-Employment Contracts." *Quarterly Journal of Economics* 98, supplement, 173–188.

Greenwald, Bruce G., and Joseph E. Stiglitz (1987). "Imperfect Information, Finance Constraints, and Business Fluctuations." In M. Kohn (ed.), *Taipei Symposium on Monetary Economics*. Oxford University Press.

Grossman, Sanford, Oliver Hart, and Eric Maskin (1983). "Unemployment with Observable Aggregate Shocks." *Journal of Political Economy* 91, 6 (Dec.), 907–928.

Gurley, John G., and Edward S. Shaw (1960). *Money in a Theory of Finance.* Washington, D.C.: Brookings Institution.

Hall, Robert (1986). "The Unit Elasticity Hypothesis and the Indeterminacy of Output." Mimeo. Stanford University. March.

Hall, Robert (1987). "A Non-Competitive, Equilibrium Model of Fluctuations." Mimeo. Stanford University. December.

Hall, Robert, and Edward Lazear (1984). "The Excess Sensitivity of Layoffs and Quits to Demand." *Journal of Labor Economics* 2, 233–257.

Hart, Oliver (1983). "Optimal Labour Contracts under Asymmetric Information: An Introduction." *Review of Economic Studies* 50, 3–35.

Hart, Oliver, and Bengt Holmstrom (1987). "The Theory of Contracts." In T. Bewley (ed.), *Advances in Economic Theory: 5th World Congress.* Cambridge University Press.

Howitt, Peter, and Preston McAfee (1987). "Costly Search and Recruiting." *International Economic Review* (Feb.), 89–107.

Howitt, Peter (1988). "Animal Spirits." Mimeo. University of Western Ontario.

Jackman, Richard, Richard Layard, and Steve Nickell (1988). "The Effect of Unions on Unemployment." Mimeo.

Jaffee, Dwight, and Franco Modigliani (1969). "A Theory and Test of Credit Rationing." *American Economic Review* 59, 5 (Dec.), 850–872.

Jaffee, Dwight, and Thomas Russell (1976). "Imperfect Information and Credit Rationing." *Quarterly Journal of Economics* 90, 4 (Nov.), 651–666.

Katz, Lawrence (1986). "Efficiency Wage Theories: A Partial Evaluation." *NBER Macroeconomics Annual*, 235–276.

Keeton, William (1979). "Equilibrium Credit Rationing." New York: Garland Press.

Kiyotaki, Nobuhiro (1987). "Multiple Expectational Equilibria under Monopolistic Competition." Mimeo. University of Wisconsin.

Layard, Richard, and Stephen Nickell (1987). "The Labour Market." In R. Dornbusch and R. Layard (eds.), *The Performance of the British Economy*, Oxford: Clarendon Press, 131–179.

Leontief, Wassily (1946). "The Pure Theory of the Guaranteed Annual Wage Contract." *Journal of Political Economy* 54, 76–79.

Lindbeck, Assar, and Dennis Snower (1986). "Wage Setting, Unemployment and Insider Outsider Relations." *American Economic Review* 76 (May), 235–239.

Lindbeck, Assar (1987). "Union Activity, Unemployment Persistence, and Wage Employment Ratchets." *European Economic Review* 31, 1/2, 157–67.

Mankiw, N. Gregory (1986). "The Allocation of Credit and Financial Collapse." *Quarterly Journal of Economics* 101 (Aug.), 455–470.

Maskin, Eric, and Jean Tirole (1986). "Dynamics of Oligopoly. Part III: Price Determination." Mimeo. MIT.

McDonald, Ian, and Robert Solow (1981). "Wage Bargaining and Employment." *American Economic Review* 71, 896–908.

Minford, Patrick (1982). *Unemployment, Cause and Cure*. Oxford: Martin Robertson.

Murphy, Kevin, Andrei Shleifer, and Robert Vishny (1987). "The Big Push." Mimeo. Chicago Business School.

Nash, John (1953). "Two-Person Cooperative Games." *Econometrica* 21, 128–140.

Nickell, Stephen (1982). "A Bargaining Model of the Phillips Curve." Discussion Paper 105. London School of Economics. Centre for Labour Economics.

Oswald, Andrew (1985). "The Economic Theory of Trade Unions: An Introductory Survey." *Scandinavian Journal of Economics* 87, 2, 160–193.

Oswald, Andrew (1987). "Efficient Contracts Are on the Labour Demand Curve: Theory and Facts." Mimeo. London School of Economics.

Pencavel, John (1985). "Wages and Employment under Trade Unionism: Microeconomic Models and Macroeconomic Applications." *Scandinavian Journal of Economics* 87, 2, 197–225.

Pigou, A. C. (1927). *Industrial Fluctuations*. London: Macmillan.

Committee on the Working of the Monetary System. Report (1959). (Radcliffe Report.) London: Her Majesty's Stationery Office.

Ramey, Valerie (1987). "Non-Convex Costs and the Behavior of Inventories." Mimeo. San Diego. December.

Ross, Arthur (1948). *Trade Union Wage Policy*. Berkeley: University of California Press.

Rotemberg, Julio (1987). "The New Keynesian Microfoundations." *NBER Macroeconomics Annual*, 69–104.

Rotemberg, Julio, and Garth Saloner (1986). "A Super Game Theoretic Model of Price Wars during Booms." *American Economic Review* 76, 3 (June), 390–407.

Rotemberg, Julio, and Garth Saloner (1987). "The Relative Rigidity of Monopoly Pricing." *American Economic Review* 77, 5 (Dec.), 917–926.

Salop, Steven (1979). "A Model of the Natural Rate of Unemployment." *American Economic Review* 69 (March), 117–125.

Shapiro, Carl, and Joseph Stiglitz (1984). "Equilibrium Unemployment as a Discipline Device." *American Economic Review* 74 (June), 433–444.

Shleifer, Andrei (1986). "Implementation Cycles." *Journal of Political Economy* 94, 6 (Dec.), 1163–1190.

Solow, Robert (1979). "Another Possible Source of Wage Stickiness." *Journal of Macroeconomics* 1, 79–82.

Stigler, George, and James Kindahl (1970). *The Behavior of Industrial Prices*. New York: National Bureau of Economic Research.

Stiglitz, Joseph (1976). "Prices and Queues as Screening Devices in Competitive Markets." IMSSS Technical Report 212. Stanford University.

Stiglitz, Joseph (1979). "Equilibrium in Product Markets with Imperfect Information." *American Economic Review* 69, 2 (May), 339–345.

Stiglitz, Joseph, and Andrew Weiss (1981). "Credit Rationing in Markets with Imperfect Information." *American Economic Review* 71, 3 (June), 393–410.

Stiglitz, Joseph (1985). "Credit Rationing and Collateral." Bell Communications Research Discussion Papers.

Stiglitz, Joseph (1986). "Theories of Wage Rigidities." In J. L. Butkiewicz et al. (eds.), *Keynes' Economic Legacy: Contemporary Economic Theories*. New York: Praeger.

Stiglitz, Joseph (1987). "Macro-Economic Equilibrium and Credit Rationing." NBER Working Paper 2164.

Tobin, James (1972). "The Wage-Price Mechanism: Overview of the Conference." In O. Eckstein (ed.), *The Econometrics of Price Determination*. Washington, D.C.: Federal Reserve System.

Townsend, Robert M. (1979). "Optimal Contracts and Competitive Markets with Costly State Verification." *Journal of Economic Theory* 21, 265–293.

Weitzman, Martin (1982). "Increasing Returns and the Foundations of Unemployment." *Economic Journal* 92, 787–804.

Williamson, Stephen D. (1986). "Costly Monitoring, Financial Intermediation, and Equilibrium Credit Rationing." *Journal of Monetary Economics* 18, 2 (Sept.), 159–180.

Woglom, Geoffrey (1982). "Underemployment with Rational Expectations." *Quarterly Journal of Economics* 97, 1 (Feb.), 89–108.

10   Some Useful Models

The range and complexity of the models developed in the previous chapters are testimony to the creativeness of macroeonomic theorists. But what good are those models for the working economist? Are they merely "mental gymnastics of a peculiarly depraved type" (Samuelson 1947), or are they useful and are they used?

In fact many of the models we have presented are used not only to clarify conceptual issues but also to explain current events and to help in the design and assessment of macroeconomic policy. In analyzing real world issues, almost all economists are eclectic, drawing on different models for different purposes. Sometimes the models we have analyzed are used as we presented them; more often the basic model has to be developed in a particular direction for the question at hand. Often the economist will use a simple *ad hoc* model, where an ad hoc model is one that emphasizes one aspect of reality and ignores others, in order to fit the purpose for which it is being used.[1]

Although it is widely adopted and almost as widely espoused, the eclectic position is not logically comfortable. It would clearly be better for economists to have an all-purpose model, derived explicitly from microfoundations and embodying all relevant imperfections, to analyze all issues in macroeconomics (or perhaps all issues in economics). We are not quite there yet. And if we ever were, we would in all likelihood have little understanding of the mechanisms at work behind the results of simulations. Thus we have no choice but to be eclectic.[2]

How does a good economist know what model to use for the question at hand? By being a good economist. Much of the art of economics lies in being able to know which unrealistic assumptions are merely peripheral to the issue at hand and which are crucial.[3]

In this chapter we present a (nonexhaustive) list of models that are useful for analyzing real world issues, and in each case we describe or present an application of the model. In the process we review many of the models we have seen, but we also introduce the workhorses of applied macroeconomics such as the IS-LM and the Mundell-Fleming models.

10.1 Equilibrium Models and Asset Pricing

If one believes that imperfections play a crucial role in macroeconomic fluctuations, why would one ever want to use the models developed in chapters 2 and 3, which assume perfectly competitive markets, or their counterparts in chapter 7, which extend the analysis to allow for the presence of uncertainty?

We can think of a number of cases in which this may be appropriate. The Ramsey model can, for example, be used in its normative interpretation. We may ask how an economy should react to an adverse technological shock, an increase in the price of its imports, or an increase in the interest rate it has to pay on its foreign debt. Should it cut consumption or investment, or should it, instead, increase its indebtedness? We have seen in chapter 2 how the open economy version of the Ramsey model can be used to analyze these issues. For issues having to do with intertemporal transfers, such as the burden of the debt and Ricardian Equivalence and the effects of pay-as-you-go social security, the two natural starting points are the Ramsey and the Diamond model with and without bequests. For these issues, imperfections in goods and labor markets may not be central, and it is a good strategy at first to leave them out.[4]

A third application is to asset pricing. Again, imperfections in goods and labor markets may not be crucial to the understanding of the relation between short- and long-term interest rates, or between returns on stocks and returns on bonds. Equilibrium business cycle models that incorporate uncertainty and asset choice by consumers provide a natural environment in which to study these issues. This is what we now do.

Let us return to the maximization problem of a consumer under uncertainty studied in chapter 6. The consumer, who has an horizon of T periods, maximizes

$$E\left[\sum_{t=0}^{T-1} (1 + \theta)^{-t} U(c_t)|0\right]. \tag{1}$$

We do not need to specify fully the dynamic budget constraint at this point. All we need to assume is that at time t the consumer can choose to carry his wealth in any of n risky assets, with a (net) stochastic rate of return z_{it},

$i = 1, \ldots, n$, and in a riskless asset, with a rate of return r_t. This implies a set of $n + 1$ first-order conditions at time t of the form

$$U'(c_t) = (1 + \theta)^{-1}E[U'(c_{t+1})(1 + z_{it})|t], \qquad i = 1, \ldots, n, \tag{2}$$

$$U'(c_t) = (1 + \theta)^{-1}(1 + r_t)E[U'(c_{t+1})|t]. \tag{3}$$

We have shown in chapter 6 how to derive these equations. Their interpretation is straightforward. The consumer must choose consumption such that, along the optimal path, marginal utility this period is equal to discounted expected marginal utility next period. This must be true at the margin no matter what asset, risky or riskless, is considered; this gives us the $n + 1$ first-order conditions. For risky assets, what matters is the expected value of the product of the marginal utility and the rate of return; both are uncertain as of time t. For the riskless asset, the rate of return, which is known at time t, can be taken out of the expectation. This gives equation (3).

The Consumption CAPM

Equations (2) and (3) give a set of joint restrictions on the processes for consumption and asset returns. In chapter 6 we thought of equations (2) and (3) as imposing restrictions on the behavior of consumption, given the process for asset returns. But we can, instead, think of them as telling us what the equilibrium asset returns must be, given the process for consumption.

By substituting (3) into (2), we obtain

$$0 = E[U'(c_{t+1})(z_{it} - r_t)|t], \qquad i = 1, \ldots, n. \tag{4}$$

Equivalently, and dropping the time index to denote conditional first and second moments (so that $E[\cdot|t]$ is denoted $E[\cdot]$, etc.),

$$0 = E[U'(c_{t+1})]E[z_{it} - r_t] + \text{cov}[U'(c_{t+1})z_{it}], \qquad i = 1, \ldots, n. \tag{5}$$

Thus the expected return on asset i in an equilibrium satisfies

$$E[z_{it}] = r_t - \frac{\text{cov}(U'(c_{t+1})z_{it})}{E[U'(c_{t+1})]}, \qquad i = 1, \ldots, n. \tag{6}$$

The higher the covariance of an asset's returns with the marginal utility of consumption, the lower is the equilibrium expected return on the asset. With diminishing marginal utility, the implication is that in equilibrium consumers are willing to accept a lower expected return on an asset that provides a hedge against low consumption by paying off more in states when consumption is low.

This equation must hold for any consumer who can freely choose between the $n + 1$ assets. If all consumers are identical and infinitely lived, then equation (6) holds, using the consumption of the representative individual, and, given a specification of utility, can be tested with data on aggregate consumption and asset returns.[5] If individuals are finitely lived but otherwise identical, we have to take into account that the consumption of those who are alive at both times t and $t + 1$ is not exactly the same as aggregate consumption at time t and $t + 1$; if we look at short intervals, however, this is unlikely to be a major issue. If individuals differ in other ways, in the form of the utility function or the presence of nondiversifiable income risk, for example, the conditions under which equation (6) can be tested using aggregate data are not likely to be satisfied (see Grossman and Shiller 1982). Nevertheless, equation (6) gives us a simple way of thinking about the determinants of asset returns.

The CAPM and Betas

Suppose that there exists an asset or a composite asset, m, whose return is perfectly negatively correlated with $U'(c_{t+1})$ [i.e., assume that $U'(c_{t+1}) = -\gamma z_{mt}$, for some γ]. It follows that for all risky assets,

$$\text{cov}[U'(c_{t+1})z_{it}] = -\gamma \, \text{cov}(z_{mt}z_{it}). \tag{7}$$

Further, for asset m, equation (6) implies that

$$E[z_{mt}] = r_t - \frac{\text{cov}[U'(c_{t+1})z_{mt}]}{E[U'(c_{t+1})]}$$

$$= r_t + \frac{\gamma \, \text{var}(z_{mt})}{E[U'(c_{t+1})]}. \tag{8}$$

By substituting (7) and (8) into (6), we obtain

$$E[z_{it}] - r_t = \left[\frac{\text{cov}(z_{it}z_{mt})}{\text{var}(z_{mt})} \right] (E[z_{mt}] - r_t), \tag{9}$$

or by defining β_i as $[\text{cov}(z_{it}z_{mt})/\text{var}(z_{mt})]$,

$$E[z_{it}] - r_t = \beta_i(E[z_{mt}] - r_t). \tag{10}$$

This equation is known in finance as the "security market line." If we interpret asset m as the asset composed of all existing tradable assets ("the market"), then equation (10) tells us that the expected return on a given asset in excess of the safe rate is proportional to the expected return on the market in excess of the safe rate. The coefficient of proportionality is equal to the coefficient β_i, which has the interpretation of a regression coefficient of z_{it} on z_{mt}.

This equation implies that a stock with a large variance of returns may or may not require a risk premium for consumers to hold it. If these variations are positively correlated with the market, the asset will have a large β and will indeed require a positive premium. If, however, the variations are uncorrelated with those of the market, the risk in holding the asset can in effect be diversified away, and the equilibrium return will be equal to the riskless rate. If a stock covaries negatively with the market, it provides a hedge, and consumers will be happy to hold it at an expected rate of return that is lower than the riskless rate.

A comparison between equations (6) and (10) shows the attractiveness of (10) for empirical purposes. The equilibrium relation in (10) between the market expected rate of return, the riskless rate, and the rate of return on any asset does not involve the specification of preferences and risk aversion. Computing the beta of a security can be done using a simple regression. As a result betas have become a standard product in applied finance. They are commercially available and are used in stock market analysis. The asset m used in the calculation of the betas is typically the entire stock market.

Although we have derived the security market line from the consumption CAPM (capital asset-pricing model) and the assumption of perfect negative correlation between the return on the market portfolio and the marginal utility of consumption, its derivation actually precedes the derivation of the consumption CAPM. It was derived, in what is now known as the standard or traditional CAPM, by Lintner (1965), Mossin (1966), and Sharpe (1964). The derivation was based on a two-period model in which utility was either defined directly over the mean and variance of portfolio returns or assumed to be quadratic. Merton (1973) showed under what conditions the standard capital asset-pricing formulas could be derived in continuous time from intertemporal optimization of consumers over portfolio choices and consumption.

In essence, the standard CAPM should be a good approximation to asset pricing when the marginal utility of consumption is highly correlated with the return on the stock market, or more generally the portfolio of tradable assets. This is more likely to be the case if most assets are tradable: the presence of a large nontradable asset such as human wealth is likely to decrease the correlation. In this case the consumption CAPM may do better.[6] In practice, however, the consumption CAPM (using data on aggregate consumption) appears to describe asset returns less accurately than the standard CAPM (Mankiw and Shapiro 1986).

The Lucas Asset-Pricing Model

In chapter 6 we thought of the first-order conditions of the consumer optimization problem as imposing restrictions on consumption given asset returns. We have used them above, instead, to think about restrictions on asset returns given consumption. In fact, though there is nothing wrong with either interpretation, both consumption and asset returns are endogenous and respond to shocks affecting the economy. Ultimately, it is these reactions to exogenous shocks that we would like to understand. This is generally very hard. Lucas (1978) cut through the difficulty by considering an exchange economy in which output each period was exogenous and perishable. This in effect makes consumption equal to output in equilibrium and thus exogenous; the first-order conditions can then be used to price assets as a function of (exogenous) consumption. Although this would appear to eliminate the difficulty rather than to solve it, the model has proved extremely useful to study a range of empirical issues. We briefly present it and discuss a few implications.

There are n risky assets in the economy, each of which generates a stochastic physical return in the form of perishable manna, equal to d_{it} per period. (The assets can usefully be thought of as trees, and output as seedless apples.) The assets are the only source of income in the economy. Denote by p_{it} the ex-dividend price of asset i in period t. Let p_t and d_t be the $n \times 1$ vectors of prices and dividends at time t.

The economy consists of identical infinitely lived consumers. The representative consumer maximizes

$$E\left[\sum_{t=0}^{\infty} (1 + \theta)^{-t} U(c_t) | 0\right].$$

In any period the consumer receives dividends on the assets that he holds. He then decides how much to consume and what assets to hold into the next period. Let x_{it} be the quantity of asset i that the consumer holds between t and $t + 1$. Let x_t be the $n \times 1$ vector of x_{it}. The budget constraint can then be written as

$$c_t + p_t'x_t = (p_t + d_t)'x_{t-1}.$$

The right-hand side gives the value of the portfolio chosen at time $t - 1$, as of time t, including dividends. The left-hand side is equal to consumption plus the value of the portfolio chosen at time t. The first-order conditions are

$$p_{it} U'(c_t) = (1 + \theta)^{-1} E[U'(c_{t+1})(p_{it+1} + d_{it+1})|t], \qquad i = 1, \dots, n. \qquad (11)$$

For market equilibrium, the quantities of each asset demanded must be equal to the exogenous supply. Assuming that there is one unit of each asset, equilibrium implies that $x_{it} = 1$ for all i, t. From the budget constraint this implies that $c_t = \sum d_{it}$: consumption must be equal to output, which is the sum of dividends. Thus equation (11) gives us a recursive relation determining the price of the asset as a function of exogenous variables, the d_{it}'s. We can solve equation (11) forward to get, assuming no bubbles,

$$p_{it} = E\left[\sum_{j=1}^{\infty} (1 + \theta)^{-j} \left(\frac{U'(c_{t+j})}{U'(c_t)} \right) d_{it+j} | t \right]. \qquad (12)$$

The price is equal to the expected present discounted value of dividends, where the discount rate used for $t + j$ is the marginal rate of substitution between consumption at time $t + j$ and consumption at time t. Although the right-hand side only depends on the joint distribution of endowments and is exogenous, it is far from easy to see how it behaves over time. To go further, it is necessary to make assumptions about either the utility function or the distribution of returns.

Assume first that consumers are risk neutral so that $U'(c)$ is constant. Then the price is given by

$$p_{it} = E\left[\sum_{j=1}^{\infty} (1 + \theta)^{-j} d_{it+j} | t \right]. \qquad (13)$$

This is a familiar formula from chapter 5. The price is equal to the present discounted value of expected dividends, discounted at a constant rate, which is the subjective discount rate of consumers. Movements in prices come from movements in expected dividends. It is this pricing formula that is often tested in the volatility tests described in chapter 5.

Assume, instead, that consumers are risk averse. Assume that there is only one asset (or equivalently that we are looking at the price of the market portfolio), with dividend d_t, so that $c_t = d_t$. Assume further that utility is logarithmic. Then the price p_t of the single asset is given by

$$p_t = E\left[\sum_{j=1}^{\infty} (1 + \theta)^{-j} \left(\frac{d_t}{d_{t+j}} \right) d_{t+j} | t \right] = \left(\frac{1}{\theta} \right) d_t.$$

In this case the price of the stock depends only on the current dividend, and not on future expected dividends. This is in sharp contrast with the previous case. Two things happen when consumers expect higher dividends at time $t + j$. The first is, as before, that at given marginal rates of substitution, higher dividends increase the price. But higher dividends also mean higher consumption, and thus lower marginal utility: other things being equal, dividends are valued less when times are good and consumption is high. Put another way, higher dividends in this case are associated with increases in interest rates. The result, in the logarithmic utility case, is to leave prices unchanged. This example is a useful, if somewhat extreme, counterexample to the idea that higher expected dividends necessarily increase prices.

Why is the Lucas model of more than academic interest? Because equation (12) holds whether or not the economy is an exchange economy. If the representative agent assumption is correct or, more generally, if aggregation conditions are satisfied, equation (12) holds, given the process for aggregate consumption, so long as agents can freely choose the composition of their portfolio. Thus substantial research has gone into asking whether, given the actual process followed by aggregate consumption, the pricing of assets is roughly consistent with equation (12). Campbell (1986), for example, has used this model to study how the process for consumption determines the term structure of interest rates, that is, the relation between yields to maturity on bonds of different duration. Mehra and Prescott (1985) have examined whether this model can explain the large premium of average stock returns over riskless bonds, which for the United States has been historically around 6%.[7] They parameterize the consumption process as a Markov process for the growth rate of consumption so as to fit the postwar process for consumption. They then derive the risk premium and the riskless rate as a function of alternative values of the discount rate and the degree of relative risk aversion. Their conclusion is that there is no set of parameters that can explain both the riskless rate and the the equity premium. The size of the equity premium is much larger than can be obtained from any plausible estimate of risk aversion. This result has triggered further research on how heterogeneity in consumers may explain the empirical premium (e.g., Mankiw 1986). This research has potentially important implications, for example, on how to think about the golden rule under uncertainty.

10.2 Money Demand Models, Deficits, Seigniorage, and Inflation

We used money demand models in chapter 4 to study the dynamics of inflation. We argued there that the use of such ad hoc models, which implicitly assume that real variables are either constant or move slowly

Table 10.1
Deficit/GNP ratio and inflation in Israel, 1974–1986

	1974	1975	1976	1977	1978	1979	1980
Deficit/GNP (%)	18.8	23.5	12.1	14.9	18.2	11.1	11.6
Inflation (%)	56	23	38	43	48	111	133

	1981	1982	1983	1984	1985	1986
Deficit/GNP	20.6	11.3	4.9	16.9	4.2	−7.1
Inflation	101	131	191	445	185	20

Note: Inflation = rate of change of the CPI.

enough compared to nominal variables that their movement can be ignored, could be appropriate when the focus is on times of high inflation. We now extend our earlier analysis of the relation between deficits and inflation.

Students of hyperinflation (e.g., Sargent 1982; Dornbusch and Fischer 1986) often stress the role of the budget deficit in the inflationary process, reporting that fiscal reform seems, in practice, to be an essential component of a stabilization program. A common criticism of this stress on the budget deficit is that the data rarely show a strong positive association between the size of the budget deficit and the inflation rate. Table 10.1 illustrates this fact with annual data on the budget deficit as a percentage of GNP and the inflation rate in Israel over the period 1974 to 1986.

One possible explanation is that deficits are in fact associated, at different times, with different expectations of money growth in the future. In the face of high deficits, people may anticipate that the government will have no choice but to increase its use of seigniorage. Or they may expect that under such pressure the government will be forced to introduce drastic fiscal reform and to reestablish budget balance through higher taxes. These are likely to lead to different inflation rates today. This argument is explored by Drazen and Helpman (1988) and has the following structure:[8]

Consider an economy in which money demand is given by

$$\frac{M}{PY} = \phi(r + \pi^*),\tag{14}$$

where Y is output, r is the real rate of interest, and π^* is the expected rate of inflation; both Y and r are assumed to be constant in what follows. Money demand is decreasing in the nominal interest rate: $\phi'(\ ) < 0$. Furthermore it is assumed that $\pi\phi(r + \pi)$ is increasing in π for $\pi < \pi'$ and decreasing in π for $\pi > \pi'$. This implies that the graph of seigniorage revenue against the inflation rate has the Laffer curve property.

The government is running a deficit equal to δ (as a ratio to GNP). The primary deficit, δ_0, is assumed to be constant and positive so that the deficit follows

$$\delta = \delta_0 + rb, \tag{15}$$

where b is the ratio of government bonds to GNP. The higher the government debt, the larger are the interest payments on the debt and the higher is the deficit.

The government finances the deficit by both money creation and the issue of bonds. It finances a share α of the deficit by printing money and a share $1 - \alpha$ by borrowing. Thus

$$\frac{dM/dt}{PY} = \alpha\delta \tag{16}$$

and

$$\frac{db}{dt} = (1 - \alpha)\delta. \tag{17}$$

By substituting (15) into (17), we see clearly that debt dynamics are unstable:

$$\frac{db}{dt} = (1 - \alpha)[\delta_0 + rb]. \tag{18}$$

Thus the financing of the budget has to change at some point. The simplest (if not the most realistic) assumption is that it is known that fiscal reform will take place at time T and that it will take one of two forms. The first is that the government will move entirely to money financing of the deficit;[9] the other is that it will close the budget gap through increased taxes and no longer use seigniorage. We examine the dynamics of inflation under these alternative assumptions.

Money Financing

By differentiating (14) with respect to time, assuming perfect foresight, $\pi = \pi^*$, and substituting in (16), we obtain

$$\phi'(r + \pi)\left(\frac{d\pi}{dt}\right) = \alpha(\delta_0 + rb) - \pi\phi(r + \pi). \tag{19}$$

Equations (18) and (19) characterize the dynamics of inflation and debt (before time T). We plot these dynamics in the (π, b) space in figure 10.1.

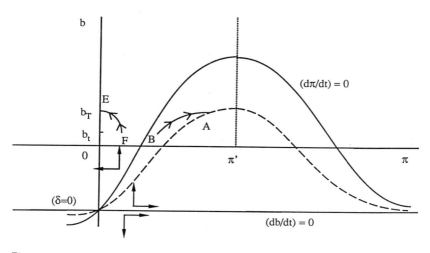

Figure 10.1
Dynamics of inflation and debt

From (19) the locus $d\pi/dt = 0$ is such that seigniorage, $\alpha(\delta_0 + rb)$, is equal to the inflation tax, $\pi\phi(r + \pi)$. Given our assumptions on money demand, for low levels of inflation, an increase in inflation increases the inflation tax and thus increases the feasible level of debt. When $\pi = \pi'$, seigniorage is maximized: this gives us the highest level of debt consistent with constant inflation. As we consider higher levels of inflation, seigniorage declines, and so does the level of sustainable debt. Given that δ_0 is positive, if inflation and thus the inflation tax are equal to zero, the government must be a net creditor: interest payments have to offset the primary deficit.

The locus $db/dt = 0$ is the horizontal line on which $\delta = 0$. This again requires the government to be a net creditor and to earn sufficient interest to offset the positive primary deficit.

The equations of motion are shown by the arrows: debt is increasing above the line $\delta = 0$ and decreasing below that line; from (19) the inflation rate is increasing below the locus $d\pi/dt = 0$ and decreasing above it. These dynamics are unlike any we have seen until now. If the economy does not start at $\delta = \pi = 0$, it does not converge. It is also unclear how inflation is determined. Although b is clearly given at any point in time, how are we to choose the inflation rate? (The assumption we have used many times that the economy chooses the saddle point path is not useful here: there is no saddle point path.)

Both problems reflect the same underlying fact: in the absence of a change in policy, debt will increase without bounds. It is precisely the expectation of a change in policy that ties down the dynamics of inflation. Consider the case where it is believed that the government will take action at time T to stop debt accumulation by switching to complete money financing of the deficit: By integrating (18) from t to T, we can calculate the value of the debt at T given the value of debt at time t, the primary deficit, and the interest rate. Call this value b_T. Given this value b_T, we can compute the inflation rate that is consistent from time T on with full financing of the deficit by money creation, thus with debt stabilization at level b_T from time T on. From equation (19), with $\alpha = 1$, this inflation rate is given by

$$\pi\phi(r + \pi) = \delta_0 + rb_T.$$

The locus of inflation rates as a function of b_T is drawn in figure 10.1. It coincides with the $d\pi/dt = 0$ locus for $\delta = 0$. It is then strictly below it for values of δ: if money creation has to finance the whole deficit, rather than just a fraction α of it, a given rate of money creation can only sustain a lower level of debt. This locus also reaches a maximum at π'.

We can now characterize the dynamics of inflation. Assume that b_T is at the level drawn in figure 10.1. At that level of debt there are two possible inflation rates.[10] Suppose that it is believed that the economy will converge to the lower inflation rate.[11] Then, given b_T, the point to which the economy must converge at time T is determined. That is the point A in figure 10.1. This in turn determines inflation at time t: Given debt at time t, say, b_t, the inflation rate at time t must be such that if the economy follows the equations of motion (18) and (19), it ends up at point A at time T.[12] This determines uniquely the inflation rate at time t. We show such a path starting at B. Clearly on this path the inflation rate is increasing over time along with the debt. With the debt rising, the deficit is also increasing. Thus under the assumption that the fiscal change will involve a shift to complete money financing of the deficit, the inflation rate and the deficit increase together over time until the stabilization takes place at T.

The analysis raises an interesting possibility that is examined by Sargent and Wallace (1981). Suppose that the government decreases the share of the deficit financed by money creation. By itself this would tend to decrease inflation. But, if the government is expected to shift to full money financing at time T, lower money creation means faster accumulation of debt between now and T and higher money creation after T; anticipations of high money growth in the future imply higher inflation today. Sargent and Wallace, using the Cagan money demand function, show the effect to be ambiguous: it is possible in this case for inflation to increase in response to lower money creation today.

Tax Financing

Alternatively, suppose that the stabilization program, when it comes, is expected to involve an increase in taxes. That means that the inflation rate will not be used at all and that the steady state inflation rate will be zero. The economy will accordingly end at the point E in figure 10.1. Starting from b_t, the initial inflation rate has to be such that the economy converges to point E at time T. In figure 10.1 the starting point is F, from which the economy converges to E over time, with an increasing debt, and therefore an increasing deficit, but a declining inflation rate. On the path FE the deficit is rising, but the inflation rate is falling. Thus on this path there is a negative correlation between the inflation rate and the deficit. The reason is that the current inflation rate is affected by future (expected) inflation rates and that the closer the economy comes to time T, the closer it comes to an expected inflation rate of zero.

Drazen and Helpman's (1988) explanation of the empirical failure to find an association between the budget deficit and inflation is that expectations of how the deficit will be closed may change during the course of the inflationary process. Early in the inflation it is entirely possible that in-dividuals believe that the accumulating debt will lead to greater inflation in the future. But then as the debt becomes large, individuals may believe that a comprehensive fiscal package, possibly setting the inflation rate to zero, is virtually essential. If the time of stabilization, T, occurs when the debt has passed the level at which the maximal steady state seigniorage is too small to pay the interest, then it is certain that the stabilization will have to include a fiscal element. Thus it is quite possible that even with an increasing deficit and national debt, the inflation rate will fall over time as the prospect that the budget deficit will be cut increases.

One other aspect of the adjustment paths in figure 10.1 deserves attention: seigniorage revenue at each moment of time would be same on path BA as on FE. Thus by comparing two economies, one with a rising and one with a falling inflation rate, we can observe exactly the same seigniorage revenue being collected in each.

Finally, we note that the precise paths followed by inflation and bonds depend on the assumptions made about deficit financing. Where we have as-sume constant shares of the deficit financed by borrowing and seigniorage, Drazen and Helpman assume a constant growth rate of money, with the remainder financed by borrowing; another possibility is that the government collects a constant amount of seigniorage revenue and finances the re-mainder by borrowing.

10.3 Aggregate Supply and Demand, Wage Indexation, and Supply Shocks

The following model has played a central role in the analysis of economic fluctuations in the presence of nominal rigidities:

$$y^d = m - p + v, \tag{20}$$

$$y^s = \beta(p - w + u), \qquad \beta > 0, \tag{21}$$

$$n^d = \gamma(p - w + \alpha u), \qquad \gamma > 0, 0 \leqslant \alpha \leqslant 1, \tag{22}$$

$$n^s = \delta(w - p), \qquad \delta \geqslant 0, \tag{23}$$

$$w \mid En^d = En^s, \qquad n = n^d. \tag{24}$$

Here y, n, w, and p are the logarithms of aggregate output, employment, the nominal wage, and the price level, respectively, and u and v are supply and demand shocks. Constants are ignored for notational simplicity, and all variables are implicitly indexed by t. For any variable x, Ex denotes $E[x|u(-i), v(-i), i = 1, \ldots, \infty]$; it is the expectation of x conditional on lagged, but not on current, values of u and v.

The simplest motivation for equation (20), aggregate demand, is simply as a statement of the quantity theory equation or the Clower constraint, with velocity assumed to be exogenous.

The next two equations give output supply and labor demand as functions of the real wage and a technological shock. They can be derived frc_n profit maximization under perfect competition. As we saw in chapter 8, they can also be derived as implicit supply and demand functions under imperfect competition; equation (21) can be inverted to give the price set by firms given the nominal wage, the technological shock, and the level of output. The parameters β, γ, and α depend on the technology and are likely to be related; we do not specify this relation here.[13] An interesting special case, which we considered at various points in chapter 9, is that of constant returns to labor in which the price depends only on the wage and the technological shock, and not on the level of output.

The last two equations characterize wage setting. Equation (23) is labor supply. Equation (24) specifies the nature of the nominal rigidity: the nominal wage is set so as to equalize expected labor demand and expected labor supply. Given the nominal wage, employment is determined by labor demand. Again, as we saw in chapter 9, the behavior of the nominal wage implied by (23) and (24) can be given noncompetitive interpretations. The wage may be set by bargaining between firms and workers, with the nominal wage set one period in advance. Or the wage may be set by firms, based on efficiency wage considerations, and again set one period in advance.

The model can be simplified further. By substituting (22) and (23) into (24) and taking expectations conditional on the information set, we obtain the nominal wage:

$$w = Ep + \left(\frac{\alpha\gamma}{\delta + \gamma}\right) Eu. \tag{25}$$

The nominal wage is equal to the expected price level plus a non-decreasing function of the expected technological shock. Unless labor supply is perfectly elastic, an expected positive shock leads to an increase in both employment and wages. Replacing in equation (21), and utilizing equation (20), gives

$$y^d = m - p + v, \tag{20}$$

$$y^s = \beta(p - Ep) + \beta(u - aEu), \tag{26}$$

$$a \equiv \frac{\alpha\gamma}{\delta + \gamma}.$$

The output supplied depends on the unexpected movement in the price level as well as on the actual and the expected technological shock. The reason for the presence of the last term is that an anticipated positive technological shock leads workers to increase their real wage demands, thus decreasing its effect on equilibrium output. The coefficient a is between zero and one. It is equal to zero only when labor supply is perfectly elastic (or more generally when wage-setters want to set a constant real wage, regardless of the level of employment), if δ is infinite. Note also the similarity of equations (20) and (26) with the equilibrium model of Lucas analyzed in chapter 7. The Lucas supply curve is also given by equation (26) (except for the productivity terms). In that model suppliers react, under imperfect information, to perceived relative price differentials. Although the mechanism is different, the equations are the same.

Equations (20) and (26) give us a simple aggregate demand-aggregate supply system. Stripped down as this model is, it has nevertheless been immensely useful. It was particularly helpful in understanding the basic effects of supply shocks and the pros and cons of wage indexation in the 1970s.[14]

Supply Shocks, Output, and Inflation

The first oil shock of 1973 presented an analytic problem to economists who up to that point were used to thinking of most shocks as coming from the demand side. The analytic problem was to explain the simultaneous existence of high inflation and recession.

The supply-demand system gives a simple answer. Figure 10.2 shows the aggregate demand curve, given money and velocity, and the aggregate supply curve, given the expected price level and the expected value of the supply shock as embodied in the nominal wage. Aggregate demand is downward sloping, and aggregate supply upward sloping. An unexpected adverse supply shock shifts the aggregate supply curve to the left, to AS', shifting the economy's equilibrium to E', with a higher price level and a lower level of output. Given the past price level, a higher price level means higher inflation. This is a strikingly simple explanation for simultaneous high inflation and low output.

The figure also makes clear the well-known dilemma of aggregate demand policy confronted with an adverse supply shock: any attempt to fight the higher price level by reducing the money supply further reduces output, but trying to maintain the level of output with an expansionary monetary policy means a higher price level. This, however, raises another more basic question: Should demand policy actually be used (assuming that it can be used) to stabilize output in the presence of such shocks?

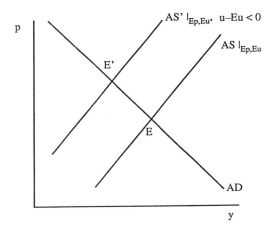

Figure 10.2
Effects of an adverse supply shock

A good starting point is to compare the response of output to supply shocks in the presence and absence of nominal rigidities. Suppose first that there were no nominal rigidities, that, for example, wages could be set after observing the shock. In this case, from (26), output would react to the supply shock according to

$$y = \beta(1 - a)u, \tag{27}$$

or equivalently

$$y = \beta(1 - a)(u - Eu) + \beta(1 - a)Eu.$$

In the presence of nominal rigidities, we must first solve for the expected price level and then for the actual price level and output. Eliminating output between (20) and (26) and taking expectations gives

$$Ep = Em + Ev - \beta(1 - a)Eu.$$

Replacing this in (26) and solving for output gives

$$y = \left(\frac{\beta}{1 + \beta}\right)(m - Em + v - Ev + u - Eu) + \beta(1 - a)Eu. \tag{28}$$

The response of output to expected supply shocks is, not surprisingly, the same in both cases. Whether nominal rigidities increase the response of output to unexpected supply shocks is, however, ambiguous and depends on whether $1/(1 + \beta)$ exceeds $1 - a$. If labor supply is completely elastic, or equivalently if wage-setters desire a constant expected real wage that is independent of employment, then $a = 0$, and output moves less in the presence of nominal rigidities. The more inelastic is labor supply, the higher is a, and the lower will be the variability of output without nominal rigidities (i.e., the more likely are nominal rigidities to destabilize output in the presence of supply shocks).

The intuition for this result can be derived from figure 10.3. Figure 10.3a plots supply and demand, absent nominal rigidities, and shows the effects of an adverse unexpected supply shock. The shift in the vertical supply curve is equal to $\beta(1 - a)(u - Eu)$. Unless $a = 1$, an adverse supply shock leads to lower output even in the absence of nominal rigidities: y declines to y'. Figure 10.3b plots supply and demand under nominal rigidities. The supply curve, equation (26), is now upward sloping, with slope β. An adverse unexpected supply shock shifts the supply curve by $\beta(u - Eu)$, decreasing output from y to y''. Whether y' is smaller than y'' is ambiguous, since there are two effects at work. Because wages are set in advance, they can respond

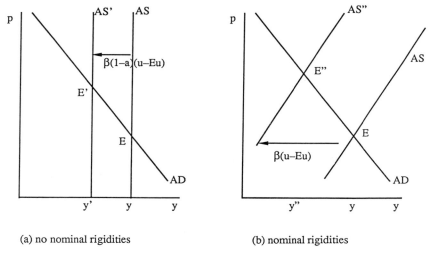

(a) no nominal rigidities   (b) nominal rigidities

Figure 10.3
Effects of an adverse supply shock, with or without nominal rigidities

neither to unexpected movements in the supply shock nor to those in the price level. That they cannot respond to the supply shock is (unless $a = 1$) unambiguously destabilizing: if they could adjust, wages would decrease in response to the adverse shock, mitigating the effect of the shock on output. That they cannot respond to the price level is, however, stabilizing: an adverse supply shock increases the price level, thus automatically decreasing real wages. Whether this second effect leads to a sufficient decrease in real wages is doubtful, and it depends, as we have seen, on the parameters of the model.

We therefore do not get an unambiguous answer to the first question. But suppose that the answer was, for example, that nominal rigidities led to more fluctuations in output in response to supply shocks. Would this imply that trying to stabilize output by the use of, say, monetary policy is desirable? The answer to this second question is equally ambiguous but for a different set of reasons. If apart from the nominal rigidity the economy were otherwise undistorted, then there would be a strong case for trying to achieve the same outcome as would arise without nominal rigidities. Thus, if output responded excessively to a real disturbance—drought, an earthquake, or an oil price shock, for example—there would be a strong case for using nominal money to decrease, though not to eliminate, the effects of the disturbance on output. But the presence of other distortions complicates the answer. If, for example, considerations of efficiency wages are important in the labor market, there is no reason to give much normative significance to the no-nominal-rigidity equilibrium. Or shocks may reflect nontechnological factors, such as a push for higher wages, coming from a stronger bargaining position of insiders. The best policy in this case may well be to negate the effect of the shock on output and employment by an expansion of the money stock.[15] When these considerations are important, as we have argued that they are, the model presented above can no longer help us to assess what policy should try to achieve. A normative analysis must start much closer to microfoundations, that is, from the models reviewed in chapters 8 and 9.

Wage Indexation

A very similar set of issues arises in the context of wage indexation. Although wage indexation had been widely thought to be attractive in protecting workers' real wages from unanticipated inflation and in reducing the effects of nominal fluctuations on output, its desirability was questioned in the 1970s in the face of the large supply shocks. Analyses of the implications of wage indexation under different types of shocks were provided by Gray (1976) and Fischer (1977). The above model provides a convenient framework to use in thinking about the issues.

Suppose that wages, instead of being predetermined, can be partially or fully indexed to the price level. That is, instead of being determined by equation (25), wages are given by

$$w = \left[Ep + \left(\frac{\alpha\gamma}{\delta + \gamma} \right) Eu \right] + \lambda(p - Ep). \tag{25'}$$

The coefficient λ is the degree of indexation. There is full indexation when $\lambda = 1$, and no indexation when $\lambda = 0$. Note that in accordance with reality, indexation does not allow wages to respond to other variables than the price level; in particular, it does not allow for a direct response to unexpected supply shocks. Substituting (25') into (21) gives us a modified aggregate demand-supply system:

$$y^d = m - p + v, \tag{20}$$

$$y^s = \beta(1 - \lambda)(p - Ep) + \beta(u - aEu). \tag{26'}$$

The effect of unanticipated movements in the price level on output is inversely related to the degree of indexation. Under full indexation output is unaffected by unexpected price level movements.

To study the effects of wage indexation, we solve for output and the price level. To simplify notation, we assume that v is identically equal to zero and that both m and u are white noise so that Em and Eu are equal to zero. Given these assumptions, we obtain

$$p = \left[\frac{1}{1 + \beta(1 - \lambda)}\right](m - \beta u), \tag{29}$$

$$y = \left[\frac{1}{1 + \beta(1 - \lambda)}\right][\beta(1 - \lambda)m + \beta u]. \tag{30}$$

Higher indexing (a higher value of λ) unambiguously increases the variance of the price level, increasing its response to both money and supply shocks. The effects of indexing on the variance of output depend on the source of shocks. By making wages respond, through the price level, to nominal disturbances, indexing decreases the real effects of money on output. But by decreasing the response of real wages to supply shocks, indexing increases the response of output to supply shocks. The mechanisms at work are the same as those described earlier.

What is therefore the optimal degree of indexing? This question gets us back into the issues discussed above. It requires us to specify what we think the optimal response of output should be to supply shocks, something we cannot answer without being much more specific about the nature of shocks and distortions in the economy.

Suppose, for example, that nominal rigidities are the only source of distortions. We may want to look at the variation in output around its value in the absence of nominal rigidities, $y^* = \beta(1 - a)u$. We briefly consider this case. Suppose that we give no weight to price fluctuations and thus try to minimize the variance of $y - y^*$. What is then the optimal degree of indexation? From (30),

$$y - y^* = \left[\frac{1}{1 + \beta(1 - \lambda)}\right]\beta(1 - \lambda)m + \beta\left\{\left[\frac{1}{1 + \beta(1 - \lambda)}\right] - (1 - a)\right\}u.$$

Minimizing the variance of $y - y^*$ gives us an optimal value for λ. Rather than writing down the solution, we consider two special cases. If the variance of supply shocks is equal to zero (if $u \equiv 0$), then $\lambda^* = 1$. In an economy in which nominal disturbances dominate, full indexing is optimal. If the variance of nominal shocks is equal to zero (if $m \equiv 0$), then $\lambda^* = 1 - [a/(1 - a)\beta] < 1$. It is optimal to let the real wage decrease in response to adverse supply shocks and thus to have less than full indexing. In the general case it is easy to show that the optimal degree of indexation is a decreasing function of the variance of supply shocks relative to that of monetary shocks. Thus, to the extent that the 1970s were a period of large supply shocks, full indexation was indeed a bad idea.

Research on indexation has considerably progressed since those early papers (e.g., see Dornbusch and Simonsen 1983). It has studied why wages are indexed only to the price level and whether indexation to other aggregates might not dominate price level indexation. It has examined the implications of actual indexing rules in which wages do not respond to current but to past inflation developments. It has studied how indexation changes the rules of the policy game and optimal monetary policy. But the basic model is still at the core of current developments.

Learning about Permanent and Transitory Shocks

It was frequently argued in 1973 that the oil price shock was transitory, likely to last about six months; in fact, it was simply not clear at the time whether the shock was permanent or transitory. Uncertainty about the permanence of the shock must have slowed real adjustment to it, for instance, the adaptation of the capital stock to the higher price of energy. We now show, using the above model, how this uncertainty may have contributed to the dynamics of price level and output adjustment. By using this otherwise static model, we isolate most clearly this particular source of dynamics. In what follows, we draw on an important article by Muth (1960) on the formation of expectations.

Suppose that the supply shock, u_t (we now reintroduce the time index), is the sum of two components, one that displays persistence and follows a random walk and another that is white noise:

$$u_t = e_{1t} + e_{2t},$$
$$e_{1t} = e_{1t-1} + \varepsilon_{1t},$$

$$(31)$$

where ε_{1t} and e_{2t} are uncorrelated and both white noise, with zero mean and variances σ_1^2 and σ_2^2, respectively. The only information available to individuals is past values of u_t; even ex post they cannot observe separately the two components of u, e_1, and e_2.

The key result on which we draw is that

$$E[u_t|t] \equiv E[u_t|u_{t-j}, j = 1, 2, \ldots] = \sum_{j=1}^{\infty} \theta_j u_{t-j},$$

$$(32)$$

where

$$\theta_j \equiv (1 - \lambda)\lambda^{j-1}, \qquad j = 1, 2, \ldots,$$

$$\lambda \equiv \frac{z - \sqrt{(z^2 - 4)}}{2}, \qquad \text{with } z \equiv 2 + \left(\frac{\sigma_1^2}{\sigma_2^2}\right)$$

so that

$$1 > \lambda > 0, \qquad \frac{\partial \lambda}{\partial(\sigma_1^2/\sigma_2^2)} < 0.$$

The result is that the expectation of the supply shock, u, in the next period, conditional on past values of u, is a distributed lag on past values of u, with weights that decline exponentially. If the variance of the innovation of the permanent component is large, then λ is close to zero, and $E[u_t|t]$ is close to u_{t-1}. But if the innovation of the transitory component is large, individuals put less weight on the last value of u and more weight on values further lagged. Note also that (32) is just like adaptive expectations and can be rewritten as

$$E[u_t|t] - E[u_{t-1}|t - 1] = (1 - \lambda)(u_{t-1} - E[u_{t-1}|t - 1]).$$

The demonstration that adaptive expectations were indeed rational in this case was an important contribution of Muth (1960).

We now trace the effects of transitory and permanent shocks on output. (Remember that in doing so, we know more about the nature of the shock than the individuals themselves, who only observe the sum of the two.) Assume for simplicity that wage-setters desire a constant real wage so that $a = 0$ in equation (26). Assume also, for notational simplicity, that there are no unanticipated money or velocity shocks. Under these assumptions and full information, output would be given by $y_t = \beta u_t$. Under our assumption that the current shock u is not observable when wages are set, output is given by equation (28), which now has the form:

$$y_t = \left(\frac{\beta}{1 + \beta}\right)(u_t - E[u_t|t]) + \beta E[u_t|t]. \tag{33}$$

To characterize the effects on output of a transitory adverse supply shock, we consider the effects of the sequence $u_{t-i} = 0$, for $i > 0$, $u_t = e_{2t} < 0$, and $u_{t+i} = 0$, for $i > 0$, on output. From (32) we know that individuals will form expectations according to

$$E[u_t|t] = 0,$$

$$E[u_{t+1}|t + 1] = (1 - \lambda)e_{2t},$$

$$E[u_{t+i}|t + i] = (1 - \lambda)\lambda^{i-1}e_{2t}.$$

In period t they do not anticipate the shock. In following periods, because they do not know that the shock in period t was transitory, they expect a negative value of u which they revise toward zero as time passes. Replacing in (33) gives the output:

$$y_t = \left(\frac{\beta}{1 + \beta}\right) e_{2t},$$

$$y_{t+i} = \left(\frac{\beta^2}{1 + \beta}\right)(1 - \lambda)\lambda^{i-1} e_{2t}.$$

Although the supply shock is gone after one period, its effects last much longer. The initial effect of the shock is to decrease output. In following periods wage-setters continue to anticipate a negative value of u, knowing that this will imply a high price level. This leads them to ask for high nominal wages, resulting in low output. But as expectations are revised, output returns to normal over time. The path of output is drawn in figure 10.4a.

A similar analysis applies to permanent shocks. Consider the effects of the sequence $u_{t-i} = 0$, for $i > 0$, and $u_{t+i} = \varepsilon_{1t} < 0$, for $i \geqslant 0$. From (32) we know that individuals will revise their expectations over time according to

$$E[u_t | t] = 0,$$

$$E[u_{t+1} | t + 1] = (1 - \lambda)\varepsilon_{1t},$$

$$E[u_{t+i} | t + i] = (1 - \lambda^i)\varepsilon_{1t}.$$

Individuals will slowly adjust their expectations to the new level of e_{1t}. Output will therefore be given by

$$y_t = \left(\frac{\beta}{1 + \beta}\right) \varepsilon_{1t},$$

$$y_{t+i} = \beta\varepsilon_{1t} - \left(\frac{\beta^2}{1 + \beta}\right)\lambda^i\varepsilon_{1t}.$$

The path of output is drawn in figure 10.4b. The response of output at time t to a shock is the same whether the shock is transitory or permanent. Thereafter the effect of the permanent adverse shock on output steadily increases over time. This is because, in period $t + 1$ and after, wage-setters underestimate the size of the adverse shock and thus underestimate the price level in setting the nominal wage. This underestimation leads to higher output than would happen under perfect information. Over time

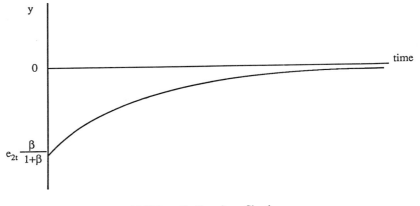

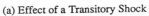

(a) Effect of a Transitory Shock

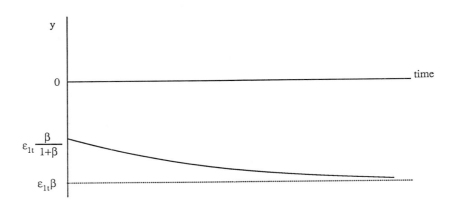

(b) Effect of a Permanent Shock

Figure 10.4
Effects of transitory and permanent shocks on output

wage-setters steadily revise their estimate of the shock, and with it their expectation of the price level. As a result output decreases to its new steady state value.

This model generates interesting dynamics of output adjustment in response to shocks. It would appear, however, that agents make serially correlated mistakes in response to shocks and thus do not have rational expectations. This is not true. Individuals within the economy do not know what type of shock has occurred. Their expectations are rational and, given their information, *on average* correct: they tend to overpredict the price level when a supply shock is transitory and underpredict it when a shock is permanent. The weights on past shocks in equation (32) are chosen so that on average the overpredictions balance the underpredictions. Output is not on average serially correlated to a greater extent than the underlying supply shock, even though the response to a particular shock implies a prolonged and gradual adjustment.

This first aggregate supply-demand model makes for a powerful first model to analyze many issues. But its neglect of dynamics is obviously both a strength and a weakness. We now turn to aggregate demand-supply models that focus on dynamics from the demand side and/or the supply side.

10.4 The Dynamics of Demand: The IS-LM and Mundell-Fleming Models

The IS-LM model was invented by Hicks (1937) to summarize the analytical contents of Keynes' *General Theory*. Whether or not it does so,[16] it has become one of the basic macroeconomic models. The demand side of large macroeconometric models is merely the IS-LM model writ large, and despite criticisms, the model survives in use past its fiftieth year.

The IS-LM, Fiscal Policy, Output, and the Term Structure

In its simplest version the IS-LM model includes an equation representing asset markets equilibrium, the LM (liquidity preference equals money),

$$\frac{M}{P} = L(i, Y),$$

$$\frac{\partial L}{\partial i} < 0, \tag{34}$$

$$\frac{\partial L}{\partial Y} > 0,$$

where i is the nominal interest rate, Y real output, and L the demand for money. The goods market equilibrium equation, the IS (investment equals saving), is

$$Y = A(r, Y, F),$$

$$\frac{\partial A}{\partial r} < 0,$$

$$1 > \frac{\partial A}{\partial Y} > 0, \tag{35}$$

$$\frac{\partial A}{\partial F} > 0.$$

Here r is the real interest rate and F is an index of fiscal policy, for instance, the full employment deficit. The demand for goods is a decreasing function of the real interest rate, both because a higher interest rate reduces investment demand and because it may increase saving; the demand for goods increases with income through its effect on consumption and investment decisions.

In the full employment version, wages and prices are fully flexible, and the level of output is determined by labor market equilibrium. The IS curve is the locus on which the demand for goods is equal to full employment output.[17] This determines the real interest rate, which must therefore be such as to reconcile saving and investment decisions at full employment. The nominal rate is then equal to the real rate plus inflationary expectations, and the LM determines the price level.

We concentrate, instead, on the fixed price level version of the model. In this case output is determined by aggregate demand at a given price level. The implicit assumption is therefore that even if prices adjust, they do so sufficiently slowly for one to take them as given and assume demand determination of output for some period of time.[18] Given the price level and inflationary expectations so that $r = i - \pi^*$, the IS and LM curves can be drawn in (Y, i) or in the (Y, r) space, as in the familiar figure 10.5. In this form the model can be used as it is in textbooks to analyze the effects of changes in the money stock and fiscal policy on the level of output, with multipliers giving the derivatives of output with respect to the policy variable.

Two main types of criticism have been leveled at the fixed price level version of the IS-LM.[19] The first is that when considering output dynamics, it is not appropriate to ignore the supply side of the economy. If one takes

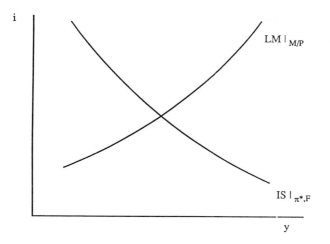

Figure 10.5
IS-LM curves

the view that prices and wages are flexible and that output dynamics are
the result of equilibrium business cycle fluctuations, it indeed makes little
sense to first look at output dynamics assuming a perfectly elastic supply
curve for goods. Variables that affect the demand for goods may well also
affect the supply of labor and the supply of goods. In this case studying
responses of output within the IS-LM framework is at best a potentially
misleading detour on the way to characterizing equilibrium.

We have made it clear, however, that this is not our characterization of
fluctuations and that movements in aggregate demand appear to be initially
accommodated mostly by movements in output and employment rather
than by movements in prices. The asymmetry in the treatment of supply
and demand decisions may well be intellectually unappealing, and we have
spent most of chapters 8 and 9 worrying about it, but it appears to be an
accurate description of reality. It is then appropriate for us to use the IS-LM
for the study of short-run adjustments. How short is the short run? To that
question, there is no easy answer. It is clear that using the fixed price IS-LM
model to study medium- or long-run effects of policy or that maintaining
the assumption of fixed prices while allowing for dynamics of capital
accumulation, for example, is at best inappropriate. In that case one must
embed the IS-LM in a model that allows for an explicit treatment of
aggregate supply and of price and wage adjustment. We will see examples
of such models in the following sections.

The second set of criticisms focuses on the specification of the IS and LM equations. The demand for money in the LM curve is actually quite consistent with the demand for money that emerges from the models studied in chapter 4. But the demand for goods in equation (35) is only a pale reflection of our analysis of optimal behavior under uncertainty in chapter 6. The treatment of fiscal policy as a single index is an equally drastic simplification of the way fiscal policy affects consumption or investment behavior. These flaws, however, are flaws of the simplest textbook version. Keynes' analysis relied heavily on expectations and their effects on aggregate demand. Large macroeconometric models allow for wealth effects, expectations, and complex lag structures and, except for rational expectations, capture most of the effects characterized in chapter 6. Many analytical extensions also study the potential role of expectations in the transmission of policy changes to output. We present one such version now.[20]

Policy, Anticipations, Recessions, and the Term Structure

It has been argued[21] that the tax cuts passed in 1981 may have been recessionary. Most of the tax cuts were promised for future years, and future tax cuts may reduce current aggregate demand. To analyze this proposition, we adapt the IS-LM model in the following way:

First, we introduce the distinction between short and long real rates, r and R, respectively. We recognize that investment, as well as consumption, should be affected by the long-term real interest rate, R, rather than by the short real rate, r. Thus we write the demand for goods as a function of the long rate, income, and the index of fiscal policy $A(R, Y, F)$. To the extent that long rates depend on current and future expected short rates, this introduces a channel for expectations of future events to affect current output. It is obviously not the only way expectations of the future may affect current decisions, and we will return to the issue later.

Second, we assume that the adjustment of output to movements in demand takes time. Namely, we assume that

$$\frac{dY}{dt} = \phi[A(R, Y, F) - Y]$$
$$= \phi(R, Y, F), \qquad \phi_R < 0, \phi_Y < 0, \phi_F > 0. \tag{37}$$

Note that $\phi_Y < 0$ follows from the earlier assumption that $A_Y < 1$. There are two possible justifications for this equation. The first is that spending adjusts slowly to its underlying determinants given by $A(Y, R, F)$. The other is that spending is equal to $A(Y, R, F)$ but that firms respond to aggregate demand movements first by drawing down inventories and then by increasing output. Both motivations raise issues of their own, many of which were discussed in chapter 6.[22]

Third, we have to establish the links between nominal and real and between short- and long-term interest rates. Assume that there are two types of bonds in the economy, short (or more precisely instantaneous) nominal bonds, that pay a nominal interest rate of i and real consols that promise to pay one good per instant forever, with consol rate R.[23] The real rate of return on short bonds is equal to $r = i - \pi^*$, where π^* is the expected instantaneous rate of inflation. Let Q be the real price of a consol, and let R be the consol rate, the inverse of the price of the consol. The instantaneous real rate of return on the consol is equal to $1/Q + (dQ/dt)/Q$ which in turn is equal to $R - (dR/dt)/R$. The first term is the coupon payment, and the second the rate of capital gain. When the long rate increases, the price of the consol decreases, creating a capital loss.

Assume that asset holders equalize rates of return on both consols and instantaneous bonds up to a constant risk premium.[24] Then, under the perfect foresight assumption, expected and actual rates are equal (except when an unanticipated change in policy occurs) up to the constant risk premium, α:

$$R - \frac{dR/dt}{R} = r + \alpha = i - \pi^* + \alpha. \tag{38}$$

Finally, the short-term nominal rate is determined by the LM relation given output and real money balances:

$$\frac{M}{P} = L(i, Y). \tag{39}$$

The rate appropriate to the choice between money and bonds, be it short bonds or consols, is the short-term nominal rate.

This extension gives some flavor of the complexity of the interactions between asset markets and goods markets. Given output, real money balances determine the short-term nominal rate. Given inflation expectations, this determines the short real rate. Anticipations of current and future real rates determine the long real rate, which affects spending and output. This complex transmission mechanism is central to a macroeconometric model such as the MPS model (e.g., see Modigliani 1971, who gives estimated empirical counterparts to the equations specified above and draws their implications).

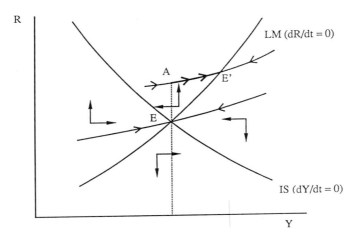

Figure 10.6
Effects of an unanticipated increase in F

Figure 10.6 shows the two loci on which Y and R, respectively, are not changing. The $dY/dt = 0$ locus is derived from (37); this is simply the IS curve of figure 10.5, for on that schedule output is equal to spending. The $dR/dt = 0$ locus is derived from the LM relationship, by substituting for i from (38) into (39); this represents the LM schedule of figure 10.5, for when $dR/dt = 0$, the short nominal rate is equal to the consol rate, up to expected inflation and a risk premium, both of which we treat as constant. The equation is

$$\frac{M}{P} = L\left(R - \frac{dR/dt}{R} + \pi^* - \alpha, Y\right). \tag{40}$$

The arrows represent dynamic behavior. To the right of the IS curve spending is below output, and output is therefore falling. The direction of the vertical arrows is most easily seen by moving to the right of the LM curve; this increases the demand for real balances, which from (40) has to be offset by a decrease in dR/dt. The equilibrium is accordingly a saddle point. Given Y at any point in time, the assumption that the economy converges to the steady state determines the long real rate uniquely. This assumption of convergence in effect rules out bubbles; these issues were discussed in chapter 5.

We can now use this model to study the effects of a change in fiscal policy such as the 1981–1983 tax cuts, voted in 1981 to be implemented over the

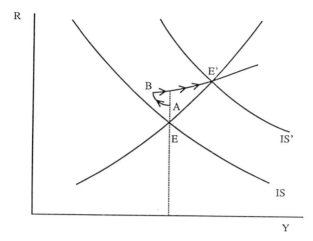

Figure 10.7
Effects of an anticipated increase in F

next three years. Throughout we assume that for some reason left un-specified (failure of Ricardian equivalence, or anticipations of lower govern-ment spending rather than of higher taxes later), the decrease in taxes increases the index F, and thus increases aggregate demand and equilibrium output.

Consider first an unanticipated increase in F, that shifts the IS curve to the right (not shown), moving the steady state from E to a point like E' in figure 10.6. The dynamic adjustment is shown on the path AE'. The fiscal expansion increases aggregate demand, and output therefore begins to grow. The long-term interest rate rises, with the short rate initially remaining constant because output has not changed yet [note from (40) that given M/P and Y, the interest rate i has to remain unchanged]. The long rate continues rising with output, and the short rate rises as well. In the new equilibrium, output is higher, as are both long and short interest rates.

A more relevant exercise in terms of the 1981–1983 tax cuts is to look at the effect of a fiscal expansion that is announced (and believed) at time t_0, to be undertaken at some time t_1 in the future. Figure 10.7 illustrates the dynamics of adjustment. The initial equilibrium is shown at point E. Once fiscal policy has changed, the new steady state is at E', where the new IS curve, IS', intersects the LM curve. At time t_1 the economy must be on the saddle path associated with E'; otherwise, the economy would never con-verge to the new equilibrium. Prior to t_1, dynamics are determined by the equations of motion associated with E. At time t_0, Y is given. Finally, the adjustment path must be such that there be no expected discrete change in R (the consol rate) during the adjustment process. If such a change were expected, the price of consols would be expected to change by a discrete amount, generating the possibility of arbitrarily large capital gains per unit time. Accordingly, the adjustment path is one that follows the dynamics dictated by the arrows around E until fiscal policy actually changes; precisely at that moment the adjustment path has to hit the saddle path leading to E'. Such a path is shown by ABE' in figure 10.7.

Upon the announcement of the expected policy change, the long-term interest rate rises. Because F (fiscal policy) has not yet changed, there is no pressure increasing aggregate demand while the higher long rate reduces demand and output. The short-term interest rate starts falling along with output, though the long rate is rising in anticipation of the policy change. When fiscal policy eventually changes, output begins to rise and the short rate rises with it. In the adjustment from B to E', output and both interest rates are rising. The interesting part of the adjustment process is the segment AB where the prospect of higher future interest rates raises the current long rate and thus reduces investment. Accordingly, in this model the anticipation of an expansionary fiscal policy is itself contractionary. Interestingly also, from t_0 to t_1, the term structure twists, with long rates increasing while short rates are decreasing.

Obviously, many caveats must be given concerning the result that anticipated fiscal expansion is contractionary. There are other channels than interest rates through which expectations affect current decisions. Expectations of lower future taxes and of future income may offset the contractionary effects of higher real rates and lead to expansion rather than contraction. On the other hand, when account is taken of price adjustment over time, fiscal expansion may lead individuals to expect fiscal expansion to have more effect on real rates and less on output and income, since these have to return eventually to their full employment values; this makes contraction more likely.[25] The treatment of fiscal policy by a single index is a shortcut which becomes unacceptable when deficits lead over time to significant changes in debt, for example. In this case we can shift to the model developed in chapter 3 to analyze the long-run effects of deficits, or we can integrate the two. It is the beauty of the IS-LM model that this can be done; the main reason for the success of the IS-LM model is indeed its versatility, the fact that it can readily be adapted to analyze a wide variety of policy and other issues.

The Mundell-Fleming Model, Monetary Policy, and Exchange Rates

Although this book follows tradition in largely ignoring open economy aspects of macroeconomics, it is not possible to ignore international trade in goods and assets when analyzing the actual behavior of any economy. There are only three serious excuses for not making all of macroeconomics explicitly open economy. First, the world economy is closed, and the conditions for aggregating over the whole world are for some issues, such as growth, no more rigorous than those needed to aggregate within an economy. Second, for some questions the rest of the world is not central and can be treated as just another source of disturbances, and third, it is difficult. In particular, because two-variable systems are much easier to analyze and understand than higher-order systems,[26] adding the exchange rate to a model usually exacts a price in the need to simplify elsewhere in the model.

The open economy version (extension) of the IS-LM is the Mundell-Fleming model, which was developed in the contributions made by Robert Mundell and Marcus Fleming in the early 1960s.[27] We first present the simplest comparative static version of the model, and show how the openness of the economy affects conclusions about the operation of monetary and fiscal policy. We then extend it to study the effects of monetary policy and demonstrate the classic Dornbusch (1976) overshooting of exchange rates result.

Extending the fixed price IS-LM model, the Mundell-Fleming model assumes fixed price levels at home and abroad. In addition it assumes that domestic and foreign goods are imperfect substitutes but that domestic and foreign assets are perfect substitutes and command the same expected rate of return. Finally, it also assumes that the country is small enough that it can take foreign variables as given and unaffected by its actions. The model can be used to study equilibrium under either fixed or flexible exchange rates. We limit ourselves to the flexible case.

The LM relation remains unchanged. The implicit assumption is that there is no currency substitution. Thus

$$\frac{M}{P} = L(Y, i), \tag{34}$$

or, in inverse form (this will be convenient later),

$$i = i\left(\frac{M}{P}, Y\right),$$

$$\frac{\partial i}{\partial (M/P)} < 0,$$

$$\frac{\partial i}{\partial Y} > 0. \tag{41}$$

Let e be the nominal exchange rate, the price of foreign currency in terms of domestic currency, and let i' be the foreign interest rate.[28] By arbitrage, domestic bonds and foreign bonds must pay the same expected rate of return. Thus

$$i = i' + \frac{(de/dt)^*}{e}. \tag{42}$$

If the domestic interest rate exceeds the foreign interest rate, our currency must be expected to depreciate vis-à-vis the foreign currency, that is, e must be expected to increase.

The IS curve must take into account the effect of exports and imports. Letting P and P' represent the domestic and foreign price levels, the IS relation is rewritten as

$$Y = A\left(i - \pi^*, Y, \frac{eP'}{P}, F\right),$$

$$\frac{\partial A}{\partial (eP'/P)} > 0. \tag{43}$$

The demand for goods depends on the real rate of interest, on income, on the real exchange rate, and on the index of fiscal policy. A real depreciation is assumed to increase aggregate demand. The other derivatives are as before. Given that prices are fixed, π^* is taken to be equal to zero in what follows.

We start by examining the determination of the exchange rate in the static equilibrium, that is, when $de/dt = (de/dt)^* = 0$. If the exchange rate is constant, the domestic interest rate must be equal to the world rate. Thus equilibrium is characterized as

$$\frac{M}{P} = L(Y, i') \tag{44}$$

and

$$Y = A\left(i', Y, \frac{eP'}{P}, F\right). \tag{45}$$

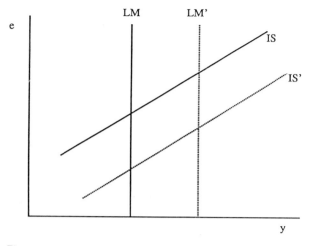

Figure 10.8
The Mundell-Fleming model

These two loci are drawn in the (e, Y) space in figure 10.8. The LM locus is vertical: given M/P and i', there is a unique value of Y that satisfies the LM relation. The IS relation is upward sloping. A depreciation leads to an increase in demand and in equilibrium output.

This equilibrium has strong implications as to the effectiveness of monetary and fiscal policy. An increase in the money stock shifts the LM curve to LM', causing an increase in output and a depreciation of the exchange rate. Expansionary fiscal policy shifts the IS curve to the right, to IS', causing an appreciation of the currency but not affecting the level of output.

The keys to understanding these results are the fixed price level and interest rate. The interest rate fixes the velocity of circulation, and with the price level fixed, any increase in money translates into real output changes. With higher real output, the exchange rate must depreciate to generate the demand that supports the higher level of output. There are two ways of explaining the fiscal policy result. With fixed output, the increase in aggregate demand generated by a fiscal expansion has to be offset by a fall in net exports, which requires an appreciation. An explanation with more intuitive appeal is that whereas ordinarily a fiscal expansion with fixed money stock would set off an increase in the interest rate, here any potential increase in the interest rate generates a capital inflow that causes the currency to appreciate until the decrease in net exports offsets the initial increase in aggregate demand; the net capital inflow is precisely equal to the required increase in the current account deficit.

Like its IS-LM cousin, the static Mundell-Fleming model is both simple and, in its simplest version, of limited applicability. Like the IS-LM model, it can easily be refined to accommodate expectations, accumulation, and price adjustment over time. For example, we have learned that the result that fiscal policy leads to appreciation is not very robust. When domestic and foreign assets are not perfect substitutes, once a route is found for fiscal expansion to increase the level of income, the trade balance tends to worsen and the exchange rate may correspondingly depreciate rather than appreciate. We now present one of the most interesting and important extensions of the Mundell-Fleming model, developed by Dornbusch (1976).

Exchange Rate Overshooting and Asset Price Volatility

Among the many surprises in the operation of the floating exchange rate system is the volatility of nominal exchange rates. Dornbusch (1976), using the Mundell-Fleming model, showed how this could be explained. We first provide a slightly modified version of his argument.

Suppose that we modify our initial model to recognize, as before, that output adjusts slowly to spending.[29] Further, and only to simplify the algebra, we assume that the real interest rate does not directly affect spending. Equilibrium is then characterized by

$$\frac{(de/dt)^*}{e} = i\left(\frac{M}{P}, Y\right) - i',$$

$$\frac{dY}{dt} = \phi\left[A\left(Y, \frac{eP'}{P}, F\right) - Y\right].$$

The first equation combines the arbitrage equation and the inverted LM curve. The second states that output adjusts slowly to movements in spending. The dynamics of the system are characterized in figure 10.9. The locus where the exchange rate does not change is the LM locus of figure 10.8. The locus where output does not change is the IS locus of figure 10.8. To the right of the LM, the domestic interest rate exceeds the foreign rate, and the exchange rate must be depreciating. An increase in output starting from a point on the IS implies excess supply and thus that output is decreasing. The equilibrium is, not surprisingly, saddle point stable; the saddle path is downward sloping.

Now suppose the money stock is increased. Then, in figure 10.10, the new equilibrium is E'. The path of adjustment is a jump in the exchange rate from E to A and an adjustment of output and the exchange rate over time

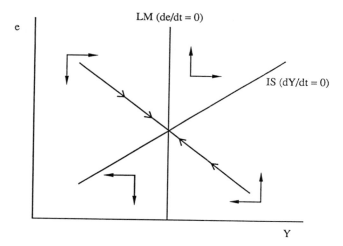

Figure 10.9

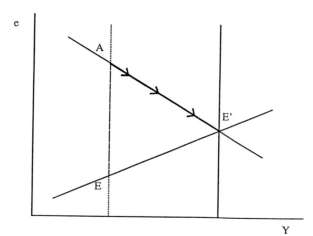

Figure 10.10
Effects of an increase in money

along AE'. Thus the exchange rate overshoots its long-run level, and the currency experiences a large depreciation followed by appreciation. The intuition is simple. At the time of the increase in money, output (as well as the price level) is fixed, so that the nominal rate must decrease. The interest differential generates capital outflows and depreciation. The currency keeps depreciating until it is expected to appreciate at a rate that makes domestic and foreign bonds equally attractive. This happens at point A in figure 10.10. The fact that there must be expected appreciation clearly implies an initial depreciation in excess of that required in the new equilibrium.

Dornbusch looked, instead, at the effects of slow price level adjustment in response to movements in nominal money. His conclusion was the same, that increases in nominal money would lead to a large nominal and real depreciation followed by a return to the same real exchange rate in the new steady state (with price flexibility in the long run, money is again neutral). The intuition for his result is exactly the same as that given above, but with the price level replacing output. He also found that the slower the price level adjusts to movements in aggregate demand, the larger was the size of overshooting at the time of the change in money. This result that more rigidity in the prices of goods is likely to be associated with more volatility in asset prices (exchange rates here) in the presence of nominal shocks is an important one. Further research has shown that the overshooting result can be overturned, but the basic insight remains.

10.5 Dynamics of Aggregate Supply

The Wage-Price Mechanism

Nearly two decades ago Tobin (1972) gave a summary of the then prevailing view of the dynamics of aggregate supply. The "wage-price mechanism" described by Tobin consisted of two equations, a price, or "markup," equation and a wage equation, the "Phillips curve":

$$\frac{dp}{dt} = \frac{dw}{dt} - a + f(u), \qquad \frac{df}{du} \leqslant 0, \tag{46}$$

$$\frac{dw}{dt} = \alpha \frac{dp^*}{dt} + g\left(u, \frac{du}{dt}\right), \qquad \frac{dg}{du} \leqslant 0, \frac{dg}{du/dt} \leqslant 0, \tag{47}$$

where p and w are the logarithms of the price level and the nominal wage, a is the rate of change of labor productivity, and u is the unemployment rate. The asterisk denotes an expectation.

The markup equation gave the behavior of prices, or the implicit supply curve of firms. Prices were a markup over unit labor costs, with wages adjusted for labor productivity. Unemployment in equation (46) stands as a proxy for the level of output compared to capacity; the actual equations used a variety of measures, from a deviation of output from trend to capacity utilization or the output capital ratio. The general conclusion was, however, the same across estimated equations: firms appeared to satisfy demand at a roughly constant markup, so df/du was close or equal to zero. This roughly constant markup was the explanation for the acyclical movement in the real wage.

The Phillips curve gave the behavior of nominal wages. The rate of wage inflation depended on expected price inflation as well as on the level and possibly the rate of change of unemployment. As of 1970 the issue of whether α was equal to or less than one was far from settled. The issue was an important one, because the existence of a long-run trade-off between unemployment and inflation depended on α being less than unity. Econometric estimates at the time were in the range of 0.4 to 0.8, although sometimes not significantly different from one. As these estimates increased in the 1970s, the Phillips curve came to be specified with α equal to unity. It is safe to say, though, that most economists who came to accept the view that there was no long-run trade-off between inflation and unemployment were more affected by a priori argument than by empirical evidence. That argument, made by Friedman (1968) and Phelps (1968), was that labor market equilibrium eventually determined real, not nominal wages, that there was no long-run money illusion and therefore α had to be unity. In addition to expected price inflation, wage inflation depended inversely on both the level of unemployment and its rate of change. The effect of the level of unemployment on wage inflation was the central contribution of Phillips' (1958). That changes in unemployment (du/dt) affected wage inflation had been noted by Lipsey (1960) and was embodied in most econometric specifications.

Combining the markup and the Phillips curve relations, assuming $\alpha = 1$, gives a relation between price inflation and unemployment:

$$\frac{dp}{dt} = \frac{dp^*}{dt} - a + f(u) + g\left(u, \frac{du}{dt}\right). \tag{48}$$

Given a specification of expectations, this equation gives a simple characterization of the change in the price level as a function of unemployment. In textbooks it is often combined with the IS-LM model in order to characterize the dynamic effects of policy on output and prices.

Equation (48) in turn implies, for a given rate of growth of productivity, a long-run equilibrium value for the unemployment rate. Assuming that $dp^*/dt = dp/dt$ and $du/dt = 0$, the equilibrium value of u was given by

$$f(u) + g(u, 0) = a. \tag{49}$$

This rate, which has come to be known as the natural rate of unemployment, or more accurately but less elegantly as the "nonaccelerating inflation rate of unemployment," or NAIRU, depends on the rate of productivity growth as well as on the implicit determinants of the functions $f(\cdot)$ and $g(\cdot, \cdot)$. Lower productivity growth requires an increase in equilibrium unemployment. Similarly, higher unemployment benefits or more militant unions could well increase the NAIRU by affecting $g(\cdot, \cdot)$.

The Issues

An increasing proportion of macroeconomists, even among those who believe in the importance of nominal and real rigidities, has become uncomfortable with the wage-price mechanism as described by Tobin. The reasons have more to do with the theoretical underpinnings of the price and wage equations than with their empirical performance.

Indeed the equations described above have performed reasonably well over the last 15 years, at least in the United States. Over those years standard specifications have been extended to allow for a direct effect of primary input prices in the price equation, the distinction between the price index which is relevant for workers, such as the CPI, and the price index corresponding to domestic output, such as the GNP deflator, and for refinements in the unemployment measure used in the Phillips curve. The system so extended has been fairly successful at tracking the disinflationary effects of unemployment in the 1980s.[30] The Phillips curve has been much less successful in Europe, however, where the current high unemployment is not associated with decreasing inflation.[31] This failure appears to be a general characteristic of times of sustained high unemployment: Samuelson and Solow (1960) had noted the same breakdown of the Phillips curve relation during the Great Depression.

But the main source of dissatisfaction stems from theoretical concerns. Some of the characteristics of the Phillips curve are theoretically puzzling. Perhaps the main one is the rate-of-change specification of the wage and price equations. To see this, rewrite the Phillips curve (with $\alpha = 1$), substracting price inflation from both sides, as

$$\frac{dw}{dt} - \frac{dp}{dt} = \frac{dp^*}{dt} - \frac{dp}{dt} + g\left(u, \frac{du}{dt}\right). \tag{47'}$$

The left-hand side of (47') is the rate of growth of real wages. Both unanticipated inflation and higher unemployment reduce the current real wage. If thereafter inflation is always at the expected level and u is at the natural rate, the real wage will remain permanently lower as a result of current shocks. Thus the rate-of-change formulation of the Phillips curve implies that transitory disturbances have permanent effects on the real wage. Since most micro-based theories do not generate such permanent effects of shocks on real wages, this appears to be an unduly strong a priori restriction. Another feature is the treatment of productivity growth. The standard Phillips curve does not allow for a response of wages directly to the rate of productivity growth: thus a slowdown in productivity growth, which leads (from pricing) to higher price inflation given wage inflation, requires higher unemployment to reconcile workers with the lower rate of wage inflation given price inflation. If, however, we think of wages as being set in part by bargaining, it is quite conceivable that workers will accept a lower rate of real wage growth without being forced into it by higher unemployment. A final feature, and one that was emphasized by the Lucas critique of the Phillips curve, is the ambiguity associated with the exact interpretation of "expected inflation" in the Phillips curve. Does p^* stand, for example, for current expectations of p or instead for a distributed lag of past expectations of p, as embodied in the existing set of labor contracts?

For all these reasons the "wage price mechanism," although it remains a central feature of large macroeconometric models, has lost its status as the agreed model of aggregate supply. Our description of current research on nominal rigidities, and goods and labor markets in chapters 8 and 9, makes clear that there is at this stage no consensus on what such a standard model should be. We have not yet sorted out the respective role of nominal price versus wage rigidities, the role of increasing returns in production and pricing, the relative importance of efficiency wages versus membership effects, and so on. The Taylor model, which captures both nominal rigidities and allows for a low elasticity of wages to unemployment, has proved very useful in analyzing many issues. We have developed and used it in chapter 8. We use two of its variants below to analyze the issue of whether price flexibility may in fact be destabilizing and to characterize the dynamic effects of a change in money growth. The Taylor model is not well suited for other tasks, however, such as the study of how fluctuations in productivity and changes in taxation or in unemployment benefits affect employment, wages, and prices over time. We present in the last part of this section a model developed by Layard and Nickell (1987) to explain movements in U.K. unemployment.

Price Flexibility and Output Variability

In the simplest classical textbook model, price and wage flexibility success-fully keep the economy continuously at full employment. By implication, it seems, wage or price inflexibility must increase divergences in output from the full employment level. However, it has long been argued that price flexibility may in fact *de*stabilize output. Irving Fisher (1920) attributed the trade cycle to price movements, stating that neither interest rates nor wages typically succeed in anticipating price movements adequately. Fisher also emphasized that price movements cause income and wealth redistributions, with deflation causing bankruptcies for those unable to meet nominally fixed debts. Keynes (1936, ch. 19) discussed how wage flexibility could destabilize rather than stabilize output in response to movements in aggregate demand. Not only would a strong deflation, in response to a decrease in out-put, transfer income away from workers, and away from entrepreneurs to rentiers, decreasing aggregate demand, but anticipated deflation would also increase real rates of interest, further decreasing demand and output.

This last effect was emphasized again by Mundell (1968) and Tobin (1975).[32] Assuming slow price adjustment and adaptive expectations, Tobin showed that if a decrease in output led to anticipations of a strong deflation, this could indeed increase real rates of interest, leading to further deflation and a major depression. The argument was recast in a Taylor-type model with rational expectations by DeLong and Summers (1986). Driskill and Sheffrin (1986) had shown that increases in flexibility (a stronger elasticity of wages to output) necessarily decrease the variance in output when shocks come from wage setting. Delong and Summers showed, however, that when shocks come from aggregate demand and are serially correlated, increases in the responsiveness of wages to demand conditions can actually increase the variance of output. They argued further that given plausible parameter values, this outcome is likely to be the rule rather than the exception. Although the argument can be made analytically in the full-fledged Taylor model, we present it in a simpler version that captures the essence of the argument.[33]

Consider the IS-LM model, with the nominal rate of interest affecting money demand and the real rate affecting the demand for goods. An increase in the price level decreases real money balances and the demand for goods.

An increase in expected inflation decreases the real rate given the nominal rate, and thus leads to an increase in the demand for goods. We capture these two effects by specifying aggregate demand as

$$y_t = -p_t + aE[p_{t+1}|t] + u_t, \qquad 0 < a < 1,$$

$$u_t = \rho u_{t-1} + e_t, \qquad 0 < \rho < 1, \tag{50}$$

where y and p are the logarithms of output and the price level. u_t is a disturbance term that reflects the effects of all other variables in the IS-LM model and is assumed to follow a first-order autoregressive process. e_t is white, with mean zero. The information set at time t includes current and past values of u. The coefficient on p is normalized to be one for notational simplicity. The restriction on a is implied by the fact that a proportional increase in the price today and in the price expected next period (which leaves the expected rate of inflation unchanged) decreases equilibrium output.

On the supply side we want to capture the fact that nominal prices both have some inertia and respond more or less strongly to movements in output. We assume that nominal wages at time t are given by

$$w_t = cE[y_t|t - 1], \tag{51}$$

where w is the logarithm of the nominal wage. We assume that wages are predetermined at time t and depend on expected output at time t. We will interpret the coefficient c as the degree of wage flexibility. The important assumption is an implicit one: the wage does not depend on the expected price level at time t. Equivalently, the nominal wage depends on the unconditional expected value of the price level, which in this model is equal to zero. This is where we take a shortcut. We need to have some degree of nominal wage inertia: the overlapping Taylor model delivers this implication by making w_t a function of w_{t-1}, but does so at some cost in terms of simplicity. Our formalization achieves the same result in a simpler and cruder way.

Finally, prices are a markup over wages. Thus

$$p_t = w_t = cE[y_t|t - 1]. \tag{52}$$

We now solve for equilibrium output when the economy is characterized by equations (50) and (52). First, by taking expectations conditional on information at time $t - 1$ in both equations, and solving, we get

$$E[y_t|t - 1] = \left[\frac{1}{1 + c(1 - a\rho)} \right] \rho u_{t-1}. \tag{53}$$

So far this result does not support the position that flexibility is destabilizing. An increase in flexibility, an increase in c, clearly decreases the variance of $E[y_t|t-1]$. This is because if wages respond strongly to expected output, a positive nominal disturbance today—which, if ρ is positive, implies an expected positive disturbance next period—is expected to be offset by higher wages and thus higher prices. This result is, however, about expected output, not actual output. Replacing (53), and the associated value of $E[p_{t+1}|t]$ in (51), gives actual output:

$$ y_t = E[y_t|t-1] + \left[1 + \frac{ac\rho}{1 + c(1 - a\rho)} \right] e_t. \tag{54} $$

The second term is the contemporaneous response of output to unexpected nominal disturbances. If ρ is positive, the coefficient is an increasing function of c. Thus the higher the degree of flexibility, the *stronger* is the effect of unexpected demand shocks on output. The intuition behind this result is simple. The greater the flexibility, the larger is the anticipated decrease in prices next period (prices are predetermined today) in response to a negative demand shock today, the stronger is the anticipated deflation, the larger the real rate and thus the larger the decrease in output today. This is indeed just the Keynes-Mundell-Tobin effect.

On net, flexibility has two effects: it increases the contemporaneous response of output to shocks but decreases the persistence of these effects on output. The net effect is generally ambiguous. The model makes the important point that wage flexibility is not necessarily desirable. In the process of formalization, some of the insights of Fisher and Tobin may, however, have been lost: in this model, wage flexibility leads to deeper but shorter fluctuations, not to the long-lasting depressions that both Fisher and Tobin were trying to explain.

Dynamic Effects of Changes in Money Growth

We now use a continuous time version of the Taylor model, due to Calvo (1983), to study the dynamic effects of money growth on output.

There is a continuum of identical price-setting firms.[34] Each firm changes its price with constant probability δ at any point in time. Thus the variable "time until the next change" has density function $\delta \exp(-\delta h)$, $\delta > 0$.[35] Denote by x_t the (log of the) price set at t by a firm that changes its price at t. In setting its price, the firm takes into account both the price level and the level of aggregate demand expected to prevail during the period until its next price change. The assumed price-setting rule is

$$x_t = \delta \int_t^{\infty} [p_s^* + \beta y_s^*] \exp[-\delta(s - t)] \, ds, \qquad \beta > 0, \tag{55}$$

where p and y are the logarithms of the price level and aggregate output, respectively; the asterisk denotes an expectation.

Assuming that changes are uncorrelated across price-setters, the proportion of prices at time t that were set at time $t - s$ is $\delta \exp[\delta(t - s)]$. Thus, if we define the price level as a weighted average of prices currently in existence, we get

$$p_t = \delta \int_{-\infty}^{t} x_s \exp[-\delta(t - s)] \, ds. \tag{56}$$

Note that the price dynamics are very similar to those of the Taylor model, in that the price level today is a weighted average of prices set in the past but each individual price, when set, is set in a forward-looking manner. Note also that x can jump at time t, but the price level itself cannot. By differentiating (55) and (56) with respect to time, we obtain

$$\frac{dx}{dt} = \delta(x_t - p_t - \beta y_t),$$

$$\frac{dp}{dt} = \delta(x_t - p_t). \tag{57}$$

This set of equations gives us the dynamics of x and p, given y. If our interest were, for example, in the effects of a change in the money stock, we could use these two equations together with a specification of aggregate demand and solve for the dynamics of x and p. However, we are interested here in the effects of a change in the rate of growth of money. To do so, we need to manipulate these equations further. Define π as the rate of inflation, dp/dt. Then, differentiating (57) yields

$$\frac{d\pi}{dt} = \delta \left(\frac{dx}{dt} - \frac{dp}{dt} \right) = -\delta^2 \beta y_t. \tag{58}$$

Equation (58) gives us a relation between the change in inflation and the level of output, which must hold at all times except at times of unexpected changes in the exogenous variables in the system.

To close the model, we specify aggregate demand as the reduced form of an IS-LM model, allowing y to depend positively on both real money balances and on expected inflation:

$$y_t = a(m_t - p_t) + b\pi_t^*. \tag{59}$$

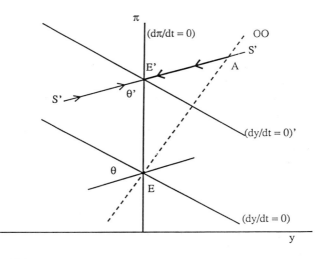

Figure 10.11
Effects of an increase in money growth

Note that since aggregate demand is a function of the price level, p_t, we are implicitly assuming that the rate of purchases is unaffected by the dispersion of prices.[36] Differentiating with respect to time, denoting the rate of nominal money growth by θ, using (58), and assuming perfect foresight gives

$$\frac{dy}{dt} = a(\theta - \pi) - b\delta^2\beta y. \tag{60}$$

Figure 10.11 characterizes the dynamics in (y, π) space. The constant inflation locus, given by (58), is the vertical axis. The constant output locus, given by (60), is downward sloping. The equilibrium values of y and π are zero and θ, respectively, and the equilibrium is saddle point stable.

Consider now the effects of an increase in money growth, which shifts the long-run equilibrium from E to E'. The new saddle path is given by $S'S'$. The question arises where we jump at the time of the change. The answer is given in equation (59): at the time of the increase in money growth, neither m nor p change, so any change in y and π must satisfy $dy = bd\pi$. We represent this relationship by the dashed line OO (to indicate that it determines the initial conditions), that goes through point E. We assume it intersects the saddle path at point A, thereby determining the starting point for the dynamic adjustment to E'. Thus the path of adjustment is a jump from E to A followed by a movement over time from A to E'.

The adjustment path can be explained as follows: At the initial level of output, the increase in the growth rate of money causes a higher expected rate of inflation, thereby reducing the real interest rate (the nominal interest rate is fixed, given $m - p$ and y), and thereby increasing aggregate demand. Since output is determined by demand, the level of output increases discretely, the inflation rate changing by the amount that ensures the economy starts on the saddle path.

Thus, when the growth rate of money increases, the inflation rate initially increases by more than its new steady state level, the level of output jumps, and thereafter both output and the inflation rate decline toward their steady state values. Note that if expected inflation did not affect aggregate demand, a change in money growth would be matched by a simultaneous increase in inflation, with no effects on real output: this would be the case although most individual prices would not move at the time of the change. The result is reminiscent of the Caplin-Spulber results (although not identical since we consider changes in the rate of growth, not in the level of money) derived in chapter 8 and is another warning that individual price stickiness does not necessarily imply nonneutrality of nominal money.

Wage and Price Dynamics Revisited

European unemployment, which had remained very low from the end of World War II until 1970, increased steadily in the 1970s and further increased in the first half of the 1980s. It is currently stable, but at very high levels; in 1987 the unemployment rate stood at 10% in the U.K., at 10.5% in France. Contrary to at least simple versions of the natural rate hypothesis, this high level of unemployment is no longer associated with decreases in inflation. In a series of contributions (1986, 1987), Layard and Nickell have constructed an empirical model aimed at explaining this evolution.[37]

Their model is conceptually similar in structure to models we saw in chapters 8 and 9. Firms are imperfectly competitive, setting nominal prices based on costs and demand. The characterization of nominal wage determination is susceptible of alternative interpretations, from bargaining to efficiency wages. The model of aggregate supply is composed of three equations: a price equation and two equations giving wages. They are estimated using annual data from 1956 to 1983 and have the following form:[38]

$$p - w = a - 0.61\Delta^2 w - 0.51\Delta^2 w(-1) - 0.253u + 0.075\Delta u$$

$$- 0.338\Delta^2 u - 1.07(k - l) + e_p, \tag{61}$$

$$w - p = b - 0.36\Delta^2 p - 0.104 \log(u) + 0.212R$$

$$+ 1.07(k - l) + z + e_w, \tag{62}$$

$$R = 0.054 + 0.061R(-1) - 2.41u + 5.58u(-1) - 2.18u(-2) + e_R.$$

The variables are defined as follows: p and w are the logarithms of the value added price deflator and of hourly labor cost, respectively. u is the unemployment rate, defined as $l - n$, where l and n are the logarithms of the labor force and employment, respectively. k is the logarithm of the capital stock. z is a set of exogenous variables, which includes variables measuring mismatch, employment protection, the ratio of unemployment benefits to the wage, the degree of union power, income policy variables, and the relative price of imports and employers' labor taxes. Finally, R is the proportion of unemployed out of work for a year or more. The notation $\Delta^n x$ denotes the nth difference of variable x.

The *price equation*, equation (61), gives the price set by firms and allows for two types of dynamics. First, the nominal price does not respond instantaneously to the nominal wage; this is captured by the terms $\Delta^2 w$ and $\Delta^2 w(-1)$. Second, the equation implies a dynamic relation between employment (remember that u is $l - n$) and the markup, $p - w$. To examine it further, ignore the nominal rigidities and interpret (61) as an inverted labor demand function. We may then compute the short-run and long-run elasticities of employment with respect to the real wage given $(k - l)$:

$$\frac{dn^d}{d(w - p)}\bigg|_{k-l, n(-1), n(-2)} = -\frac{1}{(0.516)} = -1.93,$$

$$\frac{dn^d}{d(w - p)}\bigg|_{k-l} = -\frac{1}{(0.253)} = -3.95.$$

One interpretation of these dynamics is that they are generated by costs of adjustment of employment, which lead to a higher increase in the markup in the short run than in the long run in response to an increase in demand and employment.[39] Although Layard and Nickell allow productivity to enter the price equation, they find it to be empirically insignificant and drop it from their specification.[40]

The *wage equation* (62) gives the nominal wage chosen in wage setting and also allows for two types of dynamics. The nominal wage adjusts to price level changes over a period of two years, with the adjustment being 64% complete within the year. The wage responds to the unemployment rate: the logarithmic specification implies that the effect of unemployment on wage demands decreases with the level of unemployment. The wage depends positively on the proportion of long-term unemployed. For a given unemployment rate, the higher the proportion of long-term unemployed, the higher the wage chosen in wage setting. This is an important effect that can be justified either through membership effects, that is, from the fact that the employed do not represent the interests of the long-term unemployed in bargaining (an idea explored in chapter 9) or from the fact that the long-term unemployed stop searching, stop being active participants in the labor market, so that they have no impact on wage setting. The dynamics between R and u imply a complex relation between the real wage in (62) and unemployment. An increase in unemployment due to a larger inflow into unemployment initially decreases R; both lead to a decrease in the wage. Over time R increases, thus decreasing the pressure of unemployment on the wage. The variables in z affect the wage through various channels. For example, an increase in the replacement ratio, the ratio of unemployment benefits to the wage, decreases search, strengthens the position of labor in bargaining, and forces firms that pay efficiency wages to increase wages. An increase in the mismatch of jobs and workers across skills, regions, or industries increases the amount of reallocation unemployment, along the lines developed in chapter 7.

In the long run, given z and given $k - l$, these two equations determine equilibrium unemployment and real wages. Ignoring lags, equations (61) and (62) become, replacing R by its value from the second equation in (62),

$$p - w = a_0 - 0.253u - 1.07(k - l), \tag{63}$$

$$w - p = b_0 - 0.104 \log(u) + 0.232u + 1.07(k - l) + z. \tag{64}$$

Layard and Nickell call the real wage implied by the first equation, the "feasible real wage," the real wage that firms can afford to pay given their technology and a specific level of employment. They call the real wage implied by the second equation the "target real wage," the real wage consistent with wage bargaining for a given level of unemployment. In equilibrium the two must be consistent. Equilibrium is represented in figure 10.12, using 1985 values for z.[41] An interesting aspect of the figure is that the target real wage, which is a decreasing function of unemployment for values of unemployment below 12%, becomes an increasing function of unemployment above 12%. The reason is that as unemployment increases, the direct effect of unemployment decreases (this comes from the logarithmic specification), and the proportion of long-term unemployed increases.[42] Eventually the second effect dominates the first. This is an interesting but

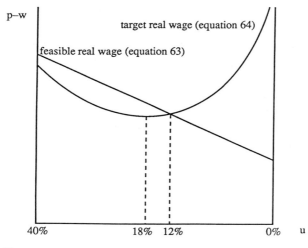

Figure 10.12
Equilibrium unemployment

perhaps not a very robust result, for it depends on the logarithmic rather than linear specification of the direct effect of unemployment.

In the long run, equilibrium unemployment only depends on z. (The model is constrained so that the unemployment rate is unaffected by the ratio of labor force to capital, $k - l$.) In the short run, however, unemployment can deviate from that value. In effect, in the short run, unemployment is determined by aggregate demand, and the price and wage equations determine the movement in wages and prices. An increase in aggregate demand increases employment. This leads to increases in both nominal prices and wages as firms attempt to increase their desired markup, and wage bargains attempt to increase the real wage. The dynamic effects of aggregate demand depend on both the dynamic nominal interactions and the dynamic relations among employment, markups, and desired real wages. In particular, a decrease in demand, leading to an increase in unemployment, has a strong initial impact on wages and prices. If unemployment remains high, the pressure on wages and prices decreases: the proportion of long-term unemployed increases, decreasing wage pressure given prices; firms ride out costs of adjustment, decreasing their desired markup.

How do Layard and Nickell explain the increase in unemployment in Europe within their model? They point to increases in the elements of z during the 1970s as the main cause of actual as well as equilibrium unemployment. They emphasize increased union militancy, higher primary input prices, and increases in employers' taxes and social security. They conclude that equilibrium and actual unemployment increased in tandem during the 1970s. In the 1980s, however, all these factors have reversed course and thus cannot explain the further increase in unemployment. Layard and Nickell explain most of the increase in unemployment of the 1980s by adverse shifts in aggregate demand. Given the prolonged high level of unemployment, however, and the high proportion of long-term unemployed, there is little downward pressure on inflation. Trying to reduce unemployment too fast could be inflationary.

The Layard-Nickell model provides an example of how to relate the theories developed in this book to the data. It suggests a complex set of causes for high unemployment in which both demand and supply factors play a role and the labor market's own dynamics explain the persistence of high unemployment with nearly stable inflation.

Problems

1. *Asset pricing in the consumption CAPM. (This follows Hansen and Singleton 1983.)*

Consider the first-order condition satisfied by optimal plans of consumers, equation (2) in the text:

$$1 = (1 + \theta)^{-1} E\left[\left(\frac{U'(c_{t+1})}{U'(c_t)}\right)(1 + z_{it}) \middle| t\right].$$

Assume that utility is CRRA, with a coefficient of relative risk aversion of γ. Assume also that the rate of growth of consumption, defined as $\log(c_{t+1}) - \log(c_t)$, and the net rate of return on asset i, defined as $\log(1 + z_{it})$, are conditionally joint normally distributed, with mean g and x and covariance matrix V. Derive the equilibrium rate of return x as a function of θ, γ, g, and the elements of V. Interpret.

2. *The term structure of interest rates. (This is a simplified version of Campbell 1986.)*

Consider the Lucas asset-pricing model, with only one asset. Assume that the dividend on the asset follows

$$\log(d_t) = g + \log(d_{t-1}) + e_t,$$

where e_t is normally distributed, white noise, with mean zero and variance σ^2. Assume that utility is CRRA, with a coefficient of relative risk aversion of γ.
(a) Consider an i-period pure discount bond at time t, a bond that pays one unit of the good at time $t + i$ and has price p_{it}. Derive the equilibrium value of p_{it}.
(b) Define the yield to maturity on an i-period pure discount bond as r_{it}, such that $(1 + r_{it})^{-i} = p_{it}$. Characterize the term structure of yields to maturity at time t. Is it upward or downward sloping? Explain.
(c) How would we have to change the model to explain why the term structure is sometimes upward and sometimes downward sloping?

3. *Dynamic effects of demand and supply shocks in a model with nominal rigidities.*

Consider the following model of the economy:

$$y_t = m_t - p_t,$$

$$y_t = a(p_t - w_t + u_t),$$

$$w_t = p_{t-1},$$

$$m_t = m_{t-1} + e_{mt},$$

$$u_t = u_{t-1} + e_{ut},$$

where all notation is standard. The two sources of shocks are nominal money and productivity; both follow random walks.

(a) Characterize the dynamic effects of a shock to nominal money, e_{mt}, on prices, real wages, and output.

(b) Characterize the dynamic effects of a shock to productivity, e_{ut}, on prices, real wages, and output.

(c) Compare your results to the results of the Blanchard-Quah decomposition of output movements reported in chapter 1.

(d) Derive the correlation between real wages and output implied by this model. Can it be reconciled with the stylized facts given in chapter 1?

(e) (This is harder.) Derive the univariate representation of output, given the relative variance of e_m and e_u and assuming that they are uncorrelated.

(f) "The increasing evidence supporting the view that the U.S. GNP series contains a unit root implies that any model which is to explain the nature of observed fluctuations must be essentially driven by productivity shocks." Comment.

4. *Output and the Stock Market.*

Consider the following modification of the dynamic IS-LM model presented in section 10.4:

(IS) $\dfrac{dy}{dt} = \sigma(d - y),$ $\sigma > 0,$

        $d = aq + by + g,$ $a > 0, 0 < b < 1,$

(LM) $r = cy - h(m - p),$ $c > 0, h > 0,$

(ARB) $\dfrac{(dq/dt)^*}{q} + \dfrac{\pi}{q} = r,$

        $\pi = \alpha_0 + \alpha_1 y,$ $\alpha_1 > 0.$

y is output, d is aggregate demand, q is the value of firms on the stock market (the implicit assumption is one of pure equity finance), and g is a variable reflecting the effects of fiscal policy on aggregate demand. The variable r is the short real rate of interest; inflation, actual and expected, is equal to zero so that r is also the nominal rate of interest. $m - p$ is the logarithm of real money. π is profit. Asterisks denote expectations.

(a) Explain the rationale behind each of these equations. Show that the third equation (ARB), together with the assumption of no bubbles, implies that the market value of firms is equal to the present discounted value of expected profits.

(b) Reduce the system to a dynamic system in q and y. Characterize the conditions on the coefficients under which the equilibrium, for given values of m, p, and g, is a saddle point equilibrium under perfect foresight. Assume in what follows that these conditions hold.

(c) Show the dynamic effects of an unanticipated permanent increase in g on the stock market and output. Why is the initial effect on the stock market ambiguous?

(d) Show the effects of an anticipated increase in g on the stock market and output. Can an expansionary fiscal policy decrease output? Why?

(e) Describe (in words) the dynamic effects of a bubble on the stock market and output in this economy.

5. *Overshooting and price adjustment.*

Consider the following version of the dynamic Mundell-Fleming model. Instead of assuming, as in the text, that the price level is fixed and that output adjusts slowly, assume that in response to a change in money, output remains constant and prices adjust slowly. (The only reason for not having both output and prices adjust slowly is to avoid a three-dimensional system.) Thus the dynamics of the economy are given by

$$\frac{(de/dt)^*}{e} = i\left(\frac{M}{P}, \bar{Y}\right) - i',$$

$$\frac{dP}{dt} = \phi\left[A\left(\bar{Y}, \frac{eP'}{P}, F\right) - \bar{Y}\right],$$

where $\bar{Y}$ is full employment and actual output.

(a) Characterize the equilibrium in the (e, P) space.

(b) Characterize the dynamic effects of an unanticipated increase in the nominal money stock on nominal and real exchange rates. Explain your results.

(c) Compare your results to those obtained in the text.

6. *In the Calvo model of section 10.5, characterize the dynamic effects of*

(a) an unanticipated increase in the level of the money stock,

(b) an anticipated increase in the level of the money stock.

7. *Staggered contracts in the open economy.*

Consider the following economy:

$$y_t = a(e_t - p_t) + b(m_t - p_t) + v_t, \tag{1}$$

$$p_t = \left(\frac{1}{2}\right)\phi(w_t + w_{t-1}) + (1 - \phi)e_t, \qquad 0 < \phi < 1, \tag{2}$$

$$w_t = \left(\frac{1}{2}\right)(w_{t-1} + E[w_{t+1}|t]) + \gamma(y_t + E[y_{t+1}|t]) + u_t, \qquad \gamma > 0. \tag{3}$$

The policy rules are

$$m_t = \beta p_t \qquad \text{and} \qquad e_t = \alpha p_t. \tag{4}$$

Both u and v are white noise, uncorrelated with each other and with variance σ_u^2 and σ_v^2. The information set at time t includes past, but not current, values of u and v.

(a) Interpret these equations. What is the interpretation of ϕ? Can the policymaker really use separate policy rules for exchange rates and money? Is equation (3) reasonable in an open economy?

(b) Solve, under rational expectations, for p and y as functions of current and lagged realizations of u and v.

(c) Describe the response of p and y to u and v. How do the parameters ϕ, γ, α, and β affect the magnitude and the persistence of these responses?

Notes

1. The practice of using simple ad hoc models is common. Among well-known examples are Lucas (1973), who used a simple aggregate supply-aggregate demand model presented in chapter 7; Barro and Gordon (1983), who used a single equation aggregate supply model which we will use in chapter 11; and Sargent and Wallace (1981), who used simple demand-for-money equations to analyze the link between deficit finance and inflation.

2. Since we are on the subject of methodology, we will mention two related issues that often come up in this context.

Building ad hoc models does not mean limiting oneself to small analytical models that admit explicit solutions. Although this is what we do in this book, there is no reason to make it a general principle. Improvements in computing power have made it much easier to use by way of simulations models that cannot be solved analytically. Large macroeconometric models that allow combinations of many more dynamic mechanisms than any analytical model have a long history of use and usefulness in many parts of macroeconomics. The problem of communicating results and their robustness to readers is, however, more difficult when simulations have to be used than when explicit solutions can be presented.

Nor does building ad hoc models mean systematically eschewing the rigor of deriving the model from first principles. The costs and benefits of deriving a model from first principles—explicit utility and profit maximization, and explicit treatment of market structure—must be weighed case by case. Explicit derivation forces one to think more precisely about the specification one intends to use. It may lead, however, for reasons of analytical tractability, to specifications which are unpleasantly contorted and leave out important complexities of the issues at hand.

3. We have already gone further into methodology than might be wise, but we should note that we are disagreeing here with Friedman's (1953) argument that models should be judged solely by their predictions.

4. In each case the reader will probably think of many reasons why leaving out imperfections may in fact be misleading. In the case of foreign borrowing, for example, issues of repudiation, which are left out of chapter 2, have turned out to be crucial in the current debt crisis. In the case of Ricardian equivalence, uncertainty and the functioning of credit markets under incomplete information, which we studied in chapter 9, turn out to be relevant for the question whether and when individuals can undo the government's actions. The conclusion is that no model is ever complete; progress is achieved by introducing new elements that were left out of previous models and turn out to be important.

5. See, for example, Hansen and Singleton (1983).

6. Note that equation (6), which uses individual consumption, does not require, for example, that human wealth be tradable. But if human wealth is not tradable, aggregation problems are likely to be more severe.

7. This premium appears to have dramatically decreased in the 1980s and is now apparently much smaller. The word "apparently" needs to be used because the expected rate of return on stocks is not observable.

8. The model and policy analysis that follow are not exactly those of Drazen and Helpman. They start from a maximizing model, making assumptions that enable them to work in reduced form with a demand for money function plus budget constraints; in addition they formally analyze debt dynamics when there are changing probabilities of the type of stabilization that will eventually be undertaken.

The dynamics presented in this section are more intricate than those presented in section 4.7, which the reader may want to review first.

9. For this to be a feasible policy shift, required seigniorage has to be less than the maximal amount, which is attained at inflation rate π'.

10. This argument assumes that b_T is less than the maximum feasible level of debt given the seigniorage function. If this were not the case, the government program would not be feasible and thus not credible.

11. This raises the question how this belief is formed. The answer cannot be found within the model as it has been presented here. We have discussed closely related issues in our analysis of learning in chapter 5.

12. This is a key assumption, equivalent to the assumption that the inflation rate is not expected to jump both on the dynamic path and at the moment of the change in policy. The basis for this assumption is that the money stock is itself continuous; therefore if the inflation rate were expected to jump, the stock of real balances would jump and so would the price level, imposing large instantaneous capital gains or losses on money holders. To rule out such expected infinite instantaneous capital gains or losses, the path of the inflation rate has to contain no expected jumps.

13. The reader may want to derive them, for example, from a Cobb-Douglas specification with multiplicative technological shocks, $Y = (NU)^a$.

14. See, for example, Bruno and Sachs (1985) for an analysis of the effects of supply shocks on the OECD countries within that broad framework.

15. It is clear that we are then describing a game between wage-setters and the monetary authority. Wage-setters are likely to understand how the monetary authority will react to their wage demands. This raises many important issues, which we will analyze in the next chapter.

16. Hicks has subsequently expressed doubts about the faithfulness with which the apparatus reflects Keynes' macroeconomic theories. We believe it is actually a good representation.

17. This assumes that the interest rate affects neither labor supply nor labor demand so that the labor market determines the level of output. If this were not the case—if, for example, one believes along the lines explored in chapter 7 that interest rates affect labor supply decisions—one must solve for labor, goods, and assets market equilibrium simultaneously rather than recursively.

18. The assumption is more likely to be right if there is sufficient slack in the labor markets and in capacity that movements in aggregate demand can easily be accommodated, such as during depressions. Hicks (1937) wrote: "So the General Theory of Employment is the Economics of Depression."

19. This statement is clearly not right. Like any successful benchmark model, the IS-LM has been subjected to an unending litany of criticisms, many of which belong to the history of thought. We concentrate on those we find relevant at this stage.

20. This follows Blanchard (1981), whose focus is on the interaction between the stock market and output rather than on the interaction between long-term interest rates and output with which we are concerned here.

21. See Blanchard and Dornbusch (1983), and Branson, Fraga, and Johnson (1985).

22. To mention a few, our characterization of optimal consumption, as well as the empirical evidence, does not suggest long lags in the adjustment of consumption. Likewise, the evidence on inventory behavior is not suggestive of strong smoothing effects of production in response to demand shocks. Also, if firms initially deplete inventories, they should later increase production not only to meet demand but also to return to their desired level. This leads to a more complex dynamic characterization than (37).

23. Such bonds do not exist in most countries, but the analysis remains appropriate even so.

24. Here again, chapter 6 and the first section of this chapter make clear what issues lie behind such an arbitrage assumption. Under risk neutrality (and additive separability) expected rates of return are equalized, but they must all be equal to the subjective discount rate. If they are not, aggregate consumption becomes infinitely positive or negative. Under risk aversion we do not expect the premium to be exactly constant or invariant to changes in policy.

25. These issues are studied in Blanchard (1981).

26. In the words of Robert Solow, "If the Lord had intended us to analyze three variable systems, she would have made the page three dimensional."

27. Mundell wrote a series of papers on this subject, collected in *International Economics* (1968). Dornbusch (1980) presents a very clear exposition. Frenkel and Razin (1987) summarize and extend the basic model.

28. The tradition is to denote foreign variables by an asterisk. However, we are already using that symbol to denote expectations.

29. Dornbusch (1976) specifies a slow price adjustment. We maintain the assumption of constant prices but return to discuss the issue at the end of this section.

30. See Englander and Los (1983) and Blinder (1988). However, Gordon (1988) finds in effect large negative residuals in the wage equation and large offsetting positive residuals in the price equation over the period.

31. See Blanchard and Summers (1986).

32. We mentioned modern versions of the distribution effects of deflation in our analysis of credit markets in chapter 9. Those versions emphasized the effects of deflation on the optimal investment decisions of firms.

33. The following model is a simplified version of the appendix in Fischer (1977).

34. An alternative interpretation is that there is a continuum of wage-setters; x denotes the wage chosen by a wage-setter, and p the price chosen by firms who mark up over the average wage.

35. The formal similarity between this model and the finite horizon model developed in chapter 3 should not escape the reader. This is no accident: the Poisson distribution, which is heavily used in both cases, is extremely convenient for purposes of aggregation. Here, just as there, the assumption is not particularly realistic. If firms choose their price at random times, we would expect these changes to happen at times where money is changing, along the lines developed in chapter 8 in analyzing state-dependent rules, as we would expect the timing of changes not to be independent across firms.

36. Calvo (1983) assumes the existence of an agency that in effect equalizes purchasing prices to the average price level.

37. Ray Fair (e.g., 1984) uses a similar approach in developing a macroeconometric model of the United States.

38. These are simplified versions of their empirical specifications. See Layard and Nickell (1986, 1987) for details.

39. Note that this result is at odds with the stylized fact, from studies of price behavior in the United States, that firms accommodate fluctuations in demand in the short run with no or little adjustment in their price. We have unfortunately no reconciliation to offer.

40. Layard and Nickell's (1987) explanation is that the effect of productivity on employment, given the real wage and the capital stock, depends on whether the elasticity of employment with respect to the real wage is greater or less than one.

They conclude that to the extent that this elasticity is not very different from one, one may not find an effect on productivity. In view of their estimated elasticity, their argument is not fully persuasive.

41. This figure is taken from Layard and Nickell (1987).

42. This opens up the possibility of multiple equilibria, with both a low and a high unemployment equilibrium, as we had in the Diamond model of chapter 9. For estimated parameter values, however, there appears to be another equilibrium value of unemployment in figure 10.12, but it is close to 100%.

References

Barro, Robert, and David Gordon (1983). "A Positive Theory of Monetary Policy in a Natural Rate Model." *Journal of Political Economy* 91 (Aug.), 589–610.

Blanchard, Olivier (1981). "Output, the Stock Market, and Interest Rates." *American Economic Review* 71, 1 (March), 132–143.

Blanchard, Olivier, and Dornbusch, Rudiger (1983). "US Deficits, the Dollar and Europe." Reprinted in O. Blanchard, R. Dornbusch, and R. Layard (eds.), *Restoring Europe's Prosperity*. Cambridge, MA: MIT Press, 1986.

Blanchard, Olivier, and Lawrence Summers (1986). "Hysteresis and the European Unemployment Problem." *NBER Macroeconomics Annual* 1, 15–78.

Blinder, Alan (1988). "The Challenge of Unemployment." Richard T. Ely Lecture. *American Economic Association Papers and Proceedings* 78 (May), forthcoming.

Branson, William, Arminio Fraga, and Robert Johnson (1985). "Expected Fiscal Policy and the Recession of 1982." NBER Working Paper 1784. December.

Bruno, Michael, and Jeffrey Sachs (1985). *Economics of Worldwide Stagflation*. Cambridge, MA: Harvard University Press.

Calvo, Guillermo (1983). "Staggered Prices in a Utility-Maximizing Framework." *Journal of Monetary Economics* 12, 3 (Sept.), 383–398.

Campbell, John (1986). "Bond and Stock Returns in a Simple Exchange Model." *Quarterly Journal of Economics* 101 (Nov.), 785–804.

De Long, J. Bradford, and Lawrence H. Summers (1986). "Is Increased Price Flexibility Stabilizing?" *American Economic Review* 76, 5 (Dec.), 1031–1044.

Dornbusch, Rudiger (1976). "Expectations and Exchange Rate Dynamics." *Journal of Political Economy* 84, 1161–1176.

Dornbusch, Rudiger (1980). *Open Economy Macroeconomics*. New York: Basic Books.

Dornbusch, Rudiger, and Stanley Fischer (1986). "Stopping Hyperinflations Past and Present." *Weltwirtschaftliches Archiv* 122, 1, 1–47.

Dornbusch, Rudiger, and Mario Henrique Simonsen (1983). *Inflation Debt and Indexation*. Cambridge, MA: MIT Press.

Drazen, Allan, and Elhanan Helpman (1988). "Inflationary Consequences of Anticipated Macroeconomic Policies." *Quarterly Journal of Economics*, forthcoming.

Driskill, Robert, and Steven Sheffrin (1986). "Is Price Flexibility Destabilizing?" *American Economic Review* 76, 4 (Sept.), 802–807.

Englander, Steven, and Cornelis Los (1983). "The Stability of the Phillips Curve and Its Implications for the 1980s." Research paper. Federal Reserve Bank of New York. January.

Fair, Ray (1984). "Estimated Trade-offs between Unemployment and Inflation." NBER Working Paper 1377. June.

Fischer, Stanley (1977). "Wage Indexation and Macroeconomic Stability." Reprinted in S. Fischer, *Indexing, Inflation and Economic Policy*. Cambridge, MA: MIT Press, 1986.

Fisher, Irving (1920). *Stabilizing the Dollar*. New York: Macmillan.

Fleming, J. Marcus (1962). "Domestic Financial Policies Under Fixed and Under Floating Exchange Rates." IMF *Staff Papers* 9, 3 (Nov.), 369–379.

Frenkel, Jacob A., and Assaf Razin (1987). "The Mundell-Fleming Model: A Quarter Century Later." NBER Working Paper 2321.

Friedman, Milton (1953). "The Methodology of Positive Economics." In his *Essays in Positive Economics*. University of Chicago Press.

Friedman, Milton (1968). "The Role of Monetary Policy." *American Economic Review* 58, 1 (March), 1–17.

Gordon, Robert J. (1988). "The Role of Wages in the Inflation Process." *American Economic Association Papers and Proceedings* 78 (May), forthcoming.

Gray, JoAnna (1976). "Wage Indexation: A Macroeconomic Approach." *Journal of Monetary Economics* 2, 221–235.

Grossman, Sanford, and Robert J. Shiller (1982). "Consumption Correlatedness and Risk Measurement in Economies with Nontraded Assets and Heterogenous Information." *Journal of Financial Economics* 10, 195–21ᴄ.

Hansen, Lars, and Kenneth Singleton (1983). "Stochastic Consumption, Risk Aversion and the Temporal Behavior of Asset Prices." *Journal of Political Economy* (April), 249–266.

Hicks, John R. (1937). "Mr. Keynes and the 'Classics': A Suggested Interpretation." *Econometrica*. Reprinted in J. R. Hicks, *Critical Essays in Monetary Theory*. Oxford University Press, 1967.

Keynes, John M. (1936). *The General Theory of Employment, Interest and Money*. Reprinted Harbinger, Harcourt Brace and World, 1964.

Layard, Richard, and Stephen Nickell (1986). "The Performance of the British Labour Market." Centre for Labour Studies. London School of Economics Discussion Paper 249.

Layard, Richard, and Stephen Nickell (1987). "The Labour Market." In R. Dornbusch and R. Layard (eds.), *The Performance of the British Economy*. Oxford: Clarendon Press, 131–179.

Lintner, John (1965). "The Valuation of Risk Assets and the Selection of Risky Investments in Stock Portfolios and Capital Budgets." *Review of Economics and Statistics* 47, 13–37.

Lipsey, Richard (1960). "The Relation between Unemployment and the Rate of Change of Money Wage Rates in the United Kingdom 1962–1957: A Further Analysis." *Economica* 27, (Feb.), 1–31.

Lucas, Robert, E., (1973). "Some International Evidence on Output-Inflation Trade-offs." *American Economic Review* 63 (June), 326–334.

Lucas, Robert E., Jr. (1978). "Asset Prices in an Exchange Economy." *Econometrica* 46, 6 (Dec.), 1426–1445.

Mankiw, N. Gregory, and Matthew Shapiro (1986). "Risk and Return, Consumption Beta versus Market Beta." *Review of Economics and Statistics* 68, 3 (Aug.), 452–459.

Mankiw, N. Gregory (1986). "The Equity Premium and the Concentration of Aggregate Shocks." NBER Working Paper 1788. January.

Mehra, Rajnish, and Edward Prescott (1985). "The Equity Premium: A Puzzle." *Journal of Monetary Economics* 15, 2 (March), 145–162.

Merton, Robert C. (1973). "An Intertemporal Capital Asset Pricing Model." *Econometrica* 41, 5 (Sept.), 867–888.

Modigliani, Franco (1971). "Monetary Policy and Consumption." In *Consumer Spending and Monetary Policy: the Linkages*. Federal Reserve Bank of Boston Conference Series, 5 (June), 9–97.

Mossin, Jan (1966). "Equilibrium in a Capital Asset Market." *Econometrica* 34, 768–783.

Mundell, Robert A. (1968). *International Economics*. New York: Macmillan.

Muth, John F. (1960). "Optimal Properties of Exponentially Weighted Forecasts." Reprinted in R. E. Lucas and T. J. Sargent (eds.), *Rational Expectations and Econometric Practice*. Minneapolis, MN: University of Minnesota Press, 1981.

Perry, George L. (1966). *Unemployment, Money Wage Rates, and Inflation*. Cambridge, MA: MIT Press.

Phelps, Edmund S. (1968). "Money-Wage Dynamics and Labor-Market Equilibrium." *Journal of Political Economy* 76, 4, part II (July–Aug.), 678–711.

Phillips, A. W. (1958). "The Relation between Unemployment and the Rate of Change of the Money Wage Rates in the United Kingdom." *Economica* 25 (Nov.), 283–299.

Samuelson, Paul A. (1947). *Foundations of Economic Analysis.* Cambridge, MA: Harvard University Press.

Samuelson, Paul, and Robert Solow (1960). "Analytical Aspects of Anti-Inflation Policy." *American Economic Review* 50, 5, 177–194.

Sargent, Thomas J. (1982). "The Ends of Four Big Hyperinflations." In R. E. Hall (ed.), *Inflation.* University of Chicago Press.

Sargent, Thomas, and Neil Wallace (1981). "Some Unpleasant Monetarist Arithmetic." *Federal Reserve Bank of Minneapolis Quarterly Review* 5, 1–17.

Sharpe, William F. (1964). "Capital Asset Prices: A Theory of Market Equilibrium under Conditions of Risk." *Journal of Finance* 19, 425–442.

Tobin, James (1972). "The Wage-Price Mechanism: Overview of the Conference." In O. Eckstein (ed.), *The Econometrics of Price Determination Conference.* Washington, D.C.: Federal Reserve System.

Tobin, James (1975). "Keynesian Models of Recession and Depression." *American Economic Review* 65 (May), 195–202. Reprinted in J. Tobin, *Essays in Economics Policy and Practice.* Cambridge, MA: MIT Press, 1982.

11   Monetary and Fiscal Policy Issues

Although contention about the appropriate model of the economy and its microeconomic foundations continues, macroeconomic policy decisions have to be made. Central banks have to decide how to control the money supply and interest rates (if they can), and whether to fix the exchange rate or let it float. Governments have to decide how much to spend and how to finance their spending through taxes, borrowing, or printing money.

In this chapter we use simple macroeconomic models to analyze monetary and fiscal policy issues. Although it seems natural to argue that policy should be inactive or neutral in the face of uncertainties about the structure of the economy and the operation of policy, this would not provide a concrete description of any policy. Is an inactive monetary policy one that keeps the money base, or M1 or M2 constant, or is it a policy that keeps nominal interest rates constant? Does an inactive fiscal policy fix government spending at a constant level or as a constant proportion of GNP? Does it hold tax rates or total tax revenue constant? And so on.

Likewise, this chapter does not address the tactics of economic policy—for instance, the question of how much the money base should rise in a particular month—because such questions cannot be answered without the use of a specific and detailed macroeconometric model. Policy simulations, or derivations of optimal policies given specified welfare functions, provide the answers to the detailed questions and are an input into the decision-making processes of both the Fed and the Congress. Rather we concentrate on the strategic issues, on such questions as whether the money stock (or its growth rate) should be held fixed or should instead respond to new information, or whether a policy of targeting interest rates leaves the price level undetermined (and what that might mean), or whether tax rates should be varied over the course of the business cycle.

Before getting down to the issues, we briefly discuss alternative views of the goals of policy. We start on the policy issues by discussing the conduct of monetary policy in a fiat money world. We then go on to examine fiscal policy questions and conclude with an examination of the important problem of dynamic inconsistency in policymaking.

11.1 The Goals of Economic Policy

In analyzing issues of macroeconomic policy, be it deriving an optimal policy or simply judging outcomes of alternative policies, what objective function should we assign to policymakers?

The traditional approach is to assume that the policymaker maximizes a *social welfare function*. If the economy has identical infinitely long-lived individuals, the social welfare function naturally coincides with the utility function of these individuals. Even if policymakers and individuals have the same objective function, there may still be room for the policymaker to improve the allocation as long as markets are imperfect; the policymaker must still decide how to minimize the tax burden needed to finance government spending. When, however, the economy is composed of individuals who differ in many ways and who may not have infinite horizons, defining the social welfare function becomes more difficult. One might appeal, as we did in chapter 3, to some implicit social contract across generations, born and unborn. Or, one might limit oneself to checking whether existing allocations are Pareto optimal, an approach that we also followed in chapter 3 and that leads to the golden rule result of capital accumulation.

An alternative approach is to take into account some of the political or institutional realities that further constrain actual policy. Or going even further, one might want to take into account that policymakers have their own agenda, their own objective function. Policymakers may represent the interests of particular groups. At the same time they care about remaining in power, either because they want to be able to implement their political agenda or simply because they enjoy it. Thus an alternative starting point is to derive the relevant objective function from the incentives and constraints faced by politicians. In the limit this approach becomes a purely positive analysis of policy in which the goal becomes one of explaining existing policy rather than to recommend changes.

Economists have, for the most part, ignored these incentives and constraints and have analyzed optimal policy starting from a social welfare function, leaving to political scientists the job of explaining the characteristics of existing policy.[1] This is not a completely satisfactory division of labor, nor is it strictly enforced: we shall see below that standard characterizations of the policymaker's objective function put more weight on the costs of inflation than is suggested by our understanding of the effects of inflation; in doing so, they probably reflect political realities and the heavy political costs of high inflation.

The other issue we face is more mundane but extremely important nevertheless. Evaluating the full-fledged social welfare function, which is likely to depend on the utilities of current and prospective members of society, under alternative policies, rapidly becomes analytically untractable. Thus we often have to rely on a simpler objective function, a *macro welfare function*, defined directly over a few macroeconomic variables such as output, unemployment, inflation, or the current account. This approach goes back explicitly at least to Tinbergen (1952) and implicitly much further, to earlier authors who discussed policies to stabilize the trade cycle. One such macro welfare function that has played an important role in the literature, and which we will use heavily below is the following loss function:

$$L = E\left[\sum_0^\infty (1 + \theta)^{-t}(w_p(\pi_t - \bar{\pi}_t)^2 + w_y(y_t - \bar{y}_t)^2) \middle| 0 \right]. \tag{1}$$

The loss function is quadratic in the expected deviations of both the inflation rate and the level of output from their target values, $\bar{\pi}_t$ and $\bar{y}_t$, and discounts future deviations at the rate θ. We briefly discuss each of the terms in that function.

Consider first the term in output. The quadratic term can be interpreted as a quadratic approximation to the welfare loss of being away from $\bar{y}$, the equilibrium level of output absent distortions and rigidities. The target level of output $\bar{y}_t$ has a time index to take into account the desirability of some changes in output, for example, those in response to changes in productivity. In the representative-agent competitive-equilibrium business cycle models of chapter 7, all variations in output were indeed variations in $\bar{y}_t$. But in the sticky price Keynesian models of chapters 8 and 9 there were further deviations of output from the full employment level in response to shocks, which were not warranted. In these models also, even in the absence of shocks, $\bar{y}$ is not the equilibrium level of output. In the presence of monopoly power by firms, for example, as in the model of chapter 8, the equilibrium output is too low. In that case the loss function should not penalize deviations of output around the full employment level symmetrically; rather output that is a given percentage below the full employment level is penalized more heavily than output that is the same percentage above the full employment level.

How do we justify the quadratic term in inflation? What are the welfare costs of inflation? The literature suggests a distinction between the costs of anticipated and unanticipated inflation. Anticipated inflation is socially costly because it causes unnecessary economizing on real balances (as implied by the optimum quantity of money result of chapter 4), generates costs of price change, and even increases endogenous relative price uncertainty (Benabou 1988). Unanticipated inflation is costly because it increases relative price variability (Cukierman 1984) and costs of information gathering. The redistributions of income and wealth associated with unanticipated inflation can also be regarded as socially undesirable. Despite an impressive array of models in which inflation is socially costly, there appears to be professional consensus (which we believe is less justified than it was a decade ago) that economics cannot justify the weight put on low inflation as a goal of policy.[2] Its presence as the only macroeconomic variable in addition to output in the loss function reflects in part the fact that, right or wrong, inflation is perceived as costly by people and is costly for policymakers to ignore.

Finally, what determines the discount rate in (1)? This may be the discount rate that individuals use to discount their future. Or it may be smaller, reflecting the concern of the policymaker for generations yet unborn. Or, it is sometimes argued, it may be larger than the private discount rate: because of the shortness of the typical government's horizon, its discount rate θ is likely to be above the correct social discount rate. This brings us back to our earlier remarks as to the normative-descriptive ambiguity in the interpretation of (1).

11.2 Monetary Policy

In a pure commodity money system, money looks after itself. The flow supply of the commodity, a durable such as gold, is determined by costs of production, and the demand is generally determined by both its monetary and nonmonetary uses. Under the gold standard a certain weight of gold is the numeraire, and the price level is the inverse of the relative price of gold. The price level is determined at each moment by the demand for the stock of gold (including jewelry demand) and the supply, which is the existing stock. Changes in the price level over time are determined by changes in the stock demand and by changes in net supply, which is dependent on the costs of producing gold, its rate of use as an input in production, and its rate of depreciation.[3]

A commodity money system could operate completely automatically. There is no record of how a pure system without inside money has worked. The evidence from the gold standard period, however, gives no reason to think that a pure commodity money system would ensure either more price level stability or fewer financial panics than modern fiat money systems,[4] except for the important fact that the long-run inflation rate during the gold standard period was lower than it has been subsequently. In any event, given the resource savings of using a token money, commodity money systems have been replaced by fiat money systems .

As banking and paper money developed in the nineteenth century, governments were forced to deal with the question of how to control the monetary system, in general, and the quantity of paper money, in particular. For want of space, we will not review the fascinating history of thought on money, banking, and monetary policy[5] but will rather turn directly to monetary policy issues that arise in fiat money systems.

In all cases we assume that the central bank controls the quantity of money, and we will examine the effects on output and price level behavior of alternative operating rules of monetary policy under the maintained assumption that there are nominal rigidities. In doing so, we narrow the discussion in several respects. First, by using models in which monetary policy has real effects because prices or wages are sticky, or because the monetary authority can react more quickly to disturbances than the private sector, we prejudge the question of whether monetary policy can have real effects. Further we restrict the mechanism through which monetary policy affects the economy.[6] We view these as reasonable assumptions. Second, by assuming that the government controls money, we do not discuss the issues introduced by the presence of inside money in the conduct of monetary policy.[7] Third, by omitting details of central bank–commercial bank interactions, we pass over the role of the central bank as lender of last resort and preventer of panics and bank runs.[8]

We focus on a number of issues, all of which have figured prominently in discussions of monetary policy. We start by examining the trade-off between output and price or inflation stability, and the accelerationist hypothesis, due to Friedman (1968) and Phelps (1968). We then study the case for the use of interest rates versus money to control output. Finally, we consider the case for and the implications of alternative simple rules of monetary conduct, from nominal interest rate pegging to constant money growth or nominal income targeting.

Output versus Price Stability

The simplest model to discuss the trade-offs involved in output versus inflation stabilization is the first model of aggregate demand and aggregate supply introduced in the previous chapter, namely,

$$y_t = m_t - p_t + v_t,$$ (1)

$$y_t = \beta(p_t - p_t^*) + \beta u_t.$$ (2)

All variables are in logarithms. The first equation gives aggregate demand, the second aggregate supply.[9] p_t^* is the expected price level at time t, based on information available at time $t - 1$. v_t and u_t are demand and supply shocks, both following AR(1) processes:

$$v_t = \rho_1 v_{t-1} + \varepsilon_{1t}, \qquad 0 \leqslant \rho_1 < 1,$$

$$u_t = \rho_2 u_{t-1} + \varepsilon_{2t}, \qquad 0 \leqslant \rho_2 < 1.$$ (3)

The monetary authority is assumed to have the loss function:

$$L = E\left[\sum_0^\infty (1 + \theta)^{-t}(w_p \pi_t)^2 + w_y(y_t - \bar{y})^2) \Big| 0 \right].$$ (4)

Thus the monetary authority dislikes deviations of inflation from zero. In addition its target level of output is constant. This is an important assumption, with important implications later: if we think of u as an adverse technological shock, we will expect $\bar{y}$ to move with u. Thus one possible interpretation of u is rather as a wage push, or an increase in profit margins of firms that the monetary authority does not want to accommodate. Finally, $\bar{y}$ is allowed to be different from zero, the equilibrium output in the absence of disturbances.

Money in period t is chosen with knowledge of the current values of v and u. This gives monetary policy the opportunity of reacting to information that becomes available after some private sector decisions have already been made.[10] We now consider the implications of alternative rules for money. Throughout this section we assume that the policymaker can precommit to following its rule in period t. In this way we avoid the issue of time inconsistency, which we will defer until section 11.3.

It is instructive to start by assuming adaptive expectations on the part of individuals. Once this is done, we will turn to the implications of rational expectations.

Adaptive Expectations
Assume that expectations of the *inflation rate* are adaptive[11] and are determined by

$$\pi_t^* - \pi_{t-1}^* = (1 - \gamma)(\pi_{t-1} - \pi_{t-1}^*), \qquad 0 < \gamma \leqslant 1.$$ (5)

By solving recursively backward, we get expected inflation as a distributed lag of past inflation, with weights declining at rate γ. For our convenience later, we write (5) using the lag operator L, as

$$(1 - \gamma L)\pi_t^* = (1 - \gamma)L\pi_t. \tag{5'}$$

Subtracting p_{t-1} from both p_t and p_t^* in (2) yields output as a function of actual minus expected inflation, and the supply shock:

$$y_t = \beta(\pi_t - \pi_t^*) + \beta u_t. \tag{2'}$$

Replacing π_t^* from (5') and rearranging gives

$$y_t = \beta\left(\frac{1 - L}{1 - \gamma L}\right)\pi_t + \beta u_t. \tag{6}$$

Under adaptive expectations output depends on the supply shock and on a distributed lag of changes in the rate of inflation.

Suppose first that w_p in the loss function is zero so that the goal of monetary policy is simply to keep output constant at $\bar{y}$. It is clear from (6) that monetary policy is capable of setting output exactly at $\bar{y}$ each period. The implied behavior of the inflation rate, obtained from (6) with $y_t = \bar{y}$, is

$$(1 - L)\pi_t = \frac{(1 - \gamma L)(\bar{y} - \beta u_t)}{\beta}. \tag{7}$$

Note that the process for inflation has a unit root. Given this process for inflation, equation (1) gives us the implied process for money.

We interpret (7) in two parts. First, we ignore the u_t component and ask what happens if $\bar{y}$ exceeds zero, the natural rate of output when u is zero. In that case $\pi_t - \pi_{t-1} = (1 - \gamma)\bar{y}/\beta$, and the inflation rate is increasing by the amount $(1 - \gamma)\bar{y}/\beta$ in each period. This is the famous *accelerationist* result derived by Friedman (1968) and Phelps (1968), using their Phillips curve together with the adaptive expectations assumption. The explanation is simple: if the government is trying to keep output above the natural rate, it has to produce inflation at a higher rate than expected each period. Since the expected inflation rate is a weighted average of past inflation rates, the actual rate must be increasing. Second, we consider the stochastic component, u_t. Whenever there is a supply shock in the current period, the government moves the inflation rate to offset the output effects of that shock. The change in the inflation rate gets built into expectations, with the result that future changes in inflation rates are set off by the current supply shock, and there is no force in the system tending to bring it back to any constant inflation rate.[12]

Of course, if the government has an inflation target as well as an output target, the accelerationist problem does not arise in this model. In the extreme case in which w_y is zero, and the government is concerned only about inflation, it can use monetary policy to set $\pi_t = 0$ in each period and leave output to be determined by (2'), given initial conditions. Eventually, expected inflation too becomes equal to 0 and in steady state $y_t = \beta u_t$.

Thus in the two extreme cases the government can stabilize the level of output completely at the cost of the inflation rate increasing forever, or it can stabilize the inflation rate completely with output eventually becoming equal to βu_t. In the general case the government maximizes (4), with both w_p and w_y nonzero. If an adverse supply shock hits, the government has to decide whether to increase the inflation rate (undertake expansionary monetary policy) to offset the effect of the shock on output. But it faces two penalties if it does so. First, it will move the current inflation rate above the level where it would have been otherwise; second, it will increase expected inflation in all future periods, thereby tending to reduce output as of a given inflation rate. It will thus certainly not entirely offset the adverse shock but rather accommodate it only partially. In this case, however, the stochastic processes for both the inflation rate and the level of output will be stable.[13]

One lesson of this adaptive expectations example is that the government will eventually lose control of nominal variables unless it has a nominal target. Where it is concerned only with keeping output at a target level ($w_p = 0$), the inflation rate is either ever-accelerating or can wander anywhere. So long as there is any weight on inflation in the loss function ($w_p > 0$), the inflation rate becomes a stationary process. Note, however, that the conditional expectation of the inflation rate is always well defined even when $w_p = 0$; given the history of inflation, the inflation rate will not move far off except in the long run.

Rational Expectations

Assume, instead, that expectations are rational. p_t^* is now $E[p_t|t - 1]$, the mathematical expectation of p_t based on information up and including time $t - 1$. We now switch gears and assume that the loss function includes a price *level* target rather than an inflation rate target. Thus π in (4) is replaced by p. For notational convenience, assume that the target price level is equal to zero. A price level target is not the same as a zero inflation rate target; the latter leads to a unit root in the process for the price level since we have no intention of reversing the unanticipated price level disturbances that occur within a given period. We switch to a price level target mainly because we will be discussing the issue of price level determinacy.

Consider again the case where the only goal of policy is to stabilize output. From (1) to (3) and the assumption of rational expectations,

$$y_t = \left(\frac{\beta}{1+\beta}\right)(m_t - E[m_t|t-1] + \varepsilon_{1t} + \varepsilon_{2t}) + \beta\rho_2 u_{t-1}. \tag{8}$$

The monetary rule which minimizes the variance of y around $\mathbf{y}$ is given by

$$m_t = E[m_t|t-1] - \varepsilon_{1t} - \varepsilon_{2t}.$$

Under that rule output and the price level are given by

$$y_t = \beta\rho_2 u_{t-1},$$

$$p_t = E[m_t|t-1] + \rho_1 v_{t-1} - \beta\rho_2 u_{t-1} - \varepsilon_{2t}. \tag{9}$$

Compare these results with those obtained under adaptive expectations. Under adaptive expectations, the monetary authority can achieve a level of output $\bar{y}$ higher than the natural rate, albeit at the cost of accelerating inflation. Under rational expectations, this simply becomes impossible: monetary policy cannot affect the average level of output. Thus the accelerationist result becomes an impossibility result. Similarly, monetary policy cannot eliminate the effects of anticipated supply shocks on output.[14] Monetary policy can, however, modify the effects of unexpected shocks, which in this case would mean canceling their effects on output.

Under adaptive expectations the inflation rate became unstable when the goal of policy was purely to stabilize output. Is the price level determinate in this case? The simple answer is no: equation (9) does not imply a determinate price level. Depending on the value of $E[m_t|t-1]$, the money supply and the price level could be anything. Formally, the attempt to fix a real variable produces price level indeterminacy, a result akin to the instability of the inflation process under adaptive expectations. But the cure for the indeterminacy is here quite obvious: set a base level for m_t, from which deviations will take place. Call that m, replace $E[m_t|t-1]$ in (9) by m, and the price level becomes determinate.[15]

Thus, provided the monetary authority has some nominal anchor, the price level will be determinate even when it concentrates policy entirely on stabilizing the level of output.

In cases where both w_p and w_y are nonzero, there is a trade-off between the goals of price level and output stabilization. The optimal monetary rule in this case is[16]

$$m_t = -v_t + \left(\frac{w_p - w_y\beta}{w_p + w_y\beta^2}\right)\beta\varepsilon_{2t} + \beta\rho_2 u_{t-1}. \tag{10}$$

Monetary policy completely offsets the effects of the lagged supply shock on prices, as well as current velocity shocks v_t.

The response of the money stock to a current supply shock is ambiguous, however, depending on the sign of $(w_p - w_y\beta)$. A favorable supply shock, ε_{2t}, tends to reduce the price level and increase output. If w_p is large, monetary policy offsets the price effect of the shock, tending to accentuate its effect on output; this is because a large w_p means that the loss function puts relatively heavy weight on price level behavior. For a large w_y monetary policy also offsets the output effect of the shock.

Interest Rate versus Money Targeting

Having examined the general issues involved in using money to achieve output or/and price stability, we go one level down and look at how monetary policy should be implemented. A long-standing discussion in monetary policy concerns whether the monetary authority should use money or interest rates to control output or/and prices. Within the framework we have developed above, this question does not make much sense, for two reasons. The first is quite simply that we have not introduced interest rates explicitly into the analysis: this is easily remedied by extending the analysis to include an IS and an LM relation. The second is more fundamental, however. Had we extended the analysis to allow for interest rates, we would have derived an optimal rule for money as a function of current and past disturbances. Corresponding to that rule for money, we could have derived a corresponding rule for the interest rate, also as a function of current and past disturbances. And either rule would have had the same outcome for output. Within that framework, using a money rule would have been equivalent to using an interest rule .

In an important article Poole (1970) suggested that the issue was in fact that, within a period, the monetary authority did not know what the disturbances were and could not observe output. Thus, within a period, it had the choice between fixing the level of money or fixing the level of interest rates, accommodating any movement in money demand at the given rate. Poole sought the conditions under which pegging money or interest rates would be appropriate. Poole used an IS-LM model without the aggregate supply side and offered the following answer: if disturbances originate primarily in the demand for money (v_t), hold the interest rate constant; if they originate in the goods market (z_t), hold the money stock constant.[17]

We present a simple extension of his analysis, introducing the aggregate supply side.

Consider the following model, which was introduced in chapter 10:

$$y_t = \beta(p_t - E[p_t|t-1] + u_t), \tag{11}$$

$$m_t - p_t = y_t - ai_t - v_t, \tag{12}$$

$$y_t = -br_t + z_t, \qquad r_t = i_t - (E[p_{t+1}|t] - p_t). \tag{13}$$

The first equation represents aggregate supply. The second is the LM equation, and the third is the IS equation, with the demand for goods depending on the real interest rate. The real interest rate is equal to the nominal rate minus expected inflation.[18]

Because we are interested in the response of output to unexpected disturbances under a money or an interest rule, let us assume that all three shocks are white noise. Furthermore we will assume that money is always expected to be equal to zero so that under either rule, $E[p_t|t-1]$ and $E[p_{t+1}|t]$ are both equal to zero. Solving for output gives

$$y_t(m) = [a\beta + b\beta + b + ba]^{-1}\{\beta b v_t + b(1+a)\beta u_t + a\beta z_t\}$$

when the money stock is fixed (at $m = 0$), and

$$y_t(i) = (\beta + b)^{-1}\{b\beta u_t + \beta z_t\}$$

when the nominal interest rate is fixed (at $i = 0$).

Poole's basic result still comes through: when the goal is to reduce fluctuations in output, and if the main source of uncertainty consists of shocks to the demand for money, an interest rule clearly dominates a money rule because velocity shocks do not affect output under such a rule.

Poole's results should also imply that the response of $y(i)$ to a change in z is larger than the response of $y(m)$ to a change in z, a shock to the demand for goods. This is likewise unambiguously the case. Thus that result is confirmed in the present rational expectations context. The logic is simple: if the money stock is held constant, the effects of the increase in aggregate demand caused by z are partly offset by a rise in interest rates, which cannot occur when the interest rate is held constant.

In addition we can examine the relative responses of $y(i)$ and $y(m)$ to a supply shock. The response of output to a supply shock will be greater under interest rate pegging if $b > 1$. This is because the aggregate demand curve in (p, y) space is flatter under interest rate pegging if that condition is satisfied.

The Poole model has led to a voluminous body of research that has examined alternative specifications of the timing of expectations, alternative goals of the monetary authority, and so on.[19] Its basic insight remains central to the understanding of the choice between money and interest rate targeting.

The Dangers of Nominal Interest Rate Pegging

Although we have concentrated on the derivation of optimal rules, much of the discussion of monetary policy has focused on the operating character-istics of simple rules, such as constant money growth or nominal interest pegging. We leave aside for the moment the question of why one would want to settle for such rules and examine, instead, the implications of interest rate pegging, of keeping the nominal interest rate constant at some level i.[20]

The Federal Reserve agreed during World War II to hold the three-month Treasury bill rate at 0.375%, and this level was maintained from 1943 to 1946. Although the Fed feared the inflationary consequences of holding the nominal rate low, Treasury pressure ensured that it had risen only to 1.5% by 1951, at which time the famous Treasury-Fed accord gave the Fed more freedom to adjust the interest rate. A similar cheap money episode in Britain broke down in 1947 as the government attempted to move the consol rate down from 2.5% to 2%.

Wicksell ([1898] 1965) had already argued that a policy that set the interest rate at an incorrect level could generate inflation or deflation. The intuition is that when interest rates are pegged, every increase in the demand for money is accommodated so that there is nothing to tie down the price level. We now make that intuition more precise. We use the model de-veloped just above, which includes an IS, an LM, and an aggregate supply relation. Again, we start with adaptive expectations and then turn to rational expectations.

Adaptive Expectations
Rewrite (11) to (13) as

$$y_t = \beta(\pi_t - \pi_t^* + u_t), \tag{14}$$

$$m_t - p_t = y_t - ai_t - v_t, \tag{15}$$

$$y_t = -br_t + z_t, \qquad r_t = i_t - \pi_{t+1}^*, \tag{16}$$

and under adaptive expectations

$$\pi_t^* - \pi_{t-1}^* = (1 - \gamma)(\pi_{t-1} - \pi_{t-1}^*), \tag{17}$$

Suppose now that the nominal interest rate is pegged at $\overline{i}$. Replacing π_{t+1}^* in (16), using (17), and eliminating y_t between (14) and (16) gives

$$-b\overline{i} + b[\gamma\pi_t^* + (1 - \gamma)\pi_t] + z_t = \beta(\pi_t - \pi_t^* + u_t). \tag{18}$$

The right-hand side gives aggregate supply, and the left-hand side aggregate demand. Inflation increases aggregate supply; it also increases aggregate demand by increasing expected inflation from t to $t + 1$, decreasing the real rate of interest given the pegged nominal rate. We assume that the effect of an increase in prices at time t is to increase supply more than demand [i.e., that $\beta > b(1 - \gamma)$].[21] By using (17) to eliminate π_t^* and rearranging, we get

$$\{[\beta - b(1 - \gamma)] - \beta L\}\pi_t = -b(1 - \gamma)\overline{i} + (1 - \gamma L)(z_t - \beta u_t). \tag{19}$$

This is an unstable equation. Given the nominal rate, an increase in expected inflation decreases the real rate, leading to higher output and higher inflation. This leads to higher expected inflation in the next period, an even lower real rate, further increasing output and inflation, and so on. In the background, if we look at (15), the monetary authority is running an accommodating monetary policy. To maintain the nominal interest rate, it has to accommodate any change in either the price level or the demand for real money balances. Since output and inflation rise simultaneously, the government has to keep increasing money.

Thus under adaptive expectations, if the monetary authority commits itself to a constant nominal interest rate forever, it loses control not only over the price level but also over the inflation rate. This was the second major point made by Friedman (1968). Plausible as the adaptive expectations formulation may be in a reasonably stable environment, it is nonetheless hard to believe that individuals continue to form expectations of inflation adaptively if the inflation rate is ever-accelerating. Thus we now look at how conclusions derived using adaptive expectations have to be amended when expectations are rational.

Rational Expectations
We return to equations (11) and (13) and assume rational expectations, Rewriting the equations for convenience, with the nominal rate pegged at $\overline{i}$,

$$y_t = \beta(p_t - E[p_t|t - 1] + u_t), \tag{11}$$

$$m_t - p_t = y_t - a\overline{i} - v_t, \tag{12'}$$

$$y_t = -b\{\overline{i} - (E[p_{t+1}|t] - p_t)\} + z_t. \tag{13'}$$

The price level appears to be indeterminate under rational expectations. For with rational expectations and no uncertainty, $p_t = E[p_t|t-1]$, implying from (11) that output is βu_t. From (12') we then obtain a determinate level of real balances corresponding to $\bar{i}$ given y_t and v_t, and from (13') we obtain a determinate level of the expected inflation rate given y_t, $\bar{i}$, and z_t. But knowing real balances is not sufficient to tie down the price level.[22] Once again (see our earlier results about output stabilization), the accelerationist result obtained under adaptive expectations becomes an indeterminacy result under rational expectations. This result was first derived by Sargent and Wallace (1975).

But, as in the case of output stabilization considered earlier, this indeterminacy is easily removed. All that is needed to tie down the price level is some initial level of the money stock. Assume for computational simplicity that the three shocks u, v, and z are white noise. If period t is the period in which the interest rate policy is first begun, let the monetary authority announce that it intends to stabilize the nominal interest rate each period by the following policy:

$$m_t = \bar{m}_t + \psi_1 v_t + \psi_2 u_t + \psi_3 z_t, \tag{20}$$

where $\bar{m}_t$ is arbitrary. Future values of $\bar{m}$ (i.e., $\bar{m}_{t+i}$ for i positive) consistent with the interest rate target can be announced at the same time, as can the ψ_i's.

The values are[23]

$$\bar{m}_{t+1} = \bar{m}_t + \frac{(b+a)\bar{i}}{b},$$

$$\psi_1 = -1,$$

$$\psi_2 = \frac{\beta(b-1)}{\beta+b}, \tag{21}$$

$$\psi_3 = \frac{1+\beta}{\beta+b}.$$

The expected money stock $\bar{m}$ follows a deterministic path, increasing steadily over time. The response to a velocity shock (ψ_1) is negative because the money stock is reduced to compensate for higher velocity, which would otherwise reduce the interest rate. The response of money to a supply shock (ψ_2) is ambiguous: an increase in aggregate supply decreases prices and increases output. The first effect tends to reduce interest rates, leading to a reduction in the money stock. The second increases the demand for real money balances, leading to an increase in the money stock. The money stock is increased in response to aggregate demand shocks that would otherwise tend to raise the nominal interest rate ($\psi_3 > 0$).

Thus, although there is a sense in which the price level is indeterminate with interest rate fixing under rational expectations, that indeterminacy can be removed by specifying the base level of the money stock (Canzoneri et al. 1983). Note that this is exactly what we did in our analysis of interest versus money targeting earlier: we assumed that in every period expected money was equal to a fixed value, namely, zero. In this model the price level in future periods will then fluctuate around a deterministic path. The fact of a deterministic path is special, however, a result of the assumption that shocks are serially uncorrelated and that, in general, the price level may follow a random walk with drift.

To summarize, while there are dangers associated with a pegged nominal interest rate policy, these dangers are not inherent to such a policy. The policy can, in principle, be designed so as to maintain (limited) control over the money supply.

The Case for Simple Rules

We have just examined a simple rule, nominal interest rate pegging, and concluded that it could be used without necessarily leading to runaway inflation or other catastrophes. Nominal interest rate pegging is only one of many simple rules that at one time or another have been put forward by monetary economists or practitioners. Another currently popular proposal is that of nominal income targeting. The precise meaning of the proposal is not clear. One interpretation is that it is a statement about the macro welfare function, advocating a linear trade-off between real output and price level deviations from target. Monetary policy would then be faced with the task of minimizing that loss function. An alternative interpretation is that nominal income is an intermediate target of the monetary authority. Yet another interpretation is that like nominal interest rates or high powered money in the Poole model, nominal income is an instrument that the monetary authority can set every period. This last interpretation is hardly realistic, but it is the one that has been most thoroughly analyzed, with an interesting conclusion: if interest rate targeting in the face of supply shocks is better than money targeting, then nominal GNP targeting may be even better.[24] Yet another simple rule is that of constant money growth, advocated by Friedman.[25]

This enumeration of rules raises a basic question. Why should policy restrict itself to such simple rules? Friedman, in making the argument for constant money growth, emphasized both that monetary policy should be fixed by a rule and that it should not respond to disturbances. These are two separate arguments. The first rules out discretion, that is, letting the monetary authority decide in each period what is best. It does not exclude, for example, rules such as (21), for a monetary rule could still be specified in feedback form like (21) above. We address the rule-versus-discretion issues in the last part of this chapter, where we discuss the dynamic inconsistency of policy. This notion, formalized in macroeconomics by Kydland and Prescott in 1977, can be detected in Friedman's 1950s arguments for a monetary rule. We discuss here the second part of the argument, which argues for simple or nonactivist rules.

Friedman's formal analysis was based on the idea that because the lags of monetary policy are long and variable, activist policy might destabilize the economy rather than stabilize it.

The arguments can be made using a single-equation reduced form in which a target variable, say, output is related to money by an equation of the form

$$y_t = a(L)y_{t-1} + b(L)m_t + \varepsilon_t, \tag{22}$$

where ε_t is, for convenience, white noise, and $a(L)$ and $b(L)$ are lag polynomials. This equation differs from the reduced forms that would be derived in the earlier simple models because it has more lags; such lags are typically found in econometric investigations of the dynamic multipliers of policy.

Suppose that the target level of y_t is 0, that the money stock can only be set on the basis of information up to time $t-1$, and consider the role of lags. First, in the absence of lags, there may be no role for policy. If the a_i in $a(L)$ were all zero, active policy could not reduce the variance in GNP. Since active policy can only react to events occurring before t and since output without active policy would be $y_t = \varepsilon_t$, any active use of policy could only increase the variance in output.

If there are lags (nonzero a_i) and if the coefficients in (22) are known, then optimal monetary policy could exactly offset the lagged effects of earlier disturbances and monetary policy by setting

$$m_t = -b(L)^{-1}a(L)y_{t-1}. \tag{23}$$

Under this policy GNP is as close to target as possible. In (23) long lags appear to be no deterrent at all to an active policy.

However, policy (23) may be very active indeed, to the point that it could produce *instrument instability*, requiring ever larger changes in the money

stock to offset its own lagged effects (Holbrook 1972).[26] Instrument instability occurs when the current effects of a given change in the money stock
are small and the lagged effects large: then a large change in the money
stock is needed today to offset the effects of the most recent shock, but these
large effects later come back to require even larger changes in money.

Instrument instability is clearly one reason to avoid too active a use of
policy and is thus an argument moving in the direction of a constant growth
rate rule. Formally, the problem of instrument instability can be handled by
including costs of instrument instability in the loss function. At a deeper
level the reason to ascribe costs to large movements of instruments is a lack
of confidence in the underlying models: it is quite certain that existing
relationships will break down if policies require changes in instruments that
are outside the range of historical experience.

This points to a more powerful argument for inactive policy—the existence of uncertainty about the structural coefficients in a model. This is what
Friedman means by variable lags. Suppose that the b_j parameters in (23)
were stochastic. Then to the extent that the stock of money departs from
zero, any active use of policy adds variability to output. It is easy to show
in an equation like (23) that uncertainty about the multipliers, the b_j's, leads
to an optimal policy that is less active (Brainard 1967). As the variance of
the multiplier rises, the output variance-minimizing policy tends toward
setting $m = 0$ in all periods.

In the Brainard example uncertainty leads one to choose values of m closer
to zero. But it raises the question of what is the corresponding monetary policy in practice (Diamond 1985). Statistical inference would place the minimum
uncertainty at the historical average level of the monetary variable in the
regression.[27] More generally, uncertainty is likely to be smaller the smaller
the difference between the new policy being contemplated and past policy.

In any case there is little technical basis for the notion that a strict constant
growth rate rule would be optimal. That it should be less active than implied
by equation (23)—which attempts to hit the target period by period—is
obvious, but that it should go all the way to inactivity is not. Perhaps the
best argument that could be made is that since there is so much disagreement
among economists about the appropriate model of the economy, estimates
of optimal policy derived from any one model are bound to understate the
true uncertainty about the effects of policy. Nevertheless, it has been
possible to find simple active feedback rules for monetary policy that
performs well in a variety of models.

In the final section of this chapter we will see that the possibility of
dynamic inconsistency provides arguments for rules, but not for inactive
rules.

11.3 Fiscal Policy

Fiscal policy raises many of the same issues as monetary policy. In an economy in which fluctuations are partly due to the combination of aggregate demand effects and nominal rigidities, fiscal policy also has the potential to reduce fluctuations in aggregate demand and thus increase welfare. This has long been a theme of Keynesian macroeconomics. Whereas for monetary policy the major trade-off is between price and output stability, the trade-off for fiscal policy is between output stabilization and the distortions from tax and spending policies. This points, however, to an important difference between fiscal and monetary policy. Even in the absence of nominal rigidities and other imperfections, fiscal policy has important effects on the macroeconomy. It is these implications that we briefly review in this section.[28] We focus on two issues. The first is that of the effects and the optimal use of deficits and debt policy. The second is that of optimal taxation and business cycles, when taxes are distortionary.

Debt Policy

Much of the ground on this issue has already been covered, and the two basic results were derived in chapter 3. When individuals have finite horizons, the economy may be inefficient: it may have a capital stock that exceeds the golden rule level. The government can then use deficit and debt policy to reduce the capital stock and make all generations better off. We showed how the government, by maximizing a social welfare function, would choose the optimal path of capital accumulation to the modified golden rule steady state. Although we did not spell out the sequence of taxes that would support this path we examined the effects of deficits, and of unfunded social security programs in both the Diamond and the Blanchard models (for further analysis of optimal taxation in OLG models, see, in particular, Ordover and Phelps 1979; Atkinson and Sandmo 1980; King 1980; Calvo and Obstfeld 1987). In chapter 4 and again in chapter 10, we examined the relation between deficits, money finance, and inflation, although we did not focus on welfare implications.

Romer (1988) has used the model of perpetual youth of chapter 3 to assess the social welfare costs of protracted deficits when the economy is below the modified golden rule capital stock. The argument has been made that the tax cuts of the early 1980s in the United States were in part implemented to force reductions in spending, through the political pressure resulting from large deficits. One may ask what the welfare cost of these deficits may be, if these reductions do not lead to decreased spending but have to be financed by higher taxes later. Romer derives the following result: consider the following changes in (lump-sum) taxes, starting from a balanced budget and steady state:

$$\frac{dB}{dt} = \Delta T, \qquad 0 \leqslant t < H,$$

$$= -a \exp[-a(t - H)]H\Delta T, \qquad t \geqslant H,$$

where B is government debt and T is taxes. Taxes are reduced so as to increase the deficit by a constant amount ΔT for a length of time H. (Note that as interest payments increase over time, taxes are implicitly raised between 0 and H to maintain a constant deficit; this assumption is made for convenience.) Thereafter taxes are raised so as to return debt to its original level: debt is retired at rate a. If $a = 0$, the debt is maintained at the higher level forever. Romer shows that if r^* is the modified golden rule interest rate corresponding to the objective function of the policymaker, the welfare loss in terms of consumption is given, to a second-order approximation, by

$$L = \left(\frac{r - r^*}{a + r^*}\right) H \left[\frac{\Delta T}{C(0)}\right],$$

where r is the actual rate of interest, and $C(0)$ the initial level of aggregate consumption. This formula has various interesting aspects. The welfare loss is proportional to the distance of the interest rate from the modified golden rule rate. The farther away the interest rate is from the modified golden rule, the more costly it is to reallocate consumption from future generations to those currently alive. Also whether debt is repaid, and at what rate, makes a substantial difference to the welfare cost of deficits policies. Debt that is quickly repaid has a lower welfare cost.[29] Romer then uses various empirical counterparts to the variables in the formula to compute potential welfare effects of deficits. One is struck, however, at how difficult this quantification is: once more, when uncertainty is introduced, we have to confront the problem of deciding what the appropriate counterpart to r is, not to say anything about r^* which reflects the appropriate discount rate in the social welfare function. We discussed the issue of the golden rule under uncertainty in chapter 7, but more to register our limited knowledge of the answers than to give a clear lead as to what rate to use in such a case.

The presence of uncertainty, together with imperfections in credit markets, introduces additional channels through which deficit policy can affect welfare, even when individuals have infinite horizons. Liquidity constraints are often mentioned as implying a role for deficits in increasing both aggregate demand and, potentially, welfare. Tobin (1972) showed how, when individuals face a higher rate for borrowing than for lending, they face a kinked budget constraint; thus intertemporal reallocations of taxes can affect spending and increase utility. But more recent work which endogenizes liquidity or credit constraints along the lines described in chapter 9 has qualified these conclusions. Imperfect credit markets do not necessarily imply a role for deficit policy (see Hayashi 1986; Yotsuzuka 1987; Rotemberg 1988). A different channel for tax reallocations has been explored by Barsky, Mankiw, and Zeldes (1986): if labor income is not fully diversifiable, and taxes are proportional to income, higher taxes in the future can, by reducing the variance in aftertax income, lead to a decrease in precautionary saving and an increase in consumption.[30]

Distortionary Taxes, Government Spending, and Business Cycles

Buchanan and Wagner (1977) argued that the pre-Keynesian presumption that the budget should at all times be balanced was replaced by Keynes with an agnosticism that permitted deficits to become arbitrarily large—which, with a remarkably long lag, they duly became in the 1980s in the United States. In fact Keynesians and others (e.g., Friedman 1948) have argued for a cyclically balanced budget, with deficits in recessions offset by surpluses in booms. We now look at the implications of the very non-Keynesian view that cycles are equilibrium responses to productivity shocks.

Suppose that all fluctuations are equilibrium fluctuations in response to shifts in technology, and that all individuals have infinite horizons so that Ricardian equivalence holds. But assume that taxes are distortionary and that government spending affects activity. Should the government run a balanced budget or keep tax rates constant, leading—just as in the Keynesian prescription but for very different reasons—to countercyclical deficit policies? The question is an important one since it does not go away when we allow for additional imperfections; it just becomes more complicated. Unfortunately, even in the simplest case, it is already a difficult question to answer. We now review what is known.

Optimal Taxation in the Atemporal Economy

The strategy in deriving optimal taxation in the intertemporal context has been to adapt the results from the theory of optimal taxation in the standard atemporal model. In that model the government, subject to a revenue requirement, has to find the set of taxes that maximizes the social welfare function. Following Ramsey (1927), the optimal tax literature has derived formulae for tax rates as functions of compensated elasticities of demand in conditions where lump-sum taxes are unavailable.[31] A basic result is the following:

Consider a consumer who earns labor income which he spends on n commodities. The government can potentially tax his labor income and all of his n commodities, but because only the ratio of aftertax prices to aftertax wages affects consumer decisions, it needs only n taxes to achieve any given allocation. If labor income remains untaxed and the price of good i is p_i, the n ad valorem commodity taxes, τ_i, are given by the solution to[32]

$$\sum_{i=1}^{n} \tau_i p_i S_{ki} = -\theta x_k, \qquad k = 1, \ldots, n. \tag{24}$$

Here τ_i are the tax rates on the n goods, x_k are purchases of good k, S_{ki} are compensated (Slutsky) derivatives $(\partial x_k / \partial p_i$, on an indifference surface), and θ is a parameter that is a function of the government's revenue requirement.

The literature has concentrated on finding conditions under which the tax rates on the n commodities are the same. In this case an income tax or uniform commodity taxation can achieve the second-best optimum that usually requires n different tax rates. Various separability restrictions permit uniform taxation, taking prices as given. In particular, Deaton (1981) shows that if the utility function can be written as

$$U(z, X) = V[z, \phi(X)], \tag{25}$$

where z is leisure and $X = [x_1, x_2, \ldots, x_n]$, and ϕ is homothetic in X, then uniform commodity taxation satisfies (24).[33]

Optimal Taxation in an Intertemporal Equilibrium Model
With some care the results from the atemporal case can be applied to the intertemporal context, with the budget constraint now being the intertemporal budget constraint of the representative consumer.

Assume that the government only has labor taxation at its disposal. Suppose, to start with, that the consumer consumes goods only in the first period, and consumes leisure in all periods. Then by reinterpreting (somewhat awkwardly) leisure in the atemporal model as consumption here and consumption goods in the atemporal model as leisure in different periods here, we can use the Deaton result. In particular, if utility is separable in consumption and leisure and satisfies condition (25), uniform labor taxation is optimal. This will be the case, for example, if utility is additively separable in time, as well as in consumption and leisure, with the utility being isoelastic in leisure.

The restriction that consumption occur only in the first period is easily relaxed. Because labor income taxes do not affect the relative price of consumption across periods, we can aggregate consumption in a consumption index. If utility, defined over this consumption index and leisure in different periods satisfies the Deaton conditions, uniform taxation is again optimal.[34] The utility function given in the previous paragraph satisfies these conditions.

This uniform taxation result, in an intertemporal context, is known as *tax smoothing*. As the above argument makes clear, it is not a general result. However, it is difficult to establish any presumption about the direction in which tax rates should deviate from constancy over the cycle, when the cycle is characterized by changes in productivity. This suggests an ignorance argument for tax smoothing. Put another way, there is surely no theoretical argument in favor of balancing the budget in every period, of having countercyclical taxes.

Tax Smoothing, Deficits, and the Behavior of Debt
Given the difficulty associated with deriving optimal taxation from fundamentals, some economists have taken a shortcut, setting up the problem in such a way that tax smoothing is clearly optimal. For example, Barro (1979a) derives the tax-smoothing result by assuming that the costs of revenue collection per period are given by a time-invariant first-degree homogeneous function of tax collection and the level of output:

$$Z_t = F(T_t, Y_t) = Y_t f(\tau_t), \tag{26}$$

where T is total tax revenue, Y is the level of output, and τ is the average tax rate.

The present value of collection costs is then minimized subject to a given path of government spending, G_t, and the government budget constraint,

$$G_t + RB_{t-1} = T_t + B_t, \tag{27}$$

where R is $1 + r$, with r the interest rate (assumed constant, and not taxed), and B_{t-1} is the stock of debt at the beginning of period t. Minimization of the present value of costs of collection subject to (27) implies a constant tax rate. Obviously, the tax-smoothing result emerges from the properties of the cost-of-collection function, particularly the fact that it is invariant to the shocks that cause cycles.

In an uncertain multiperiod world, Barro (1979a) interprets the tax-smoothing result as implying a martingale for the tax rate. Whenever new information becomes available—for instance, that government spending has to rise or that the rate of growth of productivity has slowed—the tax rate is adjusted so as to remain constant in expected value thereafter.

If government spending is constant or countercyclical, then the tax-smoothing argument suggests a countercyclical pattern of deficits in response to anticipated or transitory changes in output (Barro 1979). The following simple model gives a framework for thinking about the cyclical behavior of the deficit:

By solving (27) forward, and assuming the no-Ponzi-game condition that the present value of terminal debt goes to zero, we obtain

$$B_{t-1} = \sum_{i=0}^{\infty} \frac{T_{t+i} - G_{t+i}}{R^{i+1}}.$$

(28)

This is a familiar condition from chapter 3, which has to hold for realized values of T and G: the present value of primary surpluses will eventually be sufficient to pay off the existing debt.

The condition (28) can be seen as a statement that on average the budget will be balanced, no matter what. The terms in (28) represent *actual* future taxes and spending, whether or not they are anticipated as of time t. For instance, the budget balance may be attained by an unexpected capital levy, or inflation, or outright repudiation of the debt.[35] But if the transversality condition is satisfied, the present value of future primary surpluses is equal to the current outstanding debt.

By assuming that taxes are proportional to income and that the tax rate, τ_t is such that if it remained in place from t on, equation (2ʒ) would be satisfied in expected value, we have[36]

$$\tau_t = \frac{B_{t-1} + E\left[\sum_{i=0}^{\infty} (G_{t+i}/R^{i+1}) \Big| t\right]}{E\left[\sum_{i=0}^{\infty} Y_{t+i}/R^{i+1} \Big| t\right]}.$$

(29)

Suppose for the sake of concreteness that aggregate output Y follows a first-order autoregressive process and that government spending G moves in the same direction as Y—as it should do when G enters individual utility functions as a consumption good. Thus

$$Y_t = (1 - \rho)\bar{Y} + \rho Y_{t-1} + v_t, \qquad 0 \leqslant \rho \leqslant 1,$$

(30)

$$G_t = \bar{G} + gY_t + u_t, \qquad g \geqslant 0, \tag{31}$$

where $\bar{Y}$ and $\bar{G}$ are constants and u and v are mutually uncorrelated white noise.

By taking expectations in (29), we obtain

$$E\left[\sum_0^\infty \frac{Y_{t+i}}{R^{i+1}}\bigg|t\right] = \frac{Y_t - \bar{Y}}{R - \rho} + \frac{\bar{Y}}{r} \tag{32}$$

and

$$E\left[\sum_0^\infty \frac{G_{t+i}}{R^{i+1}}\bigg|t\right] = \frac{\bar{G}}{r} + \frac{u_t}{R} + g\left(\frac{Y_t - \bar{Y}}{R - \rho} + \frac{\bar{Y}}{r}\right). \tag{33}$$

The tax rate is accordingly

$$\tau_t = g + \frac{B_{t-1} + u_t/R + \bar{G}/r}{(Y_t - \bar{Y})/(R - \rho) + \bar{Y}/r}. \tag{34}$$

The deficit, D_t, equal to $B_t - B_{t-1}$, is given by

$$D_t = rB_{t-1} + \bar{G} + u_t - \frac{Y_t(B_{t-1} + u_t/R + \bar{G}/r)}{(Y_t - \bar{Y})/(R - \rho) + \bar{Y}/r}. \tag{35}$$

The deficit will in this case be countercyclical as a result of tax smoothing. The explanation is that taxes are set to balance the budget on average; when output is high today, tax revenue will be above average. This holds even if government spending is procyclical ($g > 0$) since, from (34), total taxes move with income in a way that offsets the effects of (linearly) procyclical government spending on the deficit.

The implied behavior of the budget, if GNP follows a random walk, can be obtained by setting ρ equal to one in (35). In that case the deficit is white noise,

$$D_t = u_t/R, \tag{36}$$

and the debt then also follows a random walk,

$$B_t = B_{t-1} + D_t. \tag{37}$$

The above argument is normative, but Barro (1987) has argued that the behavior of the British government from 1701 to 1918 was consistent with the tax-smoothing model.

The issue of optimal deficits has also been studied by Lucas and Stokey (1983) and Flemming (1987). In the Lucas-Stokey model consumers make a labor–leisure choice and a consumption decision in each period. Taxes are levied on labor income. There is no capital, so all saving takes the form of purchases from or sales to the government of state-contingent payoff bonds. The payoffs are contingent on the only exogenous stochastic variable in model, government spending. For instance, a particular debt instrument may specify that in period t the government will make payments to the consumers if there is no war but will collect payments (on the debt) from consumers if there is a war.

Lucas and Stokey present several interesting examples of optimal taxes and financing. In one case government spending is zero in all periods except period T. In period T the government has to spend a positive amount, say for a war. The tax rate, consumption, and labor input will each be constant in all nonwar periods.[37] Before the war the government uses the proceeds of the taxes to buy bonds from consumers, building up a war chest. When the war comes, the government uses the bonds it has bought to pay for part of the war. It also borrows, its tax revenues after the war being just sufficient to pay the interest each period. Depending on parameter values, labor may be either taxed or subsidized in period T, but in any case more work will be done. The budget is thus in surplus before the war, in deficit during the war, and balanced after the war. Since output is higher during the war, the deficit is procyclical, but this is because the high income is associated with a temporarily high level of government spending.

In another example, the setting is identical except that the period-T war is not certain: there is a probability α of war in period T, necessitating positive government spending; if there is no war, there will be no government spending at T. In all periods when there is no war (including period T), private consumption and labor supply are the same. If there is a war, however, consumption of goods and leisure are both reduced as production is diverted to war use.

The government levies taxes in each period. Before the potential war it uses the revenue to buy bonds issued by consumers that pay a fixed amount every period except in period T when the payment is contingent on whether there is a war. We can think of these bonds as involving a period-T payment from consumers to the government if there is a war, and from the government to consumers (for the insurance they have provided) if there is no war. In addition the government sells bonds to the private sector in period T, using future taxes to just pay the interest each period, and thereby ensuring that the tax rate is the same in all periods during which there is no war.

In this example too the government runs a surplus before the potential war, a deficit in period T, and a balanced budget in each subsequent period.

Optimal Government Spending
The standard assumption in the macroeconomic literature on optimal taxes (e.g., Barro, 1979a; Lucas and Stokey 1983) is that government spending is exogenous, and perhaps also stochastic. The fact that large changes in government spending (on goods and services) have taken place in wartime justifies this as a first approach.

It is also clear, however, that elements of government spending are endogenous. For instance, in a model where public goods are consumption goods, with the representative agent having the felicity function $U(c_t, z_t, g_t)$, where z is leisure and g the supply of public goods (or other goods on which government spends), and with all goods normal, government spending would normally be procyclical.[38] The level of government spending should also be affected by the marginal cost of collecting taxes. If some of government spending is on investment goods (infrastructure), then this too would be expected to be responsive to the shocks hitting the economy. Still, in the equilibrium context some components of government spending may operate as a current input into production. The cyclical pattern of this component of government spending would depend on whether it was a complement or substitute for that factor or factors whose current productivity is affected by current disturbances.[39]

Optimal Government Asset Supplies
Assuming that the government decides to borrow, what form should these liabilities take? The convention in theoretical models is that the government issues price level indexed debt; in practice, governments usually issue nominal debt, but only occasionally they issue indexed bonds.

If some markets are missing, then the government may be able to increase efficiency by issuing a particular type of debt. If, however, there is an asset market inefficiency that the government can cure, it may well be able to do so by acting as a financial intermediary independently of the state of the deficit.

Another reason why the government may care about the maturity of its debt is as a way of establishing credibility of a particular policy. A government that issues nominal bonds with long maturities has a strong incentive to use unexpected inflation as a way of reducing its debt commitment. Lucas and Stokey (1983) show in their model that the government can choose the maturity structure of its debt so as to make it optimal not to change policy later. This takes us to issues of dynamic inconsistency, to which we now turn.

11.4 Dynamic Inconsistency

A policy is dynamically inconsistent when a future policy decision that forms part of an optimal plan formulated at an initial date is no longer optimal from the viewpoint of a later date, even though no relevant new information has appeared in the meantime.[40] The problem and its implications have been the subject of extensive, mainly theoretical, research since Kydland and Prescott (1977) first showed that optimal macroeconomic policies could well be dynamically inconsistent.[41]

An example of dynamic inconsistency drawn from Kydland and Prescott (1977), which we develop below, is that of optimal taxation in an economy with capital accumulation. Under rational expectations the solution gives tax rates that are optimal, conditional on their being expected by private agents. But once capital is in place, its supply is inelastic, and a government acting to maximize the welfare of the representative individual would tax capital more heavily. Precisely the same problem occurs with the optimal inflation tax and money holdings (Calvo 1978); the monetary authority can always impose a lump-sum tax by discretely increasing the money supply and, once the private sector has formed expectations, is tempted to do so.[42]

The basic issue is that of the costs for a government of not being able to precommit itself to carry out promised policy actions, or of the virtues of policy rules over discretion. A precommitted government, such as one following policy rules, will carry out the policy that is optimal given that it is expected. A government with discretion may under rational expectations be expected to make the short-run optimal decision every time it can. Therefore it gains nothing from its opportunism and on average produces a worse outcome than would a government able to tie its hands.

There has been far less empirical than theoretical work on the implications of dynamic inconsistency. There are two questions. First, do governments in fact act in a dynamically inconsistent fashion—or equivalently, do societies suffer as a result of their governments' inability to precommit themselves to policies? And second, if not, why not—that is, what institutions or constraints on behavior exist or can be created to mitigate the problem?

In this section we first present two simple examples of dynamic inconsistency, and then ask whether the phenomenon to which it points should be taken seriously. We next turn to proposed solutions, which either suggest mechanisms to prevent dynamic inconsistency or argue that the problem is less serious than it seems. We conclude with an application to the problem of disinflation.

An Optimal Tax Example

About the simplest example of dynamic inconsistency in an optimal tax problem occurs in the following two-period model: Individuals consume in two periods, work only in the second, and have an initial endowment of capital, k_1. Government spends only in period two. The government does not levy taxes in period one; in period two it will levy taxes on labor and capital to pay for its spending. It is assumed not to have lump-sum taxes at its command. Equivalently, it cannot buy or tax capital in the first period.

The utility of the representative individual is

$$U(\ ) = \ln c_1 + (1 + \theta)^{-1}[\ln c_2 + \alpha \ln(n - n_2) + \beta \ln g_2], \tag{38}$$

where c_i is consumption in period i, and n_2 and g_2 are period two work and government spending, respectively.

The production function is linear with

$$c_1 + k_2 = Rk_1,$$
$$c_2 + g_2 = an_2 + Rk_2. \tag{39}$$

The Command Optimum
The central planner's objective function is the utility of the representative individual. We examine four different solutions to the planner's problem, each corresponding to different constraints imposed on its behavior.

The command optimum is the first-best solution, attained when the planner determines quantities directly by maximizing (38) subject to the economy's production possibilities (39). This implies that

$$c_1 = \left[1 + \frac{1 + \alpha + \beta}{1 + \theta}\right]^{-1}\left(Rk_1 + \frac{an}{R}\right),$$

$$c_2 = \frac{Rc_1}{1 + \theta},$$

$$n_2 = n - \frac{\alpha c_2}{a}, \tag{40}$$

$$g_2 = \beta c_2.$$

The command optimum does not exhibit dynamic inconsistency. Given the choice of k_2 implied by the first-period consumption decision, the government will still choose the values of c_2, n_2, and g_2 in (40) when period two arrives. We denote the level of utility associated with the command optimum by U^*.

The Precommitted Optimal Tax Solution
Suppose next that the government has to use distortionary taxes to fund government spending. In the precommitted solution the government formulates an optimal plan in period one and is expected to (and does) continue with that plan in period two. As we shall see below, the government has to find some way of tying its hands if it is indeed to carry through on the plan.

Assume that the government can tax both labor and capital in the second period but can neither tax nor borrow in the first period.[43] The private sector maximizes subject to the constraint

$$c_1 + \frac{c_2}{R_2} = Rk_1 + \frac{a(1 - \tau_2)n_2}{R_2},$$ (41)

where R_2 is the aftertax return to capital in period two and τ_2 is the rate of taxation of second-period labor income. The government budget constraint in turn is

$$g_2 = a\tau_2 n_2 + (R - R_2)k_2.$$ (42)

In order to make its first-period consumption decision, the private sector has to form expectations of second-period tax rates. We assume that expectations are rational so that the tax rates expected by the public are precisely those that the government chooses when solving its optimal tax problem at time one. The rates that it will impose are announced, and the announcement believed. In general, both capital and labor income will be taxed. The conditions for optimal taxes are sufficiently nonlinear that no convenient formulae for the optimal rates emerge.[44] We denote the utility level attained in this case as U_p, where the subscript p stands for precommittment.

The Consistent Solution
The precommitted solution is time inconsistent. In period one the government announces that both capital and labor income will be taxed in period two. When period two arrives, however, the capital is already in place and can be taxed without creating any distortion. But taxation of labor creates a distortion. The government, *acting in the best interest of its citizens,* will

therefore tax only capital, unless of course its precommittment prevents its doing so.

But given that the public knows the government will be tempted in period two to tax only capital, it may well believe this is what will happen. If the public does not believe any period-one announcements, it will calculate its optimal saving decision in period one on the assumption that only capital is taxed in period two.

The *consistent* or *dynamic programming* solution obtains when the government uses and is expected to use dynamic programming to make its decisions.[45] In this case it will in period two take the existing stock of capital as given, and tax only capital. Since it is expected to do so, and since it has no incentive not to make that decision when period two arrives, the solution is time consistent.

The consistent solution is obtained by maximizing backward in time. Start in period two with a one-period optimal tax problem for the government, taking k_2 as given. This leads to a zero rate of labor income tax and a positive rate of taxation of capital. Then, taking that tax rate on capital as given, go back one period to solve the consumer's problem, which yields the second-period capital stock as a function of the expected (and actual) rate of taxation of capital in period two.

The consistent solution is generally described as the discretionary solution that emerges when the policymaker is free to optimize in each period. But it prejudges the question whether a government given the freedom to reoptimize each period will operate in a short-sighted way. Thus we refer to the consistent solution as the short-sighted rather than the discretionary solution.

Because capital is taxed heavily in period two, capital accumulation is lower in the consistent solution than in the precommitted solution to the optimal tax problem. Accordingly, utility in this case is lower too. We denote the utility level in the consistent solution by U_s, where the subscript s represents "shortsightedness."

Time Inconsistent Solutions
There is also a class of time inconsistent solutions that obtain when expectations and actions do not coincide. The utility level will depend on private sector expectations. One solution to consider obtains when the private sector expects the government to carry out the optimal precommitted policy, but the government in period two regards itself as not bound by that belief. We can call this *the* time inconsistent solution, with utility level

U_f (for fooling), while recognizing that there are many inconsistent solutions. Indeed, if the government is free to manipulate expectations, it can attain the command optimum by inducing the right set of beliefs.[46]

The Problem of Dynamic Inconsistency
The utility levels corresponding to these different solutions can be ordered

$$U^* > U_f > U_p > U_s. \tag{43}$$

The first two inequalities follow directly from the differing constraints that are imposed. First-best is best, accounting for the first inequality; the second occurs because the government, having induced a given set of beliefs, is free to reoptimize in the second period under the time inconsistent solution.

The last inequality shows that a government that can precommit itself to carrying out a policy will produce a better outcome than one that short-sightedly reoptimizes each period. The second inequality, however, points out the problem posed by dynamic inconsistency: if the government can fool people into believing it will be consistent, it can then cheat them for their own good. This is a result of the distortions present in the optimal tax problem.

The assumption that the government and private agents have the same utility function is made here to show the dynamic inconsistency phenomenon in the cleanest possible setting.[47] But much interesting work has developed from models in which the policymaker and private agents may have different loss functions or in which it is necessary to specify only a policymaker loss function and a private sector reaction function. We now present the best-known such case, the Phillips curve monetary policy game introduced by Kydland and Prescott (1977) and developed by Barro and Gordon (1983, 1983a), Backus and Driffill (1985, 1985a), Canzoneri (1985), Rogoff (1985), and others.

The Expectational Phillips Curve Example

Suppose that the single-period loss function of the policymaker is quadratic in the rate of inflation, π, and in the deviation of output, y, from a target level:

$$M(\ ) = w\pi^2 + (y - k\overline{y})^2, \qquad w > 0, \quad k > 1. \tag{44}$$

Here $\overline{y}$ can be interpreted as full employment output. Thus the target level of output exceeds the natural rate. The assumption that $k > 1$ is crucial. We discussed possible reasons for this in section 11.1. The most plausible justification is the presence of distortions or imperfections that causes the natural rate of employment to be too low. This justification allows the loss function $M(\ )$ to be consistent with the single-period utility function of private agents. Another is that the government's objective function as shaped by the electoral process leads the government to seek to raise output above the natural rate.[48]

As in section 11.2, an expectational Phillips curve describes the relationship between output and inflation in each period:

$$y = \bar{y} + \beta(\pi - \pi^*),\tag{45}$$

where π^* is the expected rate of inflation. In the context of the present model the expectational Phillips curve must result from wage or price stickiness rather than from imperfect information. π^* may, for example, reflect expectations of inflation as embodied in predetermined nominal wages.

We consider first a one-period game. The policymaker sets the inflation rate, given π^*, so as to minimize $M(\ )$.[49] From (44), π is given by

$$\pi = (w + \beta^2)^{-1}\beta[(k - 1)\bar{y} + \beta\pi^*].\tag{46}$$

Figure 11.1 shows the actual inflation rate as a function of the expected inflation rate. This represents the government's reaction function to the private sector's decisions as embodied in wage contracts, for example.

The only point at which expectations are rational is at A in figure 11.1. At that point the inflation rate is

$$\pi_s = w^{-1}\beta(k - 1)\bar{y}.\tag{47}$$

Note that the larger the β (i.e., the greater the output gain from unanticipated

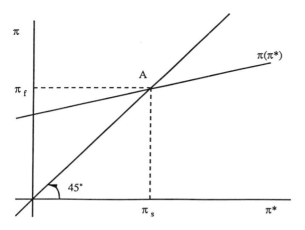

Figure 11.1
Expected and actual inflation

inflation), the larger the distortion $k - 1$, and the smaller the w (the less costly the inflation), the higher is the inflation rate.

The implied value of the loss function in the one-period optimization is

$$M_s = (k - 1)^2 \bar{y}^2 (1 + w^{-1} \beta^2). \tag{48}$$

This equilibrium, which is equivalent to the consistent or shortsighted solution in the tax case, is evidently worse for the government (and, if it has the same utility function, for the private sector) than a zero-inflation equilibrium. The zero-inflation equilibrium, the precommitment solution, gives a value of the loss function equal to

$$M_p = (k - 1)^2 \bar{y}^2. \tag{49}$$

Why in this game does the government not choose an inflation rate of zero, thereby attaining M_p rather than M_s? Under the rules of the game, in which the private sector chooses π^* first, $\pi = \pi^* = 0$ is not a Nash equilibrium. Once the private sector has committed itself to $\pi^* = 0$, the government will choose the positive rate of inflation implied by (46). The inflation rate π in (47) is a Nash equilibrium that, if expected by the private sector, will be implemented by the government.[50] If the government could somehow commit itself to choosing $\pi = 0$, it could obtain the distorted second-best outcome M_p.

In order to discuss the reputational equilibrium, we want also to calculate the inflation rate and value of the utility function in the fooling solution in which individuals expect the policymaker to create zero inflation, but he instead acts opportunistically. With $\pi^* = 0$, the optimal discretionary rate of inflation is, from (46),

$$\pi_f = (w + \beta^2)^{-1} [\beta(k - 1)\bar{y}]. \tag{50}$$

The corresponding value of the loss function is

$$M_f = (1 + w^{-1} \beta^2)^{-1} (k - 1)^2 \bar{y}^2. \tag{51}$$

Thus

$$M_f = (1 + w^{-1} \beta^2)^{-1} M_p \equiv (1 + \xi)^{-1} M_p,$$
$$M_s = (1 + w^{-1} \beta^2) M_p = (1 + \xi) M_p. \tag{52}$$

Note that $\xi = \beta^2 / w$ is, loosely, a measure of the utility gain from unexpected inflation: β gives the increase in output and w the utility loss from higher inflation. As in (43), this time with $M(\ )$ as a loss function,

$$M_f < M_p < M_s. \tag{53}$$

Dealing with Inconsistency

How seriously should we take the problem of dynamic inconsistency? It is clear that societies do find ways to deal with situations in which dynamic inconsistency could occur. So do individuals.[51] Wealth, in general, and the national debt, in particular, are standing invitations to surprise taxation, which is rarely explicitly imposed. Implicit social security obligations are honored and protected. Property rights are protected by law and understood to be essential to economic efficiency in a market environment.[52]

Dynamic inconsistency has been invoked most often in macroeconomics to explain an alleged inflationary bias in macroeconomic policymaking. Such a bias emerges clearly in the expectational Phillips curve example, which is certainly suggestive as a description of government behavior in the United States and Britain in the 1960s and 1970s. It is less suggestive of government behavior in the 1980s and the 1930s, or of German and Swiss government behavior in the 1970s, so the inflationary bias cannot be regarded as inevitable.[53]

Nevertheless, the question remains of how societies deal with potentially dynamically inconsistent situations. If standard models, such as the optimal tax model, suggest that governments will be tempted to behave inconsistently, and they do not, then something is missing from the models.

Reputation
Reputation is the most interesting and persuasive explanation of how governments avoid dynamic inconsistency. Governments know that they can do better than the shortsighted solution over the long run. They hope, by acting consistently over long periods, to build up a reputation that will cause the private sector to believe their announcements. We will examine models of reputation in some detail later. Before that we consider other solutions.

Bonding
Hughes Hallett (1986) argues that dynamically inconsistent behavior cannot occur because the public, knowing that the government will be tempted to renege, will not believe any announcements except those derived from the consistent or dynamic programming solution. With those expectations the government will in fact undertake the dynamic programming solution. In terms of figure 11.1 he argues that the public will not believe any announcement other than π_s, and given that belief, that is what will happen.

Knowing that, the government can, however, do better than the consistent solution by posting a bond that penalizes it for not carrying out the first-best (in figure 11.1, zero inflation) outcome. So long as the value of the bond exceeds the gain to the government from moving from $\pi = 0$ to π_f in figure 11.1 (the inflation rate that is optimal for the government when the private sector expects zero inflation), it will carry out the zero inflation rate. That way everyone is better off.

It is not clear what such a bond might be. Hallett argues that the government's reputation is one such bond, and we shall see below that the analogy is close. Equivalently, the bond might be a campaign promise, which, if not executed, brings punishment at the next election. Or, as in the models of Lucas and Stokey (1983) and Persson, Persson, and Svensson (1987), the government may structure the debt in such a way that it penalizes itself by not following through on its announced plans. For instance, by becoming a nominal creditor, the government can penalize itself for creating unexpected inflation.[54]

Of course, the bonding solution raises very delicate issues, too. Dynamic inconsistency does not disappear. Rather the solution assumes that the government will not violate certain explicit obligations, such as paying the bond, even though there is an incentive to do so. Without a theory of reputation such solutions have to be regarded as incomplete.

The Law

The law, constitutional or less fundamental, is obviously one solution to the dynamic inconsistency problem. In the perfect certainty environment of the optimal tax and monetary policy games, or assuming the equivalent uncertain environment with a complete description of states of nature, it would be possible to prescribe dynamically inconsistent policymaking by law.

But not all potential dynamic inconsistency situations can be dealt with by the law. This raises the questions of which issues are and should be handled through the law and which by discretionary policymaking. The ability to describe future contingencies fully must be an important element in this choice.

A potentially fruitful way of thinking about the constitutional law-law-rule-discretion continuum is to view policies as involving a trade-off between the benefits of flexibility and the costs of dynamic inconsistency.[55] Depending on the policy, the legal system makes an *ex ante* choice of the costs that should be attached to attempts to change it. Discretionary policies, such as monetary policy, can be changed at low cost; rules fixed by law, such as much of fiscal policy, are changeable at greater cost; rules fixed by constitutional law such as the rights of private property or interstate commerce are in principle also changeable but at yet greater cost.[56]

Kotlikoff, Persson, and Svensson (1986) in an overlapping generations model resolve a potential dynamic inconsistency by having the optimal policy enshrined in a law that the older generation can sell to the younger. If the older generation violates the law, it cannot sell it. The younger generation has the alternative of setting up its own law, but by assumption doing that is more expensive than buying the used law. It therefore buys the law from the older generation, and the game continues, ensuring dynamic consistency. The real world analogy of the sale of laws is not obvious but may be related to legislative logrolling.

Conservative Policymakers

Rogoff (1985) points out that the inflationary bias of the Phillips curve example can be reduced by appointing conservative policymakers.

Suppose society's loss function is $M(\ )$. Let w_b (b for banker) be the policymaker's weight on inflation in his personal loss function. Giving such an individual full discretion results in a loss for society of

$$M_b = \left(1 + \frac{\beta^2}{w_b}\right) M_p. \tag{54}$$

The more conservative the policymaker, the closer the society comes to achieving the precommitted equilibrium.

The notion of appointing conservative central bankers is certainly suggestive. Further reasons to appoint them relate to the benefits of reputation, to be examined below.

Vulnerability as a Defense

If the government cannot precommit so that the discretionary outcome obtains, the value of the loss function is, as we have seen,

$$M_s = (1 + w^{-1}\beta^2)(k - 1)^2 \bar{y}^2. \tag{51}$$

The parameter w is a measure of the cost of inflation to individuals. Any move that reduces the costs of inflation (relative to the costs of deviations of output from the target level) would reduce w. Indexation (e.g., of the tax system) might be regarded in this way.

But now observe that a reduction in w *increases* M_s. Although the marginal cost of inflation falls at a given inflation rate, the "equilibrium" inflation rate rises enough, from (46), to actually increase the total cost.[57]

This result is possible only because the discretionary solution is not first-best. Because the outcome is distorted and because the policymaker is trying to maximize the welfare of the representative individual, it is possible by increasing the costs of the distortion (inflation) to the representative individual to make him better off.

The result provides some justification for the standard view of committees of inquiry that by reducing inhibitions against inflation, indexation would only make the situation worse.[58] Note, though, that this would not hold for wage indexation, which by reducing the effects of unanticipated inflation on output, reduces the parameter β.

Reputational Equilibria

Can reputation sustain the optimal policy? The key to the answer is the specification of private sector expectations, of how the public reacts to broken promises.

Suppose that the horizon is infinite and that policymakers have the intertemporal loss function L_t:

$$L_t = E\left[\sum_0^\infty (1 + \theta)^{-i}(w\pi_{t+i}^2 + (y_{t+i} - k\bar{y})^2)\bigg| t\right]. \tag{55}$$

The loss function in each period is the same as in equation (44) earlier. We denote the inflation rate (47) associated with consistent (shortsighted) policy in the one-period problem by π_s. The inflation rate associated with the precommitted monetary policy is $\pi_p = 0$.

The Simplest Nonstochastic Case
We start with expectations based on the private sector's viewing the policymaker as either reliable or opportunistic. If the inflation rate has ever been anything other than the precommitted rate of zero, the expected inflation rate from then on will be π_s from (47). If the government has hitherto produced the precommitted inflation rate, $\pi_s = 0$, it is expected to continue doing so.

Why these particular expectations? They will turn out to be justified, or rational. But in many cases they are not the only rational expectations or in game theory terminology, not the only *perfect* equilibrium. The problem of multiple rational expectations solutions to repeated games is well known, and there is as yet no good way of choosing among alternative perfect solutions.[59]

Given these expectations, consider a government that has always produced zero inflation, now considering whether to continue producing zero inflation or whether instead to fool the public. If it cheats, it gains in that period:

$$\text{temptation} = M_p - M_f = \frac{\xi M_p}{1 + \xi}. \tag{56}$$

It then has to pay for its cheating by being expected to produce the discretionary solution forever.[60] If that is what is expected, that is the best thing for the government to do. The loss from discretionary policy in one period relative to the precommitted equilibrium is

$$\text{loss} = M_s - M_p = \xi M_p. \tag{57}$$

Note that both the temptation and the loss are increasing in ξ.

The gain from acting opportunistically is then equal to the temptation minus the present discounted value of the loss that starts a period later:

$$\text{gain from opportunism} = \text{temptation} - \frac{\text{loss}}{\theta}$$

$$= \xi M_p [(\theta - (1 + \xi)][\theta(1 + \xi)]^{-1}. \tag{58}$$

The government will act opportunistically if it has a very high discount rate, and it will then be expected to behave (and will behave) that way in every succeeding period. It will keep the inflation rate at zero if the discount rate is low or if ξ is high. The role of ξ in determining whether the government keeps inflation at zero appears paradoxical in that when ξ is high, the short-run gain from unanticipated inflation is high. Thus, if anything, a low ξ would be expected to produce low inflation. But since both the gain and the loss are increasing in ξ, the net effect is a priori indeterminate, and it depends on the curvature of the loss function.

Note that in this certainty setting, a reputational equilibrium is possible only if the horizon is infinite. Otherwise, the government would be sure in the last period to produce the discretionary outcome whatever the private sector's expectation and, working backward, would be expected to do the same in the first period.

The Barro-Gordon Example
Another perfect equilibrium in this type of model has been derived by Barro and Gordon (1983a). Their expectations assumption is that if the government fails to produce the expected inflation rate this period, the private sector expects the one-period inflation rate π_s next period; if they produce the expected inflation rate this period, they regain credibility.

For a low discount rate, zero inflation can be shown to be an equilibrium in this model.[61] For higher discount rates, Barro and Gordon find a reputational equilibrium by solving for the inflation rate at which the government just acts in accordance with expectations. Solutions exist only if $\xi\theta < 1$, that is, only if the government is not too impatient. If it is, it will go to the one-period solution. Otherwise, the solution for the consistent inflation rate is between 0 and π_s.

Thus, depending on the parameters, this reputational model may produce an inflation rate anywhere between (and including) the optimal precommitted rate and the optimal shortsighted rate.

The nature of the equilibrium in both of these examples is that so long as it does not miscalculate, the government will carry out its announced policy because there is no advantage to not doing so. In the Barro-Gordon model, if it should by miscalculation deviate, then it will implement π_s next period, given that it is expected to do so. It regains credibility and thereafter is happy to return to the reputational equilibrium inflation rate. In the first model, if it ever miscalculates, it thereafter implements π_s forever after. In each case the equilibrium is perfect—though, as the two examples illustrate, it is obviously not unique.

Multiple Equilibria

Perhaps there are many possible equilibria in the real world, and it is pure accident that a particular situation exists. Nevertheless, it would be preferable if theory could narrow down the range of possibilities.

The description of the private sector's response to the government's deviation as a punishment raises the hope that the design of an optimal punishment strategy will reduce the multiplicity of equilibria. But unless the private sector is thought of as a single union, or as otherwise capable of highly coordinated actions, it is difficult conceive how it can select that set of expectations that leads to optimal punishment.

The Kreps-Wilson Reputation Model

If reputation is important, might a government have an incentive to build up its reputation in order to harvest the benefits at some point in time? This problem, in the context of inflation, has been studied by Tabellini (1983, 1985), Backus and Driffill (1985a, 1985b), and Barro (1986), using a model of reputation due to Kreps and Wilson (1982). Tabellini and Backus-Driffill consider a monopoly union that sets wages in a game with a monetary authority.[62] The alternative assumption, made by Barro, is that private agents are homogeneous and not engaged in strategic considerations vis-à-vis the policymaker. The union-versus-central bank game may be appropriate for Europe, but in the U.S. context the notion that private agents cannot combine against the monetary authority is more attractive than the alternative.

The horizon is finite. The public believes there are two possible types of policymaker, the strong and the weak. The strong never inflates. The weak is always tempted to produce unanticipated inflation but, by pretending to be strong, can build up a reputation for strength. The weak policymaker potentially engages in a mixed (randomizing) strategy, picking a probability of acting tough (or alternately, producing inflation) in each period and letting the dice decide the policy choice. If in any period the dice make him act weak, the public understands he is weak, and in each subsequent period he obtains only the discretionary outcome.

To simplify calculations, we switch to the government utility function used by Backus-Driffill and Barro-Gordon and present only a two-period illustration. Suppose that the government has the single-period utility function[63]

$$W = -\left(\frac{a}{2}\right)\pi^2 + b(\pi - \pi^*). \tag{59}$$

At the beginning of the game (time zero) the policymaker has a reputation, defined by the probability q_0 that he is tough (that $b = 0$). The policy choices and outcome if the policymaker is indeed tough are simply to always choose zero inflation. Thus we focus attention on the more interesting problem of the lamb in wolf's clothing.

One key to the structure of the game is that reputation evolves according to Bayes' rule. Let y_t denote the probability that the (weak) policymaker chooses to play tough in period t. Let x_t denote the public's view of the probability that the policymaker chooses to act tough given that he is weak. In equilibrium we will require $x_t = y_t$, but the government cannot manipulate x_t by its choice of y_t.

The prior reputation is q_t. In the next period, by Bayes' rule, the reputation will be, if there is no inflation,

$$q_{t+1} = \frac{q_t}{q_t + (1 - q_t)x_t} > q_t. \tag{60}$$

The term $(1 - q_t)x_t$ in the denominator is the joint probability that the outcome is zero inflation and the policymaker is weak.[64] Thus, if it sees no inflation, the private sector will increase its probability that it is dealing with a strong government.

We illustrate the solution in a two-period $(T - 1$ and $T)$ model. Note that the inflation rate that maximizes (59) is

$$\pi_s = \frac{b}{a} = 1, \tag{61}$$

where for convenience we set both b and a at unity. In the last period, T, the weak policymaker will certainly inflate, setting $\pi = 1$. Private agents expect inflation to be zero with probability q_T, and one with probability $1 - q_T$, implying that $\pi_T^* = 1 - q_T$. The value of the utility function in the last period, if the weak policymaker has made it this far without creating inflation, is thus

$$W_T = -(\tfrac{1}{2})\pi^2 + (\pi - \pi^*) = q_T - \tfrac{1}{2}. \tag{62}$$

Note that the last-period utility is increasing in reputation, and this is the incentive for good behavior in earlier periods. Note also that if the policy-maker is known to be weak he will inflate without obtaining any output benefit, and have a utility level in the last period of $-1/2$.

In the previous period the policymaker chooses the probability of con-tinuing to be strong. At that point, q_{T-1}, his period $T-1$ reputation is given. The expected inflation rate is given by

$$\pi_{T-1}^* = 1 \cdot (1 - q_{T-1})(1 - x_{T-1}), \tag{63}$$

which is the private sector's probability that inflation occurs (i.e., that the policymaker is weak *and* plays weak) times the one-shot optimal inflation rate for the weak government, which is equal to one.

If he plays strong, his one-period utility at $T-1$ is just $-\pi_{T-1}^*$. But individuals, seeing no inflation, revise q_T for period T according to (60). If he plays weak, his one-period utility is $(1/2) - \pi_{T-1}^*$. But individuals, seeing inflation at $T-1$, realize that the government is weak and enter period T with $q_T = 0$. Thus, if the policymaker chooses a probability y_{T-1} of playing strong, his expected utility is given by

$$J_{T-1}(y_{T-1}; q_{T-1}) = y_{T-1}[-\pi_{T-1}^* + (1 + \theta)^{-1}(q_T - \tfrac{1}{2})]$$

$$+ (1 - y_{T-1})[(\tfrac{1}{2}) - \pi_{T-1}^* - (1 + \theta)^{-1}(\tfrac{1}{2})]. \tag{64}$$

The first expression in square brackets is the utility derived by not inflating in this period and then inflating in the last period; the contents of the second expression in square brackets is the utility from inflating now and then inflating when expected to in the last period.

If he maximizes (64) with respect to y_{T-1}, the first-order condition for an interior maximum ($0 < y < 1$) is

$$q_T = (\tfrac{1}{2})(1 + \theta). \tag{65}$$

If q_T is given by (65), then by (60), x_{T-1} is given by

$$x_{T-1} = \frac{(1 - \theta)q_{T-1}}{(1 + \theta)(1 - q_{T-1})}. \tag{66}$$

With rational expectations x and y must coincide so that $y_{T-1} = x_{T-1}$. This determines the equilibrium value of y at time $T - 1$.

The probability of playing tough in the second-to-last period is thus increasing in reputation and decreasing in the discount rate.

Note that for $\theta < 1$, the solution is definitely interior for any reputation less than 0.5; someone with a poor reputation will randomize. A weak policymaker with a good reputation, however, will play tough for sure, keeping the bonanza to the end. For instance, for $\theta = 0$, any reputation greater than one-half will result in the policymaker playing strong.

The general form of the solution as the number of periods rises is described by Barro (1986); the method of deriving the solution can be inferred from the above two-period example. For a long-horizon problem, the policymaker will start out by not randomizing at all, thus not producing inflation. Because private agents are uncertain of the policymaker's type, inflation is below its expected level during this whole time, causing a small recession. Eventually, the end beckons, and the policymaker begins to randomize. During this period his reputation improves, and the probability of playing strong falls. Then toward the end, maybe only in the last period, he inflates for sure.

One result that emerges from this framework is that as the horizon goes to infinity, and provided the discount rate is low, the reputational equilibrium with zero inflation is attained. The reasoning is similar to that above: the penalty for revealing your weakness is a very long period of inferior performance.

Neither the elegance nor the suggestiveness of the Kreps-Wilson construct can be denied. But the analysis, by focusing entirely on the weak policymaker who has made it through without inflating, draws attention away from the implausibility of the view that the policymaker makes decisions by randomizing.[65]

Exogenous Uncertainty

None of the models presented so far has dealt with exogenous uncertainty. The uncertainty in the Kreps-Wilson reputation model is entirely endogenous. We examine uncertainty in three contexts: uncertainty about the tastes of the policymaker, uncertainty about the environment, and uncertainty about the information available to the policymaker.[66]

Political Uncertainty

Alesina (1987) nicely produces a political business cycle out of private sector uncertainty over the outcome of elections. Suppose there are two political parties with different utility functions. In particular, using the convenient utility function (59), the shortsighted inflation rates for parties D and R are π_s^D and π_s^R:

$$\pi_s^D = \frac{b^D}{a^D} > \pi_s^R = \frac{b^R}{a^R}. \tag{67}$$

Suppose that elections are held at fixed intervals and, for simplicity, that the probability of victory for the D's is given and equal to q. Suppose also that neither party is capable of precommitting on the inflation rate and thus that each will produce its own discretionary rate of inflation. Then immediately before the election the expected rate of inflation is

$$\pi^* = q\pi_s^D + (1 - q)\pi_s^R. \tag{68}$$

This means that in the period after the D's win an election, the actual rate of inflation will be higher than the rate that had been expected, and by the same token unanticipated inflation will be negative after the R's win. Accordingly, the D's will start their terms with a boom, thereafter reverting to high inflation without a boom, and the R's will start with a recession, thereafter reverting to a low rate of inflation without a recession. The D's justify their reputation as a party of expansion and high inflation, and the R's justify theirs as the party of recession and low inflation, even though it is known precisely what each will do if elected. Obviously, the ability of the parties or their policymakers to affect output depends on the lack of wage contracts contingent on the election outcome or, more simply in this model, on the absence of price-indexed contracts.

Alesina generalizes his analysis to include reputational effects of the Barro-Gordon (1983a) type, without significantly affecting the nature of the results. Alesina (1988) presents empirical results on economic performance following presidential elections in the United States that tend to support his model.

Flexible Policy

The Phillips curve models underlying most of the dynamic inconsistency–inflation literature sector implicitly have a one-period lag in wage or price setting. That suggests the opportunity for discretionary policymakers to respond rapidly to disturbances that would otherwise have real effects, as in the models of section 11.2. Indeed, one of the most serious arguments for discretionary policy is that the policymakers can handle certain disturbances more rapidly and more cheaply than can myriad private agents around the economy, an argument we explored in chapter 8. For instance, there is no reason why a shift in the demand for money should be transmitted to prices, causing all economic agents to make some adjustment when the money-creating authorities can respond instead.

Rogoff (1985) develops a model in which, as noted above, a conservative policymaker helps to reduce the costs of dynamic inconsistency by not being tempted excessively by the lure of inflation. But he also shows why such a solution can go too far. The point can be demonstrated in the inflation example above, with the output supply function generalized to

$$y = \bar{y} + \beta(\pi - \pi^* + u). \tag{69}$$

Here u is a white noise disturbance that is not known to private agents when they make their wage decisions. (We do not show time subscripts.) We denote the variance of u by σ^2. The social loss function is now the expectation of $M(\ )$ in equation (44).

The monetary authority is in a position to respond to realizations of u, but π^*, representing wage setting, is determined before u is known. There is no precommitment, so the consistent or shortsighted solution is chosen each period. The inflation rate is

$$\pi = (w + \beta^2)^{-1}\beta[(k-1)\bar{y} + \beta\pi^* - \beta u], \tag{70}$$

implying that π^* is the same as under certainty, namely,

$$\pi^* = \left(\frac{\beta}{w}\right)(k-1)\bar{y}$$

and

$$\pi = \left(\frac{\beta}{w}\right)(k-1)\bar{y} - (w + \beta^2)^{-1}\beta^2 u. \tag{70'}$$

In this solution the monetary authority responds to supply shocks, allowing them to affect both output and inflation: an adverse supply shock both raises the inflation rate and reduces output below the natural rate.[67]

The expected value of the loss function under these conditions is calculated as

$$E(M) = (1 + \xi)(k - 1)^2\bar{y}^2 + (1 + \xi)^{-1}\beta^2\sigma^2, \qquad \xi \equiv \frac{\beta^2}{w}. \tag{71}$$

The nature of the flexibility-consistency trade-off emerges clearly. By installing a conservative policymaker with a large w, the loss from the first component (due to the inability to precommit) is reduced. But at the same time the loss from the second component is increased because the policymaker's distorted tastes prevent his responding flexibly to supply shocks. The need for flexibility makes it undesirable to have a monomaniacal inflation-fighter at the central bank.[68]

The presence of exogenous uncertainty also modifies the analysis of the reputational equilibrium in the Kreps-Wilson model. Suppose, for instance, that the government cannot control the inflation rate exactly and that the public's only information about the government's type has to be deduced from the behavior of the inflation rate. Then a government trying to develop a reputation for toughness has to take into account the possibility that an adverse draw of the inflation rate will destroy its reputation.[69]

Private Information
Canzoneri (1985) and Cukierman (1986) both discuss the implications for monetary policy of the monetary authority having private information. In Canzoneri's model the private information is a forecast of money demand disturbances, that the policymaker in an ideal setting would want to offset. In Cukierman's analysis the central bank has private information about its tastes in the current period and future periods, as well as about disturbances.

The aim is to find arrangements in which the policymaker produces the optimal precommitted policy in the face of disturbances. The discretionary solution with conservative policymaker, which Rogoff chooses, does not fully resolve the inflationary bias from dynamic inconsistency problem. The optimal policy given the disturbances in the output supply function is to produce $\pi^* = 0$ and to have the central bank only offset u disturbances around that mean rate of inflation. The implied feedback policy is

$$\pi = -\frac{\beta^2 u}{w + \beta^2}, \qquad \text{with } y = \bar{y} + \frac{w\beta u}{w + \beta^2}. \tag{72}$$

The implied value of the loss function is

$$E(M_p) = (k - 1)^2\bar{y}^2 + \frac{\beta^2\sigma^2}{1 + \xi} \tag{73}$$

which is below the value in (71), as should be expected from the fact that this corresponds to the precommitted equilibrium.

The policymaker's actions can be monitored *ex post* if the values of u are known. But suppose the Fed has to take action based on a forecast of u and that the forecast is private information. Then, if the private sector believes the central bank may act inconsistently, the Fed will not credibly be able to convey its private information about the disturbance. Any time the Fed takes big actions, even if it is in truth reacting to a forecast, it will most likely be suspected of cheating by trying to produce the preferred outcome with higher output.[70]

An equilibrium exists in which individuals establish confidence intervals, for example, for the inflation rate, and revert to expecting the central bank to act opportunistically if inflation goes above the interval. There is a trade-off for the Fed between flexibility and credibility. Further, confidence might be lost even when the Fed is doing its job.[71] The notion that confidence breaks down occasionally is one that Canzoneri recommends, on the grounds that other reputational equilibria are too stable.[72]

It seems clear that with private information it will never be possible to stop the Fed from cheating in every single instance. But it is certainly possible to keep it from cheating on average, since the average rate of inflation is supposed to be zero in this framework and can easily be monitored. Of course, if the Fed and private individuals have the same utility function, the cheating is in a good cause and does harm only if it adversely affects their reputation.

Cukierman (1985) describes a model in which the central bank has different goals than those of the public and also has changing tastes. The public does not know the parameters of the central bank's utility function and only slowly learns about them. In this context the central bank prefers the private sector to be uncertain of its actions, to the extent that it prefers imprecise to precise methods of monetary control. Cukierman argues that such considerations explain central banks' penchant for secrecy.

Disinflation

We now briefly show how a government may be caught in a high-inflation equilibrium in the following sense: given expectations, it does not want to move from the high-inflation equilibrium; but if it were at a zero-inflation equilibrium, it would stay there.

Suppose a government has been inflating at the expected rate π_s. The public does not believe any announcements by the government. Suppose that the public's expectations are that if the government produced an inflation rate of π_s last period it will do so this period; if it produced an inflation rate of zero last period, it will do so in the next period.[73]

Then the government, in weighing the possibility of disinflating, knows that it will pay the price of a one-period recession. We now return to the loss function (44). With the public expecting $\pi_s = \beta(k - 1)\bar{y}/w$, the one-period loss from a zero-inflation rate is

$$M(\pi = 0 | \pi^* = \pi_s) = M_p(1 + \xi)^2,$$

where we are using terms defined in equations (49) and (52). The net loss from reducing the inflation rate from π_s to 0 is therefore

$$\text{first-period loss} = M_p(1 + \xi)\xi. \tag{74}$$

The gain from disinflating is equal to the present discounted value of the reduced losses from the next period on. They result from the difference between the loss when $\pi = \pi^* = 0$ and $\pi = \pi^* = \pi_s$, respectively, which is equal to

$$\text{gain} = \frac{\xi M_p}{\theta}. \tag{75}$$

The government will not disinflate if the loss outweighs the gain, that is, if

$$\theta(1 + \xi) > 1. \tag{76}$$

If (76) is satisfied, the government will stay at the high-inflation equilibrium.

Suppose, alternatively, that the government starts at a zero-inflation equilibrium. It considers surprising the public to obtain a one-period gain in utility. The price it pays is then that in the next period the private sector believes it will produce the inflation rate π_s, and it does so. We assume that thereafter it stays at the high-inflation equilibrium (i.e., it satisfies 76).

A government contemplating inflating from the zero-inflation equilibrium gains in the first period by producing a boom. It pays later by producing the inflation rate π_s rather than zero. By calculating the optimal inflation rate when $\pi^* = 0$, we can show that the one-period gain from producing the surprise inflation is

$$\text{gain} = \frac{\xi M_p}{1 + \xi}. \tag{77}$$

The loss in this case is that the government thereafter produces π_s instead of zero; this amount is given by the gain in (75).

Accordingly, if the government faces an expected inflation rate of zero, it will not inflate so long as

$$\frac{1}{\theta} > (1 + \xi)^{-1},$$

or equivalently,

$$1 + \xi > \theta. \tag{78}$$

There is a set of values of θ and ξ for which both inequalities (76) and (78) can be satisfied simultaneously, namely, if

$$(1 + \xi) > \theta > (1 + \xi)^{-1}. \tag{79}$$

When these inequalities are satisfied, a government that is expected to produce high inflation will do so because it is not willing to pay the transitional cost of the recession needed to move to a zero-inflation equilibrium. But if it were at zero inflation, it would not want to move to a higher equilibrium.

It is under such conditions that governments may resort to wage and price controls as a means of forcing inflation down for a transitional period during which it has time to prove that it has indeed changed its policies— which will be clear if the wage and price controls operate without causing significant shortages.[74]

Rules versus Discretion

The concept of dynamic inconsistency brought a new perspective on the rules versus discretion debate. The pre-1977 case for rules outlined in section 11.2, however suggestive it may have been, was vulnerable to the simple criticism that any good rule can always be operated by discretion—and that discretion therefore always dominates rules.[75]

Kydland and Prescott (1977) identified the precommitted solution with a rule and the dynamic programming solution with discretion, thereby making a stronger case for rules than for discretion. Of course, the case is not one for a constant growth rate rule in preference to any other rule, but for precommitment over shortsighted policymaking.

Models of reputation suggest that discretionary policymaking may be less irresponsible than the short-run optimization implied by the dynamic programming or consistent solution. Taking into account the benefits of flexibility, however, the case for rules over discretion again becomes ambiguous, a matter to be judged case by case. This is hardly satisfactory as a means of deciding a priori what sort of policy regime to install, but this cannot be helped.

Economic Policy and Game Theory

Although game theory entered the theory of economic policy along with dynamic inconsistency, it has an independent value in studying policy. The game-theoretic approach points strongly toward the crucial role of expectations,[76] as well as the incompleteness of the rational expectations concept. The multiple equilibria of the reputational games are all rational expectations equilibria. What is urgently needed is to find ways of selecting from among the many equilibria those that are likely to be selected in practice. Since in practice there is never certainty about the government's intentions (even within the government) and about the relationship between outcomes and intentions, it is quite likely that the relevant equilibria will involve learning and the use of Bayes' rule, which is to say that in many circumstances rational expectations will resemble adaptive expectations.

11.5 Conclusions

Economists study the economy both for the sheer intellectual pleasure of trying to understand the world in which they live and with the hope that improved knowledge will lead to better economic policy and performance. That there is nevertheless some distance between the theory of economic policy as outlined in this chapter and actual policy should be obvious. To go from here to actual policy, one must not only confront the issues emphasized in this chapter but also have a view as to the causes and the mechanisms of economic fluctuations (which is what the rest of this book was about), a sense of the limitations imposed by the political process, and enough knowledge of facts and institutions to translate general recommendations into actual policy measures. This is why macroeconomic policy is never easy.

Problems

1. *The gold standard as a monetary rule.*

The following is a loglinear model of an economy in which gold is held as an asset:

$$m_t^d = p_t + y_t - a_1(E[p_{t+1}|t] - p_t) - a_2(E[q_{t+1}|t] - q_t) + \eta_t, \tag{1}$$

$$m_t^s = \lambda + g_t^m + q_t + \theta_t, \tag{2}$$

$$m_t^s = m_t^d. \tag{3}$$

In these equations p_t is the price level and q_t is the price of gold; both are measured in terms of the numeraire (dollar). η and θ are disturbances, m is the money stock, g^m is the stock of monetary gold (the monetary base), and y_t is real output.

The stock demand for nonmonetary gold is given by

$$g_t^{nm} = b_1(p_t - q_t) - b_2(E[p_{t+1}|t] - E[q_{t+1}|t] - (p_t - q_t)) + u_t \tag{4}$$

and

$$g_t^m = g - g_t^{nm}$$

where g is the total stock of gold, assumed to be constant, and u is a disturbance term.

Finally, the supply of output is given by

$$y_t = h(p_t - E[p_t|t - 1]) + v_t, \tag{5}$$

where v is a disturbance.

(a) Explain briefly the rationale behind these equations.

(b) Assume that the government runs a gold standard monetary policy, with $q_t = 0$ for all t. Compute the variances of p_t and y_t under the assumptions that all disturbances have zero serial and cross correlation.

(c) Suppose, instead, that the government can successfully fix $p_t = 0$ for all t by allowing q_t to vary. Under what conditions is output more stable?

(d) Suppose that all disturbances follow first-order autoregressive processes. How is your previous answer affected?

2. *Nominal income targeting.*

Consider the simple macroeconomic model

$$m_t + v_t = p_t + y_t,$$

$$v_t = ai_t + by_t + \varepsilon_t,$$

$$y_t = -c\{i_t - (E[p_{t+1}|t] - p_t)\} + \theta_t,$$

$$p_t = E[p_t|t - 1] + dy_t + \eta_t,$$

where v is velocity, ε, θ, and η are disturbances with zero serial and cross correlation, and all other variables are standard. The information set at time t includes current and past values of ε, θ, and η.

(a) Derive output under a fixed money rule and a fixed nominal income rule.

(b) Under what conditions does a nominal income rule dominate a fixed money rule? What objective function should you use to answer that question?

3. *Indexation and inflation.*

Suppose that the government maximizes $L = a\pi^2 + (y - ky)^2$, $k > 1$, subject to the Phillips curve relation $y = \bar{y} + b(\pi - \pi^*)$.

(a) Compute the equilibrium inflation rate in the absence of commitment.

(b) Suppose that the degree of indexation of wages increases. What happens to the coefficients a and b? Under the assumption that only b changes, what happens to equilibrium inflation? What happens to the value of the loss function?

(c) Suppose that indexation of financial instruments becomes more widespread. What happens to the coefficients a and b? Under the assumption that only a changes, what happens to equilibrium inflation and the value of the loss function?

(d) "Indexation is likely to lead to more inflation. Thus it should generally be resisted." Discuss this statement.

(e) How would you modify your analysis if money affects activity through balance sheet effects, as described at the end of chapter 9?

4. *Exogenous uncertainty in a reputation model. (This is adapted from Hoshi 1988.)*

This problem introduces exogeneous uncertainty into the Kreps-Wilson model studied in this chapter. As in the text, the (weak) government has a one-period utility function defined by equation (59), and the public thinks that the government is strong with probability q_t. We assume, however, that the government (weak or strong) cannot control the inflation rate exactly. For simplicity, we assume that the weak government can only choose one of two values for the inflation rate, the one-shot optimal inflation rate, b/a, or zero inflation. Then, with some small probability $1 - p$, the government fails to obtain its desired inflation rate. Thus, it if tries to choose zero inflation, it ends up with inflation of b/a with probability $1 - p$. If, instead, it tries to choose inflation of b/a, it ends up with zero inflation with probability $1 - p$. p is assumed to be greater than 1/2.

(a) Assume $a = b = 1$. Compute the public's expectation of inflation in the last period, T, assuming that the type of government has not been revealed by that time. Observe that the expectation is decreasing in q_T.

(b) Noting that the government cannot control inflation perfectly, compute the expected utility for the weak government in the last period, given q_T. Observe that it is increasing in q_T. Also observe that the marginal contribution of q_T is smaller in the presence of exogenous uncertainty.

(c) Compute the expected utility of the weak government if if chooses a probability y_{T-1} of playing strong in period $T - 1$. Note that playing strong leads to zero inflation only with probability p. In order to have an interior maximum $(0 < y_{T-1} < 1)$, what condition must q_T satisfy? Observe that the presence of uncertainty makes q_T larger.

(d) Write down the Bayes relation that relates q_T to q_{T-1}, x_{T-1} (the public view of the probability that the weak government acts tough) and p. Solve for x_{T-1}. Given p, observe that x_{T-1} is a decreasing function of q_T.

(e) Show that the above relation implies that $q_T > q_{T-1}$ if $p > 1/2$. Given q_T, show that x_{T-1} is increasing in p.

(f) Using the results in (d) and (e), discuss the effects of exogenous uncertainty on the reputational equilibrium (note that in equilibrium $x_{T-1} = y_{T-1}$).

5. *Policy in a two-party system. (This follows Alesina 1987.)*

The setup is the same as in section 11.4. Suppose, however, that elections take place every n periods. The outcome of an election is an i.i.d. random variable, and the probability that D wins is given by q. A party gets utility level $-Z$ when not in office. Using equation (68), note that people must form inflation expectations for the election year as they are not sure of which party will win the election. Both parties are assumed to have infinite horizons and discount the future at rate θ.

(a) Compute the expected utility for each party, when each party follows its shortsighted stragegy, equation (67).

(b) Compute the expected utility for each party, when both parties choose zero inflation every period.

(c) Show that for party R, the expected utility in (b) is always larger than the utility in (a). Under what condition does the expected utility for D become larger under (b) than under (a)?

(d) Consider the following strategies for both parties. If the party in power has produced zero inflation throughout its incumbency, the other party chooses zero inflation if elected. If the party in power has produced positive inflation, the other party chooses, from then on, its shortsighted inflation rate if elected. Can these strategies sustain the zero-inflation equilibrium?

6. *Disinflation.*

We saw in section 11.4 how a government may be caught in a high-inflation trap. Instead of assuming that the one-period loss function is given by equation (44), assume that the government has the one-period loss function given by equation (59), namely,

$$W = -\left(\frac{a}{2}\right)\pi^2 + b(\pi - \pi^*).$$

(a) Suppose that a government has been inflating at the rate $\pi^s = b/a$. We assume that expectations are such that if the government has inflated at rate π^s last period, it is expected to do so in the next, and that if the inflation rate was equal to zero last period, it is expected to be again equal to zero this period. Under these assumptions show that the government will always disinflate so long as $\theta \leqslant 1$.

(b) Suppose, alternatively, that the government started at zero inflation. Show that it would never want to inflate.

(c) Compare your results with those in the text. How do you explain the difference?

(d) Suppose now that the public forms expectations as follows: If inflation has been equal to zero for the last n periods, it is expected to be equal to zero in the next. Otherwise, expectations are equal to π^s. Show that the government can be caught in the high-inflation trap if n is large enough.

Notes

1. This has changed in the last ten years. Economists have come closer to building models to explain the behavior of policymakers and its implications for policy. See Alesina (1988) for a survey.

2. See Fischer and Modigliani (1978) for a list of the costs of inflation, and Fischer (1981) for an attempt to measure some of these costs.

3. Formal models of price level determination under the gold standard are contained in Barro (1979), Fischer (1986), and Barsky and Summers (1988). The "cost of production" theory of the price level has a long tradition. See, for instance, the discussion in Wicksell ([1898] 1965, ch. 4).

4. Although a pure commodity money system would, by definition, avoid bank runs, credit is bound to exist in any reasonably sophisticated financial system, creating the potential for financial panics.

5. Mints (1945) provides a good introduction.

6. We reviewed in chapter 4 channels other than nominal rigidities through which changes in money could have real effects and concluded that those channels are likely to be quantitatively unimportant.

7. We also do not discuss the issues raised by a pure credit, inside money, system. We briefly did so in chapter 4.

8. Diamond and Dybvig (1983) develop a model of bank runs.

9. Note that equation (2) replicates equation (26) of chapter 10, with a equal to zero in (2). We do this for simplicity. As we saw in that chapter, a is equal to zero if workers desire a constant real wage.

10. Very similar results would be obtained if we assumed two-period labor contracts and required the money supply decision at time t to be based on information available only up to the end of period $t - 1$.

11. It makes a significant difference to the results below whether expectations are formed adaptively about the price level or about the inflation rate. In the absence of a more closely specified model of expectations, there is no general basis for assuming one form rather than the other, or indeed more sophisticated expectations hypotheses such as the adaptive-regressive formulation (Frenkel 1975).

12. We have assumed that the target rate of output does not respond to u_t. The unit root result goes through, however, as long as the policymaker wants smaller fluctuations in output in response to u_t than would be the outcome under flexible prices.

13. The optimal solution can be derived by using (6) to substitute for y_t in the loss function, and then solving for π_t and for the implied path of money from (1). The solution gives only one insight beyond those noted in the above paragraph: the unconditional expectation of the inflation rate is equal to

$$\frac{\bar{y}\beta w_y \theta}{w_p(1 + \theta - \gamma)}.$$

Thus on average the bigger the $\bar{y}$, the greater the relative weight on output in the loss function (w_y/w_p), the greater the output bang per unit of inflation in the Phillips curve, β, the greater the discount rate, and the larger the γ, the higher is the inflation rate. These effects are entirely intuitive.

14. If the supply function was such that u_t was white noise and serial correlation was generated, instead, by a lagged output term in the supply equation, (as in Lucas 1973) output could be fully stabilized.

15. See Canzoneri et al. (1983). A related point is made by McCallum (1981) in the context of interest rate pegging under rational expectations, as we shall see later.

16. The optimal rule is derived by assuming that it takes the form

$$m_t = \hat{m} + \psi_1\varepsilon_{1t} + \psi_2\varepsilon_{2t} + \psi_3 v_{t-1} + \psi_4 u_{t-1},$$

and by solving for the unknown parameters $\hat{m}$ and ψ_i's.

17. As the textbooks show, this conclusion can easily be understood using an IS-LM diagram.

18. The specification of expected inflation implies that participants in asset markets know the current shocks and the current price level. Alternative specifications of information can be and have been explored.

19. See, for example, Canzoneri, Henderson, and Rogoff (1983) or Dotsey and King (1986).

20. The question is different from that studied earlier in which we examined the implications of setting the nominal interest rate at some level i within each period. The two are, however, related, as we shall show later.

21. We discussed the potentially destabilizing effects of inflation in chapter 10, section 10.3.

22. This point can be shown more formally by solving the implied expectational difference equation for p_t:

$$(\beta + b)p_t = \beta E[p_t|t - 1] + bE[p_{t+1}|t] - b\bar{i} + z_t - \beta u_t.$$

Consider some arbitrary solution to the equation. Another solution is given if any constant is added to each of p_t, $E[p_t|t - 1]$, and $E[p_{t+1}|t]$. Since these variables are logarithms of prices, adding a constant to each of them is equivalent to increasing all prices proportionately, implying that the price level path is indeterminate.

23. Here is the calculation. Substitute (11) into (12)′ and take expectations to obtain $E[p_t|t - 1] = \bar{m}_t + \bar{a}\bar{i}$. When updated a period, this equation gives the expectation of p_{t+1}.

Next substitute (20) and $E[p_t|t - 1]$ into the equation for p_t obtained by combining (11) and (12)′. Then substitute that equation and the expression for $E[p_{t+1}|t]$ into (13)′, after substituting out for y_t. Finally, equate coefficients and solve for $\bar{m}_{t+1}$ and the ψ_i.

24. This is shown by Bean (1984), who also shows that in his framework the same basic results are obtained even when the government cannot hit the nominal income target exactly. West (1986) shows that the result is not robust to various changes in lag structure and assumptions about expectation formation.

25. Friedman (1959) presents a complete exposition of ideas developed over the course of a decade. Clark Warburton (1952) and E. S. Shaw (1950) were other early proponents of fixed or nearly fixed money growth rules. Simons (1948) proposed a price stabilization rule. Since the monetary authority does not directly control the price level, the Simons rule in effect specifies the target of monetary policy rather than the actions of the central bank.

26. For example, if $a_i = 0$ for all $i > 0$ and $b_i = 0$ for $i > 1$, but $b_1 > b_0$ (and both are positive), then

$$m_t = -(b_0)^{-1}[b_1 m_{t-1} + a_0 \varepsilon_{t-1}],$$

which is an unstable first-order difference equation.

27. The relevant equation might be in first difference form, in which case setting money growth at its historical average may minimize uncertainty.

28. One reason for not focusing on fiscal policy as a stabilizer in models with imperfections is that there has been surprisingly little recent work in that mode.

29. The loss goes to zero as a goes to infinity, but this is misleading because the quality of the second-order approximation to the loss function deteriorates as a gets very large.

30. See Bernheim (1987) for a general assessment of the effects of deficit policies.

31. Atkinson and Stiglitz (1980) present a full discussion of the basic approach and generalizations. See particularly material on the Ramsey problem in Lecture 12, and the discussion of intertemporal taxation in Lecture 14, pp. 442–451.

32. The derivation is in Atkinson and Stiglitz (1980, p. 372).

33. This is a sufficient condition. Deaton shows that a necessary and sufficient condition is that U be quasi-, or implicitly, separable in z and X. See also Sadka (1977).

34. See Aschauer and Greenwood (1985) and Kremers (1985) for related results.

35. If the debt is rising rapidly, the assumption of a fixed interest rate becomes untenable at some point.

36. Another shortcut is taken here. We are in effect solving for t as if it were certain that future tax rates were going to be equal to τ. This is clearly not true, since news about income and spending would change the tax rate in future periods.

37. This result would not occur if there were capital; in that case the economy could smooth consumption during the war by increasing the capital stock in preparation for that (possible) event.

38. Flemming (1987) presents an interesting model with endogenous government spending and stochastic wages.

39. The following oversimplified model is a case where government spending is countercylical. Suppose that gross output, y_t, is given by:

$$y_t = (g_t + \alpha + \varepsilon_t)^\beta,$$

where g_t is government spending, α is a constant, and ε_t is a disturbance. Output is used either for consumption or for government spending on the input.

Consumption ($c_t = y_t - g_t$) is maximized by allowing g to rise when ε falls, that is, when there is a negative productivity shock. At the same time c_t falls. Thus government spending would be countercyclical in this case.

40. Dynamic consistency is equivalent to the game-theoretic notion of subgame perfection. For a 1977 treatment of game theory, see James Friedman; more recent surveys of particular aspects and applications are by Fudenberg and Tirole (1983) and Roberts (1985).

41. Cukierman (1986), Rogoff (1987), and Alesina (1988) provide useful surveys; this section draws on Fischer (1986a).

42. In a perceptive early paper, Auernheimer (1974) discussed the optimal inflation tax under the constraint that the government was not allowed to produce discrete changes in the price level. He was thus close to requiring the government to pursue a dynamically consistent policy. Turnovsky and Brock (1980) state that dynamic inconsistency does not obtain in their model—which has money in the utility function—with respect to monetary policy, though it does with respect to fiscal instruments. The reason appears to be that in their model the government is able to attain, through a time zero money blip, a first-best equilibrium in which it owns claims on the private sector equal to the present value of its future spending.

43. If the government could tax capital in the first period, it would in effect have a lump-sum tax at its disposal (since the capital is already there) and could achieve the command optimum.

44. The first-order conditions are presented in Fischer (1980).

45. The optimality principle in dynamic programming asserts that at every stage of an optimal program, the optimizer will do what is best from that point on, taking as given the results of earlier decisions.

46. Obviously, this is not always true in optimal tax problems. Distortions generally remain even in the single-period optimal tax formulation. The first-best optimum is attainable in this case because there is no taxation in the first period.

47. Lucas and Stokey (1983), Persson and Svensson (1984), and Turnovsky and Brock (1980), among others, have studied dynamic inconsistency in a similar representative agent optimal tax setting.

48. This argument suggests, however, that one major difference between the government and individuals is in their discount rates. For the moment, however, we limit ourselves to a one-period model. Cukierman (1986) provides an extended discussion of these points.

49. The policymaker sets money, which in turn affects the inflation rate. It is simpler to think of the policymaker as choosing inflation directly.

50. It is also the only Nash equilibrium. When speaking of the private sector "moving first," it is tempting to think of it setting its expectation strategically. If π^* was a private sector strategic variable, it could be set at the value that would from (46) induce $\pi = 0$. Algebraically, that would result in $y = k\bar{y}$ and produce a first-best solution. But that would not be an equilibrium because π and π^* would be different. In other words, it is inconsistent to argue that the public "sets" π^* at a negative number in order to achieve $\pi = 0$.

51. Elster (1979) and Schelling (1984) are stimulating references, dealing in part with individual inconsistencies and problems of self-control.

52. The patent example pointed to by Kydland and Prescott (1977) and Taylor (1983) is an interesting special case of the protection of property rights.

53. Further back in history, there seems to have been a deflationary bias. At the ends of the Napoleonic and Civil wars, and World War I, Britain and the United States deflated to get back to fixed gold parities.

54. The general principle explained by Persson and Svensson (1984) is to place the successor government in a situation where the penalty for deviating from the precommitted consistent plan balances at the margin the benefit of doing so. In principle, such arrangements can be made in any situation where the full set of states of nature can be specified ex ante.

55. Rogoff (1985) suggests this trade-off; we present his analysis later in this chapter. Cukierman and Meltzer (1986) include similar considerations in their analysis of a government's choice between discretion and rules.

56. If there is no legal basis for changing certain laws, the society has decided that the cost of change is a revolution.

57. This outcome is utility or loss function dependent and can be overturned.

58. Reputational considerations are also typically part of the anti-indexation argument.

59. Rogoff (1987) emphasizes that multiple equilibria are a serious problem for whatever positive theories might be derived from such games.

60. Hallett's suggestion that the government's reputation acts as a bond can be seen in this calculation.

61. In the original Barro-Gordon model zero inflation is not an equilibrium, because of differing assumptions on the utility function.

62. Several authors, including Driffill, study (fiscal) policymaking in a similar context in the *Scandinavian Journal of Economics* 87, 2 (1985). Calmfors' introduction is particularly useful.

63. The benefit of using (59) will be seen to be that the inflation rate under discretion is independent of the expected inflation rate, thus substantially simplifying calculations.

64. Bayes' rule implies that

$$\text{Prob}(S|\pi = 0) = \frac{\text{Prob}(\pi = 0|S) \cdot \text{Prob}(S)}{\text{Prob}(\pi = 0|S) \cdot \text{Prob}(S) + \text{Prob}(\pi = 0|W) \cdot \text{Prob}(W)},$$

where S is strong and W is weak.

65. Rogoff (1987) sets up a reputational model with a continuum of policymakers, in which optimal policy is not randomized.

66. This covers work by Alesina (1987), Rogoff (1985), Canzoneri (1985), and Cukierman and Meltzer (1986).

67. We are assuming that the target level of output does not change with the supply shock. That assumption does not affect the basic point being made here.

68. Rogoff also discusses the choice among different policy instruments in the presence of uncertainty.

69. In the Barro (1986) model the strong government always chooses a zero inflation rate. To imitate it, the weak government has also to produce a zero inflation rate. If the strong government, rather than not caring at all about inflation, merely cares more than the weak government, it may seek to differentiate itself from the weaker government by choosing a lower inflation rate than its one shot optimum. Hoshi (1988) examines this possibility, finding circumstances under which there is a pooling equilibrium in which the two types of government produce the same inflation rate in earlier periods, as well as conditions for a separating equilibrium in which their earlier period inflation rates differ. He also studies the effects of exogenous uncertainty—the government cannot exactly control the inflation rate—on these equilibria.

70. In the Canzoneri model the policymaker and private agents have different utility functions. This is not necessary.

71. Porter (1983) shows that a cartel may break down occasionally even when no one is cheating because firms in the industry have a signal extraction problem and interpret a low industry price as a signal that other firms may be price cutting.

72. Rogoff (1987) discusses the Canzoneri results, emphasizing the multiplicity of equilibria and asking why the public should converge on this one; he also points out that the public finds itself "punishing" the central bank even though it knows it never cheats.

73. This is an extreme form of adaptive expectations.

74. The preceding analysis does not explain how the government got itself to the high equilibrium inflation in the first place. A fuller model of the disinflation process

may include the assumption that the disinflating government is one whose w (in the loss function) has risen and whose task now is to communicate that information to the public.

75. However, a careful reading of Friedman's case for rules (1959) suggests that he was reaching for a concept like dynamic inconsistency; for instance, he discusses why a constitutional guarantee of free speech is better than a case-by-case approach.

76. To some extent this is misleading: the models used in game-theoretic analyses of policy typically are stripped down to the point where it is virtually only expectations that yield interesting dynamics. In more complete models, both structural lags and expectational sources of dynamics affect the performance of policy.

References

Alesina, Alberto (1987). "Macroeconomic Policy in a Two-Party System as a Repeated Game." *Quarterly Journal of Economics* 102 (Aug.), 651–678.

Alesina, Alberto (1988). "Macroeconomics and Politics." *NBER Macroeconomics Annual*, 13–52.

Aschauer, David, and Jeremy Greenwood (1985). "Macroeconomic Effects of Fiscal Policy." In K. Brunner and A. Meltzer (eds.), Carnegie-Rochester Conference Series on Public Policy. Vol. 23 (Autumn), 91–138.

Atkinson, Anthony B., and Joseph E. Stiglitz (1980). *Lectures on Public Economics.* New York: McGraw-Hill.

Atkinson, Anthony B., and Agnar Sandmo (1980). "Welfare Implications of the Taxation of Savings." *Economic Journal* 90 (Sept.), 529–549.

Auernheimer, Leonardo (1974). "The Honest Government's Guide to the Revenue from the Creation of Money." *Journal of Political Economy* 82, 3 (May–June), 598–606.

Backus, David, and John Driffill (1985). "Rational Expectations and Policy Credibility Following a Change in Regime." *Review of Economic Studies* 52, 2 (April), 211–222.

Backus, David, and John Driffill (1985a). "Inflation and Reputation." *American Economic Review* 75 (June), 530–538.

Barro, Robert J. (1979). "Money and the Price Level under the Gold Standard." *Economic Journal* (Mar.), 13–33.

Barro, Robert J. (1979a). "On the Determination of the Public Debt." *Journal of Political Economy* 87, 5 (Oct.), 940–971.

Barro, Robert J. (1983a). " Rules, Discretion and Reputation in a Model of Monetary Policy." *Journal of Monetary Economics* 12, 1 (July), 101–122.

Barro, Robert J. (1986). "Reputation in a Model of Monetary Policy with Incomplete Information." *Journal of Monetary Economics* 17, 1 (Jan.), 3–20.

Barro, Robert J. (1987). "Government Spending, Interest Rates, Prices, and Budget Deficits in the United Kingdom, 1701–1918." *Journal of Monetary Economics* 20, 2 (Sept.), 221–248.

Barro, Robert J., and David Gordon (1983). "A Positive Theory of Monetary Policy in a Natural Rate Model." *Journal of Political Economy* 91, 4 (Aug.), 589–610.

Barsky, Robert (1985). "Three Interest Rate Paradoxes." Ph.D. dissertation. MIT.

Barsky, Robert, N. Gregory Mankiw, and Stephen Zeldes (1986). "Ricardian Consumers with Keynesian Propensities." *American Economic Review* 76, 4 (Sept.), 676–691.

Barsky, Robert, and Lawrence H. Summers (1988). "Gibson's Paradox and the Gold Standard." *Journal of Political Economy* 96, 3 (June), 528–550.

Bean, Charles R. (1984). "Targeting Nominal Income: An Appraisal." *Economic Journal* 93 (Dec.), 806–819.

Benabou, Roland (1988). "Optimal Price Dynamics and Speculation with a Storable Good." *Econometrica*, forthcoming.

Bernheim, Douglas (1987). "Ricardian Equivalence: An Evaluation of Theory and Evidence." *NBER Macroeconomics Annual* 2, 263–303.

Brainard, William (1967). "Uncertainty and the Effectiveness of Policy." *American Economic Review, Papers and Proceedings* 57, 2 (May), 411–425.

Buchanan, James, and Richard Wagner (1977). *Democracy in Deficit: The Political Legacy of Lord Keynes*. New York: Academic Press.

Calvo, Guillermo (1978). "On the Time Consistency of Optimal Policy in a Monetary Economy." *Econometrica* 46, 6 (Nov.), 1411–1428.

Calvo, Guillermo, and Maurice Obstfeld (1987). "Optimal Time-Consistent Fiscal Policy with Finite Lifetimes: Analysis and Extensions." CARESS Working Paper 97–09, University of Pennsylvania.

Canzoneri, Matthew B. (1985). "Monetary Policy Games and the Role of Private Information." *American Economic Review* 75, 5 (Dec.), 1056–1070.

Canzoneri, Matthew B., Dale W. Henderson, and Kenneth Rogoff (1983). "The Information Content of the Interest Rate and Optimal Monetary Policy." *Quarterly Journal of Economics* 98, 4 (Nov.), 545–566.

Cukierman, Alex (1984). *Inflation, Stagflation, Relative Prices, and Imperfect Information*. Cambridge: Cambridge University Press.

Cukierman, Alex (1986). "Central Bank Behavior and Credibility—Some Recent Developments." *Federal Reserve Bank of St. Louis Review* 68, 5–17.

Cukierman, Alex, and Allan H. Meltzer (1986). "A Positive Theory of Discretionary Policy, the Cost of Democratic Government and the Benefits of a Constitution." *Economic Inquiry* 24, 3 (July), 367–388.

Deaton, Angus (1979). "The Distance Function in Consumer Behavior with Applications to Index Numbers and Optimal Taxation." *Review of Economic Studies* 46, 3 (July), 391–405.

Deaton, Angus (1981). "Optimal Taxes and the Structure of Preferences." *Econometrica* 49, 5 (Sept.), 1245–1260.

Diamond, Douglas W., and Philip H. Dybvig (1983). "Bank Runs, Deposit Insurance, and Liquidity." *Journal of Political Economy* 91, 3 (June), 401–419.

Diamond, Peter A. (1985). "Ignorance and Monetary Policy." Mimeo. MIT.

Dotsey, Michael, and Robert King (1986). "Informational Implications of Interest Rate Rules." *American Economic Review* 76, 1, 33–42

Elster, Jon (1979). *Ulysses and the Sirens.* Cambridge: Cambridge University Press.

Fischer, Stanley (1980). "Dynamic Inconsistency, Cooperation and the Benevolent Dissembling Government." *Journal of Economic Dynamics and Control* 2, 1 (Feb.), 93–107.

Fischer, Stanley (1981). "Toward an Understanding of the Costs of Inflation: II." In Karl Brunner and Allan Meltzer, (eds.), *The Costs and Consequences of Inflation,* Carnegie-Rochester Conference Series on Public Policy, Vol. 15.

Fischer, Stanley (1986). "Monetary Rules and Commodity Money Schemes Under Uncertainty." *Journal of Monetary Economics* 17, 21–35.

Fischer, Stanley (1986a). "Time Consistent Monetary and Fiscal Policies: A Survey." Mimeo. MIT.

Fischer, Stanley, and Franco Modigliani (1978). "Toward an Understanding of the Real Effects and Costs of Inflation." *Weltwirtschaftliches Archiv* 114, 810–833.

Fisher, Irving (1920). *Stabilizing the Dollar.* London: Macmillan.

Flemming, John S. (1987). "Debt and Taxes in War and Peace: The Case of a Small Open Economy." In M. J. Boskin, J. S. Flemming, and S. Gorini (eds.), *Private Saving and Public Debt.* Oxford: Basil Blackwell.

Frenkel, Jacob (1975). "Inflation and the Formation of Expectations." *Journal of Monetary Economics* 1, 403–421.

Friedman, Benjamin M. (1975). "Targets, Instruments, and Indicators of Monetary Policy." *Journal of Monetary Economics* 1, 442–473.

Friedman, James W. (1977). *Oligopoly and the Theory of Games,* Amsterdam: North-Holland.

Friedman, Milton (1948). "A Monetary and Fiscal Framework for Economic Stability." Reprinted in Milton Friedman, *Essays in Positive Economics*. University of Chicago Press, 1953.

Friedman, Milton (1959). *A Program for Monetary Stability*. New York: Fordham University Press.

Friedman, Milton (1962). "Should There Be an Independent Monetary Authority?" In Leland B. Yeager (ed.), *In Search of a Monetary Constitution*. Cambridge, MA: Harvard University Press.

Friedman, Milton (1968). "The Role of Monetary Policy." *American Economic Review* 58, 1 (Mar.), 1–17.

Fudenberg, Drew, and Jean Tirole (1983). "Dynamic Models of Oligopoly." Unpublished manuscript. MIT.

Hallett, A. J. Hughes (1986). "Is Time Inconsistent Behavior Really Possible?." Centre for Economic Policy Research Discussion Paper 138. London.

Hayashi, Fumio (1986). "Tests for Liquidity Constraints: A Critical Survey." NBER Working Paper 1720.

Holbrook, R. S. (1972). "Optimal Economic Policy and the Problem of Instrument Instability." *American Economic Review* 62, 1 (March), 57–65.

Hoshi, Takeo (1988). "Government Reputation and Monetary Policy." Ph.D. dissertation. MIT, ch. 3.

King, Mervyn A. (1980). "Savings and Taxation." In G. A. Hughes and G. M. Heal (eds.), *Public Policy and the Tax System*. London: George Allen & Unwin.

Kotlikoff, Laurence J., Torsten Persson, and Lars E. O. Svensson (1986). "Laws as Assets: A Possible Solution to the Time Consistency Problem." NBER Working Paper.

Kremers, Jeroen J. M. (1985). "Is Dynamic Tax Smoothing an Optimal Public Financial Policy?" Unpublished manuscript, Nuffield College.

Kreps, David, and Robert Wilson (1982). "Reputation and Imperfect Competition." *Journal of Economic Theory* 27, 2 (Aug.), 253–279.

Kydland, Finn E., and Edward C. Prescott (1977). "Rules Rather than Discretion: The Inconsistency of Optimal Plans." *Journal of Political Economy* 85, 3 (June), 473–492.

Kydland, Finn E., and Edward C. Prescott (1980). "A Competitive Theory of Fluctuations and the Feasibility and Desirability of Stabilization Policy." In Stanley Fischer (ed.), *Rational Expectations and Economic Policy*. University of Chicago Press.

Lucas, Robert E. (1973). "Some International Evidence on Output-Inflation Trade-offs." *American Economic Review* 63 (June), 326–334.

Lucas, Robert E., and Nancy L. Stokey (1983). "Optimal Fiscal and Monetary Policy in an Economy without Capital." *Journal of Monetary Economics* 12, 1 (July), 55–94.

McCallum, Bennett T. (1981). "Price Level Determinacy with an Interest Rate Rule and Rational Expectations." *Journal of Monetary Economics* 8, 3 (Nov.), 319–329.

McCallum, Bennett T. (1985). "Bank Deregulation, Accounting Systems of Exchange, and the Unit of Account: A Critical Review." In K. Brunner and A. Meltzer (eds.), *The 'New Monetary Economics,' Fiscal Issues and Unemployment*. Carnegie-Rochester Conference Series on Public Policy. Vol. 23 (Autumn).

Mints, Lloyd (1975). *A History of Banking Theory*. University of Chicago Press.

Ordover, Janusz A., and Edmund S. Phelps (1979). "The Concept of Optimal Taxation in the Overlapping-Generations Model of Capital and Wealth." *Journal of Public Economics* 12, 1 (Aug.), 1–26.

Persson, Torsten, and Lars E. O. Svensson (1984). "Time-Consistent Fiscal Policy and Government Cash-Flow." *Journal of Monetary Economics* 14, 3 (Nov.), 365–374.

Persson, Mats, Torsten Persson, and Lars E. O. Svensson (1987). "Time Consistency of Monetary and Fiscal Policy." *Econometrica* 55, 6 (Nov.), 1249–1273.

Phelps, Edmund S. (1968). "Money-Wage Dynamics and Labor Market Equilibrium." *Journal of Political Economy* 76, 4 (part 2), 678–711.

Poole, William (1970). "Optimal Choice of Monetary Policy Instruments in a Simple Stochastic Macro Model." *Quarterly Journal of Economics* 84 (May), 197–216.

Porter, Robert H. (1983). "Optimal Cartel Trigger Price Strategies." *Journal of Economic Theory* 29, 2 (April), 313–338.

Ramsey, Frank P. (1927). "A Contribution to the Theory of Taxation." *Economic Journal* 37, 47–61.

Roberts, John (1985). "Battles for Market Share: Incomplete Information, Aggressive Strategic Pricing, and Competitive Dynamics." Unpublished manuscript. Stanford University.

Rogoff, Kenneth (1985). "The Optimal Degree of Commitment to an Intermediate Monetary Target." *Quarterly Journal of Economics* 100, 4 (Nov.), 1169–1190.

Rogoff, Kenneth (1987). "Reputational Constraints on Monetary Policy." In Karl Brunner and Allan Meltzer (eds.), *Bubbles and Other Essays*. Carnegie-Rochester Conference Series. Vol. 26.

Romer, David (1988). "What Are the Costs of Excessive Deficits?" *NBER Macroeconomics Annual*, 63–98.

Rotemberg, Julio (1988). "Moral Hazard, Borrowing, Lending and Ricardian Equivalence." Mimeo. MIT.

Sadka, Efraim (1977). "A Theorem on Uniform Taxation." *Journal of Public Economics* 7, 3 (June), 387–392.

Sargent, Thomas J., and Neil Wallace (1975). " 'Rational' Expectations, the Optimal Monetary Instrument, and the Optimal Money Supply Rule." *Journal of Political Economy* 83, 2 (April), 241–254.

Schelling, Thomas C. (1984). *Choice and Consequence.* Cambridge, MA: Harvard University Press.

Shaw, Edward S. (1950). *Money, Income and Monetary Policy.* University of Chicago Press.

Simons, Henry C. (1948). *Economic Policy for a Free Society.* University of Chicago Press.

Tabellini, Guido (1983). "Accommodative Monetary Policy and Central Bank Reputation." Unpublished manuscript. University of California, Los Angeles.

Tabellini, Guido (1985). "Centralized Wage Setting and Monetary Policy in a Reputational Equilibrium." Unpublished manuscript. University of California, Los Angeles.

Taylor, John B. (1983). "Comment." *Journal of Monetary Economics* 12, 1 (July), 123–125.

Tinbergen, Jan (1952). *On the Theory of Economic Policy.* Amsterdam: Elsevier.

Tobin, James (1972). "Wealth, Liquidity and the Propensity to Consume." In B. Strumple, J. Morgan and E. Zahn (eds.), *Human Behavior in Economic Affairs; Essays in Honor of George Katona.* Amsterdam: Elsevier.

Turnovsky, Stephen J., and William A. Brock (1980). "Time Consistency and Optimal Government Policies in Perfect Foresight Equilibrium." *Journal of Public Economics* 13, 183–212.

Warburton, Clark (1952). "How Much Variation in the Quantity of Money Is Needed?" *Southern Economic Journal* 18, 4 (April), 495–509.

Weil, Philippe (1987). "Permanent Budget Deficits and Inflation." *Journal of Monetary Economics* 20, 2 (Sept.), 393–410.

West, Kenneth D. (1986). "Targeting Nominal Income: A Note." *Economic Journal* 96 (Dec.), 1077–1083.

Wicksell, Knut (1965). *Interest and Prices.* New York: Augustus M. Kelley. Reprints of Economic Classics.

Yotsuzuka, Toshiki (1987). "Ricardian Equivalence in the Presence of Capital Market Imperfections." *Journal of Monetary Economics* 20, 411–436.

Name Index

Subject Index

Nominal money. *See* Money, nominal
Nominal rigidities, 373–374, 375, 386,
  414, 418n.5, 489
  in aggregate supply-demand model, 518,
  521–523, 524
  and efficiency wages, 461
  in financial markets, 488
  and labor contracts, 432–433
  in prices, 386, 413, 434
  and union/employment model, 454
  in wages, 434, 462
Nonaccelerating inflation rate of
  unemployment (NAIRU), 544
Nonhuman wealth, 121
Nonlinear dynamics, and simple linear
  difference equations, 225–226
Nonmonetary economies, 208n.19
  consumption in, 172–174
  wealth in, 174
No-Ponzi-game (NPG) condition, 49–50,
  80, 87n.47
  enforcement of, 84n.24
  and perpetual youth model, 118
  in Sidrauski model, 189

Offer curve, 246–252
Oil prices, and recessions, 19
Oil shock (1973), 373, 520, 525
Okun's law, 8–9, 364–365n.27, 464–465
OLG model. *See* Overlapping generations
  model
Open economy macroeconomics, 29,
  537
  and intertemporal allocation (Ramsey
  model), 58–69, 76–78, 506
  staggered contracts in, 557–558
Open market operations (OMO), and
  money growth, 181–188
Optimal capital, 296–297
Optimal government asset supplies, 591
Optimal government spending, 591
Optimal inflation rate, 181, 191
Optimal punishment, 604
Optimal quantity of money, 181, 191
Optimal taxation
  in atemporal economy, 585–586
  in intertemporal equilibrium model,
  586–587
Output. *See also* GNP
  in aggregate supply-demand model, 518,
  520–523, 526–529
  booms and recessions in, 6–7

and demand, 375, 379, 382, 386–387,
  388, 413–414, 427, 463, 531, 546–
  548
and demand (Lucas model), 356–360
and employment fluctuations, 337–346
and IS-LM model, 529–531
in loss function, 568
and money, 355–356, 375, 382,
  396–398, 402, 411
in monopolistic competition model, 377,
  379–381, 382, 387, 388
and price flexibility, 546–548
vs. price stability, 570–575
and shocks, 12–15, 325, 326, 356–357,
  359, 526–529, 548
stabilization of, 393–394
and stock market, 556–557
trends vs. cycles in, 7–15
variability of, 546–548
Output, labor. *See* Productivity, labor
Output growth. *See* Growth
Outside money, 193–194
Overemployment, and labor contract,
  437–438
Overlapping generations (OLG) model, 91,
  489
  and fiscal policy, 126–135
  and perpetual youth model, 115–126,
  138–141
  and Ramsey model, 91, 92, 106, 116, 126,
  132
  and social security effects, 110–114
  with two-period lives, 92–110, 137–138,
  141
Overlapping generations model with
  money, 154–155, 156–164,
  and interest, 182
  and multiple equilibria, 245–256
  and simple linear difference equation, 217,
  224, 239
  and transaction services, 234
Overtime wages, 465, 497n.43

Permanent vs. transitory shocks, 7–8, 288,
  525–529
Perpetual youth model, 115–126
  and saving–interest rate relation,
  138–141
Perpetuities, and bubbles, 223
Phase diagrams, 79, 83n.16
Phillips curve, 19, 358, 542–543, 544–545,
  572, 596–598, 599